Evaluation
Defines and talks of Educational Theater

Area
Speech Education

Look at closely

HISTORY OF
SPEECH EDUCATION
IN AMERICA

History of
Speech Education in America

BACKGROUND STUDIES

....

PREPARED UNDER THE AUSPICES OF THE
Speech Association of America

KARL R. WALLACE, *Editor*

WARREN GUTHRIE

FREDERICK W. HABERMAN   HAROLD WESTLAKE

BARNARD HEWITT   CLAUDE M. WISE

Editorial Board

New York
APPLETON-CENTURY-CROFTS, INC.

PREFACE

....

This volume of studies was undertaken early in 1948 with the official sanction of the Speech Association of America. Since the early 1930's, the Association's Committee on the History of Speech Education, under the leadership of Giles Gray, A. M. Drummond, and Bert Emsley, helped to secure the interest of scholars and teachers in the history and tradition of the field of Speech as it has unfolded in the United States. Committee members themselves engaged in historical studies, and some of their own labors are represented in this volume. They cajoled an occasional graduate student into unearthing materials and preparing theses that helped to reveal the foundations of old meaning and to beget new vigor for modern precept and practice. By mid-1947 the Committee—and many other persons concerned with the backgrounds of pedagogy—believed that the time had come for a joint, systematic project of considerable magnitude. The early studies had not only provided valuable information about the teaching of Speech in America; they pointed to bibliographic resources and suggested many directions of profitable research. In December, 1947, upon recommendation of the Committee, the Association authorized this volume of papers and selected the Editorial Board.

For six years this book has been in preparation. Aided by the Committee, the Board set up a chronological list of topics. The list gave some system to the project and the topics are reflected, for the most part, in the chapter headings. Readers, however, should not regard the chronological progression as an attempt to write definitive history. Before a "final" history of speech education can be prepared, we need the work of many future scholars who will furnish the facts as to who taught what, and where, and how. We believe, nevertheless, that the studies included here supply significant information and afford interpretations which must be reckoned with by future historians of the subject. They organize much that has already been done; they offer much that is new.

The scope of the studies covers American speech education from Colonial times to about 1925. But because most of the streams in

American education have their tributaries in English and classical sources, three articles focus on the springs and currents which flowed long before New England and Virginia schools and colleges were established.

The main current bears the formal label of Rhetoric, the art of verbal communication. We are mainly concerned in this book, not with writing, but with speaking—with the use of speech in socially significant situations and the attempts to teach the art of oral communication in a formal educational environment. Rhetoric so conceived gave rise to a number of branches of study. It gave impetus to the study of style and speech composition, to the study of elocution and delivery, to the analysis of speech sounds, and to phonetics and pronunciation. It gave considerable impetus, also, to the art of composition and delivery in the theatre. If these may be thought of as the chief branches of rhetoric, it seems clear that the branches divide and subdivide, gathering strength in studies other than rhetoric, until they establish their own currents which we designate today by such terms as speech correction and pathology, oral interpretation, educational dramatics, and the arts of mass communication—radio and television.

About all of these branches, except radio and television, this book has something to say. In other words, it focuses upon systematic education in speech as it has been manifested in the college and the school.

The terminal date, 1925, has not emerged inviolate. In some ways it provided a logical stopping point, for by the 1920's the basic lines of speech instruction had been recognized academically, at least in the American college. The study of phonetics and speech correction, both in course and in clinic, had taken root; dramatics had found its niche; oral interpretation had its ally in literature; public speaking and discussion had been taught effectively outside of the traditional courses in English composition; undergraduate and graduate majors in speech had been formally established. By and large, what has happened since the 1920's in the field of Speech reflects the influence of increasing specialization and the application of basic knowledges and skills to meet professional requirements in a professionally minded society. An account of such developments, especially in education for radio and television, will have to be told later. The reader will discover, furthermore, that in a few instances, chiefly in the article dealing with intercollegiate debating and in the chapters treating of the professional societies, which did much to foster speech education, the significant story had to include certain events in the 1930's and the 1940's. The character of the American Educational Theatre Association, for example, did not emerge clearly until the last decade.

The Editorial Board fully acknowledges the fine co-operation of the contributors. Many of them are recognized as authorities in their lines of study. They were asked to take a fresh look at their materials, to extend their research, and to prepare new studies. This they gladly did. A few of the authors were asked to undertake what to them were new lines of investigation. They, too, responded superbly. The results, we feel, are worth the close observation and critical analysis which both mature scholars and graduate students in Speech can exercise.

We are grateful to our publishers and their editorial assistants whose faith in this venture is as great as ours. The Speech Association of America stands in heavy debt to members of the Editorial Board, particularly Professor Hewitt, whose labors were often beyond routine endeavor. To Professor Haberman goes deep appreciation for the preparation of the index. And to the contributors, I express my personal respect and admiration. Many of them have graciously borne our editorial suggestions, requests, revisions, liberties, and idiosyncrasies. Such credit as this work may deserve belongs entirely to them. I alone must bear its shortcomings.

KARL R. WALLACE

CONTENTS

....

ix

PART III

THE EDUCATIONAL THEATRE

PART I

The Heritage

1 English Backgrounds of Rhetoric

WILBUR SAMUEL HOWELL

....

I

The present volume aims to describe America's experience in educating citizens for the duties of oral communication. This experience is part of the history of education in the new world; it is also a commentary upon our cultural and political history in every period of our development from colonial community to continental nation. Several articles in the ensuing pages will examine the various theories that have guided American educators in preparing students to speak in public. Still other articles will discuss that strange phenomenon, the "elocutionary" movement in Britain and America during the nineteenth century. Still other articles will explore American contributions to phonetics and lexicography; American experiments with theatre arts as an academic study; American interest in intercollegiate debating; and American regard for the college literary and forensic society as the nurse of future statesmen, educators, lawyers, preachers. The reader of these pages will encounter names already well known to him: John Witherspoon, signer of the Declaration of Independence, who was professor of rhetorical studies in eighteenth-century Princeton, and who lectured on eloquence to James Madison and a generation that was to give us our present nation; John Quincy Adams, sixth president of the United States, who as first Boylston Professor of Rhetoric and Oratory at Harvard brought to his students a gifted revaluation of the rhetorical teachings of Cicero and Quintilian; Woodrow Wilson, who coached debating teams at Princeton during his career as professor of politics. There are other famous names in these pages, Noah Webster and Henry Ward Beecher, for example, not to mention men and women prominent as public readers, lecturers, actors, and teachers of dramatics. These and many others will receive attention here, as their part in the development of rhetorical education in America is noticed.

My purpose in this first essay of the present volume is to describe the main works on rhetoric written in England before the beginnings of higher education in the new world.¹ These English works began to be produced when higher education first flowered in England during the lifetime of the Venerable Bede (673-735). I shall trace them from that epoch to the date of the first Commencement at Harvard in 1642, when higher learning became a native product in what is now the United States.

English rhetoric in these nine hundred odd years is of course not exclusively or even mainly an Anglo-Saxon invention. It is instead a commodity developed by the English people from ancient Roman rhetorical theory, even as Roman theory in its turn had been derived from materials first consciously systematized in early Greece and Sicily. Thus the main works with which I shall deal in this article are descended through Cicero and Quintilian from the rhetorical writings of Plato and Aristotle, even though the line of descent may appear at times to begin with some lesser intermediate authority.

English rhetoric between the eighth and the seventeenth century is perhaps best described in round terms as a mosaic with five dominant patterns. One of these patterns may be called the Ciceronian. This pattern became a part of the English record in the generation that followed Bede, and it was still flourishing in England in 1642. Another of these patterns may be called the stylistic. Bede himself was the first Englishman to contribute to this pattern, which, as we shall see, involved an emphasis upon the third of the main divisions of Ciceronian rhetoric. The stylistic pattern was still in existence at the time of the first Commencement at Harvard; thus it is the oldest form of rhetorical theory to be dealt with in this article, although for convenience I shall discuss it after the Ciceronian pattern has been examined. The third pattern of English rhetoric, which may be called the formulary pattern, dates from the middle years of the sixteenth century, so far as the printed English record is concerned. It too was still in existence when Harvard was founded, although it must be regarded as a minor development in the period now under discussion. The fourth pattern of English rhetoric may be called the Ramistic. This originated in the efforts of the French philosopher, Pierre de la Ramée, usually called by his Latin name Ramus, to reform the liberal arts during the sixteenth century. Ramus' *Dialecticae Libri Duo*, which states the basic tenets of his reform of the liberal arts, was first translated into English in 1574. Ramistic rhetoric stems from these tenets, but it was actually formulated into a system by Ramus' close friend and colleague, Audomarus Talaeus, or Omer Talon, whose *Rhetorica* was first translated into English in 1584. At the time of the first Commencement at Harvard fifty-eight years later, Ramistic rhetoric, as we shall see, was the dominant pattern of rhetorical theory in New England. The fifth and final pattern of English rhetoric to receive attention in the present article is the Baconian. The Baconian pattern begins officially with the publication in 1605 of Francis Bacon's *Advancement of Learning*. This remarkable philosophy of learning was only thirty-seven years old when Harvard held her first Commencement, but it had already had a profound effect upon seventeenth-century thought, and what it had to say about rhetoric must be considered here as part of the inheritance which American rhetorical education received from the motherland.

Each of these five patterns will now be considered in turn.

II

Ciceronian rhetoric in the form which it assumes in Cicero's own works is best described as an art made up of five arts. These five arts, as five procedures which constitute the complex act of preparing and delivering a communication, are designated by Cicero as Invention, Arrangement, Style, Memory, and Delivery. In *De Inventione*, the first work which Cicero wrote on the subject of rhetoric, he defined these five procedures as he and his later disciples generally conceived of them, and these definitions are brief enough for quotation here:

Invention is the discovery of valid or seemingly valid arguments to render one's cause plausible. Arrangement is the distribution of arguments thus dis-covered in the proper order. Expression [that is, *elocutio*, Cicero's term for style] is the fitting of the proper language to the invented matter. Memory is the firm mental grasp of matter and words. Delivery is the control of voice and body in a manner suitable to the dignity of the subject matter and the style.[2]

Cicero's *De Inventione* discusses only the first of these five pro-cedures, although, had it been completed, it would have covered the others as well. The earliest Roman treatment of the five terms as a whole is found in a work entitled *Ad C. Herennium Libri Quattuor De Arte Rhetorica*, usually called the *Rhetorica ad Herennium*. During the Middle Ages the *Rhetorica ad Herennium* was ascribed to Cicero. Nowadays it is not accepted as Cicero's work, but nobody disputes the great similarity between it and Cicero's *De Inventione*. Nor is it unfair to assume that the two works would have been closely alike through-out, if Cicero had completed *De Inventione*. In all his other major writings on rhetoric, Cicero holds to the five procedures as his basic terms, whether he deals with them all, as in *De Oratore* and *De Parti-tione Oratoria*, or mainly with the third one, Style, as in *Orator*.[3] The following words from his *Brutus*, spoken by himself as he and Atticus and Brutus converse about rhetoric on the lawn near a statue of Plato,

show his enduring regard for eloquence as the product of these five
faculties:

Well then, . . . to praise eloquence, to set forth its power and the honours
which it brings to those who have it, is not my present purpose, nor is it necessary. However, this one thing I venture to affirm without fear of contradic-
tion, that whether it is a product of rules and theory, or a technique dependent on practice, or on natural gifts, it is one attainment amongst all others of
unique difficulty. For of the five elements of which, as we say, it is made up,
each one is in its own right a great art. One may guess therefore what power
is inherent in an art made up of five great arts, and what difficulty it presents.[4]

An art made up of five great arts—this is the Ciceronian thesis about
rhetoric. The most thorough commentary in classical Roman times upon
these five arts, as treated by Cicero and many lesser writers, is Quintilian's *Institutio Oratoria,* a work of great scholarship and genuine
human interest. These five arts in Cicero and Quintilian have an
elaborate subject matter, which cannot at this time be explained. Some
of this subject matter will become apparent as my discussion proceeds.
Most of it will have to be treated here in round terms, if space is to be
conserved for the main topics of this essay. It may for the moment be
sufficient to say that the first of these terms, Invention, stands for the
processes of analysis by which the speaker finds material for his
speeches, whereas the second term, Arrangement, means the processes
of synthesis or combination by which material is put into order for
presentation. The other terms, Style, Memory, and Delivery, have a
more obvious application to the speaker's total problem, and they need
not be made the subject of special explanation now.

Many English rhetorics in the period of my present discussion recognize these five terms of Ciceronian rhetoric as the major heads of the
theory of communication. Other English rhetorics recognize three or
four of these terms. Whenever these terms or a majority of them are
mentioned by Englishmen as the basic concepts of rhetorical theory,
and are then treated in such a way as to stress the priority of Invention
above the others, the rhetoric thus created becomes Ciceronian in the
present sense in which I am using the word.

This Ciceronian pattern of English rhetoric begins historically with
Alcuin, the first Englishman to compose a rhetorical work with Cicero's
five procedures explicitly enumerated and discussed in the traditional
way. Alcuin was born in the year 735, the date of Bede's death, and he
was educated in England under scholars who had known and admired
Bede. The fame of the new English learning, to which Bede had greatly
contributed, was recognized throughout Europe during the eighth century; so recognized, indeed, that Alcuin was invited at length to France

by Charlemagne, and there given the task of establishing a system of education for the emerging French nation. Alcuin's *De Rhetorica,* composed in Latin in the year 794 as a dialogue between himself and his royal patron, is one of the works he produced in carrying out his educational mission; [5] another is his *De Dialectica,* the first work by an Englishman on that subject.

Alcuin's *De Rhetorica* devotes most of its space to Invention, which Cicero had considered to be of overwhelming importance to oratory. Ciceronian Invention, as I suggested above, is the process by which a speaker analyzes his subject and thus determines the subject matter of his speech. This process involves several steps. One step consists in deciding whether the prospective speech is to be Ceremonial, Deliberative, or Forensic; this decision teaches the speaker whether to emphasize honor, expediency, or justice in his speech, and once he knows which of these to emphasize, he has some of the subject matter he needs. Another step consists in placing his prospective subject within one of the nine postures or positions that controversies occupy, to the end that he may use the lines of argument naturally available in that particular position. These nine positions cannot here be explained; but they involve the Latin concept of *constitutio* or *status,* and are in rhetorical theory equivalent to the concept of topics or places in dialectical theory as expounded in Cicero's *Topics* and Aristotle's similar work.[6] The third step in the process of devising subject matter for a speech consists in thinking of possible materials to be used in getting attention during the Introduction, and of possible materials to be used in each one of the other five standard parts of the classical oration. Now these three steps involve the largest part of Cicero's theory of rhetorical Invention; and Alcuin's *De Rhetorica* covers the subject of Invention in the same terms.

Alcuin gives almost no space to Arrangement, the second of the conventional topics, thanks to the fact that in Ciceronian theory Invention covers part of Arrangement by dealing with the six standard parts of the oration, and Style covers another part by dealing with the ordering of words in sentences. As for Style, Alcuin speaks of it in such fashion as to indicate only a fraction of that part of Ciceronian theory, but, even so, Style ranks next after Invention in the amount of space he devotes to it. He gives none of the lore of Memory as set forth in such works as the *Rhetorica ad Herennium;* he merely quotes Cicero's definition of it as given in *De Oratore,* and warns that it is improved by exercise and harmed by drunkenness. To Delivery, the fifth part of the Ciceronian system, Alcuin devotes about half as much space as he had given to Style. Thereafter he ends the dialogue by speaking briefly of the four cardinal virtues in relation to the Christian concept of love.

Alcuin's *De Rhetorica* is not merely a treatise based upon Cicero. It is rather an abridged edition of *De Inventione,* so far as its treatment of the first part of rhetoric is concerned; and a mosaic of phrases from *De Oratore* and *Orator,* so far as the other parts are concerned. These phrases from the two latter works probably came to Alcuin from Julius Victor, a rhetorician of the fourth century A. D., whose *Ars Rhetorica* bases itself more broadly in Ciceronian theory than does Alcuin's *De Rhetorica.*[7] Despite his unwillingness to venture away from his sources, Alcuin deserves credit for his skilful summary of the important parts of the ancient scheme. His *De Rhetorica* is an attractive little work, quite apart from the interest it holds as the first statement by an Englishman of the five procedures of Cicero's theory of communication.

"With the death of Alcuin," remarks Atkins, "the tradition of learning in England underwent a prolonged eclipse."[8] This observation applies with particular force to Ciceronian rhetoric, for it was several centuries after Alcuin that interest in the five procedures began to reassert itself. In fact, this interest does not seem to reappear among English writers until the early thirteenth century, when Geoffrey of Vinsauf used Cicero's terms as the basis of his *Poetria Nova.*[9] We shall have occasion later to examine Geoffrey's use of these terms in poetical theory when we discuss Stephen Hawes' *The Pastime of Pleasure,* a poetical work of the early sixteenth century, which also treats the art of poetry as a manifestation of Ciceronian rhetoric. Hawes is the first Englishman to make his own language deliver Cicero's five terms. This fact may remind us of the acceptance of English in the fourteenth century as the official medium of instruction in Britain[10]—a development which hastened the rise of vernacular learning.

Before we reach the sixteenth century and the complete vernacularization of Ciceronian rhetoric, a Latin work in Cicero's idiom should be mentioned as part of the history of rhetoric in England, even though its author was an Italian. This work, usually called the *Nova Rhetorica,* has the distinction of being the first work on rhetoric ever to be printed in England. It appeared at Caxton's press in Westminster about 1479; another edition dated 1480 bears the imprint of St. Albans, and is regarded as no doubt the first book to be printed at that press by Caxton's contemporary, "the Schoolmaster Printer."[11]

The *Nova Rhetorica* is the work of Lorenzo Guglielmo Traversagni. Traversagni was descended from a wealthy and noble family in Savona, Italy, and became a member of the Franciscan order in that town at the age of twenty. He received instruction and the title of doctor from his teachers at the monastery, one of whom was Francesco dalla Rovere, later Pope Sixtus IV. His active years were spent as a traveling scholar: he studied logic, philosophy, theology, and canon law at Padua and Bologna; he later lectured on theology at Cambridge, Paris, and Toulouse. It was during his sojourn at Cambridge that he composed his *Nova Rhetorica;* in fact, he tells us at the conclusion of that work of his having finished it July 6, 1478, at Cambridge. At that time he was fifty-six years of age. His teaching career in foreign parts ended at Toulouse when he was seventy. Thereafter he lived at the Franciscan monastery in his native Savona, where he spent his last years writing, teaching, collecting books, and bestowing benefactions upon his cloister. He died March 5, 1503, at the age of eighty-one, leaving behind many works in manuscript, and one published work, the *Nova Rhetorica.*[12]

The *Nova Rhetorica* is thoroughly Ciceronian in the sense in which that term is here being used. It contains an introduction and three books of doctrine. The introduction recalls the benefit, the splendor, and the glory conferred in past time upon wise men and great commonwealths by copiousness in speaking. The following books treat the five topics of Cicero's rhetoric. In Book I Invention is discussed as it pertains to the conventional six parts of the Forensic oration; and in the first pages of Book II, as it pertains to Deliberative and Ceremonial speaking. The topic of Arrangement occupies the closing pages of Book II. The final book is devoted mainly to Style, although Memory and Delivery are each given more than a merely perfunctory recognition. A student of English rhetoric describes the *Nova Rhetorica* as "scholastic in tone, with frequent reference to the fathers of the Church, as St. Bernard, St. Anselm, St. Basil, Beda, etc." [13] This remark applies particularly to Traversagni's analysis of Style, where by mentioning the fathers and by making frequent quotations from the Bible, he indicates the special applicability of pagan rhetoric to preaching.

Traversagni uses the terms of Ciceronian rhetoric in Cicero's native language, as Alcuin had done. Six years after Traversagni's death, those terms spoke English for the first time. As I mentioned before, the responsible agent in this development was Stephen Hawes' *Pastime of Pleasure,* an attractive allegory of learning written in verse and published in 1509.[14] The *Pastime* is modeled upon an earlier verse allegory in English, *The Court of Sapience,* which Hawes himself believed to be the work of Lydgate,[15] and which had been published by Caxton around 1481. There are two interesting differences between the treatment of rhetoric in the *Court* and in the *Pastime,* despite the influence of the former upon the latter. The *Court* devotes only six seven-line stanzas to rhetoric, whereas the *Pastime* devotes to that subject ninety-two seven-line stanzas; and the *Court* discusses rhetoric in stylistic terms, referring the reader meanwhile to Balbus de Janua's *Catholicon* and Geoffrey of Vinsauf's *Poetria Nova* for further information, whereas the *Pastime* discusses rhetoric in terms of the five procedures of the Ciceronian tradition, and uses the *Poetria Nova* for material relating to those terms. Thus the *Court* stands as the earliest English version of the philosophy behind stylistic rhetoric, and will be referred to again when I discuss that pattern. The *Pastime,* however, can claim to be the earliest version in English of the basic pattern which Alcuin and Traversagni had followed.

The *Pastime,* which runs to 5816 lines of verse arranged into forty-six chapters or cantos, tells the story of the poet, La Graunde Amoure, in quest of a beautiful lady, La Bell Pucell. The quest requires the poet to visit the Tower of Doctrine and the Tower of Chivalry on his way to the Tower Perilous, where dwells the lady. In the Tower of Doctrine he receives essential preparation for his quest in the form of instruction in the seven liberal arts, third of which is rhetoric. Lady "Rethoryke" instructs the poet in her art and with dramatic propriety gives him the sort of instruction that more befits the poet than the orator. Nevertheless, she explains her subject as if Cicero were outlining the steps in oratorical composition.[16]

First she speaks of "inuencyon." This she describes as the product of five faculties: common wit, imagination, fantasy, judgment, memory. Her description of these faculties does not depend upon anything from the accepted explanation of rhetorical Invention as set forth, for example, by Alcuin; for she is bent upon making rhetorical theory help in the composition of poetry as well as prose, or of poetry more than prose. Still, she keeps the name of rhetoric, and she sets forth the first division of her subject under the term sanctioned by Cicero.

The second division of her subject she calls "dysposycyon." Here she speaks of ways to organize narrative and argumentative compositions. *Narratio* is a standard part of the classical oration described in Ciceronian rhetoric, and the theory of *narratio* in oratory is applicable to poetry. Thus Lady "Rethoryke" is not outside Ciceronian rhetoric on this topic, although her emphasis is not upon oratory.

Her third topic is "elocucyon." She begins this as if she were going to enumerate and discuss the schemes and tropes of oratorical style; but she soon deserts this line of procedure and speaks instead of the theory of interpreting fables and figures so as to perceive the essential truth conveyed in them. Thus Style becomes for her the art of interpreting poetic fictions, not the art of clothing in language the arguments and persuasions of oratory.

"Pronuncyacyon," her next topic, is interesting as perhaps the first theory of oral reading or oral interpretation in the English language. She is thinking of the poet reciting his poems, not of the orator delivering a speech, and she proceeds accordingly.

Her final topic is "memoratyfe." The theory of memory, as set forth in the *Rhetorica ad Herennium* and usually mentioned and discussed in other works of the Ciceronian rhetorical tradition, involved the notion that the speaker could remember his speech by associating its ideas with a system of images of his own choosing, and by visualizing those images as arranged in a system of localities or places familiar to himself. Lady "Rethoryke" explains this ancient theory by suggesting that the "orature" associate the tales he wants to remember with appropriate images, and envisage those images as arranged within his leathern wallet. Her words are:

> Yf to the orature many a sundry tale
> One after other treatably be tolde
> Than sundry ymages in his closed male
> Eche for a mater he doth than well holde
> Lyke to the tale he doth than so beholde
> And inwarde a recapytulacyon
> Of eche ymage the moralyzacyon. . . .[17]

So does Lady "Rethoryke" combine the terms of Ciceronian rhetoric with the requirements of a poet's profession, as Geoffrey of Vinsauf had no doubt taught her to do by the *Poetria Nova*, and as the *Rhetorica ad Herennium* had in turn taught Geoffrey to do, when he decided to analyze the problem of poetic communication.

In his pioneering essay on sixteenth-century English rhetorics prefixed to his edition of Leonard Cox's *The Arte or Crafte of Rhethoryke*, Frederic Ives Carpenter implies that Caxton's translation of the *Mirrour of the World* is perhaps the first printed account of Cicero's five terms to appear in English.[18] The *Mirrour* appeared first around 1481, and in a second edition around 1490. If either of these editions had contained a discussion of rhetoric in Cicero's five terms, Carpenter's implication would be perfectly justified. But the discussion of rhetoric in the two fifteenth-century editions of the *Mirrour* amounts only to fifteen lines in Oliver H. Prior's reprint of those works,[19] and those lines are devoted to general comments on the relation between rhetoric and the moral and political sciences. It is in the third edition of the *Mirrour* that the account of rhetoric is expanded to include brief passages on "inuencion," "disposicion," and "eloquens," followed by some few comments on Memory and Delivery. These are the passages noticed by Carpenter; but they appeared first in print around 1527, and by that time Hawes' *Pastime* had been issued in its second edition. Caxton's *Mirrour* must be relegated to second place in numbering the appearances of Ciceronian rhetoric in English versions.

In third place belongs Leonard Cox's *The Arte or Crafte of Rhethoryke*, although in a sense it is first, for it is the earliest rhetorical schoolbook published in English, and it is the earliest systematic attempt to acquaint English readers with the original rhetorical content of the Ciceronian concept of Invention. Cox's *Rhethoryke* appeared in its first edition in London around 1529, and in its second edition at the same place in 1532.

At that time, Cox was a schoolmaster at Reading. As he himself informs us, he had been thinking long and hard on a way to occupy himself in the service of his patron, the Abbot Hugh Faringdon. He finally had decided, he says, that it would be best for young students if he wrote "some proper worke of the ryght pleasaunt and parsuadyble arte of Rhetoryke." [20] He envisaged rhetoric, he goes on, as "very necessary to all suche as wyll eyther be aduocates and proctoures in the lawe, or els apte to be sente in theyr prynces Ambassades or to be techars of goddes worde in suche maner as maye be moste sensible and accepte to their audience: And finally to all them that haue any thynge to prepose or to speke afore any companye, what someuer they be." [21] He believed, he adds, that there was "no scyence that is les taught." [22] Then he proceeds to remark upon the faults in a society unschooled in rhetoric.

In brief, Cox finds three such faults. First is rude utterance, which, when prevalent in legal speaking, impairs the client's cause. Second is inept disposition in sermons; this has the effect of confounding the hearer's memory. Great tediousness in discourse is third. Cox implies that this is very common, and that it arises from the speaker's lack of invention, order, and proper style. He adds that it ends in driving hearers away or putting them to sleep.

The remedy for these shortcomings, Cox implies, can be provided by proper instruction in rhetoric. His treatise, which, as he declares, is "partely traunslatyd out of a werke of Rhethoryke wrytten in the lattyn tongue, and partely compyled of myne owne," [23] provides that instruction. Incidentally, one Latin source acknowledged by Cox himself in his treatise is Cicero's *De Inventione*.[24] But, as Carpenter was the first to point out, Cox's real source is the *Institutiones Rhetoricae* of Melanchthon.[25]

Melanchthon's *Institutiones Rhetoricae* partitions rhetoric under the topics of Invention, Judgment, Disposition, and Style.[26] Now the second of these terms seems out of place in a treatise on Ciceronian rhetoric as I have been describing it. In actual fact, however, the term is not so much out of place as unnecessary. It appears to have come to Melanchthon from dialectical theory. In dialectical theory, as standardized by Cicero's *Topics* from Aristotle's similar work, there are two main topics, Invention and Judgment,[27] roughly parallel in intent to the first two procedures of Ciceronian rhetoric. It is never surprising when pieces of the machinery of dialectical invention and judgment turn up in treatises on rhetoric by disciples of Cicero. In fact, we shall observe later that pieces of the machinery of dialectical invention appear in Thomas Wilson's *Arte of Rhetorique*. Melanchthon's use of the word Judgment as a main process in rhetoric seems to be merely an illustration that a piece of the machinery of dialectical disposition has turned up where it does not belong if the concept of arrangement is meanwhile being recognized.

Cox defines rhetoric as having the four procedures enumerated by Melanchthon.[28] He limits himself to Invention, however, commenting both at the beginning and end of his work that Invention is the hardest of the four to master.[29] He takes the trouble to point out, moreover, that in thus limiting himself he has "folowed the facion of Tully who made a seuetall werke of inuencion."[30] Actually, of course, he treats Invention by speaking of it as in part the process of finding material for the divisions of the oration, with the result that his treatise, like Cicero's, covers Arrangement as well as Invention, despite its seeming limitation to the latter topic.

Cox mentions in a letter dated May 23, 1540, that he is planning a work on rhetoric to be called the *Erotemata Rhetorica*.[31] Possibly that would have been more complete than his *Rhethoryke;* possibly also it would have been a further translation from Melanchthon, since Cox's projected title suggests his desire to identify his work with the latter, who had entitled one of his works the *Erotemata Dialectices*. But Cox's second work on rhetoric appears never to have been published.

Next after Cox's *Rhethoryke* in the sequence of English versions of Ciceronian theory is Thomas Wilson's *The Arte of Rhetorique*, the greatest work in this tradition by an Englishman. Wilson produces a systematic, learned, and lively account of each of the five procedures of Cicero's theory of oratory. To Invention he devotes 68 per cent of his total space; to Arrangement, a little less than 2 per cent; to Style, slightly more than 21 per cent; to Memory, about 4 per cent; and to Delivery, about 2 per cent. These proportions are not greatly different from those in the *Rhetorica ad Herennium*, which gives 43 per cent of its space to *inventio*, 2 per cent to *dispositio*, 45 per cent to *elocutio*, 6 per cent to *memoria*, and 4 per cent to *pronuntiatio*.

In his study of the sources of Wilson's *Rhetorique*, Russell H. Wagner states that the *Rhetorica ad Herennium*, doubtless considered by Wilson to be Cicero's, was one of Wilson's chief authorities, and that Wilson also went to Erasmus "for leading ideals, for detailed matter, and for examples and critical dicta"; Wagner indicates, moreover, that Wilson draws to some extent upon Quintilian's *Institutio Oratoria*, upon Cicero's *De Inventione, De Oratore, De Partitione Oratoria*, and *Brutus*, and possibly also upon Cox's *Rhethoryke*.[32] To these sources I would want to add Richard Sherry's *A Treatise of Schemes and Tropes*, which

I shall discuss later as the first treatise in English on the actual terms of what is here being called stylistic rhetoric. Wilson relies upon Sherry for English phraseology or for illustrations in his discussion of the three kinds of style, in his definition of figure, of scheme, of *gradatio*, and in his clarification of such stylistic concepts as aptness, metaphor, metonymy, transumption, periphrasis, epenthesis, syncope, proparalepsis, apocope, *extenuatio*, and *dissolutum*.[33]

"The finding out of apt matter, called otherwise Inuention, is a searching out of things true, or things likely, the which may reasonablie set forth a matter, and make it appeare probable." [34] With these words Wilson opens his discussion of the first part of Ciceronian rhetoric. He adds at once, "The places of *Logique*, giue good occasion to finde out plentifull matter." These places, as set forth in Wilson's *Rule of Reason*, the first logic in English, are sixteen in number. They constitute in the aggregate a machinery for the analysis of dialectical questions, even as the nine positions of argument, to which reference was made in the discussion of Alcuin's *De Rhetorica*, constitute a machinery of analysis for rhetorical questions. Now Wilson does not expect the reader of his *Rhetorique* to make use of all sixteen of the places of logic in conducting a rhetorical analysis of a subject. He indicates instead that six of them are particularly helpful to the orator, and he enumerates those six.[35] In addition, he sets forth the nine positions associated traditionally with rhetoric, and discusses them.[36] Thus his discussion of Invention in rhetoric overlaps his discussion of Invention in dialectic—an untidiness that Ramus was at that very moment condemning as it had appeared in continental rhetorics earlier in the sixteenth century.

Wilson also permits his discussion of Arrangement to overlap Invention. Under Invention, as Cicero had sanctioned, Wilson discusses the standard parts of the classical oration, and the materials appropriate to each.[37] Thus when he comes to Arrangement, where the parts of the oration might logically be discussed, he sees that he has already said most of what is needed for this topic. He contents himself with a summary of what he had discussed as he spoke of the parts of the oration, and with a bit of advice on the necessity for constant discretion in arranging materials for audiences.[38]

This brief discussion of Wilson's *Rhetorique* will have to suffice at this time. It does scant justice to a work of ingenuity, good sense, and learning. It also does not even suggest how far Wilson went in naturalizing Ciceronian theory, and in giving it an English habitation and a name. It does not indicate how seriously Wilson looked at the English bar and pulpit of his time, and how vigorously he strove to make Ciceronian rhetoric applicable to their problems. Nor does it comment upon Wilson's analysis of the ancient memory system devised with special reference to oratory and explained in essential terms in the *Rhetorica ad Herennium*. Wilson gives this oddity of Roman times a noteworthy treatment and thus anglicizes it more completely than Hawes had done in the *Pastime of Pleasure*. Wilson also gives Style a noteworthy treatment as the third part of rhetoric. His famous protest against the use of dark words and "ynkehorne termes" [39] occurs in this part of his treatise. Style he defines attractively as follows: "Elocution getteth words to set forth inuention, and with such beautie commendeth the matter, that reason semeth to be clad in Purple, walking afore both bare and naked." [40] The true heads of his subsequent discussion are "Plainnesse," "Aptnesse," "Composition," "Exornation"; [41] and his analysis of each is much more than a perfunctory attempt to get Latin ideas into English. These and many other special points of distinction make Wilson's *Rhetorique* one of the great books in its field, and are reasons why I regret the brevity of this review of it.

Beginning in 1553, when it was first published in London, Wilson's *Rhetorique* enjoyed great popularity for an entire generation. It appeared in a second edition in 1560, in a third in 1562, in a fourth in 1563, and in a fifth in 1567. Then for a while there seems to have been a slackening market for it. But after a lapse of thirteen years, successive reprintings again occurred in 1580, 1584, and 1585. [42] By that time, the first English translation of the main terms of Ramistic rhetoric had just appeared, and Ramus' famous *Dialecticae Libri Duo* had been available in an English translation for eleven years. Thus the absence of interest in Thomas Wilson's *Rhetorique* after 1585 may be explained by the rise of interest in Ramus' reformed version of Ciceronian rhetorical and dialectical theory.

Thirty-six years after Wilson's *Rhetorique* had had what appears to be its last sixteenth-century edition, the tradition which it had so well represented was again revived. Its revival occurred in textbooks written in Latin for students in the public schools. Thus the circulation of the theory of Ciceronian rhetoric was confined in the early seventeenth century to the younger segment of the population of England, and to the atmosphere of the classroom and the study hall. Wilson had had more ambitious plans for his work, as anyone who reads it will notice.

The first seventeenth-century textbook devoted to the revival of Ciceronian rhetoric was written by Thomas Vicars and published at London in 1621 under a Greek and Latin title, the χειραγωγία *Manvdvctio ad Artem Rhetoricam*, that is, *Guide to the Art of Rhetoric*. In its first edition the *Guide* contained an enumeration and discussion of the five main procedures of Ciceronian rhetoric. A later edition dated 1628 at London adds a second book in which selected Ciceronian orations are analyzed according to the terms of the five procedures as set forth in Book I. The difference between the two parts of this 1628 work is indicated as that between the genesis of the oration and its analysis. The difference between rhetoric and logic is stated on the title page in a conceit based upon Zeno's ancient epigram: "Rhetorica est palmae similis, Dialectica pugno; Haec pugnat, palmam sed tamen illa refert." [43]

Two other Latin rhetorical handbooks appeared soon after that of Vicars. One was Thomas Farnaby's *Index Rhetoricus,* first published at London in 1625, and reprinted many times in the seventeenth century. It limits itself on its title page to the schools and to the instructing of those of the tenderer ages; its doctrine is set forth in terms of four of Cicero's five procedures, Memory being omitted altogether. Similar to it is William Pemble's *Enchiridion Oratorium,* that is, *Oratorical Manual,* published at Oxford in 1633,—except that Pemble limits himself to Invention and Arrangement, after recognizing rhetoric to consist of these two parts and Style and Delivery as well. [44]

Thus the Ciceronian rhetorical tradition was in being at the time of Harvard's first Commencement, even if it had tended after the great work of Thomas Wilson to be eclipsed by Ramistic rhetoric and to be revived later in the form of Latin manuals for schoolboys. Let us now examine the second pattern of English rhetoric, called here the stylistic, to see what had happened to it during the period between the seventh and the seventeenth century.

III

Stylistic rhetoric as a recognizable and distinctive tradition in rhetorical theory in England has two main characteristics. First of all, it is openly committed to the doctrine of Style as the most important part of the five-part scheme just discussed. Secondly, it is openly mindful that Invention, Arrangement, Memory, and Delivery, or combinations of two or more of these other parts of rhetoric, are also legitimate topics in the full rhetorical discipline. Readers of Cicero's *Orator* will recall that its major emphasis is upon Style, although it gives some degree of recognition to the other parts of rhetoric. [45] Thus the *Orator* is important as a source book in the history of stylistic rhetoric, although the fourth book of the *Rhetorica ad Herennium,* the third book of Cicero's *De Oratore,* and the eighth and ninth books of Quintilian's *Institutio Oratoria* all contain a full treatment of Style as the verbal aspect of the speaker's total problem, and all are sources of this or that work in the post-classical development of the rhetoric I am now describing.

The first treatise by an Englishman in the field of stylistic rhetoric is the Venerable Bede's *Liber de Schematibus et Tropis.* [46] Bede is presumed to have written this work in 701 or 702. [47] His immediate sources are chapters 36 and 37 of Book I of Isidore's *Etymologiae*,[48] where Isidore is discussing grammar on his way to a treatment of rhetoric and dialectic in Book II.[49] The fact that Bede's treatise on the schemes and tropes is taken from Isidore's *De Grammatica* rather than from his *De Rhetorica* might lead one to suppose that Bede is not to be classed among rhetoricians but among grammarians. Indeed, Halm admits Bede's *Liber* with great reluctance to a place in his collection of minor Latin rhetorics, saying that he would willingly have left it out if his plan did not seem to require him to accept all the items previously allowed within that particular tradition.[50] In other words, Halm seems embarrassed by the nonrhetorical content of the *Liber* and by the uncritical acceptance of that work as a rhetoric by his predecessors, Pithou and Capperonnier, both of whom had included it in their *Antiqui Rhetores Latini*. But students of the history of rhetoric have to accustom themselves not to be embarrassed when a given rhetoric contains material that appears elsewhere in grammars or dialectics. They have to learn to argue that, if Bede's definitions of the schemes and tropes come from a treatise on grammar by Isidore, and if Isidore in turn got those definitions in part from the grammars of Donatus and Charisius, one can nevertheless find the same materials in such still older works as the *Rhetorica ad Herennium* and the *Institutio Oratoria*. Thus Bede's *Liber* need not occasion apologies when we accept it among stylistic rhetorics.

The method followed by Bede in treating the schemes and tropes is simple: he enumerates seventeen schemes; he defines each and illustrates it from the Bible, except in one case, where his example is from the Christian poet Sedulius [51]; then he enumerates thirteen tropes, defining each later and illustrating again from the Bible. His guiding conception of these two big divisions of Style is clearly indicated in his opening words:

On many occasions in writings it is customary for the sake of elegance that the order of words as they are formulated should be contrived in some other way than that adhered to by the people in their speech. These contrivances the Greek grammarians call schemes, whereas we may rightly term them attire or form or figure, because through them as a distinct method speech may be dressed up and adorned. On other occasions, it is customary for a locution called trope to be devised. This is done by changing a word from its proper signification to an unaccustomed but similar case on account of necessity or adornment. And indeed the Greeks pride themselves upon having been the discoverers of such schemes and tropes.[52]

Bede does not deal with any other topics of the complete Ciceronian doctrine of style, nor does he specifically recognize in his *Liber* that Style is only one of the five parts of rhetoric. But he surely was well acquainted with the five-part division of Ciceronian rhetorical theory. He probably did not have any of Cicero's rhetorical writings in his own library, but he did of course have Isidore's *Etymologiae*,[53] and Isidore lists the five conventional parts of rhetorical theory in his own treatise on rhetoric a few pages beyond his disquisition on the schemes and tropes.

Stylistic rhetoric appears to have been the most popular form of rhetorical theory in England between the eighth and the fifteenth century. Space does not permit us to examine here the various Latin writings on this subject by Englishmen. A few representative authors should, however, be mentioned. One of the foremost is John of Salisbury, whose *Metalogicon,* as Atkins has observed, deals with rhetoric less as a matter of Invention and Arrangement than of Style.[54] Another is Geoffrey of Vinsauf. His *Poetria Nova,* as I indicated earlier, recognizes the five procedures of Ciceronian rhetoric and thus belongs to my first category; but his *Summa de Coloribus Rhetoricis* is plainly in the stylistic tradition.[55] Still another medieval Latin work in this tradition by an Englishman is John of Garland's *Exempla Honestae Vitae,* which Atkins describes as "a text-book treating of the use of the rhetorical figures." [56] These are all works in a class with Bede's *Liber,* and they were produced at a time when the full Ciceronian theory of rhetoric was being little used, except by Geoffrey of Vinsauf as the framework for a treatise on poetry.

The first printed English account of the stylistic aspect of rhetoric occurred around 1481 with the publication at Caxton's press in Westminster of a learned poetic allegory, *The Court of Sapience,*[57] to which I have already made brief reference as a work which influenced Hawes and was attributed by Hawes to John Lydgate. Modern scholarship doubts that Lydgate wrote the *Court,* but not that Hawes imitated it. As I said of it earlier, however, its treatment of rhetoric is briefer than that in Hawes' work, and more in the stylistic tradition.

The *Court* recounts the poet's dream of a journey under the guidance of Sapience. The final stages of the journey take the poet to the castle of Sapience, where he visits the seven ladies, that is, the seven liberal arts. Six seven-line stanzas are devoted to "Dame Rethoryke, Modyr of Eloquence," or as a Latin headnote has it, to a "breuis tractatus de Rethorica." [58] This brief tractate does not consist in an enumeration of the schemes and tropes. But it does characterize Dame Rhetoric as if her chief concern were the stylistic aspects of composition. Thus the function of rhetoric is described as that of teaching what vices in style to avoid, what gay colors are included in the rhetorician's knowledge of his craft, what differences there are among these colors, what properties they have, how each thing declared may be painted, what distinctions

exist between "coma, colon, periodus," [59] and what works may be consulted for information about the colors. Cicero is called "The chosyn
spowse vnto thys lady fre"; in his works is found "Thys gyltyd craft of
glory"; other authors who would teach of the colors are "Galfryde" and
"Januense," that is, Geoffrey of Vinsauf and Balbus de Janua, the latter
of whom is mentioned especially for the fourth book of his *Catholicon*.[60]
It is specifically indicated that the springs of eloquence are in sound
knowledge of the Code, the three Digests, the books of law and of
natural philosophy—a recognition, of course, of the underlying importance of Invention in the theory of discourse. The closing stanza gives
Dame Rhetoric jurisdiction over "prose and metyr," and lists those who
have excelled in each of these forms.

It was almost seventy years after the first edition of the *Court,* when
the sixteenth century had reached its midpoint, that the schemes and
tropes of the stylistic tradition appeared for the first time in the English
language. The work which features them thus is Richard Sherry's *A
Treatise of Schemes and Tropes,* published at London in 1550. As I have
already indicated, this work influenced the phraseology and illustrations
of Thomas Wilson's treatment of Style in his famous *Rhetorique* published three years later, as one pioneering work is likely to influence
another if the later author has access to the earlier.

Sherry realized that his work was something new in the English
literary tradition—that it had no vernacular prototype. In fact, his dedicatory epistle "To the ryght worshypful Master Thomas Brooke Es-
quire" anticipates a public reaction made up of initial bewilderment:

I doubt not but that the title of this treatise all straunge vnto our Englyshe
eares, wil cause some men at the fyrst syghte to maruayle what the matter of
it should meane: yea, and peraduenture if they be rashe of iudgement, to cal
it some newe fangle, and so casting it hastily from them, wil not once vouch
safe to reade it: and if they do, yet perceiuynge nothing to be therin that
pleaseth their phansy, wyl count it but a tryfle, and a tale of Robynhoode.[61]

"These words, *Scheme* and *Trope*," he goes on, "are not vsed in our Englishe tongue, neither bene they Englyshe wordes." [62] I got acquainted
with them, he says later, when I read them to others in Latin (Sherry
was a schoolmaster in Magdalene College school in Oxford from 1534
to 1540); and, he declares, since they helped me very much in the
exposition of good authors, "I was so muche the more ready to make
them speak English." [63] He wants them to speak English, moreover,
because the English language is being enriched, English literature is
becoming famous, and English learning needs these terms. It needs
them especially because "no lerned nacion hath there bene but ȳ
learned in it haue written of schemes & fygures, which thei wold not
haue don, except thei had perceyued the valewe." [64]

On three occasions Sherry makes it plain that he is dealing with Style, not as the only part of rhetoric, but as the third part in the traditional Ciceronian pattern. The first occasion arises when he reminds serious readers that it is their obligation to know the schemes and tropes:

For thys darre I saye, no eloquente wryter maye be perceiued as he shulde be, wythoute the knowledge of them: for asmuche as al togethers they belonge to Eloquucion, whyche is the thyrde and pryncipall parte of rhetorique.[65]

The second occasion arises when he has finished his dedicatory letter and is about to begin his treatise. The following headnote at this point carries us into the text:

Schemes and Tropes. A briefe note of eloquciō, the third parte of Rhetoricke, wherunto all Figures and Tropes be referred.[66]

On the third occasion, Sherry mentions explicitly two of the other procedures of Ciceronian rhetoric that lie adjacent to style. Tully and Quintilian, he says at this point, thought that Invention and Arrangement were marks of prudence and wit in any kind of composition, but that Style was the peculiar mark of the orator as man of eloquence.[67]

As for the theory behind the schemes and tropes, Sherry takes the same position that Bede had taken: that there is a normal, plain, and ordinary way of speaking, used among the populace, and an unusual, uncommon, extraordinary way, used among the elegant and educated. This latter way is described by the schemes and the tropes, taken collectively. These contrivances amount to all possible extraordinary patterns of language which men can devise as a system of substitutes for pedestrian, everyday patterns. Here are Sherry's key definitions:

Scheme is a Greke worde, and signifyeth properlye the maner of gesture that daunsers vse to make, when they haue won the best game, but by translacion is taken for the fourme, fashion, and shape of anye thynge expressed in wrytynge or payntinge; and is taken here now of vs for the fashion of a word, sayynge, or sentence, otherwyse wrytten or spoken then after the vulgar and comen vsage. . . .[68]

Fygure, of Scheme ȳ fyrst part, is a behaueoure, maner, or fashion, eyther of sentence, oracion, or wordes after some new wyse, other then men do commenlye vse to wryte or speake . . . .[69]

Emonge authors manye tymes vnder the name of figures, Tropes also be comprehended: Neuerthelesse ther is a notable difference betwixt them. In figure is no alteracion in the wordes from their proper significacions, but only is the oracion and sentence made by them more plesaunt, sharpe and vehement, after ȳ affeccion of him that speketh or writeth: to ȳ which vse although tropes also do serue, yet properlye be they so called, because in them for necessitye or garnyshynge, there is a mouynge and chaungynge of a worde and sentence, from theyr owne significacion into another, whych may agre wyth it by a similitude.[70]

A change from the common pattern—this, then, is the concept behind the schemes and the tropes. Thus if one says, "I was berattled," instead of "I was rattled," he has changed the common pattern of a word without changing its literal meaning, and the scheme thus created is called *Prosthesis* or *Appositio.*[71] The purpose of this scheme is to call strong attention to one's thought (or one's self) by adding some unusual element to a familiar pattern. Now if one says, "I have but lately tasted the Hebrew tongue," he has taken the word *taste* from its routine orbit and transferred it to a different but analogous orbit, with the result that the change thus produced, which constitutes a trope called *Metaphora,* also calls memorable attention to one's thought.[72]

It would be suggestive to speculate upon a theory of communication which emphasizes that true excellence is achieved only by a departure from the natural pattern of everyday speech. That theory would appear to be congenial to a society in which the holders of power and privilege are hereditary aristocrats, who do not have to use speech to gain anything for themselves. In such a society, the commoners, who do have to use speech as one of their instruments in the quest for privilege, would consider that the unusual pattern of communication might impress the aristocrat and distinguish the commoners from the herd. Perhaps considerations like these explain the enormous popularity of the schemes and tropes as an element in education in the sixteenth century.

Sherry's treatment of the schemes and tropes is orderly and thorough. I shall not have time, however, to comment further upon it here. It might be mentioned as I leave it that Sherry is quite explicit about the sources upon which his work is based. He speaks in his dedicatory letter of having prepared himself for his present task by reading sundry treatises, some written long ago, and some in his own day.[73] He declares that these he did not translate but drew upon.[74] From the authors explicitly mentioned by him then and later, it would appear that he places primary reliance upon such modern works as Rudolphus Agricola's *De Inventione Dialectica,* Petrus Mosellanus' *Tabulae de Schematibus et Tropis,* Thomas Linacre's *Rudimentes Grammatices,* and Erasmus' *De Duplici Copia Verborum ac Rerum;* whereas for the ancients he goes to Quintilian's *Institutio Oratoria,* to Cicero's *Orator, De Oratore,* and *De Partitione Oratoria,* and to Aristotle's *Topics* and *Rhetoric.*

Sherry uses at one point in his *Treatise* the image of a man getting true pleasure from a goodly garden garnished with flowers only when he knows the names and properties of what he sees therein.[75] This image may have suggested something to Henry Peacham. At any rate, Peacham published at London in 1577 a work in the same field as Sherry's entitled *The Garden of Eloquence Conteyning the Figures of Grammer and Rhetorick.* This work is more extensive than the one just discussed, more extensive, too, than Sherry's revised edition of 1555, published at London as *A Treatise of the Figures of Grammer and Rhetorike* [76]; and it represents English stylistic rhetoric in full maturity.

Now, the *Garden of Eloquence* draws heavily upon Sherry's earlier work, particularly upon the first edition. Space does not permit me to set forth passages in Peacham that have a counterpart in Sherry. The reader who wishes to assure himself of the similarity between Sherry's edition of 1550 and Peacham's work might compare the discussion of Expolition in the one treatise with that in the other.[77] As for the similarity between Sherry's revised edition and Peacham's work, the reader might compare what the former and what the latter say about Partition.[78] These resemblances indicate, of course, that Peacham and Sherry are in the same rhetorical tradition, and must be considered together. But the one thing that brings them finally together, and dissociates them forever from the Ramists, who were then coming into fashion, is that Sherry and Peacham treat the schemes and tropes as in part the concern of grammar and in part the concern of rhetoric, whereas the Ramists, as we shall see, insisted that grammar and rhetoric must not be allowed to overlap, and that the schemes and tropes belonged only to rhetoric.

Two other stylistic rhetorics in the tradition of Sherry and Peacham were composed in the last decade of the sixteenth century. Incidentally, a second edition of Peacham appeared in 1593, and may be taken as evidence of the continuing interest in his elaborate work. But a more popular work in his field appeared at London in 1592 with the publication of a new and augmented edition of Angel Day's *The English Secretorie*. This enlarged edition of a work which had first come out six years before contained a treatise on the tropes, figures, and schemes. Day is no Ramist; he allows the schemes to be shared by grammar as well as by rhetoric. But for those who wanted the tropes and figures without the special context and treatment required by the Ramists, Day's work was as good as any other, and it continued to be reprinted during the next forty-five years.

The last stylistic rhetoric to require mention here is John Hoskins' *Directions for Speech and Style*. This work is believed to have been composed in the year 1599; portions of it were embedded in Ben Jonson's *Timber* (1641), and a large part of it was printed without acknowledgment in Thomas Blount's *Academie of Eloquence* (1654) and in John Smith's *Mysterie of Rhetorique Unvail'd* (1657); but it did not achieve an edition under its own author's name until 1935, when the late Professor Hoyt H. Hudson brought it out in company with an excellent introduction and notes.[79] Like other rhetoricians in the stylistic tradition, Hoskins emphasizes the tropes and figures; but he does not do so

in the manner of the Ramists, for they would not permit recognition of
Invention and Disposition as parts of rhetoric, whereas Hoskins cheer-
fully begins with a nod at these two procedures. Hoskins might have
been expected to be a Ramist, too; Talaeus, Ramus' close collaborator,
and Sturm, the teacher of Ramus, are the only two modern authorities
whom he names in the list of authors used by him as sources.[80]

In the period between 1599 and 1642, four successive editions of
Angel Day's *English Secretorie* testify to the continuing interest of
Englishmen in stylistic rhetoric. But the tropes and figures, as a main
ingredient of that rhetoric, had meanwhile been appropriated by the
Ramists, as I have already suggested, and as I shall have occasion later
to discuss. Thus at the time of the first Commencement at Harvard,
only an acute observer, aware of the history of rhetoric during the hundred years just past, would have been able to disentangle the old
stylistic rhetoric from the newer Ramistic rhetoric and to explain the
differences between them. But the fact is that, even if the old stylistic
rhetoric of Bede, Sherry, and Peacham had merged with Ramistic
rhetoric by 1642, the stylistic tradition itself in its substantive aspect
was at that date still very much alive, thanks to the special help it had
had from the Ramists.

✗ IV

The formulary pattern of English rhetoric before 1642 has to be mentioned by any historian of early rhetorical theory in England who is
striving to tell his story completely. Yet that historian also has to
acknowledge that of all segments of the English theory of communication, formulary rhetoric was the least popular, so far, at any rate, as the
sixteenth and early seventeenth century are concerned.

In essence, formulary rhetoric in the period now under consideration
is illustrated by those works which consist of a series of model compositions or model parts of compositions for guiding students in the practice of communication.

Rhetorical education has always rested upon the assumption that
practice in communication is necessary for the development of proficiency, and that practice must involve experience with the typical
patterns of communication in civilized life. Sometimes rhetorical practice is regulated in the classroom by the study of models, sometimes by
the study of rhetorical theory, and occasionally by the whims and
vagaries of instructor or student. This third method of regulation is
usually permitted only in education as a private venture or in public
education at the higher levels of instruction. The second method of
regulation, where the study of theory accompanies practice, is perhaps

the most widely used of all methods on the middle and upper levels of the educational process. The patterns of theory which I am explaining in this paper are all relevant to this second method. The first method, that of regulating practice by the study of models, is usually most popular on the lower levels of instruction or in the elementary phases of the mastery of the act of communication. Thus formulary rhetorics, which implement this method, ordinarily envisage the schoolboy as their reader, and ordinarily involve rhetorical theory only so far as a few basic terms are necessary in giving directions for schoolboy practice.

Formulary rhetoric is of course a part of the two streams of rhetorical theory just discussed. Thomas Wilson's *Rhetorique,* for example, contains model compositions to illustrate the theory of such standard communications as the deliberative discourse, the letter of consolation, and the legal argument.[81] The same impulse to provide models in connection with theoretical terms is shown by Richard Sherry, who attaches to his *Treatise of Schemes and Tropes* a "declamacion of a briefe theme, by Erasmus of Roterodame." [82]

Formulary rhetoric as an entity by itself begins to be a vernacular development in England in the second quarter of the sixteenth century. At first, however, it is a thing of shreds and patches, not a full-grown pattern. Its beginnings are found in several popular collections of passages from the classics as published at English presses: Nicholas Udall's translation of excerpts from Terence, called *Floures for Latine Spekynge* (London, 1533); Richard Taverner's translation of selections from the *Apophthegmata* of Erasmus, called *The Garden of Wysdom* (London, 1539); the same Taverner's translations from the *Chiliades* of Erasmus, called *Prouerbes or Adagies* (London, 1539). These collections, however, are more in the nature of commonplace books than of formulary rhetorics. Their interest is centered in the thoughts conveyed by the passages they contain, not in the rhetorical forms illustrated by those passages. Moreover, they were probably often used as reference books by preachers and writers in search of classical utterances on common topics, and thus they would be more of a guide to the content than to the method of a given discourse. The true formulary rhetoric differs from them in having its interest centered in rhetorical forms, and in having its selections cover a variety of occasions for discourse.

The first fully developed formulary rhetoric to appear in English, and the best example of this type of rhetoric in the period here under discussion, is Richard Rainolde's *Foundacion of Rhetorike.*[83] This work, as Professor Johnson has shown, is mainly an English adaptation of Reinhard Lorich's Latin version of Aphthonius' *Progymnasmata.*[84] Aphthonius is one of the three great names in the field of ancient formulary rhetoric, the others being Theon and Hermogenes.[85] Theon is supposed to have lived in the first half of the second century A. D.; Hermogenes, in the second half of the same century; and Aphthonius, towards the end of the fourth century. Not Aphthonius alone, but all of them, composed works called *Progymnasmata* for rhetorical instruction.[86]

Rainolde, like Sherry, sees himself as a pioneer in his particular field. But it is Wilson and not Sherry to whom he refers as he speaks in his preface "To the Reader" of himself as innovator. He begins this preface with mention of Aphthonius and Hermogenes, among others. He then says that he has prepared the present work "because as yet the verie grounde of Rhetorike, is not heretofore intreated of, as concernyng these exercises, though in fewe yeres past, a learned woorke of Rhetorike is compiled and made in the Englishe toungue, of one, who floweth in all excellencie of arte, who in iudgement is profounde, in wisedome and eloquence moste famous."

Rainolde's method of procedure in his work is to provide orations upon the typical patterns of discourse. Before he does this, however, he makes a few introductory comments. His distinction between logic and rhetoric follows that in Thomas Wilson's *The Rule of Reason* and amounts, as Wilson's had, to an expansion of Zeno's epigram about logic being the closed fist and rhetoric the open hand.[87] Few, he observes, possess both of these arts to perfection; those who do are most noble and excellent. He names the famous orators of Greece and Rome, and after some comment upon them he returns to Demosthenes, whom he recalls as having once framed an oration upon a fable.[88] This leads him to define fables, to distinguish three types of them, and to comment upon their use by orators and poets.[89] He mentions Bishop Morton as using a fable of Aesop to answer his jailer, Buckingham; also Bishop Fisher as using one in a speech in Parliament.[90] Then he indicates that an oration may be made upon a fable, and upon the following other patterns: a Narration, a *Chria*, a Sentence, a Refutation, a Proof, a Commonplace, a Praising, a Dispraising, a Comparison, an *Ethopeia*, a Description, a Thesis, and a Law.[91] Making orations upon these patterns, he goes on, is called "of the Grekes *Progimnasmata*, of the Latines, profitable introduccions, or fore exercises, to attain greater arte and knowlege in *Rhetorike*. . . ." [92] "Therefore," he adds, "I title this booke, to bee the foundaciō of *Rhetorike*, the exercises being *Progimnasmata*." [93]

The exercises which follow are model speeches upon each of the fourteen patterns previously enumerated. There are two speeches to illustrate the Fable; five to illustrate Narration; and one to illustrate each of the other patterns. Some of the model speeches run to

nine or ten pages; others, to six or eight; the shortest, to a half-page.
Each model is preceded by comments on the composition of that particular form. Also, most models are divided into clearly marked sections or parts. The speech to illustrate Refutation, for example, is on the
subject, "It is not like to be true, that is said of the battaill of Troie," [94]
and it is divided into six parts. The first censures all poets as liars; the
second states Homer's theory of the cause of the Trojan war; the third
reduces that theory to a matter of doubt; the fourth, to an incredibility;
the fifth, to an impossibility and an unlikelihood; and the sixth, makes
out Homer's explanation of the cause of the war to be an unseemly and
unprofitable notion.

Rainolde's *Foundacion,* published in 1563, appears not to have had
a second edition until 1945, the date of Professor Johnson's facsimile
reprint. Nevertheless, interest in formulary rhetoric did not completely
disappear in England during the closing years of the sixteenth century.
Angel Day's *The English Secretorie,* already mentioned as a stylistic
rhetoric of the fifteen-nineties, is also a formulary rhetoric by virtue of
the fact that it contains specimens of the various kinds of letters
expected of a practicing secretary. Two other works of the last decade
of the sixteenth century must likewise be remembered as collections of
exercises for speakers and writers. One of these works is Anthony
Mundy's *The Defence of Contraries* (London, 1593); the other, Lazarus
Piot's *The Orator* (London, 1596).

Mundy's *Defence of Contraries,* which declares itself in the preface
to be designed to show lawyers how to assemble proofs in support of
causes ordinarily considered indefensible, contains twelve declamations
on themes antagonistic to common opinion. In the first declamation,
poverty is held to be better than riches; in the second, beauty is proved
inferior to ugliness; in the third, ignorance is given a higher rating than
knowledge; in the seventh, drunkenness is declared better than sobriety;
and so on. Following the index of contents at the end of the work is "A
Table of such Paradoxes, as are handled in the Second Volume, which
vpon the good acceptation of this first Booke, shall the sooner be published." The fourteenth and last declamation in this projected volume
promises to uphold the thesis "that a Lawyer is a most profitable member in a Commonwealth." Apparently, however, Mundy never added
these fourteen declamations to his original twelve. The entire group of
twenty-six paradoxes, as Mundy knew them, were in a work published
at Paris in 1553 under the title, *Paradoxes, ce sont propos contre la
comune opinion, debatus en forme de declamations forēses: pour exer-
citer les jeunes aduocats en causes difficiles.* But Mundy may not have
known that this French work was a translation by Charles Estienne of
twenty-six of the thirty declamations which had been originally com-

posed in Italian by Ortensio Landi and published at Lyons in 1543 as *Paradossi cioè sententie fuori del comun parere.*

Lazarus Piot's *The Orator,* like Mundy's *Defence of Contraries,* is an importation from abroad. Its title page indicates that it was "written in French by Alexander Siluayn, and Englished by L. P." Siluayn turns out to be Alexandre van den Busche; the French work in question turns out to be *Epitomes de Cent Histoires Tragicques;* and "L. P." is identified in the dedicatory letter of *The Orator* as Lazarus Piot. Until recently, scholarship has considered Piot to be Anthony Mundy, and *The Orator* to be an expansion of the *Defence of Contraries.* But in actual fact, as Celeste Turner has shown in her *Anthony Mundy An Elizabethan Man of Letters,* Piot was a literary rival of Mundy in the field of translating, and *The Orator* does not bear the slightest relation to the *Defence of Contraries,* except that both works are formulary rhetorics. Piot's *The Orator* contains a preface "To the Reader" introducing his hundred "Rhethoricall Declamations," and asserting that their use by "euery member in our Commonweale, is as necessary, as the abuse of wilfull ignorance is odious." He then specifies the readers whom he wants for his declamations: "If thou studie law, they may helpe thy pleadings, or if diuinitie (the reformer of law) they may perfect they [sic] persuasions. In reasoning of priuate debates, here maiest thou find apt metaphors, in incouraging thy souldiours fit motiues." The hundred declamations that make up Piot's collection are organized thus: the number and title of the declamation are first given; then in italic type is a brief statement of its occasion; then in roman type is the declamation in two parts, one part being the speech made in accusation, the other, the speech made in reply. Declamation 95 will serve to illustrate how the two speeches relate to each other in every one of the exercises. In the first speech of this Declamation, a Jew contests a judicial ruling that he must on pain of death take no more or no less than an exact pound of flesh as bond for the debt which a Christian had not paid on the proper date. The other speech, by the Christian, claims that the original bond should not be required because of his present willingness to pay the debt in money. Declamation 95 is of interest to Shakespearean scholars, some of whom suggest that Shakespeare derived hints from it for his famous scene in *The Merchant of Venice,* and that the earliest possible date of composition of that play may thus be fixed at 1596, when Piot's *The Orator* was published.

In the forty-six years between 1596 and 1642, formulary rhetorics in the tradition of Rainolde, Mundy, and Piot appear to have gained more of a foothold in English secondary education than they had been able to do previously. I shall enumerate the chief works in this growing movement towards the use of the rhetorical model, although the discussion of them must await another occasion. Perhaps first in time was John Clarke's *Transitionum Rhetoricarum Formulae, in Usum Scholarum* (London, 1628). But the same author's *Formulae Oratoriae,* which had reached a fourth edition by 1632, appears to have been the most influential work in the field of formulary rhetoric in the period before the first Commencement at Harvard. Thomas Farnaby's *Index Rhetoricus,* already mentioned in connection with the revival of interest in Ciceronian rhetoric during the first half of the seventeenth century, should now be listed among formulary rhetorics of that period; for by 1633 the *Index* had acquired a section of "Formulae Oratoriae" to go with its exposition of four of the topics of Cicero's theory. The third and last of the formulary rhetorics to require mention here is Thomas Horne's χειραγωγία *sive Manuductio in Aedem Palladis* (London, 1641). This little book of 175 pages of text contains a general introduction on reading and writing, a series of rhetorical precepts, and a concluding section of "Exemplaria." It would seem to be the final illustration of formulary rhetoric in the period under survey here.

V

Between 1584 and 1642, the Ramistic pattern of rhetoric and of dialectic constituted the dominant theory of communication in England; and of all the theories under discussion here, it is the one which the first graduating class at Harvard understood best. We shall see later why it can be confidently asserted that that first graduating class understood best the Ramistic theory of communication. Just now it is more to the point to observe that Ramistic rhetoric and dialectic, so much a matter of intimate knowledge on the part of the educated Englishman of the period of Marlowe, Shakespeare, and Jonson, became obsolete at the end of the seventeenth century, and dropped out of sight altogether, with the result that even historians of literary theory did not until recently begin to recognize how important Ramus' version of these two arts was in its own time.[95]

The Ramistic theory of communication means two things. It means first that the three liberal arts, grammar, rhetoric, and dialectic, are severely departmentalized, and separated one from another, so that materials formerly claimed by two of them are made the exclusive and final property of one or the other. It means secondly that each of these liberal arts is arranged for the reader or student so that he encounters first the definition of the art he is mastering, then a statement dividing it into two main parts, then a treatise on one of those parts, and then a treatise on the other, each main part being divided and subdivided in its turn until finally the foundation terms and illustrations are set forth.

The first of these characteristics of Ramism can be seen in any Ramistic grammar, dialectic, and rhetoric of the period under discussion here. A Ramistic grammar is always divided into two parts, Etymology and Syntax. A Ramistic dialectic is always divided into two parts, Invention and Arrangement. A Ramistic rhetoric is always divided into two parts, Style and Delivery. Never, as in the old stylistic pattern of English rhetoric, did the Ramists permit tropes and figures to be classed as grammatical and rhetorical, for that kind of thinking suggested an untidy duplication between grammar and rhetoric, as if distinctions had become blurred and confused. Never, as in the system of scholastic learning, did the Ramists permit rhetoricians to write upon Invention and Arrangement, since that would mean a duplication between their art and dialectic, which, as we noticed earlier, also claimed Invention and Arrangement as its own. Never, as in the old Ciceronian theory of rhetoric, did the Ramists allow the theory of the parts of an oration to be covered under the topic of Invention, since that would sanction a theft by Invention of materials belonging properly to the topic of Arrangement.

The second of the two main characteristics of Ramism is also obvious in treatises on the three liberal arts in the late sixteenth and early seventeenth century. The best place to look for an illustration of this characteristic is in Ramus' own *Dialectique,* which was published at Paris in 1555 as his French version of the system also stated in his *Dialecticae Libri Duo* (Paris, 1556). The text proper of the *Dialectique* begins with a definition: Dialectic is the art of disputing well. Next comes a brief comment on this definition, with citations from Plato and Aristotle. Next comes the partition: Dialectic has two parts, Invention and Arrangement. Each of these terms is at once defined, the definitions crisply discussed, and the lines of difference between them established. Invention is then made to assume the duty of explaining what arguments are and where they dwell. Arguments are then classified as artificial or inartificial; artificial arguments are divided into the primary and the derivative primary; primary arguments are at once given four species; the first species is at once given four aspects. Now, these four aspects constitute the first cluster of Ramus' foundation terms. By this time we have reached page 6 of a treatise which runs to 140 pages, and Ramus' analysis of the forms of argument is ready to begin. The rest of this work is as severely schematized as the part I have just described. Divisions of material are always enumerated with mathematical precision; transitions are always marked, although abruptly, and without grace; illustrations for each basic term appear with the regularity of the refrain at the end of stanzas of a song.

These two characteristics of Ramism are derived from laws which

Ramus thought to be the great controlling principles of the philosophy of learning. He applied these principles in the first instance to the relations between subject and predicate in any given logical proposition,[96] because of course the logical proposition was the form in which knowledge got itself expressed, and thus the laws governing those propositions were in reality the very determinants of knowledge. But as time went on, these principles came to be applied to the relations between one statement and another in a given structure of statements. In this latter environment these principles are customarily called by the Ramists the law of justice, the law of truth, and the law of wisdom.[97]

The law of justice is perhaps best explained as a prohibition against allowing a learned treatise to deal with more than one field of knowledge. Thus if the subject of a treatise is logic, no statements belonging to rhetoric or grammar should be made therein. The law of truth is a prohibition against allowing a learned treatise to contain statements only partly true or true only on occasion. A statement on dialectic in a treatise on dialectic, for example, must not be subject to exceptions or to occasional applications to other disciplines. The law of wisdom is a prohibition against allowing a learned treatise to be a disorderly mixture of general principles, particular statements, and specific cases. Definitions, which by nature are general, belong, that is, on one plane, Partitions on a lower, Subdivisions on a still lower, and so on.

Roland MacIlmaine, first Briton to translate Ramus' dialectical theory into English, prefaced that work with an "Epistle to the Reader," in which he shows the exuberance of the Ramists as they contemplated the workings of their master's three rules upon Aristotelian dialectic and upon what I have been calling here the Ciceronian theory of rhetoric. My little book, says MacIlmaine, contains all the logical doctrine to be found anywhere in Aristotle, and all the logical doctrine to be found anywhere in Cicero or Quintilian.[98] Here are the words used by MacIlmaine to describe how the application of Ramus' three rules to the logical and rhetorical writings of these three great ancients will result in a reformed dialectic or logic:

Take the forenamed bookes, and with thy rule of iustice geue to euery arte his owne, and surely if my iudgement dothe not farre deceaue me, thou must geue some thing to the Arte of Grammer, some thing to Rethoricke, some thing to the fower mathematicall artes, Arithemeticke, Geometrie, Astrologie and Musicke, some thing also (althoughe but litle) to Phisicke, naturall Philosophie, and diuinitie. And yet all that is in these bookes (only the fore said digressions excepted) dothe appartaine eyther to the inuention of Logicke, or els to the iudgemente. Now gather togeather that wich remainethe, after euery arte hathe receiued his owne, and see if there be any false, ambiguous or vncertein thing amongest it, and yf there be (as in dede there is some) take thy document of veritie, and put out all suche sophis-

ticall speakinges. And last perceiue if all thinges be handled according to
their nature, the generall generallye, and the particuler particulerlie, if not,
take thy rule of wysdome, and do according as the third documente teach-
ethe thee: abolyshe all tautalogies and vayne repetitions, and so thus muche
being done, thou shalt comprehende the rest into a litle rome.[99]

Now, Ramus' reformed rhetoric, which began on the assumption that
Invention and Arrangement belonged to dialectic, and continued on the
assumption that Style and Delivery were purely and properly rhetorical,
was written out by his good friend and colleague, Audomarus Talaeus,
as I indicated earlier. Talaeus' rhetorical system, published at Paris in
1544 as the *Institutiones Oratoriae,* and later as the *Rhetorica,* accepts
explicitly these two assumptions of Ramus,[100] and proceeds to reduce
Style as the first part of the new rhetoric to Tropes and Figures, whereas
Delivery, the second part of the new rhetoric, is made to consist of
Voice and Gesture. In this form the rhetorical aspect of Ramus' theory
of communication was introduced into England.

The story of Ramus' influence upon English rhetoric has already been
sketched in another place,[101] and only a few points need be repeated
here. One is that, after MacIlmaine gave Ramus' *Dialecticae Libri Duo*
its first Latin edition on English soil in 1574, and its first English translation that same year, Ciceronian rhetoric went into an eclipse in England for a half-century, its ancient procedures being carried on in part
by Ramistic dialectic and in part by Ramistic rhetoric.[102] Another point
to be remembered is that many other Englishmen besides MacIlmaine
had an important role in making the Ramistic theory of communication
popular in England before 1642. Chief among these are Dudley Fenner,
Abraham Fraunce, Charles Butler, Samuel Wotton, Thomas Spencer,
Alexander Richardson, Robert Fage, and John Barton.

Dudley Fenner's importance lies in the fact that his *Artes of Logike
and Rethorike,* published anonymously at a continental press in Mid-
delburg in 1584, and in a second edition under Fenner's name at the
same place four years later, is the first one-volume English translation
of the main heads both of Ramus' *Dialecticae Libri Duo* and Talaeus'
Rhetorica. Fenner does not acknowledge his work as a translation of
these two authors, an indication, no doubt, that, to all of his contemporaries at all interested in logic and rhetoric, such an acknowledgment
would be superfluous.

Abraham Fraunce is important as the second English translator of
the main heads of both the *Dialecticae Libri Duo* and the *Rhetorica.*
Unlike Fenner, however, Fraunce published his translations separately,
the first as *The Lawiers Logike* (London, 1588), and the other at the
same place and in the same year as *The Arcadian Rhetorike.*[103] *The
Arcadian Rhetorike* differs in two ways at least from Fenner's similar

work: it translates the major points of Talaeus' doctrine of Delivery, whereas Fenner had not; and it provides its illustrations from among standard classical and modern authors, including Sidney, whereas Fenner had found his illustrations in the Bible. *The Lawiers Logike* also differs from Fenner's similar work in placing a heavy emphasis not only upon the relation between logic and law but also upon the exposition of leading points of Ramistic doctrine.

Charles Butler is an important figure in the history of Ramistic rhetoric on two counts. First, his *Rhetoricae Libri Duo,* first published in 1597,[104] carried Ramistic rhetoric into the public schools of England, and enjoyed a phenomenal success, being still mentioned as a popular book in 1659.[105] Secondly, his *Oratoriae Libri Duo,* first published at Oxford in 1629, pays a handsome tribute to Ramus' reform of the liberal arts, and at the same time proceeds to violate one of the cardinal tenets of that reform by offering a theory of Invention, Arrangement, and Memory, as if the first two of these terms were no longer the exclusive property of logic.[106] Butler's tribute to Ramus occurs as he is making ready to adapt to the needs of oratory Ramus' doctrine of the places of dialectical Invention. Says he:

These brief and methodical precepts concerning the places or kinds of arguments are supplied from Peter Ramus, whose singular acuteness in rebuilding the Arts I am never able to admire enough; and they are not so much assembled in part as adopted in full. Except some in Ramus are brought forth somewhat differently here, to the end that they may be adapted to the use of oratory. But not of course in any wrong sense. For whatever cannot be set forth in a better fashion, why should it be made worse by change? [107]

When Butler uttered these words in 1629, he apparently was not aware that fifty-five years before a good English Ramist would have considered it improper to treat the places of Invention anywhere but in a treatise on dialectic. In fact, Roland MacIlmaine, whose enthusiasm for Ramism has already been noticed, said in the prefatory "Epistle to the Reader" accompanying his translation of 1574 that any learned writer must avoid the very thing Butler later did. MacIlmaine's words are:

Is he not worthie to be mocked of all men, that purposethe to wryte of Grammer, and in euery other chapiter mynglethe something of Logicke, and some thing of Rethoricke: and contrarie when he purposethe to write of Logicke dothe speake of Grammer and Rethoricke.[108]

Samuel Wotton, Thomas Spencer, and Robert Fage are worthy of mention in a history of Ramism in England because each of them published a translation of Ramus' *Dialecticae Libri Duo* in the six years between 1626 and 1632, when interest in that work appears to have been especially strong.[109] Alexander Richardson is of importance for his

English commentary on Ramistic dialectic, published at London in 1629 as *The Logicians School-Master: or, A Comment vpon Ramvs Logicke.* John Barton is of importance because his *Art of Rhetorick Concisely and Compleatly Handled,* which appeared at London in 1634, is thoroughly Ramistic in its treatment of rhetoric, even though Barton shows some tendency in his preface, "To the Reader," to question whether Style and Delivery are the only concerns of rhetorical theory.[110] Barton opens the actual text of his treatise with the following words:

Rhetorick is the skill of using daintie words, and comely deliverie, whereby to work upon mens affections. It hath two parts, *Adornation* and *Action.*[111]

Thereafter Barton discusses Adornation as an exclusive product of the tropes and figures, whereas Action is to him a matter of gesture and utterance. The English text of his work runs to thirty-five pages, after which is a Latin translation of it, entitled "Rhetorices Enchiridion."

Barton's *Art of Rhetorick* is the last example of Ramistic theory to receive consideration here, where I am limiting myself to the period before Harvard's first Commencement. Ramistic theory still had vitality by 1642, and it was to exercise a continuing influence upon English rhetoric during the remainder of the seventeenth century. But forces were beginning to work against it by 1642, and they were ultimately to make it look obsolete, even as at first it had made Ciceronian rhetoric look cumbersome, redundant, and medieval. One of the forces working against Ramism in the latter part of the sixteen-hundreds had been set in motion by the publication of Francis Bacon's philosophical writings in the early years of that very century, and to that author we must now turn for a rhetorical theory that stands as a counterpoise to the existing theories of its time.

VI

Francis Bacon's complete theory of rhetoric exists in passages scattered throughout his many works. I shall not attempt here to reconstruct that theory, because in the first place I would not have room to do so, and in the second place that very subject has already received a full measure of attention and an able treatment by Professor Karl Wallace.[112] What I shall do here is to confine myself to the *Advancement of Learning,* which between 1605 and 1642 received at English presses four editions in English and one in Latin [113]; and to show that Bacon's excellent discussion of rhetorical theory in that work is not only an express reaction to stylistic, Ciceronian, formulary, and Ramistic rhetoric, but also an indication of a new future for the theory of communication.

Stylistic rhetoric, with its preponderant emphasis upon the third part of the Ciceronian program, and with its delight in enumerating the tropes and figures as standard ways in which verbal expression could depart from the ordinary patterns of speech, receives attention in Book I of the *Advancement of Learning*, where Bacon is speaking of the three diseases which had beset learning in the preceding century. One of these diseases Bacon calls "delicate learning,"—learning that strives for "vain affectations." [114] This particular disease turns out in Bacon's description to be an excessive addiction to stylistic rhetoric.

Bacon explains the origin of this malady of culture by saying that Martin Luther, as a member of the party of reform in his own time, had summoned ancient authors to bear witness against that time, and thus had encouraged an exact study of the language of those authors, and "a delight in their manner of style and phrase." [115] Meanwhile, the old party, the schoolmen, "whose writings were altogether in a differing style and form," [116] had offered opposition to the new party. The people, who were the prize of war in the struggle between the two parties, and whom both parties were bent upon winning and persuading, caused the development of a type of eloquence in which variety of discourse was thought "the fittest and forciblest access into the capacity of the vulgar sort." [117] What Bacon adds at this point may be quoted to show that these pressures led to the partial eclipse of the rhetoric of Invention and Arrangement and to the overemphasis upon the rhetoric of Style:

So that these four causes concurring, the admiration of ancient authors, the hate of the schoolmen, the exact study of languages, and the efficacy of preaching, did bring in an affectionate study of eloquence and copie of speech, which then began to flourish. This grew speedily to an excess; for men began to hunt more after words than matter; and more after the choiceness of the phrase, and the round and clean composition of the sentence, and the sweet falling of the clauses, and the varying and illustration of their works with tropes and figures, than after the weight of matter, worth of subject, soundness of argument, life of invention, or depth of judgment.[118]

In the list of authors cited immediately by Bacon to illustrate excessive devotion to the stylistic aspect of communication, we find critics of Ramism like Ascham, and precursors of Ramism like Sturm, whom Ramus himself acknowledges as his teacher.[119] Thus Bacon's disapproval of stylistic rhetoric may be accepted as criticism of the Sherry-Peacham-Hoskins tradition as well as criticism of Talaeus, Fenner, and Fraunce. To both traditions the following words of Bacon apply as he summarizes the first disease of learning:

Here therefore the first distemper of learning, when men study words and not matter: whereof though I have represented an example of late times, yet it hath been and will be *secundum majus et minus* in all time. . . . It seems to me that Pygmalion's frenzy is a good emblem or portraiture of this vanity: for words are but the images of matter; and except they have life of reason and invention, to fall in love with them is all one as to fall in love with a picture.[120]

Towards the Ciceronian tradition Bacon shows more respect than he does towards stylistic rhetoric. As he discusses Natural Philosophy in Book II of the *Advancement of Learning*, he speaks of his intention to use the word Metaphysic in a sense of his own; but he says he hopes men of judgment will see "that in this and other particulars, wheresoever my conception and notion may differ from the ancient, yet I am studious to keep the ancient terms." [121] Bacon is indeed studious to keep the ancient terms of Ciceronian rhetoric within his philosophy of learning. He is also studious, of course, to show wherein his own conceptions differ from the ancient. Thus he gives the five procedures of Cicero's rhetorical theory a place in learning, not when he speaks of rhetoric itself, but as he approaches that subject.

These five procedures, condensed into four, appear as he begins his discussion of the Intellectual Arts. Here are his own words:

The Arts Intellectual are four in number; divided according to the ends whereunto they are referred: for man's labour is to *invent* that which is *sought* or *propounded;* or to *judge* that which is *invented;* or to *retain* that which is *judged;* or to *deliver over* that which is *retained.* So as the arts must be four; Art of Inquiry or Invention: Art of Examination or Judgment; Art of Custody or Memory; and Art of Elocution or Tradition.[122]

A few pages later, Bacon defines "Tradition" as "Delivery"—"the expressing or transferring our knowledge to others." [123] Thus to him the terms Style and Delivery of Ciceronian rhetoric become a single term, Tradition; and Tradition stands for the process of communication, to which grammar, logic, and rhetoric make their distinctive contributions. At the end of Book I of the *Advancement of Learning* Bacon speaks of books under the image of ships which "pass through the vast seas of time, and make ages so distant to participate of the wisdom, illuminations, and inventions, the one of the other." [124] These books, these communications, are the product of the great Intellectual Art, Tradition; and, in Bacon's analysis, grammar contributes to Tradition by supplying knowledge of speech and words, logic, by supplying knowledge of the method of presentation, and rhetoric, by supplying knowledge of the means by which thoughts may be vividly represented to man's imagination.[125]

Before Bacon discusses Tradition as the fourth Intellectual Art, he speaks of the other three. He finds the first one, Invention, to be deficient so far as it might address itself to a technique by which new knowledge is discovered. He finds it more than sufficient, however, in respect to speech or argument, although, as he emphasizes, this sort of invention is not properly invention in the sense of the discovery of something new, but invention only in the sense of a resummoning of what we already know.[126] He indicates two existing mechanisms for assisting invention in this latter sense: the promptuaries, and the topics.[127] The promptuaries include the doctrine of positions in Ciceronian rhetoric, and collections of such ready-made devices as speech introductions.[128] The topics are made up of the places of logic.[129]

Bacon's treatment of Invention may well be the first important reinterpretation of the theory of rhetorical invention to be made in the Christian era. It indicates that the classical theory carries the speaker back to all the general wisdom which, on the one hand, is relevant to his subject, and, on the other, is known already. It also indicates that, good as the classical theory is for its purposes, it cannot give the speaker new facts about his subject, for these new facts come only as that subject is studied in and for itself. Thus Bacon's criticism of Invention may be taken in historical perspective to suggest the ultimate disappearance from rhetorical theory of the elaborate Latin doctrine of postures or positions of argument, and the ultimate emergence in rhetorical theory of the doctrine that the speaker learns what to say only by the most conscientious study of the facts of the matter with which his speech deals.

Bacon's discussion of Judgment and Memory as the second and third of the Intellectual Arts need not be summarized here. I should only like to say that, when Bacon speaks of Memory, he shows his knowledge of the memory system I have mentioned before in connection with my account of Hawes and Wilson.[130]

When Bacon comes to discuss rhetoric as the third science in the process of Delivery or Tradition, grammar and logic being, as I have said, the other two, he begins with these words:

Now we descend to that part which concerneth the Illustration of Tradition, comprehended in that science which we call Rhetoric, or Art of Eloquence; a science excellent, and excellently well laboured.[131]

He then mentions the rhetorics of Aristotle and Cicero as works in which those writers "exceed themselves." [132] As for his own conception of this science, his words cut through to the very essentials:

The duty and office of Rhetoric is *to apply Reason to Imagination* for the better moving of the will.[133]

In his ensuing elaboration of this thesis, he says in effect: if speakers take the truth and state it merely in terms of "naked propositions and proofs," [134] the Reason of man may accept it, and want to follow it; but the Passions or Affections of man, a rebellious and unruly faculty, may not accept it as truth, may want to follow something else; in this conflict between Reason and the Affections, a victory for the Passions would be inevitable, "if Eloquence of Persuasions did not practise and win the Imagination from the Affection's part, and contract a confederacy between the Reason and Imagination against the Affections." [135] In other words, Rhetoric becomes the means by which man appeals to the Imagination, and wins this faculty to the support of Reason, so that both faculties together can nullify the disruptive effects of the Passions, and can thus control the Will.

Shot full as it is with the imagery of statecraft and faculty psychology, this theory of rhetoric nevertheless seems suddenly to reach back through the centuries to the pre-Ciceronian era, when Plato was discussing rhetoric in *Phaedrus* and was analyzing the soul of man under the figure of the charioteer and the two horses. That Bacon had been reading *Phaedrus* before he wrote his account of rhetoric in the *Advancement of Learning* is proved by the fact that he quotes that work shortly after his admiring references to the rhetorics of Cicero and Aristotle.[136] Another proof of the influence of Plato upon Bacon in the field of rhetoric comes when Bacon suggests that the proofs of rhetoric must differ according to the auditors, and that this notion "in perfection of idea, ought to extend so far, that if a man should speak of the same thing to several persons, he should speak to them all respectively and several ways"—a suggestion that Plato makes much of in *Phaedrus*.[137] Incidentally, it is this Platonic notion that Bacon recommends for further inquiry by the coming generation of rhetoricians.[138]

Thus far this discussion of Bacon's rhetorical theory has involved an analysis of his disapproval of stylistic rhetoric, whether in the traditional or the Ramistic pattern, and an analysis of his wish at once to preserve and to reinterpret the chief terms of Ciceronian rhetoric. It has been emphasized that Bacon's reinterpretation of the term Invention looks toward, although it does not predict, the disappearance of the doctrine of positions from rhetorical theory. It has also been indicated that Bacon's reinterpretation of Delivery as Elocution or Tradition, and of rhetoric as the "Illustration of Tradition," restores to rhetoric its communicative function and gives it, not by implication but expressly, the task of reaching and persuading men. It has also been shown that Bacon thinks of a future rhetoric given partly to the study of the relation between speech forms and audience reactions. Let us now briefly examine Bacon's reaction to Ramistic logic and to formulary rhetoric.

Ramus had conceived of the process of communication as a whole to which dialectic contributed Invention and Arrangement, and to which rhetoric contributed Style and Delivery. Moreover, Arrangement was to Ramus a term which included the whole subject of method in discourse. His theory of method was that a learned treatise should be organized by a procedure of definition, partition, and illustration, with bipartite divisions of subject matter wherever possible. A popular treatise, he thought, could be organized less severely, but his followers tended to slight this aspect of his theory, and to emphasize the other.[139]

When Bacon comes to discuss method as the second of the three arts of Tradition or communication, he makes it a part of logic, as Ramus had done. He says that the subject of method "hath moved a controversy in our time"[140]—an obvious reference to the dispute between Ramists and the scholastics upon this matter. Then he indicates what to him is the difference between one sort of communicative method and the other:

And therefore the most real diversity of method is of method referred to Use, and method referred to Progression; whereof the one may be termed Magistral, and the other of Probation.[141]

The first of these methods Bacon explains obliquely as that form of presentation which is best for making knowledge believed; the second, as that form of presentation which is best for getting knowledge examined. He finds this second method to be neglected in his time.[142] The first method, which was precisely what Ramus regarded as the method for the learned treatise, Bacon finds to be misused in the truly scientific discourse, and to be more appropriate to the teacher.

Thus Bacon differs from Ramus on the question of the method to be followed in organizing a work of science or learning. Ramus wants a dogmatic method, Bacon a suggestive. But Bacon has one further objection to Ramus' concept of method in communication: he believes that Ramus' three laws are excellent, but that the application of the law of wisdom to the learned treatise has produced a "canker of Epitomes," and a "uniform method and dichotomies," the result of which has been that "the kernels and grains of the sciences leap out, and they are left with nothing in their grasp but the dry and barren husks."[143]

One other difference between Bacon and Ramus should be noted. It concerns the relation of logic to rhetoric. Whereas Ramus believed these two arts to be divided in respect to subject matter, so that logic would always discuss Invention and Arrangement, with rhetoric always limited to Style and Delivery, Bacon sees the two arts as operating in two different spheres of communication, one sphere being the world of learning, the other, the world of practical affairs. Says Bacon:

It appeareth also that Logic differeth from Rhetoric, not only as the fist from the palm, the one close the other at large; but much more in this, that Logic handleth reason exact and in truth, and Rhetoric handleth it as it is planted in popular opinions and manners. And therefore Aristotle doth wisely place Rhetoric as between Logic on the one side and moral or civil knowledge on the other, as participating of both. . . .[144]

Bacon closes his account of rhetoric with a note about its present deficiencies, and it is here that he mentions formulary rhetoric. He had touched upon it before in his remarks upon Invention, as my discussion of his attitude toward promptuaries has shown. Now he suggests that a preparatory store of theses should be made up for the use of speakers and that a collection of formulas representing introductions, conclusions, digressions, transitions, and excusations should be undertaken.[145] Thus he wants formulary rhetoric enriched, and this enrichment came later, as we have seen, in the works of Clarke, Farnaby, and Horne.

Bacon's rhetorical theory did not replace the theories which had flourished in England during the sixteenth century. Indeed, as I have shown, Ciceronian rhetoric was revised by Vicars, Farnaby, and Pemble in the period between 1620 and 1640; and that was the time when the *Advancement of Learning* was being given four separate editions. Meanwhile, Ramistic rhetoric was merging with the older English stylistic rhetoric, without loss to the popularity of the tropes and the figures. And in the same period, formulary rhetoric was being improved in the direction which Bacon had indicated. But Bacon's theory had three advantages over its rivals. First, it was stated in a work that exercised a profound influence upon the intellectual life of the seventeenth century. Secondly, it brought to rhetorical theory the stimulating influence of Plato and Aristotle at a time when traditional English theory had hardened into perfunctory conventions. Thirdly, it was formulated, not in what Bacon somewhat scornfully terms the Magistral method, but in what he approvingly calls the method of Probation. That is to say, it was stated to invite further inquiry rather than to force assent. In Book I of the *Advancement of Learning*, Bacon had observed that "knowledge, while it is in aphorisms and observations, it is in growth; but when it once is comprehended in exact methods, it may perchance be further polished and illustrate, and accommodated for use and practice; but it increaseth no more in bulk and substance." [146] This latter method Bacon did not allow to enter into his rhetorical theory. He fashioned his theory in aphorisms and observations, and so left it in growth.

How far English rhetoric developed in the seventeenth century towards a new theory of communication is a subject which lies outside the scope of my present essay. But such a development did take place. It can be seen taking place in the decision of the Royal Society to keep out of their scientific writing "these specious Tropes and Figures," to keep out also "all the amplifications, digressions, and swellings of style," and to exact "from all their members, a close, naked, natural way of speaking." [147] It can be seen taking place in the renewed interest in Aristotle's *Rhetoric* among Englishmen during the seventeenth century, as evidenced especially by Thomas Hobbes' English abridgement of that work, published about 1637 under the title, *A Briefe of the Art of Rhetorique*. It can be seen taking place in Joseph Glanvill's *An Essay Concerning Preaching*, published at London in 1678. And it can be seen taking place in the interest shown in the first English translation of *The Port Royal Logic* in 1685.[148] But these developments occurred after the first Commencement at Harvard, and thus were not part of the English record at the time when higher learning began in New England.

VII

On September 23, 1642, Harvard College held her first Commencement and graduated nine young men.[149] These young men were more heavily committed to the Ramistic theory of communication than to any of the other theories I have discussed. After all, the program of that first Commencement lists the theses which the graduates were prepared to defend as a result of their training under Henry Dunster, and the rhetorical and logical theses on that program are heavily Ramistic. The twelfth logical thesis, for example, is an invitation to the graduates to discuss Ramus' three laws: "Praecepta Artium debent esse κατὰ πάντος, καθ' αὐτό, καθ' ὅλου πρῶτον." [150] Moreover, in the library which John Harvard had bequeathed in 1638 to the college subsequently named for him, there was a copy of Ramus' *Dialecticae Libri Duo* and Talaeus' *Rhetorica*—the two works suited before all others to give those nine first graduates a command of the Ramistic theory of communication.[151] We may be sure that the graduates knew how Ramus had assigned Invention and Arrangement to dialectic, Style and Delivery to rhetoric, as part of his program of giving each art what properly belonged to it under the law of justice. Thus we may also be sure that the four main terms of Ciceronian rhetoric were familiar to New England's first college graduates, even if those terms came to them in the reformed system of Ramus.

But there is a strong likelihood that those terms were also known to that graduating class from non-Ramistic sources. John Harvard's library contained the *Rhetoricorum Libri Quinque* of Georgius Trapezuntius, a scholar of the fifteenth century; [152] and that work is an excellent and ample treatise on the five procedures anciently assigned by Cicero to rhetoric, with definitions of them from the *Rhetorica ad Herennium* and *De Inventione*. Possibly the first graduating class could have learned these five procedures directly from Cicero, if the copy of Cicero's *Opera Omnia* in John Harvard's library happened to include the rhetorical works.[153] As for the pre-Ramistic rhetoric of tropes and figures, the graduates could have mastered that in Henry Peacham's *Garden of Eloquence*, a copy of which was in John Harvard's library, possibly as a relic of his own school days in England.[154] John Harvard's library also contained a copy of the *Advancement of Learning*,[155] and thus the graduates had access to the new learning and to the rhetorical theory framed to suit it. It would be strange indeed if by Commencement Day that year they had not yet read that already famous work. Only the formulary rhetorics appear not to have been represented in John Harvard's library, except in such collections of phrases and proverbs as Grynaeus' *Adagia*, Draxe's *Calliepeia*, and Lycosthenes' *Apophthegmata*.[156] But these rhetorics, of course, would not have assisted disputants at a college ceremony to examine questions of rhetorical theory. They would have provided models for practice, and hence would have been found on a lower level of education than that occupied by the first graduates of Harvard.

Notes

1. For a representative selection of other accounts of English rhetoric in this period, see the following: E. E. Hale, Jr., "Ideas on Rhetoric in the Sixteenth Century," *PMLA*, XVIII (1903), 424-444; R. C. Jebb, "Rhetoric," in *The Encyclopaedia Britannica*, 11th ed.; Donald Lemen Clark, *Rhetoric and Poetry in the Renaissance* (New York, 1922); Charles Sears Baldwin, *Medieval Rhetoric and Poetic (to 1400)* (New York, 1928); William Phillips Sandford, *English Theories of Public Address, 1530-1828* (The Ohio State University, 1929); Lee Sisson Hultzén, *Aristotle's "Rhetoric" in England to 1600*, unpublished Ph.D. dissertation, Cornell University, 1932; William Garrett Crane, *Wit and Rhetoric in the Renaissance* (New York, 1937); T. W. Baldwin, *William Shakspere's Small Latine & Lesse Greeke* (Urbana, 1944), II, 1-68; J. W. H. Atkins, *English Literary Criticism: The Renascence* (London, 1947), pp. 66-101.
2. Cicero, *De Inventione*, 1. 7. 9, trans. H. M. Hubbell (The Loeb Classical Library, Cambridge, Mass. and London, 1949), pp. 19-21.
3. For indications of Cicero's constant reference to these five major terms, see *De Oratore*, 1. 28. 128; 1. 31. 142; 1. 42. 187; 2. 19. 79; 2. 85. 350; see also *De Partitione Oratoria*, 1. 3, and *Orator*, 14. 43-55.
4. *Brutus*, 6. 25, trans. G. L. Hendrickson (The Loeb Classical Library, Cambridge, Mass. and London, 1939), pp. 35-37.
5. The Latin text and an English translation of this work, formally called *Disputatio de Rhetorica et de Virtutibus Sapientissimi Regis Karli et Albini Magistri*, may be found in Wilbur Samuel Howell, *The Rhetoric of Alcuin and Charlemagne* (Princeton, 1941). The Latin text is also found in J.-P. Migne, *Patrologia Latina* (Paris, 1844-1864), CI, 919-950; and in Carolus Halm, *Rhetores Latini Minores* (Leipzig, 1863), pp. 523-550.
6. See Howell, *Rhetoric of Alcuin*, pp. 33-61.
7. *Ibid.*, pp. 22-33. For the text of Victor's *Ars Rhetorica*, see Halm, *Rhetores Latini Minores*, pp. 371-448.
8. J. W. H. Atkins, *English Literary Criticism: The Medieval Phase* (New York and Cambridge, England, 1943), p. 59.

9. The text of the *Poetria Nova* is found in Edmond Faral, *Les Arts Poétiques du XIIe et du XIIIe Siècle* (Paris, 1924), pp. 197-262; see the same work, pp. 194-197, for an analysis of the *Poetria Nova,* and pp. 15-33 for a discussion of Geoffrey of Vinsauf; see pp. 28-33 for an analysis of the question of the date of the *Poetria Nova,* which Faral finally places between 1208 and 1213.

10. Atkins, *The Medieval Phase,* p. 142.

11. See William Blades, *The Biography and Typography of William Caxton, England's First Printer* (London and Strassburg, 1877), pp. 216-219; also E. Gordon Duff, *Fifteenth Century English Books* ([Oxford], 1917), p. 102; also Isak Collijn, *Kataloge der Inkunabeln der Schwedischen Öffentlichen Bibliotheken II. Katalog der Inkunabeln der Kgl. Universitäts-Bibliothek zu Uppsala* (Uppsala, 1907), p. 232; also *British Museum General Catalogue of Printed Books* s. v. "Traversanus (Laurentius Gulielmus)." My present discussion of the *Nova Rhetorica* is based upon the Huntington Library's microfilm copy of the St. Albans edition of 1480.

12. This sketch of Traversagni is given here because of the difficulty the reader might otherwise have in learning something of him. A brief account of him is found in Blades, pp. 218-219. By far the best accounts, one in Italian and the other in Latin, are found in Giovanni Vincenzo Verzellino, *Delle Memorie Particolari e Specialmente Degli Uomini Illustri della Città di Savona,* ed. Andrea Astengo (Savona, 1890), pp. 400-401, 520-521; upon these I have relied almost completely. See also Lucas Waddingus, *Scriptores Ordinis Minorum,* editio novissima (Rome, 1906), p. 158.

13. Frederic Ives Carpenter, *Leonard Cox The Arte or Crafte of Rhethoryke A Reprint Edited with an Introduction, Notes, and Glossarial Index* (Chicago, 1899), p. 25.

14. Stephen Hawes, *The Pastime of Pleasure,* ed. William Edward Mead, Early English Text Society (London, 1928 [for 1927]); see especially pp. xxix-xxx for a discussion of the edition of 1509.

15. *Ibid.,* p. 56, line 1357. According to Whitney Wells, "Stephen Hawes and *The Court of Sapience,*" *The Review of English Studies,* VI (1930), 284-294, the *Court* influenced Hawes' *The Example of Virtue,* which in turn provided the pattern for the *Pastime.*

16. *Pastime,* ed. Mead, pp. 30-54 [lines 652-1295].

17. *Ibid.,* p. 52 [lines 1247-1253].

18. P. 25. Carpenter calls Caxton's *Mirrour* a translation of the French version of the *Speculum Mundi.* Actually, the work is a translation of the *Image du Monde,* a French encyclopedia perhaps best attributed to Gossouin, and probably completed in January, 1245 (O.S.); see Oliver H. Prior, *Caxton's Mirrour of the World,* Early English Text Society (London, 1913 [for 1912]), pp. vii-xi.

19. *Caxton's Mirrour,* ed. Prior, pp. 35-36.

20. Cox, *Rhethoryke,* ed. Carpenter, p. 41.

21. *Ibid.,* pp. 41-42.

22. *Ibid.,* p. 42.

23. *Ibid.,* p. 42.

24. *Ibid.,* pp. 81, 87.

25. *Ibid.,* p. 29.

26. *Ibid.,* p. 91; Carpenter reprints extracts from Melanchthon's *Institutiones Rhetoricae* on pp. 91-102.

27. Cicero, *Topica,* 1. 1-5; 2. 6-7.

28. Cox, *Rhethoryke,* ed. Carpenter, p. 43.

29. *Ibid.,* pp. 43, 87.

30. *Ibid.,* p. 87.

31. *Ibid.,* pp. 15-16, 21.

32. Russell H. Wagner, "Wilson and His Sources," *Quarterly Journal of Speech,* XV (1929), 530-532.

33. The following table, based upon *Wilson's Arte of Rhetorique 1560*, ed. G. H. Mair (Oxford, 1909), and upon Richard Sherry, *A Treatise of Schemes and Tropes* ([London], [1550]), indicates the chief points of similarity between the two works:

Topic	Wilson	Sherry
"audience of sheepe"	p. 166	sig. C 2 r °
"three maner of stiles"	p. 169	sig. B 3 r °
"figure"	p. 170	sig. B 5 r °
"metaphore"	pp. 172-173	sig. C 4 v °—C 5 r °
"abusion"	pp. 174-175	sig. C 5 r °
"metonymia"	p. 175	sig. C 5 v °
"transumption"	p. 175	sig. C 5 r °—C 5 v °
"periphrasis"	pp. 175-176	sig. C 6 v °
"scheme"	p. 176	sig. B 5 r °
"epenthesis"	p. 177	sig. B 6 r °
"syncope"	p. 177	sig. B 6 r °
"proparalepsis"	p. 177	sig. B 6 r °
"apocope"	p. 177	sig. B 6 r °
"extenuatio"	pp. 180-181	sig. D 7 r °*
"gradatio"	p. 204	sig. D 5 v °
"dissolutum"	p. 205	sig. D 6 r °

* Wilson illustrates "extenuatio" with the form used by Sherry to illustrate "diminutio."

34. Wilson, *Rhetorique*, ed. Mair, p. 6.
35. *Ibid.*, p. 23.
36. *Ibid.*, pp. 86-97.
37. *Ibid.*, pp. 99-116.
38. *Ibid.*, pp. 158-160.
39. *Ibid.*, pp. 162-164.
40. *Ibid.*, p. 160.
41. *Ibid.*, p. 162.
42. This list of editions of Wilson's *Rhetorique* is based upon the entries in the *Short-Title Catalogue* s. v. "Wilson, Sir Thomas."
43. For a discussion of another occurrence of this epigram in the seventeenth century, see Wilbur Samuel Howell, "Nathaniel Carpenter's Place in the Controversy between Dialectic and Rhetoric," *Speech Monographs*, I (1934), 20-41.
44. William Pemble, *Enchiridion Oratorivm* (Oxford, 1633), p. 2.
45. See Cicero, *Orator*, 14. 43-44; 15. 50-53; 17. 54-61.
46. For the text of this little work, see Halm, *Rhetores Latini Minores,* pp. 607-618; also Migne, *Patrologia Latina*, XC, 175-186.
47. The evidence on this matter is presented in M. L. W. Laistner, *A Hand-List of Bede Manuscripts* (Ithaca, 1943), pp. 131-132.
48. See M. L. W. Laistner, "The Library of the Venerable Bede," in *Bede his Life, Times, and Writings*, ed. A. Hamilton Thompson (Oxford, 1935), p. 241.
49. For Isidore's *De Grammatica* and *De Rhetorica*, see Migne, *Patrologia Latina*, LXXXII, 73-124, 123-140; for his *De Rhetorica* alone, see Halm, *Rhetores Latini Minores*, pp. 505-522.
50. Halm, p. xv.
51. Laistner, "The Library of the Venerable Bede," in Thompson, p. 241.
52. Bede, *Liber de Schematibus et Tropis*, ed. Halm, p. 607; translation by the present author.
53. Laistner, "The Library of the Venerable Bede," in Thompson, pp. 263-266.
54. Atkins, *The Medieval Phase*, p. 75.
55. An analysis of this work and typical extracts from it are found in Faral, *Les Arts Poétiques*, pp. 321-327.

56. Atkins, *The Medieval Phase*, p. 97.

57. The only modern edition is by Spindler; see *The Court of Sapience,* ed. Robert Spindler, *Beiträge zur Englischen Philologie,* VI (Leipsiz, 1927). Its first edition is usually listed under the title *De Curia Sapientiae* or *Curia Sapientiae,* although the work is in English.

58. *The Court of Sapience,* ed. Spindler, pp. 198-200.

59. *Ibid.,* p. 199, line 1911. Bühler thinks these three terms belong to punctuation; he finds their inclusion as a part of rhetoric unusual, although he indicates that the author of the *Court* is probably following Isidore and Balbus in including them in rhetoric. See Curt Ferdinand Bühler, "The Sources of the Court of Sapience," *Beiträge zur Englischen Philologie,* XXIII (Leipzig, 1932), 75. Actually, however, these terms belong, not to punctuation, but to the theory of oratorical style. They may be found in Cicero, *Orator,* 61. 204-206; 62. 211-214; 66. 223-226; also Quintilian, *Institutio Oratoria,* 9. 4. 22-45, 122-130.

60. Bühler, *op. cit.,* p. 75, shows that the author of the *Court* depends also upon the *Laborintus* of Évrard l'Allemand.

61. Sig. A 1 v °–A 2 r °.

62. Sig. A 2 r °.

63. Sig. A 4 v °.

64. Sig. A 5 r °.

65. Sig. A 6 v °.

66. Sig. B 1 r °.

67. Sig. B 1 v °.

68. Sig. B 5 r °.

69. Sig. B 5 r °.

70. Sig. C 4 r °–C 4 v °.

71. My illustration is modeled upon that in Wilson, *Rhetorique,* ed. Mair, p. 177. For Sherry's less telling illustration, see *Treatise of Schemes & Tropes,* sig. B 5 v °.

72. This illustration is from Sherry, sig. C 4 v °.

73. Sig. A 5 r °.

74. Sig. A 6 r °.

75. Sig. A 8 r °–A 8 v °.

76. The second edition of Sherry's work abandons his earlier distinction between Schemes and Tropes and substitutes for it the distinction between figures of grammar and figures of rhetoric, tropes being given a place under the latter heading. The second edition is also a mixture of Latin and English; most topics are explained in both languages in the course of the treatise.

77. Cf. Sherry (1550), sig. F 7 r °–F 8 v °, and Peacham, sig. Q 1 r °–Q 2 r °.

78. Cf. Sherry (1555), fol. XLI r °–XLI v °, and Peacham, sig. R 3 v °.

79. See John Hoskins, *Directions for Speech and Style,* ed. Hoyt Hopewell Hudson, Princeton Studies in English, XII (Princeton, 1935); see especially pp. xiv-xv for a discussion of the date of Hoskins' work, and pp. xxvii-xxxviii for an examination of the use of the *Directions* by Jonson, Blount, and Smith.

80. Hoskins, ed. Hudson, p. 3; for a full discussion of the sources of the *Directions,* see pp. xxii-xxvii.

81. Mair, pp. 39-63, 66-85, 92-94.

82. Sig. G 1 r °.

83. Its title and imprint are as follows: *A booke called the Foundacion of Rhetorike, because all other partes of Rhetorike are grounded thereupon, euery parte sette forthe in an Oracion vpon questions, verie profitable to bee knowen and redde,* Made by Richard Rainolde (London, 1563).

84. See Francis R. Johnson, *The Foundacion of Rhetorike by Richard Rainolde with an Introduction* (New York: Scholars' Facsimiles and Reprints, 1945), p. xiv.

85. For sketches of these three rhetoricians, see *Dictionary of Greek and Roman Biography and Mythology,* ed. William Smith, s. v. "Aphthonius of Antioch," "Hermogenes 6," and "Theon, literary 5."

86. See John Edwin Sandys, *A History of Classical Scholarship,* 2nd ed. (Cambridge, England, 1906), I, 318-319, 381.

87. Fol. 1 r °–1 v °; see also above, note 43.

88. Fol. 2 v °.

89. Fol. 2 v °–3 r °.

90. Fol. 3 v °–4 r °.

91. Fol. 4 r °.

92. Fol. 4 r °.

93. Fol. 4 v °.

94. Fol. 25 r °.

95. The recent works specifically recognizing the forgotten importance of Ramus are as follows: Hardin Craig, *The Enchanted Glass* (New York, 1936); William Garrett Crane, *Wit and Rhetoric in the Renaissance* (New York, 1937); Perry Miller, *The New England Mind* (New York, 1939); Sister Miriam Joseph, *Shakespeare's Use of the Arts of Language* (New York, 1947); Rosemond Tuve, *Elizabethan and Metaphysical Imagery* (Chicago, 1947); Donald Lemen Clark, *John Milton at St. Paul's School* (New York, 1948).

96. See the *Dialectiqve de Pierre de la Ramee* (Paris, 1555), pp. 84-85. Ramus' three laws are derived from Aristotle's discussion of the premises of demonstration in the *Analytica Posteriora,* 1.4. For the Greek terms for these laws, see below, p. 57.

97. For a list of the works in which Ramus and his interpreters discuss these three laws, see Wilbur Samuel Howell, *Fénelon's Dialogues on Eloquence* (Princeton, 1951), pp. 8-9.

98. Roland MacIlmaine, *The Logike of the moste Excellent Philosopher P. Ramus Martyr* (London, 1574), pp. 7-8.

99. *Ibid.,* pp. 11-12.

100. See Talaeus' prefaces to the first and a later edition of his *Rhetorica* in *Petri Rami Professoris Regii, & Audomari Talaei Collectaneae Praefationes, Epistolae, Orationes* (Marburg, 1599), pp. 14-16.

101. See Wilbur Samuel Howell, "Ramus and English Rhetoric: 1574-1681," *QJS,* XXXVII (1951), pp. 299-310. A complete account of the English Ramists, with special attention to Chaderton, Harvey, Temple, John Milton, and many others, will be found in my forthcoming book on logic and rhetoric in the English Renaissance.

102. Of the five parts of Ciceronian rhetoric, only Memory failed to find a place in Ramistic dialectic or rhetoric. Ramus believed that Memory was not an explicit topic for either art to deal with, but, as a faculty of the mind, was assisted and strengthened by what dialectic had to say about Arrangement. See *P. Rami Scholarum Dialecticarum, seu Animadversionum in Organum Aristotelis, libri xx,* ed. Joannes Piscator (Frankfurt, 1581), p. 593. See also *P. Rami & A. Talaei Collectaneae Praefationes,* p. 15, where Talaeus expresses his view on this subject.

103. For a recent edition of this latter work, and a careful commentary upon it, see *The Arcadian Rhetorike by Abraham Fraunce,* ed. Ethel Seaton (Oxford: Published for the Luttrell Society by Basil Blackwell, 1950).

104. The first edition bears the following title: *Rameae Rhetoricae Libri Dvo. In vsvm Scholarvm* (Oxford, 1597); the second edition (1598) and later ones were entitled *Rhetoricae Libri Dvo,* Ramus' name being no longer included on the title page.

105. See Charles Hoole, *A New Discovery Of the old Art of Teaching Schoole,* ed. E. T. Campagnac (Liverpool and London, 1913), "The Masters Method," p. 132.

106. For an English translation of the section on Memory in the *Oratoriae Libri Duo,* see Lee Sisson Hultzén, "Charles Butler on Memory," *SM,* VI (1939), 44-65.

107. *Oratoriae Libri Dvo* (Oxford, 1629), sig. L 1 r °. Translation by the present author.

108. MacIlmaine, p. 9.

109. The titles of these three translations are given in full in the present author's "Ramus and English Rhetoric: 1574-1681," *op. cit.,* p. 306.

110. The title page of this work identifies the author as "J. B. Master of the free-school of *Kinfare* in *Straffordshire*." The dedicatory epistle identifies J. B. as John Barton, as does the epistle "To the Reader."

111. Barton, *Art of Rhetorick*, p. 1.

112. See Karl R. Wallace, *Francis Bacon on Communication & Rhetoric or: The Art of Applying Reason to Imagination for the Better Moving of the Will* (Chapel Hill, 1943).

113. See R. W. Gibson, *Francis Bacon A Bibliography of his Works and of Baconiana to the year 1750* (Oxford: At the Scrivener Press, 1950), pp. xiv-xv; 72-73, 108-109, 118-124.

114. *The Works of Francis Bacon*, ed. James Spedding, Robert Leslie Ellis, and Douglas Denon Heath (Boston, 1860-1864), VI, 117, hereafter cited as *Works*.

115. *Works*, VI, 118.

116. *Ibid.*, VI, 118.

117. *Ibid.*, VI, 119.

118. *Ibid.*, VI, 119.

119. *Ibid.*, VI, 119. For an illustration of Ascham's criticism of Ramus, see Roger Ascham, *The Scholemaster*, ed. John E. B. Mayor (London, 1863), pp. 101-102. For Ramus' tribute to Sturm, see *P. Rami & A. Talaei Collectaneae Praefationes, Epistolae, Orationes*, p. 67.

120. *Works*, VI, 120.

121. *Ibid.*, VI, 215.

122. *Ibid.*, VI, 260-261.

123. *Ibid.*, VI, 282.

124. *Ibid.*, VI, 169

125. *Ibid.*, VI, 285, 288, 297.

126. *Ibid.*, VI, 261, 268-269.

127. In the English version of the *Advancement of Learning*, Bacon's terms for these two aids are "Preparation" and "Suggestion." In the Latin version, the terms are "Promptuaria" and "Topica." Cf. *Works*, II, 386, and VI, 269.

128. *Works*, VI, 269-270.

129. *Ibid.*, VI, 270-272.

130. *Ibid.*, VI, 281-282.

131. *Ibid.*, VI, 296.

132. *Ibid.*, VI, 297.

133. *Ibid.*, VI, 297.

134. *Ibid.*, VI, 299.

135. *Ibid.*, VI, 299.

136. *Ibid.*, VI, 298. Bacon says: "And therefore as Plato said elegantly, *That virtue, if she could be seen, would move great love and affection*." This quotation is from *Phaedrus*, 250. See Lane Cooper, *Plato Phaedrus, Ion, Gorgias, and Symposium, with passages from the Republic and Laws* (London, New York, Toronto, 1938), p. 34. Cooper translates the passage thus: "O what amazing love would Wisdom cause in us if she sent forth an image of herself that entered the sight, as the image of Beauty does."

137. Cf. *Works*, VI, 300, and *Phaedrus*, 271-272, 277; for a translation of the Platonic passages, see Cooper, pp. 61, 68.

138. *Works*, VI, 300.

139. For a discussion of this matter, see the present author's *Fénelon's Dialogues on Eloquence*, pp. 14-16. For Ramus' discussion of Method, see *Dialectiqve* (1555), pp. 120-135.

140. *Works*, VI, 288.

141. *Ibid.*, VI, 289.

142. *Ibid.*, VI, 289.

143. *Ibid.*, VI, 294; IX, 128, 122; II, 434, 427-428.

144. *Ibid.*, VI, 300.

145. *Ibid.*, VI, 302-303.

146. *Ibid.*, VI, 131.

147. Thomas Sprat, *The History of the Royal-Society of London* (London, 1667), pp. 112, 113.

148. This work was first translated into English under the title, *Logic; Or, The Art of Thinking* (London, 1685).

149. For a full account of this historic ceremony, see Samuel Eliot Morison, *The Founding of Harvard College* (Cambridge, Mass., 1935), pp. 257-262.

150. Morison, p. 439. For a thorough discussion of the influence of Ramus at Harvard during the seventeenth century, see Miller, *The New England Mind*, pp. 115-156, 312-330, 493-501.

151. See Alfred C. Potter, "Catalogue of John Harvard's Library," *Publications of the Colonial Society of Massachusetts*, XXI (1919), 219-220.

152. *Ibid.*, p. 224.

153. *Ibid.*, p. 225. According to Potter, John Harvard's library contained Cicero's *Operum Omnium tomus* 1-3 (Basel, 1528), but I do not know the precise contents of that particular edition.

154. *Ibid.*, pp. 192, 208.

155. *Ibid.*, p. 198.

156. *Ibid.*, pp. 199, 202, 213.

2 Rhetorical Theory in Colonial America

WARREN GUTHRIE

....

Basic to the later development of speech education in America was the foundation on which that development was built—the rhetorical theory studied and taught in the colonies. We will examine briefly the pattern and growth of that rhetorical theory.

The Rhetoric of Style

During the first century of American colonization the educational doctrine and some of the writings of Peter Ramus [1] seemed almost to dominate the thinking of the colonists. Ramean works on grammar and dialectic were included in John Harvard's bequest to the colonies' first college. Leonard Hoar, writing to his nephew, Josiah Flynt, a freshman at Harvard, in 1661, refers to the "Incomparable P. Ramus," and further adds that Josiah should "make use of the grand Mr. Ramus in Grammar, Rhetorique, Logick." [2] Cotton Mather reported that in Harvard "the Ramean discipline be . . . preferred unto the Aristotelian." [3] In 1693 thirteen copies of "Rami Logica" were imported into Boston. [4] The 1723 catalogue of the Harvard Library lists his *Scholia in 3 primas liberales artes*.

Although Ramus wrote no formal rhetoric as a separate treatise, certain concepts are clear in his writings. His feeling was that rhetoric was the least important member of the trivium, since it was concerned only with ornamenting those ideas given by logic, and already expressed correctly with the aid of grammar. Much of what was formerly rhetorical doctrine in the classical conception was thus imported into logic or dialectic. Especially was this true of invention and arrangement. Rhetoric was left only with style and delivery as Ramean logic became to a considerable extent a "rhetorical logic"; although it retained the typical syllogistic doctrine, it added much of the material and point of view of classical *inventio*.

Thus, the period of Ramean rhetoric in America, continuing until

48

c. 1730, was a period of rhetorical decadence, far from the active elements of the art which the ancients had considered the very heart of rhetorical doctrine.

The following will indicate the general scheme of Ramus' rhetoric: [5]

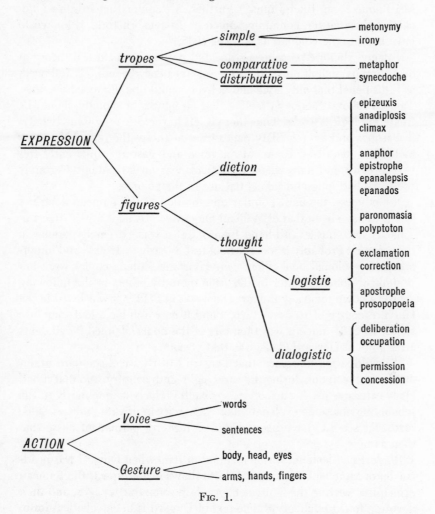

FIG. 1.

Since Ramus himself wrote no rhetoric, it was from a number of works in the Ramean tradition that his doctrine was circulated in the colonies. Perhaps the most "official" one—it was highly praised by Ramus in its preface—was the text written by Omer Talon. His *Rhetorica* [6] was one of the works used for the teaching of rhetoric at Harvard College, and the book had considerable circulation in the colonies. John Harvard's bequest contained a copy,[7] and another was in the library of Increase Mather.[8] A copy which is bound together with Ramus's *Dialectics and Greek Grammar* to make one volume is inscribed by Dudley Bradstreet with the date 1694.[9] Bradstreet was graduated by Harvard in 1698. (One recalls the reference of Mr. Hoar to the "grand Mr. Ramus . . . in Rhetorique.") Further, Alexander Richardson's *Logician's Schoolmaster*, containing much of Talaeus' rhetoric, is known to have been in the colonies as early as 1635.[10]

Talaeus' rhetoric presents a truncated pattern of rhetorical theory at best. Ramus' definition, "Rhetorica est ars bene dicendi," is followed, as is his belief that only style and delivery should be discussed. Further, Talaeus follows Ramus in feeling that all figures of thought should be treated in logical works. Thus there is left to rhetoric only some twenty-five tropes and figures. Sixty pages treat of these—the rest of the work includes generalized comment on voice and gesture. Apparently this very brevity and narrowness of outlook was an advantage. Certainly the work had long and influential use in the colonies.

Nonetheless, the most popular presentation of the Ramean doctrines seems to have been that of William Dugard.[11] His book was a digest of Talaeus, and thus a third-hand Ramus, but it was extremely popular in the colonies. Probably it was a school text as early as 1690,[12] and importations by colonial booksellers were constant. Fifteen copies were imported by Robert Boulter in 1682; ten more by others in the following year.[13] Known to be a grammar school text in 1712,[14] it was listed in the Harvard course of study in 1726,[15] and it may still have had some use as late as 1764, since it was then one of the books claimed by students after a fire at Harvard College in that year.[16]

It would seem, therefore, that Dugard's work was a standard grammar school textbook during the early eighteenth century, and that it had fairly extensive use in the colleges as well. Perhaps its popularity in the schools may be some explanation of its scarcity in private libraries, since textbooks seem to have been valued as little for permanent possession then as now.

Rhetorices Elementa was first issued in 1650 when Dugard was headmaster of Merchant Taylors school. It follows in all respects the Ramean principles, treating the figures of speech in some thirty pages, and then devoting four to delivery.[17] The text of Dugard is in catechetical form, and, as the title advertises, is so arranged that if the questions are omitted the answers will give a complete foundation in rhetoric for beginners. A notation from the opening will give some picture of the method and scope of the book: [18]

Quaest.   1. *Quid est Rhetorica?*
Rhetorica est ars ornate dicendi.

2. *Quot sunt partes Rhetorices?*

Partes Rhetorices   Elocutio, &
   duae sunt: Pronuntiatio

Following the definitions there is a list of the Ramean figures of speech, each illustrated from Latin literature. Brief as this treatment of style is, it is detailed in contrast with the very brief and perfunctory treatment of delivery which follows. The discussion of delivery gives only a few suggestions concerning the proper "voice" for the various parts of an oration, and some general advice on the movement of the whole body and its parts.

Thus the book features concise definitions of the standard Ramean tropes and figures, with a minimum of illustrative material. While its contribution to the development of rhetorical theory must be adjudged slight, it was compact and doubtless useful to both grammar school and college students. At any rate, it represents the rhetorical doctrine taught the colonists before 1730 in its most popular form.

Perhaps the strongest competition to the Ramean concept of rhetoric in the early colonies came from the followers of the great Dutch philosopher, Gerhard Johann Vossius. Vossius' own rhetoric,[19] had some circulation in the colonies. Listed as in the Harvard Library in 1724, it was starred as especially useful for upperclassmen in Yale in 1743.[20]

Vossius' rhetoric treated of an art much more closely allied to classical concepts than did the rhetoric of Ramus—a much fuller art than Ramus was willing to concede. Although Vossius, too, treats mostly of trope and figure, there is a fairly adequate discussion of invention, disposition, and pronunciation as well.

Actually, Vossius' views were most popularly presented to the colonies through the works of Thomas Farnaby.[21] References to the *Index* are numerous,[22] and all seem to indicate that Farnaby, with Dugard, was one of the most popular of the rhetoricians influencing early American rhetorical thought.

Farnaby's writings reflect his association with Vossius, and they may have been influenced by the Jesuit teaching in the classical tradition which he had experienced as well. His definition of rhetoric is not "ars ornate dicendi," but "facultas de unaquaque re dicendi bene, & ad persuadenum accomodate." [23]

The organization of Farnaby's book also tends toward the classical tradition. In schematic form, relying largely on bracketed tables, Farnaby treats of invention, disposition, elocution, and pronunciation, thus at least mentioning all of the orthodox points of classical rhetoric except *memoria*. But when one considers that he treats invention in ten pages and disposition in nine, it can be seen that the discussions are relatively brief compared with the emphasis given to these same matters in classical rhetoric. The treatment of elocution or style is more detailed, the qualities of language being treated, as well as the movement of sentences, periods, and rhythms, and all of the Ramean tropes and figures.

The second part of the work is a handbook of composition with brief advice and specimen phrases and forms to use in the various parts of a theme. Also are included heads for a commonplace book in which quotations may be filed for use in writing and speaking—four pages of topics running from "Abstinentia, Abusus," to "Vultus, Uxer."

There is frequent reference to classical sources, and on the whole the book seems vastly superior to Dugard's digest.[24] It balances the divisions of rhetoric well enough that it would seem to offer, in the hands of a capable tutor or scholar, a chance for a rhetoric filled with some of its old-time vitality. Its use in the colonies would seem to indicate, however, that it was applied much as was Dugard.[25] One finds little evidence to show that the sketchy treatments of invention and arrangement influenced practice in any substantial way. Perhaps the most that can be said is that it served as a reminder of the full tradition of rhetoric during a time when the Ramean concept was the more popular.[26]

A number of other rhetorical works were available to the colonists, of course. They range from collections of commonplaces or formulae for the writing of themes or orations, to reference books,[27] and their influence is difficult to assess.

One type of the rhetoric of trope and figure, the so-called "rhetorics of the scriptures," should be noted. Largely in the Ramean tradition as to content, this class of rhetorics illustrated the traditional list of figures with quotations from the Bible. The most popular of this group seems to have been the work of John Smith.[28] Available in America as early as 1683, the work is frequently referred to in early colonial writings, and was highly recommended by Samuel Johnson as late as the middle of the eighteenth century.[29] Some idea of the philosophy of the book may be gained from the introduction:

[Rhetoric] hath two parts, *viz.*

1. Garnishing of Speech, called *Elocution.*
2. Garnishing of the manner of utterance, called *Pronunciation* (which this treatise is not principally aimed at).

Elocution, or the garnishing of speech, is the first and principal part of Rhetorique, whereby the speech itself is beautified and made fine: And this is either
   The fine manner of words called a Trope: or
   The fine shape or frame of speech, called a Figure.[30]

One of the earliest inquiries into the scientific nature of speech was also in the colonies, John Winthrop receiving from the Royal Society of London in 1670 a copy of William Holders' *Elements of Speech.*[31] The book was a forerunner of many of the later works in phonetics, for it makes a strong attempt to popularize a phonetic alphabet, suggesting that the use of a universal sound alphabet would simplify all teaching, and that such an alphabet is absolutely necessary in training the deaf to speak.

The material is interesting, and undoubtedly significant for the historian in voice science, but the single copy found in the preparation of this study would not seem to indicate important influence in the colonies.

Outstanding is the almost complete lack of the classical influence in early rhetorical teaching in America. Although most of the evidence is negative, it seems clear that Aristotle, Cicero, and Quintilian exerted little influence on the beginnings of American rhetorical theory; similarly, Cox [32] and Wilson,[33] frequently hailed by students of English rhetorical theory, seem to have had no direct influence on the colonies. No record has been found in any library, public or private, which would indicate that either of these two works was in the colonies before 1730.

The Classical Tradition

Despite this domination by Ramean rhetoric during the earliest period in American history, by 1730 there were growing indications of a turn toward the classical tradition. The so called *"Port Royal Art of Speaking"* [34] enjoyed some vogue by 1750, and represented almost a complete departure from Ramean concepts. First known to be in the colonies in 1716,[35] the *Art of Speaking* exerted vital influence in the development of American rhetorical theory.

The 1696 edition is actually two books bound into one—an Art of Speaking and an Art of Persuasion.

The "Art of Speaking" opens with a discussion of the formation of the organs of speech. Then, following chapters on grammar and vocabulary, there is detailed consideration of trope and figure. Although this would seem to be a consideration of those same aspects of rhetoric which engrossed the Ramean school, the emphasis is clearly on a new concept: although one's style should be ornamental, this is never the end of style. Rather, style is always subservient to the end of the speech.

The second book of the work, the "Art of Persuasion," carries forward the emphasis indicated in the earlier section. Dividing the art into five parts, "Invention of the proper Means, Disposition of these means, Elocution, Memory and Pronunciation,[36] the work shows a clear empha-

sis on rhetoric as an active art, concerned with the moving and influencing of men.

The general treatment is Ciceronian and the entire work is a keystone
in the bridge between the truncated rhetoric earlier prevalent in the
colonies and the full classical approach which was soon to become
dominant. Interestingly enough, the work also offers a foretaste of the
coming emphasis in American education on "belles lettres." Specialized
discussions of the style of the historian and of the poet are provided.
Within a few years belles lettres emerges as a separate discipline—and
eventually leads to the creation of departments of English Language
and Literature in American colleges and universities.

Along with the growing interest in the more complete rhetoric represented by the *Art of Speaking*, there were increasing signs of the use
of the classical rhetorics, especially Cicero, in the colonies. Although
Aristotle's works are infrequently mentioned, Cicero's *De Oratore*
became one of the most popular works on speech in mid-eighteenth
century America. In the Yale library "6 dupl." copies were available in
1743; the charging lists of the Harvard library from 1762 to 1770 show
its use with constant regularity. Quintilian also was in wide circulation.
A part of the University of Pennsylvania course of study in 1756,[37] it
was in the curriculum of Washington College in Maryland in 1783.[38]

In addition to this growing interest in the classical authors, a number of English works in the classical tradition were imported into the
colonies after 1730. Since most of these works have been discussed in
other studies,[39] only brief comment seems required here. Suffice it to
say that every important rhetoric published in England during the
eighteenth century found its way into one or more of the large American libraries.

One of these English rhetorics, however, merits special attention.
It is John Ward's *A System of Oratory*.[40] Called the "most complete
statement of classical rhetoric written in the English tongue," [41] Ward's
System exerted wide influence in America. Dominant in the college field
until 1780, it was in general circulation as well. Only the works of
Campbell and Blair were to destroy its influence.

Much has been written about Ward's rhetorical theory and its influence on American speech education,[42] and an especially helpful discussion by Douglas Ehninger summarizes this material as follows:

The work clearly has historical importance, and in a very real fashion contributed to the development of modern rhetorical theory. For, though later
writers may have departed from classicism, unless the full scope of the classical rhetoric had been firmly established they hardly could have advanced
beyond it. It was Ward's ultimate contribution—and one for which he was
eminently fitted—to sweep away once and for all the last vestiges of the

Ramean apostasy, and thus help pave the way for the great creative rhetorics of the eighteenth century.[43]

Rhetoric and Belles Lettres

Along with the growth of the classical tradition in America was a corresponding increase in interest in the new rhetorics of style which were being sent to the colonies. Such works as Anthony Blackwell's *Introduction to the Classics,* first published in London in 1718,[44] and copied almost without change by Robert Dodsley for *The Preceptor,*[45] were popular in America very soon after publication. *The Preceptor,* for example, was read by Samuel Johnson in 1749,[46] and was later used at both Pennsylvania and Harvard.[47] Some editions contained only the Blackwell material on style; others reprinted John Mason's *Essay on Elocution,* giving that work wide circulation in America.

Other contemporary rhetorics of style known to have been circulated in America include John Stirling's *A System of Rhetoric,* probably first published in London in 1733, and Thomas Gibbon's *Rhetoric; or a view of its principal Tropes and Figures* (London, 1767).

Of greatest importance, in terms of later trends in rhetorical theory, however, is the work on taste and composition written by Henry Home, Lord Kames. Within a few months after publication the three volumes comprising *The Elements of Criticism* [48] were shipped to Harvard College,[49] and copies were soon found all through the colonies.

The book is an effort to investigate, systematically, the metaphysical principles of the fine arts. Home discards the accepted authoritarian rules for literary composition, and builds instead new rules based on human nature. Thus it is a philosophical treatment of taste and criticism rather than a rhetoric in the sense that that term has been used in this discussion, but it presages an era to follow.[50] In only a few years rhetoric and belles lettres were to be decisively linked by Hugh Blair, and rhetoricians to become steadily less interested in oratory and public address and more concerned with "English Language and Literature."

The Elocution Movement

Still a third major development in rhetorical theory as it affected America was taking place during the latter half of the eighteenth century—the growth of the elocution movement. Beginning in England, where criticisms of the delivery of English orators had become especcially severe by 1750, special training in "elocution," or delivery, was soon widely popular both in England and the United States. John Mason, mentioned above, seems to have been the first writer to justify the use of the term *elocution* to describe delivery. He offers no explanation for the growth of the "vulgar" use of elocution as applied to delivery rather than style, although a footnote to his work explains his usage.[51]

From almost the beginning the elocutionists were divided into two schools—the "naturalistic" and the "mechanistic."[52] The naturalists believed that basic principles of effective delivery came from nature herself, and so their system of elocution was based on large precepts and on the speaker's understanding of the thoughts read or spoken. In contrast, the mechanists, while they too wanted the "natural" orator, felt that true naturalness could only come from a study of the rules implicit within nature. Thus they offered elaborate systems for acquiring naturalness.

Almost every elocution book written and published in England seems to have circulated in America, and in terms of library requests in the colleges, many were more widely read than the more complete rhetorics we have mentioned. Soon the largest number of rhetorical works written by Americans were to be on elocution.[53]

Beginnings of American Rhetoric

Clearly, the dominant influence in the development of American rhetorical theory came from England. The growth of an indigenous American rhetoric was slow—its fruits came some years after the period covered in this essay. Nonetheless, even during the colonial and revolutionary years, some contribution to the theory of rhetorical prose was made in America.

Just as in England, where many encyclopedic works were written during the eighteenth century, in the colonies similar volumes were published. It is difficult to determine the first editions of many of these works, but *The Young Secretary's Guide* was in its sixth edition by 1727, and *The American Instructor, or Young Man's Best Companion* had a ninth edition published in Philadelphia in 1748. This work defined rhetoric as "the Art of Speaking in the most elegant and persuasive manner; or as my Lord *Bacon* defines it, the Art of applying and addressing the Dictates of Reason to the Fancy, and of recommending them there so as to attract the Will and Desires."[54]

Actually, the first complete American rhetoric was that of John Witherspoon.[55] Although Witherspoon was educated in Scotland, and contemporary Scottish influences are apparent in his writing, the *Lectures* constitute a genuine American rhetoric. Based primarily on classical rhetoric, Witherspoon interpreted these principles in the light of the philosophy of his own time.

Wilson Paul summarizes Witherspoon's contribution to the development of speech education in America:

John Witherspoon holds a key position in the transition from the colonial oratory of the clergymen, to the American oratory of the statesman. His lectures led the way for the introduction into America of the British eighteenth century school of rhetoric furthered by John Quincy Adams. In a nation torn by war and internal confusion, he carried the banner of theoretical enlightenment and practical improvement of public speaking.[56]

Despite its nineteenth-century dominance in American speech education, no substantial contribution to elocutionary theory was made in America prior to 1785. In that year Noah Webster published the third section of his *Grammatical Institute of the English Language*,[57] but its material on theory was taken largely from Burgh and is only some ten pages of the two hundred included in the volume. Actually, Webster's only plea for this study in preference to the *Art of Speaking, The Preceptor*, or Scott's *Lessons*, is that it is an American work.[58]

Rhetorical theory in colonial America was rhetorical theory in transition. Ramean in the earliest years, American rhetoric felt the growth of the classical tradition bringing with it renewed interest in the classics themselves, and new interest in the contemporary writings of English rhetoricians. Increased interest in taste and criticism during the period reflected English thinking in most respects, and in America, as in England, the elocution movement was well established by 1785. Although few contributions of an original sort have come from colonial America, the foundation is laid for the productive and creative era ahead.

Notes

1. Pierre de la Ramee, also known by the Latinized Petrus Ramus (1515-1572). One of the most helpful biographies is that by Frank P. Graves, *Peter Ramus and the Educational Reformation of the Sixteenth Century* (New York, 1912).
2. Quoted in Perry Miller and T. H. Johnson, *The Puritans* (New York, 1938), pp. 709-710.
3. Cotton Mather, *Magnalia Christi Americana* (Hartford, 1853), II, p. 21.
4. W. C. Ford, *The Boston Book Market, 1679-1700* (Boston, 1917), p. 131.
5. Graves, *op. cit.*, p. 138.
6. Audemari Talaei, *Rhetorica, e. P. Rami Regii Professoris Praelectionibus Observata* (Antwerp, 1582).
7. *Harvard College Records* (MSS), I, p. 261.
8. Julius H. Tuttle, "The Libraries of the Mathers," *American Antiquarian Society*, New Series, XX, p. 288.
9. Arthur O. Norton, "Harvard Text Books and Reference Books of the 17th Century," *Publications of the Colonial Society of Massachusetts*, XXVIII (1930-1933), 424.
10. C. F. and R. Robinson, "Three Early Massachusetts Libraries," *Publ. Col. Soc. Mass.*, XXVIII (1930-1933), 133.
11. William Dugard (1606-1662). *Rhetorices Elementa* was first issued in 1650; by 1673 it had passed through seven editions.

12. Norton, *op. cit.*, p. 366.

13. Ford, *op. cit.*, pp. 126-150.

14. R. F. Seybolt, *Public Schools of Colonial Boston* (Cambridge, 1935), p. 71.

15. *Benjamin Wadsworth's Book Relating to College Affairs* (MS), p. 28. Report of tutors Flynt and Welstead.

16. R. F. Seybolt, "Student Libraries at Harvard, 1763-64," *Publ. Col. Soc. Mass.*, XXVIII (1930-1933), 454.

17. William Dugard, *Rhetorices Elementa Quaestionibus et Responsionibus Explicata*, Editio Tricesima (Londini, 1705).

18. Dugard, *op. cit.*, p. 1.

19. Ger. Jo. Vossii, *Elementa Rhetorica Oratoriis Ejusdem Partitionibus Accomodata, Inque Usum Scholarum Hollandiae & Westfrisial Emendatus Edita* (Londini, 1739) is the edition now in the Harvard Library.

20. *A Catalogue of the Library of Yale College in New-Haven* (New London, 1743).

21. Thomas Farnaby (1575?-1647). By 1639, famous as a schoolmaster and classical scholar, he was in repeated correspondence with Vossius. *Index Rhetoricus* was first issued in 1625, and was revised to the *Index Rhetoricus et Oratoribus* in 1646. The following notes are from the London edition of 1654.

22. Listed for sale by Robert Chisholm in Boston in 1680, other specific references to the work appear in 1693, 1702, 1705, and 1721. The *Index* was a part of the Harvard course of study in 1726, listed in the Yale catalogue of 1743, and was among the books claimed lost by Harvard students after the fire of 1764.

23. Farnaby, *Index Rhetoricus et Oratoribus*, p. 2.

24. Among the sources cited by Farnaby are Aristotle, Hermogenes, Dionysius, Longinus, Aphthonius, Cicero, Quintilian, Capella, Trapezuntius, Ramus, L. Vives, Alsted, Caussinus, Vossius, and others. Foster Watson calls Farnaby "one of the greatest of the schoolmaster editors of the classics," and this contact with the classical authors is obvious (*op. cit.*, p. 350). The *Index* is called by Mair in his introduction to Thomas Wilson: "a small but exceedingly well-constructed book." (*Arte of Rhetorique* [Oxford, 1909]), p. xix.

25. The phrasing in the Harvard records was "Dugard's *or* Farnaby's Rhetoric" (italics mine), Wadsworth, *op. cit.*, p. 28.

26. Donald Lemon Clark, *Rhetoric and Poetry in the Renaissance* (New York, 1922), p. 62, makes the point that Farnaby "gives a fairly proportional treatment of *inventio, dispositio, elocutio,* and *actio. Memoria* he omits, following here, as elsewhere, the sound leadership of Vossius."

27. Typical are John Clarke, *Formulae Oratoriae* ... (London, 1639); and Nicolaus Caussinus, *De Eloquentia* ... (London, 1651).

28. *The Mysterie of Rhetorique Unveil'd* (London, 1665).

29. *Samuel Johnson, President of King's College: His Career and Writings*, ed. Herbert and Carol Schneider, 4 vols. (New York, 1929), I, p. 317.

30. Smith, *op. cit.*, p. 1.

31. William Holders, *The Elements of Speech: an essay of inquiry into the natural production of letters, with an appendix concerning persons Deaf and Dumb* (London, 1669). The book was sent Winthrop with the thanks of the Society for certain items which he had sent to London. ("Correspondence of the Founders of the Royal Society with Governor Winthrop of Connecticut," *Massachusetts Historical Society Proceedings*, 1st series, XVI [1878], 244.)

32. Leonard Cox, *Arte or Crafte of Rhetoryke* (London, 1524).

33. Thomas Wilson, *Arte of Rhetorique* (London, 1553).

34. Bernard Lamy was the author of the work published under the following title: *The Art of Speaking Written in French by Messieurs Du Port Royal in Pursuance of a Former Treatise, Entitled, The Art of Thinking Rendered into English* (London, 1696).

35. A copy now in the Harvard library is inscribed, "Edward Wigglesworth, 1716." Wigglesworth was graduated by Harvard in 1712. Other specific references

have been found to the work in 1722, 1726, 1742 and 1748, and it seems to have been considered by Benjamin Franklin for use in his "English School."

36. Lamy, *op. cit.*, "The Art of Persuasion," p. 268.

37. T. H. Montgomery, *A History of the University of Pennsylvania from Its Foundation to AD 1770* (Philadelphia, 1900), pp. 238-239.

38. William Parker, *An Account of Washington College in the State of Maryland* (Philadelphia, 1789), p. 41.

39. See especially Warren Guthrie, "The Development of Rhetorical Theory in America," *Speech Monographs*, XIV (1947), 41-47.

40. London, 1759.

41. W. P. Sandford, *English Theories of Public Address, 1530-1828* (Columbus, 1928), p. 110.

42. See especially Sandford, *op. cit.*, pp. 107-110; H. F. Harding, "English Rhetorical Theory, 1750-1800," unpublished Ph.D. dissertation, Cornell University, 1937, pp. 40-48 and ff.; Guthrie, *op. cit.*, pp. 44-47.

43. Douglas Ehninger, "John Ward and his Rhetoric," *Speech Monographs*, XVII (1951), 16.

44. The subtitle is descriptive of the work: *An Essay on the Nature of Those Emphatical and Beautiful Figures Which Give Strength and Ornament to Writing.*

45. (London, 1748).

46. *Career and Writings*, Appendix.

47. Its use at Pennsylvania was along with Longinus and Quintilian. At Harvard the rhetoric from the *Preceptor* was an official "reciting book" in 1786, and an American edition was published "for the use of the University in Cambridge."

48. The first edition was published in London, 1762. Seven editions were published before 1790, and an American edition was published in 1796.

49. *Harvard College Papers*, 1650-1753 (MSS), I, p. 296.

50. For further comment on Kames, see S. Austin Alliborne, *A Critical Dictionary of English Literature and British and American Authors* (Philadelphia, 1891), I, 870-874.

51. For further discussion of the changes and the meanings of "elocution," "pronuntiatio," etc., see F. W. Haberman, "The Elocution Movement in England, 1750-1785," unpublished Ph.D. dissertation, Cornell University, 1947.

52. Incidentally, each called itself natural. Contemporary argument continues over just what is "natural" and what is "mechanical." For illustration see recent writings by Parrish, Van Dragen, Winans, and others in the *Quarterly Journal of Speech*.

53. Many studies have been done of the elocution movement. One especially helpful to the student of the period is Haberman's, *op. cit.*

54. George Fisher, *The American Instructor*, p. 302. It may be of interest to note that the first use of "elocution" to describe delivery that I have found is in this work. The parts of logic are given as Invention, Judgment, Memory, and "the Art of Elocution or Delivering."

55. John Witherspoon, *Lectures on Moral Philosophy and Eloquence* (Woodward's 3rd ed.; Philadelphia, 1810). Witherspoon was president of Princeton from 1768 to 1794, and the *Lectures* were delivered during that time. They were never planned for publication, but were first published with Witherspoon's collected writings after his death, and later reprinted as a separate volume.

56. For a complete analysis of Witherspoon, see Wilson B. Paul, "John Witherspoon's Theory and Practice of Public Speaking," unpublished Ph.D. dissertation, Iowa, 1940.

57. *An American Selection of Lessons in Reading and Speaking* (Hartford, 1785).

58. Webster was especially filled with patriotic fervor and was attempting to establish a distinctively "American" language. Thus his three volume *Grammatical Institute*, and the strongly nationalistic flavor of the selections chosen for Vol. III.

3 Rhetorical Practice in Colonial America

GEORGE V. BOHMAN

....

Much of higher education in Colonial times was conducted orally, not only as lectures and recitations, but prescribed as formal original speeches, as declamations, disputations, commonplacing, and dramatic dialogues, and as essays and poems read aloud. To understand the place of rhetoric in such education and the accumulated customs of the first one hundred forty years of training in speaking in American colleges, one must consider three major questions: What was the pattern of public programs and curricular exercises in speaking at the close of the Revolution? How did this pattern develop in American colleges? What were the principal values and disadvantages of the most common forms of rhetorical training?

Pattern of Rhetorical Training at the Close of the Revolution

For the purposes of this study, rhetorical training may be divided into (1) the public programs of the colleges in which student speakers participated and (2) the regular requirements and practices in the curriculum and in student clubs and societies.

Speaking in Public College Exercises

By the end of the Revolution, guests were ordinarily invited to almost any exercise which involved orations and disputations so that students often had audiences composed of others than students and faculty at monthly and quarterly exercises, senior examinations, commencements, and special academic occasions such as the inauguration of a president or professor, commemorations, and official visits of dignitaries.

In 1786, young John Quincy Adams wrote from Harvard that at the next commencement "there will be delivered two English poems, two English orations, two Latin orations, a Greek dialogue, three forensic

60

disputes, and an English dialogue between four." [1] At Yale, in 1785, orations in Hebrew, Greek, and Latin, an English oration on eloquence, a dialogue, syllogistic disputes, and two forensic disputes did the candidates "great Honor with the Literati, & gave universal Satisfaction to the most respectable & splendid Assembly." [2] At Rhode Island College, commencement included orations in Greek, Latin, and English, a poem, and usually both syllogistic and forensic disputes. [3] For almost five hours at the Princeton commencement of 1784, Stiles heard sixteen graduates of the College of New Jersey deliver orations in English—salutatory, valedictory, gratulatory, serious, and humorous. [4] In typical postwar commencements, the syllogistic disputations were disappearing and forensic disputes, English orations, and occasional student "dialogues" together with some poems and essays read aloud became the fare which was, as always, well interlarded with reunions over food and drink.

During an academic year, however, commencement was only the climax of a series of exhibitions and examinations of the oral prowess of college students. At least by 1778, Yale concluded the traditional oral examinations of the senior class with a program of orations. Stiles described it:

The Senior Tutor thereupon made a very eloquent Latin Speech & presented the Candidates for the Honors of the College. This Present^a the Pres^t in a Latin Speech accepted, & addressed the Gentlemen Examiners & gave the latter Lib^y to return home till Comm.

The exercises after the tutor's speech consisted of a cliosophic oration in Latin, 11 minutes; a poetical composition in English, 12 minutes; an English dialogue, 9 minutes; a cliosophic oration in English, 16 minutes; disputations in English, 11, 8, and 7 minutes; a valedictory oration in English, 22 minutes; and an anthem. [5]

In 1771, President Witherspoon of the College of New Jersey had introduced prize contests in speaking on the day preceding commencement. These included reading English, Latin, and Greek aloud "with propriety and grace and being able to answer all questions on its orthography and grammar," speaking Latin, and pronouncing English orations. In the last contest, "the preference was determined by ballot, and all present were permitted to vote who were graduates of this or any other College." Reporting on the first year of these contests, the *Pennsylvania Chronicle* said that "in public speaking the competitors were numerous, and it was very difficult to decide the pre-eminence." In 1774, the oratorical prizes were won by Charles Lee and John Rogers, "each adjudged by seven Gentlemen." A biographer has suggested that H. H. Brackenridge not only became known as an eloquent undergraduate orator at Princeton, but wrote speeches for others, once to be rewarded by a much needed "handsome suit of clothes and a cocked hat." [6]

On a variety of other occasions during the academic year, such as quarter-days, semiannual exhibitions, and sometimes monthly programs, outsiders were invited to hear disputes, orations, and dialogues presented by students. Regarding quarter-days at Yale in 1784 and 1785, Stiles noted: "Present 100 Ladies & Gentlemen. a crouded Assembly" and "A Full Assembly of Scholars, Gent. & Ladies." A student called the exercises, which were usually held in the comparatively small college hall or chapel, "very clever & humorous." In 1780, Stiles described the program as "anthem; dialogue; oration; anthem." On December 11, 1782, "the Seniors exhibited the usual academic Entertainments. viz a Latin oration, an English Dialogue between Gen Warren, Gov Hutchinson & Count Pulaski all in the Shades. And English Oration." With his customary precision, Stiles recorded the lengths of the various items on some programs:

July 16, 1783. Cliosophic Oration English 11', Forensic Dispute, about 50', English Dialogue, 20', Valedictory Oration in Latin, 26', Address to the Candidates by Tutor Meigs; he as all others speaking on the stage 16'.

Mar. 9, 1785. Latin Oration, 15', Dialogue 33', English Orations 8'. [7]

On commemorative occasions, colleges usually included some student speaking on the programs. At Yale in the 1770's and 1780's, classmates delivered memorial orations for deceased students. These speeches compounded large quantities of general philosophy on death and religion with personal recollections and tributes and long, sentimental conclusions which were usually adorned with elegiac poetry. [8] At Stiles' inaugural, a "senior Bachelor ascended the Stage & delivered ƒ congratulatory Oration in Latin." [9] Students of the College of Willia ı and Mary sometimes spoke on founders' day. Following a custom at Oxford and Cambridge when the Tudor sovereigns visited, junior or senior orators at Harvard pronounced Latin orations before the visiting governor. [10]

Speaking in the Curriculum and in Literary and Debating Societies

From the use of different forms of speaking in public academic exercises, we gain some insight into the pattern of training and certainly can observe administrative emphases or the suitability of the different forms for public use. But the major evidence of the pattern of rhetorical training may be found in the weekly and yearly requirements of the curriculum and in the extracurricular activities of students in literary and debating societies.

Although the curriculum was still strongly classical in content, by the mid-1780's the Latin and Greek languages were less used in oral exercises than ever before and by the end of the eighteenth century even Latin syllogistic disputations had disappeared from the public exercises in all the colleges but Rhode Island and from practically all training programs. Logic, formerly a required freshman course which served as a basis for the syllogistic disputes, had generally become part of the junior or senior curriculum. Interest in English language and literature seemed to develop in various directions. The forensic disputes which replaced the syllogistic were in English. Although the learned languages were still employed in original speaking, the number of English orations greatly increased. A revival of interest in declamations and the institution of contests in reading aloud at the College of New Jersey probably motivated drill in oral delivery. To some extent, this may indicate awareness of the expanding literature of the elocutionists. At Harvard, the Overseers had for some years considered dramatic dialogues and other experiments in theatrical performances as desirable oral training. However, emphasis on writing English also was increasing and the appearance of both dialogues and the longer commencement and quarter-day pieces called "essays" on public programs seem partly an oral increment derived from the new attention to "belles lettres."

Another change which was far advanced in the 1780's in the colleges was the abandonment of the class tutor system for more specialized tutors and professors. However, at Harvard, for example, all tutors were still expected to teach writing and speaking in addition to a specialty. Many tutors were young and inexperienced in teaching and by no means specialists in rhetoric. Only President Witherspoon's lectures on rhetoric in the postwar period provided notable, expert guidance for training in speaking.

The pattern of rhetorical instruction continued to consist of weekly attendance at lectures and exercises by classes. In some colleges, only the two upper classes participated in disputations and orations. President Madison thus described the requirements at William and Mary:

The public exercises are, 1st, weekly, the Whole University in a convenient apartment, one of the Society presiding. Questions are previously prepared and then debated. 2 Monthly, for the students in Law. And annually when subjects are given to deliver Orations, which, if deserving, are printed.[11]

At Harvard, John Quincy Adams, who was well impressed with the training in speaking, wrote:

... speaking in the Chapel, before all the classes, which I shall have to do in my turn four or five times before we leave college. Such also are the forensic disputations, one of which we are to have tomorrow. A question is given out by the tutor in metaphysics, for the whole class to dispute upon. They alternately affirm or deny the questions, and write, each, two or three pages for or against, which is read in the Chapel before the tutor, who finally gives his opinion concerning the question. We have two or three questions every quarter. That for tomorrow is, whether the immortality of the human soul is probable from natural reason? It comes in course for me to affirm, and in this case it makes the task much easier. It so happens that whatever the question may be, I must support it.[12]

In Stiles' *College Memoranda* of 1783, some speaking is indicated for each class, usually once or at the most twice during the week. Seniors and juniors disputed Mondays and Tuesdays. Juniors also spoke in chapel part of Thursday afternoons. Sophomores spoke in chapel Saturday afternoons. The amount of freshman time for speaking is not clear.[13] In general, the number of opportunities for each student to speak was not large. Although most of the compositions were usually written out before delivery, the amount of criticism both in written and oral forms and, indeed, the effort put upon the composition and performance by students are factors not clarified in contemporary accounts.

That there were numerous students who sought more rather than less opportunities to speak is suggested by the existence of literary and debating societies in the colleges. Particularly at New Jersey, Yale, Harvard, Dartmouth, and William and Mary, student members of such clubs indulged in frequent programs which emphasized all the types of speaking that were included in the curricular exercises. In addition, business sessions and extempore disputes as well as some dramatizations provided even greater variety. Mutual criticism and competition stimulated improved performances. At William and Mary, the able George Wythe also sponsored moot courts for would-be lawyers at which some deliberative as well as strictly legal problems were debated.[14]

Such was the nature of student training and activities in speaking just after the Revolution. The training consisted primarily of lectures and readings in rhetorical theory and related subjects, together with regular exercises in original speaking, declamation, and disputation which gave a few opportunities annually for each student to speak before his class and tutors and for selected students to speak at quarter-days, examinations, prize contests, and commencements. As purely extracurricular enterprises, speaking and debating flourished, sometimes on a competitive basis, in literary and debating societies. The quality of all these aspects of rhetorical training varied considerably from one college to another. The quality of instruction was apparently superior under the aegis of President Witherspoon, George Wythe, and perhaps under Ezra Stiles and the Yale tutors.

The Development of Rhetorical Training in Early American Colleges

The manner in which rhetorical training developed may be seen in three stages. The first was the pattern used at Harvard College in the seventeenth century. In a second stage, with minor changes, the Harvard pattern was adopted at Yale and the College of William and Mary. During the middle decades of the eighteenth century, the College of New Jersey, the College of Philadelphia, King's College, Dartmouth College, and Rhode Island College instituted programs which contained many of the same elements, but showed considerable individuality. In a third stage, more significant changes in the traditional pattern of Tudor and Continental education resulted from demands for functional training in the speaking of English which began with the planning of the College of Philadelphia at mid-century and permeated all the colleges.

In 1642, when Harvard set up laws to guide students, it required declamations, syllogistic disputations, orations, and commonplacing. All these had been similarly practiced in Britain and Europe. The rules of syllogistic disputation had changed little since Abelard's day and for centuries formal declamations and orations had been exhibited by British university students at commencements and state visits.[15] In the early laws, Harvard undergraduates and bachelors were required to "repeate Sermons in ye Hall whenever they are called forth," "untill they have Commonplaced," although the purpose seemed not so much rhetorical as that "with reverence & Love they may retaine God & his truths in their minds." Commonplacing was generally scheduled for nine and ten o'clock Saturday mornings.[16] Declamations for first, second, and third year men were held at nine and ten on Fridays. At first, "publique declamations in Latine and Greeke" were planned for each student monthly, but these were reduced to bimonthly in 1655. The declamations, contrary to frequent usage, seem generally to have been original orations and sometimes were delivered in English instead of a classical language.[17] Practice in disputation, supervised by the president, occupied an hour for each class on Monday and Tuesday afternoons. Finally, the whole college heard the president lecture on rhetoric from eight to nine Friday mornings and, after declamations, rhetoric was to be studied the rest of the day. In this plan of 1642, syllogistic disputations provided practice in logic, but the subjects which were chosen ranged through all the areas of study. Likewise, declamations or orations represented practice in rhetoric, which for the followers of Ramus it will be recalled meant the canons of *elocutio* and *pronuntiatio*. To a marked extent, pedagogy also followed the Ramist procedure of one subject a day, taught by successive periods of lecture, study, quiz, and oral applications of what was learned in one or more of the prescribed rhetorical exercises.[18]

Disputations and orations constituted the main fare at seventeenth century commencements. Before as many critical Harvard alumni, admiring parents, and curious townsfolk as could come, the young men showed their skills in logic and rhetoric and made their first promising public impressions upon future colleagues in the ministry and leaders in both church and politics.[19]

When the College of William and Mary and Yale College were founded near the opening of the eighteenth century and even at mid-century when the College of New Jersey and King's College were planned, the Harvard pattern (or perhaps more accurately, the traditional university pattern) of rhetorical training was used. Thus, at the beginning of these colleges, the Latin syllogistic disputations, declamations, and orations predominated.[20]

By mid-century, however, various forces were challenging the dominance of the Latin language, the Ramist views of rhetoric and logic, and consequently the nature of the rhetorical exercises. Demands for more functional training in the English language led to more orations in English and contributed to the substitution of the forensic for the syllogistic disputation. Under President Finley, the College of New Jersey required some declamations "to display the various passions, and exemplify the graces of utterance and gesture." At Yale and other colleges, Latin orations appeared on commencement programs until the end of the period.[21] During the last half of the century, the colleges permitted forensic disputations to become increasingly prominent both in the classroom exercises and in public exhibitions. The syllogistic form appeared last at commencements at New Jersey in 1774, Philadelphia in 1775, and King's in 1770. The forensic form was used in the 1760's at commencements by all except Dartmouth, Rutgers, and possibly William and Mary. The forensic gained ground until, prior to the outbreak of the Revolution, Harvard, Yale, King's, Philadelphia, Rhode Island College, and the College of New Jersey required forensic disputation, usually weekly, by the two upper classes. By the 1790's, the syllogistic form had practically disappeared from the requirements of American colleges.[22]

Benjamin Franklin's *Proposals Relating to the Education of Youth in Pennsilvania* (1744) and the *Idea of the English School* (ca. 1751) widely publicized a point of view that was gaining favor particularly in urban areas. Franklin demanded the training of youth in the English tongue:

Thus instructed, Youth will come out of this School fitted for learning any Business, Calling, or Profession, except wherein Languages are required; and tho' unacquainted with any antient or foreign Tongue, they will be masters of their own, which is more immediate and general Use....[23]

Both in the *Proposals* and the *Idea of the English School*, he outlined courses which emphasized speaking and reading skills. He wanted youth to develop clarity and conciseness, to pronounce distinctly, and "to form their own Stiles." In his plans, he did not overlook the study of model speeches, the elements of rhetoric and logic, translations of the classics, and the latest British literature of Milton, Locke, Addison, Pope, and Swift or the use of the dictionary; for, he wrote:

It is impossible a Reader should give due Modulation to his Voice, and pronounce properly, unless his understanding goes before his Tongue.... Declarations, repeating Speeches, delivering Orations, ... [and] Public Disputes warm the Imagination, whet the Industry, and strengthen the Natural Abilities.[24]

This broad concept of a program of speech training grew out of Franklin's wide acquaintance with the needs of professional and business men, his interest in contemporary literature and writers, his belief in the doctrine of good works, and awareness of the special dialectal problems of the middle colonies. Franklin was a clear spokesman for the awakened interest in public speaking that was developing out of the religious revivals, the rise of the lawyer class, and the formation of business and trade organizations in which he himself had taken the lead. Political agitation in the ensuing decades intensified this interest in speaking well.

Although Franklin actually met with only partial and irregular success in his effort to establish speaking training primarily in English at the new college, in other colleges students were demanding exercises in English and governing boards were not completely unsympathetic. In October, 1754, the Harvard Board of Overseers selected a committee "to project some new method to promote oratory." In June, 1755, the Corporation approved an ingenious plan to substitute dialogues for the usual declamation. The materials were to be chosen and translated from standard Latin authors, each student to impersonate a part and then deliver his part in translation as an oration. In May, 1757, the Corporation directed the tutors to spend Friday mornings, except when formal declamations were being held, helping freshmen and sophomores with their elocution or pronunciation of Latin or English orations, speeches, or dialogues. In addition, once a month the two senior classes were to hold disputations "in English in the forensic manner without being confined to syllogisms." For ten years the Overseers were concerned with the enforcement of these major changes by semiannual visitations and exhibitions.[25]

Probably the College of New Jersey developed the most ambitious programs of original orations. According to the *Account* of 1764, seniors gave original orations at monthly oration-days and the three other classes alternately delivered original orations and declamations from other authors. Apparently, Witherspoon's arrival as president accentuated President Davies' program and the new president soon instituted the annual prize contests which have been described. In 1772, Witherspoon described the curricular requirements in oratory:

> During the whole course of their studies, the three younger classes, two every evening formerly, and now three, because of their increased number, pronounce an oration, on the stage erected for that purpose in the hall, immediately after prayers; that they may learn, by early habit, presence of mind, and proper pronunciation and gesture in public speaking. This excellent practice, which has been kept up almost from the first foundation of the College, has had the most admirable effects. The senior scholars, every five or six weeks, pronounce orations of their own composition, to which all persons of any note in the neighborhood are invited or admitted.[26]

At King's, the formal laws produced little enlargement of original speaking. At Philadelphia, with Professor Kinnersley's departure in 1772, oratorical exercises declined.[27] At Rhode Island College, both forensic disputations and English orations appeared on the first commencement programs. In 1774, the two upper classes were required to attend weekly forensic disputes.[28] At Dartmouth, the first commencement of 1771 included one English oration, two orations in Latin, a syllogistic dispute, but no forensic disputation occurred prior to 1774. In the laws of 1782, the first Wednesday of each month was devoted to forensic disputes by seniors.[29]

As previously noted, another change which occurred as the Ramist system of logic and rhetoric gave way to classical rhetorical theory and use of the native tongue was the employment of professorial lecturers or special tutors in rhetoric and allied fields in a few colleges. Such experts as William Small at William and Mary, Kinnersley at the College of Philadelphia, and Witherspoon at the College of New Jersey became noted lecturers, though it may be doubted that they were superior to President Dunster and other teacher-presidents of Harvard in the seventeenth and early eighteenth centuries who personally conducted the lectures as did Witherspoon in this later period.

Several colleges experimented with dialogues and with poems, essays, and other written compositions of a literary nature which were read aloud as part of the speaking exercises. These appeared on commencement programs in 1762 at Philadelphia, 1764 at Princeton, 1773 at Harvard, and at other colleges thereafter. Was direct instruction given in these exercises? The essays and poems read aloud may have been part of the training in declamation. Although the Harvard Overseers blessed the teaching of dramatic dialogues in 1755, the chief evidence of training in such exercises is in the literary clubs.

At Harvard, Yale, New Jersey, William and Mary, King's, Dartmouth, and perhaps at the other colleges to a lesser degree, societies were organized at various times during the eighteenth century, which utilized disputations, orations, and other types of speaking as major items on their programs, although religious and social activities and society libraries were also important incentives for students to join. Many societies did not outlive the student generation which organized them, but by mid-century a few organizations achieved a degree of permanence. Critonian at Yale lasted from 1750 to 1772. In 1753, Fellowship Club, later Linonian, and in 1768 Brothers in Unity were founded. At William and Mary in 1776 the first chapter of Phi Beta Kappa was formed. It later organized chapters at other colleges. In the same year, Rutgers men founded the Athenian society. In the 1780's at Dartmouth, three major societies, the Social Friends, the United Fraternity, and the local chapter of Phi Beta Kappa began. At the College of New Jersey, the earlier Well-Meaning and Plain-Dealing societies were disbanded in 1768 but the next year the famous American Whig and Cliosophic societies arose to create a strong competition in varied programs which included debates, disputations, occasional orations, "Harangues," and reading aloud. In Clio, "correctors of speaking" and "correctors of composition" became regularly elected officers. At King's, Rhode Island College, and the College of Philadelphia the societies appear to have been less influential in student life.[30]

Values of Major Forms of Rhetorical Training

What were the principal values and some of the disadvantages of the major forms of rhetorical training which were used in the early American colleges? For purposes of general criticism and evaluation, we shall consider here only the syllogistic disputation, the forensic disputation, and the oration which persisted as an exercise throughout the period. The unusual opportunities for more flexible forms of speaking which the student societies made possible we shall mention but briefly. David Potter treats of the literary society later in this volume.

Syllogistic Disputations

In an era in which most students at Harvard were planning to be ministers, the sifting and defense of "truth" by categorical forms of logic offered advantages, particularly if audiences were accustomed to the "plain style" of pulpit address in which concise, didactic, and closely reasoned discourse was predominant. Aside from some abstract speculation, the purpose of formal logic was not primarily to develop and project new solutions for problems. As syllogistic disputation was practiced, the topics or theses were drawn from the curriculum of ethics, philosophy, politics, theology, grammar, rhetoric, mathematics, and ancient languages. What the student studied he could formally defend or attack. If the "truth" seemed to be wanting adequate defense, the tutor or president-moderator, except at public occasions, would intervene and suggest arguments. Either intervention or a decision on the "truth" by the moderator could assist the lone respondent if he were overwhelmed by several opponents.

Despite efforts to insure the victory or at least an adequate defense of accepted truths, extreme conservatives, such as the Boston minister Crosswell, charged that graduates were forced to deny theses that were true and that the "Spirit of Atheism is thereby diffused." In an answer to Crosswell's charges, President Holyoke chiefly relied upon the century-old tradition behind this type of thesis. He made no formal Aristotelian justification of the exercise, but pointed to its use in all Protestant universities and especially at Harvard under Chauncy, Oakes, and Mather, who "were as jealous of the Honour of God as you...." [31]

It was also argued against the disputes that the logical method was too intricate and made too many minor distinctions which reduced argument to "a Parcel Terms" and the "Art of Wrangling." By 1786, when this form had been abandoned at most colleges, John Quincy Adams recorded in his Harvard diary:

These syllogistics are very much despised by the scholars, and no attention seems to be paid to them by the company at Commencement. The scholars in general think that the government in giving them those parts write on their foreheads DUNCE in capital letters.

A few days later he wrote his father:

Syllogistic disputes ... are held in detestation by the scholars, and everyone thinks it a reflection upon his character as a genius and a student to have a syllogistic; this opinion is the firmer, because the best scholars almost always have the other parts. There are many disadvantages derive from these syllogisms, and I know of only one benefit, which is this. Many scholars would go through college without studying at all, but would idle away all their time, who merely from the horrors of syllogisms begin to study, acquire a fondness for it, and make a very pretty figure in college. . . .[32]

Among the few contemporary accounts of public performances of students in these disputes, the *Pennsylvania Gazette* in 1762 commented that debate at Princeton on a thesis "afforded pleasure to the learned portion of the audience." Of course Latin was understood only by the academic community, which somewhat limited the values of exercises in that language at commencements. John Macpherson complained that at the College of Philadelphia in 1767, even the Latin was "ill done . . . ill pronounced, & there was no action, for they spoke from desks." [33] Actually, if we judge from a few manuscripts and Stiles' diary, the public disputes of later years comprised only a few concise Latin sentences at a time by each speaker and interest was perforce due either to parental pride or the keenest intellectual curiosity.

The objections, then, to the syllogistic dispute were numerous. In contrast to the forensic type of disputation, the syllogistic was overly concise and brief. It limited logical reasoning to deductive, mostly categorical syllogisms. Because of the nature of the proofs, the subjects that were appropriate gave little chance to debate current policies and to project and test solutions. The structure, in which one respondent faced a number of opponents tended, many thought, to favor the opposition. The pattern was extremely stereotyped and allowed no essential adaptation for the persuasion of the audience. In this respect, the syllogistic dispute remained dialectic and therefore not rhetorical training, except for the requirement of oral presentation.[34]

Forensic Disputations

To students familiar with the syllogistic, the forensic dispute offered much more varied opportunities for using all forms of reasoning and the whole range of classical rhetorical skills from invention through delivery. The less concise and usually more familiar English language prompted fluency; it assured, too, that audiences would understand most of what was said. For students, the practice of using from two to four persons on each side in debate and the extension of the total time to forty-five minutes or more in both public and training exercises made the preparation and delivery of a forensic a major academic event in which it was an honor to participate.

The colleges turned to the forensic form just before and during the period in which students were taking an intense interest in the difficulties between the Colonies and Great Britain, which challenged men to form opinions and to debate them vigorously. Many subjects continued to be chosen from the fields of academic controversy in philosophy, rhetoric, languages, and literature. As the Revolution approached, however, students chose a large proportion of questions from the issues which sprang up between the mother country and the Colonies or from the domestic reforms advocated by the Whigs. Proposition and questions such as these illustrate the trend:

It is lawful for every man, and in many cases his indispensable duty, to hazard his life in the defence of his civil liberty. (1768)
The Non-Importation Agreement reflects a Glory on the American Merchants, and was a noble Exertion of Self-Denial and Public Spirit. (1770)
The legality of enslaving Africans.
Whether the Press ought to be free?
Whether Females ought to be admitted to public Civil Government?
Whether Representatives are to act according to their own Minds or the Minds of their Constituents? [35]

At the first commencement of Rhode Island College in 1769, James Varnum and William Williams debated "Whether the British America can, under her present circumstances, with good policy effect to become an independent state." [36] In 1773 at Harvard, Theodore Parsons and Eliphalet Pearson clashed over whether African slavery was according to the law of nature. Rather than the formal arguments, the careful persuasive approaches of the opposing speakers in this debate commanded respect. The first speaker against slavery apparently assumed considerable opposition to his position. So, with little argument and slight attention to African slaves, he talked at some length about the views of the audience on liberty in general. Then, to combat such a conciliatory approach, the second speaker in the debate asked the audience to suspend its sentiments and examine the arguments objectively. He said: "That Liberty is sweet to all, I freely own; but ... the doctrine of happiness of the whole ... requires some subordination." With this he began a long formal argument that slavery in general reflected a law of nature which was peculiarly applicable to Africans in this country. [37]

After the Revolution, Stiles recorded such timely questions for disputation as the mode of taxation for paying continental debts, private vs. public education, universal toleration of religions, the established church, Vermont statehood, a standing army, increased power for Congress, the Society of the Cincinnati, and imprisonment for debt. [38]

Contemporary comment reflected less interest in the subjects used than in the "spirit and eloquence" of the speaking. The *Pennsylvania Gazette* praised the English forensic dispute at Princeton in 1760 on the proposition that "the Elegance of the Orations consists in the Words being Consonant to the Sense" by saying that "The Respondent, Mr. Saml Blair, acquitted himself with universal applause in the elegant

Composition and Delivery of his Defence; and his Opponent answered with Humor and Pertinency." In 1767 at Philadelphia, Macpherson remarked: "We were then entertained by an English dispute, opened by Tighlman (who alone it is said composed his own piece) who was opposed by Johnson. Barkson wound up & bore the bell as the phrase is." [39]

By the end of the period the forensic dispute was adversely criticized on two points which have always demanded careful supervision and restraint. Macpherson noted that in disputes, as in oratory, some students were unwilling to make adequate preparation and either had to obtain help to prepare a speech or spoke with superficial knowledge. The second fault was that, especially in the literary and debating societies, personal abuse, exaggerated argumentum ad absurdum, and ridicule were too often rife.

On the whole, however, the forensic dispute was better adapted to the variety of secular as well as religious careers toward which students of the latter half of the eighteenth century might look. Besides the pulpit, the courtroom, the legislative hall, the town meeting, and the stump claimed as much flexibility, knowledge of current issues, and skillful speaking as the best students could learn. Their intense interest and the approval of administrations and of many leading alumni testify to the wide acceptance of the forensic dispute as a means of training leaders in the Colonies and the infant nation.

Orations

Orators were men of considerable honor in the colleges. Presumably, the curricular program prepared every man to deliver original speeches as well as declamations from other authors. In the earlier years, when classes were small, every student might get a chance to dispute or deliver an oration in a public exercise and the best were selected for the salutatory or valedictory orations at commencement or for a complimentary oration at the visit of a governor or the inauguration of a president. Later, when the orators were elected by the senior class, as at Harvard, "there was a great deal of intriguing carried on." [40] Whether by the class or the professors, the choice was announced some weeks before the oration was to be delivered. Benjamin Wadsworth's *Book* recorded notices sent between March 14 and April 15 for late June commencements. At Princeton, Witherspoon required that speeches be submitted to him for correction and approval at least four weeks before the exercises.

If orations generally were of the lengths of those preserved or whose times were recorded, they ranged from about seven to twenty-five

minutes long. Some early Latin orations may have been longer.[41] Many
of the publicly delivered orations must have been developed and first
delivered in the routine classroom exercises. Yet, some young men
found the task of composition onerous. In a letter to William Paterson,
an alumnus, student Edward Graham wrote:

I was told to entreat your assistance in my favor, to prepare me for my last
public speaking in college the next commencement. On all occasions hitherto
I have made a trial of my own abilities with a view to my own improvement. . . .
    The present Senior class in college of which I am a member consists of
about thirty, amongst whom are several excellent speakers who I suppose will
take all possible methods to make an appearance in the fall to the greatest
advantage—if it were supposed that to do this they relied only upon their own
Study and ingenuity I should consider it my interest and exert my powers to
be on a level with them. But as it is known that they depend for the most
part on the assistance of their friends of greater experience and abilities for
their commencement orations there is but little encouragement for one alone
to strive. . . .

Graham must have asked for a complete text from Paterson, for he
added: "If so if I should receive one time enough to commit well to
memory and exercise myself well in it, it will do." [42]
    Contemporary accounts provide some general criticism of the pub-
licly delivered orations. Holyoke referred to a series of Harvard valedictory orations as "tolerable," performed "pretty well," "indifferently both
as to Speech & Action," and "well." The *Pennsylvania Gazette* characterized the delivery of orations at King's College, May 18, 1773 as "elegant," "delivered with great propriety," "with more propriety of pronunciation and gracefulness of action," "elegant diction . . . received
with much applause," and "with earnestness and warmth, which never
fail to interest the passions of the hearer." In 1762, the same newspaper
had chiefly referred to elegance, graceful ease, and propriety of the
orations at the commencement of the College of New Jersey. Two years
earlier, the *Gazette* had mentioned the "very sprightly and entertaining
Manner" in which Benjamin Rush delivered "an ingenious English
harangue in Praise of Oratory." At 1768, at Princeton, William Paterson
remarked that "although the bulk of the young men made a handsom
appearance, yet some really fell short of the expectations of their
friends." Regarding the commencement of the College of Philadelphia
in 1767, John Macpherson wrote:

After prayer, Bankson pronounced a Salutatory Oration. This was one of
the best performances of the day. The Latin was well articulated, & but for
the tone that ran through the whole pronunciation, it was very compleat. . . .
White, a master of arts then pronounced an Oration. I forbear to give any
character of this, you will I dare say see one in the papers; but (if as usual)
it will be far above the merit of the piece.

In the 1780's, Chastellux heard the orations at Philadelphia and commented: "Some excellent declamations were made in Latin and in English, by no means inferior to those I have heard at Oxford and Cambridge. Their compositions in general were elegant, and their elocution easy, dignified, and manly. . . ." Chiefly, however, Chastellux was impressed that "whatever the subject, the great cause of liberty and their country was never lost sight of, nor their abhorrence of the tyranny of Great Britain." [43]

Obviously, despite regulations to encourage early preparation and careful practice in the delivery of orations, their quality varied widely. At times, perhaps more in some colleges and under some professors and tutors than others, the style of student speeches tended to be flowery, eulogistic, and hortatory. The compliments which were traditional in salutatory, gratulatory, and valedictory orations required some passages with these characteristics. The exhibitory nature of commencements and other public occasions and, particularly the stimulus which the successful end of the Revolution gave orators of the 1780's to praise victory, liberty, military heroes, and the future of the United States, were added factors which encouraged an exaggerated style. A Dartmouth orator professed, in keeping with his reading of the less sophistic classic writers, that he had "not affected a florid style, or the Beauties of Composition, but to communicate his Sentiments with the greatest Simplicity and Plainness." Yet he included such passages as these:

Just to address you on this final day, that like a veil shuts up our most pleasant scenes.

But to sum up all, education softens the rough and savage passions of the mind that are wild by nature, smoothes the boisterous and foaming seas of unbridled lust and ambition, melts the obdurate and unrelenting heart into compassion; adds sweetness to the bands of society; extends and brightens the rational faculties of the human soul . . . even next to that which is heavenly and divine.

Now to conclude in a word. How happy will be the consequences should America, while shaded with the balmy wings of freedom, cultivate and promote education. For a long time she has been drenched with scenes of blood. But do not the lamps of night begin to disappear before Aurora's blush? The auspicious morn begins to gild the western hills with its golden rays, and cheer the hearts of freedom's sons with the rising beams of a peaceful day? Therefore, O *Americans!* let your hands be strong, your influence to cultivate education; may your troubles come to a speedy end, and this land be the grand theatre, where the blessed Redeemer shall make peculiar displays of this latter day glory. [44]

The salutatory oration by Sylvanus Ripley, Dartmouth 1771, contained similar figures, alliteration, and parallelisms, and was written in a strained, amplified, exalted style, as these passages suggest:

As the welcome Approach of friendly Citizens to the cavern'd Hermit; or gradual dawn of rosy Morning to the bewilder'd Traveller; so is this pleasant arrival of the Venerable Literate to this solitary Seat of the Muses.

But without Learning, Benevolence looks like a Diamond rough in the mind that can't display itself to Advantage.

Early in the Infancy of Time Learning began to dawn in the Eastern World, & afterwards gradually shone around, to charm the Circle of the inhabited world with new-born Rays.

No sooner is the happy Stranger arriv'd on their Coasts, than Oratory breaks forth from the shades of Ignorance & the Charms of Poetry and polite Literature grace the barren mount of Parnassus.[45]

From the standpoint of a critic who is familiar with the long history of rhetoric since Corax, Ripley's style will be considered exaggerated and fulsome, his preparation probably as hasty and insufficient as that of many students through the centuries. Ripley's Dartmouth mentors doubtless applauded his style as close to the accepted taste for this kind of commencement oration. In perspective, Ripley's style is simply less mature, less smooth, less tempered by experience than the labored, published effort of Dartmouth's later son, Webster, in the peroration of the "Reply to Hayne."

In seeking to teach the major rhetorical skills, the Colonial college probably found no more effective form than the oration. Rameans and Aristotelians alike seemed to regard it highly. Under diligent tutors and professors, orations were closely supervised during preparation, revised to improve content, arrangement, and style, and polished in delivery. They were spoken in whatever languages prevailed in academic life. In these original speeches, students were generally free to discuss current public as well as academic issues and to project their thinking and talking in directions which they could follow afterwards in the ministry, law, and politics. These advantages, coupled with the usefulness of orations in competitions and their appeal to public audiences, account for the continued popularity of the oratorical form in the curriculum, the literary societies, and for public academic occasions.

Literary and Debating Societies

Primarily, the literary and debating societies which flourished, though often briefly and sporadically in the American colleges during the last three-quarters of the eighteenth century, offered additional opportunities to dispute, declaim, and deliver original speeches. Competition both within the societies and between rivals on the same campus whetted the enthusiasm of speakers. To improve the quality of speaking, largely for more effective competition it seems, "correctors of speaking" and "correctors of composition" were sometimes elected. In later years, dialogues, dramatic performances, and the reading aloud of essays and narrations were also included in society programs.

The chief additions to the kinds of rhetorical fare which the societies offered college students, however, were extempore and impromptu speeches. Nowhere else in the colleges was there occasion for such vigorous parliamentary practice as in the business sessions of the societies. Then, besides the scheduled disputations, which tended to be a series of carefully planned and written speeches with comparatively little adaptation to immediately preceding arguments, particularly when the participants were less experienced members, societies occasionally held extempore disputes in which the rather scant evidence indicates more lively give-and-take.[46] In the 1790's, at the College of New Jersey, society debates were of a parliamentary nature, in which each member was permitted a speech with no time limit in whatever order he chose to speak, with a possibility of second and third speeches of not more than ten minutes.[47]

Hence, generally, it may be argued that although social interests and intersociety rivalry seem to have dominated the societies, they stimulated much more speaking than the curriculum provided and gave some impetus to extemporaneous and impromptu debate and to parliamentary practice.[48]

Notes

1. *Writings*, ed. W. C. Ford (New York, 1913), I, 25. He added to the letter a request for Blair's *Lectures* in octavo.
2. Ezra Stiles, *Literary Diary* (New York, 1901), III, 184.
3. R. A. Guild, *History of Brown University* (Providence, 1867), pp. 348 ff.
4. Stiles, *Diary*, III, 119.
5. Stiles, *Diary*, III, 11, March 13, 1782. Cf. poem by Joel Barlow, *A Prospect for Peace* (New Haven, 1778), 12 pp., delivered at the Yale examination of that year.
6. John MacLean, *History of the College of New Jersey* (Philadelphia, 1877), I, 312, 363; *Pennsylvania Gazette*, October 13, 1773; *Pennsylvania Journal*, October 12, 1774; C. M. Newlin, *Life and Writings of H. H. Brackenridge* (Princeton, 1932), p. 9.
7. Stiles, *Diary*, II, 438; III, 11, 80, 130. "A Young Man's Journal," *New Haven Colony Historical Society Proceedings*, IV, entry of March 10, 1784. Stiles, *Diary*, III, 11, March 13, 1782 and other dates noted, with some variations in punctuation to clarify the items.
8. E.g., published pamphlets by Samuel Nott (1778), Samuel Austin (1782), Joseph Denison (1782), and Reuben Hitchcock (1786).
9. Stiles, *Diary*, II, 277.
10. *Publications of the Colonial Society of Massachusetts*, XVI, 565, 711; Josiah Quincy, *History of Harvard University* (Boston, 1860), II, 87 ff, 155; MacLean, *op. cit.*, I, 215-216.
11. *William and Mary Quarterly*, 2d series, VIII, 295, August 1, 1780.

12. *Writings,* I, 21.

13. Stiles, *Diary,* III, 99.

14. Ota Thomas, "The Theory and Practice of Disputation at Yale, Harvard, and Dartmouth, from 1750 to 1800," unpublished Ph.D. dissertation, State University of Iowa, 1941; S. E. Morison, *Three Centuries of Harvard* (Cambridge, 1936), pp. 138 ff, 180; *WMQ,* IV, 213-260, "The Original Records of the Phi Beta Kappa Society"; Stiles, *Diary,* II, 527, April 4, 1781; *WMQ,* VI, 183.

15. Karl R. Wallace, "Rhetorical Exercises in Early Tudor Education," *Quarterly Journal of Speech,* XXII (1936), 44-51; Colyer Meriwether, *Our Colonial Curriculum 1607-1775* (Washington, 1907), pp. 226 ff; S. E. Morison, *Harvard College in the Seventeenth Century* (Cambridge, 1936), I, 141 ff.

16. *PCSM,* XV, 25, Laws of 1642-46; *ibid.,* XXXI, 333, laws of 1655; Morison, *Harvard College,* I, 141.

17. Morison, *Harvard College,* I, 179-185; including contrasting texts by Michael Wigglesworth and Joseph Belcher.

18. Morison, *Harvard College,* I, 140-141. Barrett Wendell, *Cotton Mather, Puritan Priest* (Cambridge, 1926), p. 36, quoting *Paterna:* "For my Declamations I ordinarily took some Article of Natural Philosophy for my subjects, by which contrivances I did kill two birds with one Stone." David Potter, *Debating in the Colonial Chartered Colleges* (New York, 1944), p. 5 n. Quincy, *op. cit.,* II, Appendix xv, lists mulcts or fines for failure to perform rhetorical exercises: not exceeding 1/6 for not declaiming, 1/6 for bachelors neglecting disputes, 3/ for respondents neglecting. These were modified after 1761.

19. Morison, *Harvard College,* I, 465 ff.

20. Cf. Elaine Pagel, "The Theory and Practice of Disputation at Princeton, Columbia, and the University of Pennsylvania from 1750 to 1800," unpublished Ph.D. dissertation, State University of Iowa, 1943, pp. 35-36 and 150 ff. Forensic disputations appear to have been about equally used from the first at King's. Evidence is poor on early practices at William and Mary. Minor changes occurred in the Harvard laws of 1723.

21. MacLean, *op. cit.,* I, 266-267, quoting Finley's "An Account of the College of New Jersey" (1764), pp. 23-30.

22. Cf. studies of Potter, Pagel, and Thomas as well as the histories of the early colleges.

23. *Writings,* ed. A. H. Smyth (New York, 1905-1907), III, 29.

24. *Ibid.,* II, 386-396.

25. Quincy, *op. cit.,* II, 124, 127, 129, 132. The laws of 1767 carried similar provisions. "Harvard College Records," *PCSM,* XXXI, 352-353, section VII: "All the Classes shall attend with their respective Tutors on Saturday Mornings for Instruction in Theology, Elocution, Composition, Rhetoric & Belles Lettres." The semiannual exhibitions before the Overseers were abandoned in 1781 for quarterly exercises before the "President, Professors, Tutors."

26. MacLean, *op. cit.,* I, 362.

27. Pagel, *op. cit.,* pp. 88-108.

28. Guild, *op. cit.,* p. 345; Potter, *op. cit.,* p. 36.

29. *Ibid.,* p. 36.

30. Potter, *op. cit.,* pp. 66-67; Pagel, *op. cit.,* pp. 108-125.

31. *Testimony Against the Prophaneness of Some of the Public Disputes* (Boston, 1760).

32. Potter, *op. cit.,* p. 29, from the "Student Diary of John Quincy Adams" in Henry Adams, *Historical Essays,* p. 113, May 23, 1786, and J. Q. Adams, *Writings,* I, 24, June 14, 1786.

33. MacLean, *op. cit.,* pp. 253 ff; *Pennsylvania Gazette,* October 21, 1762; *Pennsylvania Magazine of History and Biography,* XXIII, 53.

34. For these criticisms in greater detail, see Potter, pp. 29-32, and the dissertations of Ota Thomas and Elaine Pagel, cited above.

35. Cf. Potter, *op. cit.,* pp. 43-47, for these and other samples of forensic theses.

36. *Rhode Island Historical Society Collections*, VII, 281-288.

37. Pamphlet (Boston, 1773). The text, pp. 3-48, suggests either a long debate or speeches amplified for publication.

38. Cf. Stiles, *Diary*, for various dates, 1779-1785.

39. MacLean, *op. cit.*, I, 216-217; *PMHB*, XXIII, 53.

40. J. Q. Adams, *Writings*, I, 27.

41. See also Stiles' timing of commencements.

42. W. J. Mills, *Glimpses of Colonial Society* (Philadelphia, 1903), pp. 156-159. Also note an essay promised in a letter of 1769 to John Davenport at Princeton, and a letter of Paterson to Aaron Burr, 1772: "Be pleased to accept of the inclosed Essay on Dancing; if you pitch upon it as the subject of your next discourse, it may perhaps furnish you with a few hints, and enable you to compose it with more facility and dispatch." *American Antiquarian Society Proceedings*, XXIX, 54.

43. *Holyoke Diaries 1709-1856* (Salem, 1911), June 27, 1766; June 29, 1765; July 5, 1767; July 1, 1768. *Pennsylvania Gazette*, May 26, 1773; October 21, 1762; MacLean, *op. cit.*, I, 253 ff; Mills, *op. cit.*, p. 60, November 16, 1768; Chastellux, *Travels in North America* (London, 1787), I, 229. Congress, the French Minister, and Pennsylvania officials were also present. *PMHB*, XXIII, 53, November 17, 1767.

44. *An Oration on Early Education* (Dresden, 1779). Spoken by Samuel Wood, who later helped prepare Daniel Webster for Dartmouth College.

45. Manuscript, Dartmouth College Archives, August 28, 1771.

46. Cf. Yale Fellowship Club, 1766; Linonia at Yale, 1783; Phi Beta Kappa, Dartmouth, 1781; and Potter, *op. cit.*, pp. 71-74.

47. Pagel, *op. cit.*, pp. 115-117.

48. Yale, Dartmouth, College of New Jersey, and Harvard had developed the stronger societies by the end of this period.

4 English Sources of Rhetorical Theory in Nineteenth-Century America

CLARENCE W. EDNEY

∙∙

English theory thoroughly permeated instruction in public address in American colleges and universities during the nineteenth century. And the English treatises that dominated the field were those of John Ward, George Campbell, Hugh Blair, and Richard Whately.[1] This paper, therefore, will review and compare the theories of these giants of the English scene, and, in order to present a complete picture of trends, will introduce comment concerning other not-to-be-neglected English writers.

General Perspective

Whereas the Ramean rhetoric of style and delivery had been favored in early American instruction,[2] the English theories that controlled the classrooms in the nineteenth century were classical in basic tendency. However, the intellectual controversies and achievements of the early modern age modified classical rhetoric in directions that cut deeply into American thought.

Ward's System of Oratory

John Ward's [3] *System of Oratory* is representative of one current of English theory that is exclusively classical in tendency.[4] Published posthumously in 1759, it is an 863 page, two volume, simplified, repetition of classical tenets. For theory, Ward leans most heavily upon Quintilian; for illustration, he depends very largely upon Cicero. He devotes one lecture to a review of the origin and development of rhetoric, one to the nature of oratory, one to the divisions of oratory, eight to invention, eight to disposition, twenty-seven to elocution (including three on the subject of history), five to pronunciation, and three to the things (nature, art, and practice) necessary to develop skill in oratory. Possibly George Campbell was thinking of the *System* when he complained that theories of rhetoric published up to his time were only the observations of classical writers "put into a modish dress and new arrangement."

Ward gathers in the thinking of both Cicero and Quintilian when he defines oratory as "the art of speaking well upon any subject in order to persuade." [5] To speak well, the orator must speak justly, methodically, floridly, and copiously.[6] And, although the principal aim of oratory is to persuade, the speaker often attempts, as subordinate objective, to delight and conciliate.[7] He limits the parts of oratory to invention, disposition, elocution, and pronunciation, including memory under pronunciation "to which it seems most properly to relate." [8]

Campbell's Philosophy of Rhetoric *and* Lectures on Pulpit Eloquence

To George Campbell [9] we are indebted for two treatises, his *Philosophy of Rhetoric,* published in 1776, and his work on homiletics published posthumously (1807) as the last twelve chapters of *Lectures on Systematic Theology and Pulpit Eloquence.* Possibly because it demands rigorous scholarship, the *Philosophy* was less popular in American colleges than Blair's *Lectures.*[10] The work on pulpit eloquence went through many editions, but we have no exact account of places or frequency of use in America.

Both treatises must be studied in order to obtain a complete view of the theories advanced by this Presbyterian divine.[11] They are written with different aims in view. The *Philosophy* attempts to ascertain "the radical principles of that art, whose object it is, by the use of language, to operate upon the soul of the hearer." [12] It is perhaps one of the most penetrating examinations of the psychological, epistemological, philosophical, and literary bases of rhetoric that has been produced in the long and proud history of the discipline, and was evaluated by Richard Whately as a work that is "incomparably superior" to that of Dr. Blair, "not only in depth of thought and ingenious original research, but also in practical utility to the student." [13] The volume on homiletics is, essentially, a handbook for the preacher who, with little training in public address, must officiate acceptably in the pulpit. Neither book attempts to provide "a full institute of rhetoric."

Campbell's definition of eloquence as "that art or talent, whereby the speech is adapted to produce in the hearer the great end which the speaker has, or at least ought to have principally in view" is stated in almost identical terminology in both works. So is his explanation of the ends of eloquence, which departs so definitely from classical concept and has had such permanent impact upon modern theories of rhetoric.

From this essential starting point, each treatise moves in the direction of its particular objective. The *Philosophy* penetrates deeply into the nature of wit, humor, and ridicule, into the sources of evidence, into a consideration of audience, into an examination of the differences in orations delivered at the bar, in the senate, and from the pulpit, and into the nature of language and its use in rhetoric. The *Lectures* are devoted primarily to lessons in pronunciation, elocution, and disposition.[14] And, because he believes that disposition is intimately connected with the intent of a speech, Campbell gives us, in the *Lectures,* a much more complete explanation of the ends of eloquence than is found in the *Philosophy.* Any given speech has, as its ultimate aim, one of four objectives: to enlighten the understanding, to please the imagination, to move the passions, or to influence the will. The understanding is reached either by a speech to inform or a speech to convince. The imagination is stimulated by discourse which exhibits "a lively and beautiful representation of a suitable object." The passions are moved by address which stimulates emotion or desire. The will is influenced by speech which concurrently moves the passions and directs these passions by means of rational appeals.

Unquestionably Campbell's analysis was influenced by the practical, epistemological, inductive character of seventeenth and eighteenth century English philosophical thought. Undoubtedly the inspiration for his orientation of rhetoric toward a "science of human nature" and his itemization of the ends of eloquence is to be found in works of Lord Kames,[15] Francis Bacon,[16] John Locke,[17] and David Hume.[18]

Blair's Lectures on Rhetoric and Belles Lettres

In 1783, after almost a quarter-century of oral presentation, Hugh Blair published his smooth-flowing *Lectures on Rhetoric and Belles Lettres.*[19] Instantly popular in American colleges, the treatise is representative of the belles lettristic-critical current of English theory.[20]

In his preface, Blair expresses the hope that the *Lectures* will provide a comprehensive work for those who "are studying to cultivate their taste, to form their style, or to prepare themselves for public speaking or composition." [21] In line with these aims, he provides the reader with four disquisitions on taste, two on the rise and progress of language, two on the structure of language, fifteen on style, eleven on eloquence, one each on historical and philosophical writing, eight on poetry, and one each on tragedy and comedy.

In typical pedagogical fashion, Blair reviews the benefits of study of rhetoric and *belles lettres.* The individual who desires to improve his eloquence is told that the rules of rhetoric will "assist genius," strengthen accuracy of thought, correct slovenly expression, and help in "distinguishing false ornament from true." The individual who does not intend to speak in public is told that the principles of *belles lettres* teach us "to admire and to blame with judgment." Attention to this "speculative science" improves our knowledge of human nature, exercises our reason without tiring it, provides employment for leisure time, refreshes the mind after the "labor of abstract study," raises the mind "above the attachments of sense," increases sensibility "to all of the tender and humane passions," weakens the more violent and fierce emotions, "disposes the heart to virtue," and furnishes material for "fashionable topics of discourse." [22]

In spite of this deflection of rhetoric in the direction of fine literature, Blair holds to a solid and defensible philosophy of the subject. If these lectures have any merit, he says, "it will consist in an endeavor to substitute the application of these principles in the place of artificial and scholastic rhetoric; in an endeavor to explode false ornament, to direct attention more towards substance than show, to recommend good sense as the foundation of all good composition, and simplicity as essential to all true ornament." [23] Moreover, he follows Campbell's lead in expanding the scope of rhetoric. "To be truly eloquent is to speak to the purpose. . . . Whenever a man speaks or writes, he is supposed, as a rational being, to have some end in view; either to inform, or to amuse, or to persuade, or, in some other way to act upon his fellow creatures." The lowest degree of eloquence is that which aims only at pleasing the hearers. A somewhat higher degree of eloquence is that through which the speaker attempts, not only to please, but to inform, to instruct, to convince. The highest degree of eloquence is that used to influence conduct and persuade to action. [24]

Whately's Elements of Logic *and* Essentials of Rhetoric

For the purpose of this study we are primarily concerned with two of Richard Whately's ninety-seven published works, his *Elements of Logic* (1826) and his *Elements of Rhetoric* (1828). [25] Undoubtedly Whately considered them companion volumes; each contains numerous cross references to the other, and the *Rhetoric*, in the section on refutation, refers the reader to the *Logic* for a discussion of fallacies.

Whately is given credit for stimulating renewed interest in the study of logic and for the feat of again raising this discipline to a high level of academic respectability. But he was deeply indebted to Edward Copleston, his undergraduate tutor at Oriel College, Oxford, for many of his ideas about it. This indebtedness he freely acknowledges in the dedicatory and prefatory pages of the *Logic* before providing the reader in Book I with an "Analytical Outline of the Science," in Book II with a "Synthetical Compendium" of principles, in Book III with an explanation "of fallacies," in Book IV with a "Dissertation on the Province of Reasoning," and, in the Appendix, with one of the very best tracts ever written "On Certain Terms Which Are Peculiarly Liable to be Used Ambiguously." [26]

Although probably less renowned for his *Rhetoric* than for his *Logic*, Whately is largely responsible for initiating that trend of theory which moved rapidly in the direction of a rhetoric of argumentation and debate. His stated objective is to treat of "argumentative composition, *generally* and *exclusively*." However, his "middle ground" becomes quite broad and he produces a text which interprets rhetoric as the art of speaking to instruct, to convince, and to persuade. Part I is devoted to a consideration "Of the Address to the Understanding, With a View to Produce Conviction (Including Instruction)," Part II is concerned with an examination "Of The Address to the Will, or Persuasion," Part III considers "Style," and Part IV philosophizes upon "Elocution or Delivery."

Whately felt a need to mitigate prejudice against instruction in rhetoric and, in the course of his effort, offers some excellent advice concerning the teaching of speech. Reasoning that prejudice stems from observation of the cramped efforts of learners, he recommends four policies: first, that topics for speaking be drawn from the studies in which the learner is engaged, from the content of conversations to which the student has listened with interest, and from the student's every-day activities; secondly, that the rules inculcated be based upon broad philosophical principles; third, that sedulous care be taken in correction; and fourth, that the teacher offer continuous encouragement. Strangely, he considers debating societies more harmful than beneficial because "students are apt, when prematurely hurried into a habit of fluent elocution, to retain through life a careless facility of pouring forth ill-digested thoughts in well-turned phrases, and an aversion to cautious reflection." [27]

There is no mistaking the fact that the *Rhetoric* is the product of a theologian who was much involved in the religious controversy of his time. In it one finds not only indications of a practical view of Christianity but the mark of a divine who would fight the Rationalists with their own weapons. Thus the *Rhetoric*, at times, seems to be overly concerned with techniques of defense. And, undoubtedly, Whately's exhaustive treatment of "testimony" and his originality in supplying us with the theory of "presumption" and "burden of proof" grew out of his unceasing effort to clarify and defend Christian evidences.[28] Perhaps, too, this devotion not only prompted but gave rigidity to his strange theory of induction.

Priestley's Course of Lectures on Oratory and Criticism

Joseph Priestley's *A Course of Lectures on Oratory and Criticism* [29] is mentioned because it is an interesting attempt to utilize David Hartley's doctrine of the association of ideas, and because some comment seems necessary in order to complete the picture of currents of theory in later English rhetoric. The work had little impact upon American instruction. And, although it must not be ignored, it obviously is the product of restless intellectual energy rather than penetrating study of the theory of rhetoric.

The salient characteristics of this work, first published in 1781, are three: the first is the reduction of all composition to two kinds, narration and argumentation; the second is the belief that the principal objective of every speaker is to "inform the judgment, and thereby direct the practice" (attempts to please and to affect are admissible only when "subservient to that design"); and the third is the treatment of all aspects of rhetoric, aside from limited discussions of *topica*, techniques of amplification, and methods of arrangement, under a broad concept of style.

Such, then, are the general points of view of the chief English rhetoricians who were well known to American students and teachers of rhetoric in the nineteenth century. We shall now compare their views of four of the five divisions of classical rhetoric. Although Ward was the only writer among this group of English rhetoricians who discussed his theory under the classical divisions of *inventio, dispositio, elocutio,* and *pronunciato*, it seems wise, for the sake of clarity, to utilize this traditional partition in this paper. Because major attention to the classical division of *memoria* virtually disappeared in the writings of these theorists, it will be noticed only in passing.

Invention

All of these writers, by implication or by direct statement, insist that broad knowledge and thorough command of subject are the sources of the materials of invention. Blair calls for a "proper acquaintance with the rest of the liberal arts." Campbell suggests that "everything that serves to improve knowledge, discernment, and good sense" is valuable to the orator. Ward declares that "great learning and extensive knowledge" as well as "a lively imagination" and "readiness of thought" are of great help in invention. Whately implies a similar point of view.[30]

Logical Proof

Without exception, the English theorists agree about the close relationship of rhetoric and logic. Whately declares that rhetoric is an "off-shoot of logic," and Campbell insists that eloquence is "but a particular application of the logician's art." Ward protests the Ramean tendency to divorce invention and disposition from rhetoric, and states emphatically that both rhetoric and logic teach us to reason from causes, effects, circumstances, etc., even though there are, between the two, differences in aim as well as in kinds of proofs used. Blair declares that reason and argument are the "foundations of eloquence." [31]

When theories are compared, however, striking differences appear in concept as well as in approach to the problem of discovering logical proofs.

Although Ward is sceptical of the worth of *topoi*, he suggests that they may lessen the difficulty of finding arguments. He divides them into internal and external topics, corresponding to Aristotle's division of proofs into artificial and inartificial. From Quintilian's list,[32] he selects sixteen internal commonplaces. He reduces the Roman rhetorician's list of external commonplaces to three forms of *human* testimony (writings, witnesses, and contracts), and adds, as a major division, *divine* testimony (which is "incontestable").[33] Also, he follows Quintilian [34] to the letter in explaining the "conjectural" state, the "definitive" state, and the state of "quality."

In line with classical theory, Ward distinguishes between the discovery of arguments and argumentation. Consequently, the "forms of reasoning used by orators" are considered in that section of his *System* devoted to *dispositio*. They are syllogism, enthymeme, induction, and example. And it is here that he displays his greatest inadequacy. His explanation of syllogism is weak and incomplete. He believes, erroneously, that the only way that enthymeme differs from syllogism is in the omission of one of the premises.[35] His illustrations of "induction" and his explanation of "example" lead one to feel that, in both cases, he is thinking in terms of literal analogy. When he states, finally, that "the whole induction or example has the nature of an enthymeme," we recognize that, had Ward been a more penetrating thinker, his theory of argumentation might have resembled that of Richard Whately.

Blair discounts completely the usefulness of the classical equipment for finding arguments. And, because he doubts if any kind of explanation will be helpful to the student, detours this particular aspect of the theory of rhetoric.

Campbell, in presenting his readers with a discussion of "logical truth" remains consistent with his desire to trace the mind's "principal

channels of perception and action, as near as possible, to their source."
He does not pretend to advance a theory of logic as such. Perhaps, as
Whately charges, he misunderstood the real nature and function of
logic. Influenced by a century of English philosophical thought, he was
very much concerned about the sources of knowledge. It is worth
mentioning that the epistemological approach to logical proof was not
unique to Campbell. Quintilian, many centuries earlier, had pointed out
that "unless there be something which is true, or what appears to be
true, and from which support may be gained for what is doubtful,
there will be no grounds on which we can prove anything." [36]

In a bold statement that disavows the whole theory of perception
through "ideas" (which lies at the heart of Hume's scepticism), and
aligns his thinking with that of Thomas Reid,[37] Campbell declares that
"logical truth" consists in "the conformity of our conceptions to their
archetypes in the nature of things." This conformity of concept and
object is perceived either "intuitively" upon bare attention or "deduc-
tively" by comparing related concepts. We arrive at "first truths" intuitively and immediately through intellection, consciousness, and common
sense.[38] We know immediately through "intellection" the truth of such
propositions as "the whole is greater than the part." We know immediately through "consciousness" the truth of the fact that we exist,
feel, think, and so forth. We know immediately through "common
sense" the truth of statements like "whatever has a beginning has a
cause." We arrive at other truths by a process of reasoning in which we
compare intuitive truth with related perceptions. These truths may be
either demonstrative (certain) or moral (probable).[39] Demonstrative
truth is derived from the "invariable properties or relations of general
ideas." Moral truth (or variant degrees of likelihood) is obtained by
comparing intuitive truth with the evidence of experience, analogy, and
testimony.[40]

In his explanation of "experience," Campbell provides us not only
with a description of the essential preliminary condition to scientific
induction which Mill calls "unscientific practice" but also with a relatively advanced view of causation in the theory of induction. And,
although he accepts the constancy of nature's laws as the fundamental
principle of induction, Campbell does not, as did Whately, jump to the
conclusion that every induction is a syllogism in which the suppressed
major premise is a proposition that declares the uniformity of nature.[41]
Both Campbell and Whately attempt to apply the mathematics of
probability to the weighing of evidence and argument in rhetoric.

Whereas Campbell is concerned with *how we know*, Whately is, in
his *Rhetoric*, concerned with *how we prove*. Investigation, he says,
should be completed and conclusions should be reached before argu-

mentative composition starts; and the first step in the process of composition, although not necessarily so in final argumentation, is to lay down these conclusions or propositions.[42]

Whereas Campbell represents an extreme position which holds that the syllogism is useless, Whately speaks for the opposite view which declares that the syllogism is the universal type of inference. It is customary, he says, "to argue in the enthymematic form, and to call ... the expressed premise of the enthymeme, the argument by which the conclusion is proved." [43]

Arguments are those propositions which serve as premises. When classified in regard to the "relation of the subject-matter of the premise to that of the conclusion" they fall into two major groups: first, those that can be used "to account for the fact or principle maintained, supposing its truth granted;" and second, "those that cannot be so used." [44]

The first class is argument from cause to effect. In saying that "if the Cause be fully *sufficient*, and no impediments intervene, the Effect in question follows certainly; and the nearer we approach to this, the stronger the argument," and also in stating that "this is the kind of argument which produces (when short of absolute certainty) that species of the Probable which is usually called the Plausible," Whately appears to include all causal argument, probable and necessary.[45] And, although he improves upon these criteria for testing causal reasoning in his analysis of the fallacy of *non causa pro causa*, the Archbishop of Dublin is to be criticized for ignoring the discussions of plurality of causes and combinations of causes and conditions which were available to him in the works of Bacon, Hobbes, Locke, Hume, Watts, and Mill.

Arguments that fall in the second major group are those of sign and example. Argument from sign is argument from an effect to a condition. It is *ratio cognescendi* or reason for knowing.[46] From some signs, we can infer either the certain or probable "cause" of an effect or phenomenon. From others, we can infer some "condition" without which the effect could not exist. Argument from testimony is a species of sign. We reason that, because testimony exists, the fact attested is true (the truth of what is attested is a "condition" of the testimony having been given). When testimony is to a matter of *fact*,[47] we evaluate it by questioning the honesty of the witness, his accuracy, and his means of getting information. When the testimony is to a matter of *opinion*,[48] it is necessary to enquire as to the ability of the individual to form a judgment. Testimony is strengthened if it is inimical to the known prejudices of the attestor, if it is corroborated by many witnesses (assuming that the testimony is original and not hearsay), if it comes through incidental hints or oblique allusions and is therefore undesigned, if it leads to a conclusion that the attestor would be unwilling to admit, if it agrees with generally known statements which remain uncontradicted, if, in case of concurrent testimony, there has been no opportunity for concert and especially when rivalry or hostility exists between the attestors, and if it is improbable that the thing attested could have been imagined or invented.[49]

Example, the second division of sign, includes arguments usually designated by the terms induction, experience, and analogy. In arguments such as these "we consider one or more, known, individual objects or instances, of a certain class, as a fair *sample*, in respect of some point or other of that class; and, consequently draw an inference from them respecting either the whole class, or other, less known, individuals of it." The term "induction" is applied to arguments that stop short at the general conclusion. Inductions can be stated in syllogistic form because, in all cases, there exists a major premise which assumes "that the instance or instances induced are sufficient to authorize the conclusion."[50] The term "experience" applies to the premises from which we argue and not to the conclusion we reach.[51] The term "analogy" is used for argument in which we reason from one thing to another thing, both of which are similar in "relation." Whately here seems to be confined to figurative analogy, and seems to have overlooked the implications of Campbell's thinking on the subject.

There is "no distinct class of refutatory argument;"[52] arguments become such because they are used either to prove the opposite of a proposition or to over-throw the arguments by which the proposition has been supported. In the first instance, the argument is only "accidentally refutatory" in that it can be developed in the absence of opposing argument. In the second instance, the argument consists of exposure of fallacies.[53]

In every fallacy, Whately writes, the conclusion either does or does not follow from the premises. Where conclusions *do not* follow, the fault is in the reasoning, and these, therefore, are called logical fallacies. They are subdivided into (1) purely logical fallacies which exhibit their fallaciousness by the bare form of the expression without respect for the meaning of terms, and (2) semi-logical fallacies which are "cases of ambiguous middle term except its non-distribution." Purely logical fallacies would include (a) undistributed middle, (b) illicit process, (c) negative premises or affirmative conclusion from a negative premise and *vice versa*, and (d) more than three terms. Semi-logical fallacies result from (a) ambiguities in language or (b) ambiguities in context.

Where the conclusion *does* follow from the premises, the fallacies are called nonlogical, or material fallacies. Of these there are two kinds: those in which the premises are such as ought not to have been assumed, and those in which the conclusion is not the one required. Nonlogical fallacies, in which the premise is unduly assumed, has two species, *petitio principii,* "in which one of the Premises either is manifestly the same in sense with the Conclusion, or is actually proved from it," and *non causa,* or false cause, in which there is "undue assumption, of a Premise that is not equivalent to, or dependent on, the Conclusion." Nonlogical fallacies in which the conclusion is irrelevant (*ignoratio elenchi*) break down into the fallacy of objections, the fallacy of shifting ground, the fallacy of using complex general terms, the fallacy of appeals to the passions (argumentum ad hominem, ad verecundiam, and so forth), and the fallacy of proving a part and suppressing the rest of the question.[54]

Whately warns his readers that, in reasoning in the realm of probabilities, there are likely to be sound arguments and valid objections on both sides of a proposition and, consequently, it is possible that solid arguments may be advanced against one that is true. Therefore, it is wise to concede the strength of objections that are unanswerable. Weak advocates can do harm to a cause for the reason that they are easily answered, leaving the impression that all arguments which could have been advanced have been destroyed. For the same reason, it is dangerous to advance more arguments than can be maintained. Psychologically, an elaborate attack upon arguments is likely to enhance their importance or to result in audience refusal of the refutatory remarks. Furthermore, it is wise to confine arguments to those that "are directly accessible to the persons addressed," and sometimes it becomes necessary to trace an erroneous opinion directly to its source.

Emotional Proof

Among the English rhetoricians, George Campbell is the only theorist who attempts a thorough and systematic examination of the pathetic. Why, he asks, does the pathetic, "which consists chiefly in exhibitions of human misery," hold our attention? What is the cause of "that pleasure which we receive from objects or representations that excite pity and other painful feelings?" After examining and expressing dissatisfaction with the hypotheses of Abbé Du Bos, Fontenelle, Hume, and Hobbes, he presents his own, and concludes that the pleasure in pity arises "from its own nature or from the nature of those passions of which it is compounded and not from any thing extrinsic or adventitious." The observations that lead him to this conclusion are, first, that all of the simple passions may be divided into two classes, the *pleasant* (love, joy, hope, gratitude, pride) and the *painful* (hatred, grief, fear, anger, shame); second, that there is "an attraction or association among the passions"; third, that "pain of every kind generally makes a deeper impression on the imagination than pleasure does, and is longer retained by memory"; fourth, that, if pleasant passions predominate among a "group" of both pleasant and painful passions, there arises often "a greater and more durable pleasure to the mind, than would result from these, if alone and unmixed"; fifth, that "under the name pity may be included all the emotions excited by tragedy"; and sixth, that "pity is not a simple passion, but a group of passions united by association, and as it were blended, by centering in the same object." [55]

Whately accepts Dugald Stewart's division of the passions into "appetites, desires, and affections," to which he adds "self-love" and "conscience." These he calls "the active principles of our nature." Ward is satisfied to speak of "commotions of the mind." [56]

Our authors are in complete agreement as to the place of emotional appeal in persuasive discourse. Ward insists that it be used only to influence men to act "agreeably to reason." Campbell, Blair, and Whately admit that there can be no persuasion without appeal to the passions but insist that, rhetorically and ethically, conviction of the understanding comes first. [57]

Talent in the use of emotional proof, says Blair, is not gained from a philosophical knowledge of the passions but rather from "a certain strong and happy sensibility of mind." He recommends that the speaker consider whether the subject will admit the pathetic, seize the critical moment that is favorable to emotion in whatever part of the discourse it occurs, paint the object of the passion in the most striking and natural manner, be moved himself, he bold and ardent, use simple and unaffected language, beware of digressions and comparisons, beware of too much reasoning, and never attempt to prolong the pathetic too far. [58]

No passion, declares Whately, is aroused by thinking about it *per se*, but "by thinking about, and attending to, such objects that are calculated to awaken it." He suggests that the speaker dwell upon the circumstances of the case at hand, use comparison, and either openly display the feeling to be conveyed or appear laboring to suppress it. In no case should address to the passions be introduced as such. If it seems unlikely that the occasion or object at hand will excite the desired emotion, the speaker may turn attention to that which will raise the feeling; once aroused, the passion may be turned in the direction required. [59]

Campbell explains that circumstances "chiefly instrumental" in operating on the passions are (1) probability, (2) plausibility, (3) importance, (4) proximity of time, (5) connection of place, (6) relation to the persons concerned, and (7) interest in the circumstances. An unfavorable passion is calmed by annihilating or diminishing the object which raised it, or by exciting some other passion that will overcome it. [60]

On the surface, Campbell, Blair, and Whately seem to dichotomize "reason" and "emotion." None of them, however, seems to think in terms of a strict division of human powers. Unquestionably, their attempt to analyze and clarify the aims of public address, as well as the limitations of language, led them to speak but not necessarily to think in terms of separate human "powers." Campbell, at least, would have been aware of Locke's warning that this way of speaking "has misled many into a confused notion of so many distinct agents in us." [61]

Ethical Proof

English concepts of ethical proof are encompassed in Ward's explanation of it as "the means by which the speaker conciliates the minds of his hearers, gains their affection, and recommends both himself and what he says to their good opinion and esteem." [62] Ward, Campbell, and Blair lean toward Quintilian's philosophy that the speaker must *be* a good man in order to recommend himself to an audience. Whately leans in the opposite direction and declares, specifically, that he is talking about "the impression produced in the minds of the hearers" rather than the real character of the speaker. [63]

Whately follows Aristotle in stating that the character to be established is that of good principle, good sense, and good will. [64] Ward insists that the speaker display the qualities of wisdom, integrity, benevolence, and modesty. [65] The speaker will more easily gain assent if he appears to be convinced of the truth of his position, [66] and if he appears to be of the same party as the hearers. [67] The speaker should express wise, amiable, and generous sentiments. [68] He should avoid inconsistency, [69] direct self-commendation, [70] and a display of oratorical skill. [71] To allay prejudice, the speaker should turn the emotion in another direction or excite a contrary state of mind. [72] Also he should make concessions, defer appropriately to the judgment of his hearers, and request that they attend exclusively to the subject. [73]

Disposition

In English theory, much of the judgment, selection, and adaptation assigned to *dispositio* by classical writers is siphoned into other divisions of rhetoric or is concentrated under a consideration of audience. In general, that which is left to *dispositio* is decision concerning the arrangement, adaptation, and proportionment of the parts of a speech. [74]

Arrangement

In general, and with only slight differences from theory to theory, the English rhetoricians choose to follow Cicero's six-part division of a speech into introduction, narration, proposition, confirmation, refutation, and conclusion. Probably the only important variation from typical instruction is Campbell's stipulation that the conclusion of every sermon should be persuasive in nature.

Audience

Probably the distinguishing characteristic of English instruction concerning adaptation to audience is location in the rhetorical systems. Campbell gives a special section of his *Philosophy* to a consideration of the audience, but the bulk of Whately's comment falls within his discussion of persuasion. Blair scatters his relatively few and general comments throughout his treatise. Ward spreads his ideas concerning adaptation into three places in his *System,* into his explanation of the use of *topoi* in commendatory and deliberative speeches, into his lectures on the passions, and into his consideration of ethical proof.

The most careful analysis of audience is found in Campbell's *Philosophy.* Drawing upon Aristotle, he declares that hearers must be considered both "as men in general" and "as men in particular" or, in other words, as men having certain general similarities and as men having certain specific differences. Men in general are endowed with understanding, imagination, memory, and passions. In adapting discourse to understanding, the speaker is concerned about the clearness and simplicity of his proofs, his reasoning, and his language. In order to stimulate imagination, he makes sure that his ideas are vivacious, beautiful, sublime, or novel. In accommodating discourse to memory, he attempts to facilitate the "association of ideas." In attempting to touch the passions, he "communicates lively and glowing ideas of the object." Men in particular are different in intellectual attainment, behavior, habit, and occupation. Also they are different from group to group.[75] All aspects of the discourse must be adapted to these specific differences.

Our other theorists contribute nothing that is not encompassed in Campbell's analysis. Whately, however, reminds his readers that, although the speaker uses "all precautions not inconsistent with his object" to avoid displeasing his hearers, "he who would claim highest rank as an orator ... must be the one who is the most successful, not in gaining popular applause, but in *carrying his point,* whatever it be."[76]

Elocution

"Elocution directs us to suit both the words and the expressions of a discourse to the nature of the subject," explains John Ward. "General elocution" is concerned with "elegance" (purity and perspicuity), "composition" (turn and harmony of periods), and "dignity" (tropes and figures) of language. "Particular elocution" makes use of the constituents of general elocution to form the low, middle, and sublime styles. To become master of a good style an orator must be endowed with a vigorous mind, a lively fancy, good judgment, and a strong memory. And style must be adapted to the subject, the time, the place, the hearers, and "other circumstances." [77]

"General elocution," as explained by Ward, conforms closely with Cicero's discussion of "embellishment of language." His division of "particular elocution" is definitely a repetition of Cicero's discussion of three "forms" or "complexions" of eloquence.[78] This comparison helps to clarify the various referents of the word "style" in the works of our English rhetoricians. Blair uses the word to encompass both of Cicero's (and Ward's) divisions of elocution. Campbell and Whately abandon Cicero's "forms" of eloquence, and limit their thinking to what Ward calls "general elocution" and Cicero labels "embellishment."

Hugh Blair defines style as "the peculiar manner in which a man expresses his conceptions, by means of language." And he divides this aspect of rhetoric into "perspicuity" and "ornament." His explanation of perspicuity is typical: words must be pure, proper, and precise; sentence structure must be clear, exact, unified, strong, and harmonious. He warns that ornament is liable to abuse, but provides a full catalog of figurative language as well as an exhaustive analysis of twelve different forms or complexions of eloquence. To this, he appends suggestions for the attainment of good style. These suggestions are perhaps Blair's most important contribution to the subject. Study the subject, he says, and "think closely" about it. Become acquainted with the style of the best authors, but remember that "servile imitation" is dangerous. Obtain frequent practice in composing, and remember that style must be adapted to both the subject and the capacity of the hearers. Above all, do not allow attention to style to take precedence over attention to thought.[79]

Campbell's treatment of elocution seems to have been influenced by four factors: first, English philosophical thought concerning the relationship of language and knowledge; second, observation of the difficulties in communication brought on by provincial dialects; third, eighteenth-century concern about the meaning of words; and fourth, Quintilian's elaborate discussion of style.

As interested as he was in the sources of knowledge, it would have been inconceivable for Campbell to neglect the nature, use, and signification of language as it relates to knowledge. Along with Bacon, Hobbes, Locke, and Hume, he insists that words, if used with meaning, must have clear reference to something. Hobbes and Campbell believe that this reference is to things actually existing and actually apprehended. Locke and Hume believe that the reference is to "ideas." The issue, is, of course, one which has to do with the reality of knowledge. There is no disagreement about the fact that unless language has distinct and specific reference to the object of which it is a sign, it is pure jargon. In the works of these men we find the basic tenets of what has, of late, come to be called general semantics.[80]

While serving in his country parish, Banchory Ternan, Campbell became concerned about dialects. And later, as a professor of pulpit eloquence at Marischal College, he warned his students that "if you attach yourself to a provincial dialect, it is a hundred to one, that many of your words and phrases will be misunderstood in the very neighboring province, district, or county." [81] To overcome the fault, he recommended that his students study the best grammarians and the best English authors.

Evidence of English interest in the meaning of words is found in the publication of dictionaries. Samuel Johnson's fascinating *Dictionary* (1755) had been followed by John Walker's *Critical Pronouncing Dictionary and Expositer of the English Language* (1791), Thomas Sheridan's *General Dictionary of the English Languages* (1780), John Ash's *New And Complete Dictionary* (1775), and William Kendrick's *New Dictionary* (1773). It had been preceded by Nathaniel Bailey's *Universal Etymological English Dictionary* (1721), Edward Phillip's *New Worlde of Wordes* (1658), and Henry Cockeram's *Dictionary* (1623).

Following the lead of Quintilian,[82] Campbell divides elocution into two kinds: "grammatical" and "rhetorical." The "grammatical art" is the foundation of the "rhetorical art." The highest aim of the former is the lowest aim of the latter. But the two overlap. Grammar looks toward "syntax" or the composition of words into one sentence. Oratory looks toward "style" or both the composition of words into sentences and the composition of many sentences into a discourse.[83] The orator must not only be master of the language he speaks but he also must be capable of adding to grammatical purity "those higher qualities of elocution, which will render his discourse graceful and energetic." In regard to grammar, Campbell designates "use" as the supreme authority over language as long as it is "reputable," "national," and "present." He provides us with nine canons by which the speaker may be guided in the selection or rejection of words and expressions. Achievement of "grammatical purity," he says, is the common aim of both grammarian and orator. Purity of the English tongue may be injured, first, by "barbarism" or the use of obsolete, new, or "new-modeled" words, second, by "solecism" or violation of the rules of syntax, and third, by "impropriety," or failure to use words to express precise meaning. In regard to style, Campbell insists that, in addition to being pure, it must be perspicuous, vivacious, elegant, animated, and musical. He elaborates upon only two of these qualities. Perspicuity is violated by speaking obscurely, ambiguously, or unintelligibly. Vivacity results from the use of language that imitates things, the use of specific terms, and the use of tropes, as well as from brevity in the use of words, variety in the arrangement of sentences, and inconspicuousness in the use of connectives.[84]

Unfortunately, Campbell became interested in botany and did not write his contemplated chapters of the *Philosophy* which, presumably, would have set forth his ideas on elegance, animation, and music in language.

Richard Whately's theory of elocution reveals six distinguishing characteristics. The first is his refusal to introduce observations concerning grammar. It is not, he says, exclusively the concern of rhetoric. The second is his limited treatment of ornament. The only aspects of language that have application to argumentative and persuasive works, he claims, are perspicuity, energy, and elegance. Perspicuity is aided by avoiding overly-long sentences, uncommon words, prolixity, and overly-concise statements. Energy is improved by choosing words carefully, by expressing ideas briefly, and, insofar as the rules of language will permit, by expressing first the ideas that occur first. Elegance is assisted by avoiding "homely and coarse words and phrases," and by using a "smooth and easy flow of words in respect of the sounds of the sentences." A third feature of Whately's theory of elocution is his emphasis upon the relativity of perspicuity. Lucidity of thought, he says, cannot be predicted without reference to the hearers and to the kind and degree of attention they will bestow upon it. A fourth distinctive element is Whately's insistence that, to achieve elegance of language, the speaker should "maintain the appearance of expressing himself, not, as if he *wanted to say something*, but as if he *had something to say*." A fifth distinguishing mark is his discussion of spurious kinds of writing and speaking in which "obscurity" rather than perspicuity is to the purpose. And a sixth is his emphasis upon differences between rhetoric and poetic. Whereas Campbell sees a close relationship between oratory and poetry, Whately discerns great unlikeness. The poet and the orator, says Campbell, make use of the same rules of composition and the same tropes and figures. Frequently, their aims coincide. Versification makes poetry only a variety of oratory and not a different form of expression.[85] To Whately, the differences stem from primacy of purpose as well as from primacy of language and form. Thought is primary in rhetoric, but subordinate in poetry. Elegant language and metre are primary in poetry, but subordinate in oratory.[86]

Pronunciation

All of these English theorists emphasize the importance of delivery. Campbell devotes one full lecture to it. Ward quotes Cicero, Demosthenes, and Quintilian in agreeing that "this is the principal part of an orator's province, from whence he is chiefly to expect success in the art of persuasion." Blair declares that "nothing is more important" in public address than delivery. Whately calls it "a most important branch of rhetoric." [87]

Principles

Although the detail devoted to the subject of pronunciation by these rhetoricians ranges from Ward's lengthy and minute explanation to Blair's few paragraphs, all are in agreement that the delivery of the speaker should be "natural." They differ, however, concerning the method of teaching delivery. Ward is neo-classical in his tendency to formulate rules, suggest models, and recommend imitation. Campbell, Blair, and Whately, on the other hand, may be classified as romanticists who confidently trusted the end result of an individual's response to his own thought-emotion. Two basic points of view seem to underlie their instruction. In the first place, the speaker should concentrate upon his subject. This point is given strong emphasis in the *Elements of Rhetoric,* and, although Whately claims some degree of originality for the idea, it is expressed or implied in the theory of each of his predecessors. Secondly, the speaker should feel independent of rules and remain confident of the effectiveness of delivery that springs spontaneously from earnest attempts to communicate. The "natural manner," says Whately, is "that which one naturally falls into who is really speaking, in earnest, and with a mind exclusively intent on what he has to say, avoiding all thoughts of self." It is "the delivery of a man of sense and taste, speaking earnestly, on a serious subject, and on a solemn occasion." When a speaker is engaged in public discourse, suggests Blair, "he ought to be then quite in earnest; wholly occupied with his subject and his sentiments; leaving nature, and previously formed habits to prompt and suggest his manner of delivery." [88]

Whately, possibly because he had been able to observe the effects of the elocutionary movement, pens not only a carefully meditated argument for the natural manner but also a castigating refutation of mechanical systems of teaching delivery. His observations are written as though they were the outgrowth of considerable discussion, and so intent is he upon establishing the soundness of his philosophy that he repetitiously writes his chapter twice. He argues that systems of analyzing and marking passages are (1) *imperfect* in that no variety of marks could be invented to indicate all the different "tones," (2) *circuitous* in that they attempt to teach the reader to do that which comes naturally, and (3) *ineffectual* because attention is focused on the voice, and the voice, therefore, becomes studied and artificial.

Voice and Articulation

The recommendations of these English rhetoricians in regard to voice and articulation hold up well when compared with modern precepts. Campbell divides delivery into "grammatical pronunciation" and "rhetorical pronunciation." These, he says, are so perfectly distinct, that "each may be found in a very eminent degree without the other." Grammatical pronunciation consists "in articulating, audibly and distinctly, the letters whether vowels or consonants, assigning to each its appropriate sound, in giving the several syllables their just quantity, and in placing the accent, or, as some call it, the syllabic emphasis, in every word on the proper syllable." Rhetorical pronunciation consists "in giving such an utterance to the several words in a sentence, as shows in the mind of the speaker a strong perception, or as it were, feeling of the truth and justness of the thought conveyed by them, and in placing the rhetorical emphasis in every sentence, on the proper word, that is, on the word which, by being pronounced emphatically, gives the greatest energy and clearness to the expression. Under this head is also comprehended gesture." [89]

Campbell warns against a forced and unnatural grammatical pronunciation and lists five potential faults: (1) straining the voice "beyond its natural key," (2) rapidity of rate, (3) a "theatrical and violent manner," (4) "insipid monotony," and (5) a "sing-song manner." In connection with this he offers four suggestions on the management of the voice: (1) avoid beginning on too high a clef, (2) preserve the same key on which you begin, (3) begin by speaking deliberately and slowly, (4) engage in frequent practice in reading, speaking, and repeating before at least one "sensible companion."

Blair approaches the matter somewhat differently and says that the speaker, in delivery, has two aims: (1) to speak so as to be fully and easily understood, and (2) to speak with grace and force. To accomplish the first objective, the speaker should (*a*) "use a due degree of loudness of voice," (*b*) use distinct articulation, giving "every sound its due proportion ... without slurring, whispering, or suppressing any of the proper sounds," (*c*) be moderate in rate, avoiding extremes of precipitancy and slowness, and (*d*) use proper pronunciation, forming each sound according to "polite usage" and giving each word its "proper accentuation." To accomplish the second objective, the speaker attends to emphasis, pauses, tones, and gesture.[90]   *1 0 02 75*

Whately tells us that three qualities of delivery fall within the province of rhetoric: (1) perspicuity, which makes the meaning fully understandable to the hearers, (2) energy, which conveys meaning forcibly, and (3) elegance, which conveys meaning agreeably. However, he does not follow through and isolate the elements that enter into these qualities; rather he attempts to establish the general principle that "nature" will spontaneously suggest the proper emphases, tones, pauses, degrees of loudness, degrees of rapidity, and so forth.

Ward treats voice under the headings "quantity" and "quality." As to quantity of voice, he recommends that the speaker "fill the place where he speaks," avoid extremes of pitch, avoid monotony and sudden variations, adapt to the nature of the subject, maintain variety in pace, give each word and syllable "its just and full sound, both as to time and accent," and attend to pausing. As to quality of voice, he asks that we make the best of what nature has bestowed upon us, and, by careful attention, improve on its strength, clearness, fullness, and smoothness.[91]

Action

Ward uses the term gesture as the label for "a suitable conformity of the motions of the countenance, and several parts of the body in speaking, to the subject matter of the discourse," and divides it into "natural" and "imitative." Natural action consists of those gestures and motions that normally accompany our words; imitative action is that which is used in describing or in personating. He provides rather elaborate advice concerning management of the head, countenance, eyes, shoulders, arms, hands, chest, and feet.[92]

The other theorists do not follow Ward's lead. Whately refuses to discuss bodily action. The situation at present, he says, "seems to be, that the disgust excited, on the one hand, by awkward and ungraceful motions, and, on the other, by studied gesticulations, has led to the general disuse of action altogether; and has induced men to form the habit ... of keeping themselves quite still, or nearly so, when speaking." [93]

Campbell includes "gesture" under the head of rhetorical pronunciation, but has little to say upon the subject.[94] Perhaps he felt, as did Whately, that "it would be inconsistent . . . to deliver any *precepts* for gesture; because the observance of even the best conceivable precepts, would, by destroying the natural appearance, be fatal to their object. . . ." [95]

Blair doubts the value of Quintilian's list of rules, and suggests that "the study of action in public speaking, consists chiefly in guarding against awkward and disagreeable motions; and in learning to perform such as are natural to the speaker in the most becoming manner." [96] Whately agrees, and argues that "no care should be taken to use graceful or appropriate action; which, if not perfectly unstudied, will always be . . . intolerable. But if any one spontaneously falls into any gestures that are unbecoming, care should *then* be taken to break the habit." [97]

Stagefright

Whately devotes considerable space to the problem of stagefright, and considers it a problem for those who drop the "sheltering veil" of an artificial mode of delivery and adopt a natural manner. Blair and Ward touch upon it in short paragraphs, and suggest that it is a problem peculiarly common to those who are just beginning to speak in public.

Whately reasons that the cause of this "embarrassed, bashful, nervous sensation" is the close relationship between audience and speaker. The speaker knows that every fault in his delivery "makes the stronger impression on each of the hearers, from their mutual sympathy, and their consciousness of it." Ward claims that the problem is related to the degree of modesty in the speaker as well as to his ambition to excel.

Both Blair and Whately offer the same advice. The speaker, suggests Blair, "will find nothing of more use to him, than to study to become wholly engaged in his subject; to be possessed with a sense of its importance or seriousness; to be concerned much more to persuade than to please." [98]

Kinds of Delivery

Ward, Campbell, and Whately list three forms of delivery: speaking extemporaneously, speaking from memory, and reading. All but Blair state unequivocally that the extempore method is the better form. Whately writes elaborately concerning the superiority of the method, and recommends that the extemporaneous speaker attempt to reach the high level of style and arrangement which, generally, characterizes written discourse.[99]

Ward suggests that speaking from memory provides more opportunity for control of the voice and for the use of bodily action than does the method of reading. Campbell recommends that the preacher read from the pulpit because speaking extempore requires a certain "original and natural talent," and because, in speaking memoriter, the voice falls into a "kind of tune." Whately suggests that, with effort, it is possible for a person to read as well as he speaks. He discusses three levels of good reading: *correct reading*, which attempts to convey the sense of the material read; *impressive reading*, which adds to correct reading "some adaptation of the tones of the voice to the character of the subject, and of the style"; and *fine reading*, which "seems to convey, in addition, a kind of admonition to the hearers respecting the feelings which the composition ought to excite in them." [100]

English theories have had strong and permanent impact upon American instruction in rhetoric. The English writers to whom we are primarily indebted are John Ward, George Campbell, Hugh Blair, and Richard Whately. All but Ward were theologians. Fundamentally and basically, the theories expounded by these writers follow in the classical tradition. Ward's *System* is representative of the many English works on rhetoric that were, with only slight deviation, exclusively classical in concept. But, of these four, Ward alone looked only behind himself. Campbell was strongly influenced by Bacon's insistence upon inductive reasoning from observed facts, and by the empirical psychology of Hobbes, Locke, Hume, and Reid. As a result, his *Philosophy* initiated a psychological-epistemological-semantic trend in rhetorical theory that had tremendous influence upon American thought. Blair added to the literature of his day still another, yet sound, treatise on genteel criticism. His *Lectures* may be described as belles lettristic-critical in trend. They isolate rhetoric from "logical and ethical disquisitions" and locate it with studies that "sooth the mind, gratify the fancy, or move the affections." Invention was the core of Whately's theory; but his philosophy of delivery was romantic-naturalistic. Consequently his *Rhetoric* may be characterized as inventional-naturalistic in trend. It initiated the rapid development of a rhetoric of argumentation and debate. Priestley's *Lectures*, mentioned here only because they round out the picture of trends in English rhetorical theory, may be labelled as associationistic. Without question, these writers bequeathed to modern scholars the very best rhetorics that had been written since the time of Quintilian.

Notes

1. See Warren Guthrie, "The Development of Rhetorical Theory In America," *Speech Monographs*, XIII (1946), 14-22; XIV (1947), 38-54; XV (1948), 61-71; XVI (1949), 98-113.

2. *Ibid.*, XIII, 16-18; Wilbur Samuel Howell, "Ramus and English Rhetoric: 1574-1681," *Quarterly Journal of Speech*, XXXVII (October, 1951), 299-310.

3. For biographical information see Douglas Ehninger, "John Ward and His Rhetoric," *SM*, XVIII (1951), 1-16.

4. Another English treatise that adhered more or less slavishly to classical doctrine and is worth mention here is John Lawson's *Lectures Concerning Oratory* (London, 1742). See Guthrie, *op. cit.*, XIV, 41-44; H. F. Harding, *English Rhetorical Theory, 1750-1800*, unpublished Ph.D. dissertation, Cornell University, 1928; W. F. Sanford, *English Theories of Public Address*, 1530-1828 (Columbus, Ohio, 1931); Douglas Ehninger, "Dominant Trends in English Rhetorical Thought," *Southern Speech Journal*, XVIII (1953), 3-12; Ray E. Keesey, "John Lawson's *Lectures Concerning Oratory*," *SM*, XX (1953), 49-57.

5. *A System of Oratory*, 2 vols. (London, 1759), p. 19. Cf. Quintilian, *Institutes of Oratory*, tr. J. S. Watson (London, 1856), ii. 15, 1-37; Cicero, *On The Character of the Orator*, tr. J. S. Watson (London, 1855), i. 31.

6. Ward, *System*, I, 21. Cf. Cicero, i. 11-15.

7. Cf. Cicero, ii. 29. Quintilian, iii. 5, 1-2.

8. Cf. Quintilian, iii. 3, 1.

9. For biographical information, see George Campbell, *Lectures on Ecclesiastical History*, ed. George Skene Keith (London, 1800), Vol. I.

10. See Guthrie, *op. cit.*, XV, 63-64.

11. See Harding, *op. cit.*, p. 140; Clarence W. Edney, "Campbell's Lectures on Pulpit Eloquence," *SM*, XIX (1952), 1-10.

12. George Campbell, *The Philosophy of Rhetoric* (Boston, 1823), Preface, p. 6; Alta B. Hall, *George Campbell's Philosophy of Rhetoric, Book I*, unpublished Ph.D. dissertation, Cornell University, 1934; Clarence W. Edney, *George Campbell's Theory of Public Address*, unpublished Ph.D. dissertation, Iowa, 1946; John Crawford, *The Rhetoric of George Campbell*, unpublished Ph.D. dissertation, Northwestern, 1947.

13. Richard Whately, *Elements of Rhetoric* (London, 1841), p. 12.

14. George Campbell, *Lectures on Systematic Theology and Pulpit Eloquence* (Boston, 1810), p. 167.

15. Henry Home of Kames, *Elements of Criticism* (Edinburgh, 1762).

16. Francis Bacon, *The Advancement of Learning* (London, 1605); *Novum Organum* (London, 1620).

17. John Locke, *An Essay Concerning Human Understanding* (London, 1690).

18. David Hume, *A Treatise of Human Nature* (London, 1730-1740).

19. For biographical information see James L. Golden, *The Rhetorical Theory and Practice of Hugh Blair*, unpublished Master's thesis, Ohio State, 1948; J. Hall, *Account of The Life and Writings of Hugh Blair* (London, 1807); the *Dictionary of National Biography;* Robert M. Schmitz, *Hugh Blair* (New York, 1948).

20. Alexander Jamieson's *Grammar of Rhetorical and Polite Literature* (London, 1818) was another English work that followed this trend and was widely used in American colleges as an introductory text.

21. (Philadelphia, 1844), p. 10.

22. *Ibid.*, pp. 11-15.

23. *Ibid.*, p. 10.

24. *Ibid.*, p. 261.

25. For biographical information see W. J. Fitzpatrick, *Memoirs of Richard Whately* (London, 1864); Reverend T. Mozley, *Reminiscences, Chiefly of Oriel College and the Oxford Movement* (Boston, 1882); W. Tuckwell, *Reminiscences*

of Oxford (London, 1907); E. Jane Whately, *Life and Correspondence of Richard Whately, D. D.* (London, 1866); the *Dictionary of National Biography.* For the chief work on Whately's rhetoric, see W. M. Parrish, "Whately and His Rhetoric," *QJS,* XV (1929), 58-79; and by the same author, "Richard Whately's Elements of Rhetoric, Parts I and II: A Critical Edition," unpublished Ph.D. dissertation, Cornell University, 1929.

26. Richard Whately, *Elements of Logic* (New York, 1864).

27. Whately, *Rhetoric,* p. 30.

28. Whately's well-known handbook on *Christian Evidences* appeared in 1837, and was translated during his lifetime into at least a dozen languages.

29. (Dublin, 1781).

30. Blair, *Belles Lettres,* p. 10; Campbell, *Lectures,* p. 179; Ward, *System,* I, 48-49; Whately, *Rhetoric,* pp. 16-32. Cf. Elbert W. Harrington, *Rhetoric and the Scientific Method of Inquiry* (Boulder, Colorado, 1948).

31. Whately, *Rhetoric,* Preface, p. x; Campbell, *Philosophy,* p. 59. Ward, *System,* I, 31-32. Blair, *Belles Lettres,* p. 12.

32. Cf. Quintilian, v. 10, 94.

33. Ward, *System,* I, 44-76.

34. Cf. Quintilian, iii. 6, 66-67.

35. Cf. James H. McBurney, "The Place of the Enthymeme in Rhetorical Theory," *SM,* III (1936), 49-74.

36. Quintilian, v. 10, 11-16.

37. Thomas Reid, *Essays on the Intellectual Powers of Man* (Edinburgh, 1785).

38. Descartes, Locke, and Mill also insisted that intuition (or perception) was the crux of any attempt to explain the sources of knowledge. Mill declared that "the truths known by intuition are the original premises from which all others are inferred." John Stuart Mill, *A System of Logic* (New York, 1873), p. 4.

39. Cf. Hume, *op. cit.,* p. 332.

40. Campbell, *Philosophy,* pp. 61-84.

41. Clarence W. Edney, "Campbell's Theory of Logical Truth," *SM,* XV (1948), 19-32.

42. *Rhetoric,* pp. 7, 36.

43. *Ibid.,* p. 39.

44. *Ibid.,* p. 48.

45. Cf. Orville L. Pence, "The Concept and Function of Logical Proof in the Rhetorical System of Richard Whately," *SM,* XX (1953), 23-38.

46. See *The Rhetoric of Aristotle,* ii. 25, tr. Lane Cooper (New York, 1932), p. 180.

47. "Something that might, conceivably, be submitted to the senses, and about which there could be no disagreement among persons who should be present and to whose senses it should be submitted." Cf., Locke, *op. cit.,* IV. 16, 5.

48. When the conclusion is one which is general in nature or which assigns causes and which has demanded an exercise of judgment.

49. Whately, *Rhetoric,* pp. 62-75. Cf. Campbell, *Rhetoric,* pp. 82-84; Locke, *op. cit.,* IV. 15, 4. Whately is indebted to Campbell.

50. Whately, *Logic,* p. 256-258. Cf. Mill, *op. cit.,* p. 225.

51. The only difference between Campbell's theory of experience and that of Whately in this instance is point-of-reference, one epistemological, the other logical.

52. Cf. Aristotle, *op. cit.,* ii. 25, p. 177. Cicero, *Rhetorical Invention,* I. 42. Quintilian, IV. 13, 1.

53. Cf. Aristotle, *op. cit.,* ii. 25, p. 177.

54. Whately, *Logic,* pp. 168-250.

55. Campbell, *Philosophy,* pp. 146-174.

56. Whately, *Rhetoric,* pp. 195-197, 207-208; Ward, *System,* I, 158.

57. Ward, *System,* I, 156-158; Campbell, *Philosophy,* p. 107; Blair, *Belles Lettres,* p. 385; Whately, *Rhetoric,* p. 195.

58. Blair, *Belles Lettres,* pp. 395-362.

59. Whately, *Rhetoric*, pp. 209-230.
60. Campbell, *Rhetoric*, pp. 111-126.
61. Locke, *Essay*, II. 21, 5-6.
62. *System*, I, 140.
63. Campbell, *Rhetoric*, p. 129; Ward, *System*, I, 141; Blair, *Belles Lettres*, p. 15; Whately, *Rhetoric*, p. 208.
64. Whately, *Rhetoric*, p. 208. Cf. Aristotle, *op. cit.*, ii. 1, p. 92.
65. *System*, I, 142-147.
66. Campbell, *Philosophy*, pp. 128-129.
67. *Ibid.*, p. 129; Whately, *Rhetoric*, pp. 246-247.
68. Whately, *Rhetoric*, p. 232.
69. *Ibid.*, p. 257.
70. *Ibid.*, p. 231; Blair, *Belles Lettres*, p. 147.
71. Whately, *Rhetoric*, p. 241.
72. *Ibid.*, pp. 260-262.
73. Campbell, *Philosophy*, p. 130.
74. Cf. Cicero, ii. 76, 77. See Russell H. Wagner, "The Meaning of *Dispositio*," in *Studies in Speech and Drama* (Ithaca, N. Y., 1944), pp. 285-294; Douglas Ehninger, *Selected Theories of Inventio in English Rhetoric*, unpublished Ph.D. dissertation, Ohio State, 1949.
75. Campbell, *Philosophy*, pp. 100-124.
76. Whately, *Rhetoric*, pp. 239.
77. Ward, *System*, pp. 110-424.
78. Cf. Cicero, iii, 52.
79. Blair, *Belles Lettres*, pp. 101-205.
80. Cf. Bacon, *op. cit.*, pp. 19-32; Hobbes, *Leviathan*, I. 4, 25; R. I. Aaron, *John Locke* (London, 1937), pp. 95-208; Hume, *op. cit.*, p. 320. See Alfred Korzybski, *Science and Sanity* (Lancaster, Pa., 1948).
81. Campbell, *Lectures*, pp. 181-200.
82. Cf. Quintilian, ix, 3, 2.
83. *Ibid.*, viii, 2, 1.
84. Campbell, *Philosophy*, pp. 175-475.
85. *Ibid.*, p. 18.
86. Whately, *Rhetoric*, pp. 263-379.
87. Blair, *Belles Lettres*, p. 365; Whately, *Rhetoric*, p. 381; Ward, *System*, I, 314-316; Campbell, *Lectures*, pp. 196-211.
88. Blair, *Belles Lettres*, p. 376; Whately, *Rhetoric*, pp. 390, 401, 410-421; Campbell, *Lectures*, p. 200; Ward, *System*, I, 319, 382-383.
89. Campbell, *Lectures*, p. 197.
90. Blair, *Belles Lettres*, pp. 366-368.
91. Ward, *System*, I, 329-343.
92. *Ibid.*, I, 344-359.
93. Whately, *Rhetoric*, p. 448.
94. Campbell, *Lectures*, p. 198.
95. Whately, *Rhetoric*, p. 451.
96. Blair, *Lectures*, p. 375.
97. Whately, *Rhetoric*, p. 450.
98. *Ibid.*, pp. 420-430; Blair, *Belles Lettres*, p. 376.
99. Ward, *System*, I, 381-384; Campbell, *Lectures*, pp. 205-208; Whately, *Rhetoric*, pp. 385-447.
100. Ward, *System*, I, 382; Campbell, *Lectures*, p. 208; Whately, *Rhetoric*, pp. 385, 404-406.

5 English Sources of American Elocution

FREDERICK W. HABERMAN

....

As a modern study elocution originated in England. In its first half
century, from 1750 to 1800, it was accepted in America as readily as in
its native land, and in the next century cultivated even more assidu-
ously. The Americans, in the early stages of the movement's history,
republished British authors, copied them with or without acknowledge-
ment, modified and adapted their teachings to meet their situations.
In the later stages, they folded in a new French influence. Meanwhile,
they were creating a movement in America which possessed attributes
of independence as well as adaptation.

In other essays in this volume may be found discussions of the development of elocution in America. We shall here be concerned with
the phenomenon of elocution in England: with the genesis of the movement; with the characteristics of the movement—its scope, methodology,
divisions, and terminology; with the authors and books which were the
substance of the elocutionary ideas; and with the host of other elocutionary books which followed in the train of the movement.

The Genesis of the Elocutionary Movement

Elocution concentrated on man speaking. It emerged from the eighteenth century as an investigation of the rhetorical canon of delivery.
Delivery, to be sure, had been studied in all ages and in all nations of
the western world prior to 1750, but the elocutionary movement was
an examination of delivery so specialized in nature and content as to
differ in kind from former studies.[1] This phenomenon was the result of
several eighteenth-century forces working in concatenation.

Just as the seventeenth century was a century of criticism of style, so
the eighteenth was one of criticism of delivery. Inevitably, the criticism
fell most heavily on the hapless occupants of the English pulpit. Richard Steele [2] in the pages of the *Spectator* wrote disparagingly of their
"rakish, negligent air" and their habit of "lolling on their books." Jon-

athan Swift, acutely aware of the layman's grumbling about the dullness of church services, laid the blame on whomever he was talking to.
To his congregation, Swift said that it was his parishioners' gluttony and
not the preacher's dullness which caused them to go to sleep; besides
that, it was absurd to expect superb oratory from all preachers on all
occasions.[3] To the clergy, however, he observed that the reading of
sermons, especially with the head "held down from the beginning to
the end, within an inch of the cushion" must be roundly condemned.[4]
A satirical poem by Dr. Byram makes the same point:

> For, what's a sermon, good, or bad,
> If a man reads it like a lad?
> To hear some people, when they preach,
> How they run o'er all parts of speech,
> And neither raise a word, nor sink;
> Our learned bishops, one would think,
> Had taken school-boys from the rod,
> To make ambassadors of God.[5]

The faults of delivery most commonly noted by the critics of the
eighteenth century were frigidity, inertness, colorlessness, vulgarity,
absent-minded reading. Lord Chesterfield, that untiring expositor of
the worldly education of the man of position, limned the ideal to be
achieved: "a most genteel figure, a graceful noble air, an harmonious
voice, an elegancy of style, and a strength of emphasis." [6]

The elocutionary movement was also a direct outgrowth of the
seventeenth- and eighteenth-century interest in the English language.
In bringing the language to full stature in the seventeenth century, the
English had discovered, somewhat to their surprise, that they could
legitimately be proud of their native tongue. Along with their pride
ran a concurrent sentiment: to make the language an even more noble
instrument by standardizing and improving it in all its aspects, both
written and spoken.

Many of those who dealt professionally with language advocated the
establishment of an English Academy which would legislate on the
purity and beauty of the tongue. In 1660 R. H., in 1679 Dryden, in 1697
Defoe, in 1712 Swift supported the founding of a society which would
"polish and refine the English tongue." [7]

The Academy was not founded until 1901, but these pleas in support
of one resulted in the making of dictionaries to increase knowledge
about the individual words that make up the language and in the making of grammars to improve the handling of words in collocation. Concern about improvement of the written aspects of the language was
matched by correlative concern over the oral aspects. John Evelyn, for

example, chairman of a committee on the improvement of the English tongue appointed by the Royal Society in 1664, proposed:

That there might be invented some new periods and accents, besides such as our gram'arians and critics use, to assist, inspirit, and modifie the pronunciation of sentences, and to stand as markes before hand how the voyce and tone is to be govern'd, as in reciting of playes, reading of verses, etc., for the varying the tone of the voyce and affections, etc.[8]

The lexicographers of the eighteenth century undertook the invention of ways to implement the first idea implied in Evelyn's proposal: the correct phonation of words in isolation. Bailey in 1731, Kenrick in 1773, and Ash in 1775 adopted devices of syllabification, accent and stress marks.[9] At this point, the elocutionists turned to lexicography. Thomas Sheridan's dictionary of 1780 was the most complete guide to pronunciation until Walker's dictionary appeared eleven years later.[10]

The study of phonation in individual words led naturally to investigation of the second idea implied in Evelyn's proposal: the devising of ways to indicate inflection, pause, force, and rate in the delivery of words in connected discourse. Such investigation resulted in the publication of treatises on voice management, complete with symbolic systems making it theoretically possible to render the language with grace and correctness. These treatises on voice management were manuals of elocution.

Another reason for the interest in delivery and for the development of the art of elocution was the perception that power in oral presentation was an instrument of public persuasion. Buffon, well known in England, said in his famous discourse of 1753 that the requisites for arousing the crowd are a "vehement and affecting tone, expressive and frequent gestures, rapid and ringing words." [11] Charles Palmer, Deputy-Sergeant to the House of Commons, wrote as one of his maxims that delivery "is the very life and soul of eloquence.... The art of oratory is never so great and potent by the things that are said, as by the manner of saying them." [12]

Not only in parliament but also in the pulpit was oral presentation thought to have a persuasive effect. Competence retained the congregations; incompetence lost them.

The parliamentary audience is a specialized one; so, in some senses, is the religious audience. But the elocutionists were aware also of the emerging mass audience in the eighteenth century, created by the immense diffusion of knowledge. Lecky says that the effect of this diffusion of knowledge was such that "all important controversies became in their style and method more popular." [13] Popularization meant that ideas addressed to this mass audience, eager for knowledge and leaders, should be invested with more immediacy, more vividness, more simplicity, and more clarity not only in composition, but also in delivery.

The general interest in delivery so noticeable after 1750 is traceable in part to the renewed popularity of the theatre, to the development of a new style of stage delivery that revealed the potentialities of the language, to the personal influence of the great actor David Garrick, to the pedagogy of the two actors, Sheridan and Walker, who adapted stage delivery to certain forms of social discourse, and to the recognition that the training of a young speaker might well include emulation of the best actors and practical exercise in dramatic presentation.[14]

Finally, the elocutionary movement arose as a response to the demands of the age for training and educating its rising generation. Good speakers were in demand; society lavished extensive favors upon those who spoke well. Burgh, headmaster of a boys' school, spoke of the need for a "competent address and readiness" in "*parliament*, at the *bar,* in the *pulpit,* at *meetings* of merchants in *committees* for managing public affairs." [15] Sheridan remarks that "promotion, or honour to individuals, is sure to attend even a moderate share of merit" in good public reading or speaking.[16] William Enfield said that "there are few persons who do not daily experience the advantages" of a "just and graceful elocution." [17]

Practical need for expertness in delivery, as presented by complaining auditors or felt by ambitious speakers; philological and linguistic investigations into pronunciation and inflectional patterns; recognition of the persuasive effect of pleasing delivery; the emergence of a new convention of dramatic presentation that invested delivery of spoken language with a new liveliness; the acknowledgment of competence in speaking as a part of general education—all these forces acting together in the eighteenth century inspired the most intensive study of delivery ever undertaken.

Characteristics of the Elocutionary Movement

Sheridan gave elocution its broadest definition, one that comprehended the work of the elocutionists for over a hundred years:

A just delivery [Sheridan says] consists in a distinct articulation of words, pronounced in proper tones, suitably varied to the sense, and the emotions of the mind; with due observation of accent; of emphasis, in its several gradations; of rests or pauses of the voice, in proper place and well measured degrees of time; and the whole accompanied with expressive looks, and significant gesture.[18]

This "just delivery" fitted either the rhetorical situation or the interpretational situation. The elocutionists, it is true, concentrated in their pedagogical techniques more upon the practice of reading aloud, than on the delivery of original speeches. Rice in 1765 and Cockin in 1775, for instance, were interested solely in the art of reading aloud.[19] There is implicit, however, in the writings of many elocutionists, the retention of a relationship between training in reading aloud and the delivery of an extemporaneous speech at the bar or from the well of a legislative assembly. Mason says that his book on elocution is "intended chiefly for the assistance of those who instruct others in the art of reading. And of those who are often called to speak in publick." [20] Walker says that "as reading is a correct and beautiful picture of speaking; speaking, it is presumed cannot be more successfully taught, than by referring us to such rules as instruct us in the art of reading." [21] Sheridan concurs. He points out that the aim of public speaking is persuasion, that persuasion cannot be accomplished without the appearance of earnestness, that earnestness of delivery can best be learned through elocution. Whether the goal of the elocutionists was the creation of the graceful reader or the persuasive speaker or both, the technique was that of supplying principles and rules and systems of notation in conjunction with a skillful teacher for the better mastery of the printed page.

The printed page, the voice, language, and the body as used in oral presentation supplied the material upon which the movement brought philosophy, rules, principles, notation, and a master's insight to bear. In devising ways to analyze these materials the elocutionists used the precepts of ancient rhetoric and the practices of the stage. But a new force, operating over a period of some decades, eventually gave the movement its distinctive turn.

That force was science. It is the elocutionists' primary claim to fame in rhetorical history that they applied the tenets of science to the physiological phenomena of spoken discourse, making great contributions to human knowledge in that process.

The spirit of the elocutionary movement, like that of science, was one of independence, of originality, of a break with tradition.

The methodology of the elocutionary movement, like that of science, was a combination of observing and recording. Just as the astronomer observed the movements of the planets and recorded them in special symbols, so the elocutionists observed certain phenomena of voice, body, and language, and recorded them in systems of notation. The elocutionists who contributed most to the movement are those whose work is characterized by exhaustive analysis based on observation, by systematic organization, and by the invention of systems of symbolic representation.

The philosophy of the elocutionary movement, like that of the scientific-rationalistic creed, was a conception of man controlled by natural law. The elocutionists believed that the nature of man was governed by the same law and order which seventeenth-century science had discovered in the nature of the universe. They could claim that their rules and principles and systems represented the order that is found in nature; they were "nature still, but nature methodized." The phrase "follow nature" meant in general that the rational order found in the universe should be reproduced in books; and it meant in the field of delivery that the laws of elocution must approximate as closely as possible the laws of life.[22]

The elocutionists of the eighteenth century generally referred to their subject as an art. Rarely did they use the word *science* or the word *scientific*. But as the century neared its completion, the subsidiary subjects investigated became more and more "scientific" in the sense that elocution tended to be concerned with speech correction, with the anatomy of vocal physiology, and with the physics of sound production. Many writers of the nineteenth century—Thelwall, Rush, Bell, Plumptre, for example—looked upon elocution as a science.[23]

Scientific or artistic, the maxims and theoretical precepts which teacher and pupil were expected to master were diverse. For convenience in examination we may profitably group the contributions of the elocutionists into four divisions.

The division of bodily action included all the signs of visual communication, such as modifications of facial expression, manner and attitude, movement of arms and legs. The qualities of gesture or of bodily action most frequently sought were those of grace and force. Though the elocutionists set up no hard and fast dichotomy of method for the attaining of these two qualities, it seems apparent that there were two levels of training in their systems. The one was that of simple practice in the use of bodily actions, such as the sweep of the arm, the pointing of the finger, the clasping of the hands. This was the gesture of technical training. The other was that of the complex action required to communicate the passions. This was the gesture of emotional expression. The elocutionists implied that the appropriate gesture of emotional expression gave force to delivery; and they inferred that studious attention to the technique of controlling bodily action lent it grace. To accompany their descriptive and sometimes prescriptive accounts of bodily actions, the elocutionists eventually invented symbols to represent them.

The division of voice management was concerned with the meaningful manipulation of English sounds. The elocutionists wished to make the voice into a resilient instrument, capable of reading with variety and effectiveness. Vocal flexibility, buoyancy, responsiveness to meaning and innuendo, control—such were the qualities which the elocutionists sought. This division included definition and expert discussion of the elements of voice management, among them accent, emphasis, pause, pitch, force, rhythm, tone; it included the formulation of bodies of principles in some instances, of bodies of rules in others, and the development of rational systems, complete with notation, for the proper handling of the voice.

The division of pronunciation took account of the actual phonation of words. In trying to ameliorate dialectal variations from the "standard" pronunciation, to excise vulgar pronunciations, and to remedy mistaken pronunciations, the elocutionists, perforce, became lexicographers. Both Walker and Sheridan, at an early date in the movement, began to work on methods for standardizing pronunciation and for devising a notation by which the correct pronunciation would be immediately apparent. In other words, they were looking for ways to systematize pronunciation just as they had systematized the management of the voice and the actions of the body. Sheridan produced a dictionary in 1780 making use of a device new to lexicography: the respelling of the word to be pronounced into a loose phonetic script. Walker, in his dictionary of 1791, says of his own method:

[It] divides the words into syllables, and marks the sounds of the vowels like Dr. Kenrick, spells the words as they are pronounced like Mr. Sheridan, and directs the inspector to the rule by the word like Mr. Nares; but, where words are subject to different pronunciations . . . produces authorities for one side and the other, and points out the pronunciation which is preferable.[24]

In the division of vocal production the elocutionists attended to the problem of the actual formation of the sounds of speech. Their insistence that oral delivery be both pleasurable and persuasive presupposed that the pupil was capable of producing speech sounds—if not pleasant sounds, at least recognizable ones. A pupil who lisped or stammered could not become a polished speaker so long as he retained his defective utterance. Of all the divisions of elocution, this one had been the least cultivated by any predecessors of the elocutionists. Little was known about the anatomy of the speech mechanism, much less about the nature of speech sounds, and virtually nothing about speech therapy. In this division, the elocutionists addressed themselves to three problems: the identification of English sounds, the manner in which those sounds were produced, and the impediments which might interfere with the production of those sounds.

The elocutionists employed terms which had long been commonplace in rhetorical history, but they used them with the new signification that emerged during the eighteenth century. The years 1625-1725

form the great divide between two periods in which the technical definitions of the terms *style, elocution,* and *pronunciation* differed significantly. Whereas *pronunciation* once embraced the whole field of delivery, it later signified the correct phonation of words in isolation.
Elocution, which once meant the manner of artistic composition, became identified with the manner of artistic delivery. *Style,* once a
subsidiary synonym for elocution, later comprehended the whole canon
of the choice and arrangement of words.

Certain characteristics of the intermediate century, 1625-1725, explain
these changes in interpretation. These years were notable for the reaction from the excesses of the rhetoric of exornation with which *elocution,* especially, was intimately identified; for the spreading influence
of the scientific method; and for the development of linguistic scholarship. These forces fused into a destructive energy that drove the theories
and practices of the rhetoric of exornation, together with its specialized
terminology, into oblivion; but at the same time, they generated a constructive impulse that led to the formulation of a new set of theories
and practices to take the place of the old.

The criticism of exornation was sharp. In 1643, Howell called it "the
disease of our time"; Wilkins, Barrow, South, Arderne, Eachard, Glanvil,
and others condemned "the hard words, abstruse and mysterious
notions, the affected use of scraps of Greek and Latin, pretty cadences,
fantastic phrases, and rhetorical figures of all kinds." [25] These attacks
doomed exornation; and *elocution,* a word frequently used as title for
this conception of rhetoric, shared the obloquy along with the subject
matter. The reaction from exornation, plus the impetus of the scientific
method, led to a re-examination of the laws of the language and the
principles and purposes of prose. In the course of this re-examination
pronunciation, style, and *elocution* obtained their new meaning and
status. Let us see briefly how these new meanings came about.

Linguistic scholars strove to solidify, purify, and standardize the
language. In that process, it became important to discover the correct
phonation for words and to employ a term that would indicate this
special province of linguistic study. The term employed, of course, was
pronunciation. The term was satisfactory in many ways: it had etymological claim to the required meaning; it had always possessed, in English rhetorical theory, a secondary definition equivalent to the new
requirement; and it was willingly given this primary meaning by the
new writers who were interested in oral presentation.

The scientific and scholarly impulses that produced these linguistic
investigations, produced also a revolutionary change in the conception
of what constituted good prose. The "vicious Abundance of Phrase,"

condemned by the Royal Society, gave way to the slide rule and geometrical unity.[26] Prose became "functional"; utility supplanted artifice. In analyzing the new prose, literary critics shifted their attention from the speaker to the writer, partly because written prose lent itself to more scientific scrutiny, and partly because these scholars were more interested in the fine art of literature than in the useful art of oratory. Having given up the term *elocution*, the critics needed a new term. *Style* was at hand. It served admirably because of its relative etymological purity, its straightforward, uncontaminated history, its intimate connection with writing, and its tenuous relation to oratory.

The new investigators of oral presentation also needed a term. Four were at hand. *Pronunciation*, the traditional term, would no longer suffice because it had been given a restricted meaning, one which the new group could use very nicely. Another term was *action*. Derived from *actio* and possessing some of the sanction of classical rhetoric, especially Cicero's,[27] the term was, however, too limited in scope. For action referred specifically to overt physical motion and tended to exclude voice management. A third term was the modern word *delivery*. But it was too modern. Adapted from the French *délivrer*, the primary signification of the word in England (as in its native land it is still the main signification) was "to set free" whether by spear, by *habeas corpus*, or by midwife. The term later achieved currency in the language of law, of sport, of physical deportment, and by 1806, in the language of rhetoric, although there are scattered examples of its use in this sense before this date. The fourth term, *elocution*, seemed satisfactory. It was etymologically pure. The sense of oral presentation of expression was, in fact, more closely related to the etymology of the word than was the sense of style or manner or composition. It was a word traditionally connected with rhetoric. It was a close relative of the word eloquence. And on the principle that respectability is determined by the company one keeps, it could shake off the disrepute of exornation when associated with the virtue of the new oral presentation.

Authors and Books

The elocutionary movement may best be understood by an examination of the books which were produced in its name. There were hundreds published. Some of them, those that contained the substance of the elocutionary ideas, established the subject. These books were originating accounts or investigative treatises, such as those by Mason, Burgh, Sheridan, Walker, Austin, and Bell. Another category was that of the manual designed for use in the professions, such as the manual

of clerical elocution. A third was that of books for school and home
use: the reasoned textbooks, the volumes containing text and illustrative anthology, and the books of elegant extracts.

Of the originating accounts, John Mason's *An Essay on Elocution, or
Pronunciation* (1748) is the first book to include the word *elocution* in
its title.[28] This short work deals with "the right Management of the
Voice in reading or speaking." [29] The author finds a difference between
the two. Reading, he says, must "express the full Sense and Spirit of
your Author" and speaking must be "suitable to the Nature and Importance of the Sentiments we deliver." [30] His advice is simultaneously
applicable to both.

Section I deals with a bad pronunciation and how to avoid it; Section II with a good pronunciation and how to attain it. Mason constantly recurs to the philosophy epitomized in a statement from Burnet's
Pastoral Care which he quotes with approval:

He that is inwardly persuaded of the Truth of what he says, and that hath
a Concern about it in his Mind, will pronounce with a natural Vehemence
that is far more lovely than all the Strains that Art can lead to. . . .[31]

Although he knows that the best advice is to "make the Ideas seem to
come from the Heart," he cannot avoid the prescriptive rules which
became a commonplace in the elocutionary movement; for example, "A
Comma stops the Voice while we may privately count *one*, a Semi-colon
two; a Colon *three:* and a Period *four*." [32]

James Burgh, the eminent headmaster of an academy at Stoke New-
ington which he founded in 1747, was a successful writer on political
philosophy whose only book on oratory was *The Art of Speaking*
(1762).[33]

Part I of this book is an essay "in which are given Rules for expressing
properly the principal Passions and Humors, which occur in Reading,
or Public Speaking." [34] Part II is an anthology of readings, with glosses
referring to the passions defined in the essay.

The essay contains directions to students on the vocal management of
certain types of sentences and certain types of material, an exposition
of physical demeanor in depicting seventy-six different "humors or
passions," [35] and some vigorously penned general observations on oratory. The most striking part of the book is the section in which Burgh
shows how the principal emotions are expressed by attitudes, looks,
gestures, and language. The opening lines of his description of *despair*
are typical of the vehemence and intensity his analyses call for:

Despair . . . bends the *eyebrows* downward; *clouds* the *forehead;* rolls the
eyes around frightfully; *opens* the *mouth* toward the ears; bites the *lips; widens*
the *nostrils; gnashes* with the *teeth,* like a fierce wild beast.[36]

The idea held by Burgh that "nature has given to every emotion of the mind its proper outward expression," [37] and the correlative idea that various physical features, such as the eye, are capable of projecting this expression, while not new in rhetorical history, were eagerly made a part of the elocutionary movement. Burgh's conception and intensive analysis of these ideas were given circulation in at least seven British editions and eight American reprintings of his work. He was read by Sheridan, paraphrased by Walker, anthologized by Scott, pirated by an American publisher,[38] quoted by Austin, and recalled in one way or another by elocutionists for over a century.

In 1756 at the age of thirty-seven, after his career as actor and stage manager had ended in failure, Thomas Sheridan found a new vocation as teacher, lecturer, and author in elocution. Aside from the *Works of Swift with Life* (1784),[39] Sheridan's publications deal with three subjects, education, pronunciation, and elocution, though these three may be considered as facets of his one main interest, speech. The central proposition of his three works on education is that oratory, properly taught (by Mr. Sheridan, of course), will eliminate the disorders in England.[40] Sheridan's two works on pronunciation, the *Dictionary* (1780) and the *Grammar* (1780),[41] fulfilled a linguistic need, advanced the theory of phonetics, and fixed pronunciation as one of the divisions of elocution.

His three works dealing more specifically with reading and speaking are published lectures. In *A Discourse being Introductory to a Course of Lectures on Elocution and the English Language*, delivered at Oxford in 1759,[42] Sheridan made a plea for the study of spoken language, for the employment of properly qualified masters of elocution in a revised educational system, and for the encouragement of research in the principles and rules of elocution. Sheridan's most important work is *Lectures on Elocution* published in 1762.[43] In this series of seven lectures, he provided the working definition of elocution, established his philosophy, and discussed articulation, pronunciation, accent, emphasis, tones or notes of the speaking voice, pauses or stops, key or pitch, management of the voice, and gesture. *Lectures on the Art of Reading* (1775)[44] repeats much of the doctrine published thirteen years earlier, but is notable for its inclusion of his simple symbolic code, and of his phonetic analysis of speech sounds.

Sheridan's ideal delivery was characterized by grace, sincerity, and naturalness. When he began his work, he leaned heavily on the teachings of Cicero and Quintilian and on the application to the lectern of his experience with the British stage. As accretions were made to the methodology of elocution, he adopted certain new techniques, among them a code of his own invention, symbolizing emphases, pauses of varying duration, rapidity, long and short syllables. Sheridan was the movement's greatest early figure. He gave definition and categories to the study; he conducted a vigorous propaganda for its acceptance, reaching large audiences through his lectures and his books; and he practiced brilliantly his own art.

Joshua Steele was a prosodist, a musical theorist, a business man, a reformer, and, by accident, an elocutionist because he wrote a book which greatly influenced the course of the movement.[45] *Prosodia Rationalis* (1775 and 1779)[46] is a series of tracts, a record of the correspondence between Lord Monboddo and Steele, both of whom were interested in the phenomena of language and speech. Steele convinced Monboddo that speech has melody and rhythm. He showed that this melody was a kind of tune or pitch pattern inherent in speech; that this rhythm was a recurrence of measured quantity which depends upon the nature of language and upon an inner understanding of context externalized by the outward manifestation of voice. To demonstrate his theses, he analyzed spoken speech according to musical principles, showing how speech moved up and down the musical scale by slides, the intervals between syllables being almost infinitesimal. By contrast the intervals between notes on a musical staff were easily distinguishable. Since speech melody could not be precisely rendered by literal musical symbolization, Steele invented a new notation for speech consisting of curved lines or slides. Having taken the initial step in the notation of voice management, he went on to design symbols for other factors of voice, including a set of phonetic characters which seem remarkable for his time.

With this system, Steele hoped that one might sight-read a discourse as he might a score of music and that one might preserve for posterity the performances of superb actors and orators. He illustrated his hopes with a transcription of a soliloquy as delivered by David Garrick, in which he used the musical staff, the clef, the time signature, and indicators for rate, pause, pitch, force, and stress. But in these aspirations he was to fail where later the phonograph, the tape recorder, and the cinema were to succeed.

Steele influenced the prosodists, among them Odell, Roe, Chapman, and Coventry Patmore,[47] as well as the elocutionists. Walker borrowed heavily from him (and with virtually no acknowledgment); Thelwall as heavily (but with acknowledgment); Austin, Smart, Barber, Rush, Comstock, Murdock—elocutionists on both sides of the Atlantic employed in one way or another his new analyses of the phonetic, dynamic, and prosodic components of speech.

John Walker, like Thomas Sheridan, was thirty-seven years old when he quit the stage and turned to teaching, lecturing, and writing on elocution to earn a livelihood. His life offers astonishing parallels to Sheridan's. Both of them were actors, theatre managers, educators, lecturers, writers, and lexicographers. But they differed in mental constitution. Sheridan was an observer, Walker a lawgiver; Sheridan formulated generalizations, Walker established a system; Sheridan was more the pleader who sought a revival of oratorical training, Walker more the pedagogue who decided the methods to be used in that training.

Walker published many works on pronunciation, elocution, and composition. In matters of pronunciation, he became the eighteenth-century embodiment of an English Academy. The principal work of his life, *A Critical Pronouncing Dictionary and Expositor of the English Language* (1791),[48] has been called "the statute book of English orthoëpy."[49] His school manuals on grammar and composition were potboilers written late in life after he had earned widespread fame as a lexicographer and elocutionist.

Walker published six books on elocution.[50] The *Exercises for Improvement in Elocution* (1777), dedicated to Garrick, is a collection of readings. The *Elements of Elocution* (1781), his most important rhetorical work, is a systematic presentation of a theory of elocution. *Hints for Improvement in the Art of Reading* (1783), is a brief summary of the *Elements*. A *Rhetorical Grammar* (1785) unites the old canons of rhetoric with the new ones of elocution. *Melody of Speaking Delineated* (1787) explains a method of teaching elocution by means of signs adapted from musical notation. *The Academic Speaker* (1789) is a book of extracts for declamatory practice, introduced by two essays on gesture and acting.

The basic idea in Walker's *Elements of Elocution* is that the reader obtains harmony of sound and achieves fidelity to the author's purpose by applying the inflections found in nature to the various grammatical forms utilized by the author. The sense, emphasis, suspension, completeness, force, and pitch contained in grammatical forms are released in spoken discourse through employment of the four inflections—rising, falling, and two circumflex inflections. Walker's exhaustive analysis of the interplay of inflection and grammatical form resulted in an elaborate system of rules governing the elements of vocal technique.

His claim that he discovered the inflection is not to be credited too seriously, for Steele wrote about upward and downward slides six years before Walker published *Elements*.[51] But his application of the theory of slides to grammatical forms is undoubtedly original. Walker profoundly influenced the elocutionary movement.

In 1806, the Reverend Gilbert Austin published *Chironomia; or a Treatise on Rhetorical Delivery*, a quarto volume of 600 pages, handsomely bound and printed, and available at £2.2s.[52] Of his seven other publications, one is a sermon, and six are on scientific and mechanical subjects such as barometers, carbonic acid gas, and condensers.

In *Chironomia*, Austin sought to give to the public some rules and precepts by which the national oratory might be improved, to compile a virtual anthology of quotations from the most renowned ancient and modern rhetoricians on the subject of delivery, to provide a scientifically exhaustive analysis of gesture, and to popularize a set of agglutinative symbols by which delivery might be recorded with brevity and precision.

When he examined the possible positions of the arms in gesture, Austin sloughed off tradition, eliminated the context of meaning in speaking, and observed only what positions the arms were capable of taking. His examination was physiological in nature; his method one of abstract spatial analysis. To obtain a pattern for the notation of arm positions, he imagined the speaker inside a sphere. Every point at intervals of 45° on this sphere had a symbol. For example, the right arm can take five positions when operating laterally from the body: Z is overhead, h is horizontal, R is straight down, d is midway between horizontal and down, e is midway between horizontal and overhead. Thus Austin could denote on a line of poetry, say, directions for arm positions in much the same way that Beethoven could place marks on a piece of paper for a pianist to follow.

In addition to the "scientific" method just described, Austin used other methods when describing gesture. For positions of the hands, he used the method of classification by categories; for gestures of head and eyes, the method of arbitrary selection; and for complicated action to express complex emotional states, the method of conventional designation.

Chironomia had only one British and no American edition, but it exerted an enormous influence upon elocutionists. In England, A. M. Hartley called it "incomparably the ablest treatise on delivery in general, that has yet appeared in our language." [53] In America, a host of writers, among them, Caldwell, Bronson, Bacon, Fulton and Trueblood, and as late as 1916, Joseph A. Mosher, were indebted to this extraordinary book.[54]

Alexander Melville Bell taught in Newfoundland, Edinburgh, London, Queens College in Canada, Lowell Institute in Boston. Acclaimed wherever he went, he seems to have been the international dean of the movement.[55]

In his forty-nine publications,[56] Bell touched almost every part of the art and science of elocution, but he made his most original and most enduring contribution to the subject in the division of vocal production.[57] In this area, he came close to realizing the hundred-year-old dream of the elocutionists—that of discovering the physiological means by which each speech sound is produced, of classifying those sounds scientifically, and of inventing a notation that would include a symbol for every sound. His task was to find a rational basis upon which to establish a symbolic system. Previous investigators had begun with sounds and then had tried to describe the physiological positions of the articulative organs when producing them. What Bell did was to begin with physiological positions of the organs and then determine what sounds he could make. Then, by modifying in a systematic way each of the articulators in turn, he obtained different sounds which formed a concatenated progression. He could thus account for any sound made by the human voice, whether an orthodox sound of a national language, or one of sneezing, snoring, grunting, or spitting. He discharged the second half of his task by inventing symbols which "depicted" the actions of the organs forming the sound, thus earning their title of "Visible Speech." Although visible speech had faults, its virtues were many, and its influence widespread.[58] It became the basis of Henry Sweet's Broad Romic which in turn became the basis of the IPA, and it earned Bell a line in George Bernard Shaw's preface to *Pygmalion*.

Elocution Manuals

The major books which we have so far examined established the basic ideas of elocution. Some of them gave definition and scope to the subject; others were investigative treatises, records of research that pushed outward the bounds of the subject and made contributions to human knowledge. Many of these books were used in the classroom, but only, of course, for mature or advanced students. So, along with the complete accounts of the subject and the detailed surveys of its divisions, another type of book appeared as a part of the movement—the manual of elocution.

There were, in general, two categories of manuals, those intended for practitioners of the professions, and those intended for school and home use.

Most numerous of the professional manuals were those written for the clergy. First to provide the application of the new theory of elocution to the various arts of the church service was Anselm Bayly in two books, *A Practical Treatise on Singing and Playing* (1771)[59] and *The Alliance of Musick, Poetry, and Oratory* (1789).[60] John Wesley's little book of a dozen pages, costing one penny, summarized much of Mason's advice and exemplified the author's profound respect for brevity and economy.[61] James Wright's *The Philosophy of Elocution* (1818),[62] contains a long elucidation of the office of the minister, 200 pages of voice management (the principles being paraphrased from Sheridan and the system of notation adapted from Walker), and 175 pages of liturgies of the church painstakingly marked for delivery. The Reverend John Henry Howlett's *Instructions in Reading the Liturgy of the United Church of England and Ireland* (1826)[63] analyzes the pitfalls of church oratory, provides sixty pages of advice on voice management, interprets and marks fifty liturgical pieces, using a notational system of commas, dashes, accents, hyphens, capitals, asterisks, circles, and superior numbers referring back to rules.

An unusual book on elocution for the clergy was *Garrick's Mode of Reading the Liturgy of the Church of England* (1840) by Richard Cull.[64] Cull's opening essay on the analogy between music and speech is written in the tradition of Joshua Steele. The rest of the book is a re-editing of material which had previously been published.[65] The general method used for explaining Garrick's technique is to quote a line of the service, and then to comment on the manner in which Garrick delivered it, or vice versa. For example:

When speaking the *three following words,* Mr. Garrick recommended a look, expressive of the utmost *suitable gravity,* to be cast slowly around the congregation, the voice rather *low,* and denoting, together with the whole manner, that *solemn* and *reverential respect* which is due to the place of public worship.

Dearly beloved brethren.

Here make a pause much longer than the comma. . . .[66]

The main objectives of the authors of manuals of clerical elocution were to provide instruction in the use of voice and body and to help in the interpretation of the various liturgies. The study of elocution may have been of some value in helping to rid church oratory of its worse external faults, such as indistinctness, monotonous droning, and inaudibility. But it must be doubted that pulpit oratory could achieve the warmth and spirit and animation so desired by the critics until there was general realization that a sermon was different from an essay—that it was hewn from granite, not delicately modeled with clay.

There were hundreds of manuals of elocution published between 1750 and 1900 which were intended primarily for use in schools but which could sometimes double for use in the home. Commonest of the school manuals was the book containing an introductory text and an anthology of pieces for reading or declaiming.

In the later eighteenth century, manuals by William Enfield, John Walker, and William Scott rolled up a wave of popularity that carried them into the nineteenth century. Enfield's *The Speaker* (1774)[67] contained 150 pieces suitable for Saturday "Speech Day," prefaced by a short essay that compressed elocution into eight rules. Scott's *Lessons in Elocution* (1779)[68] went through more than a score of editions in England and the United States. The book contained nothing original. American publishers prefaced their editions with four essays on delivery borrowed from Walker and Burgh. Walker's *Academic Speaker* (1789),[69] written for young scholars, contributed, in addition to a set of extracts, an essay on gesture copied later in many books and one on the relation between acting and speaking.

The distinctive feature of Henry Innes' *Elocution, its Principles and Practices* (c. 1834)[70] is its allotment of space in the introductory text to the division of vocal production, in which he describes the vocal mechanism, identifies, and suggests remedies for certain speech defects.

A. M. Hartley used a device that became increasingly popular during the nineteenth century. In the final part of the introductory text of *The Academic Speaker* (1846),[71] he names various emotional states and describes the physical action required to express each. In the anthology, he places superior numbers over certain words. For example, he inserts eighteen different numbers in the text of Chatham's speech against the American war. To find the name of the emotion, the reader refers to the number key in the headnote; after finding the name, he refers to the essay which describes the appropriate action. The headnote to Chatham's speech reads in part:

1. Resolute and angry remonstrance. 2. Indignant appeal to honour. 3. Lofty pride and regret. . . . 16. One of the finest strokes of oratory ever produced—finger of the right hand sublimely pointed to the tapestry of the Armada, eyes fixed on Effingham with ineffable scorn. . . .[72]

Taken all in all, these books of text and anthology surveyed the totality of the field of elocution, but few of them were complete accounts in themselves. The division given most space was that of voice management, followed far in the rear by vocal production, bodily action, and pronunciation.

Closely related to this genre and intended not only for the school, but also for the hearth where reading was a "favorite entertainment of the social circle," [73] were volumes of elegant extracts. Typical is Mrs. Fanny Palliser's *The Modern Poetical Speaker* (1845).[74] This book of five hundred pages, with a preface but no introductory text, was the first general anthology to include a good set of footnotes to explain hard passages, to identify obscure allusion, and to provide, in some cases, factual background for a proper appreciation of the piece. Furthermore, Mrs. Palliser did not alter a word without putting the substitute in italics; she always used asterisks to indicate lines deleted; and she did not "improve" the pieces according to her own lights. The practice of "improving" selections was commonplace enough. John Thelwall in his anthology, for example, quoted the first ninety-four lines of Collins' "The Passions, an Ode"; then, deleting Collins' last stanza, substituted sixty-eight lines from his own pen which differed from the pattern of the original poem in theme, cadence, and rhyme.[75]

The book of elegant extracts was executed according to an implicit code: theory must be cut to a minimum or eliminated entirely; the great masters should have a place of honor; the modern poets should be given a niche; no shocking word should pass the printer; extracts from the big three of early nineteenth-century England should be included —Mrs. Hemans, Southey, and Scott; and by and large, it was to be borne in mind that American authors were not quite ready for canonization.

The reasoned textbook of some length, the third type of manual, appealed to advanced students, mature minds, teachers, and educators; it was carefully organized and fully illustrated with examples; it might contain a relatively short set of selections; and it possessed an air of scholarship and philosophical completeness. One of the best correlated and most philosophical of the textbooks is Benjamin Humphrey Smart's *The Theory of Elocution* (1819).[76] Each of the first three chapters of *Theory* corresponds to a division of the field of elocution: "Mechanical Reading" corresponds to vocal production, the subject matter being articulation; "Significant Reading" to voice management, the subject matter being inflection; and "Impassioned Reading" to bodily action, the subject matter being looks, tones, and gestures. The last two chapters are further explorations of the implications of impassioned reading.

The purposes animating the authors of the school manuals were not always the same, and, of course, an author might have more than one purpose in his book. There were, in the main, however, three objectives that the manuals sought to achieve. The first of these was the acquisition of elocutionary effectiveness: delivery of discourse with distinct and pleasing articulation, graceful modulation, and decorous demeanor. A second purpose, overlaid, to be sure, on the first, was the inculcation of moral excellence. Toward the end of the period under consideration, there was an increasing number of authors who laid claim to the teaching of moral precepts and respectable conduct. Likewise a third purpose appeared with more and more frequency: the development of a taste for culture and quality.

Both the purposes and the books which the elocutionists wrote to accomplish them, were eagerly accepted in America. The demand for elocution in this nation being as great or even greater than it was in England, it is no wonder that the British found a market here for their books, or that piratical publishers should look for the cheapest way to capture the market, or that a band of indigenous writers should arise to challenge the supremacy of the originators of the movement and eventually to take over its direction.

Notes

1. For more complete studies of the elocutionary movement, see Mary Margaret Robb, *Oral Interpretation of Literature in American Colleges and Universities* (New York, 1941); Daniel E. Vandraegen, "The Natural School of Oral Reading in England, 1748-1828," unpublished Ph.D. dissertation, Northwestern, 1949; Harold Friend Harding, "English Rhetorical Theory, 1750-1800," unpublished Ph.D. dissertation, Cornell University, 1937; Frederick W. Haberman, "The Elocutionary Movement in England, 1750-1850," unpublished Ph.D. dissertation, Cornell University, 1947, which I have used freely; and Warren Guthrie, "The Development of Rhetorical Theory in America, 1635-1850—V: the Elocutionary Movement—England," *Speech Monographs*, XVIII (1951), 17-30.

2. *The Spectator*, No. 147 (1711). Also see Joseph Addison on this topic in No. 407 (1712).

3. "On Sleeping in Church," *The Works of Jonathan Swift*, ed. Walter Scott (Edinburgh, 1814), VIII, 143.

4. "A Letter to a Young Clergyman," *Works*, VIII, 347.

5. Quoted by James Burgh, *The Art of Speaking* (London, 1762), p. 216. Burgh obtained it from James Fordyce, *The Art of Preaching* (Glasgow, 1755).

6. *The Letters of P. D. Stanhope, Earl of Chesterfield*, ed. Lord Mahon (London, 1845-1853), I, 366. The date of this letter is 1749. For similar comments see *Letters of Philip Dormer, Fourth Earl of Chesterfield to his Godson and Successor*, ed. Earl of Carnarvon (London, 1890), p. 391; and for more complete study of his views see Donald C. Bryant, "The Earl of Chesterfield's Advice on Speaking," *Quarterly Journal of Speech*, XXXI (December, 1945), 411.

7. The quotation is from "Essays Upon Several Projects," *The Works of Daniel De Foe*, ed. William Hazlitt (London, 1840-1843), III; Swift, "A Proposal for Correcting, Improving, and Ascertaining the English Tongue," *Works*, IX, 355; John Dryden, Dedication of *Troilus and Cressida;* R. H., *New Atlantis*, cited by Edmund Freeman, "A Proposal for an English Academy in 1660," *Modern Language Review*, XIX (July, 1924), 291-300.

8. In a letter to Sir Peter Wyche, 1665. See J. E. Spingarn, *Critical Essays of the Seventeenth Century* (London, 1908), II, 310-312. In a letter to Samuel Pepys in 1689, Evelyn refers to his work on this committee and to his idea of an Academy for the "Art and Improvement of speaking and writing well" (p. 327).

9. Nathan Bailey, *Universal Etymological English Dictionary* (London, 1731); William Kenrick, *A New Dictionary* (London, 1773); John Ash, *New and Complete Dictionary of the English Language* (London, 1775).

10. Thomas Sheridan, *A General Dictionary of the English Language* (London, 1780); John Walker, *A Critical Pronouncing Dictionary and Expositor of the English Language* (London, 1791).

11. "Discourse on Style," trans. and ed. Lane Cooper in *Theories of Style* (New York, 1907), p. 171.

12. *Aphorisms and Maxims* (London, 1748), Maxim 108.

13. W. E. H. Lecky, *A History of England in the Eighteenth Century* (London, 1887), VI, 166.

14. Karl Mantzius, *A History of Theatrical Art* (London, 1909), V, 383 ff.; Joseph Knight, *David Garrick* (London, 1894), p. 25 ff.

15. Burgh, p. 154.

16. Thomas Sheridan, *Lectures on Elocution* (London, 1762), p. 1.

17. *The Speaker* (London, 1780), Introduction.

18. *Lectures*, p. 10.

19. John Rice, *An Introduction to the Art of Reading with Energy and Propriety* (London, 1765); William Cockin, *The Art of Reading Written Language; or, an Essay on Reading* (London, 1775).

20. John Mason, *An Essay on Elocution, or Pronunciation* (London, 1748), title page.

21. John Walker, *Elements of Elocution* (London, 1781), I, 2.

22. Despite the claim that they "follow nature," the elocutionists have sometimes been labeled "mechanists" as well as "naturalists." For varying interpretations on this question see James A. Winans, "Whately on Elocution," *QJS*, XXXI (February, 1945), 1-3; Charles A. Fritz, "From Sheridan to Rush," *QJS*, XVI (February, 1930), 82 ff.; Wayland Maxfield Parrish, "The Concept of 'Naturalness,'" *QJS*, XXXVII (December, 1951), 448-454; Robb, *op. cit.*, 16-69 *passim*; Haberman, *op. cit.*, 49-67 *passim*; Vandraegen, *op. cit. passim*, and his "Thomas Sheridan and the Natural School," *SM*, XX (1953), 58-64; Richard D. Harper, "The Rhetorical Theory of Thomas Sheridan," unpubl. Ph.D. dissertation, Wisconsin, 1951, pp. 200 ff.

23. John Thelwall, "Introductory Discourse on the Nature and Objects of Elocutionary Science" (London, 1805); A. S. Thelwall, *A Lecture on the Importance of Elocution in Connexion with Ministerial Usefulness* (London, 1850); James Rush, *The Philosophy of the Human Voice* (Philadelphia, 1827), Introduction; A. M. Bell, *Principles of Elocution* (Edinburgh, 1849), Preface; C. J. Plumptre, *King's College Lectures in Elocution* (London, 1881), p. 226.

24. *Critical Pronouncing Dictionary*, p. 9.

25. See Spingarn, *Critical Essays*, "IV, The Trend Toward Simplicity," pp. xxxvi-xlviii.

26. Thomas Sprat, *The History of the Royal Society of London* (London, 1667); 4th ed. (London, 1734), p. 112.

27. Quintilian, *Institutio Oratoria*, XI, iii, 2, 6; Cicero, *Brutus*, XXXVIII.

28. (London).

29. Mason, *Elocution*, p. 5.

30. *Ibid.*, p. 22.

31. *Ibid.*, p. 32.

32. *Ibid.*, pp. 23-24.

33. (London).

34. Title page.

35. Professor Parrish is the latest scholar to count them. See footnote 5 in "The Burglarizing of Burgh, or the Case of the Purloined Passions," *QJS*, XXXVIII (December, 1952), 433.

36. P. 173. Pagination refers to the edition retitled "On Public Speaking" and bound with Sheridan's *Rhetorical Grammar* (Philadelphia, 1783).

37. Burgh, p. 166.

38. See note 35, *supra*.

39. (London), 18 vols.

40. *British Education, or the Source of the Disorders of Great Britain* (London, 1756); *A General View of the Scheme for the Improvement of Education* (Dublin, 1757); *A Plan of Education for the Young Nobility and Gentry of Great Britain* (London, 1769).

41. Thomas Sheridan, *A General Dictionary of the English Language* (London, 1780), 2 vols. *A Rhetorical Grammar* was published originally in England as a preface to the *Dictionary*. It was published separately in America under the editorship of Archibald Gamble (Philadelphia, 1783). This American edition contains a seventy-page appendix entitled "On Public Speaking," a reprinting without credit of Part I of Burgh's *The Art of Speaking* (London, ed. of 1775). Several investigators, with this volume in their hands, have erroneously ascribed authorship to Sheridan.

42. (London).

43. (London).

44. (London).

45. See John B. Newman, "Joshua Steele: Prosody in Speech Education," un-published Ph.D. dissertation, New York University, 1950; by the same author, "The Phonetic Aspect of Joshua Steele's System of Prosody," *SM*, XVIII (1951), 279-287; and "The Role of Joshua Steele in the Development of Speech Education in America," *SM*, XX (1953), 65-73.

46. See Newman, "Phonetic Aspect," footnote 1, for a discussion of the title and the two editions of this book.

47. T. S. Omond, *English Metrists* (London, 1921), 94 *et passim;* George Saints-bury, *A History of English Prosody* (London, 1908), II, 548 *passim.*

48. (London), 28th ed. in 1826.

49. *DNB.*

50. Place of publication for all six is London.

51. See Newman, "Role of Joshua Steele."

52. (London).

53. *The Oratorical Class-Book* (Glasgow, 1824), p. 7.

54. Merritt Caldwell, *A Practical Manual of Elocution* (Philadelphia, 1845), Preface, v; C. P. Bronson, *Elocution; or Mental and Vocal Philosophy* (Louisville, 1845), engravings reprinted without credit; Albert M. Bacon, *A Manual of Gesture* (New York, 1872), Preface; R. I. Fulton and T. C. Trueblood, *Practical Elements of Elocution* (Boston, 1893), Preface and engravings; Joseph A. Mosher, *The Essentials of Effective Gesture* (New York, 1916), Preface.

55. Frederick W. Haberman, "The Bell Family—A Dynasty in Speech," *Southern Speech Journal*, XV (December, 1949), 112-117.

56. Two publications which contain his philosophy in briefest form are *A New Elucidation of the Principles of Speech and Elocution* (Edinburgh, 1849), 168 editions by 1892; and *Essays and Postscripts on Elocution* (New York, 1886).

57. See Estelle L. McElroy, "Alexander Melville Bell—Elocutionist and Phonetician," unpublished Ph.D. dissertation, Columbia University, 1951.

58. See Otto Jesperson, *The Articulation of Speech Sounds* (Marburg in Hessen, 1889), p. 3; Maurice Grammont, *Traité de Phonétique* (Paris, 1933), p. 13; Claude E. Kantner and Robert West, *Phonetics* (New York, 1941), p. 287.

59. (London).

60. (London).

61. "Directions Concerning Pronunciation and Gesture" (London, 1793). See *The Works of the Reverend John Wesley, A.M.* (London, 1840-1842), 4th ed., XIII, 488 ff.

62. (Oxford).

63. (London).

64. (London).

65. The notes made by the clergyman tutored by Garrick were systematized by a friend, J. W. Anderson, and published under the title *The Common Prayer, as read by the late Mr. Garrick* (London, 1797).

66. Cull, *Mode of Reading*, p. 67.

67. (London). At least eight editions by 1851. I have used an edition of 1798.

68. (Edinburgh). 12th English ed. in 1799; at least 11 American editions by 1820. I have used an edition of 1808 published at Worcester.

69. (London). At least three editions by 1801. I have used an edition of 1800 published at Dublin.

70. I have used the 9th ed., n.d. References in the *Catalogue of the British Museum* and in the *English Catalogue of Books*, which list as the main title what appears as the subtitle in the 9th ed., indicate that the 1st ed. is London, 1834.

71. (Glasgow). I have used the Glasgow, 1853 edition. *The Academic Speaker* is very similar to his *The Oratorical Class-Book* (Glasgow, 1824), 15th ed. in 1854.

72. Hartley, *Academic Speaker*, p. 68.

73. Thomas Ewing, *Principles of Elocution* (Edinburgh, 1815); 36th ed. in 1861. The quotation is from the 12th ed. (Edinburgh, 1828), Preface.

74. (London).

75. John Thelwall, *Illustrations of English Rhythms* (London, 1812).

76. (London). Smart also published a companion exercise book, *The Practice of Elocution* (London, 1820); 4th ed., 1842.

PART II

Rhetoric, Elocution, and Speech

6 American Contributions to Rhetorical Theory and Homiletics

JOHN P. HOSHOR

....

At the opening of the nineteenth century, rhetorical education in America was based largely on the classical writings on the subject—principally the works of Aristotle, Cicero, and Quintilian—and, more especially, on the works of certain English rhetoricians, notably Blair and Campbell. Their works, together with Whately's *Elements of Rhetoric,* published in 1828, were the most widely used textbooks in American colleges in the first half of the century, and continued to be an important influence throughout the century.

I

As early as 1800, however, an American rhetoric sufficiently complete to be considered a contribution to rhetorical theory made its appearance. This was the edition of the collected lectures on rhetoric by President John Witherspoon of Princeton. Lecturing at Princeton, Witherspoon emphasized two general points of view which were repeated and developed by Chauncey Goodrich lecturing a few years later at Yale. These were, first, that while some natural talent or capacity "is evidently necessary to the instruction or study of this art," the orator is essentially a product of his practice and training rather than his heredity; and, second, that the wise study and translation of great models is an invaluable aid in developing skill in the art of rhetoric.[1]

Witherspoon's theory of rhetoric is essentially classical, although he does not accord to *inventio* the prominence nor importance given this canon by the writers of antiquity. The orator, he feels, is more likely to have difficulty "in selecting what is proper, than in inventing something that seems to be tolerable."[2] In one other way Witherspoon differs somewhat from the classical tradition. He defined more clearly the objects of speech-making: information, demonstration, persuasion, or entertainment. While these are similar to Campbell's objects of oratory, they represent a sharper distinction and are developed quite differently.

In 1806, John Quincy Adams was inducted as first Boylston Professor of Rhetoric and Oratory at Harvard University, and in 1810 his lectures were published. In terms of completeness and fidelity to classical doctrines, Adams' theory of rhetoric surpasses Witherspoon's. As a part of the American development of rhetorical theory in the nineteenth century it is significant to note that Adams' lectures rely very little on the works of the great English rhetoricians of the period, such as Campbell and Blair, and almost not at all on the English elocutionists such as Sheridan, Steele, and Walker. It is noteworthy also that Adams placed emphasis on deliberative and judicial oratory because of their special importance in a free country.[3]

Adams regarded speaking as the "necessary adjunct and vehicle of reason," and the means for the conveyance of thought in "rational intercourse with his fellow creatures and of humble communion with his God." [4] He used Aristotle's division of oratory into demonstrative, deliberative, and judicial, and he added pulpit oratory.

In accordance with the instructions laid down by the Harvard Overseers in assigning the Boylston Professorship, Adams dealt in his lectures with invention, disposition, style, and pronunciation (delivery). His treatment of these canons was largely a restatement of the doctrines of Aristotle, Cicero, and Quintilian. The lectures do not treat delivery to any great extent. He referred without enthusiasm to the works of Sheridan and Walker in the field of elocution, and himself offered no program for the training of voice and action. He does, however, give rather explicit instructions as to the method of speech preparation.[5]

In conclusion, while Adams' lectures are for the most part a restatement of classical doctrines, they indicate a tendency on the part of some American rhetoricians to break away from the complete reliance on the English rhetorics. Unfortunately, however, they failed to re-establish the classical trend as a major movement—as indicated by the tremendous popularity of the elocutionary movement which was soon to follow.

At about the same time that Adams' lectures were published, Samuel Knox, the principal of Baltimore College, published A Compendious System of Rhetoric. This was for the most part an abstract of the work of Blair, with material on tropes and figures drawn from John Stirling's System of Rhetoric (1770). A little book, arranged in catechetical form, it touches upon all the divisions of rhetoric; but except for style the treatment is superficial. It is significant only in that it indicates the preoccupation with style and composition characteristic of many of the early nineteenth-century writers and teachers. Although the works of

Blair and Campbell, with their essentially classical interpretations, were dominant in American colleges at this time, Knox defined rhetoric as "the art of speaking and writing, in every species of style and composition, agreeably to the most approved taste, and literary improvement in language." [6] It was probably this emphasis on style and composition, seen also in the works of such early nineteenth century writers as Newman and Channing, that paved the way for the elocution movement of the middle part of the century which virtually divorced delivery from the other aspects of rhetoric.

Samuel P. Newman's *A Practical System of Rhetoric*, published in 1827, was the first American rhetoric to be used widely in the schools. It replaced Jamieson's *Grammar of Rhetoric and Polite Literature* in such American colleges as Bowdoin, Amherst, and Wesleyan. Newman is almost entirely concerned with written composition; persuasion as such forms no part of his rhetorical system. The instructions of rhetoric, he says, are twofold: "those which point out the excellencies of style, and those which give cautions against its most frequent faults." [7]

While this book offers little that is original, it is noteworthy in that it is probably the first American rhetoric intended strictly as a textbook, and as such is well written and supplied with ample illustrative material. It should be noted, also, as a further step by Americans toward developing an art of belles lettres distinct from elocution.

During the first half of the nineteenth century, the chairs of professor of rhetoric at three of America's leading colleges were held by men who, while they did not publish their lectures in textbook form, were presenting to their students rhetorical theories of remarkable balance and scope. They were Porter at Andover Academy, Goodrich at Yale, and Channing at Harvard. While it is difficult to assess the influence of these men in determining the development of rhetorical theory in America, it is certain that in their institutions, at least, they were highly respected. They influenced many of the men who became leaders in American life during the nineteenth century. Porter was also an important figure in the development of elocution and homiletics.

Ebenezer Porter held the Bartlett Professorship of Sacred Rhetoric at Andover Academy from 1813 to 1831. His lectures on homiletics and preaching were published in 1834, and his lectures on eloquence and style were collected by Reverend Matthews and published in 1836. [8] Like Adams at Harvard, Porter was required by the rules of his office to discuss certain specified subjects, including the importance of oratory, and the principles of invention, disposition, style, and delivery. Like Adams, also, Porter's treatment of the canons of rhetoric is essentially classical, leaning heavily on Aristotle, Cicero, and Quintilian; and on Campbell and Blair among the moderns. Except for style and delivery, the divisions of rhetoric are treated briefly. Style is treated rather fully, with the material coming almost entirely from Quintilian, Longinus, Campbell, and Blair. Delivery is discussed in seven of the lectures, and reveals Porter as an adherent of the Walker school.

From 1817 to 1839, Chauncey Allen Goodrich was Professor of Rhetoric at Yale University. His lectures, not published in the nineteenth century, probably had little direct influence on the development of rhetorical theory and training outside of Connecticut. His book *Select British Eloquence,* however, was read widely both in this country and in England; and in the course of his careful rhetorical criticism of the twenty orators, ranging from Sir John Eliot to Lord Brougham, he included most of the precepts covered in his lectures at Yale. Although we are not directly concerned here with criticism as such, it is noteworthy that Goodrich was the first rhetorical critic to recognize clearly the necessity for developing an adequate biographical-historical setting for the evaluation of a speech or a speaker. His clear delineation of the social forces which produce and are in turn molded by great speakers set a pattern for rhetorical criticism which is common today.

Goodrich's lectures are essentially classical in conception and scope, although he rarely refers to the classical rhetoricians. His lectures fall easily into the traditional divisions.

Public speaking, Goodrich said, is of utmost importance to the individual and to society. In no country, he pointed out, "is the power of impressing thought on others through the medium of language so controlling in its influence as here." [9] That Goodrich did not approve of the separation of delivery from the other parts of rhetoric by the elocutionists of his day is seen in the following paragraph from one of his introductory lectures:

The end of public speaking is *not* to be eloquent. I say this because an error on this subject has had great influence in corrupting eloquence—peculiarly in this country, because men are here peculiarly dependent on public speaking. It has produced a tendency to speak for the sake for delivery, of attracting the attention of constituents, of establishing a reputation for eloquence. But this attitude always defeats its object, produces unnatural language, strained sentiments, etc.[10]

Although his lectures contain no subdivision entitled "invention," Goodrich does, in various places, deal with choice of subject, sources of ideas and arguments, techniques of collecting evidence, tests of arguments and evidence, methods of adapting to audience interests, and techniques of making the speaker appear "wise" and "good." [11]

More than any American rhetorician of the nineteenth century, with the possible exception of Channing at Harvard, Goodrich was a student of philosophy, and to his total concept of invention may be added his significant discussion of the mental faculties which produce the great speaker. The great end of education, he says, is "to subject our faculties both intellectual and physical to a rigid course of discipline . . . making every power the ready and active instrument of the *will*. . . ." [12] Certain mental phenomena which had by various writers been designated "original" mental faculties are defined and analyzed. These include: abstraction, comprehension, generalization, judgment, reason, imagination, taste, and belief. Although his descriptions of these powers follow closely the work of the Scottish philosophers, Reid and Stewart, he differs from them in concluding that most of them are really laws of mental action, rather than original mental faculties. [13]

Goodrich's treatment of language and style reveals many of the ideas of Blair and Campbell, with some interesting additions of his own. Good style, for Goodrich, consists of any easy and perspicuous use of language, with energy of thought and richness of imagination. [14] His interest in lexicography led him to a careful study of etymology and of pronunciation standards. [15]

The "moral and intellectual principles of our nature" Goodrich considers most important for the student orator, but the cultivation of style and elocution are scarcely less important. [16] His treatment of delivery was essentially classical, with the addition of some attention to the separate discipline of elocution popular at the time. He would definitely be in the "think-the-thought" or "natural" tradition in delivery as represented in his day by the teachings of Sheridan. [17]

Goodrich's contemporary at Harvard University was Edward T. Channing, Boylston Professor of Rhetoric from 1819 to 1852. Channing did not publish his lectures until after his retirement, and he wrote no systematic treatise on the theory of rhetoric. His influence on many of the outstanding speakers and writers of the nineteenth century was undoubtedly of considerable importance, however, and his theory of rhetoric is well worth examining.

Channing is especially interesting to the student of the history of rhetorical theory for his rather unusual concept of the nature and meaning of rhetoric. At a time when there was a definite trend toward the separation of style and invention from delivery, on the one hand, and belles lettres on the other, the Harvard teacher's concept of rhetoric included aspects of all three. Rhetoric, he believed, was the fundamental art of communication, and its principles applied both to speech and to writing. As he stated it:

I am inclined to consider rhetoric when reduced to a system in books, as a body of rules derived from experience and observation, extending to all communication by language and designed to make it efficient. It does not ask whether a man is to be a speaker or writer,—a poet, philosopher, or debator;

but simply,—is it his wish to be put in the right way of communicating his mind with power to others, by words spoken or written.[18]

Belles lettres, in the sense of appreciation of the forms of writing, and analysis of their beauty, was specifically omitted from Channing's concept. Rhetoric, he said, "leaves this field of criticism to other laborers, and limits its inspection of general literature to the purpose of ascertaining and illustrating the essentials of accurate and forcible expression in all good composition." [19]

In spite of this rather unusual definition of the scope of rhetoric, however, Channing lectured on all the classical canons of rhetoric. He outlined the duties of rhetoric as being the analysis and explanation of the style or method of persuasive address, instruction in finding and arranging arguments, instruction in speaking, and instruction in the principles of composition or good style.[20]

An interesting point of difference between Channing and Goodrich was the former's distrust of the use of models by the student orator. "Minds of common cast may profit by reading and obeying, but genius suffers." [21] Goodrich, on the other hand, was a strong advocate of the use of models—particularly the classical orators—in the training of speakers. Yet Goodrich, like Channing, was interested in faculty psychology, and in particular the work of Thomas Reid. Like his Yale contemporary, Channing believed that the rhetorician was concerned with the development of the various faculties of the mind. His lectures do not include a systematic survey of the faculties; he asserted only that one purpose of rhetoric was to strengthen man's natural powers.[22]

Channing recognized more clearly than any nineteenth-century rhetorician that the orator should not be a leader of the multitude, but rather should be considered "one of the multitude, deliberating with them upon common interests, which are well understood and valued by all." [23] This view of the speaker, held the Harvard professor, does not reduce the "true dignity and resources of the art." [24]

II

In 1822, E. G. Welles published a small book of fifty-six pages entitled *The Orator's Guide; or rules for speaking and composing; from the best authorities*. This book, while it offers nothing new, is interesting as an indication of the growing attention in America to voice and gesture as separate problems. Welles was primarily interested in gesture and action, which he called pronunciation after the terminology of the classical rhetoricians. He quotes Cicero, Demosthenes, and Quintilian, out of context, to show that "Pronunciation, which was also called action, was considered by the most competent judges among the ancients, as the primary part of an Orator's province—as almost the only source from which he can hope to succeed, in the art of persuasion." [25]

The almost absurd artificiality of Welles' concept of gesture may be indicated in his own words:

The several motions of the body ought to be accommodated to the various tones and inflections of the voice. When the voice is even, and moderate, little gesture is required; and nothing can be more improper, than violent motion, in discoursing upon ordinary and familiar subjects. The motion of the body should rise, therefore, in proportion to the vehemence and energy of the sentiment, and appear to be the natural and genuine effect of it. [26]

Possibly the first book by an American bearing the title of rhetoric but devoted exclusively to writing rather than speaking was the *Elements of Rhetoric and Literary Criticism,* compiled and arranged by James R. Boyd, Principal of Jefferson County Institute. This book paid not even lip service to the tradition of rhetoric in the classical sense. That it represented a fairly common conception of the extent and scope of rhetorical training at the time is indicated by the fact that, first published in 1844, it had gone through six editions by 1848.

Boyd expressed his belief that "the labors of teachers in all our schools are directed too exclusively to the securing of correct habits in speaking and reading the language; and that altogether too limited an amount of time and share of attention are employed in teaching the art of correctly writing the language." [27] It is interesting to note Boyd's statement that "the habit of *writing* much with accuracy would greatly aid us, also, in *speaking* the language with accuracy and elegance." [28]

Part III of the book, devoted to a discussion of the different kinds of composition, discusses very briefly the traditional six parts of an oration. The remainder of the book is devoted to grammar, style, composition, the history of the English language, and a brief review of modern British and American literature.

Also in 1844 was published a very interesting translation from the German of Dr. Francis Theremin's *Eloquence A Virtue; or, Outlines of a Systematic Rhetoric.* William G. T. Shedd, the translator, was professor of English literature at the University of Vermont. His free translation of Theremin's work, his excellent preface, and his advocacy may have influenced American views of rhetoric.

In the preface Shedd restated the philosophical justification for rhetoric and presented the thesis that the end of rhetoric must be moral. The state of rhetoric at the time, he felt, called for an "infusion" of the moral element found in Theremin's treatise:

Rhetoric, in its best estate, is but the science of Form, or, to use Milton's phrase, an 'organic'—i.e. instrumental—Art. . . . Dissevered from Logic, or the necessary laws of Thought, it has become dissevered from the seat of life, and has degenerated into a mere collection of rules respecting the structure of sentences and the garnish of expression.[29]

Theremin insisted that, while the means employed by eloquence may be aesthetic and the form in which it appears artistic, the great *end* constantly aimed at must be moral, and only moral. Shedd believed that here was a rhetoric "that is not only formative and plastic, but *organific*, and has thus superinduced life upon the lifeless." [30]

Theremin's treatment of invention is particularly interesting. The purpose of eloquence, he held, was to "produce a change in the sentiments and conduct of other men." This being the case, "the inquiry after its fundamental principles, therefore, becomes changed quite naturally into this: *what are the laws according to which a free being may exert influence upon other free beings?* And the answer to this question can be derived only from ethics." [31]

Against this background, Theremin formulated the highest law of eloquence: "The particular idea which the orator wishes to realize is carried back to the necessary ideas of the hearer." These necessary "ideas" he defined broadly as being Duty, Virtue, and Happiness.[32] The orator, then, to connect the premises of his speech with these innate moral urges must conform to three subordinate methods or categories: *Truth*, showing that his idea is in fact Duty, Virtue, or Happiness; *Possibility*, showing that his idea is practicable; and *Actuality*, showing that his idea actually exists or the event has happened.

Theremin's system of invention and arrangement, though based on this ethical analysis, follows the general line of classical theory, and includes a discussion of the speaker's *ethos*, and the means of exciting the affections.

In addition to editing Theremin, Shedd did some lecturing and writing of his own on rhetoric. His most extensive statement is found in an inaugural address at Auburn Theological Seminary entitled "The Characteristics, and Importance of a Natural Rhetoric." Because its appropriate subject matter is the *form* of a discourse, rhetoric is especially liable to formalism and artificiality.[33] He appeals, therefore, for a rhetoric "that educates like nature. . . . a Rhetoric that organizes and vitalizes the material that is made over to it for purposes of form. . . ." [34]

Henry N. Day, a contemporary of Shedd, was another American rhetorician who made some original contributions—particularly to the theory of invention. In the preface of his first work, *Elements of the Art of Rhetoric*, published in 1850, Day stated what he believed to be his contribution:

First, Invention is treated as a distinct and primary department of the art of Rhetoric. From most English treatises this department has been generally excluded: and rhetoric has been generally regarded as confined almost exclusively to style.[35]

Day objected to Whately's concept of rhetoric because he felt the English writer confined himself to "mere argumentative composition, or the art of producing Belief." This view, he felt, excluded all "Explanatory Discourse" as well as all "Persuasion." His own system included explanation, conviction, excitation, and persuasion as the "possible immediate objects of all discourse."

Rhetoric, according to Day, is "the art of discourse."

The proper province of Rhetoric, as also its specific relations to other arts and sciences, are determined at once by the faculty which it immediately and exclusively respects,—the faculty of discourse, or the capacity in man of communicating his mental states to other minds by means of language.[36]

Although he discussed disposition briefly, Day ruled out delivery from his treatment of rhetoric and confined himself almost entirely to invention and style. The success of the elocutionists in establishing a separate discipline in this country by the middle of the century is evidenced by Day's statement about delivery:

The art of rhetoric cannot in strictness be regarded as having accomplished its end until the mental states to be communicated are actually conveyed to the mind addressed. It, therefore, may properly comprehend *delivery*.

The mode of communication, however, is not essential. The thought may be conveyed by the pen or by the voice. Elocution, or the vocal expression of thought, is not accordingly a necessary part of rhetoric.[37]

Rhetorical invention as such was defined by Day as "the art of supplying the requisite thought in kind and form for discourse."[38] It embraced, therefore, disposition, as well as invention proper. The parts of invention were determined by his analysis of the ends or objects of discourse, and were stated concisely:

The process by which a new conception is produced, is by *Explanation;* that by which a new judgment is produced is by *Confirmation*. A change in the sensibilities is affected by the process of *Excitation;* and in the will, by that of *Persuasion*.[39]

More than most of his contemporaries, Day was solidly in the classical tradition of purposive rhetoric. His unusual emphasis on the importance of directing discourse to a specific end, and selecting and arranging materials most effectively to accomplish that end marks him as one of the few original thinkers of his century.

Style, the other "great department" of rhetoric, Day thought to have certain absolute qualities, such as oral properties, suggestive properties, grammatical properties, subjective properties (which included significance and naturalness), and objective properties (which included clearness, energy, and elegance.)[40] Although his discussion of these properties was not original, he did a much better job than most rhetoricians of the century of relating them to the various kinds of discourse.

The next work on rhetoric to appear in America was Matthew Boyd Hope's *Princeton Textbook in Rhetoric*, published in 1859. The Princeton professor of rhetoric wrote his textbook in part to replace Whately. Whately's Rhetoric, Hope felt, was inadequate for his students "in the matter of their *Belles Lettres culture*," and Whately's work on elocution he found "not only inferior in its *method* and *handling*, but positively, and mischievously erroneous, in its theoretical principles, and consequently in its practical precepts." [41]

The art of rhetoric, the Princeton professor believed, differed from other arts in that "it uses *articulate language* as its proper instrument"; and "it has for its special object: 1, to convince, and 2, to persuade." The difference between conviction and persuasion was that "the *former*, (conviction) is an effect upon the *understanding*,—the intellectual or logical faculties,— the latter, (persuasion) is an effect upon *the will*, producing a change either of character, or conduct...." [42]

Hope's treatment of conviction does not differ significantly from Whately's. Persuasion, also, is treated in much the same way as the English rhetorician's, except that some influence of Shedd's translation of Theremin is apparent in Hope's placing of persuasion in the domain of ethics and insisting upon a high ethical standard of persuasion.

Like Day, Channing, Goodrich, and others of his contemporaries, Hope was strongly influenced by faculty psychology, and his analysis of the psychological conditions in persuasion, while not original, was more specific than most. Persuasion, he said, rests upon "the presence of some motive principle, in the active constitution of the human spirit, —and reaches the will, by kindling some *desire*, for the attainment of its object,—and 2, the conviction of the understanding, that the means proposed in persuasion, *promise to attain the end*." [43] These two conditions, Hope said, constituted a *motive;* and since man is a moral being, free and self-moved, it is by motives, in the described sense, that he is governed. His classification of the "motive principles to human action" implied in moral freedom is fairly specific, and probably quite representative of the thinking of most of his contemporaries.

The Princeton professor discussed arrangement or disposition in connection with persuasion and conviction; he wrote of style and elocution as less essential but "tributary to the end sought in rhetoric." [44] His treatment of style is brief and does not add materially to the work of Blair and Whately. As essential properties of effective style he discussed clearness, force, and beauty.

The treatment of elocution is also fairly brief and drawn from the work of Rush, whom Hope greatly admired. Austin's *Chironomia* is credited as the primary source of his brief discussion of action, although the influence of Whately is quite apparent in his summary statement about gestures: "Study the sentiment, and enter into the emotion, of what you wish to say; then be natural, earnest, simple, and as graceful as possible." [45]

Following the publication of Hope's work, there were no more American rhetorics until 1867, when *A Manual of the Art of Prose Composition* by John Mitchell Bonnell was published. This was primarily a book on composition dealing with style and with invention. There are also chapters on argument and one on the oration. Mostly a distillation of Blair, it offers little that is original, and is interesting chiefly as an example of the extent to which the delivery and the composition of speeches had become separate disciplines in America.

The following year, 1868, an interesting little book by William Pittenger entitled *Oratory Sacred and Secular: or, the Extemporaneous Speaker* was published. This was not so much an attempt to formulate a systematic theory as it was to set forth the outlines of a practical course of training for an orator. The prerequisites for being a successful orator, Pittenger said, were intellectual competency, strength of body, command of language, courage, firmness, and self-reliance. Some very general, and probably not very practical, rules are offered for acquiring these characteristics. Part III, "Secular Oratory," simply describes very briefly the different types of address: instructive, deliberative, legal, controversial, and popular.

Although he published no work on rhetoric, Ralph Waldo Emerson should be included in the list of Americans who contributed to the development of rhetorical theory. Occasional comments on rhetorical theory are found scattered throughout his writing; and in 1870 and again in 1875 he published essays, both entitled "Eloquence," in which he set forth his views on the subject.

Emerson defined eloquence as "the power to translate a truth into language perfectly intelligible to the person to whom you speak." [46] Reminiscent of his general transcendentalist philosophy is the interesting belief that every man, if properly stimulated, can rise above his mundane weaknesses, and become for the moment an orator. This latent or potential talent also, he said, accounts for the fact that assemblies of men are "susceptible." "The eloquence of one stimulates all the rest, some up to the speaking-point and all others to a degree that makes them good receivers and conductors. . . ." [47]

Emerson also contributed some ideas on audience analysis which reveal great insight. In every public assembly, he said, there are many audiences, "each of which rules in turn." [48] All of these audiences, however, "which successively appear to greet the variety of style and topic," [49] are the same persons—the same individual sometimes taking active part in them all.

He stressed the importance of accurate knowledge and personal force. The orator, he said, must first have "power of statement,—must have the fact and know how to tell it." [50]

Next in importance he placed "method," by which he apparently meant what was called *dispositio* by the classical rhetoricians: "The orator possesses no information which his hearers have not, yet he teaches them to see the thing with his eyes. By the new placing, the circumstances acquire new solidity and worth." [51]

Imagery also is considered important both as an aid to effectiveness and an aid to memory. Nothing, he said, "so works on the human mind, barbarous or civil, as a trope." [52]

Such separate parts, however, do not constitute eloquence. For genuine eloquence the speaker must be "sane," by which he meant that the speaker must be able to control his powers; and also there must be "a reinforcing of man from events, so as to give the double force of reason and destiny." [53]

A rhetorical handbook of 75 pages entitled *The Outlines of Rhetoric* was published in 1877. Joseph H. Gilmore, the author, was a professor of rhetoric at the University of Rochester. It is a closely packed, carefully prepared outline of rhetorical theories of invention and style. Written in the form of questions and answers, it quotes liberally from Aristotle, Whately, Campbell, Theremin, and Blair.

Though it probably adds nothing new to rhetorical theory, Gilmore's book is worthy of mention for its rather novel style and unusual clarity and conciseness of expression. The following quotation will serve to show the method and style of the book:

1. Define Rhetoric according to the view of Aristotle—Whately—Campbell. Which definition are you inclined to adopt; and why?

Aristotle regards Rhetoric as the Art of Persuasion; Whately, as the Art of Conviction; Campbell, as the Art of Discourse. Campbell's definition is to be preferred as more comprehensive than either of the others; although Aristotle justly emphasizes the most vital object of all Rhetorical study.[54]

In 1879, George L. Raymond published his *Orator's Manual*. This book is in the elocution tradition, and deals primarily with three aspects of delivery: voice culture, emphasis (time, pitch, force, volume), and gesture. It is of interest here because it included a seventeen-page appendix called "Hints for the Composition of Orations." It might be said, therefore, to represent the beginning of the reunion of delivery and composition of speeches which took place toward the end of the nineteenth century and has continued in the present century.

A two-volume work, *The Art of Speech,* by L. T. Townsend was published in 1880. It was used, among other places, at De Pauw University, and was reported to have had great influence on the career of Albert Beveridge.

Volume I, "Studies in Poetry and Prose," contains an interesting account of the origin and history of speech. Townsend, who was a professor of rhetoric in Boston University, concluded that "Human speech is both God-given and from human invention." [55] He struck a distinctly contemporary note by saying that thought is essentially "interior speech." Style, also considered in Volume I, is mostly drawn from Blair.

Volume II, "Studies in Eloquence and Logic," discusses definitions of oratory and eloquence by Aristotle, Cicero, Quintilian, Macaulay, Bautain, and Emerson. Townsend concludes that Eloquence as an *art* "is such a representation of thought in vocal, written, or gesture language, as is adapted to persuade. The aim in eloquence is to persuade the will and the moral faculties, rather than merely to convince the judgment." [56] Chapters IV through VII of the second volume contain a series of "Inferences" drawn from an analysis of Demosthenes' orations. In rather sketchy and poorly organized form, these chapters contain a fairly complete system of rhetoric, including invention, disposition, style, and delivery.

In the same year, 1880, *Rhetoric as an Art of Persuasion ... from the standpoint of a lawyer* was published. The frontispiece lists the author as "An Old Lawyer." His name was Daniel F. Miller. In the preface Miller stated that he had "studied many American and English authors on the subject of rhetoric, but found nothing in them to compare in usefulness and thoroughness of instruction to Quintilian's Institutes of Oratory." His system of rhetoric is largely a condensation of Quintilian with some influence from Cicero.

Though it offers little that could be called original, this work is noteworthy in at least two respects. In the first place, it is written in a very colloquial style and contains many interesting "asides" which occasionally show considerable insight. As one instance of this, in discussing induction he says that Bacon is credited with developing inductive reasoning, and Aristotle with developing the syllogism. Actually, said Miller, neither is true, induction being "the common vernacular of human speech, and, besides, there are plenty of books extant which contain numberless instances of the use both of the inductive and syllogistic styles of argument, written ages before the name of either Bacon or Aristotle adorned the pages of history." [57]

The other notable feature of this book is the inclusion of a great many examples and illustrations drawn largely from Quintilian, Lincoln, J. F. Dillon, Cicero, Plato, Erskine, Curran, Henry Clay, and Webster.

As might be expected, Miller does a good job of stating the principles and methods of invention and disposition, but the treatment of style is poorly organized, being mostly a listing of numerous figures of speech with illustrations.

III

Adams Sherman Hill, Boylston Professor of Rhetoric at Harvard, published his *Principles of Rhetoric* in 1878. It is perhaps of interest chiefly because it indicates the extent to which the Boylston Professorship had come to deal with the written rather than the spoken word. Hill defined rhetoric as "the art of efficient communication by language," [58] and although he does include the speaker as well as the writer in his concept, the book is addressed to the writer, with not even a discussion of "oratory" or public speaking in any form.

Part I of the book deals with "Composition in General," and takes up grammatical purity and choice of words. Part II deals with "Kinds of Composition," and takes up only three kinds: narrative, descriptive, and argumentative. None of this material seems to offer the student anything different from that found in Whately, Bair, and numerous other sources which were available at the time.

The subject of "Persuasion" is disposed of by Hill in seven pages as a subtopic of argumentative composition. To influence the "will," Hill said, it is necessary to influence the "active principles" of a man's nature.[59] He does not specify what these principles are, but recommends one of two courses: we may "dwell upon topics which are likely to call out the feelings" we wish to excite; or we may "express our own feelings in such a way as to communicate them to others." [60] In connection with the latter method he quotes from Aristotle to stress the importance of the speaker's reputation.

The Elements of Rhetoric, by James De Mille, was published in 1882. This is an imposing work of 564 pages, very similar in scope and method to Hill's *Principles of Rhetoric*. Unlike Hill, however, De Mille includes a brief discussion of oratory as one of the "General Departments of Literature"; the six other departments being description, narration, exposition, dialogue, drama, and poetry.

The study of rhetoric, De Mille said, "may be regarded as an analytical examination of literature." [61] Parts I, II, and III, comprising over half the book, take up style. Part IV, "Method," is a treatment of invention, largely along Aristotelian lines. Part V discusses the "Emotions" under such headings as "The Beautiful," "The Sublime," and "The

Ridiculous." Part VI takes up the "Departments of Literature" referred to above.

In the chapter dealing with oratory De Mille treats of the "Tactics of Oratory," which probably represents his chief contribution. These "tactics," he said, may be defined as "special devices employed by orators for the sake of persuading their hearers." [62] The following tactics are discussed: conciliation, emphasis, explanation, answers to objections, artifices, attack, defense, display of feeling. While this material is drawn directly from Aristotle and Cicero, De Mille illustrates it with examples drawn chiefly from British orators.[63] The examples suggest a fairly close acquaintanceship with Goodrich's *Select British Eloquence.*

The last major work of the century which attempted to present a complete system of rhetoric was John Franklin Genung's *The Practical Elements of Rhetoric,* published in 1886. He prepared a revision of the work in 1900 which he called *The Working Principles of Rhetoric.* An examination of the two works, however, fails to reveal any significant differences, and this discussion will deal only with the earlier work.

Like most of his contemporaries, Genung, who was Professor of Rhetoric at Amherst College, had accepted the separation of voice and delivery from rhetoric proper. Accordingly his book has two parts: Style and Invention.

Clearness, force, and beauty are the essential qualities of style. Its controlling principle Genung draws from Herbert Spencer: "the central principle of a good style lies in the economizing of the reader's attention." [64]

Genung's treatment of invention, while essentially classical in conception, represents a fairly original approach. He first discusses the "Basis in Mental Aptitudes and Habits," pointing out that while invention is to some extent a natural gift, it can be cultivated by the development of habits of "Observation," "Thought," and "Reading." [65]

The "General Processes in the Ordering of Material" are considered next under the headings of "Determination of the Theme," "Construction of the Plan," and "Amplification." [66]

He then takes up *Description,* which he calls "Invention dealing with Observed Objects"; *Narration,* "Invention dealing with Events"; *Exposition,* "Invention dealing with Generalizations"; *Argumentation,* "Invention dealing with Truths"; and *Persuasion,* "Invention dealing with Practical Issues." [67] In the first four of these divisions, Genung is addressing primarily the writer; and in the last division he is addressing the speaker, for persuasion "is so predominantly the work of oral communication," it "presupposes a speaker at close quarters with his audience." [68]

Genung's development of the principles of persuasion, while again

classical in conception, rests upon the idea of Bain that to be a persuasive speaker, "it is necessary to have vividly present to the view all the
leading impulses and convictions of the persons addressed, and be
ready to catch at every point of identity between these and the propositions or projects presented for their adoption." [69] In addition to Bain,
Genung draws material from many of his contemporaries—notably
Emerson and Henry Ward Beecher.

The last work of the nineteenth century to be considered here is not
strictly speaking a treatise on rhetorical theory. *The Principles of Public Speaking*, by Guy Carleton Lee, was published in 1899. It is probably
the first book by an American which could properly be called a "speech"
book in the modern sense. That is, it is primarily a book of advice and
suggestions on *how to do* such things as improve the voice, have better
bodily response, read aloud, prepare and deliver a speech, and take
part in a debate. There is a small amount of theory included, but for
the most part it is too fragmentary to be consistent.

While most of the material, particularly that dealing with voice and
gesture, would seem very artificial and impractical to the contemporary
student of speech, it is worth observing that by the end of the century
at least one professor of rhetoric had gathered together all the canons
of rhetoric and had attempted to formulate a consistent field of study
under the heading of "Public Speaking."

In conclusion, it may be said that while the nineteenth century did
not produce a notable advance in the theory of rhetoric, it did contribute some excellent restatements of the classical doctrines. The most
significant American contributions were probably the applications of
the principles of faculty psychology to rhetoric by such men as Goodrich, Channing, Day, Hope, and Genung; and the application of the
principles of ethics to rhetoric by Shedd. The classical tradition of
rhetoric as a complete field of study including all the canons was represented in the century by Witherspoon, Adams, Porter, Goodrich, Channing, Shedd, Hope, and, to some extent, Emerson, Townsend, and Lee.
The principal writers who had accepted the separation of delivery from
the other canons and centered their attention on Invention and Style
were Knox, Newman, Boyd, Day, Bonnell, Hill, De Mille, and Genung.

IV

A consideration of the development of rhetorical theory in the nineteenth century would not be complete without considering homiletics.
Many of the outstanding rhetoricians of the period—including men like
Witherspoon, Adams, Goodrich, Channing, and Porter—were also homileticians. The definition of homiletics most widely accepted, further-

more, treated it as a special branch or application of rhetoric. Shedd, for example, defined homiletics as "the term that has been chosen to denote the application of the principles of rhetoric to preaching. It is synonymous, consequently, with Sacred Rhetoric." [70] One major exception to this definition should be noted. George Hervey, in 1873, published his very interesting *System of Christian Rhetoric* [71] in which he constructed an elaborate system based solely on the Bible.

To give a detailed account of the treatment of each of the leading figures of the century would not be practical for our present purpose. Instead, the broad outlines of homiletical theory will be briefly sketched.

The purpose or goal of preaching underwent a definite change in the course of the century. At the beginning of the century, conviction and persuasion, considered as separate tasks, were quite commonly accepted as the preacher's primary goal. Tappan, for example, regarded persuasion as the end of all preaching.[72] John Q. Adams, on the other hand, said that the "means" of the sermon "are persuasion; its object, to operate upon the will of the hearers; its results, to produce action." [73] In the early years of the century, especially, there was a trend away from the debate-brief type of sermon which stressed "conviction." Channing, for example, stated that preachers "have addressed men as creatures of mere intellect; they have forgotten that the affections are essential to our nature, that reason and sensibility must operate together or we shall never act with perseverance and vigor." [74] Porter also objected to the debate-brief arrangement with its "applications," "uses," "propositions," "inferences," "counsels," and "reflections." That he was thinking in terms of the traditional conviction-persuasion goal is indicated, however, by his advocating the classical arrangement for the sermon: exordium, proposition, division, discussion or argument, and conclusion.[75]

Early in the century, however, instruction as a goal or purpose in preaching began to be emphasized. As early as 1800 Kirkland had stated that instruction is the first branch of the preacher's task. What revelation teaches concerning the origin, nature and destiny of man, that the preacher must explain.[76] Emmons expressed a growing belief when he said that to preach is to instruct and to instruct is generally to explain.[77] The controversy over doctrines, especially between the liberal and conservative Congregationalists, made it necessary for preachers to explain these doctrines clearly, and probably gave added weight to instruction as a goal.

Throughout the century doctrinal subjects were most universally in demand. Witherspoon's *Introductory Lectures on Divinity,* for example, take up the doctrine of the fall of man, sin, the covenant of grace, and kindred subjects.[78] Toward the end of the century a few authorities were recommending practical or ethical subjects—foreshadowing the twentieth-century concept that the minister should try to interpret the social and ethical problems of the day in the light of Christian principles. The great majority of authorities throughout the century, however, agreed with the statement of Edwards of Andover: "Sacred Eloquence is the art of speaking well on sacred subjects. These are subjects which relate to God, to Jesus Christ, to the Holy Ghost, to the souls of men, and to eternity." [79]

Most of the homileticians of this century discussed disposition as an essential part of their complete systems. Witherspoon, in the early period, had the most extensive discussion of it, pointing out that outlining is an aid to the memory as well as adding beauty, brevity, and force to the sermon.[80] Throughout the century, and particularly in the latter half of it, the textual type of sermon was most widely used. A representative statement of homiletic opinion is that of Spurgeon: "Although in many cases topical sermons are ... very proper, those sermons which expound the exact words of the Holy Spirit are the most useful and the most agreeable to the major part of our congregations." [81] Of disposition in this type of sermon, Pattison said, "The flavor of the text is everywhere to be detected in the sermon, as the breath of the pine forest is in every fir cone taken from it." [82] Analysis of the text to find its exact meaning is the first step recommended, to be followed by the formulation of a theme. Some authorities defined the theme as "the discourse condensed," it being essentially the "germ" of the sermon. Others agreed with Shedd that the theme is "an enunciation of the particular truth to be established in the sermon." [83] Division of the text or theme is the next step generally recommended by homileticians for this century. Divisions, said Hoppin, are "simply the different parts in which the main subject is formally separated or discussed." [84] Kidder, for example, quoted from Cicero, "It is chiefly order that gives distinctness to memory" to prove that breaking up the theme helps both the preacher and the listener to remember the sermon.[85]

The principles of division developed by the nineteenth-century homileticians were in agreement with the ones developed by logicians: no division should be coextensive with the subject; all together the divisions should exhaust the proposition; a single principle of division should be used.[86]

The nineteenth-century homileticians were much interested in the problem of sermon style. The separation of delivery from the aspects of invention, disposition, and style, which was going on at the beginning of the century probably contributed to this interest. The major writers of the period agreed with Channing that the sermon "must not be set forth and tricked out in the light drapery of artificial rhetoric, in prettiness of style, in measured sentences, with an insipid floridness, and the form of elegantly feeble essays." [87] Witherspoon, of the early writers, offered the most complete discussion of style, devoting five chapters to the three forms of style: the sublime, simple, and mixed.

The different interpretations of the meaning of style found among secular rhetoricians is also encountered among the homileticians. Hoppin, Etter, Fisk, and a few others held the position that the term "style" includes both the thought and its expression: "Style is the general term by which we designate the qualities of thought as expressed in language." [88] Most authorities in this century, however, followed the classical doctrine which makes "style" much the same as "use of language." Broadus' statement is representative of this group: "A man's style, then, is his characteristic manner of expressing his thoughts, whether in writing or in speech." [89] Indicative of the emphasis placed on style is the further statement by Broadus that style "is the glitter and polish of the warrior's sword, but it is also its keen edge. It can render mediocrity acceptable and even attractive, and power more powerful still. It can make error seductive, while truth may lie unnoticed for want of its aid." [90] Probably the outstanding treatment of style in the latter part of the century was that of Phelps. *His English Style in Public Discourse,* devoted especially to pulpit style, was widely accepted and used toward the end of the century. Phelps listed seven properties of good style: *purity,* meaning grammatical correctness; *precision,* which he distinguished from propriety (or purity) by saying: "Propriety is satisfied if we write good English: precision demands such a choice of good English as shall express our meaning"; [91] *individuality; perspicuity; energy; elegance,* which was synonymous with "beauty"; [92] and *naturalness,* by which he meant "fitness"; and made the point that style should fit the subject, the audience, and the occasion.

Dowling [93] and Taylor,[94] writing in the middle part, and Hervey [95] in the latter part of the century, presented detailed discussions of the value and technique of illustrative preaching. Dowling's *The Power of Illustration* is a short book containing excellent examples of illustrations of all kinds. It had wide use and probably added impetus to the trend toward expository preaching mentioned previously. "The great advantages," said Dowling, "resulting from the use of striking and vivid illustrations, are, that they serve (1) to attract and secure attention; (2) to afford scope for copiousness and variety, in the exhibition of truths which have long been familiar; (3) to impress the memory by their point and force; and (4) to render complex and difficult subjects easy and plain." [96]

Of all the canons of rhetoric, delivery received probably the greatest attention from homileticians during the nineteenth century. A few of them, including such leaders as Porter,[97] Ware,[98] and Russell [99] wrote texts which dealt exclusively with the delivery aspects of preaching. In general, the writers agreed that sincerity and naturalness were the primary requirements. Witherspoon advised his students to "study great sincerity, try to forget every purpose but the very end of speaking information and persuasion." [100] Dwight summarized his advice on delivery by saying, "To preach acceptably demands all the characteristics already insisted upon in this discourse; plainness, variety, boldness, solemnity, *earnestness,* and affection." [101]

From the beginning of the century, writers were pointing out the stiffness and artificiality both in style and delivery brought about in part at least by the practice of reading sermons. Griffin, for example, felt that this "abuse" was introduced by "the practice of *writing* sermons. The natural manner in which man addresses man is that which prevails in conversation and in more animated forms of speech without writing." [102] Some of the earlier writers advocated extemporaneous speaking as a remedy for this defect. Many, however, were slow to accept this change. John Q. Adams was representative of those who took a middle ground. He recognized that extemporized preaching may contain more warmth, earnestness, and force; but, he warned, "the stream which flows spontaneously, is almost always shallow, and runs forever in the same channel." [103] And as late as 1898, Thomas Pattison sounded much the same warning: "Undoubtedly extemporaneous speech is the highest form of address. But let us beware before we adopt it as our constant practice. The heights to which this method lifts us may usually be very lofty, but the depth to which it sometimes sinks are well-nigh unfathomable." [104] In 1824, however, Henry Ware published his *Hints on Extemporaneous Preaching,* and most authorities from that time accepted the belief that extempore delivery is, for most people, the most desirable. Ware emphasized earnestness as the central problem for effective delivery. Animation of manner, he said, will come if the speaker is fully imbued with his subject. There will be "more of the lighting up of the soul in the countenance and the whole mein, more freedom and meaning in the gestures; the eye speaks, and the fingers speak, and when the orator is so excited as to forget everything but the matter on which his mind and feeling are acting, the whole body is affected and helps to propagate his emotions to the hearers." [105]

Porter's *Analysis of the Principles of Rhetorical Delivery* and Russell's *Pulpit Elocution* are probably the most outstanding contributions by homileticians to the new science of elocution. Although most writers preferred to leave the actual teaching of elocution to the professional elocutionists, they agreed with Broadus that speech exists only in the act of speaking, and the sermon cannot be separated from its delivery.[106] By the middle of the century, it was commonly agreed that the voice can and should be developed and improved. As Kidder observed, "It is a very inconsistent philosophy which would educate the eye, the ear, the hand, and the brain, and yet refuse culture and training to the voice." [107]

Homiletical theory in America received a rapid and full development in the nineteenth century. Starting almost from scratch at the opening of the century, the groundwork laid by men like John Witherspoon and John Quincy Adams was rapidly developed by such scholars and teachers as William Ellery Channing, Henry Ware, Ebenezer Porter, Henry J. Ripley, William Taylor, John Dowling, George Hervey, William Russell, James Alexander, John Broadus, James Hoppin, Daniel Kidder, Austin Phelps, and William G. T. Shedd. The application of the principles of rhetoric to the art of preaching may be said to have been completed by the end of the century. The major development of the twentieth century, a trend which was just beginning at the close of the nineteenth, has been the changing conception of the purpose and function of preaching. To the homileticians of the last century, the preacher was an inspired individual whose function was primarily to interpret for his congregation the Bible and the Church, with man's salvation as the goal. In the present century, this viewpoint, while it still exists, has slowly given way to the conception of preaching as an interpretation by the minister of his congregation's social and ethical problems in the light of Christian principles.

Notes

1. John Witherspoon, *Lectures on Moral Philosophy and Eloquence,* 3rd ed. (Philadelphia, 1810), pp. 150-154. See also John P. Hoshor, "Lectures on Rhetoric and Public Speaking by Chauncey Allen Goodrich," *Speech Monographs,* XIV (1947), 5-8.
2. Witherspoon, pp. 233-234.
3. John Q. Adams, *Lectures on Rhetoric and Oratory* (Cambridge, 1810), I, 253-254, and III, 317-319.
4. *Ibid.,* I, 14.
5. *Ibid.,* I, 230.
6. *A Compendious System of Rhetoric* (Baltimore, 1809), p. 3.
7. *A Practical System of Rhetoric* (Portland, 1827), p. 1.
8. Ebenezer Porter, *Lectures on Eloquence and Style,* ed. Rev. Lyman Matthews (Andover, 1836).
9. Hoshor, p. 5.
10. *Ibid.,* p. 5.
11. *Ibid.,* p. 30.
12. See the unpublished Ph.D. dissertation (Iowa, 1947) by John P. Hoshor, "The Rhetorical Theory of Chauncey Allen Goodrich," p. 110.
13. *Ibid.,* pp. 51-71.
14. Chauncey Allen Goodrich, *Select British Eloquence* (New York, 1852), p. 209.
15. In 1846 and 1847, Goodrich revised both the unabridged and the abridged editions of Noah Webster's *Dictionary of the English Language.* To his 1856 revi-

sion of the University edition of the same work he added an exhaustive treatise on the principles of pronunciation.

16. Hoshor, p. 110.

17. *Ibid.*, p. 129.

18. Edward T. Channing, *Lectures Read to the Seniors in Harvard College* (Boston, 1856), p. 31.

19. *Ibid.*, p. 41.

20. *Ibid.*, p. 35-40.

21. *Ibid.*, p. 203-204.

22. Edward T. Channing, "Philosophical Essays. By James Ogilvie," *North American Review*, IV (March, 1817), 385, 386. See also Channing, *Lectures*, p. 31.

23. Channing, *Lectures*, p. 17.

24. *Ibid.*, p. 20.

25. *Orator's Guide* (Philadelphia, 1822), p. 5.

26. *Ibid.*, p. 22.

27. *Elements of Rhetoric and Literary Criticism*, 6th ed. (New York, 1848), p. ix.

28. *Ibid.*, p. x.

29. William G. T. Shedd, trans. *Eloquence A Virtue; or, Outlines of a Systematic Rhetoric*, by Francis Theremin (New York, 1850), p. viii.

30. *Ibid.*, p. xix.

31. *Eloquence a Virtue*, p. 69.

32. *Ibid.*, p. 71.

33. In *Discourses and Essays* (Andover, 1859), p. 91.

34. *Ibid.*, p. 92.

35. P. iii.

36. *The Art of Discourse: A System of Rhetoric*, 10th ed. (New York, 1867), p. 4.

37. *Ibid.*, p. 14.

38. *Ibid.*, p. 41.

39. *Ibid.*, p. 49.

40. Day, *Elements*, pp. 165-289.

41. *Princeton Textbook in Rhetoric* (Princeton, 1859), p. iv.

42. *Ibid.*, p. 2.

43. *Ibid.*, p. 84.

44. *Ibid.*, p. 2.

45. *Ibid.*, p. 289.

46. In *Emerson's Complete Works*, Riverside ed. (Boston, 1875), VIII, 126.

47. *Ibid.*, VII, 63.

48. *Ibid.*, p. 67.

49. *Ibid.*, p. 68.

50. *Ibid.*, p. 85.

51. *Ibid.*, p. 88.

52. *Ibid.*, p. 89.

53. *Ibid.*, p. 91.

54. *The Outlines of Rhetoric* (Rochester, New York, 1877), p. 3.

55. *The Art of Speech* (New York, 1880), I, 34.

56. *Ibid.*, II, 13.

57. *Rhetoric as an Art of Persuasion* (Des Moines, Iowa, 1880), p. 45.

58. *Principles of Rhetoric* (New York, 1889), p. iii.

59. *Ibid.*, p. 237.

60. *Ibid.*, p. 240.

61. *The Elements of Rhetoric* (New York, 1882), p. vi.

62. *Ibid.*, p. 76.

63. *Ibid.*, p. 485-503.

64. *Practical Elements of Rhetoric* (New York, 1886), pp. 19-27.

65. *Ibid.*, pp. 220-235.

66. *Ibid.*, pp. 248-302.
67. *Ibid.*, pp. 326-476.
68. *Ibid.*, p. 449.
69. *Ibid.*, p. 448.
70. *Homiletics and Pastoral Theology* (New York, 1867), p. 38.
71. (New York, 1873).
72. David N. Tappan, "A Sermon delivered at Kennebunk, September 3, 1800 at the Ordination of Reverend Nathaniel Fletcher," in Waterman Pamphlets, Vol. 128, Library of Congress.
73. Adams, *Lectures,* p. 330.
74. William Ellery Channing, "A Sermon Delivered at the Ordination of the Reverend Ezra Stiles Gannett.... June 30, 1815," in Waterman Pamphlets, Vol. 3, Library of Congress, p. 19.
75. Ebenezer Porter, *Lectures on Homiletics and Preaching, and on Public Prayer; Together with Sermons and Letters* (New York, 1834), p. 116.
76. John Kirkland, *A Sermon Preached at Taunton, January 5, 1800, at the Ordination of the Reverend John Pipon....* (Cambridge, 1800), p. 7.
77. Nathaniel F. Emmons, *A Sermon Delivered at the Ordination of the Reverend John Robinson....* January 14, 1789 (Providence, 1789), p. 4.
78. John Witherspoon, *The Works of the Reverend John Witherspoon,* ed. John Rodgers, III, 62 ff.
79. Justin Edwards, "An Address on Pulpit Eloquence," in Henry Burder, *Mental Discipline* (New York, 1830), p. 186.
80. Witherspoon, *Works,* pp. 443-446.
81. Charles Haddon Spurgeon, *Lectures to My Students* (London, 1875), p. 112.
82. Thomas Harwood Pattison, *The Making of the Sermon, For the Classroom and the Study* (Philadelphia, 1880), p. 65.
83. Shedd, *Homiletics,* p. 183.
84. James M. Hoppin, *Homiletics* (New York, 1883), p. 382.
85. Daniel P. Kidder, *A Treatise on Homiletics, Designed to Illustrate the True Theory and Practice of Preaching the Gospel* (New York, 1864), p. 215.
86. See the following: John A. Broadus, *A Treatise on the Preparation and Delivery of Sermons,* 30th ed. (New York, 1898), p. 288; Kidder, *Treatise on Homiletics,* p. 200; Hoppin, *Homiletics,* p. 389; Austin Phelps, *The Theory of Preaching* (New York, 1905), p. 391; John W. Etter, *The Preacher and His Sermon, A Treatise on Homiletics* (Dayton, Ohio, 1885), p. 192.
87. William Ellery Channing, *A Sermon Delivered at the Ordination of the Reverend Ezra Stiles Gannett....June 30th, 1824* (Boston, 1824), p. 13.
88. Hoppin, *Homiletics,* p. 2.
89. Broadus, *Treatise,* p. 340.
90. *Ibid.*, p. 342.
91. Austin Phelps, *English Style in Public Discourse, with Special Reference to the Usages of the Pulpit* (New York, 1915), p. 79.
92. *Ibid.*, pp. 6, 126-128, 202-217.
93. John Dowling, *The Power of Illustration an Element of Success in Preaching and Teaching,* 2d ed. (New York, 1847).
94. William Taylor, *The Model Preacher* (Cincinnati, 1859).
95. George W. Harvey, *A System of Christian Rhetoric for the Use of Preachers and Other Speakers* (New York, 1873).
96. Dowling, *Power of Illustration,* pp. 12-13.
97. Ebenezer Porter, *Analysis of the Principles of Rhetorical Delivery as Applied to Reading and Speaking,* 4th ed. (New York, 1831).
98. Henry Ware, *Hints on Extemporaneous Preaching* (Boston, 1824).
99. William Russell, *Pulpit Elocution* (Andover, 1846).
100. Witherspoon, *Works,* p. 455.

101. Timothy Dwight, "Sermon CLIII. The Means of Grace—Extraordinary Means of Grace—The Manner of Preaching," in Timothy Dwight, *Theology Explained* (Edinburgh, 1837), p. 798.

102. Edward Griffin, *A Sermon on the Art of Preaching, Delivered Before the Pastoral Association of Massachusetts* (Boston, 1825), p. 26.

103. Adams, *Lectures*, p. 341.

104. Pattison, *Making of the Sermon*, p. 326.

105. Ware, *Extemporaneous Preaching*, p. 6.

106. Broadus, *Treatise*, p. 480.

107. Kidder, *Treatise on Homilectics*, p. 330.

7 Rhetorical and Elocutionary Training in Nineteenth-Century Colleges

MARIE HOCHMUTH
RICHARD MURPHY

···

I

On December 8, 1819, Edward T. Channing, on being inducted into the Boylston Professorship of Rhetoric and Oratory at Harvard University, observed: "It is the spirit of the age to turn everything to account, and to let no good learning remain idle. How is it that eloquence has gone behind-hand?" [1] At that time, Channing had the distinction of being one of the few men in American colleges who were engaged solely to give rhetorical training. To understand Channing's lament, one must survey what had gone on in American Colleges before 1819.

In the eighteenth century, training in rhetoric and oratory at Harvard, and most colleges, had been provided not by one instructor especially selected for the work, but by the incidental direction of tutors giving instruction in a variety of subjects. There had been distinguished men in the eighteenth century who gave serious if not exclusive attention to rhetoric, but they were the exception to the rule. John Witherspoon had attempted systematic training at Princeton; [2] Timothy Dwight, long interested in the literary life of the country, incited interest in rhetoric at Yale, even as a tutor. By his "example and his instructions," he produced a "great reform in the style of writing and speaking." [3] He delivered to the students a series of lectures on style and composition, "on a plan very similar to that contained in Blair's lectures, which were not published until a considerable time afterward." [4] About 1770, "the art of public speaking began for the first time in the history of the college to be excited." Dwight continued his instruction after he became president of Yale in 1795. The job of giving rhetorical training to students frequently was one of the miscellaneous duties college presidents assumed.

153

Students seemed to desire rhetorical activity other than that provided by the system of syllogizing, disputation, and declamation that had been part of college training from the beginning in America. As early as 1719, the Spy Club was formed at Harvard and students instructed themselves in the art of discourse. Yale and Princeton soon followed with similar societies—the Critonian, Linonian, and Brothers in Unity at Yale, and the American Whig at Princeton. In 1770, Harvard students formed a speaking Club. There had been, they claimed, a "cold indifference to the practice of oratory." [5] But following the Boston Massacre there was a "feast of patriotic oratory"; [6] declamations and forensic disputes breathed "the spirit of liberty." [7]

Following the American Revolution, in 1798, Harvard students having become "exceedingly interested in the grave questions then before the country" sought college "sanction" for a meeting designed for the "purpose of expressing their opinions on the then existing crisis of our public affairs." [8] "Though removed from active life," they "watched with anxiety the interests of our country" and through public address solemnly offered "the unwasted ardor and unimpaired energies of our youth to the service of our country." [9] Financial difficulties in the colleges prevented adjustment of the curriculum to student interests in post-Revolution days, although college authorities realized the need for reorganization and adjustment to a new era. "College was never in a worse state than when I entered it," noted a student of the Class of 1798 at Harvard. "The old foundations of social order, loyalty, tradition, habits, reverence for antiquity, were everywhere shaken, if not subverted.... The old forms were outgrown, and new ones had not taken their place.... The system of government and instruction went on very much as it had done for years before, and the result was a state of great insubordination...." [10]

But a new culture was in the making, a culture that was to promote literary independence as well as political independence, and colleges were soon to adjust to the change. "It is high time that the young Hercules, who has strangled the serpents, should go forth in the plentitude of muscular force, and perform the mighty labors assigned him," wrote a young American college graduate while traveling in Europe in 1803. "American literature ought to bud, it ought to promise future fruits of Hesperian luxuriance." [11] In 1803, New England promulgated its first literary magazine, the *Monthly Anthology;* in 1815, it launched the *North American Review.* In the same year, two native sons, George Ticknor and Edward Everett started their *wanderjahre* in Germany, seeking inspiration and learning which were later to help stimulate the development of American letters. In 1803, the *Monthly Anthology* noted: "The fine arts, in America, have not made a very rapid progress, nor is their establishment very great in any particular State . . . it is our ardent desire to promote their progress among us. . . ." [12] Its second issue defined the ideals for eloquence: "Eloquence is not an introductory science, which youth can be taught from books. It is the glorious talent of improving all the treasures of art and of science, of history and of nature to the illumination, conviction and subjugation of the hearts of men. It is the dome of the temple, the perfection of human powers, the action of mind on mind, the lightening of the moral world." [13] In 1810, when John Quincy Adams published his *Lectures on Rhetoric and Oratory*, he did so with "an undoubting confidence that they will do good. They will excite the genius, stimulate the literary ambition, and improve the taste of the rising generation." [14] He wrote to improve the art of the forum, the art of the lawyer, the art of letters, in addition to the art of the pulpit.

The published lectures of Adams were a high point in the history of American rhetorical theory. They were made by the occupant of the first Chair of Rhetoric and Oratory in the country. The history of its establishment reveals in concrete form transitional elements from the eighteenth century and the nineteenth century. It was in 1771 that the will of Nicholas Boylston, wealthy benefactor of Harvard, revealed the possibility of a chair in rhetoric and oratory: "I give & bequeath unto the President & Fellows of Harvard College in Cambridge in the County of Middlesex the sum of one thousand five hundred Pounds lawfull money . . . toward the Support and Maintenance of some well Qualified Person who shall be elected by the President and Fellows of said College for the time being and approved of by the Overseers of said College to be the Professor of Rhetoric and Oratory. . . ." [15] But thirty years passed and nothing was done about the bequest. When suit by the heirs was threatened for the recovery of the grant,[16] Harvard bestirred itself. On June 24, 1805, the Corporation unanimously elected the Honorable John Quincy Adams, relative of the donor, United States Senator, and promising literary man, who was to become the sixth president of the United States, to the first Professorship. He gave his first lecture July 11, 1806 and noted in his diary: "I this day commenced my course of lectures on rhetoric and oratory,—an undertaking of magnitude and importance. . . . My lecture was well received, and could I hope that the issue of the whole course would bear a proportion to the effect of this introduction, I should be fully satisfied." [17] For the next three years during term, Adams appeared at ten o'clock on Friday mornings to deliver a lecture on rhetoric and at two o'clock in the afternoons to preside over student declamations.[18]

"A subject, which has exhausted the genius of Aristotle, Cicero, and Quintilian, can neither require nor admit much additional illustration," [19] observed Adams in his Inaugural lecture. Accordingly, the first American professor of rhetoric and oratory drew heavily upon the classical tradition. Many later practitioners in the nineteenth century followed his example, but there was a variety of systems. The stream of rhetorical and elocutionary training in the nineteenth century needs detailed charting. Through the age, now swift flowing, now quiescent, continued the main channel of classical rhetoric. Many tributaries fed it and at times, indeed, rivaled the main stream in size and momentum —the science of voice, the quasi-scientific elocutionary system, the combination of muscle and vocal rhythm in Delsartian systems. At times the course was narrowed to make way for an expanding curriculum and social life, for journalism, the sciences, the fraternity and athletics. But the stream flowed on, and gathering volume and momentum, at the end of the century cascaded into what we now know as the modern department of speech. It is convenient to chart this movement in periods of quarter centuries.

II
1800-1825

On the surface, rhetorical training in the first quarter of the nineteenth century did not seem to differ materially from what had been the vogue in the late eighteenth century. At Yale, Freshmen received training in Cicero's *De Oratore* and Sophomores studied Lindley Murray's *English Grammar*. All the students, regardless of class, were required in daily rotation to "exhibit" compositions of various kinds, and submit them to the instructor's criticism. Meeting in units of four, they declaimed, publicly and privately, on Tuesdays and Fridays, in English, Latin, Greek, or Hebrew; when required, each had to hand in a copy of his declamation "fairly written." Seniors and Juniors also disputed forensically before the class, twice a week, on a question approved by the instructor; when the disputants had finished, the instructor discussed the matter at length, giving his own views on the problems and on the arguments of both sides. One student assured his parents that all the disputes and compositions required "a great deal of hard thinking and also close application." [20] Programs at the other colleges were strikingly similar. Yale may have been a bit more fortunate than most schools in having Timothy Dwight, the president, handle the rhetorical training for Seniors. "Intellectually, the Senior year was the best to me," observed Lyman Beecher, a student during Dwight's first years in the presidency. "We all looked forward to Dr. Dwight's instructions with interest. We began with Blair's Rhetoric, half an hour's recitation, and an hour or hour and a half of extempore lecture. . . . On two other days we had written or extempore debates before Dr. Dwight, he summing up at the close." [21] Subjects of the debates were varied: "Ought Capital Punishment ever to be inflicted?" "Ought Foreign Immigration to be encouraged?" "Ought the Liberty of the Press to be restricted?" "Does the Mind always Think?" "Is a Public Education preferable to a private?" "Which have the greatest influence in Forming a National Character, Moral or Physical Causes?" "Ought the Clergy to be supported by Law?" Dwight obviously encouraged free discussion, even permitting the students to dispute the question, "Is the Bible the Word of God?" As one studies the record of the disputations, he notes attention to correctness of diction, pronunciation, soundness of argument, and judgment.[22] Commencement programs in the early years of the century abounded in forensic disputations, orations, dissertations, deliberative discussions, essays, and colloquies,[23] as they had done for years before.

Whereas the system seemed about the same as it was in the eighteenth century, there were, in fact, differences in goals and ends. Not only were colleges being pressed to train for professions other than the clergy for which the early system of rhetorical training was designed, but the clergy itself had begun to demand a new kind of training. "American rhetoric" in 1785 was "closely allied with oratory," observes Warren Guthrie, "but gradually moved more and more into the realm of composition and criticism—*belles lettres.*" [24] Students had always been required to write as a basis for oratorical training. One must remember that a year before John Quincy Adams became Professor of Rhetoric and Oratory at Harvard, a Unitarian, Henry Ware, had been elected Hollis Professor of Divinity,[25] and New England churches began to fill their pulpits with "liberal" ministers. In 1810, John Kirkland, a Unitarian, became president of Harvard. Unitarians shifted the emphasis in sermonizing away from the rigidly logical sermon, for which disputations had been excellent training, to the "literary sermon." [26] Sermons began to be praised for their grace and beauty, and criticized for an absence of "sound doctrine." Men like Joseph Buckminster, Edward Everett, and William Ellery Channing, superbly graceful writers and speakers, were occupying the pulpits, and crowds were responding to the new aesthetic appeal, even as the old line Calvinists were readying themselves for attack both on the new theology and the new method of sermonizing. Although Lyman Beecher believed that "the plain, simple, energetic, argumentative style of New England preaching . . . admits of becoming the best pulpit style in the world," even he, in 1820, was forced "for the sake of maintaining our ground" to go "as far as I could go to satisfy by popular oratory those who would be formed on a worse model. . . ." [27] "Time was, when the good people of this land retired silently from the sanctuary, saying little of the sermon, and more of the duty of improving it," noted a critic of New England preaching during the period. "But *now,* sermons have their day. In some of our cities and villages, it has become a point of etiquette to talk about them,—to descant on their merits and defects,—to point out the beautiful passages and the bad. . . ." "Like the last tale or poem," the sermon was "talked about" and it became "just as useless, as a 'tale that is told.' " [28] Sermons had clearly become "literary efforts" and were thought of as artistic productions, quite as much as were the essays in the *Monthly Anthology* or the *North American Review.* Eclectic in their ministerial training, many of the young clergymen were united in their enthusiasm for literature and literary study. Through their preaching they were trying to bring about new American ideals and were exemplifying habits of preaching and writing quite different from those of the eighteenth century.

It is not so much that rhetorical training was moving in the direction of written composition (for rhetorical training had always been allied with both speaking and writing), but that a new type of training had become necessary even for the sermon. "If we wished to impoverish a man's intellect," wrote the popular William Ellery Channing, brother of the Boylston Professor of Rhetoric and Oratory, "we could devise few means more effectual, than to confine him to what is called a course of theological reading." [29] In his own preparation, he strayed from conventional methods, proclaiming "I am now totally immersed in literature. I have settled a course of reading for three years. . . ." [30] Whereas oratory was being forced to give way to other types of literary art, the oration itself began to change its form and would soon appear as the "lecture."

The textbook most widely used for rhetorical training at the opening of the century and continuing for more than a quarter of a century thereafter was Hugh Blair's *Lectures on Rhetoric and Belles Lettres.* Published in 1783, it was ordered by Brown University college library in the same year and adopted by Yale as a text in 1785 and by Harvard in 1788. By 1803 it was the "most popular rhetorical work in the colleges." [31] Steeped in the classical tradition, Blair, nevertheless, did not consider rhetoric merely to be concerned with oral persuasion. "To speak or to write perspicuously and agreeably, with purity, with grace and strength, are attainments of the utmost consequence to all who propose, either by speech or writing, to address the public." [32] Blair who "would stop hounds by his eloquence" [33] was a Scottish minister whose published Sermons were "elegant and perspicuous discourses." [34] A country becoming increasingly self-conscious about its literature and a clergy moving rapidly away from old methods of sermonizing found Blair's *Lectures on Rhetoric and Belles Lettres* well adapted to their needs. "The study of composition, important in itself at all times, has acquired additional importance from the taste and manners of the present age," noted Blair. "It is an age wherein improvements, in every part of science, have been prosecuted with ardour. To all the liberal arts much attention has been paid; and to none more than to the beauty of language, and the grace and elegance of every kind of writing. The public ear is become refined. It will not easily bear what is slovenly and incorrect. Every author must aspire to some merit in expression, as well as in sentiment, if he would not incur the danger of being neglected and despised." [35] To Blair, the study of Rhetoric and Belles Lettres presupposes and requires a proper acquaintance with the rest of the liberal arts. "It embraces them all within its circle, and recommends them to the highest regard." [36] Blair concerned himself not only with instructions in speech-making but with instructions for historical writing, philosophical writing, and poetry, including the lyric, the epic, tragic drama, and comedy.

Supplementing the rhetorical program in most of the colleges at the beginning of the nineteenth century was a strongly classical program. It normally included logic, and the study of Greek and Latin. In the program usually were Cicero's and Demosthenes' orations, Cicero's *De Oratore* and Quintilian's *Institutes of Oratory*, although the latter was not available in "numbers sufficient to supply a Class" [37] in some colleges. The pattern of rhetorical training was similar in colleges throughout the country. Newly organized schools tended to draw their inspiration, their plans, and their instructors and presidents from the older colleges.[38]

Still, in 1819, at the beginning of Channing's long incumbency, there was dissatisfaction with rhetorical training, despite the fact that it was becoming more systematized than it had earlier been. By 1824, Brown, Yale, and Bowdoin had followed Harvard in establishing chairs of rhetoric. The textbooks and methods employed in teaching rhetoric threw emphasis on theory, with little distinction between the art of the speaker and the art of the writer. The public looked upon exhibitions of student speaking and found them not much better than they had been. "A branch of instruction which has been shamefully neglected (the word, I own, is a harsh one)," noted William Tudor, traveler and observer of a Harvard Commencement program, "has been oratory,—or rather, elocution. Every person who has attended a college exhibition, would see, with disgust, more than half the exhibiters speak their parts in such a slovenly, awkward manner, as would not have been tolerated in a village school. . . . There is a professorship of rhetoric and oratory, —but its principal duties are the instruction in the former, in the formation of style and the theory of speaking." [39]

Occasionally the teachers were blamed for the deficiencies. Both their methods and their emphasis were found to be at fault. "As for oratory, Mr. Channing's professorship was a sinecure," noted one of his students. "He had, as a speaker, no grace, nor any great diversity of modulation; and his gestures were awkward, seeming to denote rather his discomfort at being obliged to speak than the mood of thought or feeling to which he gave expression." [40] Channing conducted public declamations in the college chapel once a fortnight, with the whole Senior class obliged to attend. A certain number in their turn, according to alphabetical order repeated "with such show of oratory as they could severally command, pieces of their own choice in poetry or prose, oftener in poetry." Channing "listened attentively to these declamations, and marked them . . . on a scale of twenty-four; but he never made any comment, unless it were to rebuke the choice of a piece offensively coarse, or some outrageous grotesqueness in delivery." [41] Of the Boylston Professor of Rhetoric, Oliver Wendell Holmes wrote:

> Channing, with his bland, superior look,
> Cold as a moonbeam on a frozen brook. . . .[42]

Channing was rather obviously more concerned with developing the literary life of New England than in giving individual training in oral expression. He had little equipment and training for aiding students to remedy vocal deficiencies. He could help them write orations and other literary forms, but he apparently had little expertness in helping the students to speak with vocal perfection. "I am inclined to consider rhetoric when reduced to a system in books, as a body of rules derived from experience and observation, extending to all communication by language and designed to make it efficient," Channing observed in his lectures to the students. "It does not ask whether a man is to be a speaker or writer,—a poet, philosopher, or debater; but simply,—is it his wish to be put in the right way of communicating his mind with power to others, by words spoken or written." [43] Like his predecessors John Quincy Adams, and Joseph McKean, Channing leaned heavily upon the ancients. Precepts for voice training and elocutionary skill had not been detailed by the ancients, and Channing did not supply the deficiency to any great extent.[44]

Rhetorical and elocutionary training in the first quarter of the nineteenth century was built upon the habits of disputation and declamation prominent the century before. But there were two notable expansions. One came in the establishment of chairs of rhetoric, giving to the field a status in the curriculum. The other change was the attention given to developing the literary background of the orator with the purpose of making him more perspicuous and more perspicacious. But deficiencies in platform skill, in management of the voice and in general delivery, were apparent. In the next quarter century, training in voice and general elocutionary skills were accentuated to remedy the defects.

III
1825-1850

"The tongue or voyce is praise-worthie . . .," thought a contributor to the *New England Magazine* in 1832, as he voiced his complaint against the delivery of preachers and public men, urging that the colleges take notice. "It is but recently that they have given much attention to the subject of Eloquence, or elocution, as a science to be taught," he observed. "But the day is coming, and even now is, when a different course must be adopted. A taste for polite literature and the fine arts is becoming too general among the population of the country to allow the colleges to send forth their annual hosts of graduates for the pulpits and the forum, untaught in the most important accomplishment of a public man, without severe rebuke. Yale has already done something for improvement in the art of speaking; and Harvard,—good old dull and sleepy matron, is just awaking, and rubbing her eyes, and perceives the necessity of doing a little to stop the public clamor, and shield her alumni from the reproaches of common school-boys." [45] Complaints about the poor rendition of orations, debates, and disputations at exhibitions and commencements had been frequent for many years. People were sometimes amused at the "seeming torture" to which the human body could be put "without stretching it on the rack," [46] and occasionally reported on delivery that "would have done honor to an Aboriginal Sachem. . . ." [47] As manners in general became more refined, more and more pressure was put upon the schools to pay attention to the rendition of orations, debates, and declamations. Improved taste in composition was not enough. Then, too, a dying Calvinism was seeking to regain its losses by invigorating its preaching, and called upon the schools to aid in this task. "I must say I have been troubled at the complaints which have been made at the want of animation of the Andover students, and of the impression beginning to be made in favor of Princeton," wrote the Reverend Lyman Beecher to authorities at Andover, training ground for Calvinists after Harvard's adoption of Unitarianism. "I say, therefore, that you must remedy the defect, so far as it is positive. Your preachers must wake up, and lift up their voice. They must get their mouths open, and their lungs in vehement action, *there* in your little chapel, and, if need be, start the glass, and heave the swelling sides, and tear passion to a tatters." [48]

The criticism of the public performances of clergymen, lawyers, and men in public affairs, that now went on in America, had its counterpart in England a generation before. There the fifth of the classical canons of rhetoric had been isolated for special attention in the last half of the eighteenth century. A flood of essays and books on elocution had ensued. The elocutionary writings of Thomas Sheridan, James Burgh, John Walker, Joshua Steele, and Gilbert Austin were exported to America, were available in libraries, and were sometimes consulted by students in preparation of their declamations. By 1824, the Reverend Ebenezer Porter, who became Bartlett Professor of Pulpit Eloquence at Andover in 1811, published his own text, *Lectures on the Analysis of Vocal Inflection,* one of the earliest American discussions of vocal delivery. In 1827, he published *An Analysis of the Principle of Rhetorical Delivery,* and in 1831, his *Rhetorical Reader,* a practical textbook, the popularity of which is reflected in the fact that by 1858 it reached its three hundredth printing.

Gradually elocutionary training became separated from rhetorical training. By 1828, colleges such as Colby, Middlebury, South Carolina, and Yale, in assigning Richard Whately's *Rhetoric* specified "except Part IV," [49] the section which dealt with "Elocution, or Delivery." Such an exclusion suggests that elocutionary training was being thought of as a separate discipline. About 1823, Jonathan Barbour, a disciple of the English writer, Joshua Steele, author of *Prosodia Rationalis,* came to America.[50] By 1830, he was at least unofficially connected with Yale, and offering elocutionary training, as the title of his book published in 1830 indicates: *A Grammar of Elocution: Containing the Principles of the Arts of Reading and Speaking: Illustrated by Appropriate Exercises and Examples, Adapted to Colleges, Schools, and Private Instruction: The Whole Arranged in the Order in Which It is Taught in Yale College.*[51] The separation of rhetoric and elocution is clearly manifested in 1830 with the official appointment of Erasmus D. North as Instructor in Elocution at Yale.[52] Jonathan Barbour was hired by Harvard University in 1830 to supplement the work in rhetoric by giving special attention to elocution, being the "first professedly scientific teacher of elocution employed in Harvard College." [53] Barbour lost little time after coming to America in associating himself with American physicians, one of whom was James Rush who, in 1827, published *The Philosophy of the Human Voice.*[54] The book, intended for physicians, found its place among persons who had become increasingly interested in the special problems of the voice and in vocal presentation. Barbour was among those, having become acquainted with the contents of the book even before it was published.[55]

Wendell Phillips, eminent American orator, was a student of Barbour at Harvard and found his system "the best ever offered to any student."

Based on Rush, the system was "at once philosophically sound and eminently practical." Barbour's reliance "on principle, and comparative disuse of technical rules, seem to me a great advantage over all other systems with which I am acquainted." [56] But Phillips did not speak for the majority; student ridicule caused Barbour to resign his Harvard post by 1835.[57] Among devices unpleasant to students was his bamboo-slatted sphere which fitted over the practicing speaker, and enabled him to acquire with finesse all the gradations of gesture through 360°. Although elocution was late in developing in America, it became a required study in most colleges, and remained so until late in the century, when it became generally elective. And although early elocution closely followed English writers of the eighteenth century, after 1827 James Rush became the dominant influence, and remained influential through the century. James Murdoch, for example, was a devoted student of Rush. "I have labored," Murdoch wrote late in his career, "to simplify and make practical Dr. Rush's Philosophy of the Voice." [58] Murdoch taught Robert Fulton and Thomas Trueblood, eminent elocutionists at the end of the century. They dedicated their book, *Practical Elements of Elocution,*[59] to Murdoch, "whose life and work have been an abiding source of inspiration."

What has been said of the elocutionary movement in England during the eighteenth century may be said of the concern with delivery in America during the nineteenth century: "In methodology, it was characterized by the systematic ordering of certain observed phenomena of voice, body, and language, and by the invention and use of systems of notation to represent these phenomena. In philosophy, it was characterized by a mechanistic interpretation of the laws of nature. Elocution, in short, was a 'scientific' subject." [60] In the concern with the fifth canon of classical rhetoric, "a new ordering of an old subject" [61] took place. As the century advanced elocutionary training became the vogue and then the standard pattern.

In less spectacular fashion, the older training in the rhetorical canons other than delivery, continued. At Yale, for instance, while Erasmus North occupied himself with elocution, Chauncey Goodrich, appointed to the Professorship of Rhetoric in 1817, continued to pursue the older tradition: "The Sophomores were instructed by him, through the summer term, in Jamieson's Rhetoric. The Senior Classes were taught out of a text-book of higher Rhetoric and Criticism, and read Compositions before him which were afterwards criticized in private.... The importance of his instruction to the Seniors meanwhile was increased by the study of Demosthenes on the Crown, as the chef d'oeuvre of ancient eloquence, and by a very interesting course of lectures on English oratory...." [62] Goodrich had as his object, as he explains in his preface to

Select British Eloquence, "to awaken in the minds of the class that love of genuine eloquence which is the surest pledge of success" and "to initiate the pupil in those higher principles which... have always guided the great masters of the art...." [63] At Columbia "the declamations of the juniors and seniors were their own original compositions, and those of the freshmen and sophomores selected pieces." [64] At Williams, Mark Hopkins, having become president in 1836, carried on with traditional rhetorical training. [65] At Amherst, the old tradition was carried on under a grant for the endowment of a professorship of rhetoric and oratory as early as 1823. [66] At Bowdoin, Samuel Philipp Newman, elected in 1824 to the first professorship of rhetoric and oratory, in 1830 introduced his own textbook, *A Practical System of Rhetoric, or the Principles and Rules of Style,* following the older tradition. Out of this book, such men as Henry Wadsworth Longfellow, Nathaniel Hawthorne, Sargent Prentiss, and Franklin Pierce received their early instruction. [67]

Whereas classical study of rhetoric continued, it was to some extent affected both by the increased emphasis on delivery and by its separation from the classics as a discipline in its own right. Separate professorships meant the creation of a gulf between the classics and rhetoric, heretofore allied very closely. At Columbia in 1833, the professor of rhetoric, John McVickar, felt handicapped by no longer having control of materials for study in the classics. He was not satisfied with the materials being taught by the professor of classics since these materials did not furnish adequate basis for rhetorical training. "The professor would here respectfully suggest that it would greatly add to the student's ability to pursue this course [rhetoric], were the ancient Rhetoricians & critical writers read contemporaneously or rather previously in the classical course. Thus, the present Junior class knows nothing of Cicero's 'De Oratore,' Horace's 'Ars Poetica'—to all of which constant reference must be made—and an acquaintance with Longinus only so far as their present reading has carried them." [68] In addition to the changes brought about by the elocutionary movement and by the lesser support from the classics, rhetorical training became increasingly linked with belletristic study. As has been found, in terms of departmental organization, "by 1850 the grouping was not so frequently 'Rhetoric and Oratory' as 'Rhetoric and Belles Lettres,' or 'Rhetoric and composition,' with delivery now relegated to the tremendously popular 'Elocution.'" [69]

As new colleges began to spring up throughout the country, they modeled their courses of study on that of the older institutions. Illinois College, founded by Yale missionaries in 1829, specified in its laws: "The Professor of Rhetoric shall instruct in the Critical and Rhetorical study of Portions of the Latin and Greek orators and poets, and also in Composition, Translation and Declamation." [70] By 1833, it had already stated: "The students will also receive instruction in the science of elocution. . . ." [71] And Herbert E. Rhae has found that the "history of speech education in Indiana colleges followed the pattern set by eastern higher institutions. This is particularly true in the weekly memorized declamations among Freshmen and Sophomores. There was also a similarity in the continuity of the original orations and disputations for Juniors and Seniors with the practice in the East." [72]

During the second quarter of the century the classical tradition in rhetoric endured and in many places was expanded. But the innovations, and the greatest expansions, occurred in systems of elocution, with special attention to voice and gesture.

IV
1850-1875

To Henry Adams, a college student of the 1850's, being Class Day orator was "political as well as literary success." [73] "If Harvard College gave nothing else," he thought, "it gave calm. For four years each student had been obliged to figure daily before dozens of young men who knew each other to the last fibre. One had done little but read papers to Societies, or act comedy in the Hasty Pudding, not to speak of all sorts of regular exercises, and no audience in future life would ever be so intimately and terribly intelligent as these." [74] Uncertain as to whether he was getting an "education," in one respect at least, he was aware that the American university was doing something for its students that the European university was not. "Three-fourths of the graduates would rather have addressed the Council of Trent or the British Parliament than have acted Sir Anthony Absolute or Dr. Ollapod before a gala audience of the Hasty Pudding," [75] and "nothing seemed stranger" to the American college graduate than the "paroxysms of terror before the public which often overcame the graduates of European Universities." [76] Adams was "ready to stand up before any audience in America or Europe, with nerves rather steadier for the excitement," but "whether he should ever have anything to say, remained to be proved." [77]

If Henry Adams questioned whether he was receiving an education, even so did college administrators. The narrower curriculum of an earlier day was to expand with a country expanding in interest and activity. Although rhetorical training was to continue, more and more it was to give way to literature and criticism. Whereas the class orator could still believe himself to have achieved "political as well as literary success," he was more and more to share the rostrum with the poet, the essayist, and the editor of the college magazine. Henry Adams himself sought proficiency not only in oratory, but contributed to the college magazine and acquired enthusiasm for literature through private literary study with Lowell.

Surveying the decade prior to the mid-century for evidences of training in rhetoric and oratory, Coulton on examining the departmental organization of fifty-six colleges and universities observes that "Moral Science and Belles Lettres" had disappeared and there has been added in this period "English Literature," "English," and "Philosophy and Belles Lettres." [78] By the decade of 1870 and 1880, departmental organization continues with "English clearly predominating." [79] According to Samuel Eliot Morison, the advance of English as a special field which was eventually to encompass rhetorical training in many places was "in the nature of peaceful penetration." [80] The delay in getting started was due "not to opposition," but to a "general failure to see in it anything more than a minor element in the preparation for the ministry." [81] As late as the sixties at Harvard "English meant elocution and rhetoric. . . .[82] In 1858 and 1859, "the Freshmen had Lessons in Orthoepy and Lessons in Expression; the Sophomores, Lessons in Expression, Lessons in Action, Themes; the Juniors, Themes, Declamation, Rhetoric; the Seniors, Forensics; nothing more." [83] The gradual shift to an emphasis on English literature was given impetus by Francis J. Child who succeeded Channing in the Chair of Rhetoric and Oratory, for it was he who "first saw the possibilities of English as a factor in general scholarship." [84] Almost immediately after Child's succession, a "course of twelve Lectures was given to the Senior Class, on the English language." [85] Instruction was given in the second term of the Senior year to "small voluntary classes, in Anglo Saxon, and the rudiments of Icelandic." [86] In 1853, during the first term of the Senior class, students attended Lectures on the English language, and afterwards read selections from Chaucer's Canterbury Tales.[87] By 1876 Child had become "Professor of English."

During the period from 1850 to 1875, Elocution was a required subject in many colleges throughout the country. However, with pressure from an expanded curriculum, its value as a required subject was questioned. This was a period of vast expansion for the colleges. New fields of study were added as the country became increasingly rich, industrious, and populous. Columbia founded its school of mines in 1864; [88] California by 1870 had colleges of Agriculture, Mechanical Arts, Mines, and Civil Engineering in addition to the original Arts college.[89] The elective system of studies was greatly expanded to meet this pressure. Having been in practice to some extent since about 1820 at the University of Virginia,[90] it advanced rapidly after it was given new impetus

by Harvard's president Charles Eliot after 1869. The wisdom of requiring elocution was questioned. In 1873, at Harvard, elocution was
dropped to elective status.[91] The reason may be found in an observation of James Murdoch. Commenting on the value of elocution as it
was taught in the seventies and early eighties, Murdoch observes: "Elocution, as taught at present, is, in most cases, considered and treated in
theory and practice as little more than an imitative art, and as such
yields its rightful position of honor and dignity as a branch of study
based upon philosophic or scientific principles." [92] In 1875, Allegheny
College showed unrest with a program of elocutionary training by calling attention to the virtues of the system of speech training recommended by Professor Nathan Sheppard, a visiting professor from
Scotland who was giving a course of lectures in which there "is no
attempt to teach 'elocution' or any artificial system, nor is public speaking confounded with recitation, declamation, or dramatic reading."
Allegheny chose to "incorporate practically—especially in the advanced
classes—the suggestions and directions of Prof. Sheppard in the instructions of this department." [93] Even as early as 1861, Columbia readily
yielded up John H. Siddons, instructor in elocution, in order to avoid
a budgetary deficit, and made no appointment thereafter.[94]

Meanwhile, a traditionally classical approach to rhetoric continued.
Such textbooks as George Campbell's *Philosophy of Rhetoric*, Blair's
Lectures on Rhetoric and Belles Lettres, and Richard Whately's *Rhetoric* were still used. More often, however, textbooks to some extent based
on the principles of the English rhetorics but written by American
teachers were used. Henry N. Day's *Elements of the Art of Rhetoric,*
published in 1850 and later issued in 1867 as *The Art of Discourse* became popular. Adapted to American needs, Day's treatises nevertheless
were classical. Like Blair, Day treated discourse other than oratory,
but oratory remained the highest form of art. In his view oratory was
discourse for the purpose of effect; poetry was discourse for the purpose
of form; and history and treatises were discourse for the purpose of
subject matter. Other textbooks by Americans gained prominence, such
as that of G. P. Quackenbos, *Advanced Course of Composition and
Rhetoric.*

One need only look at the program of the University of California
in the early seventies to realize that the classical traditions were being
fully maintained. Fortnightly themes and forensics were required during the first, second, and third years, with theoretical study of rhetoric
confined to the third year. Whately's *Rhetoric* was used as a textbook,
supplemented by Cope's *Introduction to Aristotle's Rhetoric,* Blair's
Lectures on Rhetoric and Belles Lettres, and Campbell's *Philosophy of
Rhetoric.*[95] At Illinois College in the mid-west, Sophomores studied

Cicero's *De Oratore* for one half year; Juniors studied Day's *Rhetoric* and Seniors studied Demosthenes' "On the Crown." [96] Students had optional work in Quintilian's *Institutes of Oratory* and in the study of selections from English and American orators.[97] At Hamilton College, Anson Judd Upson and Henry Allen Fink were strengthening traditions begun at the founding of the college. The 1843 rules governing "rhetoricals" sent all students to the Chapel during the next forty years to attend public exercises of "declamations, select translations from the classics, the original essays and orations." On Wednesday noon of each week "four freshmen, four sophomores, and four juniors gave declamations before the assembled college; on Saturday noon of each week two from each lower class read essays, two juniors presented discussions, and two seniors gave orations." [98] Between 1854 and 1866 prize contests were established in both original oratory and extemporaneous debate. "No effort was spared by the instructor to bring out the characteristic powers of each speaker and to ready him for the best performance of which he was capable." [99] Although the Literary Societies at Hamilton had begun to decline about 1850,[100] a systematic training program in speaking continued to be very strong. The oration was considered to be an instrument of power and public service. In 1876, the Hamilton College orator, participating in one of the earliest intercollegiate oratorical contests, spoke before such distinguished judges as William Cullen Bryant, Whitelaw Reid, and George William Curtis on the subject "The Heroic Element in Modern Life" at the New York Academy of Music and won the prize of the day. Thereafter intercollegiate oratorical contests sprang up all over the country, serving to revitalize interest in public speaking.[101]

In the third quarter of the century, elocution lost position as a required subject, but continued as an elective. Rhetorical training persevered but it was modified in the direction of belles lettres, and frequently was identified with departments of English. The ever-enduring urge for platform expression found a new outlet in intercollegiate oratorical contests.

V

1875-1900

Bliss Perry was a student at Williams in the early part of the last quarter of the nineteenth century, with an "interest in speaking, writing, and miscellaneous reading." [102] It was "curious," he thought, that he could recall "so little" about his class work in English.[103] He was obliged to write and deliver orations once or twice a year under the supervision of the Professor of Rhetoric, Llewellyn Pratt, who gave his productions "as much attention as they deserved," but it was "very little." [104] The rhetoric text was that of D. J. Hill, *Science of Rhetoric*. But if he received little attention from his rhetoric instructor, he was helped to win the coveted Graves Prize in his senior year, largely through the assistance of George L. Raymond, who gave lessons in elocution "part of each year." [105] "No one pays much attention to such contests now," observed Perry, "but in our day crowds attended them." [106] For months he toiled away among the moth-eaten stuffed moose in Jackson Hall learning Raymond's "vocal exercises," the "trick of deep-breathing," and the "proper 'placing' of the voice" from lessons in *The Orator's Manual*.[107]

Before the century was over, Perry succeeded Raymond both at Williams and at Princeton. During his own years of service as a teacher of rhetoric he witnessed the decline of interest in oratory in the Eastern colleges, and tried to "prop up for a while a building that was doomed to fall" [108] by assisting in the development of forensics, a form of speaking stimulated by the organization of intercollegiate debate contests. In the nineties, when he was at Princeton he journeyed to New Haven and Cambridge to help organize the first intercollegiate debates between Yale, Harvard, and Princeton; and for some years they "excited great interest." [109] He matched his wits against great teachers like Hadley at Yale and George Pierce Baker at Harvard in faculty coaching of debates.

Perry's experience as a student and later as a teacher in a sense reflects the main line of development of rhetorical training and effort in the last quarter of the nineteenth century. Rhetoric was often taught in departments of English; oratory had a prominent position in colleges throughout the country but was losing vogue in some of the Eastern colleges; instruction was given in elocution in most of the colleges and was looked upon as an aid to students in their competitions for prizes in oratory; forensics courses were introduced into the college curriculum in order to meet the needs of organized intercollegiate debate and faculty coaching. Students, caught up in the enthusiasm for debate, argued its value over oratory.[110] Now and then, colleges in the West voiced the opinion that it was to be their duty and their honor to keep both oratory and debate alive. "Oratory must always be foremost," commented the Colorado Class of '99, "if our ambition for the reputation and success of our institution is to be satisfied; eastern college men have turned their attention to athletics and things athletic in their nature, and it is for western colleges and universities to keep alive the interest in debate and oratory if we would have power and prosperity." [111]

Debate in some form had been part of the college program from the beginning. The art of syllogizing was probably the earliest forebear of debate; it was succeeded in the eighteenth century by forensic disputation. More and more, disputations grew into the regular classroom debate or the argumentative discourse. Societies had begun to meet each other in debate early in the nineteenth century. Finally, in the last part of the nineteenth century, more ambitious undertakings were afoot and colleges began to meet each other in formalized debate. The curricular program adjusted itself to the needs of students. In 1885 Josiah Royce, later to become an eminent philosopher, was in charge of "forensics" at Harvard, or work in argumentative discourse. By 1888-1889, the Harvard catalog listed Ten Lectures in argumentative composition or oral discussion of topics in political economy and history as part of its curriculum.[112] At Boston University in the same year, Sophomores and Juniors had vocal and forensic training;[113] Oberlin in 1891-1892 under William B. Chamberlain, offered a course in Forensic Delivery, described as "Practical studies in Argumentation and Oratory; analysis of models with reference to an audience, and criticism upon the rendering of selected and original speeches and debates."[114] In 1893-1894, Northwestern offered a course in Forensics in which "Questions are announced and sides are taken one week before each debate, and references are given on the Library Bulletin to the available literature on the respective questions."[115] Wisconsin in the same year, under Frankenburger, had a course in Rhetoric consisting of "Exercises in debates, essays, orations, with personal criticism." An advanced course in the Philosophy of Rhetoric consisted of "Analysis of great orations, essays, and debates, with higher rhetorical and literary criticism."[116] Oregon in 1896-1897 offered two courses in Forensics and Orations, using Baker's *Specimens of Argumentation* as a textbook.[117] By the end of the century, California had four courses in Argumentation and Debate. They were devoted to preparation of briefs, practice in debate, oral debate on literary topics with analysis of stylistic features of argumentative discourse, and studies in masterpieces of argumentation. In addition, a course in Greek was devoted to a study of Plato's *Gorgias* with special reference to the Socratic method of argumentation.[118] Alabama had in 1898 as part of the English course, training in argumentative discourse.[119] Michigan in 1899 had a course in Oral Discussion which consisted of "application of the principles of formal logic and elocution in debating leading questions of the day," and preparation of briefs. This course was designed to "develop readiness of extemporization and is recommended to those who desire to enter the inter-collegiate debates."[120] And the University of Illinois offered in the department of Rhetoric and Oratory, a course in Oral Discussion, emphasizing data for discussion, with oral debates and attention to delivery.[121]

These are typical of the programs of training common throughout the country. Coaches and students alike were learning the art of formalized debate, and usually using as a basic text George Pierce Baker's *Specimens of Argumentation* or his *Principles of Argumentation,* or both. But the programs were a culmination of movements in the century. Half of the material in Baker's *Specimens* was taken from Goodrich, even to the notes. Students at the end of the century were applying the method of rhetorical criticism Goodrich had illustrated so thoroughly at mid-century.

Meanwhile, in this last quarter of the nineteenth century new developments took place in the handling of elocutionary training and in the formalization of speech programs. Itinerant teachers of elocution were gradually affixing themselves to colleges as part of a curriculum which was becoming more stabilized. In 1877 when William Jennings Bryan was a student at Illinois College, S. S. Hammill was instructing in elocution for part of the year. According to Bryan, "he rather leaned to the dramatic and recommended dramatic pieces to us. I rather preferred the oratorical style. . . . He trained us in modulation of the voice, gesticulation, etc., and I presume that his instructions were beneficial to me, although I have been so much more interested in the subject matter than in the form of presentation that my use of his advice has been unconscious rather than intentional." [122] In the summer session of 1878 Hammill attracted two students who were to carry on his work and to establish departments and schools of oratory in two leading universities. The two students were Thomas C. Trueblood and Robert I. Fulton who, after additional training with James Murdoch, established elocutionary training at the University of Michigan and at Ohio Wesleyan University, in a more formal way than it had been taught in many schools. Elocutionary training never died out of the college curriculum. After the elective system had come into use on a large scale, elocutionary training was often elective; at other places it was required but not accredited for graduation. At Michigan in 1892, Trueblood was made Professor of Elocution and launched a formalized program of speech training with full college credit attached.[123]

In the latter part of the nineteenth century, the principles of elocutionary training which had been based on Rush [124] were supplemented by a stream of thought deriving from the French music teacher and actor, Delsarte. Thus the physiological theories of Rush were united with aesthetic theories. College catalogs occasionally refer to the nature of the elocutionary training. Oregon offered at the end of the century numerous courses in elocution, indicating that "General Principles of Delsarte and Mackaye" [125] were used. At Michigan, "the Rush and Delsarte philosophies" [126] were taught. At Colorado, the instructor in oratory, W. H. Goodall, was an "enthusiastic admirer of Delsarte. . . ." [127]

Enthusiasm for the Delsarte theory of elocution sometimes meant emphasis on physical culture; at Colorado, W. H. Goodall was "proficient in elocution, gesture work and physical culture." At the University of Illinois in 1895, an instructor in Elocution and in Physical Culture for Women gave courses in Oral Rhetoric, including work in breathing and modulation, and practiced "the Delsarte Culture." [128] At Huron College at the end of the century Elbert R. Moses was listed as Director of a "Department of Oratory and Physical Culture." Exercises in club swinging, fencing, walking, and calisthenics were part of the program.[129]

At the time that Fulton and Trueblood were preparing for a life of teaching, Samuel Silas Curry was a student at Boston University, where Lewis B. Monroe, a student of Delsarte, was in charge of the School of Oratory. In 1879, when Monroe died, Curry succeeded to the position of director of oratorical training. Stimulated in part by Delsarte's theories deriving from Monroe, in part by Alexander Graham Bell's lectures on the science of the voice, and by numerous other influences both American and foreign, Curry became eclectic in his theories and teaching. Disturbed by mechanical and imitative practices, Curry formulated his own theories, and in 1891 published *Province of Expression*, stressing the need for mental training as a basis for effective delivery. Toward the end of the century Curry's theories were gaining wide currency in the schools.

Classical traditions went on in the last part of the nineteenth century, but more and more the concern in departments of English was with forms of writing other than oratory. Whereas the theory of invention was once almost exclusively oriented in oratorical discourse, more and more the orientation became that of prose composition generally. Books such as those of Quackenbos' *Advanced Course in Composition and Rhetoric* and John Franklin Genung's *The Practical Elements of Rhetoric*, and Adams Sherman Hill's *The Principles of Rhetoric* helped to establish new categories of rhetoric: narration, description, exposition, and argumentation.[130] In the last decade of the century, courses in public speaking were established and differentiated from the usual courses in rhetoric. Oral and written discourse began to be taught separately. And argumentation became almost exclusively the concern of public speaking.

VI

In his survey of rhetorical training in the colleges during a large part of the nineteenth century and the early part of the twentieth century, Thomas Coulton observed: "We seem to be dealing, then, with a discipline which came to no sudden awakening after a period of neglect, but one which, having long been maintained in its accustomed

place, was lifted on the tide of larger public interest in higher education and met the swell of this tide by offering more semesters of work
and in greater variety. Both growth and adjustment are evidenced." [131]
The consistent line of instruction throughout the century was classical
rhetorical training, both in specialized courses and in supplementary
programs in Greek and Latin. John Quincy Adams delivered the keynote for the age when he eulogized Aristotle and the ancients. In the
first quarter of the century the rambling instruction of the earlier century was systematized and ensconced in chairs of rhetoric. And the
purposes were expanded beyond eighteenth-century syllogizing and
disputing to include general training to make the orator more literate
and discerning. But Adams' suggestion that little could be added to the
classical tradition was never accepted fully. In the second quarter of
the century, particular concern was for systems of elocution, with training in voice and bodily gesture, with attempts to apply "science" to the
field of speech. In the third quarter of the century speech training
became linked with English literature, and departments of English
assumed the main responsibility for training in rhetoric. Interest in
elocution diminished, but the persistent urge of students to find artistic
oral expression sought an outlet in intercollegiate speaking contests.
In the last quarter of the century courses in public speaking and particularly in argumentation and forensic forms, became established.
Speech as a field—the classical rhetorical tradition combined with the
newer concerns of vocal and physical training—became established
clearly if not firmly. The base was supplied for the detailed structures
which were to be erected in the twentieth-century Departments of
Speech.

Notes

1. Edward T. Channing, "Inaugural Discourse, December 8, 1819" (Cambridge, 1819), p. 14.
2. Varnum Lansing Collins, *President Witherspoon* (Princeton, 1925), I,
141-143.
3. Denison Olmsted, "Timothy Dwight as a Teacher," *American Journal of
Education,* V (1858), 567-585.
4. *Ibid.*
5. Samuel Eliot Morison, *Three Centuries of Harvard, 1636-1936* (Cambridge,
1936), p. 138.
6. *Ibid.*
7. Letter of Reverend Andrew Eliot to Thomas Hollis, quoted by Morison,
p. 138.
8. *Memoir of William Ellery Channing, with Extracts from his Correspondence
and Manuscripts,* 6th ed. (Boston, 1854), I, 68.
9. *Ibid.,* I, 69, 70.
10. *Ibid.,* I, 60.
11. Letter of Arthur Walter to William Ellery Channing, April 1, 1803, quoted
in Joseph B. Felt, *Memoirs of William Smith Shaw* (Boston, 1852), pp. 167, 168.

12. *Monthly Anthology,* I (December, 1803), 51.

13. *Ibid.,* I, 62.

14. Letter of John Quincy Adams to his brother, August 7, 1809, quoted in *Writings of John Quincy Adams,* ed. Worthington Chauncey Ford (New York, 1914), III, 334.

15. Donald M. Goodfellow, "The First Boylston Professor of Rhetoric and Oratory," *New England Quarterly,* XIX (September, 1946), 373, 374.

16. *Ibid.,* pp. 372-389.

17. *The Diary of John Quincy Adams,* ed. Allan Nevins (New York, 1928), p. 42.

18. Goodfellow, *op. cit.,* pp. 372-389; Josiah Quincy, *The History of Harvard University* (Cambridge, 1840), II, 214-215, 290-291, 324, 326; Edward Everett, "A Eulogy on the Life and Character of John Quincy Adams" (Boston, 1848), pp. 33-35; Samuel Flagg Bemis, *John Quincy Adams and the Foundations of American Foreign Policy* (New York, 1949), pp. 132-134.

19. "An Inaugural Oration, Delivered at the Author's Installation as Boylston Professor of Rhetoric and Oratory," in *Lectures on Rhetoric and Oratory* (Cambridge, 1810), p. 26.

20. Charles E. Cuningham, *Timothy Dwight* (New York, 1942), p. 239.

21. *Autobiography, Correspondence, Etc., of Lyman Beecher, D. D.,* ed. Charles Beecher (New York, 1865), I, 48.

22. *President Dwight's Decisions of Questions Discussed by the Senior Class in Yale College, in 1813 and 1814* [From stenographic notes by Theodore Dwight] (New York, 1833), pp. 5, 6 ff.

23. "Harvard Commencement," *Columbian Centinel,* September 2, 1815, p. 1, col. 4.

24. Warren Guthrie, "Development of Rhetorical Theory in America, 1635-1850," *Speech Monographs,* XV (1948), 70.

25. Morison, *op. cit.,* pp. 187 ff.

26. Van Wyck Brooks, *The Flowering of New England, 1815-1865,* new and rev. ed. (New York, 1937), pp. 12 ff.

27. Letter of Dr. Beecher to Dr. Woods, November 12, 1820, quoted in *Autobiography, Correspondence, Etc., of Lyman Beecher, D. D.,* I, 436, 437.

28. "On the Relation Between the Clergy and People, and some Prevailing Misapprehensions of the Ministry," *Christian Examiner,* II (January & February, 1825), 5, 6.

29. "Remarks on the Character and Writings of Fenelon," in *The Works of William Ellery Channing,* 11th ed. (Boston, 1849), I, 167.

30. Letter of Channing to William Smith Shaw, quoted in *Memoir of William Ellery Channing,* I, 99.

31. Guthrie, *op. cit.,* 62.

32. Hugh Blair, *Lectures on Rhetoric and Belles Lettres,* Lecture 1. Numerous editions of Blair's *Lectures* have appeared since the Edinburgh edition of 1783; therefore, references to specific Lectures are more meaningful than page references and shall be used hereafter.

33. Robert Morell Schmitz, *Hugh Blair* (New York, 1948), p. 1.

34. *Ibid.,* p. 3.

35. Lecture 1.

36. *Ibid.*

37. Letter of the Columbia College Professors to the Trustees, Feb. 20, 1809, quoted in Helen P. Roach, *History of Speech Education at Columbia College, 1754-1940* (New York, 1950), p. 23.

38. Cf. Anthony F. Blanks, "An Introductory Study in the History of the Teaching of Public Speaking in the United States," unpublished Ph.D. dissertation, Stanford, 1927; Herbert Edgar Rahe, "The History of Speech Education in Ten Indiana Colleges, 1820-1938," unpublished Ph.D. dissertation, Wisconsin, 1939. Rahe (p. 384) concludes, "In general, we may concur with Blanks that the early history of

speech education in the East tended to be duplicated in later colleges in the Middle West."

39. William Tudor, *Letters on the Eastern States* (Boston, 1821), pp. 345, 346.
40. Andrew P. Peabody, *Harvard Reminiscences* (Boston, 1888), p. 88.
41. *Ibid.*, pp. 88, 89.
42. Brooks, *op. cit.*, p. 43.
43. Edward T. Channing, *Lectures Read to the Seniors in Harvard College* (Boston, 1856), p. 31.
44. See Dorothy I. Anderson, "Edward T. Channing's Philosophy and Teaching of Rhetoric," unpublished Ph.D. dissertation, Iowa, 1944; "Edward T. Channing's Definition of Rhetoric," *SM*, XIV (1947), 81-92; "Edward T. Channing's Teaching of Rhetoric," *SM*, XVI (August, 1949), 69-81.
45. "Eloquence and Eloquent Men," *New-England Magazine*, II (February, 1832), 93-100.
46. *Life and Letters of Catharine Sedgwick*, ed. Mary E. Dewey (New York, 1871), p. 121.
47. *Columbian Centinel*, July 19, 1794, p. 3.
48. Letter of Dr. Beecher to Dr. Leonard Woods, November 12, 1820, quoted in *Autobiography, Correspondence, Etc., of Lyman Beecher*, I, 436, 437.
49. Ota Thomas, "The Teaching of Rhetoric in the United States During the Classical Period of Education," in *A History and Criticism of American Public Address*, ed. William Norwood Brigance (New York, 1943), I, 205.
50. Daniel William Scully, "The Influence of James Rush, M. D. upon American Elocution Through His Immediate Followers," unpublished M.A. thesis, Louisiana, 1951, pp. 48-85.
51. (New Haven, 1830).
52. *Catalogue of the Officers and Students in Yale College, 1830-1831.*
53. Peabody, *Harvard Reminiscences*, p. 90.
54. Scully, "The Influence of James Rush," pp. 48-85.
55. *Ibid.*
56. James E. Murdoch, *A Plea for Spoken Language* (Cincinnati and New York, 1883), p. 102.
57. Peabody, *Harvard Reminiscences*, p. 91; Scully, "The Influence of James Rush," pp. 48-85.
58. *Analytic Elocution* (Cincinnati and New York, 1884), Preface, p. iv.
59. (Boston, 1893).
60. Frederick W. Haberman, "The Elocutionary Movement in England, 1750-1850," unpublished Ph.D. dissertation, Cornell University, 1947, p. 43.
61. *Ibid.*
62. T. D. Woolsey, "Address Commemorative of Chauncey Allen Goodrich," quoted in John P. Hoshor, "Lectures on Rhetoric and Public Speaking by Chauncey Allen Goodrich," *SM*, XIV (1947), 2.
63. Chauncey Goodrich, *Select British Eloquence* (New York, 1852), Preface.
64. Roach, *Speech Education at Columbia College*, p. 40.
65. George Gary Bush, *History of Higher Education in Massachusetts* (Washington, 1891), pp. 229, 232; see also Franklin Carter, *Mark Hopkins* (Boston, 1893), pp. 143, 144.
66. Bush, *Higher Education in Massachusetts*, p. 261.
67. P. M. D. Williamson, "Speech at Bowdoin," unpublished manuscript of a speech delivered at the Convention of the Speech Association of America, December, 1951.
68. "Annual Report of Professor John McVickar, 1833," and "Report of Mr. William Betts, 1830," quoted in Roach, *Speech Education at Columbia College*, pp. 48-49.
69. Guthrie, *op. cit.*, p. 69.
70. Donald Elmer Polzin, "Curricular and Extra-Curricular Speech Training at

Illinois College, 1829-1900," unpublished M.A. thesis, University of Illinois, 1952, p. 4.

71. *Ibid.,* p. 3.
72. Rahe, "Speech Education in Ten Indiana Colleges," p. 410.
73. Henry Adams, *The Education of Henry Adams* (New York, 1931), p. 66.
74. *Ibid.,* p. 69.
75. *Ibid.*
76. *Ibid.*
77. *Ibid.*
78. Thomas E. Coulton, "Trends in Speech Education in American Colleges, 1835-1935," unpublished Ph.D. dissertation, New York University, 1935, p. 43.
79. *Ibid.,* p. 46.
80. Samuel Eliot Morison, *The Development of Harvard University, 1869-1929* (Cambridge, 1930), pp. 66-67.
81. *Ibid.*
82. *Ibid.*
83. *Ibid.*
84. *Ibid.*
85. *Annual Report of the President of Harvard College, 1852-53.*
86. *Ibid.*
87. *Annual Report of the President of Harvard College, 1853-54.*
88. Roach, *Speech Education at Columbia College,* p. 73.
89. *Register of the University of California, 1870.*
90. Louis Franklin Snow, *The College Curriculum in the United States* (New York, 1907), p. 173.
91. Morison, *Development of Harvard University,* pp. 74-81.
92. Murdoch, *A Plea for Spoken Language,* p. 9.
93. *Catalog of Allegheny College, 1875-1876,* p. 32.
94. Roach, *Speech Education at Columbia College,* p. 77.
95. *Register of the University of California, 1870.*
96. Polzin, "Speech Training at Illinois College," pp. 9, 10.
97. *Ibid.,* p. 9.
98. Willard B. Marsh, "A Century and a Third of Speech Training at Hamilton College," *Quarterly Journal of Speech,* XXXIII (February, 1947), 23-27.
99. *Ibid.,* p. 26.
100. *Ibid.,* p. 23.
101. *Ibid.,* p. 27.
102. Bliss Perry, *And Gladly Teach* (Boston and New York, 1935), p. 56.
103. *Ibid.,* p. 56.
104. *Ibid.*
105. *Ibid.*
106. *Ibid.,* p. 67.
107. *Ibid.,* p. 57.
108. *Ibid.,* p. 135.
109. *Ibid.*
110. *The Silver and Gold* (University of Colorado student newspaper), Feb. 21, 1893.
111. *The Coloradoan* (1900), p. 108.
112. Bush, *Higher Education in Massachusetts,* p. 156.
113. *Ibid.,* p. 252.
114. *Catalogue of Oberlin College for the Year 1891-92.*
115. *Catalogue of Northwestern University, 1893-94.*
116. *Catalogue of the University of Wisconsin for 1893-94.*
117. *Catalogue of the University of Oregon, Eugene, 1896-97.*
118. *University of California Annual Announcement of Courses of Instruction in the College at Berkeley for the Academic Year 1899-1900.*

119. *Catalogue of the Officers and Students of the University of Alabama, for the Academic Year 1898-99.*

120. *Calendar of the University of Michigan, 1899-1900.*

121. *Catalogue of the University of Illinois, 1898-99.*

122. W. J. Bryan and Mary Baird Bryan, *The Memoirs of William Jennings Bryan* (Chicago, 1925), p. 87.

123. Thomas C. Trueblood, "Pioneering in Speech," *QJS,* XXVII (December, 1941), 503-511; see also Giles Wilkeson Gray, "Research in the History of Speech Education," *QJS,* XXXV (April, 1949), 156-163.

124. *Ibid.*

125. *Catalogue of the University of Oregon, 1896-97.*

126. *Calendar of the University of Michigan, 1899-1900.*

127. *Columbine* (University of Colorado school annual), I (1893), p. 38.

128. *Catalogue of the University of Illinois, 1893-94.*

129. *Huron College Catalogue, 1901-02.*

130. John F. Genung, *The Study of Rhetoric in the College Course* (Boston, 1892), p. 12.

131. Coulton, "Speech Education in American Colleges," p. 139.

8 The Elocutionary Movement and its Chief Figures

MARY MARGARET ROBB

....

The Elocutionary Movement in America derived from the English schools of elocution and until the beginning of the nineteenth century showed little originality. The greatest single influence upon teachers and textbook writers during this early period was Dr. James Rush who introduced scientific aspects of vocal production in his book, *Philosophy of the Human Voice,* published in 1827. Teaching of elocution was given a new impetus; it was concerned not only with the delivery of the speaker or reader as it affected the audience but with an analysis of vocal production in physiological and physical terms. Because of a demand for such training by students who planned to be ministers, lawyers, or political leaders, elocution became a part of the educational program. The organization of lyceums and reading groups, the popularity of the public lecturer and reader, and the growth of the American theatre also contributed, perhaps indirectly, to a new emphasis upon training in the effective use of voice and gesture.

I

This was an ideal time for such a movement to flourish. The country itself was expanding, pushing its physical boundaries westward and extending its mental boundaries to accommodate new and controversial ideas. It is the period often referred to as "romantic"; the potentials for the development of the greatest, free, educated people seemed self-evident.[1] Commager characterizes the American of the nineteenth century as both romantic and sentimental: "He was sentimental about Nature in her grander aspects and liked rolling rhetoric in his orators. He thought the whole history of his country romantic and heroic and on every Fourth of July and Decoration Day indulged in orgies of sentiment."[2] This was a time which demanded orators, ministers, lec-

178

turers, and actors who could make themselves heard over the noise of a lusty and vociferous populace.

The oratory of this period proclaimed the ideals of America and debated her problems; the lyceum popularized the lecturer as a form of entertainment combined with instruction; and the theatre, especially in urban centers, became an accepted part of the cultural pattern. When Puritan restraints were somewhat relaxed, the public which had been starved overlong demanded a generous and hearty dramatic fare in all public speech. In *America Learns to Play*, Dulles says: "It was an age of oratory, of theatricalism. The actors were the rivals of Clay, Calhoun, and Webster, and they tried to outdo them at their own trade." [3]

In answer to a demand for training in elocution many people became teachers (they were often trained for other professions such as medicine or the theatre) and, in step with a new interest in science, tried to add to their scientific knowledge of the vocal instrument and thus improve their methods of instruction. *The Philosophy of the Human Voice* gave them direction and inspiration. Walker's *Elements of Elocution* was the most popular English textbook used in the American colleges at the beginning of the century, but Sheridan, Steele, Austin, Burgh, Scott, and Whately all exerted an influence on these early elocutionists. However, the day of English dominance had passed and the Rush System was to stimulate many American teachers of elocution to write their own textbooks. From an examination of college catalogs, Guthrie found that the American textbooks used from 1821-1850 were those written by Ebenezer Porter, James Barber, Merritt Caldwell, and William Russell. The only textbook that rivalled them in popularity was Walker's *Elements of Elocution,* and the most used textbooks were those written by Porter.[4]

Although declamations, disputations, and training in rhetoric had been a part of the college program from the beginning, it was not until the nineteenth century that special chairs were endowed and speech training organized into different courses. Elocution, sometimes offered as a separate study, was often combined with the course in composition. At Amherst, in 1842-1843, a course was offered for Freshmen called *Elements of Orthoepy and Elocution* which was supplemented by weekly exercises in declamation and composition. At the same time, the University of Alabama was offering a course, *Elocution,* which included original compositions in Latin and English that were given publicly by the Freshmen every Wednesday. In 1861, Harvard gave a course entitled *Elocution* which included: Lessons in Orthoepy, Lessons in Expression, Lessons in Action, and Rhetorical Analysis and Reading. The Yale catalog for the same year describes a Sophomore course as *Elocution, Declamation,* and *Composition.*[5]

There was an interest in elocutionary training in the lower schools as well as in the colleges. William Russell, the first editor of the *American Journal of Education* (from 1826-1829) was particularly interested in the improvement of the "expressive faculties," regulated "by the laws of thought, as dictated by the sciences of *logic* and *grammar,* adorned by the graces of rhetoric." [6] Russell wrote many books to assist the teacher in the lower school. Some of the textbooks written by other elocutionists were shortened so that they could be used in the grammar schools; Porter's *Rhetorical Grammar* was one of of the most popular. In addition, there were innumerable "speakers" and "readers," consisting mainly of selections of poetry and prose but usually offering some elocutionary theory. The famous McGuffey readers gave credit to Walker for the elocutionary principles recommended to teacher and pupil.

Desire for education was rivalled only by the desire to be entertained. The theatre had broken through the puritanic prejudice by the end of the eighteenth century. In the first decades of the nineteenth century, the stars were usually English actors, but by mid-century native talent was recognized. The theatre circuit extended from Boston to New Orleans and on to California, and more than fifty established stock companies were scattered throughout the country in 1850. [7]

The professional readers were closely related to the theatre; most of them were actors who, when not playing in the theatre, gave programs of readings from Shakespeare or from well-known poets. This kind of entertainment was especially popular during Lent and was approved by many people who were still suspicious of the theatre as a form of entertainment. Anna Cora Mowatt, the author of *Fashion,* claims the distinction of being the first American woman to read professionally. After appearances in Boston and Providence, she appeared at Stuyvesant Institute, New York, on November 13, 1841, reading selections from Scott, Mrs. Hemans, Oliver Wendell Holmes, and Lord Byron. Shortly thereafter, there were six women elocutionists who were giving programs throughout the country. [8] Among the actors, Edwin Forrest, Edwin Booth, George Vanderhoff, and James E. Murdoch were popular readers.

During this early period in the development of elocution in America, the teacher was often an itinerant who gave lectures and programs of readings in addition to his work as an instructor. He often gave private lessons in several educational institutions in an area. Sometimes he set up his own private school of elocution.

The School of Practical Rhetoric and Oratory, organized by Russell and Murdoch, was one of the first private schools. Andrew Comstock was operating his Vocal and Polyglot Gymnasium in Philadelphia at about the same time. The National School of Elocution and Oratory was established by J. W. Shoemaker in Philadelphia in 1866. By the end of the century, the professional school had developed into an institution of importance. Four of the largest and best known schools were developed in the last quarter of the century: the School of Expression which later became Curry College, Emerson College of Oratory, the Columbia School of Expression, and the Phillips School of Oratory. The first two were in Boston, the second two in Chicago.[9]

It seems clear that professional, educational, and cultural conditions were congenial to the development of elocution. To appreciate what the elocutionists were teaching their students, attention will now be focused on several of the principal figures in the movement. Rush, himself, is reserved for special study elsewhere in this volume. We shall be concerned chiefly with: Ebenezer Porter, James Barber, William Russell, James E. Murdoch, and Samuel Silas Curry. Barber and Murdoch were devoted to the Rush system; Porter and Curry were eclectic in their theories and methods, taking what they considered best from other elocutionists and adding ideas of their own. They were all sincere in their desire to improve the speaking and reading of the American people, and they were all interested in studying the vocal mechanism so that they might evolve methods of teaching which would follow the cues that they found in nature. It is true that they often labelled current methods as "mechanical" or "natural," and that there was variety in the systems followed, but the objectives of the leaders were pretty much the same. The followers were the ones, who, by misinterpretation and lack of serious study and appreciation, sometimes brought discredit upon the elocutionary movement.

II

As in England, the century before, the clergy were among the first to emphasize the need for training in elocution. Rev. Ebenezer Porter, Bartlett Professor of Sacred Rhetoric in Andover Seminary, was one of the pioneer teachers and textbook writers. He believed that the worst faults in elocution originated from a lack of feeling but recognized also the faults of diction, monotonous inflections, inappropriate stress, and timing. Since Walker's *Elements of Elocution* did not quite satisfy his needs as a teacher, he wrote his own textbook.[10] Porter, like Rush, was interested in developing a scientific basis for voice training. Yarbrough believes him to be the first teacher to consider speech from the point of view of anatomy and physiology.[11] His *Lectures on Eloquence* includes four chapters on these aspects of speech.

Porter divided the study of elocution into five parts: articulation, inflection, accent and emphasis, modulation, and action. His approach to the problem of improving the reading and speaking of the student was an analysis of the faults as they represented deviations from good conversational speech and a program of practice to substitute good habits for the undesirable ones. Porter believed that the student should be allowed to read without interruption in class exercises. When he had finished, the teacher pointed out the mistakes, demonstrated by reading the exercise correctly, then asked the student to repeat the parts that were not well done.[12]

In his discussion of articulation, Porter attributes defective sounds to bad organs, bad habits, or difficulties of production. He also suggests that there is a connection between the temperament of the reader and his articulation.

A sluggish action of the mind imparts a correspondent character to the action of the vocal organs, and makes speech only a succession of indolent, half-formed sounds, more resembling the muttering of a dream than clear articulation. . . . Excess of vivacity, on the other hand, or excess of sensibility, often produces a hasty, confused utterance.[13]

Like many of the early elocutionists, Porter was interested in promoting good health in connection with elocutionary training. He believed that the quantity or fullness of the voice depended upon the strength of the lungs and, in turn, believed that exercises in using the voice with as much force as possible would develop the lungs. Stammering he attributed to "some infidelity of the nervous temperament"; the cure depended upon improving the bodily health as a means of giving "firmness to the nervous system." [14]

Although Porter attempted to follow Walker, he was really closer to Sheridan and other English elocutionists who placed understanding and feeling ahead of rules. A preliminary training of the voice Porter considered necessary, but the most important part of effective delivery was the emotional sincerity of the speaker:

After getting command of the voice, the great point to be steadily kept in view, is to apply the principles of emphasis and inflection, just as nature and sentiment demand. In respect to those principles of modulation, in which the power of delivery so essentially consists, we should always remember too that, as no theory of passions can teach a man to be pathetic, so no description that can be given of the inflection, emphasis, and tones, which accompany emotion, can impart this emotion, or be a substitute for it.[15]

Porter used notations for inflectional changes and to indicate modulation.[16] However, any system for the representation of sound he felt to be inadequate without the aid of the teacher's voice. The examples used were colloquial in order to encourage the reader to use conversational tones which, "being conformed to nature," were instinctively right: [17]

In contending with any bad habit of voice, let him break up the sentence on which the difficulty occurs, and throw it, if possible, into colloquial form. Let him observe in himself and others, the turns of voice which occur in speaking, familiarly and earnestly, on common occasions. Good taste will then enable him to transfer to public delivery the same turns of voice, adapting them, as he must of necessity, to the elevation of his subject.[18]

According to Porter, modulation, or variety in pitch and quantity, and inflection must conform to the sense of the material. The pitch of the voice, Porter says, should be "the middle key or that which we spontaneously adopt in earnest conversation."[19]

Porter uses the terms *emphatic stress* (including time and loudness) and *emphatic inflection,* to indicate methods of pointing up an idea or intensifying an emotion. The principle of emphatic stress, he explains, is that "it falls on a particular word, not chiefly because that word belongs to one class or another in grammar, but because, in the present case, it is important to *sense.*"

Teachers of elocution were interested in action as well as voice; many of them used the mechanical system presented in Austin's *Chironomia,* at least as a starting place. Barber states that his *Practical Treatise on Gesture* is abstracted chiefly from *Chironomia.* Russell gives credit to this source but says that he adapted the exercises to his own methods.[20] Porter in his discussion of action in terms of gesture, attitude, and expression of countenance, speaks of two extremes which should be avoided. The first encumbers the speaker with so much technical regulation that he becomes affected and mechanical in manner; the other condenses all precepts and preparatory practice into the advice, "Be natural." His attitude toward this aspect of elocution is as follows: "The body is the instrument of the soul, the medium of expressing internal emotions by external signs. The less these signs depend upon the will, on usage, or on accident, the more uniform are they, and the more certainly to be relied on." All bodily movement, he thought, should be spontaneous and reflect the speaker's mental and emotional reactions to the material.[21]

Ebenezer Porter, according to his associates in Andover Theological Seminary, was an outstanding person—an able teacher, writer, and minister. As a teacher he excelled in pointing out with precision faults in composition, enunciation, and gesticulation, and in prescribing correctives.[22] According to Rowe, he had an attractive personality and was always kindly in his class criticisms of the "crude homiletical achievements."[23]

In the *History of Andover Theological Seminary,* Dr. Porter is commended highly for his work. In 1827, he was selected by his colleagues to be the first president of the Seminary. He continued his work as professor of rhetoric until 1831; he was assisted by William Russell from 1828 to 1829, and from 1829 to 1831 by Jonathan Barber.[24]

Porter's skill in writing, no doubt, accounts in part for the popularity of his textbooks and the influence he exerted outside theological circles. In 1824, he published a pamphlet, *Analysis of Vocal Inflection as Applied in Reading and Speaking*. The textbook, *Analysis of the Principles of Rhetorical Delivery*, was published in 1827, and the shortened and simplified form designed for grammar schools, *The Rhetorical Reader*, in 1831. By 1843, it was used in the schools in every state of the Union. A new enlarged edition was published in 1848. As was stated earlier, Porter's textbooks were the most popular of the American books on elocution. Guthrie gives the following list of adoptions: Amherst 1827-1828, Brown 1826-1832, Dartmouth 1828-1840, Georgia 1844-1848, Gettysburg 1846-1849, Hampden-Sydney 1839-?, Middlebury 1828-1845, Mount Holyoke 1830-?, Wesleyan 1832-1849.[25] According to the review of the book in the *North American Review*, July, 1829, Porter's *Analysis of the Principles of Rhetorical Delivery* was the best of its kind.[26]

Ebenezer Porter contributed immeasurably to the growth of the elocutionary movement in the United States. He developed his own theories, based upon those of the English elocutionists, directed to the problems of teaching American students. He wrote in a clear precise style and attempted to select materials for reading which would develop a good conversational style. Although he was first of all a minister, he sought to improve American elocutionary training.

III

The attempt to make elocution scientific and to develop better methods of instruction led first to a study of the simplest elements, the vowel and consonant sounds, and to an emphasis upon the improvement of articulation as the beginning of all speech training. American speech may have been so careless that the need justified the great effort exerted to make students sound the "vocal elements" properly before attempting reading exercises. Barber was most emphatic in his belief that "Elocution should always attend to articulation, as the primary object; and in the first instance, it should be prosecuted alone, as a distinct branch of the art, and prosecuted until perfection in it is attained." According to Barber's *Grammar of Elocution*, there were forty-six vocal elements which depended upon certain definite positions of the organs of speech —seventeen vowels and twenty-nine consonants.[27]

In the preface to the second edition of *Philosophy of the Human Voice*, Dr. Rush states that Jonathan Barber was the first teacher to use his system of elocution. By appointing Dr. Barber to its department of elocution, Harvard became the first chartered institution that gave "influential and responsible approbation of the work." [28] Barber was an English physician who had devoted himself to elocution even before meeting Dr. Rush. He had published books of readings and recitations, and manuals for pronunciation and gesture earlier, but his most important textbooks were written when he was teaching at Yale, Harvard, and Andover Seminary. *A Grammar of Elocution* was published in 1830, and the simplified edition designed for the common schools titled, *An Introduction to the Grammar of Elocution,* in 1834. These two books rested heavily upon the theories of Rush, but credit was also given to Steele for theories concerning melody, and to Austin for those on gesture.

Barber undoubtedly developed his own methods of teaching but used Rush's terminology and based his course of training on the principles set forth in *The Philosophy of the Human Voice.* It has been mentioned that Barber emphasized training in articulation; he provided tables of the vocal elements and many exercises to be used in the practice of vowel and consonant sounds and their combinations. He believed that practice in unison, no matter how large the class, was a very effective way of teaching. "When time allows," he says, "it may be well for single scholars in turn to follow the teacher's voice, before the class make an attempt together; but the final concerted movement ought never to be dispensed with." When the class progressed to the study of sentences, they analyzed the sentence and decided upon the intonation which the idea demanded and then repeated it together.

Murdoch records that the students sometimes rebelled against the long period of practice on the elementary sounds which Barber required. However, Wendell Phillips testified that he had gained much from his class at Harvard. "Whatever I have acquired in the art of improving and managing my voice," he says, "I owe to Dr. Barber's system, suggestions, and lessons. No volume or treatise on the voice except those of Rush and Barber has ever been of any practical value to me." [29]

The following analysis of the pronunciation of the word *man* will give some idea of the meticulous way in which Barber worked:

In pronouncing the word MAN the lips are first intentionally brought together and pressed in a certain way against each other, and air being at the same time forcibly impelled from the throat, a sound is heard which somewhat resembles the lowing of an ox. The lips which before were held in somewhat forcible contact are now separated, the mouth is opened and its cavity is put into a particular shape; and air being again impelled from the throat during this position of the mouth, the sound A is heard as that letter is pronounced in the word *a-t.* Finally this last sound being completed, the tip of the tongue is carried upwards from the lower part of the mouth, and air issuing from the throat in a forcible manner during this state of the parts, the peculiar sound appropriate to the letter N is heard. In order to obtain a *demonstration* of the particulars of this description, let the word MAN be pronounced in a drawling manner, and let the process of articulation be carefully attended to during its continuance. Let the position which the lips first adopt be maintained for some time while the murmur, by which the sound M is produced, is continued from the throat; avoiding at the same time to proceed to sound A: then ceasing to sound the M, let the A be next sounded alone, observing the particular shape which the mouth assumes during the sound, as well as the character of the sound itself: after this stop again, and whilst the tip of the tongue is pressed against the roof of the mouth and the upper gums, let the N be slowly murmured through the organs. After the three sounds of the word have thus been separately pronounced, let MAN be slowly uttered, so that each separate sound and the coalescence of them with each other, may be distinctly perceived at the same time.[30]

English elocutionists, Walker, Sheridan, and Steele, were all interested in the study of sounds and of pronunciation, and in the explanation of the rhythms of prosody. Haberman states that they laid the foundation for the later development of speech therapy, voice training, and phonetics.[31] The early American elocutionists usually acknowledged their debt to these men and often used their theories and notations. Barber used Steele's notations for time and stress in *Exercises in Reading and Recitation,* and in the selections of poetry and prose in the *Grammar of Elocution.*[32]

Barber, for example, made an attempt in his later writings to explain the rhythm of speech in terms of the vocal mechanism and its adjustments for speaking. He felt that the speaker in following the rhythm of respiration would find it necessary to pause more often than punctuation indicated. A measure in speech he defined as a heavy or accented portion of a syllabic sound and a light and unaccented portion which were produced in one effect by the organ of the voice. "The larynx," he explains, "is a compound organ. It performs the function of an air tube and of a musical instrument. The first is essential to respiration, the second to speech. . . . In the production of all immediately consecutive sounds the larynx acts by alternate pulsations and remission. On this account, two heavy or accented syllables cannot be alternated with each other while a heavy and light one can." [33]

Although Barber put great emphasis upon practice of individual sounds and exercises, he stated that an effective elocutionary training could not depend upon a multiplicity of rules, and indicated that he was not in favor of Walker's rules for inflection based upon grammatical construction.[34] He believed that Dr. Rush had succeeded in making elocution a scientific study because he had described the functions of the voice and "listened to Nature as few ears have listened." He defended the system against criticisms that it was mechanical by saying that it showed the student the natural way of speaking effectively. In a pamphlet in which he criticized the review of Rush's book which appeared in the *North American Review,* he asks: "But is natural speaking any other than a right use of the functions of the voice?" [35]

IV

There were many elocutionists in this early period who were devotees of Rush and tried, as Barber did, to make his theories practical. Often they gave credit to the English elocutionists, but their interest and pride in the American scientist who had given them a physiological basis upon which to develop their methods was always evident. A few of the outstanding followers of Rush were: Merritt Caldwell, Andrew Comstock, Henry N. Day, Samuel Gummere, Dr. E. D. North, James E. Murdoch, William Russell, and George Vanderhoff.[36] They represented the fields of medicine, education, and the theatre.

William Russell taught in a variety of different schools, including Yale, Harvard, Princeton, Andover Seminary, Boston Public Latin School, and Abbott Female Seminary. He lectured in teachers' institutes all over New England and established a seminary for teachers in New Hampshire. Russell became the first editor of the *American Journal of Education* in 1826. In 1828 he assisted Dr. Porter, and again, from 1842 to 1844, he taught in Andover Theological Seminary and in the Theological Institute in East Windsor, Connecticut. In 1844 he established the School of Practical Rhetoric and Oratory with James E. Murdoch.[37]

Russell was a leader in education and wrote altogether some thirty books, sixteen of them concerned with elocution. Murdoch was an actor and reader, and together they made a good combination, the one interested primarily in improving the methods of teaching in the schools and the other in improving the public performances of speakers, readers, and actors. They were both indebted to Rush and Austin for much of their elocutionary theory, although Russell mentions Walker, especially in his early writings; and Murdoch discusses the contributions of Steele and Walker in his *Plea for the Spoken Language.* Their chief contribution is found in *Orthophony* which was written while they were working together in the school.

Russell believed that the elocutionary training should start in the lower schools. The methods that were most commonly used he thought were too literal and mechanical. "In many schools," he says, "the young pupil never has his attention called, definitely or consciously, to the fact that the letters of the alphabet are *phonetic* characters, the whole value of which consists in the *sounds* which they represent; in many, he may pass through the whole course of instruction without being once called to practice the constituent elementary sounds of his own language; in very many, there is no attempt made to exercise and develop, modify, or cultivate, in any form, the voice itself." Russell criticized also the mechanical pronunciation of words without any interpretation of the meaning of the content read. Even with quite small children, he felt that time should be spent in analyzing the meaning and pointing out the significant words.[38]

Russell was convinced that elocution should be a part of educational training but thought that it was usually taught very badly. He describes the two extremes in bad instruction in the following manner:

We have, in our current modes of instruction, little choice between the faults of style arising from what the indolent incline to term "a generous neglect" through fear of "spoiling" what they claim as "nature," and those faults, on the other hand, which are attributable to literal and mechanical modes of cultivation, and consist in the obtrusion of arbitrary details and artificial forms. Hence the results which characterize the one, in the gross errors of slovenly and low habit, coarse and disgusting manner, uncouth effect, bawling vehemence, and gesticulating violence, of what is sometimes dignified with the name of "popular oratory"; and hence the opposite traits of finical taste, affected elegance, false refinement, and studied contrivances of effect, which belong to perverted culture.[39]

Every teacher must have reasons for correcting the emphasis, the inflections, and pauses which a student uses in reading—these reasons, according to Russell, are the rules.[40]

Elocution, in the late forties, had developed to the stage of opposing theorists. It was not enough to convince educators that there was a need for elocutionary training, but it was also necessary to defend the methods used in teaching. Whately believed that rules vitiated style and insisted that nature could be depended upon to produce effective speech if the speaker or reader understood and was emotionally responsive to the content itself. Russell placed Whately in the group of extremists who did not believe in cultivation of the voice and says of him: "A true and efficient friend of education, in other respects, thus sides with the opponents of culture, by speaking from the preferences of personal taste and arbitrary opinion, instead of the laws of analogy and universal truth." [41] Russell believed the rules he used to be the "truest forms of nature embodied in practice."

Around the middle of the century, a kind of touchiness and "on the defensive" attitude is noticeable. The itinerant teacher was not always welcomed as he had been earlier. Russell was not allowed to continue teaching at Harvard; he was cordially received in 1825, but twenty years later was denied the privilege of teaching a class in elocution.[42]

Murdoch attributes the failure of their school in Boston to an announcement made in the high schools barring boys trained in private schools
from entering the declamation contests.[43] Rush and his followers were
disappointed that his system had not caught on as generally as they had
predicted.

The elocutionary movement, which had moved so rapidly, and perhaps faddishly, in the first part of the century, was beginning to meet
antagonism in academic circles. It was becoming too much the performer's art and did not meet the needs of the students who were being
trained for the professions of law and the ministry.

V

James E. Murdoch may be said to represent that phase of elocutionary training which was concerned with the training of public entertainers—readers and actors. However, he did not restrict his work to
the stage but devoted much of his time to teaching and lecturing. Murdoch was a devotee of the Rush system throughout his life. Although
he met Dr. Rush when his theories were first introduced, his interest
did not develop until advised by Edwin Forrest, the leading actor of
the day, to consult Rush for proper methods to improve the quality of
his voice. Murdoch records that he became intimately acquainted with
Dr. Rush, and received "rather in the capacity of a friend than of a
professional teacher, a practical exposition of the underlying principles
of his 'Philosophy of the Human Voice'. . . ." [44] In Murdoch's textbook,
Analytic Elocution, published in 1884, he affirms his earlier conclusions: that training the voice was the most important part of elocution,
that the speaking voice may be developed in the same strength, beauty,
and flexibility as the singing voice, and that the *Philosophy of the
Human Voice* set forth the most complete system of vocal training.
Murdoch was a leader in the elocutionary movement for fifty years.

As an actor, Murdoch toured the country from Boston to San Francisco. He appeared with the leading actors of the day, Edwin Booth,
Edwin Forrest, and Fanny Kemble. According to his critics, he lacked
the fire of Forrest or Booth and was never a favorite in tragedy although
he excelled in comedy. *The New York Herald* for September 8, 1857,
probably analyzed his acting accurately in the following criticism:
"Every scene bears marks of careful study, and is elaborated to the mi-
nutest details. . . . Nothing is slurred over, nothing is overdone. . . . But
this is all. With great natural and acquired advantages Mr. Murdoch is
not a genius. He lacks the art that conceals art and is without that happy
inspiration that gives life to the creation." [45]

It is also possible that Murdoch's career as an actor was not altogether satisfactory to him and that he sought to supplement it through teaching and lecturing. His health was not good and occasionally, as in England, he was forced to cancel engagements. The fact is that he retired from the stage from time to time and devoted himself whole-heartedly to advancing the Rush system of elocution and to giving lectures and readings. He became a very popular reader during the Civil War. As soon as he heard that his favorite son had joined the Army, he closed his engagement in the theatre in Pittsburgh and went to Washington. He gave patriotic readings in the hospitals to entertain the soldiers, in both houses of Congress to inspire patriotism, and in many Northern cities as benefit performances to raise money for the hospital fund. Odell records programs of Shakespearian readings given by Murdoch in New York as early as 1845, again in 1872 when he read in the Tabernacle and brought to the program something of the "stateliness of the old school," and as late as 1883.[46]

During the latter part of his life, Murdoch spent most of his time on his farm in Ohio, yet he participated in a Shakespearian Festival in Cincinnati Music Hall in 1883, playing Marc Antony and Hamlet. According to the *Cincinnati Commercial Gazette*, Mr. Murdoch could be heard easily and his voice had the "same ring as of yore." [47] On May 22, 1889, Murdoch played Charles Surface to Mrs. John Drew's Lady Teazle in a benefit performance of *School for Scandal* given "by the citizens of Philadelphia to their representative actor." Mrs. Drew in her autobiography testifies to his ability as an actor and to his charm as a man. She says that he never imitated Forrest but was always himself "which was rare in an American actor of that time." [48]

Murdoch believed in training the voice but not according to such arbitrary rules and prescribed grooves that the individual's characteristic speech was changed to imitate that of the teacher. In *The Stage or Recollections of Actors and Acting*, written after fifty years of experience, he deplored the neglect of training for actors:

A century ago elocution of a declamatory style was the prevailing dramatic tone, but yielding to the changes of fashion, it gradually assumed the form of what was termed natural speech; which in its turn, at the dictate of novelty became eccentric, and however paradoxical it may appear, unnatural. Of late years the elocution of the English and American stage, with but few exceptions, has been, no matter how offensive the term may be considered, rather a matter of instinct than the result of intelligent vocal culture.[49]

In *Analytic Elocution,* Murdoch defines elocution as "the art of so employing the Quality, Pitch, Force, Time, and Abruptness of the voice as to convey the sense, sentiment, and passion of composition or discourse in the fullest and most natural manner, and at the same time with the greatest possible gratification to the ear." [50] The student, according to Murdoch, should first learn to control the vocal mechanism and then to master the vocal elements.

Although Murdoch did not publish any books until between 1880-1884, most of his elocutionary theory had appeared earlier in *Orthophony* which, according to the preface, derived from the Rush system and presented the "vocal gymnastics" used by Murdoch in his teaching. Both *Orthophony* and *Analytic Elocution* present the theories of Dr. Rush in a simple, readable style. The innovations and additions which can be credited to Russell and Murdoch indicate greater precision and accuracy in isolating the sounds of the language and an awareness of the necessity of fitting the methods to the student and his needs. The following example shows their attention to the study of speech sounds:

ai, in *air*, though not recognized by Dr. Rush, nor by any other writers on elocution, as a separate element from *a*, in *ale*, is obviously a distinct sound, approaching to that of *e*, in *end*, but not forming so close a sound to the ear. . . . *o*, in *or*, and *o*, in *on*, are apparently considered by Dr. Rush and by Walker, as modifications of *a*, as in *all*. Admitting, however, the identity of quality in these elements, their obvious difference in quantity, and in the position and pressure of the muscles by which, as sounds, they are formed, together with the precision and correctness of articulation demand a separate place for them in the elementary exercises.

Further observation indicated the *a* sounds in *awe, all, arm,* and *an* were not diphthongal as Rush believed. The final *r* was distinguished from the initial *r* which was a harder sound, "executed by a forcible but brief vibration of the tip of the tongue against the first projecting ridge of the interior gum, immediately above the upper teeth." The list of the elementary sounds as given in *Orthophony* is very similar to our present classifications: oral and laryngeal sounds, a-ll, a-rm, e-ve, oo-ze, e-rr, e-nd, i-n, ai-r, u-p, o-r, o-n, a-le, i-ce, o-ld, ou-r, oi-l, u-se; labial sounds, b-a-be, p-i-pe, m-ai-m, w-oe, v-al-ve, f-i-fe; palatic sounds, c-a-ke, g-ag, y-e; dental sounds, d-i-d, t-en-t, th-in, th-ine, a-z-ure, pu-sh, cea-se, z-one, j-oy, ch-ur-ch; aspirate sounds, h-e; nasal sounds, n-u-n, s-ing, i-n-k; lingual sounds, l-u-ll, r-ap, fa-r. Although *m* is not listed as a nasal, the description of the sound indicates that Murdoch and Russell were aware of its nasal quality: "The 'subtonic' *m* is articulated by a very gentle compression of the lips, attended by a murmur in the head and chest, resembling somewhat that which forms the character of the 'subtonic' *b*, but differing from it in the sound being accompanied by a free, steady equable 'expiration' through the nostrils." [51]

The consideration of the quality of the voice was important to the early elocutionists. The "improved" quality designated by Dr. Rush as *orotund* was considered most desirable. Rush describes this quality as "sub-sonorous" and states that it was rarely heard in ordinary speech and never in its highest excellence except when cultivated. Other qualities which were heard in speaking and were useful especially in reading and acting were: *whispering, guttural, natural,* and *falsetto.*[52] *Pectoral, nasal,* and *oral* were terms used to describe the excess of a particular kind of resonance.[53]

Of all the teachers thus far mentioned, Murdoch was the one most interested in quality as an aspect of speech. He was eager to improve the quality of his own speech so that he could successfully interpret roles in both comedy and tragedy. As a result of this interest, he analyzed the voices of the actors he knew and observed many interesting vocal characteristics. For example, he observed in some voices a "vocal catch in the glottis." He attributes this peculiarity of speech to English actors, specifically Garrick, who may have imitated King George III, and was in turn imitated by Kean whose speech was then copied by McCready and Forrest. He describes it as follows:

> ... a sudden catch of the glottis, which causes a short cough-like sound, to be heard previous to the articulative movement of the voice. ... This peculiar organic act is the result of a dropping of the jaw and consequent depression of the larynx; it gives strength to the muscles which are called into play and control the organs of vocality, thus enabling the speaker to execute that abrupt movement by which he expels the vowel-sound from what may be called the cavernous parts of the mouth, that space which includes the roots of the tongue, the glottis, and pharynx. This deeply-aspirated quality of the voice is a strong element of expressive utterance of passionate language in the drama.[54]

The description suggests the characteristic of the voice which Rush termed *abruptness,* a term obviously devised to describe the stage speech then in vogue but later discarded.

Murdoch saw a close relationship between breath control and vocal quality. He explained very clearly the action of the diaphragm as "the bellows of the vocal organs," and used the terms *effusive, expulsive,* and *explosive* to designate the three forms of expiration. "The effusive breath may be said to *flow,* the expulsive to *rush,* and the explosive to *burst* into the outer air. These three forms of breathing, it will be found, when converted into vocality, represent the three forms which language assumes in its varied utterance from tranquility to passion." [55]

In *A Plea for Spoken Language,* published in 1883, and based on the lectures which Murdoch had given on elocution, he states that although elocutionists through a period of fifty years were indebted to Rush, his principles had never been accepted entirely, and hence there had been no uniformity of result. He speaks also of the "too prevalent idea on the part of school authorities that elocution, as a special study, is inexpedient; or worse that it cannot be successfully taught in connection with the multifarious studies of the schools." [56] Nevertheless, Murdoch and his co-worker, William Russell, did much to popularize the Rush system, and their influence on the development of the elocutionary movement itself is immeasurable. They were convinced that methods of teaching which were based on scientific principles were in accord with nature and, therefore, would allow the student to develop his own characteristic speech and develop it to its maximum capacity.

VI

The School of Expression, incorporated in 1888, is a fine example of a nineteenth-century private school which is alive today. Its founder, Samuel Silas Curry, through study and practice, evolved a philosophy of elocution which had a firm basis in psychology. Although he attempted to reconcile theories of elocution which seem to be contradictory, he did succeed in establishing a practical and effective method of teaching, usually known as the "think-the-thought" method.

Dr. Curry was born in 1847 in the mountains of Tennessee. He was reared in a strict, religious home and encouraged to prepare for the ministry. Following the usual pattern of education for the ministry, he studied elocution along with theology. Since Boston University was Curry's choice for his theological training, he began the study of elocution in the School of Oratory under Lewis B. Monroe, a student of Delsarte. In 1873, Dr. Alexander Graham Bell's opening lecture at the School of Oratory stimulated such an interest in the science of the voice that Curry decided to become a teacher instead of a preacher. When Dean Monroe died in 1879, Curry, who had completed his Master's degree the year before, was asked to carry on the work. In 1880, the University conferred the Ph.D. degree upon him; in 1883 he was made Snow Professor of Oratory, and in this capacity organized special classes in elocution. Five years later, the trustees allowed him to organize the institution which was called the School of Expression. Mrs. Curry, former teacher and student under Monroe, taught with him and together they made the school one of the most popular in the country. Very soon the School of Expression offered three years of training and an additional postgraduate year. Special courses were given for clergymen, teachers, and people with speech defects such as stammering.[57] Many talented students attended the School of Expression; not a small number were leaders in the reinstatement of speech in the college and university curriculum in the early part of the twentieth century.

Of the elocutionists studied, Curry was perhaps the one most eager to know all there was to be known about the functioning of the vocal mechanism and to find the best methods of teaching students to use speech effectively. He was not satisfied with any method then in use in the teaching of delivery. He sampled them all, studying with many teachers at home and abroad. In England, he studied with Emil Behnke and Lenox Brown; in France, he took lessons from Regnier, head of the National School of Acting; and in Italy he studied with Francesco Lamperti, professor of singing at the Milan Conservatory. Although he was critical of the theories of Delsarte, Curry states that he studied with all the known teachers of that system. In the United States, he studied with the following: Steele MacKaye, Alexander Graham Bell, Alexander Melville Bell, and, of course, Lewis B. Monroe.[58]

Because he had been exposed to so many different kinds of instruction, Curry's theories were eclectic and his writing often ambiguous. Altogether, Curry wrote fourteen books. *Province of Expression* and *Foundations of Expression,* published in 1891 and 1907,[59] set forth his philosophy as clearly as any of his writings. There is much repetition and elaboration of idea in all of them. Although little credit is given to the contemporary psychologists, their influence is marked. Curry's greatest emphasis was upon an active, trained mind and imagination. The necessity of working "within outward," of being a unified person in which the mind stimulated the body to natural expression, and the recognition of individual differences were all tenets of the Curry school. There was something of the crusader about Dr. Curry. He recognized the weakness of elocutionary training as he observed it in the late nineteenth century and he proposed to reform it. He articulated the principle that elocution should be primarily a training of the mind and the development of an ability to think creatively.

Curry gave credit to Rush for laying the scientific foundation for the study of the voice but contended that at least half of his system was useless. Rush made no distinction between the normal and abnormal, he said, and did not distinguish between the intentions of nature and what was merely a bad habit:

Still he did analyze correctly the length of inflections, and while his "shock of the glottis" is wrong and has been given up by the best teachers, yet that there is a stress in the speaking voice, a radical and vanish different from the singing voice, was clearly shown by him. Teaching, as he did, the importance of analyzing into its fundamental nature the speaking voice, the special incorrect physical action in faults has been found and a more radical treatment of defects made possible. The elements of melody having been partly explained, men have been set to observe more carefully the phenomena of speech; so that Rush's system has indirectly rendered important service in unfolding knowledge which must be understood in improving delivery.[60]

The followers of Rush used teaching methods which Curry found to be too unrepresentative and imitative. Some of the faults he found most distressing and contradictory to nature were: all action was merely gesture, grammatical structure dictated pauses and often inflections, and delivery revealed a lack of freedom and originality. Curry observed that mechanical methods had been tried and found wanting, most clergymen and actors having discarded the Rush system as too artificial and conventional. However, public readers, he stated, often exhibited all the undesirable characteristics of the student trained in this school. They showed no signs of "mental assimilation of the character," no indication of "dramatic instinct" but merely demonstrated elocutionary tricks of the throat which were "untrue to nature." [61]

Murdoch is mentioned by Curry as a good example of the mechanical school which was based upon Rush principles. Curry criticized him because he put too much emphasis upon the voice and because he concerned himself with the artificial tones: orotund, guttural, and aspirate. Examples are taken from Murdoch's textbook, *Analytic Elocution,* to illustrate the methods to which Curry objected. Murdoch's direction for reading the line, "Come back, come back, Horatius," states that it must be read with a rising, discreet third. According to Curry, the sentence could be read in fifty different ways but the one chosen is the most foreign to the meaning. "It could only be read so," he says, "when a man is trying to carry out a 'system' which is to him greater than nature." [62]

From a close study of Murdoch's theories of elocution, it is obvious that he too was interested in following nature. He was devoted to the Rush system not because of its mechanical aspects, but because he thought it gave him a firm scientific base from which to work to develop a natural delivery.

Curry did not approve of Whately's method and stated that the purely natural method could not work unless the student had normal speech. Whately's influence was detrimental to good speaking, according to Curry, and had encouraged the speaker to follow wild impulses thus "reducing all oratorical delivery to chaos." The indirect results of Whately's work, however, Curry thought helpful because he criticized the artificial methods and emphasized the importance of not placing the mind on "mere modes of delivery." [63]

The Delsarte System, Curry characterized as too artificial and speculative: it was not founded upon nature but was an attempt to "place upon nature a pre-conceived artificial conception." Whereas Murdoch held that pantomime should be in the background so that the voice could predominate, Curry states that Delsarte gave pantomime the most important place. "Neither is right," says Curry. "The great center of consciousness must be upon thought and action of the mind, and these two natural languages voice and action having a great element of spontaneity, must not be brought too much into the foreground of consciousness." [64]

On the other hand, Curry praised Delsarte as the most original investigator of the century and listed those parts of his theory which he had found helpful in evolving his own philosophy of speech. He makes special mention of: the preliminary training or the attuning of the whole body, the fact that Delsartian methods were always based upon principles, the belief that pantomime belonged to the whole body and was not restricted to gesture, and finally, the theory that there is an interrelationship of "co-existent and co-essential elements." [65]

Because of the association of the word *elocution* with the training and theories Curry found unsatisfactory, he used the word *expression* instead. To him it was a much bigger and more meaningful word. One cannot help wishing that he might have reinstated the original word *elocution* with its proper connotation. Yet the word *expression* he did use in a special way to indicate his philosophy of speech training. He defines it thus: "Expression implies cause, means, and effect. It is a natural effect of a natural cause, and hence is governed by all the laws of nature's processes. The cause is in the mind, the means are the voice and the body." [66]

From his wide background of experience, Curry articulated a philosophy of speech which resembled that of the first teacher mentioned, Ebenezer Porter. But because of his vantage point in the century, he was able to go beyond any of the others in charting methods of instruction which would be effective. His methods were eclectic and represented a culmination of the work of many conscientious, enthusiastic, and progressive elocutionists. Curry's belief that man must function as a unified whole made it impossible in good delivery for the voice to overbalance the action, or for the outward expression to be detached from the mental analysis of the material to be read. Communicating one's thoughts and feelings implied for Curry merely the deepening of natural processes. Following James' psychology, he stated that thinking consisted of first, concentration upon one point, and second, a leap of the mind to another point. Thus the need for training in making transitions and in using the pause effectively. [67]

While all of the older elocutionists mentioned in this chapter stressed the need for thought and feeling in the interpretation of literature, Curry was the first one to devise exercises for mental training as a necessary part of the teaching program. Training the mind, according to Curry, should supersede training of the voice and body.

Curry believed in a three-way interactionism between mind, voice, and body. Voice and action, he often reiterated, must not be left to accident but be developed into a flexible mechanism which will adequately express the mind or soul of the speaker. *Vocal training* he carefully distinguished from *vocal expression* as the "establishment of normal conditions of the body and voice." As did many of the earlier teachers, Curry placed great emphasis upon proper breathing and breathing exercises. He also advocated the use of exclamations for practice because they were closely associated with action and spontaneously established natural conditions of speaking and breathing.[68]

Training of the body as a whole was one of Curry's principles. According to his students, he devoted some time to gymnastic exercises of Delsartian design. The "decomposing exercises" were to relax the muscles so that the body could be organized around a center. The principle of functioning as a whole was never disregarded, and the exercises were always considered merely practice to enable the speaker to respond naturally and normally to mental stimulation.[69]

In vocal training, the term *tone-color* was used often by Curry; he considered it very important and difficult to attain. He defines it in *Foundations of Expression* as "the modulation of the overtones of the human voice by imagination and feeling." To discover the presence of tone-color, Curry suggests that the student read two very different passages—one didactic, the other imaginative and sympathetic. The difference in the voice—its pitch, pause, inflection, and especially its quality—gives the reading tone-color.[70]

Curry set very high requirements for the teacher—he must inspire his students as well as train them. The teacher of expression should be an educated man, he maintained, because he must be able to "penetrate the deepest needs of his students"; he must also understand "the effect upon the personality of all subjects." [71] His breadth of culture must be practical—not only scientific but literary and artistic as well. Without a love of art and literature, Curry felt it would be impossible for the teacher to inspire his students and stimulate the creative faculties of their minds. From all evaluations of his work, Curry seems to have measured up well to his own criteria.

VII

The nineteenth-century elocutionists made significant contributions to the field of speech education. As a group, they showed an amazing amount of vitality and originality. As teachers and theorists they fitted into the pattern of education which responded to the increased interest in science, emphasizing first the physiological and later the psychological aspect of speech. Because of their efforts, elocution became a part of the educational plan which enlarged the program to include practice in writing and speaking English in addition to similar courses in the classical languages. Later in the century, when, because of its tendency to become artificial and exhibitionary, it lost its place in the curricula of many of the institutions of higher learning, the study of elocution was fostered in private schools by teachers like Samuel Silas Curry.

Although some elocutionists declared the subject to be distinct from the study of rhetoric and more closely related to science than to any other subject, rhetoricians emphasized delivery during this century as an integral part of speech-making. The orator, lawyer, minister, and actor were all concerned with and characterized by their manner of speaking. Since the speech of the average American was indistinctly articulated and his taste in public speakers demanded a kind of exaggerated and florid quality, there was a great demand, especially during the first half of the nineteenth century, for elocutionary training in both the lower schools and the colleges. Many of the teachers of elocution were not on the regular faculties of these institutions but were itinerant teachers. Often they established themselves in a community and gave lessons in a number of schools in the area; sometimes they started private schools of speech. From their writings, it appears that they were interested in developing a science of speech, in correcting speech defects, in isolating the speech sounds, and in developing skills in reading and speaking. Later teachers have produced more specialized books in these same areas, but the early textbook writers did the spade work for the specialists.

The private schools multiplied during the century. Murdoch and Russell founded the School of Practical Rhetoric and Oratory (one of the first) in 1844, in Boston. Later the same city was to boast three of the best-known schools: the School of Expression, Emerson College of Oratory, and the Leland Powers School. Charles Wesley Emerson founded his school in 1891. He based his methods of vocal training upon the four stages of the natural development of the mind: the colossal, the melodramatic, the realistic, and the suggestive. Delsarte's methods were used in training the body. Leland Powers was a student of Dr. Curry and subscribed to his methods of teaching. In Chicago there were three equally famous schools: Phillips School of Oratory, Columbia School of Expression, and the School of Speech of Northwestern University founded by Robert McLean Cumnock. Arthur E. Phillips was famous for his use of *natural* or *tone* drills—a method based upon the value of paraphrasing for a clearer understanding of the material read. Mention should also be made of the Byron King School of Oratory in Pittsburgh, Pennsylvania, which was established in 1888. All these schools deserve special credit for carrying on the study of elocution and other phases of speech training when the educational institutions took little responsibility for this kind of education.

Porter, Barber, Russell, Murdoch, and Curry were leaders in the movement to make the study of vocal delivery an important part of education. They defined it as the use of voice and action to interpret ideas and emotions but were more interested in the development of the voice than in any other aspect of the speaking situation. Nevertheless, these teachers did not neglect the relationship of body to mind, and the importance of good health to the speaker.

Following the example of the English elocutionists and lexicographers, there was a definite emphasis upon individual speech sounds, and articulation exercises were the usual introduction to the study of elocution. There was a special emphasis on the analysis of vocal qualities which was not found in the teaching of elocution in England.

The early American elocutionists continued the study of inflection which had so engrossed the teachers and writers of the previous century; yet they did not follow the theory of Walker that inflection was always related to grammatical construction. The followers of Rush found inflectional changes similar to pitch changes in music and used many musical terms to describe the melody and cadences of speech. Notations that were used derived from musical notations and were similar to those used by Steele in *Prosodia Rationalis.*

The most influential elocutionists, if they can be selected according to the popularity of their textbooks, believed that elocutionary training depended upon rules, and did not agree with Whately that all rules were inimical to spontaneous and emotionally sensitive speaking and reading. They were aware of the two extremes in the theory of training and tried to stay between the two. The importance of understanding the content of the material and of feeling the emotion inherent in it, they all agreed, was of first importance, but the vocal mechanism must be so disciplined that it could respond properly.

Although the private school of elocution was destined to carry most of the responsibility for this kind of training in the latter part of the century, the teachers themselves transmitted the influence of the early elocutionists to twentieth-century speech education in America. For example, Thomas C. Trueblood, S. S. Hamill, Robert I. Fulton, and John R. Scott, who were pioneers in founding present-day speech departments, were all students of James E. Murdoch.[72] And over ten thousand students have studied in the Curry School, among them such famous teachers as: Lee Emerson Bassett, Smiley Blanton, Sara Stinchfield Hawk, Azubah Latham, and Gertrude Johnson.

The representative elocutionists considered in this chapter were agreed that an art must rest upon a science. Although they used different methods, they were all working to perfect a delivery that would reveal effectively thought and emotion. At the end of the century, because psychological inquiries had made mental processes clearer, the method of "thinking-the-thought" before reading became the most popular method. However, it is not the only one that persisted in twentieth-century teaching of delivery. Many of the theories, methods, and exercises which were advanced by the earlier elocutionists are to be found in modern textbooks.

Notes

1. Henry B. Parkes, *The American Experience* (New York, 1947), pp. 149, 187-188.

2. Henry Steele Comager, *The American Mind* (New Haven, 1950), p. 24.

3. Foster R. Dulles, *America Learns to Play* (New York, 1940), pp. 110-111.

4. Warren Guthrie, "The Development of Rhetorical Theory in America, 1635-1850," unpublished Ph.D. dissertation, Northwestern University, 1940, p. 244.

5. Thomas E. Coulton, "Trends in Speech Education in American Colleges 1835-1935," unpublished Ph.D. dissertation, New York University, 1935, pp. 70, 80.

6. William Russell, "Cultivation of the Expressive Faculties," *American Journal of Education*, III (1858), 58.

7. George R. MacMinn, *The Theatre of the Golden Era in California* (Caldwell, Ida., 1941), ch. I.

8. George C. D. Odell, *Annals of the New York Stage* (New York, 1928), IV, 586-587.

9. Mary Margaret Robb, *Oral Interpretation of Literature in American Colleges and Universities* (New York, 1941), pp. 131-132.

10. Ebenezer Porter, *Analysis of Principles of Rhetorical Delivery as Applied in Reading and Speaking* (Andover, 1836), p. 1.

11. R. Clyde Yarbrough, "Homiletical Theory and Practice of Ebenezer Porter," unpublished Ph.D. dissertation, University of Iowa, 1942, p. 140.

12. Porter, *Analysis*, p. vii.

13. *Ibid.*, pp. 23, 25.

14. *Ibid.*, pp. 109-110.

15. *Ibid.*, p. viii.

16. *Ibid.*, p. x.

17. Ebenezer Porter, *The Rhetorical Reader* (New York, 1835), pp. 28-38.

18. Porter, *Analysis*, p. 41.

19. *Ibid.*, pp. 93, 103.

20. Jonathan Barber, *Practical Treatise on Gesture* (Cambridge, 1831); William Russell, *American Elocutionist* (Boston, 1844), p. 200.

21. Porter, *Analysis*, pp. 144-147.

22. Lyman Matthews, *Memoir of the Life and Character of Ebenezer Porter, D.D.* (Boston, 1837), p. 254.

23. Henry K. Rowe, *History of Andover Theological Seminary* (Newton, Mass., 1933), p. 57.

24. General Catalogue of the Theological Seminary, Andover, Massachusetts, 1808-1908 (Boston, 1908), pp. 4, 20.

25. Guthrie, *op. cit.*, p. 200.

26. *North American Review*, XXIX (1829), 38-67.

27. Barber, *Grammar of Elocution* (New Haven, 1830), pp. 13, 19.

28. James Rush, *The Philosophy of the Human Voice* (Philadelphia, 1833), p. xlii.

29. James E. Murdoch, *A Plea for Spoken Language* (Cincinnati, 1883), p. 101.

30. Barber, *Grammar*, pp. 17-18.

31. Frederick W. Haberman, "The Elocutionary Movement in England, 1750-1850," unpublished Ph.D. dissertation, Cornell, 1947, p. 176.
32. Jonathan Barber, *Exercises in Reading and Recitation* (York, Pa., 1825).
33. Barber, *Grammar*, pp. 125-126.
34. *Ibid.*, p. 168.
35. Barber, *Strictures on Article II of the North American Review for July, 1829* (New Haven, 1829), p. 9.
36. Henry N. Day, *Art of Elocution* (New Haven, 1844); Samuel Gummere, *A Compendium of the Principles of Elocution on the Basis of Dr. Rush's Philosophy of the Human Voice* (Philadelphia, 1857); Dr. E. D. North, *Practical Speaking as Taught at Yale College* (New Haven, 1846); W. Russell and J. E. Murdoch, *Orthophony* (Boston, 1845); George Vanderhoff, *The Art of Elocution* (New York, 1847).
37. *Dictionary of American Biography* (New York, 1935) XVI, 250.
38. Russell, "Cultivation of the Expressive Qualities," Am. J. Ed., pp. 327-329.
39. *Ibid.*, pp. 332-333.
40. Russell, *American Elocutionist*, 4th ed. (Boston, 1846), p. 5.
41. See "Cultivation of the Expressive Faculties," Am. J. Ed., pp. 333-334; Richard Whately, *Elements of Rhetoric* (Boston, 1851); J. W. S. Hows, *Practical Elocutionist* (New York, 1849).
42. *Loc. cit.*
43. Murdoch, *Plea*, pp. 110-111.
44. *Ibid.*, pp. 106, 108, 109.
45. Odell, *Annals*, VII, 6; Roberta Fluitt White, "The Acting Career of James Edward Murdoch," unpublished Ph.D. dissertation, Louisiana State, 1945, p. 36.
46. Odell, *Annals*, V, 144; IX, 334-335; XII, 342.
47. White, pp. 105-108.
48. Mrs. John Drew, "Autobiographical Sketch of Mrs. John Drew," *Scribners* (November, 1899), XXVI, 566-568.
49. Murdoch, *Stage*, pp. 43, 45.
50. Murdoch, *Analytic Elocution* (Cincinnati, 1884), p. 11.
51. Russell, *Orthophony*, pp. 17-29.
52. Rush, *Philosophy*, p. 162.
53. Murdoch, *Analytic Elocution*, p. 10.
54. Murdoch, *Stage*, pp. 96-98.
55. Murdoch, *Analytic Elocution*, pp. 12, 21.
56. Murdoch, *Plea*, pp. 9, 12.
57. *Poems by S. S. Curry*, ed. Nathan Haskell Dole (Boston, 1922), pp. 1-2.
58. *Cyclopedia of American Biography*, X, 160-161.
59. Samuel Silas Curry, *Province of Expression* (Boston, 1891); *Foundations of Expression* (Boston, 1907).
60. Curry, *Province*, p. 325.
61. *Ibid.*, pp. 310-325.
62. *Ibid.*, p. 316.
63. *Ibid.*, pp. 333-334.
64. *Ibid.*, p. 350.
65. *Ibid.*, p. 358.
66. Samuel Silas Curry, *Lessons in Vocal Expression* (Boston, 1895), p. 310.
67. *Ibid.*, p. 19.
68. Curry, *Foundations*, p. 66.
69. M. Oclo Miller, "The Psychology of Dr. S. S. Curry as Revealed by His Attitude Toward the Mind-Body Problem," unpublished Ph.D. dissertation, University of Iowa, 1929, p. 41.
70. Curry, *Foundations*, p. 159.
71. Curry, *Province*, pp. 326, 418.
72. Thomas C. Trueblood, "A Chapter on the Organization of College Courses in Public Speaking," *Quarterly Journal of Speech Education*, XII (February, 1926), 3-4.

9 Steele MacKaye and the Delsartian Tradition

CLAUDE L. SHAVER

....

The work of François Delsarte, French teacher of vocal music and operatic acting in Paris from 1839 until 1871, was of great significance in speech training and the theatre in late nineteenth-century America. Although Delsarte was never in the United States and never published his theories in any form, the so-called "Delsarte System of Expression" was probably the most popular method of speech training in the United States during the thirty years from 1870 until 1900.

In spite of the popularity and prominence of the Delsarte system, no adequate formulation of its principles and practices was ever made and American teachers and actors were left largely in the dark regarding the basic principles of the system. Delsarte himself published nothing in his own name.

Many books and magazine articles were written during the thirty years of Delsarte's popularity, each purporting to present the "true" Delsarte system, yet none of these ever received the unqualified support of more than a few of those who called themselves "Delsartians." In the two decades from 1880 to 1900 the Delsarte system was a subject of perennial dispute, as witnessed by the large number of articles defending and attacking the system that appeared in *Werner's Magazine,* the leading speech publication of the period, and the numerous speeches pro and con as reported in the *Proceedings of the National Association of Elocutionists.*[1]

In the absence of any authoritative statement of the Delsarte system, it was inevitable that the system should be siezed upon, expanded and distorted to almost absurd lengths. Charles Bickford, writing in *The Voice,* commented:

Breathing exercises, as old as—well, as old as I am,—the Worcester and Webster "Key to Pronunciation," Guilmette contortions, light gymnastics, numerous systems of useful and ever popular calisthenics, Dr. Rush's theories, lessons from Murdoch and Russell, stage tricks and traditions which have been handed down for generations, and a thousand other things in heaven and earth not dreamt of in Delsarte's philosophy, have been tied on and sailed up on the tail of the dear old Frenchman's kite as if they belonged to it.[2]

The dilettantism which afflicted the system was well expressed by L. P. writing in "Letter Box" in *The Voice:*

I was interested in John Howard's remarks upon the Delsarte method, for I confess I do "leave the pages of the Delsarte method with a puzzled and dubious countenance," and wish that it could be simplified in some way. I have finally persuaded my husband to allow me to teach it as I enjoy the "art," and it is a great source of amusement to me, and so much more satisfactory than afternoon tea-parties or church-fairs.[3]

In commenting on the teaching of the Delsarte system at Chautauqua, New York, by Mrs. Emily Bishop, Elsie M. Wilbor wrote, "As presented there, the system is on a plane with the Swedish or any other purely gymnastic drill ... ," and commented later in the same article, "One point on which I take issue with Mrs. Bishop is her statement that Delsarte work reduces flesh, but will not make it. ..." [4] Here the Delsarte system had become a reducing method; the April, 1889, issue of *Werner's Voice Magazine* and several subsequent issues, carried an advertisement for "The Delsarte corset"!

In this welter of unauthorized books, misunderstandings, distortions, and quackeries, only one man was considered able to give an adequate formulation of Delsarte's principles. The man was Steele MacKaye, the man who had originally introduced the Delsarte theory to America. S. S. Curry wrote in 1891:

Mr. Steele MacKaye is thoroughly competent to give to the world an outline of the system of Delsarte, but he has allowed himself to be engrossed with other things, and neglected to give to the world an adequate presentation of the method of the master who so loved and honored him.[5]

This paper deals primarily with Steele MacKaye, the introduction of the Delsarte system into America and MacKaye's contribution to the system; secondarily it treats of other early figures in the movement, chiefly the Rev. William R. Alger, Unitarian minister, and Lewis B. Monroe, teacher, and the most influential book of the period, *Delsarte System of Oratory.* As an introduction to this material, a brief life of Delsarte and a summary of his "system" is given.

I

François Alexandre Nicholas Chéri Delsarte was born in Solesme, France, November 19, 1811.[6] Delsarte's early childhood was spent in poverty and privation, according to various factual and fictional biographies.[7] At the age of nine, he and his younger brother were taken to Paris by his mother, where she and the brother both soon died. In some way Delsarte became acquainted with a musician by the name of Père Bambini, who became his first teacher. Delsarte also studied with a M. Deshayes and a M. Choron. From 1826 to 1830 he attended the Conservatoire. He sang at l'Opéra-Comique, the Ambigu, and the Variétés, but was not a success in the theatre. He later became choir director at the church of the Abbé Chatel.[8]

The year 1839 is given as the date when Delsarte opened his school, but that he taught before this date is indicated in the biographies of two of his pupils, Darcier and Hermann-Léon. However, it is probably true that he did not open a school formally until 1839. There still exists a large book with the title *School of Moral and Scientific Singing*, which contains a "constitution" for this first school, and considerable material to indicate that the speculative philosophy on which the system was founded was well advanced and the basic structure completed by this time.[9]

Delsarte's ability as a teacher was praised by such critics as W. Warner, writing in *L'Eclair*,[10] Escudier in *La France Musicale*,[11] and Jules Janin in *Journal des Débats*.[12]

An examination of recently available material, consisting of some material in Delsarte's own handwriting, and more in the form of notes of his pupils, reveals some rather startling things.[13] First, Delsarte was not a speech teacher in any real sense of the word, but was, primarily, a teacher of instrumental and vocal music and an opera coach. In his later years, he seems to have coached some legitimate acting and to have offered instruction to clergymen. Recitation was used, but only as a method of teaching acting. Second, his system was not exactly a system of teaching either speech or music, but was a pseudo-philosophy, claiming to be a science, which organized all arts and sciences according to a plan which was based, in essence, on orthodox Catholic doctrine. In a period in which science was pushing forward rapidly, Delsarte's "System" was essentially a throwback to a conservative orthodox view under the guise of being a science. The "science" on which the system is founded is, however, purely speculative. In a brief summary of the system written by MacKaye in French, the "science" which would reveal the fixed laws of art is stated as "the possession of a criterion of examination against which no fact can protest." This criterion Delsarte found in the Holy Trinity. All things, according to the system, show a trinitary organization. For example, any object has height, width, thickness; time consists of past time, present time, future time, etc.:

The science of Mons. Delsarte consists of directing the light of this criterion of examination on all things, and in virtue of this idea of the trinity, to discover their intimate (interior) organization, and to explain the raison d'être of their external products. On this examination and on the science thus established, he bases all his art.[14]

By the use of this "system" of trinitary division, Delsarte organized all arts and sciences into an educational system and into a teaching method. Specifically, this concept was applied to music, particularly vocal music, and acting, the arts which Delsarte knew best. This trinitary division arises from the Holy Trinity, and each member of the Holy Trinity governs one of the elements of the trinity of any object or idea. Thus man is divided into life, mind, and soul. These are governed respectively by the Father, the Son, and the Holy Spirit. Life, mind, and soul are expressed by certain agents: vocal sound (apart from words) expresses life, words express mind, movement expresses soul. This concept of movement as the expression of soul possibly accounts for the emphasis put upon gesture and pantomime by American Delsartians. It seems unlikely that Delsarte placed any more emphasis on the physical aspects of his system than on the vocal, but in America, the physical aspects became the basis of the system and the Delsarte system became, essentially, a system of physical culture.

By another principle, the "principe du circumincéssion," which Curry translated as "principle of intertwining," the body expresses not only soul, but, to a degree, both life and mind.[15] Thus arises the familiar trinitary division of the zones of gesture and movement. Each of these major zones is divided into three minor zones, making in all nine zones of gesture. In addition to the zones, the movements of the body express the three essences of being, i.e., life, mind, and soul.

There are three basic forms of movement: movement about a center, called normal, which is vital and expresses life; movement away from a center, called eccentric, which is mental and expresses mind; movement toward a center, called concentric, which is moral and expresses soul. These three forms of movement mutually influence each other and thus give rise to nine forms, normo-normal, normo-eccentric, normo-concentric, eccentro-normal, eccentro-eccentric, eccentro-concentric, concentro-normal, concentro-eccentric, concentro-concentric. The forms of movement give rise to nine attitudes or states, and also to nine inflections or movements. All gestures, movements, or attitudes may be classified under these forms and each gesture, movement, or attitude has a special significance.

The vocal apparatus is also triune, and each element of the trinity expresses one of the essences of being, life, mind, or soul. Speech arises from three agents: the inciting agent, the lungs, which is the vital or life principle of sound; the resonating agent, the mouth, which is the intellectual or mind principle of sound; the vibratory agent, the larynx, which is the moral or soul principle of sound. All vocal effects, arising from these fundamental agents express life, mind, or soul, and may be so classified. In addition, the Delsarte system re-evaluates language according to the principle of the trinity and assigns degrees of value to the various parts of speech varying from one to nine.

Delsarte's "Cours D'Esthétique Appliquée" seems to have consisted of a series of public lectures and demonstrations on his theories, and a course of private instruction. The public lectures were generally nine or ten [16] in number, given weekly, and seem to have consisted of two parts, a lecture on some aspect of the system, often based on a chart or diagram, and a practical demonstration by pupils, and, at times, by Delsarte himself. Occasionally after the lecture there was a discussion. Angélique Arnaud, writing in 1882, said:

> Some years before his death Delsarte substituted for his concerts, lectures in which he explained his scientific doctrines and his philosophy of art. He also supplied the place of song by the recitation of certain fables selected from La Fontaine.[17]

In a lecture delivered before the Curry School of Expression in Boston in November, 1898, Mrs. Steele MacKaye described the morning lessons in much the same terms:

> The first part of the morning was given to the exposition of philosophy—the explanation of some theory, or chart. . . . After the exposition came the practical part: the recitation of a fable, a scene from a play, or perhaps a song, any of which was rendered sometimes by a pupil, sometimes by Delsarte himself.[18]

In addition to these lectures or lessons, Delsarte gave individual instruction. There is no material available to indicate just what happened in these sessions, which were held daily, but presumably Delsarte taught his pupils specific songs and roles and worked on articulation, movement, gesture, etc. Whether Delsarte used any kind of gymnastic exercises in his teaching was much argued later by American Delsartians. The scant evidence available would indicate that he did not. This question is discussed later in this paper.

II

A recent study of Delsarte's pupils has revealed that of fifty-four who can be classified, twenty-two were singers, twelve were instrumentalists, seven were actors, five were writers, four were composers, two were lawyers and three were painters.[19] Some of these pupils were well known; others are merely names. Of the entire list of pupils, only one, Steele MacKaye, is definitely known to be an American.[20]

James Steele MacKaye, playwright, actor, director, and theatre inventor, was born in Buffalo, New York, on June 6, 1842.[21] He first studied painting, but eventually decided on the theatre as a career. In preparation for this career, MacKaye decided to study acting in Paris. He went to Paris with the intention of studying at the Conservatoire, but was persuaded to study with M. Delsarte instead.

MacKaye began his studies in October, 1869, and lessons continued daily until July, 1870.[22] So rapid was MacKaye's progress, so quickly did he grasp the essentials of the system, and so brilliantly did he apply his knowledge, that after a few months he was accepted as a co-worker as well as a pupil and began doing a part of the teaching:

... within five months of their first meeting, at Delsarte's own desire and request, Mr. MacKaye was himself lecturing and teaching in Delsarte's Cours, with a success which aroused as much enthusiasm as astonishment in Delsarte's "lovable, loving and generous nature." [23]

Clearly Delsarte considered MacKaye a brilliant pupil and thus was established a close and significant relationship of disciple and master— a relationship understood and appreciated by both parties. MacKaye became Delsarte's chosen successor—the son who was to carry on the work of the master.[24]

This close relationship was abruptly terminated by the chaos of the Franco-Prussian war of 1871 and the resulting siege of Paris—a chaos which drove MacKaye back to America and Delsarte into refuge in his native village of Solesme where he lived in dire poverty on the charity of a cousin.[25] MacKaye, returning to America fired with enthusiasm for the Delsarte system, immediately began making plans for the introduction of the Delsarte system into America. Very shortly, however, word reached him of Delsarte's destitute condition. Two new friends, Rev. William R. Alger (the biographer of Edwin Forrest) and Prof. Lewis B. Monroe (Dean of the School of Oratory of Boston University) suggested to MacKaye that he give a lecture on Delsarte, the proceeds of which would go to Delsarte's relief.[26] MacKaye accepted this suggestion with typical enthusiasm and immediately set about preparing the lecture and arranging for its presentation. At the same time MacKaye and his friends thought of bringing Delsarte to America to found a great school of art similar to his school in Paris.

On March 21, 1871, MacKaye delivered at the St. James Hotel, Boston, his first lecture on Delsarte. This was the first time that the name and system of François Delsarte was presented to the American public.[27] In April the lecture was twice repeated in Boston at the Tremont Temple to large audiences and was given at Harvard University on April 21, 1871, with Henry W. Longfellow as the chairman.[28] Later,

MacKaye lectured at Steinway Hall in New York twice in April and several times in May. He also lectured in Brooklyn at the invitation of Henry Ward Beecher.[29]

Thus MacKaye spread the gospel of Delsarte. These lectures, and the impress of MacKaye's vivid personality, evidently made a profound impression, and the scheme for bringing Delsarte to America neared completion.

In the interim, Rev. Alger had gone abroad intending to see Delsarte. He was never to carry out this intention, however, for Delsarte died July 22, 1871, before Alger reached Paris.[30] With Delsarte's death the great incentive was gone, and the plan for an American "Cours D'Esthétique Appliquée" lost its vital force.

MacKaye lectured widely in the ensuing years. There is record of many lectures; many have been unreported. During the autumn and winter of 1874, MacKaye was on an extensive lecture tour under the aegis of James Redpath.[31] He had an engagement of twenty nights in Boston alone. Undoubtedly, Monroe and Alger were instrumental in setting up this series. Nine of these lectures were given under the general heading "Philosophy of Emotion and Its Expression." The lectures were listed as follows:

I. The Mystery of Emotion
II. Gesture As a Language
III. The Philosophy of Laughter
IV. The Mystic Law of Beauty
V. The Marvels of the Human Face and Hand
VI. Nature's Art
VII. Masks and Faces of Society
VIII. The Emotional Significance of the Serpent
IX. The Philosophy of Love [32]

For several months MacKaye appeared before audiences in many cities from Maine to Pennsylvania. Later in the winter he also seems to have lectured in the Middle West.[33]

In the spring of 1877, MacKaye established a school of expression at 23 Union Square, New York City.[34] Beginning on January 10 of the same year, he delivered a series of lectures on the Delsarte system at the studio of Mrs. George Hall, 33 East 17th Street, New York City.[35] Presumably Mrs. Hall was a teacher of elocution. The lectures were given at four o'clock in the afternoon. Some twenty-three of these lectures have been preserved in manuscript. There were at least thirty-four lectures delivered, as the last preserved manuscript is numbered thirty-four, although by its nature it seems not to be a concluding or final lecture. These lectures bear such titles as: "Philosophy—Aim of Artist, Nature of Perception," etc.; "The Trinities—Love, Wisdom and Power";

"Feet—Primary Expressions and Attitudes," etc. The manuscripts give a reasonably clear picture of MacKaye's interpretation of the Delsarte system and of his teaching of it.

In 1878 MacKaye presented a series of twelve lectures on the Philosophy of Expression in the Boston School of Oratory of Boston University of which Lewis B. Monroe was the founder and Dean. The lectures were attended by the entire school. This series seems to have been the most important of all MacKaye's lectures for they seem to have influenced directly the teaching of elocution or expression. Among the students in attendance were S. S. Curry and Franklin H. Sargent, the founder of the American Academy of Dramatic Arts. Many years later Sargent wrote:

... I took rapid notes, filling my notebook, and when, at the close, Steele MacKaye left us, I found myself left alone in the hall, meditating on the profundity of his discourse, overflowing for me with revelations. As I walked in the Dean's private office, I asked: *Prof. Monroe, what is this?* And I shall never forget the patriarchal old man, with his white hair, and glowing face, as he looked up at me and said, *My boy, this is the key to the universe!* [36]

Echoes of these lectures appear in many articles in *Werner's Magazine*. The lectures probably did more to set the pattern of Delsartism than any of MacKaye's other writings and addresses.

During the following years MacKaye continued to instruct private pupils and to make an occasional lecture tour. On several occasions he attempted to found a school similar to the "Cours D'Esthétique Appliquée," but his efforts came to naught as other interests drew him away. He also planned to write a number of volumes on the Delsarte system,[37] but aside from several articles in *Werner's Magazine* [38] nothing was written, or at least published. His death occurred February 25, 1894.[39]

In America the Delsarte system became primarily a system of physical training. An editorial in *Werner's Voice Magazine* in December, 1892, commented: "We are the first to present in a concise and comprehensive manner the practical workings, as well as the theoretical principles, of the various systems of physical culture, including the Delsarte, the Swedish, the German, the Eclectic, etc." [40] The central element of the Delsarte training lay in "harmonic gymnastics," a series of exercises of which relaxing or "decomposing" exercises seemed to be the most important. It seems difficult to determine whether these exercises were a part of the system as taught by Delsarte or whether they were added wholly or in part by MacKaye. In an early lecture MacKaye credited Delsarte with a system of exercises:

Delsarte has an adequate background for the basis of his system. His long study enables him to extend to the student of art three gifts, "(1) a simple but philosophical and effective method for the treatment and study of his subject, (2) a profound knowledge of the aesthetics, elements and principles of his art, and (3) a system of significant exercises which will develop to the utmost his executive power and give him the greatest command of his instrument." [41]

Later, however, MacKaye claimed credit for the development of the exercises and insisted that they were not a part of the system as taught by Delsarte. Writing in *Werner's Voice Magazine* for July, 1892, Mrs. Steele MacKaye said: "The whole system of aesthetic or harmonic gymnastics is, from the first word to the last, entirely of Mr. MacKaye's invention." She continued:

. . . In his first lectures, Mr. MacKaye never dreamed of separately cataloguing his own discoveries or inventions. . . . Such of Mr. MacKaye's discoveries as he was able to show Delsarte were glady accepted by him, as supplementing and developing the practical side of his own work. As they had thus become a recognized portion of the methods of the new science Mr. MacKaye was so eager to introduce . . . he made no attempt to separate his own contributions from the body of Delsarte's work.

But Mr. MacKaye has now been working and studying for 20 years, and during that time he has been constantly developing the Science and the Philosophy of Expression; at the same time building up and perfecting that system of psycho-physical training which to-day, under the name of Aesthetic or Harmonic Gymnastics, forms so large a portion of the practical training of the "Delsarte System," as it is taught in classes and in schools, and set forth in the various textbooks now published on the subject. . . . [42]

In his claim to have originated "harmonic gymnastics" MacKaye was supported by Mme. Géraldy, Delsarte's daughter. "My father taught expression," she said, ". . . he did not teach gymnastics. I do not say your relaxing exercises and posings are not valuable, for I believe they may be for certain purposes; but I do say that my father did not teach them." [43] In speaking of MacKaye she commented, "But he, like everybody else, has not been content to leave Delsarte's work as the master left it, but has added material of his own devising." [44]

On the other hand, Rev. W. R. Alger stated that Delsarte taught aesthetic gymnastics as part of his system. Alger himself studied with Gustave Delsarte during the year following the death of the elder Delsarte. Alger wrote later:

I had the privilege of studying with him [Gustave] for a season. Afterwards Mrs. Henrietta Russell studied with him for a year or more. We both found that he taught, as imparted to him by his father, the same system of expression, the same laws and rules, the same gymnastic training, given at a subsequent date by Mr. MacKaye to his pupils, and still later, published by Miss Stebbins in her books. [45]

Later in the same article Alger commented, "Steele MacKaye no doubt has corrected some errors in it, developed some portions of it further, made some additions to it, and improved the name by changing it from 'aesthetic' to 'harmonic.'" Alger gave a brief description of these exercises in his *Life of Edwin Forrest*.[46]

The weight of evidence, however, would seem to support MacKaye in his claims for inventing harmonic gymnastics. MacKaye accepted the trinitary concept of Delsarte, and, in general, the whole speculative philosophy, but being less profoundly religious than Delsarte, or at least not Catholic in religion, he was probably less interested in the philosophical implications than in the practical aspects. Thus MacKaye seems to be responsible for the emphasis on gesture in the Delsarte system as taught in America, although *Delsarte System of Oratory*, discussed later in this paper, also contributed heavily to that end. In any event, MacKaye's failure to make a clear and unambiguous statement about the system and his own contributions to it contributed to the conversion of the system into a method of physical culture.

Delsarte had been interested primarily in the training of singers. MacKaye was interested in the training of actors. Only in the hands of pupils of MacKaye and of pupils of his pupils was the system applied to "expression" or interpretation.

III

The part Mr. Steele MacKaye has taken in developing and popularizing the Delsarte system is too well known to need any explanation or defense. He, the late Prof. Lewis B. Monroe, and the Reverend William R. Alger were the great American trio to whom the expressional arts owe an immense debt of gratitude. They are the founders of the "new elocution," and were in the most intimate professional and personal relations with Delsarte.[47]

So wrote Edgar S. Werner in March of 1892. Of this trio, only Monroe was, by profession, a teacher. As a young man Monroe had suffered from poor health and had become interested in physical training. From this his interest had spread to vocal training.[48] He was one of the founders of the School of Oratory of Boston University, of which he later became Dean. Among his pupils here were Charles Wesley Emerson, founder of the Emerson College of Oratory,[49] S. S. Curry, founder of the School of Expression of Boston,[50] Franklin Sargeant, long the director of the American Academy of Dramatic Arts, and many other prominent leaders in the elocution movement. Alexander Graham Bell was a teacher in this school under Monroe's sponsorship.[51]

Monroe published a book, *Vocal and Physical Training*.[52] In it he stated his indebtedness to Rush and to the adaptation of Rush's work by Russell. However, the book also advocated a system of vocal and physical exercises to be taught in the public schools that would train the mind, body, and soul and presented a system modeled after the *Gymnase Triat* of Paris.[53]

MacKaye's lectures in 1877 had markedly influenced Monroe, but his early death, in July, 1879, at the age of fifty-four, deprived the elocution movement of a leader who might well have prevented some of the confusion that was associated with Delsarte's name.[54]

Rev. William Rounseville Alger is an entirely different case. As a popular Unitarian minister of Boston, Alger was drawn to Delsartism by the basic Christian philosophy of the system, although how a Unitarian minister was able to reconcile his own faith with a philosophical system so obviously Roman Catholic in its inception is difficult to see. Evidently Alger espoused only those elements of the system that would accord with his own religious philosophy. Fred Winslow Adams, writing in *Werner's Magazine*, says of Alger, "He speaks of Delsarte's aesthetic gymnastics as 'the basis of a new religious education, destined to perfect the children of men, abolish deformity, sickness, and crime, and redeem the earth!' " [55]

James R. Alger was born in 1823. As a boy he worked on a farm and at other occupations chiefly in Boston. He entered Pembroke Academy at Pembroke, New Hampshire, and at the age of twenty entered the theological school at Harvard University from which he was graduated in 1847. Upon graduation he became the pastor of Mt. Pleasant Church, Roxbury, where he remained for seven years. He then became pastor of the Bulfinch Street Church, where he remained for ten years. Because of poor health he took a trip abroad in 1865, and on his return he was offered the pastorate of the Music Hall society. He preached there from 1868 until 1872. In 1868 also he was made chaplain of the Massachusetts House of Representatives.[56] During these years, Alger had written and published a number of books. They were chiefly religious and philosophical pamphlets, but many of them had proved popular. At the time he appears in the Delsarte story, he was engaged in writing his *Life of Edwin Forrest*, published in 1877.

Both Monroe and Alger had become interested in Delsarte in a rather roundabout way. The two were good friends. Alger was under contract to James Oakes, publisher, and friend of Forrest. Oakes received a letter from the French correspondent, Francis Durivage, full of enthusiastic praise of Steele MacKaye and of Delsarte and his philosophy. Monroe and Alger were so impressed with the letters of Durivage that, when MacKaye returned to America, they made a special trip to New York to see him. They were even more impressed with him and his teaching than they had expected to be from Durivage's letters. Both became enthusiastic followers and pupils and helped to stimulate interest in MacKaye's first lectures. Alger, after a short period of study with

MacKaye, went to Europe with the intention of studying with Delsarte himself, a study prevented by the death of Delsarte. Madame Delsarte, however, wrote to Alger in Vienna, telling of her husband's death, and adding, "But when you arrive in Paris, our oldest son, Gustave, who inherits much of his father's genius and all of his traditions, will be quite at your service." [57] Alger accepted this offer and studied with Gustave Delsarte the better part of a year, and, presumably, from his studies with MacKaye and the younger Delsarte, acquired a good understanding of the Delsarte philosophy.

After his return from Paris for some years Alger continued to preach and, evidently, teach the Delsarte system. He lectured at various times on the basic philosophy of the system. In the final years of the nineteenth century he lectured at Curry's School of Expression on a number of occasions. On February 9, 1897, he spoke on the "Nature, Meaning, and Laws of Rhythm in Experience and Expression," and on February 16, he was scheduled to lecture on "Eighteen Forms of Emphasis." In the December, 1898, issue of *Expression Magazine,* Curry wrote:

Rev. William R. Alger has been giving a course of six lectures to the School of Expression on the "Drama of the Human Face." As the result of years of investigation, he has information and quotations gathered from wide and varied sources. He gave most profound and philosophical definitions and discriminations of the leading phases of the subject. Some of his definitions were most important. He carefully distinguished a mask from a face, and the expression of the face from grimacery. Among the most forcible parts of the lectures were the illustrations of various kinds of the faces which Mr. Alger has noted in his experience. [58]

Among the special courses listed in the School of Expression in the autumn issue of the *Expression Magazine* for 1899, course No. 6 was listed as follows:

VI. Rev. William R. Alger, the distinguished student and scholar, will give four courses in the afternoon lectures upon,
1. The Philosophy of Human Nature in the Acquisition of Experience and the Command of Expression.
2. The Ideal of Personal Perfection and the Method and the Principles of the Physical, Ethical and Aesthetic Training for Its Realization.
3. The Varieties of Human Character in All Its Types, Critically Studied, Defined, Analyzed, and Illustrated.
4. The Historic and Artistic Evolution of the Human Voice Considered in Its Successive Stages, Its Mysteries, Its Social Offices, and Its Ideal Perfection. [59]

And, in the Winter 1899-1900 issue of the same magazine, Alger's name appeared three times on a list of lectures and recitals:

Oct. 26. . . . A lecture on "The Work of Life and Its Motives." Rev. William R. Alger.

Nov. 11. . . . A lecture on "The Seven Fine Arts." Rev. William R. Alger.

Nov. 2, 9, 16, 28, Dec. 5, 12, 19. . . . Lectures on "The Philosophy of Human Nature in the Acquisition of Experience and the Command of Expression." Rev. William R. Alger.[60]

Some fifteen manuscripts of these lectures are still available and have been the subject of a special study.[61] The lectures indicate that Alger had accepted the trinitary concept as originally stated by Delsarte and the mechanical aspects arising from it, but there is a strong religious strain running through all his work. Price commented in her study of Alger:

The basic idea running through these lectures is that all heaven and earth, and all that is in them can be divided into the trinity, based upon the Holy Trinity of God, the Father; Jesus Christ, the Son; and the Holy Ghost. In man, created in the image and likeness of God, the trinity is manifest as life, mind, and soul, or the vital, mental and moral realms. . . .

Because man is created in the image and likeness of God, it should be his duty to develop his powers to the highest degree possible. He should always strive for perfection. It is possible for man to attain personal perfection if he has the will power to follow a rigorous and self-disciplinary training. . . .

Gaining control of his muscles and body is the first step in the realization of the ideal for the artist. His system of physical culture must be based upon aesthetic principles. They must combine mental, bodily, and emotional unity.[62]

Thus, after MacKaye's other interests had drawn him away from any serious advocacy of the Delsarte system, and even after MacKaye's death, Alger carried on the ideas and practices of the Delsarte system. He was the last important advocate of the system as he had been one of the earlier. He died February 7, 1905.

IV

The first and by far the most important of the many books dealing with the system was *Delsarte System of Oratory*, published by Edgar S. Werner. The book, essentially, was a translation of notes of French pupils of Delsarte. The book went through four editions, each edition presenting additional material.

L'Abbé Delaumosne, a French priest who had studied with Delsarte, published, in 1874, the notes of his studies.[63] The little book was entitled *Pratique de L'Art Oratoire de Delsarte*. It was translated by Frances A. Shaw and printed in 1882, under the title *The Art of Oratory, System of Delsarte*.[64] S. S. Curry said of this book:

After his death [Delsarte's], a priest, who had studied with Delsarte, published without any authority whatever, the notes he had taken of his lessons. The little book was published in Paris for fifty cents, but even at this price, the small first edition was not sold; a poor translation, however, by one who knew nothing of Delsarte, was published in America, and sold at two dollars a volume, greatly to the financial gain of the publisher. The book was universally condemned by everyone who knew anything of Delsarte, both in France and in this country. It was crude, and mis-represented his method.[65]

A comparison of the French original and the translation, however, shows that the translation was a satisfactory one and that Curry's criticism is not entirely justified. That the book misrepresented the Delsarte system may be more nearly true. L'Abbé Delaumosne evidently attended a *cours* planned for clergymen, or, at any rate, he took notes only on those aspects of the system that applied to oratory. There is no mention of music and little reference to acting. The preface opens with these words:

> Orators, you are called to the ministry of speech. You have fixed your choice upon the pulpit, the bar, the tribune or the stage. You will become one day, preacher, advocate, lecturer or actor; in short, you desire to embrace the orator's career.[66]

The book is divided into three parts: Part I, covering thirty-five pages in the translation, deals with voice; Part II, containing eighty pages, treats of gesture; Part III, with thirty-three pages, discusses articulate language. The emphasis on gesture is obvious. The book contains such standard items from the Delsarte system as the medallion of inflection, the nine basic attitudes of the legs [illustrated], the zones of gesture, etc. The material was undoubtedly gleaned from Delsarte's lectures and attempts by American Delsartians to discredit it in favor of their own theories and procedures must be discounted. This volume became the first edition of *Delsarte System of Oratory.*

The second edition of this work, published in 1884, added to the Delaumosne notes a translation of notes of another French pupil of Delsarte. In 1882, Angélique Arnaud, a minor French writer of sentimental novels, published in Paris a volume simply entitled *François Delsarte.*[67] The book was in two parts. The first part presented a brief biography while the second part discussed the philosophical basis of the system. It was this second part, along with "The Attributes of Reason," an essay by Delsarte himself, that was added to the original Delaumosne notes and published under the title of *Delsarte System of Oratory.* Arnaud's material is discursive and rambling, lacking the mechanical positiveness of the Delaumosne notes, but it does supplement heavily the philosophical treatment. This second edition was published in 1884. A third edition appeared in 1887 which added the biographical section of Arnaud's book and a section called "Literary Remains of François Delsarte," a translation of material purportedly purchased from Madame Delsarte. This material, as well as the Arnaud book, was translated by Abby L. Alger, daughter of Rev. Alger. The fourth edition, published in 1892, added "The Lecture and Lessons Given by Mme. Marie Géraldy [Delsarte's Daughter] in America," and some miscellaneous items.

In the absence of any published material from MacKaye's pen, this book remained the best statement of Delsartism and it had considerable authority. Undoubtedly it did more than any other to fix the zones of gesture and other mechanical details of the system in the minds of American teachers.

There were many other books on the Delsarte system, of course. Such books as Genevieve Stebbins' *Delsarte System of Dramatic Expression* and her *Society Gymnastics,* Anna Morgan's *An Hour With Delsarte,* Emily Bishop's *Self Expression and Health: Americanized Delsarte Culture,* and Moses True Brown's *The Synthetic Philosophy of Expression* were widely used and sold.

The system finally became a routine mechanical system for the teaching of the expression of emotion largely through gesture and body position, accompanied by statue posing, tableaux, etc. By 1900 the system was largely outmoded. It is now only of academic interest. Delsartism had its value, however, in the interest and activity stimulated in the whole field of speech, and out of the vitriolic arguments as to the meaning, interpretation and use of the system, there tended to develop a real interest in speech which has contributed, in some measure, to a better understanding of speech training everywhere.

Notes

1. Werner's Magazine was founded in January, 1879, under the name *The Voice* by Edgar S. Werner. In January, 1889, the name was changed to *Werner's Voice Magazine,* and in January, 1893, the word *voice* was dropped and the journal became *Werner's Magazine.* In general reference in this article the journal is called *Werner's Magazine;* in specific citation the name at the time is used.

2. Charles Bickford, "The Delsarte Delusion," *The Voice,* X (November, 1888), 177.

3. L. P., "Letter Box," *The Voice,* VI, No. 1 (January, 1884), 16.

4. Elsie M. Wilbor, "Chautauqua," *Werner's Voice Magazine,* XII (August, 1890), 195.

5. S. S. Curry, *The Province of Expression* (Boston, 1891), p. 337.

6. J. Weber, *Le Temps,* August 1, 1871.

7. Francis Durivage, "Delsarte," *The Atlantic Monthly,* XXVII (May, 1871), 615.

8. *Le Soir,* July 26, 1871.

9. George A. Neely, "The School of Delsarte: Based on An Original Notebook," unpublished M.A. thesis, Louisiana State, 1942.

10. W. Warner, "Publications Musicales," *L'Éclair,* August 28, 1839.

11. Escudier, "Chefs d'Oeuvre Lyriques des Anciens Maîtres," *La France Musicale,* February 4, 1855.

12. Jules Janin, "La Semaine Dramatique," *Journal des Debats,* August 8, 1853.

13. C. L. Shaver, "The Delsarte System of Expression as Seen Through the Notes of Steele MacKaye," unpublished Ph.D. dissertation, Wisconsin, 1937. See also: Novalyne Price, "The Delsarte Philosophy of Expression as Seen Through Certain Manuscripts of the Rev. William R. Alger," unpublished M.A. thesis, Louisiana State, 1941; Virginia Morris, "The Influence of Delsarte in America as Revealed Through the Lectures of Steele MacKaye," unpublished M.A. thesis, Louisiana State, 1941; Edwin Levy, "Delsarte's 'Cours D'Esthétique Appliquée', Based on an Original Notebook," unpublished M.A. thesis, Louisiana State, 1940; Neely, *op. cit.;* Myra White Harang, "The Public Career of François Delsarte," unpublished M.A. thesis, Louisiana State, 1945; Rayda Wallace Dillport, "The Pupils of Delsarte," unpublished M.A. thesis, Louisiana State, 1946.

14. Shaver, "Delsarte System," p. 41. The reader may wonder if there is any connection between Delsarte and Swedenborg. There may be, but there is no evidence of such connection. Swedenborg's name does not appear in any material relating to Delsarte. Delsarte's theories seem rather to arise from Catholic doctrine than from the philosophy of Swedenborg.

15. Curry, *Province of Expression,* p. 344.

16. The title page of Alphonse Paget's notebook states, "... Exposition in Nine Lessons on Art, Oratory, Painting and Music." Cf. Levy, "Delsarte's *Cours D'Esthétique Appliquée.*" Charles Boissière, in two separate articles in *La Reforme Musicale* (May 23, 1858 and July 11, 1858) indicates that the course consisted of ten lessons.

17. *Delsarte System of Oratory,* 206.

18. Percy MacKaye, *Epoch: The Life of Steele MacKaye,* 2 vols. (New York, 1927), I, 133-136. For a similar description of Delsarte's "Cours," see A. Giraudet's letter to the editor, *The Voice,* VII (January, 1885), 9-10.

19. Dillport, *Pupils of Delsarte.*

20. One of MacKaye's sisters studied singing with Delsarte. See MacKaye, *Epoch,* I, 134.

21. *Epoch,* I, 37.

22. *Epoch,* I, 135.

23. *Epoch,* I, 135-136.

24. *Epoch,* I, 134-135. It should be noted that Delsarte had several children, two of whom followed in his footsteps. His daughter, Marie, later Madame Géraldy, visited America in 1892 where she lectured and taught briefly. His son Gustave taught the system after his father's death until his own death in 1879.

25. *Epoch,* I, 141-142.

26. *Epoch,* I, 142.

27. *Epoch,* I, 150-151.

28. *Epoch,* I, 154.

29. *Epoch,* Appendix xli.

30. *Le Salut Public,* July 23, 1871.

31. *Epoch,* I, 228-232.

32. From a Redpath circular quoted in *Epoch,* I, 231.

33. *Epoch,* I, 263.

34. *Epoch,* I, 266-267.

35. Morris, *Influence of Delsarte,* p. 26.

36. *Epoch,* I, 190.

37. *Epoch,* II, 267.

38. "François Delsarte" (August, 1889), p. 149; "Expression in Nature and Expression in Art," a series of four articles, April, May, June, August, 1887.

39. *Epoch,* II, 460.

40. *Werner's Voice Magazine,* XIV (December, 1892), 373.

41. Morris, *Influence of Delsarte,* pp. 44-45.

42. Mrs. Steele MacKaye, "Steele MacKaye and François Delsarte," *Werner's Voice Magazine,* XIV (July, 1892), 187 *passim.* This article was written some two years before MacKaye's death and he must have known and approved of its state-

ments. See *Epoch*, II, 270. Interestingly enough, a footnote on page 271 states that Rev. Alger approved of the article.

43. E. Miriam Coyriere, "Mme. Géraldy's Visit to America," *Werner's Voice Magazine*, XIV (April, 1892), 103.

44. *Ibid.*

45. W. R. Alger, "The Aesthetic 'Gymnastics' of Delsarte," *Werner's Magazine*, XVI (January, 1894), 4.

46. William R. Alger, *Life of Edwin Forrest*, 2 vols. (Philadelphia, 1877), II, 659-662.

47. *Werner's Voice Magazine*, XIV (March, 1892), 59.

48. *Werner's Voice Magazine*, XI (September, 1889), 169.

49. Price, *Alger*, 2.

50. S. S. Curry, "Professor Lewis B. Monroe, Some Characteristics of His Teaching," *Expression Magazine*, I (December, 1896), 243.

51. *Epoch*, I, 152.

52. (Philadelphia, 1869).

53. *Ibid.*, 7.

54. *Werner's Voice Magazine*, XI (September, 1889), 170.

55. "William Rounseville Alger," *Werner's Magazine*, XV (March, 1893), 87.

56. This summary is taken from Alger's obituary notice in the *Boston Transcript*, February 8, 1905.

57. Alger, "The Aesthetic 'Gymnastics' of Delsarte," *Werner's Magazine*, XVI (January, 1894), 3.

58. V, 216.

59. V, 371.

60. Appendix, 9.

61. Price, *Alger*.

62. *Ibid.*, 119-122.

63. M. L'Abbé Delaumosne, *Pratique de L'Art Oratoire de Delsarte* (Paris, 1874).

64. *The Art of Oratory, System of Delsarte*, tr. Frances A. Shaw (Albany, N. Y., 1882).

65. Curry, *Province of Expression*, 335.

66. Shaw, *Art of Oratory*, preface.

67. Angélique Arnaud, *François Delsarte, ses Découvertes en Esthétique, sa Science, sa Méthode* (Paris, 1882).

10 Dr. James Rush

LESTER L. HALE

....

In examining or utilizing Dr. James Rush's contribution to speech education, not only must the most familiar product of his investigation, *The Philosophy of the Human Voice*,[1] be scrutinized, but its frame of reference should be appreciated. While Dr. Rush presented a detailed analysis of human vocal expression which since his day has set the stage for much that has been superficial in the teaching of speech, his own work was not superficial; it was based to a considerable extent on philosophical and scientific inquiry. In aiming his chief research towards a sound and satisfactory explanation of human function and physiology, he was led into a byway which captivated his attention and led him to elaborate investigation of the more tangible evidence of expressive behavior—the human voice. The results of this labor gave to the field of speech America's first comprehensive organization of vocal principles. The scope of the *Philosophy* was more inclusive and detailed than any single volume written on the subject prior to its first publication in 1827. The thoroughness of the book, its apparent and immediate usefulness to teachers, made Rush a recognized authority in the discipline of elocution. Unfortunately, superficial applications of his systematic description of expressive phenomena were drawn from his book. They bred many abridgements and abuses of his basic philosophical and physiological approach, obscuring and distorting his more significant and profound purpose. Consequently, appraisal of Rush's contribution to speech education is often colored by prejudice and presupposition. One's bias against any modern mechanistic technique which seems to resemble Rush's vocal analysis, however, must be isolated and properly evaluated before the Philadelphian can receive his due.

The *Philosophy* as a work on speech is Rush's attempt to apply medical science, as it was known to him, to the analysis of human behavior and the processes of neurological control. In Rush, medical science and speech come together.

219

I

The political freedom established by our nation's great leaders in 1776 was only one aspect of the emancipation of the American people. Perhaps one of the most vital influences in stimulating fresh points of view and unprejudiced thought came from the pen of Dr. Benjamin Rush, James Rush's father. Physician-general in the Continental Army under George Washington, signer of the Declaration of Independence and one of the most public-spirited men of the time, Dr. Benjamin Rush wrote voluminously and carefully on almost every subject which he wished to revolutionize. He wrote so defiantly and honestly that in later years it became politically hazardous for his son Richard Rush to permit the publication of his father's autobiography.[2]

Of such a father and in such a time was James Rush born on March 15, 1786. His mother, Julia Stockton, was the daughter of Richard Stockton, also a signer of the Declaration of Independence. He not only inherited the energies and purpose of the pioneer, but his father carefully schooled him in the discipline of observation and scientific inquiry. He attended the College of New Jersey (Princeton), receiving his degree in 1805. By 1809 he had secured the M. D. degree from the University of Pennsylvania. His father then financed his travel abroad and his study in Edinburgh. Throughout the years of his formal education, father and son exchanged many letters—letters which vouch for the personality and promise of the young physician whose professional life was to follow in the shadow of his father's waning popularity. When he graduated from the University of Pennsylvania his dissertation reflected the qualities of mind which his father had inculcated. This and other early efforts brought the approval of many.[3]

Dr. James Rush was honored by membership in many honorary societies, including the Institute de France, Academie Royale de Sciences, Peithessophian Society of Rutgers College, American Philosophical Society of Philadelphia, Rush Medical Society of Willoughby University, Peithessophian Society of Theological Seminary of New Brunswick. The hopes of a father for a son were being fulfilled in the achievements of James, the physician.

While leading his contemporaries in the revolt of ideas, Dr. Benjamin Rush wrote on many subjects. Among these was that of the mind and its diseases, an interest which the son, James, soon acquired. Goodman has identified Benjamin Rush as America's first psychiatrist, and the publication of his *Medical Inquiries and Observations upon the Disease of the Mind* was until 1883 the only comprehensive American treatise on the subject.[4] Before considering the diseases of the mind, he first described what he believed to be its faculties and operations:

Its faculties are: understanding, memory, imagination, passions, the principle of faith, will, the moral faculty, conscience, and the sense of Deity.

Its principle [sic] operations, after sensation, are perception, association, judgment, reasoning and volition. All of its subordinate operations, which are known by the names attention, reflection, contemplation, wit, consciousness and the like are nothing but modifications of the five principle [sic] operations that have been mentioned.

The faculties of the mind have been called, very happily, *internal* senses. They resemble the external senses in being innate, and depending wholly upon bodily impressions to produce their specific operations. These impressions are made through the medium of the external senses. As well might we attempt to excite thought in a piece of marble by striking it with our hand, as expect to produce a single operation of the mind in a person deprived of the external senses of touch, seeing, hearing, taste, and smell.
... the mind is incapable of any operations independently of impressions communicated to it through the medium of the body.[5]

While in Europe, Dr. James Rush became acquainted with the philosophy of Dugald Stewart [6] and Lord Bacon, and became irritated by the speculations of metaphysicians. Returning to America in 1811, he lectured to his father's classes in medical school at the University of Pennsylvania. The essence of his thinking at that time was that "reasoning is only a train of physical perception" and "that the mind in its outline consisted only of perception and memory." [7] He made notes on this subject in his Commonplace Book of Medicine in 1818 under the title "The Mind, Its Healthy Functions," [8] and planned a thorough analysis of the mind based upon careful observations.

The approach of father and son to investigations of mental function was to create considerable criticism of their own religious convictions. This was the price they were to pay for their new-found freedom of thought. This had serious consequences in the life of James, whose later endeavors were also to provoke misunderstanding and disapproval. Benjamin Rush was a leader in the Presbyterian faith and his reform effort was "as fundamentally religious as it was patriotic." [9] His stern faith (which it is presumed he imparted to his children) led him in later years to "part company with his Presbyterian teachers and associates" because he found them "too good to do good." [10] His letters to James often expressed hope that James would hold fast to his religious conviction. But society could not believe that scientific study of the machinery of human control would be compatible with faith in divine design. When James Rush in his turn developed a segment of the history of mind, religious indictment became intense and no doubt contributed to his retirement. Public opinion to a great extent was admittedly responsible for deferring his investigation of mind.

Research into the mind was dominated by "the privileged order of metaphysicians." [11] *Mind* was said to be *spirit* and *spirit* was an entity separated from matter and unyielding to human analysis. Accordingly, Rush's analysis of mental functions was judged atheistic. Such condemnation apparently became widespread as years passed and may have had some foundation in his general contempt for organized religious practice. Into a small note pad he penned in 1835: "The literary world have got to *worship* Shakespeare, and so forget to imitate his excellence, just as the religions of the world adore God and omit to imitate his truth and justice." [12] And in the Preface to *Rhymes of Contrast on Wisdom and Folly* in 1869 he wrote: "Our mind like the rest of physical Creation is under the necessary Rule of God and Nature; let us not try to thwart that Rule, by the metaphysical attempt to take their Law of the intellect into our own fictional hand. Follow that Law and it will keep us right, as it does the mind of the sub-animal world." [13]

James Rush was attempting to open further the door of scientific investigation of mind, following the efforts of his father. He believed firmly in the existence of an Almighty Power, or First Cause, and that science merely aided us in understanding His instruments of life. Many friends and relatives, however, feared for his soul's safety if he continued such materialistic reasoning. His cousin, Mary Rush, wrote dramatically and at great length petitioning him to give up his studies.

... look away, I pray you, from the weak and sinful creatures who now address you and remember only, that your *own soul is at stake*....

I entreat you, by all that is sacred in heaven, and by all that you value upon earth, by all that is manly and respectable and praiseworthy among men, to abandon your present delusive and soul-destroying views of religion.[14]

Although Rush's studies were to take him towards renown, he was never to know the comfort and respect of success which he sought in his own days.

Shortly after he had begun his practice of medicine following his return from Edinburgh, he married Phoebe Anne Ridgway (1819), an heiress and a brilliant leader of Philadelphia society. The early years of his marriage were apparently very happy, and his professional achievements during this time were his best. He not only had begun his investigations of mental function but attempted to prepare a medical text which he called *Novus Ordo Medicinae*.[15] This was to have been a compilation of medical case histories using not only a running account but a chart system for recording symptoms. A bound workbook of printed page-forms for this purpose is still among his manuscripts but comparatively few pages were recorded. This work, begun in 1813 and continued while he was conducting his successful medical practice, was apparently laid aside as his enthusiasm for his study of mind increased. He did not find another opportunity to return in earnest to it, for he intensified his study of mind during the years 1818-1822, which in turn led him, by 1823, into the field of creative communication.

This shift of interest so occupied his attention that his early notations on mind were left unpublished until after *The Philosophy of the Human Voice* had been in print through five revisions. However, in order to comprehend better the relationship between his vocal analysis and his description of mental process it is desirable first to follow his reasoning through to its eventual goal, *The Natural History of the Intellect,* which appeared in 1865. With appreciation for his avowed and original purpose of analyzing mental function, and an understanding of the product of this endeavor, we shall more readily recognize his vocal philosophy as the by-product of his medical research.

II

In addition to his conviction that mind consisted only of perception and memory, which Dr. Rush had arrived at prior to 1818, he had the growing belief that the manner in which mind was capable of expression was a part of mental function itself. He then began a careful experimental observation of vocal expression to discover the relationship between it and its apparent complement—perception.

Thus began a hybrid process of reasoning and experimentation which made the investigations of Rush an interesting cross between the armchair psychology of his contemporaries and the experimental psychology which followed almost fifty years later. It should be remembered that his 1818 recorded notations were contemporary with Bessel's report of the Greenwich observatory incident which called attention to individual differences and ushered in a new era in psychology. Thus, his primary postulates on mind and voice become historically significant in relation to experimental psychology as well as to speech.

Rush's first major postulate, which evolved during the half century in which he studied the functioning of mind, was that mind should be regarded as a physiological function as orderly as sensation itself and as tangible as muscle movement. His two volumes on the subject of human intellect which finally emerged are too involved and cumbersome to be reported upon in detail, but it can be seen that he started from a premise of physiologic reality:

All that man perceives, thinks, pronounces, and performs is respectively through his senses, his brain and his muscles. From these physical and directive agencies proceed his science and his art; and from their proper or improper use severally arise his good and his evil, his error and his truth.[16]

He finally saw function of mind as consisting of five "constituents," rather than three:

... First. Primary perceptions of things before the senses. Second. Memorial perceptions after their removal. Third. Joint perceptions; by which primary are compared with primary, or memorial with memorials which are called unmixed; and mixed, when these two different forms are compared with each other. Fourth. Conclusive perceptions, or those by which we come finally to a knowledge of the relationships of two or more of the primary and memorial to each other; from their agreement or identity to classify the things of nature; affirm their laws; and apply them to the purpose of science, of art, and of our physical, moral and intellectual selves. Fifth. Verbal perceptions, or vocal and written signs of all the other four different forms; without which allotted and manageable signs; or in common phrase, without language of sound, or of symbol, for thought and passion; the human mind would be as limited as that of the brute.[17]

What Rush was saying meant simply that the complicated and mysterious functioning of mind was really an orderly sequence of sensation, memory, association, conclusive perception, and muscular and verbal performance responses:

All of its [mind's] intellectual functions and products, whether of thought, or passion, properly so distinguished; or of passion carried into nervous, muscular, or vocal action, are the effects, the whole effects, and nothing but the effects of these.[18]

His effort as a physician-scientist to understand mind as a physiological phenomenon—a function of tangible matter and human material—was one of the first attempts at modern classifications in psychology.

His second contention was that thought and speech are inseparable:

The mind as we only can know it; is an indivisible compound of Thought and Speech or other sign. Which first begins, if they are not co-eval, is a point for Metaphysicians. . . .
To describe the mind, therefore, it is necessary to show the inseparable connection between thought and the voice; with their influences on each other: for they cannot, separately, be fully known.[19]

In pointing out the interdependence of thought and speech, and in demonstrating the functions of mind to be physiological phenomena, the third basic postulate becomes evident: that speech is a total mental and physical response. Although he stops the moving wheel to count its spokes, he remains constantly aware of man's dynamic nature, his integration, his existence as a unit, and his whole personality. "Wisdom, folly, virtue, and vice, with all their forms and effects are enacted by the mind," [20] he says, and what a person is, and what he will be, is determined by the cultivated use of sensation, memory, association, and the verbal resultant. Mental processes, then, are one and the same with physical sensation and expression; and speech cannot be isolated or disassociated from the physical being, or whole personality, for it is actually the fifth constituent of the mind itself. *The Natural History of the Intellect* attempts not only to develop these primary tenets, but to describe the manner in which behavior can be recognized and predicted in many of life's situations.

Although his final work on mind bears a strong resemblance to currently known neurological explanations of brain activity, his volumes on the subject were too late to be significant in the rapidly expanding scientific approaches to the subject. Furthermore, his final digest of the matter became so distorted by disappointments of his life and packed with the prejudice and disillusionment of a man "out of joint with his time," [21] that his volumes on the intellect were disregarded by scholars and served only to accent his final failure as a scientific figure.

It is not difficult today to understand how reasonable was Rush's transition from an analysis of mind to that of voice. As he observed the function of mind he became convinced he "should require further knowledge of the various departments of nature, science, art, and life" to enable him to "encompass the detail embraced by [my] practical system of Perceptions." [22] Furthermore, he did not wish to become involved in further argument concerning the question of the mind's "material, or spiritual, or any mystical or metaphysical causation." [23] He reasoned that for one successfully to submit to the public a view as controversial as his, he would first need to develop a reputation for profound thinking through more popular publications. He began to study mathematics, natural philosophy, history, metaphysics, philology, military science, and the aesthetic arts. This last interest awakened in him his early flair for rhyming and he began occasionally to write in "the brief sententious manner of early English Dramatists." [24] He reasoned that neither a textbook in medicine nor a professional dissertation on *mind* would be accepted by the hostile public until he had received acclaim in other ways. No doubt this decision led him first to complete the *Philosophy*.

Along the way he was drawn to a study of Smith's *Harmonics* [25] and was impressed by the "distinction perceived by the Greeks, between the continuous or sliding movement of the voice, in speech, and its discrete or skipping transition, by the steps of the musical scale." He sought to satisfy his curiosity concerning the variations of voice "by a strict, physical, and Baconian investigation of its phenomena, particularly as they might be connected with the working plan of the mind." [26] In 1823 he recorded some notes called "Remarks on the Human Voice in Reading." This marked the beginning of a more concentrated and systematic effort to study the voice.

He tried to free himself from the bondage of existing falsity and confusion in this field and to make his own first-hand observations of speech. In 1826 this work was accomplished, and he published in 1827 the first edition of *The Philosophy of the Human Voice.*

III

Having explained how Dr. Rush came to write on speech and voice and what major premises formed the foundation of his various writings, we are now in position to examine the original contributions he made specifically in the field of speech. But before doing so, it would be well first to look at the basic premise upon which his descriptive analysis of the speech process hinged. In writing *The Philosophy of the Human Voice,* Rush endeavored to furnish "physiological data to Rhetoricians." [27] It was not his concern to create a system of rules, but to observe nature that he might give a physiological foundation to expressive art.

The anatomy of the speech mechanism had already been described by science, but the physiology or function of the mechanism had not been detailed beyond discernment of the parts of the system that produced the sound. Rhetoricians, on the other hand, had noted the elements of voice—force, pitch, quality, rhythm—but had not identified them with the functions of anatomy. In publishing a vocal philosophy which gave a physiological foundation and explanation to vocal theory, Rush gave an entirely new and different emphasis to the study and teaching of speech. [28]

It is true he gave application to his organized arrangement and description of the vocal elements, which provided elocutionists easy access to a "system," but his major contention was that the natural phenomena of vocal expression were describable, and further, that only from such a description could students be guided in making their own analysis of nature.

> He who has a knowledge of the constituents of speech, and of their powers and uses, is the potential master of the science of Elocution; and he must then derive from his ear, his sense of propriety, and his taste, the means of actually applying it with success. [29]

He believed that an actor's or speaker's first obligation was to nature, that to be natural in all expression was the prime prerequisite, but that a student must have the cues to recognition of nature's unfoldment which a study of the *Philosophy* should give him. Furthermore, when the dictates of nature inspired a performer he must have at his command the skill of a voice potential which would serve his creative instinct. That potential could be cultivated by routine and organized exercise of the voice, unrelated to any specific performance effort. [30]

He reasoned that as a violinist must learn finger dexterity and tonal control through exercise, so should a vocalist, speaker, or singer achieve vocal capacity that would serve him satisfactorily in moments of creative expression.

In the preparation of his own treatise, Rush was apparently keenly aware of the work of many of the earlier writers. His personal library contains many such volumes, most of which are replete with his own marginal notations of occasional agreement and frequent violent disgust.[31]

We are now ready to consider the five major and original contributions of Rush to the teaching of speech. In the first place, he made a bold gesture at clarifying speech nomenclature. Such confusion had resulted from earlier writers using terms so freely and interchangeably that their concepts themselves were often obscured. Rush attempted to give rhyme and reason to the terms currently being used. For example, he drew together the "elements." He classified voice under five general heads: quality, force, time, abruptness, and pitch.[32]

Discussion of pitch became more clarified under his terminology because he used terms with parallel reference in music. Many confusions such as existed between the meanings of quality and tone, inflection and pitch, and among *quantity*, *accent* and *force*, were clarified by his recorded nomenclature and because of the popularity of his book they became accepted terms. No doubt the nomenclature described and used in the *Philosophy* has been a great influence in developing the speech terminology in use today.

The second, and without doubt the most important original contribution, was his concept of a *radical* and *vanishing* movement in the production of phonetic units. A greater part of his text is based upon this concept. Much of his work on pitch and stress appears to be more original with him than it actually was because of his use of *radical* and *vanish* to explain them. *Radical* is the beginning or *root* of each sound unit from which the *vanish* can develop all manner of movement to complete the unit. This *vanishing* movement has usually a fading effect, although in some cases the *radical* fades into a *stressed vanish*. The simplest illustration of *radical* and *vanish* is the diphthong or receding glide. In vowel movements of the word *day* Rush refers to the [e] as the *radical* and the [i] or [j] as the *vanish*. In the approaching glide [j] as in the word *yes*, the radical is the [j] and the [ɛ] the *stressed vanish*. There is no definite division of movement into two parts; rather these terms are "general reference to the two extremes of the movement."[33]

He pointed out further that when the voice moves through the *radical* and *vanish* in a smooth manner with no effort to prolong either the attack or the release of the sound, the *equable concrete* movement is formed. If the first part of the sound is prolonged and the *vanish* is terminated rapidly, the *protracted radical* is created. Likewise, the *protracted vanish* occurs when the *radical* is slighted but greater stress and duration is given the *vanish*.

Much can be explained by *radical* and *vanish*. Differences in stress and loudness occur always between the *radical* and *vanishing* movement. Between *radical* and *vanish* there must be a difference in pitch. Song is distinguished from speech in that song is characteristically a monotone. The pitch differences in song are of melodic nature, but a word or syllable sung on a single melody note is a *monotone*. Rush said there could be no such thing as a *monotone* in speech for there must be a change in pitch sometime during the *radical-vanishing* movement of each syllable. This can certainly be observed when a person speaks in a so-called *monotone*, for the monotonous effect comes from a predominant pitch or pitch pattern, while there are still present the slight pitch changes during each *radical-vanishing* movement of a syllable.

The third phase of his original work on voice was his explanation of the phonetic elements, based upon the function of *radical* and *vanish*. He not only reclassified them to avoid the inconsistencies of spelling, but also to observe the intonation of speech. He recognized thirty-five phonetic elements which he divided into three groups: the *tonics, subtonics,* and *atonics.* The *tonics* are capable of complete *radical* and *vanish* movements (vowels, glides); the *subtonics* can embrace this movement within themselves less perfectly, depending usually upon an adjacent tonic for completion (voiced consonants); and the *atonics* are incapable of employing the movement, but serve in the capacity of imitators or terminators (unvoiced consonants). The *tonics* serve best as vehicles of flexibility in intonation, the *subtonics* next best, and the *atonics* are of least value in that respect. He also described the sounds as to aspiration, abruptness, and other phonetic characteristics. His was the clearest and most reasonable phonetic analysis of his day.

The fourth original contribution was his treatment of syllabication. This again was based upon the *radical* and *vanishing* movement. A syllable depends upon the completion of the *radical* and *vanish*. When that movement has been terminated any new sound produced will of necessity initiate another syllable. The presence of a final *atonic* means that another syllable will of necessity be initiated if it is followed by a *subtonic* or *tonic* which has the capacity to begin a new *radical* and *vanish* movement. Two adjacent *atonics* prolong the syllable, but once the *vanish* is completed by an *atonic* a new movement cannot be begun without a second syllable resulting.

He showed further how varying effects of the syllables are created by combining different phonetic elements in the creation of a complete *radical-vanish* movement.

The first difference in the quality of a syllable is created by the presence of the *tonics* alone. Rush said in this case that there is no difference in the agreeableness of the sound, for the diphthongs are as pleasant as pure vowels, even though the concrete rise of a diphthong is composed of two different alphabetic elements.

The second type of syllable is one in which the *tonic* is initial and is followed by one or two *subtonics,* as in [ɛlm]. This forms an "easy mingling of their constituents" and consequently a pleasant, blending effect.[34]

The third type is that in which a *tonic* is preceded and followed by a *subtonic* as in [memz], [rɛlm]. A continuant effect is created by this combination also.

The fourth arrangement of elements is not so agreeable, Rush said, for *tonics, subtonics* and *atonics* are combined. This presence of the *atonic* prevents the equability of the concrete and consequently a less smooth effect. An example of this composite type is in *strength* [strɛŋθ].

A fifth arrangement is found in the second syllable of *little,* in which no *tonic* is present. Such a combination lacks strength, Rush said.

Rush also had a word to say about the glide, which he did not call by that name, but which he discussed in showing the "various degrees in the smoothness of the syllabic impulse." [35] For instance, in the word *flower* he shows how two syllables are created if the *w* subtonic is inserted between the two tonics. In other words, if the *o* is uttered as distinct diphthong [aʊ], with the [ʊ] as a protracted *vanish* movement, a complete *radical* and *vanish* results and a full syllable is formed. Thus when the [ɜ] is sounded a new *radical* is begun and a second syllable ensues.

Rush further said that if the *o* in rising through the concrete interval to the *vanishing* movement blends the [ʊ] of the diphthong with the final *er*, only one syllable results. The final [r] becomes the *vanish* of [a] and the word is spoken as one syllable, thus [flaʊr].

He added to the foregoing comment on the word *flower,* the explanation of how a *y* is often inserted between awkward combinations of successive tonics as in *aorta.* This reduces the necessity of a point of junction in vocality in order to start the *radical* of the second tonic after the *vanish* of the preceding tonic. If the *y* is inserted, a continuous utterance is created with the *y,* [i], becoming the vanish of the preceding tonic.

These two incidental observations of Rush demonstrate his recognition of the concept of glide on the basis of the reaction of the *radical* and *vanishing* movement to these particular alphabetic constructions.

Rush made rather significant observations in the field of phonetic analysis which apparently were of less interest to his contemporaries and followers, and consequently have not been identified among his contributions to speech pedagogy.

The fifth point of originality in Rush's vocal theory was his detailed description of the specific interval of inflection. He described the emotional and intellectual impressions created by the use of certain intervals of pitch-change in the spoken word. These vary from semi-tone changes in plaintive expression, when the change in pitch is so slight between the *radical* and *vanishing* movement that only the trained ear will recognize it as a varying pitch, to the octave inflection of interrogation and emphasis. He described the effect of these intervals as they occur in both rising or falling *slides,* in the *circumflex* and in the *step* forms. These variations are so rapid and in some cases so minute that it is difficult to recognize their existence as an important discriminating factor between speech and song. They are responsible, however, for much of the emotion and shades of meaning in speech.

These five phases of his vocal philosophy may be regarded as the most significant and original contributions of his book.

Rush made other contributions to speech education in his treatise on voice. Among them were his arrangement and treatment of vocal elements which became the pattern many teachers used in formulating their own instructional theory. Although almost all aspects of his description of vocal elements were already in literature,[36] Rush's own arrangement, terminology, and observable variations of course constituted definitive differences. His use of the concept of *radical* and *vanish* permeated his presentation and gave it original character.

Some mention should be made of Rush's treatment of vocal quality, since there appears to be some difference of opinion in later literature concerning his statement of this element and because of its relationship to the *Natural History of the Intellect.*

The chapters in the *Philosophy* which Rush subjected to greater revision than any others throughout the six editions were those dealing with verbal expression of mind and passion, and with the physiological description of voice. Rush believed one cannot understand the quality of voice without knowing what structures are involved in the production of it; hence as he attempted to give physiological description to vocal quality, he utilized what information was known factually about the anatomy of the vocal mechanism, added his own observations, and described all vocal behavior as physiological functioning of structure. Such study, evolving from his long-range intentions of discovering states of the mind, was subject to much revision and eventually produced his opinion on "Vocal Signs of Thought and Passion."[37] The relationship of his work on voice to his later volumes on intellect is more clearly seen in this aspect of voice analysis. In an attempt to understand the mind, he described in detail the peripheral, or vocal, signs of thought and feeling. After recording such observation in terms of vocal quality, inflections, changes of stress, and time, he then attempted to describe all the possible thoughts and passions which might give rise to such variety of vocal signs. Thus *The Philosophy of the Human Voice*, which was born of his medical inquiry into mind, itself became the parent of *The Natural History of the Intellect*, the product of his attempt to describe the combinations of mental functioning which give rise to vocal expression.

Throughout all the editions of Rush the total number of vocal qualities described in any way are six. Of these, the *nasal* quality is mentioned only as a *subtonic* in his classification of phonetic elements, and the *guttural* is given as a defective and unpleasant utterance already described by rhetoricians. The *whisper* is listed as a quality of voice until the sixth edition of his text, when he used the term *vocality* for *quality*, and hence the *whisper* could not qualify.

The *natural* quality of voice is that used in ordinary speaking and employs complete pitch range. It is produced by the vibration of the vocal cords and is capable of discrete, concrete and tremulous pitch motion. Lively or moderate sentiments of colloquial dialogue and of familiar lecture and discourse are expressed by this quality as Rush described it.

The *falsette* [sic] is "that peculiar voice in which the higher degrees of pitch are made, after the natural voice breaks or outruns its power." [38]

Again, all the phonetic elements may be made in the falsette (except of course, atonics) and it has the same pitch flexibility, although limited in range; it is made with the same mechanism which produces the normal voice. It is frequently used in screaming, and giving expression to pain and surprise.

The *whisper*, which is merely a continuant of atonic elements, is a form of producing speech which is used in expressing secrecy, and gives rise to the aspirated form of vocalization. The aspirate, per se, is never referred to as a quality of voice.

The *orotund* voice is "that natural or improved manner of uttering elements which exhibits them with a fullness, clearness, strength, smoothness, and a ringing or musical quality, rarely heard in ordinary speech." [39] It is obtainable, Rush believed, only after much cultivation of voice; in speech, it would require the adaptation of the "pure tone" production of singing and a more complete control of expiration. Its advantages in speaking are to give a greater fullness and smoothness to voice, to aid in distinct articulation, to give greater strength and musical value, and to maintain voice under better control. He declared it to be a most useful quality for interpretative purposes, but in no way should it detract from one's use of the normal quality.

Thus, Rush gave explanation to vocal quality—a phenomenon of voice resulting from the function of body structure under government of mind. Expression of thought, changes in emphasis, and passion itself are all evidenced as the product of changing combinations of quality, pitch, force, rhythm. Again it should be remembered that while Rush made a detailed description of the isolated speech processes, he expressed the modern viewpoint that it is the total, complete, and cumulative effect which is expressive. Each of the elements gives its share of support to the whole, but no element should itself be noticeable in the patterns of expressive communication.

IV

While the *Philosophy* became very popular with teachers of elocution after its first edition in 1827, it still did not give Rush the recognition which would have permitted his return to his earlier scientific studies. Accordingly, he felt that if he could attain a reputation as a literary writer, using his early love and aptitude for poetic composition, he might achieve the popular acclaim he needed to pave the way for his profound medical discourse. This resulted in the publication in 1834 of *Hamlet, A Dramatic Prelude in Five Acts*.[40] In this effort too, he fell short of the mark and remained obscure as a literary figure as well as a scientist.

Rush took heart, however, from the early appeal of the *Philosophy* and revised it three times before attempting to finish his work on the mind. By a few teachers such as Jonathan Barber, the *Philosophy* was held to be an unprecedented triumph. On the other hand, Barber himself suffered great social and professional reverses because of championing and even associating with a man whom society did not greatly respect.[41] Barber's *Exercises in Reading*[42] published in 1823 was entirely in accord with Rush and the two men were immediately attracted to each other. In fact, Rush attributed a large part of the *Philosophy*'s success to Jonathan Barber. Others who apparently approved were Jonathan's younger brother John,[43] a lecturer in the City of New York; Samuel Gummere,[44] then principal of a school in Burlington, New Jersey; a Mr. Dennison, an Irishman and teacher in Philadelphia; Dr. Andrew Comstock,[45] a physician who had established himself as a teacher of elocution in Philadelphia; and William Bryant, a clergyman of the Episcopal Church.

Several authors used material directly from Rush, probably without his consent. Rush had obvious reason to be incensed by plagiarisms of authors like Rev. W. B. Lacey,[46] Lyman Cobb,[47] Richard Cull,[48] and there is evidence of much unpleasant exchange of correspondence between Rush and men who were attempting to take advantage of him. He wrote Charles Whitney and accused him of unauthorized use of his name in an Albany, New York, *Evening Journal* advertisement which announced Whitney as a teacher of reading, declamation, and singing.[49]

The fact that Rush wrote at all in the field of speech was rather accidental and resulted from an unusual turn of affairs. Yet once he demonstrated that human vocal expression could be observed in minute detail and given an orderly and systematic description, he established a precedent which lesser men than he were to abuse. Rush did not plan a prescriptive system for teachers of elocution, but intended to show nature's orderly design. That he should have given impetus to a trend towards mechanical artifice of communication and aesthetic art was an unhappy ending to a noble determination to discover scientific facts about human behavior.

Many simplifications of his system were soon published by teachers who sought to present a concise outline of elocutionary art to students. These abridgements did not recognize his true purpose but prescribed the very artifices Rush had sought to remedy. In the Preface to the third edition of his *Philosophy*, Rush took occasion to condemn the practice of simplifying his system for schools:

This attempt, either by its very purpose, or by the manner of its execution has perhaps had the effect to retard the progress of our new system of the voice. For, the superficial character of these books, and the mingling of parts of the old method with parts of the new, together with an attempt to give definition and order to these scattered materials, has left the inquirer unsatisfied, if indeed, it has not brought his mind to confusion.[50]

He continues later:

One of the purposes of this work is to show, by refuting an almost universal belief to the contrary, that elocution *can* be scientifically taught, but the manner of explanation and arrangement in too many of these garbled schoolbook compilations, has gone far towards satisfying the objectors that it cannot.[51]

While his work on the voice was regarded as the first part of his greater work on mind, he felt that the *Human Intellect* was essential to the understanding of the *Philosophy* and should have been published as a companion work. And so it proved to be; for mid-twentieth century speech pedagogy, in keeping with Rush's basic views, holds speech to be a total physical reaction inseparable from thought, action, and emotion. Some teachers of speech today, however, ridicule what they believe to be the mechanical and superficial "system" he instigated, which was in reality a popular application gaining reputation before his major investigation of mind was revealed and his total philosophy of behavior understood.

After editing the *Philosophy* for the last time in 1866 (the 1879 edition was a reprint, following the terms of his will), his last publication was *Rhymes of Contrast on Wisdom and Folly,* appearing in the year of his death. It attempted to give evidence of the working principles of *The Natural History of the Intellect.* He demonstrated in his writing of the dialogue in rhyme the use of "natural or related ties" as an involuntary process of thought resulting from prior perceptions. This process of association had been described in its defective state by Dr. Benjamin Rush as "dissociations," [52] and no doubt referred to the disorder known today as "dysphasia." "It consists not in false perception ... but of an association of unrelated perceptions, or ideas, from inability of the mind to perform the operations of judgment and reason." [53]

The last years with his wife prior to her death had been under estranged conditions. This, together with his failure to obtain public approval for his work, embittered him. He retired from the society which had rejected him, to become a recluse, totally disillusioned, much misunderstood. Just prior to his death he apparently dictated a final statement to his brother-in-law, Henry J. Williams, who became executor of his estate; it read: "Dr. James Rush died in 1869 from difficulty of breathing in the eighty-fourth year of his age." [54] It was written in another hand (probably that of Mr. Williams whose initials, H. J. W., appear in the left-hand corner) but a last shaky signature of James Rush is affixed to the document. His will, among other provisions, called for the construction of a library building to be given to the Library Company of Philadelphia, and called the Ridgway Branch, in memory of his wife. In it were to be housed his entire private library and that of his father, whom he had admired and unsuccessfully imitated. This collection has served many scholars who seek after the works of Benjamin and James Rush. In a memorial tomb in the Ridgway Library, James Rush rests with his wife, uncomforted still by the "knock of friends" and too often misunderstood by a profession he accidentally came to serve.

As a medical scientist who was led to explore the entity called *mind* and as a "voice scientist" who rigorously studied vocal behavior, James

Rush was probably the first investigator to see that mind is inseparable from the physical phenomena of self-expression. His fellow scientists, hampered by their prejudices, could not fairly criticize his views. Overly-zealous teachers of elocution, misusing the information of his *Philosophy*, earned him ill repute among most modern teachers of speech. Perhaps only the speech historian of the 1950's understands that his field stands in heavy debt to Dr. Rush.

Notes

1. James Rush, *The Philosophy of the Human Voice: Embracing Its Physiological History: Together with a System of Principles by Which Criticism in the Art of Elocution May be Rendered Intelligible, and Instruction, Definite and Comprehensive. To which is added a Brief Analysis of Song and Recitative* (Philadelphia, 1827). Hereafter cited as *Philosophy*. Other editions: 1833, 1845, 1855, 1859, 1867, 1879.

2. See *The Autobiography of Benjamin Rush*, ed., George W. Corner (Princeton, 1948). Richard Rush had become Attorney General of the United States in 1813 under President Monroe and it would have been most embarrassing to him if in this year of his father's death, the autobiography were released to the public with its revelations concerning the heroic personalities of the nation's fathers. Hence Richard and James, even after much deletion and editing, agreed to prevent its publication. It has recently been published after it came into the possession of the American Philosophical Society in 1943, through the papers of Alexander Biddle, grandson of Samuel Rush, a brother of Richard and James, who had taken them "without authority" from James' Library.

3. For example, see letter of Dr. E. Miller to Benjamin Rush, New York, July 2, 1809. Rush Papers, Library Company of Philadelphia, Ridgway Branch.

4. Nathan Goodman, *Benjamin Rush, Physician and Citizen* (Philadelphia, 1934), pp. 254-255.

5. *Medical Inquiries and Observations upon the Diseases of the Mind*, 3rd ed. (Philadelphia, 1827), pp. 8-9.

6. Dugald Stewart, *Elements of the Philosophy of the Human Mind* (Brattleboro, 1808), [First ed., 1792].

7. James Rush, *A Brief Outline of the Analysis of the Human Intellect; Intended to Rectify the Scholastic and Vulgar Perversions of the Natural Purpose, and Method of Thinking; by Rejecting Altogether The Theoretic Confusion, The Unmeaning Arrangement, and Indefinite Nomenclature of the Metaphysician*, 2 vols. (Philadelphia, 1865), II, 435-436. Hereafter cited as *Human Intellect*.

8. *Ibid.*, II, 436.

9. *Letters of Benjamin Rush*, ed. L. H. Butterfield, 2 vols. (Princeton, 1951), I, p. lxix.

10. *Ibid.*, Benjamin Rush to Mrs. Rush, July 16, 1791, p. 600.

11. *Human Intellect*, II, 472.

12. Notation by Rush, in Rush Papers, December 14, 1835, Ridgway Branch, Library Company of Philadelphia.

13. James Rush, *Rhymes of Contrast on Wisdom and Folly. A Comparison Between Observant and Reflective Age, Derisively Called Fogie, and a Senseless and Unthinking American Go-Ahead. Intended to Exemplify An Important Agent in the Working Plan of the Human Intellect* (Philadelphia, 1869), p. xi.

14. Mary Rush to Rush, August 10, 1834. Rush Papers.

15. *Human Intellect*, II, 474.

16. *Ibid.*, I, 9.

17. *Human Intellect*, I, 195. Beginning with the fourth edition, 1855, of the *Philosophy*, Rush attempted to introduce the double comma as a punctuation mark to be of value between a single comma and a semi-colon.

18. *Human Intellect*, I, 189.

19. *Ibid.*, p. 4.

20. *Ibid.*, II, 1.

21. Philadelphia *Evening Bulletin*, July 12, 1900.

22. *Human Intellect*, II, 471.

23. *Ibid.*, p. 472.

24. *Ibid.*, p. 473.

25. Robert Smith, *Harmonics, or the Philosophy of Musical Sounds* (London, 1759).

26. *Human Intellect*, II, 475.

27. Rush's marginal notation in his personal copy of John Walker, *Elements of Elocution* (Boston, 1810), p. 244.

28. *Philosophy* (1845), p. 123.

29. *Philosophy* (1859), p. 503.

30. *Philosophy* (1827), pp. 548-549.

31. Among other authors whose books Rush used are: Rev. James Chapman, *The Music, or Melody and Rhythms of Language* ... (Edinburgh, 1818); William Cockin, *The Art of Delivering Written Language; or, an Essay on Reading* ... (London, 1775); John Dwyer, *An Essay on Elocution* (Cincinnati, 1824); William Enfield, *The Speaker, or Miscellaneous Pieces Selected from the Best English Writers* ... (London, 1835; Dedication dated 1774); John Foster, *An Essay on the Different Nature of Accent and Quality* ... (London, 1761); Henry Home of Kames, *Elements of Criticism*, 2 vols. (Philadelphia, 1816); John Mason, *An Essay on Elocution or Pronunciation*, ... (London, 1748), *An Essay on the Power of Numbers, and the Principles of Harmony in Poetical Composition* ... (London, 1749), *An Essay on the Power and Harmony of Prosaic Numbers* ... (London, 1749); Abbé Maury, *The Principles of Eloquence: Adapted to the Pulpit and the Bar,* tr. John Neal Lake (London, 1793); Lord Monboddo, *Essays on the Origin and Progress of Language*, 6 vols. (Edinburgh, 1774); Messieurs du Royal Port, *The Art of Speaking: In Pursuance of a Former Treatise, Intituled, The Art of Thinking* (London, 1708); Ebenezer Porter, *Analysis of the Principles of Rhetorical Delivery as Applied in Reading and Speaking* (Boston, 1827), *Art of Speaking* (Philadelphia, 1775); Thomas Sheridan, *A Rhetorical Grammar of the English Language, calculated solely for the Purposes of Teaching Propriety of Pronunciation, and Justness of Delivery* ... (Philadelphia, 1783), *A Course of Lectures on Elocution: together with Two Dissertations on Language* ... (London, 1781), *Lectures on the Art of Reading* (London, 1798); B. H. Smart, *A Practical Grammar of English Pronunciation* ... (London: John Richardson, 1810), *The Practice of Elocution,* (London, 1826), *The Theory of Elocution: to which are now added, Practical Aids for Reading the Liturgy* (London, 1826); Sir Joshua Steele, *An Essay Towards Establishing the Music and Measure of Speech to be Expressed and Perpetuated by Peculiar Symbols* (London, 1775); W. Thelwall, *Introductory Discourse on the Nature and Objects of Elocutionary Science* ... (London, 1805); John Walker, *A Key to the Classical Pronunciation* (Philadelphia, 1808), *A Rhetorical Grammar in which the Common Improprieties in Reading and Speaking are Detected* ... (Boston, 1814), *Elements of Elocution, being the Substance of a Course of Lectures on the Art of Reading* ... 2 vols. (London, 1781), *The Melody of Speaking Delineated* (London, 1787).

32. *Philosophy* (1827), p. 29 ff.

33. *Ibid.*, p. 43.

34. *Ibid.*, p. 82.

35. *Ibid.*, p. 83.

36. See note 31 for writers whose books were among those available to Rush and no doubt of service to him.

37. *Philosophy* (1859), p. 478 ff.

38. *Philosophy* (1833), p. 83.

39. *Ibid.*, p. 90.

40. (Philadelphia, 1834).

41. From a section of the Printer's Copy of the 2nd edition of the *Philosophy* which was omitted from the 1833 edition.

42. *Exercises in Reading and Recitation* (Baltimore, 1823).

43. *Exercises in Reading and Recitation* (Albany, 1828).

44. *A Compendium of the Principles of Elocution on the Basis of Dr. Rush's Philosophy of the Human Voice* (Philadelphia, 1857).

45. *Practical Elocution* (Philadelphia, 1830).

46. *Elocution* (Albany, 1828).

47. *N. A. Reader* (Zanesville, Ohio, 1836).

48. *Garrick's Mode of Reading the Liturgy of the Church of England* (London, 1840).

49. James Rush's letters, Ridgway Branch, Library Company of Philadelphia.

50. *Philosophy* (1845), p. xi.

51. *Ibid.*

52. *Medical Inquiries and Observations upon the Diseases of the Mind*, p. 257.

53. *Ibid.*

54. James Rush Papers.

11 The Literary Society [1]

DAVID POTTER

....

> When a multitude of young men, keen, open-hearted, sympathetic, and
> observant, as young men are, come together and freely mix with each
> other, they are sure to learn one from another, even if there be no one
> to teach them; the conversation of all is a series of lectures to each,
> and they gain for themselves new ideas and views, fresh matter of
> thought, and distinct principles for judging and acting, day by day.
>
> —JOHN HENRY NEWMAN, *The Idea of a University*

As the previous studies in this volume have indicated, an outstanding
characteristic of the early American college was its tightly knit and
closely regulated constitution. Indeed, one might conclude from an
examination of the college laws and regulations that the daily life,
social as well as curricular, of the student was designed "to reduce to a
minimum the time the devil might find employment for idle hands"
and idle minds. [2]

When judged by modern standards, however, the colonial student,
despite his closely supervised schedule, did not lead a particularly
strenuous life. But unless he strolled within bounds or indulged in the
mild forms of exercise not on the banned list, he had few approved
methods of consuming his surplus energy. The company of young
ladies was usually forbidden during college sessions. Organized athletics were unheard of. And even the privilege of reading contemporary
periodicals, much less current fiction, was denied him because the
ordinary college library contained few if any "authors who have wrote
within these 30 years." [3]

The company of his fellow scholars was practically the only legitimate avenue of escape from the academic routine which remained
open to the colonial student. It is to be expected, therefore, that
societies featuring jovial companionship as well as student-directed
opportunities for parliamentary practice, oratory, declamation, debate,
literary efforts, dramatic "productions," and reading material, all relatively free from faculty censorship and, usually, protected from "pry-

ing" eyes by high walls of secrecy, would come into being almost from the beginning of American higher education.

Rise of the Societies

In the North and South

Although student societies of a religious nature had existed on the American college campus at least as early as 1716, the first of the college literary and debate societies appears to have been the Spy Club of Harvard which, in its bylaws of 1722, was stipulating:

That a discourse of about Twenty minutes be made at every meeting by one of the Society on any Subject he pleaseth.

That any Difficulty may be propos'd to the Company & when propos'd the company shall Deliver their Thôts upon It.

That there be a Disputation on Two or more questions at every Meeting, one part of the Company holding the Affirmative, the other the Negative part of ye Question.[4]

By 1782, Harvard was also the site of the Philomusarian Club, concerted "in order—to Stem That Monstrous Tide of Impiety & Ignorance which is Like to Sweep all Before it & for Our Mutual advantage & Emolumᵗ....,"[5] and in 1770, of the Speaking Club of Harvard, later called the American Institute of 1770, which sternly ruled that "no Member shall speak in Latin in his turn nor at any other time without special Leave from the President."[6]

At Yale, in 1753, the long-lived Linonian Society was founded, largely through the efforts of President Clap (one of the first college administrators to recognize the importance of the societies as undergraduate safety valves as well as literary and forensic proving grounds). But even earlier, at least by 1750, an ephemeral college society, the Critonian, was conducting literary sessions in New Haven. And in 1768, the second major Yale society, the Brothers in Unity, disputed questions of its choosing.

Before the outbreak of the Revolution, other colonial chartered colleges witnessed the rise of undergraduate and graduate student societies. On November 11, 1750, the Flat Hat Club was founded at William and Mary and included Thomas Jefferson on its rolls, while on December 5, 1776, the Phi Beta Kappa society was constituted at the Williamsburg college with "Friendship for its Basis, Benevolence and Literature for its Pillars...," and with the assurance to its initiates that "now...you may for awhile disengage yourself from scholastic Laws and communicate without reserve whatever reflections you may have made upon various objects...."[7]

Princeton, then the College of New Jersey, appears to have been the scene of society rivalry early in its history. From the pioneering Plain-Dealing and Well-Meaning clubs, sprang two of our most vigorous college societies, the American Whig in 1769 and the Cliosophic in 1770.

Columbia (King's College) also had active forensic societies early in its history. On June 11, 1766, the *New York Weekly Gazette or Weekly Post Boy* informed its readers that "Several gentlemen having thought proper to form themselves into a . . . Literary Society, for the encouragement of learning, have raised a fund. . . ." It is likely that Alexander Hamilton belonged to this or similar society during his stay at King's.

Rutgers (Queen's College) also supported at least two pre-Revolutionary societies. Little is known of the Polemic other than a reference to its existence by Simeon De Witt in a letter to John Bogart dated February 14, 1778. At this time, however, another society, the Athenian, had been in existence "on the Banks" for five years, polishing the minds and beautifying the manners of a select group of students, faculty members, and townsfolk.

In the years which followed the war and particularly in the first two decades of the nineteenth century, the majority of the longer lasting societies were established at the older colleges. Such stalwarts were activated as the Hasty Pudding Club of Harvard in 1795, a society which even in its infancy mixed such stunts as the breach of promise case of Dido *vs.* Aeneas with serious debates on "questions of literature, morality and politics"; Philolexian in 1802 and Peithologian four years later at Columbia; Philoclean and Peithessophian at Rutgers by 1825; the Misokosmian (later the Philermenian) in 1794 and the United Brothers in 1806 at Brown; the Social Friends in 1783 and the United Fraternity in 1786 at Dartmouth; and the Philomathean in 1813 and Zelosophic in 1829 at Pennsylvania.

At other prominent colleges north and south of the Mason-Dixon line, strong student societies were functioning soon after college classes were formed. For example, three years after the receipt of its charter, Dickinson was the site of the Belles Lettres Society (in 1786). As early as 1795, the Debating Society, parent of the Dialectic and the Concord Societies, was featuring debating, composing, reading, speaking, and parliamentary procedure at North Carolina. In 1803, scarcely two years after the opening of the college, Demosthenians turned on their flow of oratory at the University of Georgia. At Hamilton, all students were expected to join one of the two societies, the Phoenix and the Union, which were founded in 1812, the year the college was chartered.

In the West

As higher education spread to the West, the literary and debate societies found fertile ground and were amply nourished by appreciative administrations and student bodies even after many of the older Northern and Southern organizations were in a period of decline.

At the Ohio colleges, the first student society appears to have been the Zelothean founded at Ohio University in 1812, some eight years after the organization of the college. Other Ohio campuses were even more receptive. At Western Reserve, Joseph Welch Barr, a transfer from Hamilton, helped form the Philozetian Society six weeks before the organization of a faculty at the college. In 1830, the Adelphic and Franklin Societies were founded at Reserve and from them descended Phi Delta. Oberlin, founded in 1833, had its share of vocal student organizations shortly after its doors were opened. But its most interesting claim to forensic fame lies in its fostering of the Young Ladies' Association "for the promotion of literature and religion" in 1835, the first of the female societies in our colleges. Also, in 1835, Denison, founded four years earlier, gave its support to the Calliopean Society and, in 1843, to the Franklin Literary Society, important forces in campus politics as well as in literary and forensic endeavors.

In Indiana, the colleges were as active forensically as their Ohio counterparts both in the classroom and in the "halls" of the student societies. In 1830, one year after Indiana University emerged from its Seminary days, the Athenian Society was founded, followed by the Philomathean Society in 1831. At little Wabash, the Philomatheans dated their history from 1834, the year of the college charter. In 1835, the Western Literary Society, later the Euphronean, was chartered by the state. Similarly, DePauw sponsored the Philological Society in 1870 and the co-educational Atlantis Society in 1873. And Notre Dame, while not so forensic-minded as other Indiana colleges, harbored such interesting associations as the St. Cecilia which, according to the 1870 catalog, was a dramatic and musical society as well as a debating club; and the Thespians, a pioneer among Indiana collegiate dramatic associations in 1861.

In 1850, the year the first undergraduate class was formed at the University of Wisconsin, the first of the Madison literary societies was established at a faculty-sponsored meeting. Following the advent of this organization, named the Athenian by Chancellor John Lathrop, a number of other societies were created by student groups, chief among them being the Hesperian in 1853 and the Castalia, a women's club, in 1864.

Moving farther west, the pattern was repeated at the major state supported colleges in Iowa. At the State University in 1861, but one year after the establishment of the collegiate department, the Zetagathian Society adopted its constitution, followed by the short-lived "Copperhead" splinter society, the Ciceronian, in 1862, and the Irving Institute in 1864. At Ames, the Iowa Agricultural College (Iowa State College) faculty sponsored the co-educational Philomathean Society during the pre-collegiate term in 1868 and in 1870 welcomed the Bachelor Society, which was followed in 1871 by the women's Cliolian.

As higher education was made available to the inhabitants of the far west, the majority of the college administrators followed the established practice of sponsoring literary and debating societies. Accordingly, the 1868-1869 catalog of the University of Deseret (University of Utah) declared:

Literary Societies will be found among the attractive and beneficial features of the University.
They will be organized among the students, and have for their objects a theoretical and practical training in oratory, debate, declamation, composition and parliamentary rule and order.[8]

At the "pioneer university of the west," Willamette, the Philomathean Society was incorporated by the Oregon Territorial Legislature in 1856, three years after the college was chartered. Unlike most of the societies of this period, Philomathean was established not only for students but also for faculty members and college sponsors. Within the next seventeen years, something new was added—two sets of brother and sister societies, Concordia (ladies) in 1861 and Hesperian (men) in 1865; and Alka (men) in 1866 and Atheneum (ladies) in 1870. At first, three joint meetings were held each term. By 1874, however, only one joint meeting was permitted per term and we read that "promiscuous meetings of the two sexes in the Society Halls . . . are forbidden except when some member of the Faculty is present or special permission has been granted. . . ." [9]

Moving south along the Pacific, we note that in 1857, Santa Clara sponsored the first meeting of the Literary Congress which divided its members into two houses, the Philalethic Senate and the Philhistorian House.

Thus by the time of the Civil War, the literary and debate society had extended its grasp on student extracurricular life from coast to coast.

Scope of The Societies—Debating

As their records indicate, the societies were catholic in the distribution of their energies and prescribed such varied exercises as spelling (in the old halls of Princeton) and declamation. They also sponsored magazines, imported prominent speakers, and conducted elaborate exhibitions for the edification of collegians, faculty, and townsfolk. But from the 1820's until their eventual decline, society energy, in the main, was concentrated upon society debating.

The Forensic Disputation

Until the rise of the student societies, the major or, in many instances, the only approved method of conducting academic debate in many American colleges was the Latin syllogistic disputation. Practically unchanged since its inception in the medieval universities, the Latin exercise was an important part of most early curricula and a feature of college exhibitions and commencements. Its format was strictly governed by rules laid down by the prevailing texts in logic and differed but slightly whether employed as a teaching and testing device or as a medium for academic display.

As indicated by Bartholomew Keckermann's *Systema Logicae*, popular at Harvard in the seventeenth century, and by *The Improvement of the Mind,* by the prolific eighteenth-century writer, Isaac Watts, the classroom procedure followed this regimen: a tutor or Professor, often the reverend president, selected a question in one of the arts or sciences taught in the college. A respondent was then appointed to defend the side of the question which, in the opinion of the tutor, represented truth. The remaining students in the class were then detailed to act as opponents with the express duty of raising logical objections to the question which the respondent either affirmed or denied.

The disputation was opened by the respondent who first read a carefully worded Latin discourse in which he stated the question, defined and delimited the question, and presented his strongest logically constructed arguments. Each of the opponents, then, made his objection to the case, drawn up in the form of a syllogism in which he either denied the major or minor premises or distinguished between the accepted usage of key words and the manner in which they were used by the respondent. The respondent, in turn, attempted to vindicate his argument by use of other syllogisms which the opponent denied or reinterpreted until the objections were silenced and "truth" triumphed logically. The tutor, of course, was always on hand to help out should the respondent falter in his command of logic and Latin.[10]

Founded to offset the uncompromising rigidity of the early American academic climate, the societies were quick to adopt types of debate which were more flexible and thus more suitable to the contemporary scene than the Latin syllogistics. As their minutes indicate, the "Two or more questions at every Meeting" ordered by the Spy Club constitution in 1722 were debated in English, anticipating the earliest record of curricular debating in the mother tongue by twenty-five years. It is likely, however, that the early English disputations resembled the Latin exercises insofar as they were carefully written and read or else committed to memory. They differed from the syllogistics, nevertheless, in several ways other than the linguistic. In the first place, as available examples of these English forensic disputations indicate, the use of emotional proof forbidden in the Latin exercise was not only permitted but encouraged in the newer method of argumentation. In the second place, although logic still played a prominent part in the constructive speeches of the forensic disputation, the syllogism was relegated to a minor position. And while, as we shall see, the questions discussed (or debated) were, at first, closely related to Latin theses disputed in the contemporary classrooms, a change in emphasis was not long in coming.

The Extempore Disputation

Eventually, of course, the college administrations recognized the value of the student initiated exercise. By 1747, English disputations were being held in Yale classrooms and ten years later, the president and fellows of Harvard voted "that once in a month the two sen.ʳ classes have their disputations in English & that in the forensic manner. . . ." [11] But by that time, the collegians were experimenting with something else. On November 6, 1766, for example, the Yale Fellowship Club minutes inform us that "the meeting was opened by an Extempore dispute by Bulkley, Kimberly and Lyon." [12]

By the end of the eighteenth century, many of the societies had adopted the extempore disputation as an additional form of debate, although one cannot determine what was meant by the term "extempore." At William and Mary in 1778, the minutes of Phi Beta Kappa indicate that the extempore was an impromptu exercise: "It be moreover strongly recommended to the other members *as an* additional and improving *Exercise,* to give their sentiments extempore on the same subject after hearing the others [who were assigned to forensics]." [13] But when the Phi Beta Kappa Society of Harvard introduced the extempore debate in 1785, the brothers apparently understood the term to have the meaning commonly held today, for the debaters were assigned to the exercise at a previous meeting, thus giving ample time for preparation and reasoned consideration—a provision also found in the laws of the Alpha chapter of New Hampshire in 1787 and the United Fraternity of Dartmouth in 1793.

As early as April 10, 1783, at least one society recognized the relative importance of the extempore debate to would-be lawyers and legislators. At that time, the Linonians voted that "two of the weekly meetings out of three be opened with an extempore Dispute and the third ... with a forensic Dispute. ..." [14] And by "extempore," the Yale men meant well prepared but not read or memorized constructive speeches, even though their intentions often outdistanced their performances.[15]

In 1810, the United Brothers of Brown prescribed extempore debating as *the* debating exercise of the society, a provision in force as late as July 7, 1855. In 1831, the Phi Beta Kappa Society of Harvard followed suit, and by the middle of the century, many society constitutions carried similar provisions although the forensic exercise was listed in some constitutions until the end of the nineteenth century.

Toward the middle of the century, the caliber of the forensic and extempore disputations was so high in the societies that several colleges dropped the exercises from the curriculum. Thus at Columbia, on January 4, 1837, the trustees were informed that "no exercises in extemporaneous speaking or debating were required from the Students, as there are two Societies ... of which these exercises constitute the principal objects." [16]

Intersociety Debating

At the turn of the century, the societies made another important contribution to debate history. Motivated by an intense rivalry which spurred the sister societies to extreme and, occasionally, ridiculous outbursts of energy, outstanding debaters, carefully selected and conditioned by their sponsors, "crossed" arguments at public exhibitions. As early as 1830, the Demosthenians and the Phi Kappas met at the University of Georgia. Before long, challenges and counter challenges were exchanged between the two leading societies of each college and the annual intersociety debates were a regular campus fixture.[17]

Then only a few decades after the first intersociety debates, something novel was introduced. To the best of my knowledge, it first happened at Illinois College on May 5, 1881. There, perhaps stimulated by the interstate oratorical contest held in Jacksonville early in the spring, the Phi Alpha Society of Illinois and the Adelphi Society of Knox met in a series of literary contests, Phi Alpha winning the debate, and Adelphi garnering honors in declamation, oratory, and essay writing. And the following day, at Kirkpatrick Chapel, in New Brunswick, New Jersey, the three representatives of Peithessophian (then struggling against general student inertia) successfully upheld the *status quo* against the representatives of New York University's Philomathean Society, who argued the affirmative of "Resolved that the only limitations on suffrage in the United States should be those of age and sex." Intercollegiate decision debating had arrived and, in the North, just in time to revive undergraduate and faculty interest in forensics.[18]

Debate Procedure

Because of the secret nature of the majority of the societies and because of the relative newness of academic debating in the vernacular, the early rules and regulations for the forensic and extempore exercises varied greatly from society to society and from college to college. Even toward the middle of the nineteenth century, there was little agreement among the rival organizations as to the selection of debaters and topics and as to the time and order allotted. Nor, as we shall see, was there a set pattern within the societies.

Selecting the Debaters

The majority of societies, like the Speaking Club of Harvard, rotated all exercises among the various performing classes, which, in turn, were constituted either by academic seniority or alphabetical distribution. Other groups, like the American Whigs in 1807, provided that the disputants "shall be appointed by the moderator" with the privilege of entering the discussion open to all society members after the appointed disputants had completed their arguments.[19] A few parliamentary minded organizations like the Society of Brothers in Unity in 1783, selected disputants by society nomination at the "preceding evening." [20] Societies which featured impromptu debates, like the United Fraternity in 1857, often prescribed that the disputants volunteer "as the role is called by the Secretary." [21] A farsighted variation of this method of appointing debaters was adopted by still other societies like the Linonian in 1835, when they voted that "whenever the requisite number, shall not be obtained by members voluntarily offering themselves, the deficiency, shall be supplied by appointments from the President." [22] Still another common provision in the society constitutions resembled the regulation of the Dialectic Association of Oberlin in 1839: "The Exec Committee (President, Vice-President, and Recording Secretary) shall appoint four disputants to occupy not over 15 minutes." [23]

The Number and Order of Debaters

In general, two to six debaters were appointed or volunteered for the regular debates although most societies provided for an unlimited number of volunteer debaters after the regular speakers had performed. However, one cannot generalize so easily about the order of the disputants. At Brown, for example, the Philermenian Society, in 1798, specified that "the Disputants shall speak in the following order—the first in the Affirmative shall open, the two in the Negative shall close upon him; and the second in the Affirmative shall close upon them; and then any Member may have liberty to offer his sentiments." [24] At Columbia, the society rules merely prescribed that the "President shall be empowered to select one from the Affirm. & one from the Neg. to open the debate . . ." with the order from that point on to be determined by the remaining contestants.[25] The majority of societies, however, like the Philoclean of Rutgers in 1832, required the affirmative to open the debate, each side speaking alternately.

Time Allotted for Debate

Although a few societies, like those at Georgia described by Professor Ellis M. Coulter in *College Life in the Old South*, turned on their oratory as early as nine o'clock on a Saturday morning and forgot to shut it off until the night had almost expired, the great majority of societies held their regular meetings in the evening and their constitutions strictly regulated the time allotted to the regularly appointed and the volunteer debaters. As might be expected, however, there was little agreement as to the limitations. Thus, for example, the Dialectic Association of Oberlin allotted its four disputants not over fifteen minutes in 1839. At neighboring Western Reserve in 1840, Phi Delta allowed the entire division assigned to debate an hour and a half. The Phoenix Literary Society of William and Mary in 1872, on the other hand, limited the two to four debaters (the number varied according to the desires and the persuasive powers of the president) to two speeches of not less than three minutes but not more than fifteen minutes. With presidential consent, the time could be extended to twenty minutes, beyond which society consent was required for more extensive argumentation. And the Philermenian Society of Brown, as late as June 12, 1858, ordered that the "Polemics shall speak only *once,* and only *ten minutes each,* before the question is given to the society; afterwards no member shall speak more than twice, or more than *ten* minutes at each time, without the consent of the Society." [26]

Judging the Debate

Although there was no set pattern for judging the formal society debates, most groups either provided for decisions by the president or by a specially appointed critic or board of critics, as at the United Fraternity as early as 1786 and the Linonian Society as late as 1878, or by a majority vote of the society members, as at the Cliosophic Society in 1823.

In the eighteenth century, the customary basis for the presidential or society decision was the validity or the merits of the question. Even as late as 1830, the minutes of the Philolexian Society indicate that

Columbia undergraduates were deciding debates according to the merits of the question and not according to the arguments advanced. Early in the nineteenth century, however, the societies began to provide for judging contestants according to their argumentative ability, as at the Cliosophic Society in 1823 and the Philoclean Society in 1831. By the middle of the nineteenth century, almost all the major societies provided for decisions according to the merits of the debate. But a number of the older societies, like the Brothers in Unity as late as 1861 and the Linonian Society in 1863, never broke entirely with the past and required decisions on both the merits of the question and the merits of the debate, the president determining the former, the society, the latter.

Although most of the societies followed the final rebuttal with a decision and then went on to other business, several organizations provided for a critical analysis of the debate and the debaters. In 1839, the Dialectic Association called for the president to criticize the performance of all speakers, while the American Whig Society, in 1848, stipulated that "It shall be the duty of the Sub-Committee—to sum up the arguments that have been advanced and decide the questions according to their merits. If the Committee be not unanimous then shall the Speaker decide between them stating his reasons; after which the decision of the House shall be taken." [27] And in 1875, the Cliosophic Society, which, as early as 1823, allowed any member to offer his sentiments on the debaters and the merits of the debate after the decision, wisely provided for a critic appointed at the stated meeting whose sole duty it was to give the Hall a "just and discriminating criticism upon the merits or demerits of the performance as well as upon the manner of its delivery." Then, after the critique, both the original performance and that of the critic were discussed by the brothers. [28]

Subjects Debated in the Colleges

Selecting the Topic

After the second decade of the nineteenth century, the majority of undergraduate societies solved the difficult problem of selecting the topic or topics for debate by providing for specially appointed committees which either reported to the president, who, in turn, selected the topic from a list of topics previously prepared, as at Cliosophic in 1823, or reported directly to the society, as at Peithessophian in 1827. Other societies, however, followed the pattern established by Phi Beta Kappa of Harvard in 1785 and required the president to furnish the topic, a practice retained by Philolexian as late as 1852. And several societies experimented with regulations like those adopted by the Philermenian brotherhood in 1794, repealed in 1798, and revived in 1812, which required that each member hand in two questions per term. The questions were, in turn, studied by a committee whose membership was constantly changing. Each committee then debated the question it selected.

The topics that were debated were not confined by strictly observed rules of censorship, as a rule, although the Philological Society of Pennsylvania in 1807 censored religious and political topics, the American Whig Society in 1812 decried the introduction of atheistic and deistic topics, and the Social Friends in 1834 and the Phoenix Society in 1872 warned against the use of religious subjects. In general, their minutes indicate that when societies limited the area of debate, the limitations were confined to the commonly accepted areas of the philosophical, political, and literary, as at Cliosophic in 1823 and Peithessophian in 1827.

Topics Debated

Despite the restrictions of groups like the Philological Society, the questions debated by the eighteenth-century societies often bore a startling resemblance to the metaphysical and philosophical theses defended by respondents at commencement and classroom syllogistics. Thus the Spy Club disputants in the 1720's argued: "Whether the Souls of Brutes are Immortal?" "Whether the happiness of Heaven will be progressive?" and "Whether there be any Infallable Judge of Controversies." [29]

As the passing century introduced pressing secular issues, the collegians, while retaining an interest in the philosophical and the religious, evinced an evergrowing concern over social and political as well as student problems. The following topics debated, selected at random from the records of the societies, indicate the widening range of interest:

Phi Beta Kappa of William and Mary:
  The Justice of African Slavery. February 27, 1779.
  Whether an Agrarian Law is consistent with the Principles of a wise Republic. June 5, 1779.
  Is Public or Private Education more advantageous. March 4, 1780.

Athenian Society of Rutgers:
  That Motion is the original cause of Heat. March 27, 1782.
  Whether the present Trade with the Enemy is disadvantageous to America in its present situation. July 24, 1782.
  Whether [there is] advantage arising from the Study of the dead Languages. August 7, 1782.

Linonian Society of Yale:

Whether Emigration from Europe to America would be beneficial to ye Latter. . . . March 17, 1791.

Whether a sudden emancipation of slavery would be politic in the state of Connecticut. June 19, 1794.

Brothers in Unity of Yale:

Whether women ought to be admitted to a share in civil government. July 19, 1792.

Would a separation between the Northern and Southern States be politic. . . . April 1, 1796.

Cliosophic Society of Princeton:

Whether ought Jews and Deists be admitted to all privileges of American citizens. August 5, 1792.

Whether debating or composition be more improving. May 27, 1794.

The early decades of the nineteenth century saw the trend toward the secular continue, with topics concerning national expansion, suffrage, defense, slavery, representation, international relations, crime and punishment, national economy, and educational problems predominant. Religious and "literary" topics were not, however, ignored, neither was sex. And a new ingredient, humor, began to show itself.

Representative questions with the decision of the judge or judges, whenever noted in the society records, follow:

Ought the U. States to take Possession of the Floridas? Philolexian Minutes (Columbia), November 7, 1819. Negative.

Ought the possession of property to be held indespensable to qualify a voter? United Brothers Minutes (Brown), May 1, 1813. Affirmative.

Ought representatives to be guided, in their votes, by the will of their constitutents? Cliosophic Minutes (Princeton), July 23, 1807. Affirmative. Philomathean Minutes (Pennsylvania), November 9, 1814. Negative.

Should the Slaves of the United States be emancipated? Clariosophic Minutes (South Carolina), 1812. Affirmative.

Was the conduct of the Governors of Connecticut & Massachusetts justifiable in refusing to call out the militia at the request of the general Government? Linonian Minutes (Yale), December 21, 1813. Negative.

Ought the regulations of Yale-College to be such, that students destined to different professions, might have an opportunity to pursue different courses of study. Linonian Minutes (Yale), June 7, 1810.

Is it probable that Russia will ever be able to destroy the balance of power in Europe? Philolexian Minutes (Columbia), November 13, 1819. Affirmative.

Are capital punishments beneficial or detrimental to a nation? American Whig Minutes (Princeton), February 15, 1813. Beneficial.

Whether it is just, & equitable, that old batchelors should be taxed for the support of old maids? Philolexian Minutes (Columbia), June 13, 1817. Negative.

The period 1820 to 1840 found the societies stronger than ever and rapidly multiplying in number. And as they solidified their hold on campus extracurricular life, they confidently passed judgment on most of the problems that faced their elders and on several that educators and statesmen had passed by.

Slavery and secession, of course, continued to attract much attention, particularly in light of the secessionist threats of South Carolina. Surprisingly, the records of the Southern societies indicate that the collegians did not commit themselves wholeheartedly to the cause of slavery, although one must remember that decisions were now being given, in the main, according to the merits of the debating. The following questions and decisions are representative:

> Is enslavement of human beings justifiable? Phi Kappa Minutes (Georgia), May 10, 1828. Negative.
> If South Carolina should secede from the Union ought the Southern states to assist her? Demosthenian Minutes (Georgia), September 18, 1830.

In general, although there were strong exceptions, the Northern and Western societies voted against the position of the Southern states:

> Is the holding of Slaves justifiable? American Whig Minutes (Princeton), January 17, 1820. Affirmative.
> Has a state the right to withdraw from the Union at pleasure? Linonian Minutes (Yale), April 4, 1832. Negative.
> Ought the government of the U.S. resort to force to secure the obedience of S. Carolina? Philolexian Minutes (Columbia), December 14, 1832. Affirmative.

Other national problems also occupied the attention of the undergraduate debaters. Of particular importance was westward expansion, now closely aligned with the spread of slavery. In general, the Southern societies voted for expansion if it favored the position of the South. The reaction of the rest of the collegians was mixed:

> Should Missouri be admitted to the Union, without the abolition of slavery? Cliosophic Minutes (Princeton), January 26, 1820. Negative.
> Would a peaceable accession of the Canadas be beneficial to the United States? Philomathean Minutes (Pennsylvania), March 29, 1820. Affirmative. Brothers in Unity Minutes (Yale), July 8, 1829. Negative.

Indian affairs, which previously had excited but little interest, now furnished many debate topics, especially in the North:

> Are not the insurrections of the Indians of our country justifiable on the the same grounds which prompted the Fathers of our country to revolt from the British yoke? American Whig Minutes (Princeton), November 5, 1832. Affirmative.

> Ought Georgia to extend jurisdiction over the Cherokee nation? Linonian Minutes (Yale), February 8, 1832. Negative.

Suffrage also furnished many topics for debate—with a noticeable but by no means overwhelming liberalization in attitude evinced by the critics:

> Ought the members of legislative bodies be required to possess a certain amount to Property. Euphradian Minutes (South Carolina), March 1, 1834. Negative. Cliosophic Minutes (Princeton), November 30, 1825. Affirmative.
>
> Ought the right of suffrage to be extended to citizens universally? Cliosophic Minutes (Princeton), June 6, 1832.

Education remained a popular subject. In the South, there was little change in the wording of the questions or in the recorded attitudes. In other parts of the country, however, there was an increasing scepticism toward prevailing educational practices:

> Is a classical education necessary to eminence in any profession? Adelphic Minutes (Western Reserve), June 1, 1830. Negative.
>
> Is the present system of College education calculated for entrance into practical life? Philolexian Minutes (Columbia), March 28, 1834. Negative.

As might be expected, sex was of some interest to disputants, especially in the South:

> Should seduction be considered a capital crime? Cliosophic Minutes (South Carolina), January 15, 1831. Negative.
>
> ... a man should be compelled by law to marry the victim of his seduction. Phi Kappa Minutes (Georgia), 1831. Affirmative.

International affairs still appealed to the society debaters, although not to the extent as did national issues. The following were among the many questions considered:

> Have we any cause to fear the growing power of Russia? Cliosophic Minutes (Princeton), August 23, 1820. Affirmative.
>
> Would it be prudent and politic for the United States to form a treaty offensive with the Republics of South America? Phi Kappa Minutes (Georgia), February 8, 1826. Negative.

Although religion did not enter the debate lists as in former years, except for the South, even the Northern and Western collegians were vitally concerned with such "problems" as:

> Is the increase of catholicism in the United States, ominous of evil? Adelphic Minutes (Western Reserve), October 13, 1820. Affirmative.
>
> Which has been the most prejudicial to mankind—Popery or Infidelity? Linonian Minutes (Yale), June 14, 1820. Popery.

And despite the predominance of the vital and the timely, the societies continued to debate such "old saws" as the execution of Mary of Scotland and the relative military merits of Caesar and Hannibal.

During the period 1840 to 1860, the Southern societies retained much of their vigor. The younger Western societies continued to expand. And even in the old Northern halls, where the exercises were often cancelled because of the lack of preparation, debating remained the primary exercise.

As in the previous decades, only the bounds of curiosity confined the limits of the debate topics. There was, however, a slight change in the frequency of the topics entertained. International affairs and foreign policy edged out slavery and secession in many societies as the war clouds threatened, and in the West education became increasingly popular as a source for debate topics. It is interesting, also, to note that many of the Southern societies abandoned the objectivity which marked much of their previous argumentation concerning slavery. Partisanship was generally the order after 1850 although some debaters (and some of their elders) hoped for compromise.

An idea of the interests, attitudes, and widespread intellectual curiosity of the undergraduates may be obtained from the following random listing of topics debated from 1840 to 1860:

Would a congress for international arbitration be desireable and practicable? Philermenian Minutes (Brown), April 19, 1851. Negative 11-5.

Would it be expedient for the U.S. to grant the petition of the Canadas requesting admission into the Federal Union? Phi Delta Minutes (Western Reserve), April 2, 1845. Negative.

Resolved that a dissolution of the Union would be beneficial to the South. Licivyronian Minutes (William and Mary), October 26, 1844.

Should South Carolina take the lead in the Southern cause? Euphradian Minutes (South Carolina), March 27, 1858. Affirmative.

Should Negroes be admitted to Yale College? Brothers in Unity Minutes (Yale), March 16, 1859.

Should a larger part of the college course be devoted to the study of the English language and literature? Phi Delta Minutes (Western Reserve), February 26, 1859.

Resolved that the present method of spelling is preferable to the Phonetic method. Young Ladies Literary Society Minutes (Oberlin), May 5, 1852.

Ought the U.S. Gov. to suppress Mormonism by force? Dialectic Association Minutes (Oberlin), September 10, 1844.

Are laws prohibiting immigration in any case justifiable? Clariosophic Minutes (South Carolina), January 29, 1842. Negative.

Is the tariff for manufacturing for the country's good? Erosophic Minutes (Alabama), May 31, 1845.

Resolved that the right of suffrage should be granted to females. Young Ladies Association Minutes (Oberlin), October 9, 1850.

Resolved—That the sale of ardent spirits ought to be prohibited by law. United Brothers Minutes (Brown), September 30, 1854.

Is Masonry compatible with our free institutes? Phi Delta Minutes (Western Reserve), December 23, 1840.

Although the Western societies continued to sponsor vigorous literary sessions throughout the period 1860-1881, the older societies of the South and the North were not so fortunate, and many expired during the war or shortly thereafter. Largely responsible for their decline was the rise of athletics, the popularity of the social fraternities, the competition of music clubs, dramatic clubs, and similar specialized organizations, the slow but gradual liberalization of the curriculum with a consequent influx of non-forensic minded students, the spread of the periodicals and other competing forms of communication, and the loosening of administrative regulations which removed many of the initial causes for the founding of the societies. But where the administrations were young and vigorous, as in the West, or where tradition was hallowed, as at Princeton, the societies held their own. And where the societies remained, forensics were featured.

In the South, immediately preceding the conflict, student attention, as in the period 1840 to 1860, was largely centered about the problems introduced by slavery and national policies with some attention paid to sex and the ancient academic "saws." Once the war started, however, there was relatively little time spent on vital issues. Escape topics furnished most of the subjects for what debating was done. But once the war ended, the awakening or surviving societies returned to a semblance of their former concern over national and, to a lesser degree, international affairs, and to heated discussions of the old "saws" which continued to appeal to the oratorically-minded Southern speaker.

Remaining records indicate that the Northern halls retained their interest in affairs of state throughout the entire pre-war and war years, although several societies with a large Southern membership, like Cliosophic of Princeton, eschewed the discussing of embarrassing topics until the war was almost over. For a time, the old ethical, literary, and historical questions made a strong comeback, but toward the end of the period they were greatly outnumbered by topics taken from the vital and pertinent areas of national, local, and, to a lesser degree, international affairs.

In the West, student interest in slavery and its resultant complications was sustained throughout the entire period. During the war, topics drawn from governmental policies and the field of education were particularly popular. And after the war, the period of reconstruction stimulated many debates on national policies. The problems concerning expansion and international happenings also appealed to society men.

In general, we can conclude that Northern and Western debaters, during the 1870's and the beginning of the 1880's, were primarily interested in national, local, and international policies in that order, with a range of interest that compares very favorably with that displayed today.

A sampling of the more popular topics debated by collegians throughout the country follows:

Should the South secede if Lincoln is elected? Demosthenian Minutes (Georgia), October 13, 1860.

Ought Pres. Johnson to be impeached for treason at the coming session of Congress? Linonian Minutes (Yale), October 31, 1866. Euphradian Minutes (South Carolina), February 23, 1867.

Resolved that a student should pursue his college course with reference to some profession. Dialectic Minutes (Oberlin), November 6, 1860.

Resolved that all studies should be made elective during Junior and Senior years. Philolexian Minutes (Columbia), March 9, 1871. Affirmative.

Should education be made compulsory in Alabama? Erosophic Minutes (Alabama), April, 1878.

Would a general congress of nations be expedient? Phi Delta Minutes (Western Reserve), March 14, 1860. Affirmative.

Should the negro be permitted to vote for elective offices? Demosthenian Minutes (Georgia), March 26, 1867.

Ought the United States to permit unlimited immigration? Brothers in Unity Minutes (Yale), January 11, 1870.

Resolved that athletics are carried to excess in the prominent American Colleges. Philolexian Minutes (Columbia), November 11, 1880.

Does art or nature contribute more to the beauty of the ladies of the present day? Cliosophic Minutes (Princeton), November 9, 1866.

Is language of Divine Origin? Peithessophian Minutes (Rutgers), February 4, 1870. Affirmative.

Resolved "that communism is a practical and desireable method of government." Phi Delta Minutes (Western Reserve), December 17, 1881. Negative.

Ought public opinion be regarded as the standard of right? Clariosophic Minutes (South Carolina), April 19, 1873.

Ought there to be any legislation in regard to strikes? Brothers in Unity Minutes (Yale), July 6, 1864. Negative.

Ought our Railroads to be in the hands of the Government? Phi Kappa Minutes (Georgia), March 16, 1869.

Ought the Young men of Alabama to seek their fortunes in other States? Philomathic Minutes (Alabama), April 30, 1875.

The Little Republics

We have endeavored to trace the origin of the literary and debating societies and we have examined the scope and influence of their major literary exercise, debating. From such a survey, we can readily conclude with William Jennings Bryan that the societies were "an important factor in school life...." [30] But to many college men of the eighteenth and nineteenth centuries, the societies were more than student safety valves or substitutes for inadequate contemporary curricula. They were, as to William H. Seward, by far the most important part of the educational system.[31] Although within the physical confines of the colleges and, consequently, subject to college regulations, the societies were, in many respects, little republics, possessing a student-centered and a student-administrated discipline complete with awards and punishments, carefully guarded rituals, specifically prescribed but easily amended exercises, and, frequently, comfortable and even elaborate quarters. For the Madisons, Websters, Calhouns, Choates, Evarts, Stones, Wilsons, and their contemporaries, they furnished a climate of opinion and a format for developing talents and personalities unequaled by any other facet of college life or instruction—then or now.[32]

A perusal of college histories indicates that Jacob Beam's estimation of the importance of the American Whig Society to its members during the nineteenth century could be applied to most American literary and debating societies during the eighteenth and early nineteenth centuries:

Throughout the century Whig stood to its members as something within the physical limits of the College yet above it and transcending it.... Hence, we hear with no surprise of the established principle that all collegiate exercises are to be neglected before the exercises of this institution (1813); of the debate decided, of course, in the affirmative "Are the exercises of this Hall of more importance than the studies of the College?" (1821), and the settled conviction many years later: "It is an acknowledged fact that the Hall training is as great a feature in the development of the intellectual life of the College as any two departments of instruction" (1893).[33]

Founded to circumvent the social, literary, and forensic limitations of the early American colleges, secret student clubs or societies closely followed the founding of institutions of higher learning throughout the country. Soon recognized by college administrations as valuable educational adjuncts and safety valves, the societies flourished throughout the country until the middle of the nineteenth century. Then, especially in the North, the rise of challenging extracurricular and social organizations, the gradual liberalization of the curriculum, and the changing complexion of the undergraduate body caused many of the old organizations to lessen in influence and activity. In the South, the Civil War weakened many colleges and, consequently, the college societies. After the war, the societies never attained their earlier measure of popularity. In the West, however, sponsored by strong administrative pressure, the societies continued to grow in prestige until the end of the nineteenth century, when, as in the North and South, intercollegiate debating temporarily gave the old organizations new life.

During the period of their greatest influence, the societies initiated many relatively new forms of debate and set up the framework for academic debating as we know it today. More than that, they furnished a place for college youth to try its literary, oratorical, and forensic wings under the aegis of a closely knit social organization.

To students of education in general and of speech in particular, the societies, through their records of topics debated and the methodologies involved, offer an insight into the development of important contemporary forms of debate and an understanding of the problems which faced our ancestors. To some of us, they engender nostalgia.

Notes

1. In order to prevent these notes from assuming unwieldy proportions while still retaining a primary function of indicating hard to find original sources, I have omitted all references to the histories and catalogs of colleges mentioned in the text except when material has been quoted. Also, I have eliminated references to the sources of literary society records except in the case of several direct quotations. The reader will notice that, whenever feasible, I have indicated the name of the society and the exact date of the minutes or constitution consulted, so that the original records, found for the most part in the libraries of the respective colleges, can be traced with little difficulty.

I should like to acknowledge my indebtedness to Dr. Frank B. Davis, whose "Literary Societies of Selected State Universities of the Lower South," unpublished Ph.D. dissertation, Louisiana State University, 1949, furnished the topics listed under the headings of the Clariosophic, Euphradian, Demosthenian, and Phi Kappa societies; and to Dr. Donald H. Ecroyd, who supplied the data listed under the headings of the Philomathic and Erosophic societies of Alabama.

2. Alexander Cowie, *Educational Problems at Yale College in the Eighteenth Century* (New Haven, 1936), p. 6.

3. Thomas Clap, *The Annals of Yale College* (New Haven, 1766), p. 86. See also John A. Kouwenhoven, "The New York Undergraduate 1830-50," *Columbia University Quarterly*, XXXI (June, 1930), 93-103.

4. William C. Lane, "The Telltale, 1721," *Publications of the Colonial Society of Massachusetts*, XXI, 227-228.

5. Julius H. Tuttle, "The Philomusarian Club," *Publications of the Colonial Society of Massachusetts*, XVIII, 79-84.

6. Records of the Speaking Club, 177-1781, I, 31. (MS. in the Harvard University Archives.)

7. *The Original Phi Beta Kappa Minutes*, pp. 29, 31.

8. Quoted in a letter written by Miss Lora Wheeler, Reference Librarian, University of Utah, dated November 10, 1950.

9. Robert M. Gatke, *Chronicles of Williamette* (Portland, 1943), p. 292.

10. See David Potter, *Debating in the Colonial Chartered Colleges* (New York) 1944, pp. 5-32, 128-130.

11. College Records, September 17, 1750-April 23, 1778, a Copy of College Book No. 7, p. 93. (MS. in the Harvard University Archives.)

12. Yale University Fellowship Club Records, Nov. 6, 1766-Feb. 6, 1767. (MS. in the Yale University Library.)

13. *The Original Phi Beta Kappa Minutes*, p. 22.

14. Records of the Linonian Society, 1768-1790. (MS. in the Yale University Library.)

15. Aaron Dutton (A dissertation of the manner of rendering the exercises of the Linonian Society pleasing and useful, Orations and Dissertations of the Linonian Society, 1772-1802, pp. 39-40. MS. in the Yale University Library) puts it nicely: "Extempore disputation requires as much study as written composition, & perhaps more.... [But] very many, who dispute extempore, pay little or no attention to the question, till they come into the society, & depend principally upon the arguments & observations, which the occasion shall suggest."

On the other hand, some ideas of how much time at least one forensic disputant spent on preparing his society parts can be had by noting the following entries in John Barent Johnson's diary ("Diary kept by John Johnson, April 10th, 1788 & Beginning of 1789." MS. in the Columbiana Section of the Columbia University Library):

January 16, 1789. "... home 8.—Sat up very late in writing a Dispute for Columbia Col. Society."

January 26, 1789. "... wrote part of a dispute for Theol. Society...."

January 27, 1789. "... stud Greek—& wrote a little (Disp.)...."

February 6, 1789. "Stud. Dispute for to-morrow."

16. Minutes of the Trustees of Columbia College, III, Part 2, 6 May 1828 to 4 December 1837, p. 1738. Typed MS. in Columbia University Library. See also Catalogue of the Officers and Students of Brown University ... 1829-30, p. 18.

17. E.g., Constitution of the American Whig Society, 1875, p. 204. MS. in the Princeton University Library.

18. "Friendly," or non-decision debates occurred at an even earlier date. For example, Northwestern's Hinman Society and Chicago's Tri Kappa Society first met in 1873.

19. Constitution of the American Whig Society, 1807. MS. in the Princeton University Library.

20. Constitution of the Brothers in Unity, 1783. MS. in the Yale University Library.

21. Constitution & Laws of the United Fraternity, May 29, 1857. MS. in the Dartmouth University Library.

22. Constitution of the Linonian Society, 1835, p. 11. MS. in the Yale University Library.

23. Secretary's book of the Dialectic Association, 1839-43. MS. in the Oberlin College Library.

24. Philermenian Society Records, 1798-1801. MS. in the Brown University Library.

25. Constitution of the Philolexian Society, 1820. MS. in the Columbiana, Columbia University Library.

26. Constitution of the Philermenian Society (1794-1864). MS. in the Brown University Library.

27. Constitution of the American Whig Society, 1848. MS. in the Princeton University Library.

28. Constitution of the Cliosophic Society (circa 1875). MS. in the Princeton University Library.

29. Lane, op. cit., pp. 229-230.

30. William Jennings Bryan and Mary Baird Bryan, The Memoirs of William Jennings Bryan (Philadelphia, 1925), p. 59.

31. Autobiography of William H. Seward (New York, 1877), p. 25.

32. See Hugo E. Hellman, "The Influence of the Literary Society in the Making of American Orators," Quarterly Journal of Speech, XXVIII (February, 1942), 12-14; and Harry M. Williams, "Two Mid-Nineteenth Century Student Speeches," Speech Monographs, XVII (March, 1950), 75-77.

33. Jacob N. Beams, The American Whig Society of Princeton University (Princeton, 1933), pp. 77-78.

12 Intercollegiate Debating

L. LEROY COWPERTHWAITE
A. CRAIG BAIRD

....

I

Intercollegiate debating is primarily an American institution. The "first of modern intercollegiate debates" occurred, according to Ralph Curtis Ringwalt, when Yale met Harvard University at Cambridge, January 14, 1892.[1] "Intercollegiate debating," observed Ringwalt, "arose in a natural reaction against the lax conditions of the literary societies and against the lack of genuine interest in any form of public speaking which for many years existed at Harvard and Yale, and, in fact, at almost all Eastern Colleges."[2] Ringwalt, one of the most prominent early writers to show an interest in college debating, recalls that around 1890 a group of young men who had had experience with interschool debates among preparatory schools near Boston proposed that the Harvard Union challenge other colleges to joint debates. The outcome of this proposal Mr. Ringwalt recounts:

For two years these men were voted down with considerable ridicule. In [the autumn of] 1891, however . . . Yale sent a challenge for a joint discussion, and the opponents of the scheme in the Harvard Union having been graduated or won over, the proposal was at once accepted. Representatives of the two colleges met at Springfield and arranged for two debates, the first to take place at Cambridge on January 14, 1892.

On this day, therefore, Harvard and Yale met on the platform in the first of modern intercollegiate debates. The question was "Resolved, that a young man casting his first ballot in 1892 should vote for the nominees of the Democratic Party." Yale had the affirmative. The late ex-Governor William E. Russell, of Massachusetts, acted as presiding officer. Though, in accordance with the agreement, there were no judges, and, consequently, no formal decision was given as to which side proved itself superior in the contest, the meeting was very satisfactory; the audience was large, representative, and enthusiastic, and the debating creditable.[3]

The news of these events soon reached other campuses, and within four years intercollegiate debating had spread across the entire continent. The next year, 1893, the Whig and Cliosophic literary societies of Princeton University journeyed to Yale for a debate. That same year, according to the late Thomas C. Trueblood, the Middle West caught the spirit, and Michigan and Wisconsin universities held their first joint debate.[4] Before the year was over Iowa and Minnesota participated in the first of a long and successful series of intercollegiate debates through the medium of the Iowa-Minnesota Debate League, organized at the conclusion of the first contest.[5] During the 1894-1895 academic year Pennsylvania met Cornell and Stanford debated with California. The following year, 1895-1896, Dartmouth, Bates College, Williams College, Wesleyan University, Boston University, Western Reserve, and the University of Chicago entered this new form of inter-college rivalry.

The year 1895 also brought an innovation in the structure of this new intercollegiate activity when Princeton, Harvard, and Yale established the first triangular debating league. In 1897, Michigan, Minnesota, Northwestern, and Chicago universities formed the first quadrangular league. "These universities," wrote Trueblood, "debated each other in pairs in January, and the winners of the semi-finals contests came together in a final debate in April each year." [6] This first Midwestern, multilateral debate league, which served as a model for many others, was at the end of eight years succeeded by a triangular arrangement composed of the universities of Chicago, Michigan, and Northwestern, the first of its kind to hold all debates simultaneously. According to Professor R. I. Fulton, of Ohio Wesleyan University, the Ohio Intercollegiate Debate League was organized at Delaware on January 2, 1897, and included Ohio Wesleyan, Western Reserve, Oberlin, Ohio State University. The first debates were held in May of that year.[7]

The next few years saw the rapid growth of debating in both numbers of institutions participating and the numbers of contests held. Practically all the early debates were conducted on the basis of the single debate "contract" arrangement, whereby one college challenged another, the second accepted, and a contract setting forth the rules and regulations of the contest was drawn up and signed by both parties. Typical of the intercollegiate debating experiences of colleges and universities during this early period were those of the State University of Iowa, which, during her first decade (1893-1903) of intercollegiate participation, took part in a total of eighteen annual contests with Minnesota, Wisconsin, Chicago, and Illinois. All of Iowa's debates were annual single events based on two-year "contracts."

Colleges evolved numerous rules and regulations governing the arrangement of the contests and their conduct. Customarily the rules specified the methods of selecting the question and the judges, the criteria for judging, number and length of speeches, provisions for financing the debate, and the like.

The participants agreed on a proposition, the entertaining school or the challenger usually submitting a proposal subject to objection by the opposing school. The constitution of the first debating league formed by Iowa and Minnesota at Minneapolis on May 27, 1893, for example, provided that the entertaining university should submit the question, the other school to have twelve days in which to choose the side it desired or to submit a new question.[8] Although universally practiced, this method of choosing the question frequently provoked disagreement and foul play. According to Egbert Ray Nichols, much wrangling and disagreement over meanings of terms was the usual result.[9] The subjects debated reflected clearly the political, economic, and sociological issues of the time. Questions most frequently debated during the first decade of intercollegiate activity dealt with such subjects as government ownership and operation of the telegraph system, international bimetallism, further territorial extension of the United States, municipal ownership and operation of street railways, direct election of United States senators, a federal graduated income tax, and compulsory arbitration of labor-management disputes.

The manner of selecting speakers for a debate was left to each institution. At first the literary societies selected the debaters from among their membership. Trueblood observed that by 1907 some institutions chose their representatives "by a series of class contests, others through departments, as at Yale and Illinois, others through debating societies or unions, as at Harvard, Princeton, Cornell and Wisconsin, or through both societies and departments, as at Michigan."[10] Still later, with the advent of the debate "coach," the "tryout" system became the general practice, with competition campus wide. The league constitutions and single debate "contracts" usually specified that contestants must be undergraduates currently attending the university represented.

Since early intercollege contests were characterized by a spirit of rivalry, the selection of judges became a matter of supreme importance. As in the selection of the question, the lists of judges proposed by the opposing team were almost always examined with suspicion. To secure an unprejudiced "jury," league constitutions and contractual agreements dwelt at some length on such matters as the manner of selecting the judges, their essential qualifications, and criteria for rendering a decision. It early became the practice for the entertaining college to submit a list of names from which the visiting college selected two judges; the latter submitted a second list from which the entertaining institution chose one. Emphasis was placed on securing judges prominent in their fields. During the early years some judges were among the most prominent citizens of the country. State supreme court judges, congressmen, and university professors were the most frequently chosen. Lawyers, ministers, and college presidents were also included. Sometimes an eminent judge or presiding officer proved to be a major drawing card for the contest, as, for example, when ex-President Grover Cleveland presided at one of the early debates between Yale and Princeton.[11]

Closely allied to the problem of selecting competent judges was that of deciding what criteria should govern decisions. Nichols reports that "sometimes a basis of fifty percent was suggested for argument and the same for delivery, sometimes it was sixty for argument and forty for delivery, or even seventy-five and twenty-five." [12] The first agreement between Iowa and Minnesota instructed the judges to decide the debate "solely on argument." [13] However, the constitution later drawn up by these two institutions directed that judges should decide "according to the stipulations governing the debate." [14] Subsequent contests served to establish that the framers of the Iowa-Minnesota League constitution meant that the judges were to award decisions on the merits of the debating, not on the merits of the question.

Another problem frequently arising during the first decade of intercollegiate debating was that of determining the proper order and length of speeches. Since the three-speaker team (sometimes referred to as the University Plan or Harvard Plan) was universally used throughout the early period, the length of speeches was important. During some of the early contests audiences often sat for as long as three hours before the debate could be concluded and the judges' decision read. Like many of the other rules for conducting the debates, those governing the length and order of speeches were usually stipulated in constitutions and agreements. Usually each speaker was allowed twenty minutes for constructive argument and the "leader" of each three-man team an additional ten minutes for summing up the arguments, with the affirmative speaking last. Another variation allotted the first and second speakers on each side twenty minutes; the third affirmative, twenty-two minutes; the third negative, twenty-three minutes; and finally, the affirmative a four-minute rejoinder. Still a third variation, used particularly in the Middle West, allowed affirmative speakers twenty, twenty-two and twenty-five minutes, with a four-minute "rebuttal" to close the debate. The three negative speakers had twenty, twenty-two and twenty-six minutes. By about the turn of the century most colleges had adopted the plan then in use among Eastern leagues of permitting fifteen-minute constructive speeches and five-minute rebuttals for each speaker. Nichols attributes to the Middle West the idea of placing the negative first in the rebuttal speeches.[15] Thus the first decade of intercollegiate debating witnessed the evolution of the "rebuttal" speech and a debating format used in formal college debating for many years.

Little doubt exists that intercollegiate debating was accepted with enthusiasm by both the participants and the audiences. The annual contest evoked wide public interest and a rousing display of school spirit. The general public and the average university student viewed the debate as primarily a contest—an "intellectual sport" characterized by rules and regulations and motivated by the desire for victory. George Pierce Baker of Harvard perhaps best expressed the trend of the day in an address before the Association of Colleges and Preparatory Schools of the Middle States and Maryland at Philadelphia, December 1, 1900:

At first it is, more than anything else, the fight, the spirit of the contest, the desire to show one's supremacy over someone else which interest our students in debating. . . . I believe that intercollegiate debating should be placed on the footing of an intellectual sport.[16]

The keen rivalry engendered by an intercollegiate contest made it a great event of the school year. Indeed, preparation for the annual debate greatly resembled that made for a modern athletic contest, to the point of arousing wide public interest through extensive advertising in newspapers, on billboards, and even the staging of "pep" rallies followed by parades through the city streets. Audiences were frequently large enough to necessitate the renting of a local theater or the civic opera house. When Iowa debated Wisconsin at Milwaukee on March 31, 1899, the reviews described Davidson's Theater as "overflowing with the crowd," composed in part of large delegations from nearby schools and colleges.[17] On the occasion of the Oberlin-Adelbert College (of Western Reserve University) debate, on May 5, 1897 in the Euclid Avenue Congregational Church in Cleveland, about one hundred and fifty Oberlin students and teachers travelled on a specially chartered train to Cleveland to hear the debate.[18]

Colleges vied with one another to see who could make the occasion of an intercollegiate debate the most memorable. Not infrequently, visiting debate teams found upon their arrival at the railway station special reception committees to escort them to the local hotel, where all arrangements for their stay had been made in advance. It was also the custom, in addition to the regular banquet immediately following the debate, for the president of the college or university to entertain both teams in his home. For the audiences, added attractions, such as musical selections, frequently spiced the lengthy verbal battles. The Oberlin-Adelbert debate of 1897 was described by Auer as follows: "While the Mather Glee Club and the Adelbert Mandolin Club offered selections between the speeches, the Oberlin debaters upheld the negative side of the question 'Resolved, That Trusts or Combinations which tend to monopolize any industry should be prohibited by law.'" [19]

To the literary societies must go the major credit for nurturing and loyally supporting active intercollegiate debate programs. Through the voluntary action of the societies intercollegiate debating got its start. They planned and financed the early events. Through systematic programs of training begun with the Freshman society member, the societies prepared their speakers for intercollegiate competition. In addition to providing varied opportunities for training in extemporaneous debating, the student organizations not infrequently hired at considerable expense private instructors in elocution to assist their teams with delivery. Even special research teams were sometimes appointed to assist the debaters in preparing their cases.

Although the literary societies shouldered most of the responsibilities for the preparation of debating teams, more and more the debaters themselves sought help among the faculty wherever and whenever they could get it. Thus the professor of English, history, or economics voluntarily assumed a new responsibility. Although trained faculty supervision of the debating program was not the rule until well into the second decade of intercollegiate competition, the "coaching system" began to appear by the close of the first decade. A few institutions, notably the universities of Michigan, Illinois, and Iowa, had by the turn of the century organized "departments" of speech, but the departments had little or nothing to do with intercollegiate debating, which existed purely as an extracurricular activity. Not until well into the second decade of intercollegiate debating did speech departments begin to assume responsibility for or jurisdiction over this popular "intellectual sport."

II

In the period 1904-1913, intercollegiate debating continued to expand rapidly and at the same time sought to improve itself.

Debating leagues increased in number and variety. With the Chicago-Michigan-Northwestern triangular experiment as a pattern, many new leagues sprang up across the country. Typical was the "I-M-I League," composed of the universities of Iowa, Minnesota, and Illinois.

Quadrangular leagues were also to be found during this second decade, that of Swarthmore, Franklin and Marshall, Dickinson, and Pennsylvania State College being among the best known. When the Chicago-Michigan-Minnesota-Northwestern league broke up in 1906, Minnesota joined the universities of Iowa, Illinois, Wisconsin and Nebraska to form the Central Debating League of America, popularly referred to as the "Five-Cornered," "Quintangular," and "Pentangular" league. This new plan amounted to a double triangular arrangement, in which, if the affirmative and negative teams each debated twice, each member institution could meet the others annually. This fact was probably responsible for the immediate popularity of the five-member leagues organized across the country. Typical of these pentangular arrangements was the league composed of the universities of Arkansas, Mississippi, Tennessee, Louisiana, and Texas. The universities of Georgia, Virginia, and North Carolina joined with Tulane and Vanderbilt in a similar organization.

Also from the basic triangular plan emerged yet another type of debating arrangement. The triangular league required each member institution to prepare teams on both sides of the question—a significant departure from the old single-debate contract plan. Hence, when one member of the league defaulted, the two remaining members, rather than be deprived of debating opportunities for one of their teams, simply matched these teams against one another on the same evening as in the triangular arrangement. This "dual plan" survived all other, more complex procedures.

Although the single-debate contract plan continued in use through the second decade of intercollegiate debating, the various league arrangements rapidly became popular, possibly because they effectively solved such problems as the choice of a question and of sides, the time and place of contests, and similar difficulties that had long been the source of dispute and friction under the single-debate contract procedure. Nichols also alleges that those responsible for debating activities saw a boon to debate preparation in the league requirement that each institution make ready teams on both sides of the question.[20]

The road of rapidly expanding intercollegiate debate activity was not altogether smooth. One of the many difficulties was that of finance. During the first decade, when intercollegiate activity was limited in most universities and colleges to one or two engagements per year, the literary societies managed to meet expenses from their regular treasuries, supplemented frequently by small admission charges to the debates. Increased activity, however, required additional funds. Since debate was definitely outside the regular curriculum, appeals to administrative authorities for assistance were usually without success. In search of supplementary sources of revenue, literary societies sponsored university lecture series, plays, and musical concerts. For many groups, debating was financed through the student activity fee, devised early in the century, which the student, upon matriculating, paid in a lump sum for his admission to athletic events, plays, and debates, and for his subscription to the college paper. If only partial and sometimes transitory, these "solutions" to financial problems opened the way for even larger debate schedules and also made possible later the "guarantee" to the visiting team with the advent of the debate trip.

Perhaps the chief characteristic of the second decade was a concerted effort to improve the quality of intercollegiate debating. In large measure, improvement manifested itself in four areas: (1) the struggle for academic recognition, (2) development of improved methods of debate preparation and delivery, (3) the devising of means for rewarding proficiency in the art of debating, and (4) the administration of the intercollegiate forensic program.

By the second decade, student debate leaders were successful in their efforts to persuade a member of the faculty to assume the extra duty of "coaching" intercollegiate teams in the final stages of their preparation for debate contests.[21] The next stage of the evolutionary process found the "coach" assisting in the selection of the debaters by the "tryout" system. Soon there appeared on every campus that relatively small group of ardent debaters referred to as the "debate squad." With the rapid increase in the number of annual intercollegiate contests came what seemed the inevitable student demand for academic credit. As a result, many "coaches" organized courses in argumentation and debate; the intercollegiate participant enrolled and thus received credit. A few institutions allowed credit specifically for intercollegiate participation by a vote of the faculty upon recommendation of the "coach." Thus, although intercollegiate debating continued to be thought of as an "outside" activity, in the second decade it gained curriculum status.

In keeping with academic associations, the best debates received publication and were thus available for study and criticism. In 1908 Harvard and the University of Chicago published full-length debates in pamphlet form. That same year the H. W. Wilson Company of Minneapolis started the *Debate Handbook Series,* followed a few years later by the *University Debater's Annual* and the *Reference Shelf* series. In 1909 Professor Paul M. Pearson, editor of *The Speaker,* compiled and edited the first volume of *Intercollegiate Debates,* consisting of a condensation of the arguments of twenty-three college debates and of one debate carried in full. In 1911, Brookings and Ringwalt's *Briefs for Debate* appeared.

The advent of the faculty director or "coach" brought decided improvement in methods of preparation and delivery. Many of the earliest intercollegiate contests had little of the extemporaneous adaptation characteristic of debate in later years. The general practice was for each speaker to write his speech in full, commit it to memory, and, at the proper time, recite it much as he would an oration. Not infrequently the cases of opposing teams failed to "clash," and the result was, according to Nichols, "an exhibition of adroit maneuvering, clever interpretation, and carefully planned strategy to avoid pitfalls and to force the opposition to defend its weaknesses and to meet the strong point of its antagonists." [22] Even the rebuttal speeches were "canned." To correct these defects, the coaches instituted what came to be popularly known as the "block system" of speech preparation. With this method, all debaters, except the first affirmative speakers, were directed to prepare paragraphs or "blocks" of arguments on all the conceivably important issues that might arise during a debate. By committing these "blocks" to memory, the debater could, during the course of the debate, select and assemble such "blocks" as would result in a direct challenge to the opponents' case. Blocked rebuttal answers were likewise prepared in advance. Before long, however, the tediousness of the block method led both coaches and students to move further in the direction of extemporaneous debating. Progress was manifest during the second decade, when debaters began allotting time for preliminary extempore refutation at the beginning of constructive speeches. Some coaches directed the first two speakers on each side to present the prepared constructive case, leaving the third speaker free to extemporize and thus try to insure a direct clash of arguments.

Another factor leading to the improvement of debating was the interest shown by colleges, and especially by university extension divisions, in high-school debating and debaters. Seeing the high schools as an excellent source of college debaters, many colleges and universities encouraged the formation of high-school debate leagues. The leagues were later amalgamated into state-wide organizations. Local, district, and finally state debate championships were determined under the auspices of the sponsoring university. Thus, during the second decade of intercollegiate debating, students who had received debate training in high school began to enter the ranks of the college debate squads.

As a further inducement to better debating, many institutions early adopted the practice of awarding cash prizes, cups, and plaques for individual achievement. Some colleges instituted "presentation day" at the end of the debating season. On this occasion, debaters received medals and a college letter to be worn on the coat or sweater.

Another form of recognition for excellence in intercollegiate forensics which had its roots in this early period was the forensic honor society. Desiring to give appropriate recognition for work of merit in intercollegiate debating, Professors E. E. McDermott, of the University of Wisconsin, and H. E. Gordon, of the State University of Iowa, proposed in November, 1904, a national forensic honor society patterned in the Phi Beta Kappa tradition. In April, 1906, representatives from the universities of Michigan, Minnesota, Illinois, Nebraska, Iowa, Wisconsin, Chicago, and Northwestern met at the Victoria Hotel in Chicago and organized Delta Sigma Rho, the first honor society of its kind in the United States. Provisions were made to establish chapters in each of the member schools with charter membership limited to those institutions represented at the founders' meeting. By the close of the decade, Delta Sigma Rho could boast twenty-five chapters limited mainly to the large universities.[23] In 1908 a second national forensic honor society, Tau Kappa Alpha, was organized at Butler College, Indianapolis, by representatives of Butler, Wabash, and Depauw. Organized at first on the basis of state chapters to which forensic honor students of the various colleges within each state might belong, Tau Kappa Alpha later reorganized to permit a local chapter in each college. By the end of the decade the third honor society, Pi Kappa Delta, was founded. According to Professor Nichols, one of its founders, it met the demand of the small colleges for an honor award and organization.[24] Election to membership in one of these forensic honor societies, which carried with it the privilege of wearing the society key, became the highest honor that could be conferred upon an intercollegiate debater.

Although the early intercollegiate debates were held under the names of institutions, they were not in reality contests between universities or colleges. Actually they were conceived, planned, and carried out by and among the various literary societies on the campuses. However, as the responsibilities for administering an ever-expanding intercollegiate program reached proportions too great for the societies independently or collectively to handle, administration was gradually shifted to a central agency representative of the institution as a whole. Hence, the second decade witnessed the rise of the university or college Forensic Association or Debate Council, which, in conjunction with the "coach," assumed the responsibilities of administering all intercollegiate debate activities. Intercollegiate debating was then no longer restricted to literary society members; any undergraduate in good standing was eligible to participate as a representative of the university or college. The "tryout" system further broadened the field of selection, thus sharpening the competition for a place on the "varsity" team and improving the general quality of debating.

III

The third decade of intercollegiate debating in the United States (1914-1923) was a period of further growth and expansion characterized by experimentation with new forms and methods. Although temporarily retarded by World War I, the general trend in intercollegiate debating pointed toward increased activity, culminating in a program whose magnitude and substance reflected the far-reaching effects of forensic endeavor on both the national and international scene.

Influenced perhaps in part by a desire to meet debate teams from more distant places and by the urge to use a laboriously prepared debate case in more than one or two debates, coaches and debaters were not content with the two or three annual contests provided by league arrangements. The interstate character of some of the triangular and other multilateral leagues had already introduced the idea of a "debate trip." The University of Denver was the first institution to schedule more than one debate on a trip into neighboring states. In 1913 a Denver team journeyed to Kansas and debated Ottawa University on April 16, and to Missouri for an engagement with William Jewell College on April 18.[25] Almost immediately other colleges and universities began sending teams on cross country tours until by 1916 the debate trip had become a popular feature.

World War I drastically curtailed intercollegiate debating. Men's literary societies suspended activities, and in the 1917-1918 academic year, college debating, along with most extracurricular pursuits, virtually ceased.

Postwar intercollegiate debating assumed a new dimension when, in 1921, debaters of Bates College, Lewiston, Maine, gained national attention by conceiving and carrying out the first international debate, a trip to Oxford University, England.[26] The debate took place before the Oxford Union on June 16, 1921, with the Bates College team upholding the affirmative of the proposition, "Resolved, that this House approves the American policy of non-intervention in European affairs." [27] The following year, 1922, Oxford reciprocated by sending a team to the United States for a return engagement with Bates College and for additional debates with Swarthmore, Columbia, Yale, Harvard, Princeton, and the University of Pennsylvania.

The third decade of intercollegiate debating witnessed expansion in another direction when women were admitted to the platform. In January, 1897, the University of Wisconsin, in reply to a challenge from the University of Iowa, had refused to permit her young ladies to participate in an intercollegiate debate, giving as her reason that ". . . ladies in that capacity do no credit either to themselves or to co-education in general." [28] Throughout the early years of intercollegiate forensic competition the appearance of women upon the public platform continued to be viewed with disfavor.

Women's societies began in earnest to promote debating activities at about the beginning of the third decade of intercollegiate forensics. Not until the postwar period, however, did appreciable numbers of women debaters actually appear on the intercollegiate platform. On May 12, 1921, purportedly the first women's intercollegiate debate in the Middle West occurred when a women's team from the University of Indiana visited the campus of the State University of Iowa to debate the issue of Philippine independence.[29] By 1923 college women, particularly in the Midwest, were debating along with men.

College debating was not without its critics. As early as 1913 debate and debating practices as they had developed in the colleges and universities over the previous twenty years became the object of widespread criticism from the public at large and from academic circles as well. Public criticism, led by persons no less prominent than Theodore Roosevelt and William Jennings Bryan, questioned the moral soundness of coaching methods, then prevalent, of requiring college debaters to argue on both sides of a question without regard for their personal convictions.[30] Although the friends and defenders of college debating managed to withstand public censure, academic criticism led to changes. Educators centered on what many of them thought to be an unhealthy stress upon winning the judges' decisions. Widespread dissatisfaction was expressed also over the choice of judges and judging methods.

The first noticeable reaction in debating circles to criticism of judged debates was the complete abolition of the decision. According to H. S. Woodward, the first non-decision debates were held in Ohio in 1914-1915.[31] Later a further innovation was added to the "judgeless" debate when members of the audience were invited to express opinions on the issue under discussion at the close of the formal debate. Thus was born the "open forum discussion."

Directors of debating argued heatedly on the issue of decision versus non-decision debates. According to Enid Miller, this argument and the dispute over methods of judging occupied more space than any other questions in the literature of speech education immediately following World War I.[32] Early issues of the *Quarterly Journal of Public Speaking* carried numerous articles, most notable of which was a series of written debates between Professor H. N. Wells of the University of Southern California Law School and Professor James M. O'Neill of the University of Wisconsin Department of Speech.[33]

By the spring of 1920 the popularity of open forum, non-decision debating had spread through the Middle West. Many of the debate leagues adopted this system, among them the "I-M-I League," all of whose debates during the 1920-1921 season were of the "judgeless," audience-participation type. Renewed debate contracts often specified the use of the non-decision method. Although this new emphasis on decisionless debating continued to be popular through the remainder of the third decade, the issue of decision versus non-decision debates was by no means resolved, as later developments reveal.[34]

Although the open forum debate proved to be popular with audiences, many debaters and debate directors believed that the judges' decision was essential to effective debating. To them the logical alternative to the old three-judge panel with its admitted evils was the expert critic judge. First used in the high-school debating leagues of Kansas and Iowa in 1915-1916, the critic judge quickly found favor. He was an "expert" in debate technique and methodology; at the close of debate he announced which team had done the more effective debating and went on to explain in a short critique the reasons for his decision. The critic judge was usually a director of debate or teacher of public speaking from a neutral or disinterested institution.[35]

As the pendulum had swung in the two years following World War I from decision to non-decision debating, by the 1922-1923 debating season it had swung back again in the direction of contest debating with the expert critic judge as referee. Thus, after nearly three decades marked with controversies as to the eligibility, even the integrity, of judges, and with the virtual elimination of judges' decisions, most of the advocates of intercollegiate debating, in the Middle West at any rate, finally settled upon the critic judge as the best solution to their problems. Despite the competitive motive, which emerged repeatedly in the intercollegiate debate program, the critic judge worked well and won the confidence of coaches and debaters for fair and equitable decisions. Furthermore, from his explanation and criticism, everyone could profit. He fitted into a system that was more interested in education than in sport.

In the last years of the third decade, American debaters were influenced by the English style of debating. Characterized by its conversational mode, wittiness, and its stress upon audience persuasion, the Oxford, or British, style of debating had a significant and profound effect in tempering the legalistic formalism of American debating.[36] Also the Oxford "split team" system—each team of two members made up of one debater from each of the participating institutions— probably helped to minimize the "sport" aspect of American debating sometimes evident in a "support the home team" attitude among audiences. The British debaters, stressing the importance of audience persuasion and unfamiliar with the American custom of awarding a decision on the merits of the debating, usually requested that audiences be permitted to vote on the merits of the question instead. Hence, the close of the third decade of intercollegiate debating saw the appearance of the "audience decision" debate. In some instances, audiences were asked to vote on the question both before and after the formal debate with a "shift-of-opinion" ballot replacing the judge's formal decision.

Thus, by the end of the third decade intercollegiate debating had taken on a new character and vitality. The dormant position into which debating had slumped during World War I gave place to renewed interest, both on the part of debaters and the general public. Audience participation, while not generally thought to be a prime motive for increased student interest, nevertheless materially transformed traditional debating from an intellectual sport characterized by a legalistic formalism designed to win victories over opponents, to a more realistic means of presenting live issues to interested listeners and of helping college youth to speak well.

IV

By 1923 college debating had seen most of its major developments. In conclusion we need only to observe now that the forces which established intercollegiate debate have been vigorous enough to keep it in good health. International debating continued to expand. New adaptations were introduced—cross-examination, direct-clash, and heckling debates—and radio enabled the debater to reach larger audiences. The most important new direction was the debate tournament, which allowed debaters to meet several colleges at one location with minimum expense. Colleges experimented also with legislative assemblies as a realistic setting for the student speaker. Although audiences have dwindled since the early years, debate has adjusted its methods to appeal to young men and women who are interested in broad and rigorous educational experience, who find pleasure in intellectual competition with their peers, and who wish to develop some facility in the adaptation of facts and arguments on public questions to the occasion and audience.

The immediate success and popularity enjoyed by the first debates with British teams soon led to the sponsorship of international debating by the Institute of International Education, which assumed the responsibility for arranging tours both in the United States and abroad. Teams from Oxford, Cambridge, and many municipal universities alternated in making annual pilgrimages to the United States. Beginning in the 1920's, debate teams from Australia, Ireland, Turkey, Germany, and the Philippine Islands appeared on American platforms. Not to be outdone by their foreign competitors, American debaters traveled abroad in ever increasing numbers. In 1927, the University of Oregon sent a team on a tour westward around the world, visiting Hawaii, Australia, India, and England en route. The following spring the Bates College debaters traveled westward across the continent and on around the world. The next year a State University of Iowa team made a two weeks' tour of eighteen British colleges and universities. Except for a temporary interruption by World War II, international debating continued to flourish under the administrative responsibility of the International Institute of Education, with the Committee on International Debate of the Speech Association of America acting as a liaison agency for the selection of debaters on a nation-wide basis to represent American colleges and universities abroad. Although considerable controversy developed concerning the educational justification of these exchange debates, few would argue that international debating failed to live up to the function envisioned by its sponsors, namely, that of fostering international good will and understanding.[37]

With the widespread use of the radio came further opportunity for the expansion and development of college debating. At first, those institutions fortunate enough to be near commercial broadcasting stations experimented with educational programs, among which were frequent college debates. Within a few years many of the larger institutions had their own broadcasting stations through which numerous intercollegiate debates were "aired." Perhaps the outstanding radio debate of the early period occurred when Iowa, the Western Conference League "champion" of 1932-1933, met Bates College, Eastern Intercollegiate League winners, on October 28, 1933. The debate was broadcast over the WJZ chain of the National Broadcasting Company, with the Iowa debaters speaking from a Chicago studio and the Bates team from a Boston station. With the rapid growth in the number of educational broadcasting units on college and university campuses, more and more debates were arranged for broadcasting. The influence exerted by this important medium upon the general quality and nature of debating would be difficult to assess. The presence of an unseen audience representing a cross section of the population necessitated more concentrated training in adapting to listeners' needs and interests as well as in improved techniques of delivery.

Mounting dissatisfaction among debate directors with the traditional form of college debating led to further experimentation with new forms and methods. Non-decision and open forum debating accompanied by the use of the "shift-of-opinion" ballot became increasingly popular. The "split-team" procedure to direct attention to the issues rather than to the speakers was also widely employed. Among the most frequently used of the new forms was the "Oregon Plan," which featured cross-examination of each speaker by a member of the opposing team at the close of each constructive speech.[38] Still another innovation was the "direct clash" method, which called for the thorough threshing out of each major issue in the debate by both sides before proceeding to the next. Quite popular for a time was the "heckling" debate, which, as its title implies, was designed to discourage memorized speeches by permitting a debater to be interrupted for questioning by an opponent. All of these innovations were designed to encourage an extemporaneous style of debating.

Probably the most significant of the later developments in intercollegiate debating was the inauguration of the debate tournament, which allegedly originated in 1923 at Southwestern College, Winfield, Kansas.[39] This new method of conducting intercollegiate debates called for the converging of several debate teams upon one college or university campus for a period of one or more days. It achieved almost immediate popularity. The earliest tournaments were of the "invitational" type, in which a particular college, upon deciding to sponsor such an event, invited a number of other schools to send participants and usually judges as well. The first national tournament, according to Nichols, was sponsored by Pi Kappa Delta at its national convention in Estes Park, Colorado, in 1926.[40] Soon the tournament idea spread over the West and Middle West and then over the nation.

Besides greatly enhancing opportunities for increased numbers of intercollegiate debates at minimum expense, the tournament brought significant changes in debating methods and techniques—changes that largely determined the character and scope of college debating. In order to hold several "rounds" of debate in one or two days, the length of speeches was reduced to ten minutes for constructive and five minutes for rebuttal speeches. Although early tournaments made use of the traditional three-speaker team, tournament efficiency was in large measure responsible for the advent of the two-speaker system. With the national tournament came the necessity for selecting a national debate question. Finally, the tournament brought a renewed emphasis on contest debating, even though many non-decision or "practice" tournaments were held. Tournament debating also meant speaking almost entirely without popular audiences; indeed, the real audience was often the critic judge.

Yet another highly significant trend in modern debating practice was the emergence of parliamentary debating carried out as a student legislative assembly.[41] In invitational forensic conferences across the land students proposed resolutions and "bills," discussed them in committee and conferences, and emerged from the final stages of a "discussion progression" with a series of resolutions introduced in the form of bills and debated by the entire assembly sitting as a legislature. Sponsors of these legislative sessions held that in addition to providing excellent opportunities for training in extemporaneous, problem-solving debating, they served also to increase student interest in social-political problems, to equip them further for the responsibilities of leadership in civic affairs, and to show relationships between discussion and advocacy in the deliberative process.

Although the competitive elements continued to evoke enthusiasm among superior debaters, the tendency of colleges and universities was to relate forensics more and more closely to general educational aims and classroom instruction. The educational values of the forensic program for the functions and purposes of a democratic society were recognized as playing an indispensable role in the struggle for survival. If free speech, basic to the American system, is to serve democracy properly, discussion and debate will continue as essential educational disciplines.

Notes

1. Ralph Curtis Ringwalt, "Intercollegiate Debating," *Forum*, XXII (January, 1897), 633.

According to Ewbank and Auer, "the first intercollegiate debate seems to have taken place in 1883 between Knox College and the Rockford Female Seminary on the 'Social benefits and evils of the lavish expenditure of wealth by the rich.' "—Henry Lee Ewbank and J. Jeffery Auer, *Discussion and Debate: Tools of a Democracy* (New York, 1951), p. 383.

2. Ringwalt, *op. cit.*, p. 633.
3. *Ibid.*
4. "Forensic Training in Colleges," *Education*, XXVII (March, 1907), 387.
5. *Vidette-Reporter* (Iowa City), June 3, 1893.
6. Trueblood, *op. cit.*, p. 387.
7. Roy Diem, "History of Intercollegiate Debating in Ohio," *Central States Speech Journal*, XX (November, 1949), 633.
8. *Vidette-Reporter* (Iowa City), November 16, 1893.
9. "The college submitting the question often cast it in trick form, hoping the challenged debaters would choose before discovering any jokers or technical flaws in the statement."—Egbert Ray Nichols, "A Historical Sketch of Intercollegiate Debating: I," *Quarterly Journal of Speech*, XXII (April, 1936), 218.
10. Trueblood, *op. cit.*, p. 387.
11. *Ibid.*, p. 390.
12. Nichols, *op. cit.*, p. 218.
13. *Vidette-Reporter* (Iowa City), April 15, 1893.
14. *Vidette-Reporter* (Iowa City), November 16, 1893.
15. Nichols, *op. cit.*, p. 217.
16. "Intercollegiate Debating," *Educational Review*, XXI (March, 1901), 245.
17. *Daily Iowan* (Iowa City), April 1, 1899.
18. J. Jeffery Auer, "Debate Goes to Town," *Oberlin Alumni Magazine*, XXXV (May, 1939), 8.
19. *Ibid.*
20. Egbert Ray Nichols, "A Historical Sketch of Intercollegiate Debating: II," *QJS*, XXII (December, 1936), 591.
21. Coaching had become so general by 1915 that Professor Frank H. Lane of the University of Pittsburgh felt moved to contribute an article for the first issue of the *Quarterly Journal of Public Speaking* asking just how far the faculty member should go in aiding the student debater. "Faculty Help in Intercollegiate Contests," *Quarterly Journal of Public Speaking*, I (April, 1915), 9-16.
22. *Ibid.*, pp. 595-596.

23. For a detailed account of the history of Delta Sigma Rho see *The National Society of Delta Sigma Rho: History, Constitution, General Regulations* (rev. to 1949).

24. *The Forensic* (March, 1923).

25. *Intercollegiate Debates*, IV, 429.

26. *Editor's Note:* Professor A. Craig Baird, co-author of this article, as director of forensics at Bates College in 1921, was responsible for this first international debate.

27. For a detailed account of this first international debate see *The Gavel* of Delta Sigma Rho, IV (October, 1921), 6.

28. *Vidette-Reporter* Iowa City), January 14, 1897.

29. *Iowa Alumnus* (Iowa City), XVIII (May, 1921), 252.

30. For a review of earlier Roosevelt and Bryan criticisms see F. G. Moore's "Where Men Debate Beliefs Not Statistics," *The Outlook*, CXXXII (1922), 55-56.

31. H. S. Woodward, "Debating Without Judges," *QJPS*, I (October, 1915), 229-233.

32. "Development of Intercollegiate Debating in the United States, Including a Specific Study in Northwestern and Chicago Universities," unpublished M.A. thesis, Northwestern, 1926.

33. For a summary of the Wells-O'Neill discussion see H. N. Wells and J. M. O'Neill, "Judging Debates," *Quarterly Journal of Speech Education*, IV (January, 1918), 76-92.

34. For a discussion of open forum, decisionless debating as practiced throughout the Middle West during the period immediately following World War I see "The Decisionless Debate with the Open Forum," *QJSE*, VII (June, 1921), 279-291.

35. For a review of the arguments advanced in favor of the "expert critic judge" method by its chief advocate, see L. R. Sarett, "The Expert Judge of Debate," *QJPS*, III (April, 1917), 135-139.

36. For an analysis and comparison of the American and British styles of debating see A. Craig Baird, "Shall American Universities Adopt the British System of Debating?" *QJSE*, IX (June, 1923), 215-222.

37. For a discussion of the educational values of international debating see A. Craig Baird, "How Can We Improve International Debating?" *QJS*, XXXIV (April, 1948), 228-230.

38. For a detailed explanation of the "Oregon Plan" by its founder see J. S. Gray, "The Oregon Plan of Debating," *QJSE*, XII (April, 1926), 175-180.

39. F. B. Ross, "A New Departure in Forensics," *The Forensic of Pi Kappa Delta* (November, 1923).

40. Nichols, *op. cit.*, p. 272.

41. Syracuse University, according to Nichols, first used this technique during the 1933-1934 season. Soon thereafter Pi Kappa Delta began sponsoring a student legislative assembly as a regular feature of its national conventions.—Nichols, *op. cit.*, pp. 277-278.

In the spring of 1939 Delta Sigma Rho staged in Washington, D. C., the first of a continuing series of national student congresses, held biennially.

13 Speech Education in Nineteenth-Century Schools

GLADYS L. BORCHERS
LILLIAN R. WAGNER

....

The history of education during the nineteenth century in the United States presents an interesting story of changing philosophies and methods which in many respects seems to reflect European patterns of education. The nineteenth century witnessed the rise of the public school system as we know it today, but neither its development nor the part played in it by speech education can be understood without a glance at American education prior to 1800.

Seventeenth and Eighteenth Centuries

New Englanders, who from the seventeenth through the nineteenth centuries led the country in most educational innovations and improvements, had a deep respect and zeal for learning as a "bulwark of Church and State." Hence they confronted the problem of establishing a system of education which would perpetuate their faith both by training young men for the ministry and by educating all children for membership in a sect. The colonists set up an educational system typically British; it consisted of some training in religion and reading by the parents or the apprentice-master (later by a town school master), a Latin grammar-school in larger places, and an English-type college to prepare students for the ministry. "As in England also, the system was voluntary, the deep religious interest which had brought the congregation to America being depended upon to insure all the necessary education and religious training." [1]

The famous Massachusetts Laws of 1642 and 1647 are considered basic to the foundation of our national system. The first merely required the councilmen to check from time to time to see if the children were being taught to "read and understand the principles of religion and the capital laws of the country." The second, based upon German and Dutch precedent rather than upon English, made the building of schools mandatory. Accordingly, Massachusetts soon had elementary schools for all its children and secondary schools in larger towns. Other New England states soon followed this example. George Martin, late nineteenth-century historian, says that the ideal was neither paternalistic nor socialistic:

The child is to be educated, not to advance his personal interest, but because the State will suffer if he is not educated. The State does not provide schools to relieve the parent, nor because it can educate better than the parent can, but because it can thereby enforce the obligation it imposes.[2]

Elsewhere the American pattern varied. The Middle Atlantic states favored the parochial type of school and later offered more opposition to the establishment of the public school system. In the South, the wealthy were largely instructed by private tutor and then sent to England for their college years while the poor received their only instruction at home or in charity schools. Cubberley states that "classes in society and negro slavery made common schools impossible, and the lack of city life and manufacturing made them seem largely unnecessary."[3]

During the Revolutionary period most grammar schools, academies, and colleges were closed or were kept open only intermittently. Not until the 1820's do we find any appreciable consciousness of education. Horace Mann accounted for the hiatus by noting that the talents of our most able men had been engrossed in the details of our struggle for existence and the problems of setting up a new government without precedence in the world.[4] Furthermore, an agricultural society was far more concerned with survival than with education or leisure. After the War of 1812 Americans began to think of themselves as a definite, dynamic, democratic nation and to take cognizance of the value of education. In this respect, however, neither the people nor the states were as farsighted as the federal government had been. The Land Ordinance of 1785 and later Congressional acts had given 80,000,000 acres of land to the public schools; yet even in the early decades of the nineteenth-century education was left largely in the hands of the church or of private individuals. Any new interest in education led to the establishment of academies and colleges rather than of schools for the general public.

Educational Importations During the Nineteenth Century

Although contemporary educational thinking in Europe had been affected by the philosophies of Rousseau, Locke, Pestalozzi, and others, the only American importations during 1800-1820 were those concerned with the inexpensive expansion of educational opportunities rather than with the improvement of teaching methods and techniques. Chief among these importations were the Infant School, the English charity-school subscription societies, and the Lancasterian system. The Infant School gradually replaced the older Dame Schools and finally led to our public school primary departments; the school societies played a sizeable rôle in our educational history until the middle of the century; and the Lancasterian system, or monitorial school as it was usually termed in the United States, maintained a certain popularity for a quarter of a century. Because of its extremely low cost (about $1 to $3 per pupil per year), it made education for all men within the reach of the populace.[5] From such beginnings, education in the nineteenth century developed. Although teachers and schools differed in their philosophies and methods, one is able to discern certain overall trends apparent during the century.

Common Schools from 1800 to 1825

During this period the common schools, i.e., what today we call the elementary system, represented approximately the same type of education found in the early colonies as well as in Europe under the Reformation several centuries earlier. Actually the times demanded no more than this.[6]

Usually the schools and their equipment were of the poorest type. Many of the teachers were extremely young, untrained, and inexperienced. The entire curriculum of most schools consisted of reading, writing, spelling, and sometimes a little arithmetic, all taught in the language of the people. Many parents considered any further education "highly injurious for practical life."[7]

Reports on early schools indicated that most of the day was devoted to reading and spelling, for, as Boone remarks, "Spelling at first was not distinct from reading; or rather, reading was not differentiated from spelling."[8] Furthermore, all reading remained essentially oral until the twentieth century. Thus speech education in elementary classes was associated with oral reading where the greatest emphasis was consistently placed upon aspects of audibility, articulation, enunciation, and pronunciation. Bodily action received very little attention. Toward the middle of the century we find an emphasis being placed upon understanding the material read.

Emphasis Upon Reading

Some conception of the importance of reading in the grades may be gained from the following quotation from the 1821 course of study for primary grades in Boston:

The fourth or youngest class shall stand up with due ceremony at as great a distance from the instructor as possible, and read with a distinct and audible tone of voice in words of one syllable. No one of this class shall be advanced to the third or higher class who cannot read deliberately and correctly in words of one or two syllables.

No one in the third class shall be advanced to the second who cannot spell with ease and propriety words of three, four, and five syllables, and read all the reading lessons in Kelly's Spelling-book.

No one of the second class shall be advanced to the first class who has not learned perfectly by heart, and recited, as far as practical, all the reading lessons in Kelly's Spelling-book, the Commandments, and the Lord's Prayer; all the stops and marks, and their uses in reading; and in Bingham's Spelling-book the use of common abbreviations . . . the use of numbers and letters used for numbers in reading; the catalogue of words of similar sound, but different in spelling and signification; the catalogue of vulgarisms, such as chimney, not chimbley—vinegar, not winegar, etc.

Not one of the first class shall be recommended by the examining committee to be received into the English grammar schools, unless he or she can spell correctly, read fluently in the New Testament, and has learned the several branches taught in the second class; and also the use and nature of pauses, and is of good behavior. And each of the scholars, before being recommended, shall be able to read deliberately and audibly, so as to be heard in any part of the grammar schools.[9]

Children were taught to read by the slow and painful process of mastering the alphabet, the ab's (ab, eb, ib, ob, ub, ac, ec, ic, etc.), then words of one syllable, of two, of three, etc. The best description we found of this process was quoted from Rev. Burton's *The District School as It Was*.[10]

Procedures in oral reading seem to have been just as mechanical, for skill in performance was gauged not by the ability to convey meaning but by the ability to "speak up loud" and "mind the stops and marks." This last expression, frequently found in the literature, meant that the child was taught to pause long enough to count one at a comma, two at a semi-colon, three at a colon, and four at a period. Such an impersonal procedure undoubtedly served a utilitarian purpose because frequently the entire class read aloud together. Reading in unison may have been the outgrowth of a similar and popular method of teaching spelling, for the two were always closely integrated. In addition to the two injunctions previously mentioned, the children were also taught to pay careful attention to pronunciation and enunciation and to read fast enough to cover a sizeable amount of material. Such were the "guide posts" to good oral reading in the early part of the nineteenth century.[11] Samuel G. Goodrich in his memoirs of this period notes that such reading generally was performed "without a hint from the master" and that "repetition, drilling, line upon line, precept upon precept, with here and there a little touch of the birch—constituted the entire system."[12]

Much of the responsibility for this mechanical approach should be placed upon the inadequacy of teachers and the barren curriculum which reflected not only the earlier European pattern but also a pioneer life which offered few cultural advantages. Textbooks used at the time placed considerable emphasis upon delivery. Marceline Erickson who analyzed 152 readers used from 1785 to 1885 found that a large number of them placed major importance upon pronunciation and voice.[13] The elocutionary movement of the eighteenth and nineteeth centuries played its part also. The elocutionists stressed the importance of oral presentation in delivery and felt that it should be of primary concern to the teacher.[14] In addition, the popular monitorial plan, by which the teacher instructed the older children, each of whom in turn taught the younger ones, may have encouraged the teaching of delivery. When a teacher keeps but one step ahead of his class, he must have very definite information about what and how he will teach. For such young instructors, drill procedures in pronunciation and enunciation should not have presented real difficulty. Neither would the injunction to "speak up loud" and to cover a large amount of material have proved troublesome. If we may accept contemporary reports, presentation of the thought or mood of a selection was never a major concern except in a few schools and therefore it placed no stumbling block in the path of the neophyte teacher. What could be simpler then than to confine one's helpful comments to "Pause for the count of one at a comma, two at a semicolon, etc."?

New Authors in the Nineteenth Century

A survey of textbooks used in the early days would indicate some of the emphases we have suggested. Noah Webster, in a letter to Henry Barnard, stated that before his reader was published in 1785 most of the books used had been the Bible, Testament, Psalter, and Thomas Dilworth's Spellingbook, originally issued in 1740.[15] William B. Fowle also mentioned the reading lessons found in early spellers by Moore, Fenning, and Perry.[16] The highly moral content of readers undoubtedly can be traced to the early religious fervor of the colonists as well as to the great religious awakening in England and America. The following reading lesson, which followed the mastering of one-syllable words in

Dilworth's speller, will indicate how textbooks fulfilled their moral obligation:

> No Man may put off the Law of God
> The Way of God is no ill Way.
> My Joy is in God all the Day
> A bad Man is a Foe to God.

Most of the eighteenth-century readers had been by English authors but William B. Fowle noted that, during the revival of common schools following the Revolution, textbooks by Webster and Bingham superseded all previous ones. Martin accounts for their popularity by saying that both their titles and their content appealed to the national spirit fostered in America.[17] Although these authors remained extremely popular far into the nineteenth century, other authors appeared upon the scene, including Fowle, Enfield, Murray, Scott, Leavitt, Adams, Pierpont, and Cooke. The 1832 *American Annals of Education* listed 28 readers published before 1804 and 102 readers published by 1832.[18]

If the schools had followed the better textbooks of the period, mechanical and stereotyped procedures might not have dominated. For example, the popular *Columbian Orator* by Caleb Bingham suggested among other things that the initial impression of voice and body was important to an audience, that one should adjust the voice to the size of the room and vary both the rate and pitch so as to avoid monotony and an affected variety, that one should have variety in position and use gesture, and that one should read as he would speak if he "could arrive at that exactness." Unfortunately, not many teachers followed such precepts in their classes; practice was not as good as precept.

Secondary Schools from 1800 to 1825

Secondary schools continued to reveal a wide variance from the elementary in curriculum offerings and in opportunities—a condition which had also existed under the European church-controlled system both before and after the Reformation. The influence of European humanism was evident in the emphasis given to Latin, Greek, classical literature, and rhetoric. These studies, prominent in the early Latin grammar schools, continued as the staples of our educational system well into the nineteenth century. This type of classical education, which had been established within two decades after the landing of the Pilgrims, undoubtedly reflected popular demand. In 1640 one out of every two hundred persons in New England was a college graduate![19]

The academies, started about 1750 and reaching their peak of importance during the 1820's, reflected the later humanism of northern

Europe, a humanism essentially more democratic both in curricular programming and in its aim at improving the lives of more than merely the select few. This type of secondary education was devoted less to the training for the ministry than to preparation for more ordinary vocations. It reflected, more than the Latin grammar school had done, the general secularization of the Renaissance as apart from one of its phases, the Reformation. If the realism and rationalism of the seventeenth and eighteenth centuries influenced our educational system, the effects are probably to be seen in the academies. We believe, however, that their broadened curriculums were more directly the outgrowth of American minds, like Franklin's, which recognized the need for a type of training directly useful to the citizens of our continent.

A few examples drawn from school statutes show the trend and character of formal education in speaking and reading. The "Regulations for Government of the School on Federal Street" stated that "public Reading and Recitation be instituted," and that "a Public Speaking [be held] as often as the Trustees shall see fit to order or permit them." The 1832 printed regulations for the Boston Latin Grammar School required that "Reading English, both in prose and verse, with readiness and propriety, shall be considered essential to every class." "Oratory" and "declamation and exercises of a forensic kind" were taught at Exeter while at Leicester "Reading and spelling were strongly recommended... as at least a weekly exercise in the upper school" and public speaking was "among the first branches taught in the English department." Here Scott's Lessons in Elocution was used for the first class mentioned and Blair for the second.[20]

The constitution of Andover for 1808 gives an indication of what was to be taught in such courses when it specifically mentions invention, disposition, style, delivery, and memory. Ebenezer Porter, who held the Bartlett Professorship of Sacred Rhetoric at Andover from 1813 to 1831, indicates that his textbook, An Analysis of the Principles of Rhetorical Delivery, was based upon the requirements of 1808. Walker's classical Key was used at the Boston Latin Grammar School and Blair's rhetoric in Miss Pierce's academy at Litchfield.[21]

Instruction in oral reading claimed a larger proportion of time in elementary studies than instruction in all aspects of speaking and reading in the secondary school. Nevertheless, speech training in the secondary schools may have been superior in quality for at least four reasons: the teachers were better educated (many academy teachers had M.A.'s); on the whole the teachers had a more professional attitude, first in the Latin grammar schools and later in the academies; secondary speech programs were not limited merely to oral reading (Leicester Academy had "the art of speaking" and Exeter had "exercises of a forensic kind," to mention only two); and the philosophies basic to secondary schools indicated an approach to education which differed from that in the common schools. The college influence upon the grammar school gave it a somewhat classical slant; on the other hand, the original concept of education which had promoted the academy produced a more utilitarian type of speech training. The close integration of lyceums with academies in the second quarter of the century is but one example of school training being put to practical use.

Extracurricular Programs from 1800 to 1825

Almost all schools employed some kind of extracurricular performances which had their place in speech training. The nature of the performances varied with the individual schools and reflected the age, interests, and abilities of the students as well as the capabilities of the instructors. Content ran the gamut from spell-downs, or similar performances of skill in arithmetic, to declamations (original or not), to debating, dialogues, and plays.

Although prizes and awards for outstanding performance may have been common, we found only one instance where ribbon awards were given annually for superior ability in reading. Humphrey reported informal gatherings of pupils from two schools, but "Quarterdays" were far more common. At times these were held at individual schools while in other places several schools combined their talents.[22]

Some critics felt that these "exhibitions" were excellent because they "kept up interest all winter and stimulated both teachers and scholars to do their best in the way of preparation" while others felt that the students were "encouraged to most vehement and obstreperous manifestations." Many persons objected when the schools put on dialogues and dramas because their "theatrical cast" was considered immoral in several sections of the country. Often the program included a variety of events—original and non-original declamations, dialogues, and plays. We found some records which indicated that a complete day was used for such an extensive program. In addition to these forms of entertainment, many academies had debating and rhetorical societies.[23]

1825 to 1855—Education for All

This period witnessed the culmination of a general belief in, and a demand for, common education for all. As a result, the structural form of our public school system as we know it today was achieved by the middle of the century. The same forces which helped to produce this result also affected the speech training offered in the elementary and secondary schools. Earlier the Lancaster system, the Infant School, the Sunday School, and the City School Societies had accustomed the populace to the idea of common schools for all. This idea, intensified by certain political, economic, and social changes which began in the first quarter of the century, gave a permanent cast to American education by 1855.

After about 1815 the country moved towards the abolition of class rule and political inequalities—a movement which started in the Western states where men were accepted for their individual worth rather than for their social standing or for their property. Politically, the phrase, "dignity and worth of the individual" took on new meaning. With the extension of suffrage to all men, rich and poor, came the realization that education was necessary to train men as citizens, and not merely as members of the Church or for the ministry or because they belonged to a particular class.[24]

During this same period the growth of manufacturing increased the size, number, and importance of cities whose populations then grew more diversified in economic, religious, and social patterns. Accordingly, the country witnessed the beginnings of a change from an agricultural to an urban society, and this shift, coincident with the desire for class equality, brought demands from newly formed labor organizations and other groups for a further expansion of educational opportunities and for improved curriculums. The second quarter of the century witnessed the long and successful struggle for a tax-supported school system—a struggle which was directly tied up with the battle to eliminate pauper or charity schools and church control over education —both of which were deemed inconsistent with the national consciousness of equality and of non-sectarianism in a democracy.[25] Such changes in the American scene were of course reflected in educational philosophy. Educators began to popularize the needs of man as an articulate person in his practical world; and they saw man as a citizen speaking as well as reading.

Other forces gave impetus and new significance to education in speaking and reading. The Lyceum movement, the growth of American literature, and the expansion of both school and public libraries reflected a maturing interest in information and culture.[26] In the schools, accordingly, teaching methods began to emphasize full and accurate understanding of the printed page. Under the influence of Pestalozzi, Mann, Barnard, and others, there were evident, also, new directions in pedagogy itself. Teachers began to see the child as a many-sided being, not as a moral being only. They reasoned that he should understand the basis of health, and offered him physical training and courses in physiology; they believed he should understand the world about him, and began to introduce courses in science into the curriculum. Education took on an "intellectual" objective.

Changes in Speech Education

These objectives in turn influenced class method and procedures. "Defining" was introduced so that the child could be taught "the habit of carrying this sense along with the letters of the word"; spelling and reading were integrated more meaningfully, with spelling losing its former place of importance and becoming an adjunct of reading; in grammar, the common dependence upon memorization of rules with little attention to transfer of training was decried and teachers suggested teaching a practical grammar and composition from everyday situations. They favored greater emphasis upon usage in both oral and written language. Journals carried many articles on vulgarisms, provincialisms, and improprieties as well as some upon regional differences. They urged teachers to be as careful of their own speech as of their students' since it was their duty to preserve the "purity of the English language." [27]

The interest in object lessons and visual education was based upon the philosophy that learning should be integrated with the child's experience and his everyday language, methods in keeping with contemporary European thinking. The same ideas were reflected in textbooks and material written for the more formal subjects as well as in juvenile newspapers, question and answer periods, and class discussions. This appearance of discussion, designed to develop one's ability to think on one's feet, was the first indication of interest in good listening habits and conversational ability. The picture of classroom activity, then, indicates a definite trend toward speech training in a broader and more practical sense than that implied in the teaching of oral reading and declamation.

The schools, nevertheless, retained their interest in reading, which continued to be essentially oral reading; articulation, enunciation, and pronunciation remained important and show the influence both of the elocutionary movement, as based upon the work of Walker, Steele and others, and also of the American concern with literature and culture. The interest in culture and the elocutionary movement probably helped to popularize dictionaries, and Walker's, which followed Johnson's *Dictionary of the English Language* (1755), was long the recognized authority. Gradually, however, Webster's and Worcester's superseded it.

The phonetic method of teaching reading came into favor in the lower grades and may have accentuated the emphasis upon articulation in the upper grades. Teachers were warned to be neither "culpably negligent ... or fastidiously anxious about a literal copy of Walker's ortheopy" and that "pedantry in pronunciation is more offensive than vulgarity." While regional differences were recognized, instructors were cautioned to teach pupils to avoid "all the provincialisms which may prevail in the community in which they have been brought up." To achieve these goals, teachers used various methods. Some favored daily phonetic drill to prevent "mumbling, clipping, skipping habits which are so universal and so destructive to all good reading"; others depended upon having students correct their own errors through the use of the dictionary; still others suggested the value of developing habits of careful listening to make students aware of articulation, or of using music, a new school subject, or of meticulous drill with the teacher and pupil in turn reading the sentence.[28]

Many teachers, school committees, and others interested in the schools of the period maintained that the teaching of reading should stress the understanding and communicating of thought more than correct pronunciation, articulation, enunciation, and modulation. The two phrases which appeared most frequently in pedagogy were "Read as you speak" and "Convey the sentiment of the author." These injunctions seemed to be centered on the key desire for understanding by both the performer and the listener, and to indicate a deeper recognition of the relationship of oral reading and speaking in the training of a literate populace. The older emphasis upon quantity of material was replaced in many instances by an almost fanatical attention to quality, and some teachers would spend a half hour on a few lines. The pupils would "*spell* and *define* the words; tell their *synonyms* and *opposites; write* and *paraphrase* the sentence or paragraph; *analyze* the words; parse the whole sentence or paragraph; recite the *history, geography, biography,* etc. to which there may be a reference in the sentence." [29] Comments by teachers and students were to be given not only upon "faults in pronunciation, pauses, inflections, tone; in omitting, substituting, or putting in words" but also upon "any fault in regard to the general style and execution of the reading, as affecting the meaning, strength, or beauty of the passage." [30]

In general, there seems to have been a gradually improving attitude toward rules. "P," for example, suggested that instead of the old "Mind your stops," the teacher should say, "Mind the sense; read to the sense"; others maintained that children needed "few rules and directions to guide them in the utterance of sentiments and emotions which they understand and feel." The stress upon a conscious carry-over from the style of everyday speaking into reading, the emphasis upon habits of "good listening" as an aid to improving reading and in developing the individual, and the oft-reiterated caution to have a "perfect conception of the piece" or to convey "the sentiment of the author," all indicate a great improvement in the teaching of reading. Perhaps the basis for these changes in methods is to be found in the new interest in the development of the individual and the recognition of the fact that he should be taught to think as well as merely to absorb what others have thought. Nevertheless, many critics continued to maintain that in all too many schools the children did not understand what they read and that they were "engaged exclusively with sounds, mere words without ideas." [31]

Textbooks of the Period

Although the old favorites by Bingham, Webster, and Murray remained in general use, many new textbooks appeared during this period. Primers by Gaullaudet, Worcester, and Parkhurst were highly recommended; readers by Leavitt, Russell, Pierpont, Swan, Fowle, Snow, Emerson, Abbot, and Angell were also popular. The famous McGuffey readers, which were still in use during the twentieth century, appeared in the 1830's. Among textbooks for upper grades and secondary schools which provided for speech training we should mention those by Walker, Barber, Emerson, Parker, Putnam, Kelly, Swan, and Mandeville. Marceline Erickson's thesis reviews some of these as well as others in the period.

Conversation

Perhaps another forerunner of modern speech training in the schools was "conversation." This could be "taught in connection with the ordinary recitation exercise . . . or we may make it a distinct exercise, giving out a subject as for composition." [32]

This second, and less prevalent, type of "conversation" may have developed because of the opportunities for participation in actual discussions in the lyceums and because the new school libraries opened vistas beyond the confines of ordinary textbooks. Both undoubtedly enlarged the horizons of at least some of the students.

"Oral instruction" was another term with seemingly the same connotation as that of conversation, "taught in connection with the ordinary recitation exercise." It bore some resemblance to the "class discussion" of today although the nineteenth-century pedagogues seemed more concerned with its value as speech training than seems the case today. Such class procedure led students not only to a greater understanding of material, but also "into the habit of thinking and reasoning upon everything they learn." [33] McGuffey maintained that unless the child were able to

. . . think without embarrassment in any situation in which he may probably be placed . . . express his thoughts on any subject with which he is acquainted with accuracy, and without hesitation ... generalize his knowledge with rapidity, so as to construct an argument, or a defence ... he is not educated; at least he is not educated suitably for this country, and especially for the West.[34]

We mentioned the fact that the new libraries and the lyceums probably encouraged "conversation" by providing material for discussion and opportunities for participation. It is also probably true that the general emphasis upon understanding as contrasted with rote learning served as a basis for the introduction of "oral instruction" as a teaching technique and for the occasional emphasis upon listening. The attention paid to European philosophy, the broadened curriculum, and the new interest in the child as a complete being were probably other factors which encouraged attention to conversation.[35] "Oral instruction" or "conversation," in turn, may have also influenced the teaching of reading, for certainly the injunction, "Read as you speak," must have become more meaningful to students.

We consider the 1820 to 1855 period significant even though the only "speech" courses as such were entitled declamation and usually appeared in the upper grades or in secondary programs.

The Secondary Program

The same forces which affected changes in the common schools also influenced the secondary programs of the Latin grammar schools, the academies, and the public high schools. Challenging the position of the academies during the 1820's the public high schools appeared to satisfy the needs of a democratic society and "represented a cooperative effort on the part of the people to provide something for themselves." In general, the high schools proposed to prepare youths for commercial pursuits and general living; the earliest ones "were entirely unrelated to the grammar schools ... and to the colleges." By the mid-century mark, however, they had begun to base their entrance examinations upon grammar-school subjects and during the 1870's college entrance tests were such that a "good high school course was practically essential." [36]

All three types of secondary schools offered a better type of speech training than that usually found in the common schools. Elocution and declamation were often listed as class subjects. In some instances, daily classes were held; in others, weekly, bi-weekly, or monthly exercises were the rule. At times a subject was listed simply as a "course in Blair's lectures"—distinctly a speech textbook. "Rhetoric" was also frequently listed as a class subject but the same connotation was not always given to the term. The commissioners of Massachusetts said, "by *rhetoric,* including *reading,* is here meant the art of public speaking," but a tendency more and more evident toward the half-century mark was to "deal with the oral aspects of composition as elocution and to confine rhetoric largely to written composition and criticism." This was in keeping with the general movement towards belles lettres.[37] Courses in "criticism" or in "criticism of the best English authors" probably were similar to such rhetoric courses. One encounters classes in "Logical exercises, in other words, *conversation*" and we can assume a form of speech training in such classes. The term "elocution," which had made its initial appearance in England nearly a century before, seemed to grow more popular and to appear in both academies and public high schools.[38] Among elocution textbooks, those by Mandeville, Barber, Enfield, and Porter were widely used. Blair's book seems to have been the one most frequently used in advanced courses; Walker's and Campbell's textbooks followed next in line. Russell's *Rudiments of Gesture* seems to have been the most used book on action although the more expensive Austin's was mentioned at times. Later in this period Jamieson's and Newman's textbooks, both reflecting the belles lettres movement, exceeded Blair's in popularity.

Extracurricular Programs

Throughout the period students in upper grades, especially in secondary schools, participated in varying degrees in speech activities. Exhibitions, often now with "musical exercises interspersed," continued to be prominent. The programs varied, but there seems to have been much emphasis upon declamation of all types. At times declamation exercises were held as regular classes; at other times the entire school met for the performance; occasionally the public was invited. Usually the selections were memorized, with original pieces growing in prominence during the later part of the period. The Latin grammar schools and some academies were apt to have "translations from and into French, Latin, and Greek languages."[39] Wednesdays, Fridays, or Saturdays seem to have been the preferred days for declamation classes.

Whenever we found adverse criticism of declamation, it seemed to be concerned with the methods used more than with the activity itself. It was criticized as being either unnatural and utterly devoid of imagination or of allowing the imagination to "run riot on the surface of style"; it was also accused of inculcating poor speaking habits in students because too often the selections were not prepared under constant supervision. Exhibitions were often criticized for their "theatrical cast" which at the time did not seem quite moral enough for the public. On the other hand, some persons believed that exhibitions could do much good for "improvement in public speaking."[40]

Throughout the period, pupils were able to participate in discussions, plays, debates, and individual performances in addition to declamation classes. Most of the extracurricular activities directly connected with the schools were held on "Quarterdays" or "Exhibitions." Indirectly the secondary schools, especially the academies, offered additional speech experiences to their students by encouraging the growth of lyceums and literary societies in the local communities. Many biographies of the period tell of the great personal gains achieved through such groups. Some of the societies furnished training in parliamentary procedure.[41] Although some lyceums were established specifically for school age people, most of them were general community projects. In either case, participation by school students was encouraged. The period, 1825 to 1855, also showed some concern for those afflicted with certain speech defects.[42]

1855 to 1900

During this period, progress in speech education seems less rapid and changes less unusual. It may well be that by the mid-century mark, our educational system had met the most urgent demands of the populace and thus the general public, engrossed in national economic and social problems brought about by the Civil War, the reconstruction period, the influx of immigrants, and the general growth of the country, were content to let educators take over the chief responsibility for education. Perhaps our system had reached a stage in its development where those skilled in the profession were best able to instigate changes. Froebel's influence brought the addition of the kindergarten, the only change in external form; Pestalozzi's influence, noted earlier, became widespread after the 1860's; and national uniformity was brought about by the increase in city superintendencies and the establishment of the U. S. Commission of Education. Finally, Herbartianism played a part in education during the 1890's and, although later superseded by other philosophies, it paved the way for changes which we have seen take place in our own times.

In one sense, almost every elementary teacher in the early part of the century could have been considered a speech teacher because most instruction had centered on oral reading; historical changes in the second quarter made the populace aware of the need for an articulate citizenry and this affected speech training in ways we have already mentioned. These factors, plus increased demands made upon citizens during the last half of the century, seemed to make teachers realize that students needed general knowledge and understanding of man and nature. With the resultant broadening of the curriculum in both elementary and secondary schools, less time was allotted to oral reading. The last half of the century, accordingly, represents a regrouping of forces —a consolidation of gains which had gradually appeared during earlier times—for the new push into twentieth-century education.

Courses in Curriculums from 1855 to 1880

Inspection of curriculums reveals that reading was still the backbone of the elementary program. Such courses as "enunciation," "elementary sounds," and "phonetics" suggest direct instruction in both speech and oral reading. In addition, declamation, conversation, object teaching, and grammar, which was becoming more concerned with usage, appeared in curricular listings.

The number of subjects offered in high schools had nearly doubled within three decades. Reports on secondary curriculums in thirty large cities scattered throughout the country indicate that reading and declamation were taught in about half while elocution was listed in a number of cases. Rhetoric was offered in almost every school, but we cannot classify this as speech training since there remained the tendency to emphasize written rather than oral composition.[43]

Indirectly the educational philosophy of Pestalozzi played an important part in speech education after 1860. The salesmanship and entrepreneurship of Mr. Sheldon at Oswego Normal were important factors in its dissemination. Hundreds of Normal graduates taught in nearly every state of the Union. The natural outcome of the "object lessons" and "oral discussions" which they advocated was an increase in emphasis upon class discussion and upon the teaching of correct usage instead of formal grammar.[44]

For this period, then, most of the school emphasis upon speaking seems to have centered in two classes—the object class, paying particular attention to the expression of ideas, and the grammar class, dwelling upon correct usage. Where conversation classes were taught, both correct usage and adequate expression of ideas were included among the goals. There were still criticisms of the too prevalent dependence upon rules and some educators blamed the high-school admission tests for this emphasis.[45]

When Wells, president of the National Teachers Association, spoke in 1864, he stressed the need for "the acquisition of language ... especially by natural conversation." We shall quote one sentence from this speech because it seems to foreshadow the type of speech training found today in many elementary and secondary schools:

The time will never come when analysis and parsing will be dispensed with; but the time will come surely when instruction in "the art of speaking" will consist mainly of lessons which embrace *actual speaking;* of exercises designed to cultivate the art of conversation, of narration, and other forms of speech, by constant and careful practice in the use of these forms.[46]

Object lessons did not usually appear on secondary curricular programs, but there seemed to be a desire to encourage students to examine what they read more carefully and this, of necessity, must have resulted in more thoughtful class discussions. One teacher reported composing two hundred questions based on the first four lines of Gray's Elegy. These, he said, were later included in a popular rhetoric. Perhaps the most stimulating class reported by a former student was Dr. Taylor's lesson on the first seven lines of Homer's *Iliad*.[47]

Reading Remains Oral

As a classroom subject, reading remained oral. Each of the methods of teaching reading—the alphabet method, the whole word method, the phonic method—had its advocates. While articulation, enunciation, pronunciation, and so forth, remained paramount in importance, some educators continued to stress the need for conveying the meaning and sentiment of the author. The attainment of a "good English tone ... clear and full ... correct in quality, i.e., attuned to the normal sound" was important.[48] The ability to read orally seemed essential not merely as training in an art but for everyday life.

The famous McGuffey readers, whose sale was undoubtedly greater than that of any other series over three quarters of a century, were very popular in the Middle West and South. Perhaps more articles and books have been written about McGuffey and his readers than about any other textbook author.[49] Gail Tousey's article in the *Quarterly Journal of Speech* is accurate, but we believe that Tousey, like some other commentators, gives McGuffey more credit than he deserves in the total picture of education. His books were not too different from many other good readers although probably he and Russell used material more nearly adapted to children's abilities, experiences, and interests than most other school authors. Tousey stressed the rhetorical elements found in McGuffey and by implication seems to account for their popularity in this manner. However we are inclined to agree with Vail who, after a half century acquaintance with the readers as teacher and as editor, wrote that their popularity was to a large measure dependent upon the energetic work of the publisher and the fact that "their greatest value consisted in the choice of masterpieces in literature which by their comments taught morality and patriotism and by their beauty served as a gateway to pure literature."[50] It should be stated here in passing that the readers reflected a changing attitude towards teaching concepts of morality.[51]

Reports from states like California, Wisconsin, and New York indicate that among the popular textbooks were those by Webster, Sanders, Willson, Sargeant, Webb, Hilliard, Howe, Parker and Watson, and Mandeville. Comments upon these as well as upon the Russell and Goodrich series and other readers of the period may be found in Marceline Erickson's dissertation.

The term *elocution* appeared more frequently in the last half of the century than it had previously. Probably William Russell's definition exemplifies some of the thinking of the time in differentiating elocution from speech, enunciation, usage, or reading in its initial stages:

Elocution—In the secondary and in the more advanced stages of education, the discipline of the ear should be extended, so as to embrace all the refining and highly intellectual influences of music and poetry as combined in elocution.

Intellect, feeling, and imagination, are all inseparably united in the appropriate expression of sentiment, as embodied in the language of oratory and poetry; and their finest effects in utterance depend upon a nice susceptibility of ear, which culture only can secure to full extent.[52]

Debating

Various forms of spelling-bees and other local and interschool activities continued during 1855-1880. Debate presented perhaps one of the more popular forms of intellectual entertainment. The lyceums continued to play a part in encouraging such activity. Actually the debating societies in these years were seldom directly connected with secondary schools or colleges, but they seemed to mushroom around such institutions. Some educators felt that if the school would assume a more direct responsibility for debating the effects would be more beneficial and some of the prevalent abuses would disappear.[53]

1880 to 1900

Although reading remained the backbone of elementary education during the last two decades of the century, possibly less class time was given to it than before and more time was devoted to silent reading, both in the class and without. In the first place, the number of circulating libraries, of newspapers, magazines, and periodicals increased rapidly so that more people needed skill in silent reading. Secondly, the enlargement of the school curriculums had added extra courses of study, with added reading assignments. Prior to 1880 we found only one or two references to reading which did not specifically mean oral reading. References to silent reading increased after 1880 and a very small number of scientific studies were made concerning rate and comprehension in oral and silent reading.[54] The influence of Herbart, Froebel, and Pestalozzi undoubtedly was responsible for this new direction in education.

The school superintendent at Quincy might declare that "the custom of making oral reading the principal and almost the only means of teaching reading has led to many errors prevalent today," [55] yet despite all indications of change, reading continued to be the staple of grammar school education, especially in smaller localities. Mark Sullivan's observation is typical:

> Our progress in school was measured by graduation from First Reader to Fifth. We described ourselves as "in the Second Reader" or "in the Third Reader." The "readers" were the backbone of education, in East Grove and throughout the nation; they were to America of the 1880's what the "New England Primer" had been to the America of the preceding century.
> The series of readers used at East Grove was Barnes'. They were an imitation of but inferior to McGuffey's which were the standard readers throughout most of America.[56]

Essentially, reading remained oral reading in the grades; that is what most teachers considered it to be. In those schools which received special commendation reading emphasized the understanding and communication of thought.[57] In such schools, moreover, additional speech training was provided through reformed grammar classes or the addition of classes in conversation or "daily exercises in talking."

On the secondary level, however, reading as a classroom subject was definitely being eliminated from the program. In reports on curriculums and suggested curriculums, reading was not mentioned.[58]

In this period, also, it seems evident that reading and its methods were set off from elocution. The *Cyclopedia of Education* and the *Dictionary of Education and Its Instruction* agree with others who differentiate reading from elocution by limiting reading to certain methods (the alphabetical, word, phonic, and phonetic) while they list articulation, pronunciation, emphasis, voice inflection and tones for elocution. They further state:

> In modern times [1880's], rhetoric as an art treats of all composition, whether spoken or written. . . . The practice, at present, which seems to be increasing in favor with teachers, is to omit elocution, or training in mere delivery, and to extend the importance of invention beyond that assigned to it by Whately.[59]

A few schoolmen deplored the separation of reading and elocution, as did the superintendent of schools at Salem:

> I must confess, however, that I am not entirely satisfied with the methods of instruction today in the upper grades of our schools in teaching the use of the voice and how to apply it in effective reading to others. . . .

By the books in use from 1830 to 1860 and after, the directions mentioned above [articulation, enunciation, pronunciation, vowels and consonants, accent, emphasis, inflections, tones and modulations, and in some books many other topics] for training the voice were enforced in the daily lessons. Now much less attention is paid to these matters. The method today seems to be to read good literature, books by the best authors. Doubtless this improves thought and the written forms of expression, but it lacks the power of expressing that thought by the vocal organs. We have in these days "Schools of Expression," "Schools of Oratory," and similar institutions by other names, but where do we find the same excellence of teaching tone and pitch, force and emphasis, articulation and pronunciation, as was common in the best schools a half century and more ago? [60]

Seemingly debate remained one of the most popular forms of speaking activity in the country. This was true in the West as well as the East. Furthermore, it had a place as an activity in many schools. Cordell Hull who attended secondary school in the 1880's wrote:

The parents of the Willow Grove section were generally farmers, with very limited education, but they were deadly in earnest that their children should get the utmost from their schooling.
It was they who established a debating society at the schoolhouse so that their children could develop themselves in debate. They attended the debates and followed the arguments closely and seriously. They would not stand for levity. I remember that at one of the debates various parents rose and protested that some of us had not fully prepared our arguments.[61]

William Jennings Bryan writes in his memoirs, "In the high school I . . . went a step forward in the art of declamation in the literary society. . . . We had a debating club in the high school." [62] George W. Norris claims that what he learned of parliamentary procedure and human nature in debating on the Ohio frontier later helped him as a U.S. Senator. He records his appreciation for the activity in the following manner:

I remember that during the summer months when the society met I worked hard in the harvest fields all day; and when daylight faded, walked to Clyde, then three miles away, for the debates, and was back in the fields soon after daylight the next morning. It was not difficult; it was a great privilege, and a great pleasure.[63]

In conclusion, we observe that the first quarter century pictures an extremely meager general education, especially on lower levels, and that almost the sole method of teaching was that of oral reading. The 1825-1855 period is the most interesting and shows signs of a decided improvement in speech training and in education in general; in the face of social changes, public school education became broader and its methods, in addition to those of oral reading and elocution, made a place for discussion and conversation. The last half of the century, taken as a whole, shows consolidation and refinement of gains made during earlier years, while the final two decades witness the distinction between reading and elocution, the rise of silent reading, the virtual disappearance of oral reading from secondary schools, and the appearance of debate activity. The forms and methods of reading and speaking in nineteenth-century schools were to be shaped and channeled into courses and activities labeled "speech" in the twentieth-century public school.

Notes

1. E. P. Cubberley, *The History of Education* (New York, 1942), p. 364.
2. *The Evolution of the Massachusetts Public School System* (New York, 1894), p. 16.
3. Cubberley, *History*, p. 653.
4. Horace Mann, "Causes Which Have Contributed to an Abatement of Interest in our Common Schools," *Connecticut School Journal*, I (1838-1839), p. 51.
5. Cubberley, *History*, pp. 661, 667-668; Josiah Quincy, *Municipal History of the Town and City of Boston* (Boston, 1830), p. 21; "Free School Society," *American Journal of Education*, XIX (1869), 509; J. P. Blanchard, "Report of the Committee Appointed to Make an Experiment of Introducing the Monitorial System into the Primary Schools of the City [Boston]," *Am. J. Ed.*, III (1828), 135-145.
6. Samuel G. Goodrich, *Recollections of a Lifetime*, I (New York and Auburn, 1857), 38.
7. *Ibid.*, pp. 33-35; Thomas Low Nichols, *Forty Years of American Life* (New York, 1937), p. 36; Charles Beecher, ed., *Autobiography of Lyman Beecher, D.D.*, I (London, 1836), p. 20; Sophia Hayes Wyatt, *Autobiography of a Landlady of the Old School* (Boston, 1854), pp. 16-17; Jacob Abbott, *New England and Her Institutions* (Boston, 1835), p. 269; Prof. Olmsted, extracts from a lecture, in *American Annals of Education*, IX (1839), 171; John Neal, *Wandering Recollections of a Somewhat Busy Life* (Boston, 1869), p. 105; A., "Colleges and Common Schools," *Am. An. Ed.*, III (Boston, 1833), 259.
8. Richard G. Boone, *Education in the United States* (New York, 1889), p. 66.
9. "The Course and Mode of Instruction to be Pursued in the Primary Schools in 1821," quoted in "Subjects and Courses of Public Instruction in Cities, Boston, Massachusetts," *Am. J. Ed.*, XIX (1869), 471.
10. Quoted by Pres. Dwight in "Remarks on Early Education," *Am. An. Ed.*, III (Boston, 1833), 307-309.
11. "History of Common Schools in Connecticut," *Am. J. Ed.*, V (1858), 145-146; Joseph T. Buckingham, letter to Henry Barnard, December 10, 1860, quoted in *Am. J. Ed.*, XIII (1863), 131; Rev. Burton, *District School*, p. 109.
12. Goodrich, *Recollections*, p. 144.
13. Marceline Erickson, "Speech Training in the Common Schools, Academies, and High Schools from 1785 to 1885 as Revealed by a Study of the Books Used in the Schools," unpublished Ph.D. dissertation, University of Wisconsin, 1948.
14. Regulations of 1823 for the Boston Latin School, quoted in "Subjects and Courses of Instruction in Cities, Boston, Massachusetts," *Am. J. Ed.*, XIX (1869), 489; Emory Washburn, *History of Leicester Academy* (Boston, 1855), p. 31; "School Books in the United States," *Am. An. Ed.*, II (1832), 371-384.
15. Quoted in *Am. J. Ed.*, XIII (1863), 123-134.
16. "Memoir of Caleb Bingham," *Am. J. Ed.*, V (1858), 339.
17. *Ibid.*; George Martin, *Evolution*, p. 100.
18. See "American Text Books," *Am. J. Ed.*, XIII (1863), 211-222, 401-408, 626-640; XIV (1864), 601-607, 751-777; XV (1865), 539-575.

19. "The American Education Society," *Am. J. Ed.*, XIV (1864), 367.

20. *Regulations for the Government of the School on Federal Street* (Boston, 1797), Articles XV, XVI, XXVII; A. Winterbotham, "View of the United States of America, London, 1796," as quoted in *Am. J. Ed.*, XXIV (1873), 139; "Regulations of 1823 for the Boston Latin School," *op. cit.*, p. 489; Elmer H. Wilds, "Public Speaking in the Early Colleges and Schools," *Quarterly Journal of Speech*, II (1916), 37; Emory Washburn, *History*, p. 31.

21. *The Constitution and Associate Statutes of the Theological Seminary in Andover with a Sketch of Its Rise and Progress* (Andover, 1808), p. 17; Warren Guthrie, "The Development of Rhetorical Theory in America, 1635-1850," *Speech Monographs*, XVI (August, 1949), 104-105; "Regulations of 1823 for the Boston Latin Grammar School," *op. cit.*, p. 489; Alain Campbell White, *History of Litchfield, Connecticut, 1720-1920* (Litchfield, 1920), p. 114.

22. Thomas C. Simonds, *History of South Boston* (Boston, 1857), pp. 116-117; Heman Humphrey, letter to Henry Barnard, *Am. J. Ed.*, XIII (1863), 127-128; Alain C. White, *History*, p. 122; Sophia H. Wyatt, *Autobiography*, p. 79.

23. John Neal, *Recollections*, p. 29; David L. Dodge, *Memorial, Consisting of an Autobiography* (Boston, 1854), pp. 49-50; James A. Woodburn, *Life of Thaddeus Stevens* (Indianapolis, 1913), p. 5.

24. Every new state admitted east of the Mississippi, except Ohio and Louisiana, granted full manhood suffrage at the time it came into the Union.

25. Cubberley, *History*, p. 672; "Increasing Attention to the Subject of Education," *Am. J. Ed.*, I (1826), 379; F. Eby and C. F. Arrowood, *The Development of Modern Education* (New York, 1945), p. 713; Governor Clinton, "Extracts from a Speech to the New York Legislature at Albany" quoted in *Am. J. Ed.*, III (1828), 125; "Extracts from Governor Morton's Inaugural Address," quoted in *Common School Journal*, II (1840), 48.

26. "American Lyceum," quoted from the *American Traveller* in *Am. J. Ed.*, III (1828), 633; "Popular Improvement," *Am. J. Ed.*, III (1828), 377-378; Horace Mann, "Third Annual Report of the Secretary of the Board of Education," *Com. Sch. J.*, II (1840), 122; George De Mille, *Literary Criticism in America* (New York, 1931), 31; the *American Traveller* quoted in "American Lyceum," *Am. J. Ed.*, III (1828), 702; A. B. Alcott, "Outline of Instruction as Conducted in Cheshire Primary School No. 1, Winter Term, 1826-27," *ibid.*, p. 93; "District School Libraries," *Com. Sch. J.*, II (1840), 66; VI (1844), 212; "Resolves Concerning School District Libraries (Chapter 113)," *Com. Sch. J.*, VII (1845), 369-370; "District School Libraries," *Com. Sch. J.*, II (1840), 66; "The School Library," *ibid.*, pp. 106-112.

27. Professor [sic] Pillans, "Account of the Method of Teaching to Read in the Sessional Schools," *Am. An. Ed.*, I (1831), 71; P., "Spelling," *Com. Sch. J.*, II (1840), 155-157; O.C.E., "Spelling," *ibid.*, pp. 15-16; E.M.G., "Spelling," *Com. Sch. J.*, III (1841), 51-52; T. Parsons, S. Howe, R. Neals, "Report on Grammar and Writing Schools in Boston," *Com. Sch. J.*, VII (1845), 298; "Vulgarisms," *Com. Sch. J.*, II (1840), 160; "Barbarisms, Solecisms, Improprieties," *Com. Sch. J.*, IV (1842), 81-84; "Foreign Words and Phrases," *Com. Sch. J.*, XI (1849), 25-26; "Provincialisms," *ibid.*, pp. 190-191; "Both, Each, Either," *ibid.*, pp. 312-314; "English Grammar," *ibid.*, pp. 374-375; Thrifty, "To the Editor of the Cabinet and Visiter," *Com. Sch. J.* III (1841), 31-32; VII (1845), 196; "Practice vs. Precept," *Com. Sch. J.*, VII (1845), 225.

28. "Review of Ebenezer Porter's *Principles of Rhetorical Delivery*," *Am. J. Ed.*, II (1827), 357; "Pronunciation," *Com. Sch. J.*, I (1839), 167; Thomas L. Nichols, *Forty Years*, p. 65; "On Teaching Reading, No. XII," *Com. Sch. J.*, VI (1844), 364, 367; Utopia, "Letters to a Primary School Teacher," quoted from *Newburyport Herald, Com. Sch. J.*, VI (1844), 56; "Reading," *Com. Sch. J.*, V (1843, 98; "Singing in the Common Schools," Extracts from Boston School Committee Report, *Com. Sch. J.*, III (1841), 189.

29. William C. Woodbridge, "Reading," *Am. An. Ed.*, II (1832), 59.

30. "On Teaching Reading, No. XII," *Com. Sch. J.*, VI (1844), 365.

31. P., "How to Teach Reading, No. XIII," *Com. Sch. J.*, VI (1846), 386; A. B. Alcott, "Common Education: Elementary Instruction," *Am. J. Ed.*, III (1828), 372; A School Committee Man, "Reading," *Com. Sch. J.*, I (1839), 158; Derby, "Individual Development," *Am. An. Ed.*, IV (1834), 367-370; George R. Hand, "Report on a Course of Instruction for Common Schools," *Western Literary Institute and College of Professional Teachers*, XI (1841), 240; Horace Mann, "Second Annual Report of the Secretary of the Board of Education," *Life and Works of Horace Mann*, II (1891), 532; Thomas H. Palmer, "The Essentials of Education," *American Institute of Instruction*, XX (1849), 85.

32. P., "Description of a Good School," *Com. Sch. J.*, VIII (1846), 71-74.

33. R., "Limited Recitations," *Com. Sch. J.*, IV (1842), 263; Extracts from "Report of a Committee on the Subject of Schools in Rhode Island, May 17, 1832," *Am. An. Ed.*, III (1833), 282-284.

34. William H. McGuffey, "Examinations," *Western Literary Institute and College of Professional Teachers*, VI (Cincinnati, 1836), 241.

35. P., "Description of a Good School," *Com. Sch. J., op. cit.*, 71-74; Horace Mann, "Seventh Annual Report of the Secretary of the Board of Education," *Com. Sch. J.*, VI (1844), 120.

36. Cubberley, *History*, p. 699; Eby and Arrowood, *History*, pp. 748, 751.

37. Extracts from "Report of Commissioners, appointed by a Resolve of the Legislature, passed on 22nd February, 1825," *Am. J. Ed.*, I (1826), 90; Warren Guthrie, "The Development of Rhetorical Theory in America, 1635-1850," *SM*, XV (1948), 70; Horace Mann, "Seventh Annual Report," *Com. Sch. J.*, VI (1844), 93.

38. "Public High Schools of Salem," *Am. J. Ed.*, III (1828), 492; "Reports on Providence High Schools," *ibid.*, p. 429; Extracts from Prospectus of "High School of Buffalo, New York," *ibid.*, pp. 233-235; "Courses of Education in the New York High School," *Am. J. Ed.*, I (1826), 26; John Griscom, "Monitorial Instruction," *ibid.*, 50-52.

39. "Musical Lecture and Exhibitions," *Am. An. Ed.*, V (1835), 91.

40. "On the Cultivation of Imagination and Taste as Aids to Expression," *Am. An. Ed.*, IV (1834), 306-309; W. Baird, "Examinations and Exhibitions," *Am. An. Ed.*, IV (1834), 374-375.

41. S. C. Phillips, "On the Usefulness of Lyceums," *American Institute of Instruction*, II (1832), 76; Allen Johnson, *Stephen Douglass* (New York, 1908), p. 16; Extracts from a letter by Joseph Harrington, 1849, in Thomas C. Simonds, *History of South Boston* (Boston, 1857), p. 128.

42. "Motives to Study in the Ipswich Female Seminary," *Am. An. Ed.*, III (1833), 76; "On Stammering," *Am. An. Ed.*, V (1835), 456-461.

43. "Subjects and Courses of Public Instruction in Cities," *Am. J. Ed.*, XIX (1869), 77-144, 463, 469-576.

44. W. P. Atkinson, "The Defects of Our School System," *American Institute of Instruction*, XXXIX (1869), 41; S. S. Greene, "The Elementary Study of the English Language," *ibid.*, pp. 59-64; M. H. Buckham, Letter to Henry Barnard, *Am. J. Ed.*, XVI (1866), 555-556; Cubberley, *History*, pp. 388-392; Richard E. Thursfield, *Henry Barnard's American Journal of Education* (Baltimore, 1945), pp. 204-211.

45. H. F. Harrington, "Remarks," *Am. I. Instr.*, XL (Boston, 1870), 68.

46. W. H. Wells, "Methods of Teaching English Grammar," *Am. J. Ed.*, XV (1865), 149.

47. William A. Mowry, *Recollections of a New England Educator* (New York, 1908), pp. 78-80, 115.

48. M. H. Buckham, "The English Language in Society and in the School," *Am. J. Ed.*, XIV (1864), 352; Joel Parker, "Reading as an Art," *American Journal of Education and College Review*, II (1856), 193-207; William H. Wells, "Report to the Chicago Board of Education," *Am. J. Ed.*, VIII (1860), 530-540;

Gideon F. Thayer, "XIII. Letters to a Young Teacher," *Am. J. Ed.*, IV (1857), 219-227; "Phonetics," *Cyclopedia of Education* (New York, 1877), 699-701; Edward P. Weston, "Extremes in Education," *Am. I. Instr.*, XXXV (1864), 18-24; William Russell, "The Cultivation of the Expressive Faculties," *Am. J. Ed.*, III (1857), 321-345; Francis T. Russell, "On the Use of Rules in Teaching Reading," *Am. I. Instr.*, XXV (1855), 53-75; Fannie Lindsley, "Course of Reading for Primary Grades," *The Chicago Schoolmaster*, IV (1871), 38-42; George S. Boutwell, *Educational Topics and Instruction* (Boston, 1859), pp. 144-148; 230; John W. Hoyt, *Report on Education* (Washington, 1870), p. 60; C. E. Stowe, "Teachers Seminaries or Normal Schools in the U.S.," *Am. J. Ed.*, XV (1865), 692; Dr. Ellis, "Dedication of Quincy School House," *Am. J. Ed.*, XII (1862), 712; M. H. Buckham, Letter to Henry Barnard, *Am. J. Ed.*, XVI (1866), 555-556.

49. Harvey C. Minnich, *William McGuffey and His Readers* (New York, 1936), pp. 195-200.

50. Henry V. Vail, *A History of the McGuffey Readers* (Cleveland, 1910), pp. 62, 69; Gail J. Tousey, "McGuffey's Elocutionary Teachings," *QJS*, XXXIV (February, 1948), 80-87.

51. Richard E. Thursfield, *Henry Barnard's Journal*, pp. 217-219.

52. William Russell, "Intellectual Education—Perceptive Faculties," *Am. J. Ed.*, II (1856), 137.

53. "History of Public High Schools of Hartford, Connecticut," *Am. J. Ed.*, XXII (1871), 346; James N. McElligott, "Debating, a Means of Educational Discipline," *Am. J. Ed.*, I (1855), 495-514; Catharine McKeen, "Mental Education of Women," *ibid.*, 577-578.

54. William S. Gray, *Summary of Investigations Relating to Reading* (Chicago, 1925), p. 5; Ada V. Hyatt, *The Place of Oral Reading in the School Program. Its History from 1880-1941* (New York, 1943), pp. 15-16; Cubberley, *History*, p. 402.

55. Hyatt, *Reading*, p. 14.

56. Mark Sullivan, *Education of an American* (New York, 1938), p. 61.

57. W. H. Holmes, "Individual Instruction in Reading in the Higher Grades," *Educational Work*, I-II (Worcester, 1906), 207-210; Walter Kunce, "The Art of Reading," *The Educator Journal*, VI (1905-1906), 97-99; Albert Marble, "On Teaching the Effective Use of English," *Educational Review*, III (1892), 22-30; S. S. Block, "The Science and Art of Reading," *Am. I. Instr.*, LII (Boston, 1881), 156-173; James L. Hughes, "Objective Methods of Teaching Elementary Reading," *Education Review*, II (1891), 162-168; George E. Hardy, "The Function of Literature in the Elementary Grades," *Education Review*, II (1891), 140-150; B. G. Northrop, "The Quincy Method," *Am. I. Instr.*, LI (1880), 3-22; R. C. Metcalf, "The Public Library as an Auxiliary to the Public Schools," *ibid.*, 46-48; Charles Eliot, quoted in Edgar W. Knight, *Fifty Years of American Education* (New York, 1952), pp. 41-42.

58. Ray G. Huling, "The American High School," *Educational Review*, II (1891), 40-56; *Report of the Committee of Ten On Secondary School Studies, Washington, United States Bureau of Education, 1893*, quoted in Edgar W. Knight and Clifton L. Hall, *Readings in American Education History* (New York, 1951), pp. 555-556.

59. H. Kiddle and A. J. Schem, *Dictionary of Education and Instruction* (New York, 1881), pp. 105-206, 245-246, 252-253, 290; *Cyclopedia of Education* (New York, 1877), pp. 257, 721, 733, 847.

60. William A. Mowry, *Recollections*, pp. 28, 267.

61. *Memoirs of Cordell Hull*, I (New York, 1948), 14.

62. W. J. Bryan and Mary B. Bryan, *The Memoirs of William Jennings Bryan* (Chicago, 1925), p. 42.

63. *Fighting Liberal, the Autobiography of George W. Norris* (New York, 1945), pp. 23-26, 27.

14 Five Private Schools of Speech

EDYTH RENSHAW

....

American life after the Civil War was characterized throughout the North by a decidedly greater prosperity and comfort than ever before. It is true that the panic of 1873 brought privation into millions of homes, but gradually business not only recovered but real wealth was greater than before the war. Men had money to spend without knowing very well how to spend it.[1]

Nothing had ever succeeded like America. Success tended to give a materialistic cast to an American's view of his world. He required that even his culture serve some useful purpose. He wanted poetry that taught a lesson, tunes that he could whistle, and paintings that told a story. His attitude toward culture was both suspicious and indulgent. Culture was tolerated only for leisure hours and even then it was chiefly for womenfolk.

The American's passion for education was unique. His public school system was the oldest in the world. He was the first to establish public libraries. He was the first to open colleges to women. Every school, library, lyceum, and chautauqua advertised the American's eager desire for self-improvement.

The postwar period of self-improvement, of popularization of culture, and of general prosperity was a time ripe for development in a field long popular with Americans, the field of oratory. In fact eloquence— the art of the pulpit, of the forum, and of the tribunal—was the only literary art which performed a vital function in the early nineteenth century.[2] Later in the century, oratory (and rhetoric in the classical sense) was to make a place for a new and less original art. It was a re-creative art—the oral interpretation of literature.

What better cities to develop the new art than Philadelphia and Boston? Oratory had long been popular in both. Both cities were known throughout the country as cultural centers. The first of the well-known and long-popular private schools of speech was established in Philadelphia, although many students and young people who sought

301

careers on the lyceum circuits flocked to Boston. And in Boston the forerunner of the private speech schools opened in 1872 when the newly-founded Boston University included the first university school of oratory. To this school, as to the rest of the university, women were admitted on equal footing with men. Although the school did not gain the future which had been dreamed for it, from its early students came some of the men and women who were later to become outstanding leaders in speech education.

Lewis Baxter Monroe was the first head of the Boston University School of Oratory, with the title of Snow Professor of Oratory. At the time of his appointment Monroe was at the height of his career as an educator. He had been supervisor of reading in the city of Boston and was the author of a set of readers which were clearly in the vein of interpretative reading. In addition he was a platform reader of note throughout New England. Monroe was a pioneer credited with exerting power in changing the emphasis in oratory and declamation from the display of technique to the communication of ideas.

Before Monroe studied with Steele Mackaye [3] (the American teacher of Delsarte methods) he was familiar with Swedenborg's philosophy. Moreover, Monroe had already worked out theories similar to those of Delsarte; accordingly he found the ideas of Delsarte congenial and taught them in his classes.[4]

Shortly after his death in 1879 the *Boston Herald* bestowed considerable praise on Monroe as an educator who exerted great influence in the field of elocution.[5] According to the article there were 5000 students of oratory and elocution in Boston. Monroe is mentioned as a "leading influence." Among his students who later became prominent were Charles Wesley Emerson, Samuel Silas Curry, Anna Baright Curry, Leland T. Powers, Elizabeth Harwood, Moses True Brown, Edward N. Kirby, Franklin Sargent, Mary A. Currier, and Robert Raymond.[6] Emerson, Curry, Powers, and Sargent were among the distinguished men who lauded Monroe's effectiveness as a teacher and his influence in awakening his students to the practical use of the imagination in elocution. According to Sargent, Monroe was the originator of the transcendental school of thought in American elocution theory.[7] Doubtless he may be called the original force which found its outlet in the five schools we consider here.

The Five Private Schools

The National School of Elocution and Oratory

After his release from the Union Army, J. W. Shoemaker,[8] a young Pennsylvanian who had taught school a few years prior to the war, moved to Philadelphia. He had already made some slight reputation as a platform reader and lecturer and was seeking advancement in those fields. Shoemaker taught private classes in elocution in Philadelphia and continued his platform work. In 1867 he married Rachel Hinkle who had been a fellow student at the State Normal School from which both had been graduated. The two gave programs throughout Pennsylvania and were also associated in various schools.

Their first school was the School for Elocution and Penmanship. Subsequently they operated the Philadelphia Institute for Elocution and Languages and finally the National School of Elocution and Oratory. The National School, opening on September 1, 1873,[9] was formally chartered by the state in 1875.[10] Its proprietors claimed that it was the first school of its kind to be chartered in the United States. The National School, always with a member of the Shoemaker family at its head, remained in continuous operation with an average enrollment of about two hundred until 1943 when it was forced by war conditions to close.[11]

In their first published catalogue (1874) the Shoemakers called attention to the fact that, though they were beginning a new school, "work bearing directly upon the present organization was commenced ... on the sixth of August, 1866. ... It is estimated that not less than three thousand students have been under instruction since the commencement of the work. At least six hundred Lectures and Readings before educational bodies, lyceums, and promiscuous assemblies have been given in the same time. Students from the Institution are actively engaged as teachers in eight States of the Union." [12] Thus the institution was actually beginning with the support of a large alumni and a seven-year history.

When the National School of Elocution and Oratory was formally established, there were four full-time teachers and four part-time lecturers on special subjects for approximately ninety students. The following year another lecturer was added and the student body enlarged to about one hundred twenty-five. The size of the faculty increased as the school slowly grew. When Shoemaker died in 1880 there were twelve teachers and two hundred students. In the next five years the school achieved its maximum size with about two hundred and fifty students.[13] From that time until Mrs. Shoemaker's death in 1915, although the size of the school fluctuated, the average student body numbered around two hundred and the faculty approximately ten.

In the beginning the school offered a two-year course. Students who finished the course, passed the examination, and deposited a thesis were awarded a diploma of graduation.[14] By 1878 the degree of Bachelor of Oratory was substituted for the simple diploma and a plan for giving the Master's degree was announced. It was to be conferred on any holder of the Bachelor's degree who at the expiration of three years passed a satisfactory examination upon the course of reading prescribed by the school.[15] These requirements for both degrees remained much the same until the school ceased to operate.

The Emerson College of Oratory

In 1880 when Charles Wesley Emerson opened his speech classes in Boston, he named his school The Monroe Conservatory in honor of his former teacher.[16] Emerson, a retired minister, had entered Boston University in 1872 to study law and oratory.[17] As long as Monroe taught, Emerson continued to study with him. After Monroe's death, Emerson himself began teaching, and in a few years changed the name of his school to the Monroe College of Oratory. Not until 1891 was Emerson's name used instead of Monroe's. From that date on, though the title has since been shortened to Emerson College, the school has always been called by its founder's name.

The first year Emerson had only about a dozen students. By 1891 over five hundred students were enrolled. By this time Emerson had associated with him fifteen regular faculty members, eight regular lecturers on special subjects, and other occasional lecturers and platform readers. The summer school on Martha's Vineyard in 1892 included seven hundred students from every state in the Union.[18]

In 1894 Emerson College of Oratory affiliated with a small, private school owned by Moses True Brown, a former student of Monroe's. Brown sold his property, the Boston School of Oratory, to Henry Lawrence Southwick, a teacher in Emerson College, and its secretary.[19] For a time the two schools used the same facilities, but issued separate diplomas. Within a few years Brown's school was absorbed in name as well as in fact by Emerson's.

Southwick and his wife, the former Jessie Eldridge, had been among Emerson's first students. Throughout their lifetime they were associated with the school, first as teachers and then as part owners and administrators. When Emerson retired in 1903, the Southwicks were chiefly responsible for carrying on the school in much the same spirit as that of its founder.

During the twentieth century, when standards for teachers' certificates were raised, Emerson College teachers studied in local universities largely because of Southwick's insistence on a well-educated faculty. In 1909 Emerson graduates were granted teachers' certificates without examination. Several colleges accredited work taken at Emerson.[20] By 1919 the Emerson college curriculum, facilities, and faculty met state requirements, and the legislature extended to the college the power to grant degrees.[21] From 1880 to 1919 Emerson College of Oratory was a private school of speech under the direct supervision of Emerson or those who had been his close professional associates.

The influence of the college was extended by the participation of its teachers in special summer schools and in training schools for teachers. The popularity of at least six of the Emerson teachers on the national entertainment circuit, as well as others in a more limited area, attracted many students. The influence of the college was still further extended through the loyalty of its former students.

The Columbia School of Oratory

In 1890 two graduates of Emerson College, Mary Blood and Ida Riley, established the Columbia School of Oratory, Physical Culture, and Dramatic Art in Chicago with the stated purpose of teaching Emerson principles by Emerson methods. The school was successful and enjoyed a national reputation for years.

Within five years, although there were only eighty-five students, two office assistants and five additional teachers were employed. As extra attractions, the school offered lectures by five educators in special fields, recitals by the faculty, and Leland Powers as a guest reader.[22] The practice of presenting special lecturers was continued and Powers read at Columbia every year until 1905.

By 1895 Columbia was offering a four-year course leading to a professional diploma. Thirteen were granted that year. Before 1900, however, the school had settled down to having a two-year course of study, a third year of postgraduate work, and extra evening and summer sessions. The average enrollment for the regular session was about a hundred, and about fifty each for the other two sessions.[23] After Ida Riley's death in 1904, the school was incorporated under the short title of the Columbia School of Expression. It retained its essential original character until after Miss Blood retired in 1927.

The announced purpose of the school was to train public readers, teachers of oratory and dramatic art, and to cultivate the graces of expression. The acknowledged authority for the theories and methods used was that of Charles W. Emerson. Until after Emerson's retirement in 1903, the Columbia catalogs announced that the physical culture course was the one taught originally by him. His textbooks were assigned as supplementary reading even after Blood and Riley published their own works modeled on the master's. The Columbia School may, therefore, be considered an extension of its Boston prototype.

The School of Expression

A few years after the founding of Emerson College two other students of Monroe formed a partnership in Boston. Anna Baright merged her School of Elocution and Expression with S. S. Curry's private classes. The new venture was called simply The School of Expression.[24]

Both Anna Baright and Curry were advanced students when they enrolled in Boston University.[25] Miss Baright had been graduated from Cook's College Institute in 1873. After four years' study with Monroe she became one of his assistants. Upon Monroe's death in 1879, she opened a private school of speech. Curry had been graduated from Grant College in Tennessee before he enrolled in the university's first class. He worked with Monroe while he acquired the M.A., B.D., and Ph.D. degress. After Monroe's death when the university's School of Oratory was reduced to a department in the School of All Sciences, Curry succeeded Monroe as Snow Professor of Oratory. This position he held until 1888, although he was also teaching in his own private school which he had started in 1883 after his marriage to Anna Baright.

The first catalog of the School of Expression was printed in 1885; in 1888 the school was incorporated. In 1895 it absorbed the Boston College of Oratory.[26] Authority to grant degrees was obtained in 1938, when a four-year college curriculum was introduced. In 1943 the corporate name of the institution was changed to Curry College. Altogether the school has been in continuous operation almost seventy years. For over forty years the Currys served as administrative officers and teachers in the School of Expression.

The Leland Powers School of the Spoken Word

Another one of Monroe's students who became prominent in the teaching of speech was Leland Todd Powers. Twenty years younger than Emerson, and ten years younger than Curry, Powers entered Boston University in 1878 when he was twenty-one years old. He remained at the University after Monroe's death and was graduated two years later.[27] While there he was a fellow student of Emerson and a pupil of Curry. He also studied in Anna Baright's private school.

A talented reader, Powers was placed under contract to the Redpath Lyceum Bureau early in his career. Under its management he began a series of engagements which in a few years included appearances in a dozen states.[28] For many years he made an annual transcontinental tour. He was a popular recitalist at the Emerson, the Curry, and Columbia schools. According to some of his contemporaries, he was the most popular reader of his day.[29]

Though Powers' chief occupation was that of a dramatic reader, he was engaged as a teacher by both Emerson College and the School of Expression. First he taught for Emerson, then for Curry; later he taught a graduate course in platform art for Emerson College before he opened his own school in 1904.[30] Apparently Powers' work was harmonious with the teachings of both these schools although each claimed to be original and individual.

According to those associated with Powers as teachers in the early days of his own school, Powers was not happy in the other schools. As a very young man he had developed an individual technique of impersonating all the characters in a play or story. This style, which he called "monacting," he taught for Emerson and Curry. Although his teaching was acceptable to both schools, he was not satisfied. During his career as reader and teacher he had been formulating his own philosophy of speech education from which he believed all speech arts should be taught.[31]

When Powers and his wife, Carol Hoyt Powers, organized the School of the Spoken Word, it was their intention to maintain a small enrollment and to do a large part of the teaching themselves. They bought a house in a Boston residential district, remodeled it for a school, and never allowed the institution to outgrow its home. At first they taught six sections of fourteen students each. Later, when they had some capable graduates to employ as teachers, they added more sections, but the enrollment never exceeded two hundred. From the beginning, students were carefully selected. Since the aim was to develop artistic platform readers, a student was not permitted to return unless he showed talent and satisfactory progress.[32] From 1904 to his death in 1920, Leland Powers was active as a teacher and administrator in the school he founded.

Chief Similarities Among the Schools [33]

Curry reduced the formula for improvement of expression to three basic methods: stimulating the "cause," developing the organic means, and securing a better knowledge of the right modes of execution. Although none of the others stated these principles so succinctly, the Shoemakers, Emerson and his followers, and Powers agreed with these basic methods in theory and practice. The spokesmen for all five schools described the "cause" of expression as mental. They advocated freeing the voice and body from habit and making them responsive agents of the "mental cause." They all recommended practicing basic exercises for voice, action, and interpretation which were believed to give the student mastery of essential forms of experience and corresponding actions for communication. They were alike in explaining that all faults of delivery, all faults of voice can be traced directly or indirectly to wrong actions of the mind. To them it was axiomatic that expression is the result not of physical, but of psychic action at the moment of utterance.

In the teaching of voice development, all five schools showed an advance over purely mechanical techniques. The kind and amount of voice training differed somewhat from school to school, but in general the training consisted of drill routine to establish good habits of posture, relaxation, breathing, and articulation. In addition the students recited much lyric poetry selected for its affective and imaginative content to stimulate vocal responsiveness. Voice practice also included saying conversational sentences. Apparently the teachers recognized that there was no automatic carry-over from drill on isolated syllables and lyric poetry to everyday speech.

Another important similarity among the schools is that Delsarte's charts formed the basis of action study. There was, however, more change within the schools in the way action was taught than in any

CENTER OF WEIGHT ⌐►	HEEL	CENTER	TOE	CORRESPONDING ASPECT OF MAN'S BEING
BACK FOOT	SUDDEN WEAKNESS OR DEPRESSION	REFLECTION	DEFIANCE	MENTAL
BOTH FEET	SUBSERVIENCE	PHYSICAL EASE	HESITATION	MORAL
FRONT FOOT	ARRESTED INTENTION	ANIMATED ATTENTION OR INTEREST	VEHEMENCE	VITAL

Delsarte's Foot Chart as Taught by Emerson and Curry.

CENTER OF WEIGHT ⌐▼	HEEL	ARCH	BALL	
BACK FOOT	PROSTRATION	REFLECTION	DEFIANCE	MENTAL
BOTH FEET	RESPECT	VULGAR EASE	INDECISION	MORAL
FRONT FOOT	SUSPENSE	ANIMATED ATTENTION	EXPLOSION	VITAL
	MENTAL	MORAL	VITAL	◄┘ DOMINANT ELEMENT OF TRINITY OF CAUSE

Fig. 2. Delsarte's Foot Chart as Taught by Powers.

other single area of instruction. The Shoemaker school, opening before MacKaye had taught Delsarte's theories in America, at first taught physical education as a way of developing health, freedom, and poise; later it added Delsarte's systematic instruction. Emerson, Blood and Riley, and Curry, all had studied Delsarte before they opened their schools. Each of them, however, tried teaching according to Delsarte's principles and attempted to stimulate proper physical responses indirectly before they changed their methods and taught the charts as such. Powers, who founded his school after the others had begun specific instruction in Delsarte, taught only the action charts. Each school modified the charts in a few details, but none of them made fundamental changes. All of them claimed that the Delsarte exercises were practiced to free the body from restrictive habits so that it could respond freely and spontaneously to what they termed "mental cause."

As for oral interpretation, the schools agreed on at least these seven principles. First, for true expression, the whole man must speak through all his being. Second, the powers of his mind must act simultaneously and spontaneously at the moment of expression. Third, the voice and actions must be responsive and subservient to the idea being expressed. Fourth, technique must, therefore, be developed through careful practice. Fifth, problems to challenge the students' thinking should be assigned. Sixth, principles should be explained only after the student has already demonstrated them through a process of trial and error. And, finally, although these teachers believed in the existence of a sort of Platonic ideal standard, they repeatedly emphasized the importance of individual differences.

As there was agreement about what constituted desirable delivery, so was there agreement about what constituted undesirable delivery. The teachers in the five schools looked with complete disfavor on a mechanical style in which the speaker used artificial voice patterns or stereotyped postures. While they all believed that students could be stimulated by observing a good performance, they frowned on the copying of external forms.

The favorite adjective used by the spokesmen for these schools to describe desirable delivery was "natural." As they used the word, "natural" meant a quality like that of conversation. It also meant a style in which the speaker was free from personal eccentricities and obtrusive habits; it did not, however, preclude a studied technique.

In each school the criteria for satisfactory performance were said to be simplicity and directness. It must be recognized, of course, that what is simple and direct to one person may not seem so to another, or to a person of another time. Accordingly they taught principles which they believed facilitated the use of speech as a social art. None of them prescribed rules. Instead, they advocated genuine responsiveness to active and present motivations.

Principles of the Schools

The Shoemakers

J. W. Shoemaker approached his work, not as an artist or an educational philosopher, but as a working teacher. He was not trying to create something new; he was trying to use the best pedagogical methods he knew. In his only major publication *Practical Elocution*,[34] Shoemaker defined elocution as the natural expression of thought by speech and gesture. In a comparatively brief, simply written textbook, he attempted to explain the principles and methods of effective expression.

The point of departure in Shoemaker's book is the one most familiar today: all speech style should be based on that of conversation. As Shoemaker expressed it, conversation contains "the germs of all speech and action, and therefore constitutes the basis of oratorical and dramatic delivery."[35] The habits acquired in daily conversation are consequently of the utmost importance and if any habits of voice, articulation, or action are faulty they must be corrected. Proceeding on the belief that reading and public address should be "noble conversation,"[36] Shoemaker devoted one section of his book to explaining principles of voice, gesture, and oral interpretation and the brief section following to methods of instruction. The third section is an anthology of prose and poetry for oral reading.

One idea fundamental to all the Shoemaker teachings is that "correct elocutionary training is the subordination of the entire physical being to the service of mind and spirit, *thought* being the product of the inner or spiritual man, and *speech* and *gesture* its natural outlet through the exterior or physical man."[37]

In explaining both theory and methods, Shoemaker followed this basic premise. In each phase of study he described the normal physical and psychological condition and then explained how to develop skill in communication. Hence the section on voice study included the structure of the instrument, its use, management, anatomy, physiology, and hygiene. The aims listed for vocal development were to secure purity, power, and flexibility. Shoemaker taught that gesture should follow not rules, but natural laws. Its purpose is to supplement speech and by its added grace, emphasis, and illustration, furnish a complete thought to the hearers.[38] While Shoemaker advocated the development of technique in the use of voice and body for oral expression, he also cautioned his students that no skill, however artful, can substitute for intelligence and spirit in oral expression. He therefore recommended that each selection be thoroughly analyzed as to language and purpose. The student should be able to answer questions such as the following: What is the principal thought? What are the subordinate ideas and how are they related to the principal thought? What was the probable state of the author's mind when he expressed the thought? How should the student himself feel, and how would he have expressed the same sentiments in similar circumstances? [39] It was Shoemaker's thesis that in answering these questions the student would develop the comprehension and sympathy necessary for interpreting literature.

The approach and content of *Practical Elocution* actually represents the school's teaching. Similar ideas are presented in explanatory essays in many of the school's annual catalogs.[40] The volume itself was used as a textbook until the school was disbanded.[41]

Although there is much the same basic philosophy in *Advanced Elocution*,[42] the only textbook written by Mrs. J. W. Shoemaker, the book lacks the simple directness of *Practical Elocution*. The later volume was written to supplement, not to supersede, the earlier. In the introductory explanation of expression, Mrs. Shoemaker used a Delsartian description of the three-sided nature of man.[43] Moses True Brown, who had taught briefly at the National School, was cited as the authority on Delsarte. In applying the idea of the trinity of man to expression, Mrs. Shoemaker explained that through the sensitive or physical phase, man receives impressions; through the intellectual and spiritual phases, man interprets impressions in the light of experience. These impressions in turn are communicated through the physical body by means of voice and action.

Advanced Elocution is divided into four sections. The first two treat voice, the third is devoted to action, and the fourth is an anthology of selections. The aim of the drills and exercises was to enable the speaker to convey to others "what he himself understands, feels, and desires; for the agents of Expression are now supposed to act reciprocally with Intellect, Sensibility, and Will." [44] In explaining voice exercises and in giving directions for educational gymnastics Mrs. Shoemaker wrote what could be considered mechanical drills. Her introduction, however, indicates that vocal drill, like physical drill, should not be divorced from meaning. The aim of all practice should be to make the communication truly expressive of the speaker's impression.[45] Perhaps her attitude toward these drills was more scientific than mechanical. A description of the voice class given in an 1884 catalog indicates that the aim of developing the several qualities of voice, such as orotund and pectoral and of practicing effusive and explosive breathing,[46] was to secure the most thorough command of the vocal instrument.[47] Drills on basic bodily positions, attitudes and gestures,[48] however mechanical the printed descriptions, were taught for the stated purpose of developing the vigor, freedom, and control needed by the body as an instrument of expression.[49]

Fɪɢ. 3. Delsartian body poses to express sentiment as taught at the National School. Taken from *Advanced Elocution*, pp. 234-235.

Emerson

Emerson and his immediate successor, Henry Lawrence Southwick, became identified with Emerson's theories of the evolution of expression and with the series of textbooks called *The Evolution of Expression*.[50] According to Emerson, all art reveals the development of the mind of the race and that of each individual in the race. It is evident that he borrowed and rephrased Haeckel's theory that the individual in its ontogony recapitulates its philogony.

Emerson's theory of evolution was that the mind (and hence all art) develops in four stages or planes. Each plane consists of four steps. But each of these four steps is made up of the same four steps. A rough analogy can be made to a picture which contains a smaller representation of the same picture. As long as another picture can be discerned there is a repetition on a different scale of the first picture.

Emerson's system of evolution, accordingly, contains sixteen steps, the four basic planes of which are: animation or the whole; attraction or the parts; selection or relation of parts to the whole; and separation or relation of part to part. On each of the four levels these same four stages were supposedly further refined as the student developed his power to understand and express.

IV PART TO PART

4. SEPARATION	INTELLECT	4. PART TO PART
3. SELECTION	WILL	3. PART TO WHOLE
2. ATTRACTION	FEELINGS	2. PART
1. ANIMATION	CONSCIOUSNESS	1. WHOLE

III PART TO WHOLE

4. SEPARATION	INTELLECT	4. PART TO PART
3. SELECTION	WILL	3. PART TO WHOLE
2. ATTRACTION	FEELINGS	2. PART
1. ANIMATION	CONSCIOUSNESS	1. WHOLE

II PART

4. SEPARATION	INTELLECT	4. PART TO PART
3. SELECTION	WILL	3. PART TO WHOLE
2. ATTRACTION	FEELINGS	2. PART
1. ANIMATION	CONSCIOUSNESS	1. WHOLE

I WHOLE

4. SEPARATION	INTELLECT	4. PART TO PART
3. SELECTION	WILL	3. PART TO WHOLE
2. ATTRACTION	FEELINGS	2. PART
1. ANIMATION	CONSCIOUSNESS	1. WHOLE

FIG. 4. Emerson's Evolution of Expression.

Basic to Emerson's theory was the belief that expression is necessary for impression just as impression is necessary for expression. He believed that in the act of expresion the student gained insight as well as technique, and through insight was self-propelled to the next stage of evolution.

The criterion for choosing the literary selections in Emerson's textbooks was provided by his transcendental philosophy that a person becomes what he thinks. Emerson, therefore, chose didactic material which he believed would enrich personality and would help the soul evolve closer to the Over-Soul.[51] Each step in the preparation and delivery of the proper kind of literature was supposed to contribute to evolutionary growth.

Emerson wanted to elevate elocution from the level of a parlor trick to a social art. For that reason he christened his work with the more reputable, though misleading, title of "oratory." Both students and teachers, however, customarily used the word "rendering" when speaking of oral interpretation.

In addition to the four books in *The Evolution of Expression* series, Emerson later published four books called *The Perfective Laws of Art*.[52] These books were little used as textbooks in the school. Their significance now lies not in what they say, but rather in Emerson's stated purpose in preparing them. His avowed, if unfulfilled, intention was to show his concern with the fullest development of the individual and not with a set of rules.

Emerson's style in these books was a barrier to the achievement of his purpose even among those who believed in his evolutionary theory of art. His extravagantly mystic terminology has to be accepted more in faith than by reason. Although Emerson's writings may not be entirely clear to the modern reader, they reveal the sincerity of his efforts to stimulate his students to meticulous analysis and responsive interpretation of literature.

The Emerson system of voice training is based on his general theory of growth. In accordance with his stages of growth in oral interpretation, he divided his voice work into four parts.[53] In the first stage the work was to develop freedom, support, openness, and correct formation of speech sounds. In the second stage there were exercises for two kinds of inflections and for what he called "elasticity" or "flexibility," and for power. In these two stages Emerson intended to show the relation of physiology to voice. In the next two he attempted to show the relation of psychology to voice. In them were to be developed facility in combining elements of speech and responsiveness in musical quality. Although Emerson never published an explanation of the details of his method, he claimed to be able to induce in the student such states of mind as would operate through the cranial nerves directly on the vocal organs and instantly control their activity.[54] The voice obeyed the mind.

In agreement with one of the main tenets of his educational philosophy, Emerson's central theory of body culture was that thought has the power to mould outward form.[55] In his school three kinds of physical culture were taught. All were supposed to develop bodily responsiveness. All of them were based on principles of Delsarte, but only after Emerson's retirement was a course taught which used the Delsarte charts.[56] Even then the instructors made a conscious effort to avoid the recognized danger of mechanical gesture. They believed that if gesture were taught in accordance with a sound pedagogy based on art, psychology, and the best practices of physical training no artificiality would result.

Blood and Riley

Closest to Emerson College from point of view of educational theories is the Columbia School of Oratory. Its educational philosophy, psychology, and teaching methods were closely patterned on the parent institution. *The Evolution of Expression* was the basis for the teaching of courses in oral interpretation which were called "rendering" and "progressive steps in rendering." [57] After 1900 "literary interpretation" took the place of "rendering" in course titles, but the latter term remained in use as a synonym in course descriptions.

In 1894 Emerson's books were supplemented by *The Psychological Development of Expression,*[58] a four-volume series edited by Blood and Riley. It copied Emerson, but the authors did attempt to modernize the terminology and explanations. Their continued use of the basic premise that all education has four planes of four steps each prevented their making any significant advancement.

The only difference between the Columbia system and that of Emerson was in terminology. The Columbia authors renamed the four planes as follows: intellect, emotion, will, and physique. In each plane these classifications were given secondary explanatory heads. But as in the Emerson explanations, mental growth was said to begin with interest in communicating simple ideas and images chiefly for entertainment and to progress to the highest stage which was inspiring belief in moral concepts. Emerson insisted that his chapter headings were to be used only by the teacher as criteria in judging the pupil's development. Blood and Riley, however, proposed to make their topics direct goals for the student himself. Each chapter has an explanation concerning "desired action of the student's mind" and "desired effect upon the student's rendering." Their attitude was more realistic than that of Emerson, for in both schools the books were in the possession of the students. Most of the explanatory subtopics in *The Psychological Development of Expression* are readily intelligible. Two representative examples are "The seeing of images while speaking" and "Comparative directness—Simple colloquial form." Blood and Riley, furthermore, attempted to use standard psychological terminology. Occasionally, especially in volume four, Emerson's vague, transcendental terms were used, as for example: "suggestiveness" and "radiation through body and voice."

Curry

Curry, like Emerson, tried to base his philosophy of art on nature. He, however, borrowed not from the natural scientists, but from philosophers. He drew ideas from Plato, Schiller, Spencer, Hegel, Kant,

Comenius, Pestalozzi, and Froebel. These ideas were freely adapted and interpreted to suit his purposes and needs. Curry's central belief was that there is a direct correspondence between art and nature.[59]

According to this theory, growth in art, as in nature, takes place in accordance with four principles: unity, freedom, harmony, and originality. By unity, he meant growth from one center, from one impression.[60] By freedom, he meant the spontaneous impulse to unfold.[61] By harmony, he meant the co-ordination of the spontaneous impulse.[62] And by originality, he meant the correspondence between inner activity and outer motion.[63]

While Curry believed that art is innate and developed out of the play impulse, he also insisted that art must be play under the influence of order. Curry classified vocal expression, when not perverted, as art because like all true arts it reveals the human soul. But unlike some of the arts, vocal expression reveals the soul directly. Like the other arts it is founded on communion of minds. By means of it, one man can awaken in another the same faculties which are active in his own. When the speaker appeals to the imagination and sympathy of his hearers he awakens their creative ability.

According to one of Curry's early graduates,[64] the heart of Curry's method lay in the study of the imagination and what he called "dramatic instinct." Much of the student's ability to interpret, Curry believed, depended on his power of creating images in his own mind and on his power of identifying himself with the literature being read.

Curry's general principles are explained in *The Province of Expression*. Many other theories regarding specific application to oral interpretation are set forth in his other nine major textbooks. Since he had no methodic system, he published no simple exposition of his teaching methods, as Emerson did in *Evolution of Expression*. Since he wrote so many books and wrote them while teaching in several schools and while being engaged in lecturing and in other enterprises, Curry's publications suffer from repetition, obscurity, and over-elaboration.

As explained in several of his books, and particularly in *Mind and Voice*, Curry believed that the voice as a natural agent should be characterized by spontaneity, freedom, simplicity, and unity.[65] As he saw it, such characteristics can be achieved only when there is spontaneous action of the faculties. Hence, Curry worked out what he believed to be a psychological, not merely a technical, method of developing the voice. He was an advocate of using literary passages which stimulate emotions of pleasurable intensity which in turn create conditions favorable to good tone. Material evoking joy and laughter was supposed to bring about centrality of motor power and unconscious coordination of parts. Practice of such material was said to develop mental as well as physical habits to bring about retention of breath, an open tone passage, and co-ordination with the vocal bands. When properly trained, the voice, according to Curry, suggests the activities of thought, imagination and feeling.[66]

To establish normal conditions of the body Curry stated that the student must understand three truths. Action is spontaneous. It precedes speech. It is not necessarily motion or gestures; it may be attitudes and bearing.[67] Furthermore, no rules should be made for the kind of gestures for certain classes of ideas. All action is personal. If a student is freed from repressions and if "dramatic instinct" is awakened, he will gain greater expressive action of the body. While Curry rejected Delsarte's "science" of the trinities in action training, he accepted Delsarte's two principles of body training. Following Delsarte he taught that the whole body must be trained and that work must be given in the fundamentals of each agent of bodily expression.[68]

Powers

Powers' school differed from those of his former associates, Curry and Emerson, in the extent to which his philosophy was based on the supposed correspondence between the infinite and the finite. Powers believed that infinite wisdom, love, and power are reflected in man and in the manifestations of his mind: "if we can agree that the universe rightly understood is an expression of its Cause[69] and that it reflects or indicates method or activity or correspondency . . . again manifested in our own minds and thought-processes and their expressional activities, then we can . . . accept this discovered method as obedient to universal law." [70] Everything that Powers wrote is an explanation or an elaboration of this statement. In it are indicated his philosophy, his psychological theories, and his ideas of the cause, nature, and technique of expression.

Because Powers believed that the universe had a three-fold nature in which the elements were co-existent, co-operative, and co-essential, his explanations, like his trinities, have no beginning or end. Typical of his reasoning in a circle is his attempt to define the nature of expression. He dogmatically asserted that "expression must necessarily be mental because its cause is in mind." [71] Then, instead of offering evidence to support his second premise, Powers merely reversed the order of the propositions and asserted that "Cause is in the mind because expression is mental." [72]

The most peculiar aspect of Powers' philosophy of education lay in his belief that every individual possesses at birth all the knowledge he will ever possess.[73] Powers therefore argued that speech education must be a process freeing the avenues of expression and eliminating the barriers to clear expression. The study of expression must be training in a few fundamentals concerning the nature of thought and how it is embodied in other minds. Since in oral interpretation the media of expression are voice and body, Powers asserted that technical training must have the aim of "dematerializing" these physical agents.[74] He did not believe in a partnership between the mind and body. In philosophy Powers was an idealistic monist. His explanation was that though the material senses recognize the body, the mind recognizes only the embodiment of an idea.[75]

For Powers the art of oral interpretation was the art of embodying the spirit and essence of literature. Such embodiment he believed possible only when the interpreter understood the thoughts and feelings recorded in his material and when the mental concept was carried out through the trained and obedient voice and body.[76] For him the concept and the expression were essentially the same, each incomplete without the other.[77]

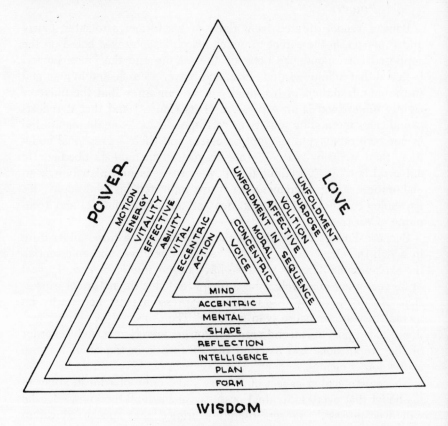

FIG. 5. Powers' Trinities of Cause.

Powers explained that all literature is the written embodiment of the three factors of thought's trinity. All mental activity reflects the same factors: the reflective factor, which conceives or plans; the affective factor, which chooses and purposes; and the effective factor which carries the plan and purpose to fulfillment. In any piece of literature one factor is dominant and the other two subordinate. As he saw it, the function of the interpreter is to reveal this relationship.[78]

The prime purpose of the course in interpretation at Powers' school was to awaken the student's vitality of thought. To begin with, there was drill on literature written to arouse people to action. Such drill would, Powers held, automatically stir vitality of thought because of the doctrine of correspondences. According to this doctrine, the author's vital purpose would stimulate the vital factor in the reader's mind.[79] He believed, too, that the development of any ability can come only through practice. His motto was "To do is to know." [80]

Powers taught that through technique and skill, the voice and body became obedient to thought.[81] In advocating technique, Powers did not deny the value of spontaneity. But he insisted that the in-

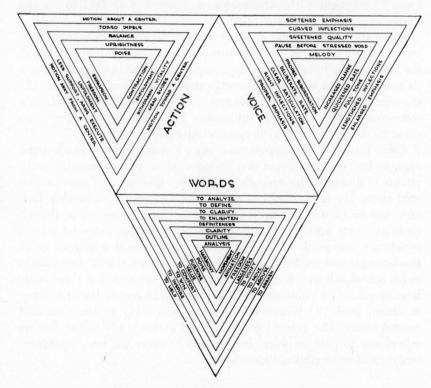

FIG. 6. Powers' Trinities of Manifestation.

terpreter, like any artist, can be spontaneous only after he has mastered his tools—his voice and body.[82]

A good voice, according to Powers, is latent in every individual; therefore voice training is essentially voice freeing. In such training the teacher must work personally with the student. Powers believed that little should be written about voice training because such writing is too open to misunderstanding.[83]

The teacher's function in voice training, as Powers expounded it, is to explain every exercise and see that it is correctly practiced. The teacher, also, can help free the student of fear and of bad habits.[84] The teacher should watch for and encourage signs of vitality of thought, and by encouraging a repetition of vital expression help make the student's material agent, the voice, obey his mind.[85]

Three conditions which Powers held to be indispensable to proper voice production were correct breath control, voice support, and proper direction of tone. The latter, he admitted, was inaccurate, but he believed the concept useful in freeing the tone. Together these three could, by stimulating the imagination, turn the student's attention away from possible throat-consciousness which was said to be the source of many vocal disturbances.[86]

The body, as the second medium through which the oral interpreter must embody his ideas, presents three major technical difficulties: (1) the body claims to have an existence apart from the mind; accordingly its sensations and nerve excitements produce unnecessary actions; (2) the inertia of the body resists thought; (3) fear causes too much bodily relaxation or tension. These difficulties, Powers held, could be overcome by drilling according to certain universal principles.

These principles Powers adapted from Delsarte, but he made some changes because he thought that Delsarte had confused sensation with vitality of thought. The strength of Delsarte's theories, as Powers evaluated them, lay in their philosophy of correspondences. Another Delsarte theory to which Powers ascribed importance was that, though there are many accidental actions, there are a few fundamental actions which are universal. Upon the theory of universal applicability of fundamental actions, Powers built the action charts which were taught in his school. All the charts were supposed to illustrate the three basic laws of action: (1) unfoldment in sequence; (2) opposition or balance in action; and (3) direction of motion according to the dominant mental factor. The general purpose of all action study in the Powers school was to gain technical facility and to make the body spontaneously obedient to vitalized thought.

Aims and Methods

The founders and proprietors of the five leading speech schools in the United States between 1870 and 1920 appropriated a watered-down transcendentalism for their philosophy; they adapted the psychological theories of the mid-nineteenth century for their pedagogical principles. Then, on the basis of their own backgrounds and interests, four of the five developed the theories with which their schools became identified. The fifth was a western offspring of its Bostonian parent institution.

The chief aims of the five schools were alike. They agreed that the general ends of all education should be development of character and enrichment of personality. They further agreed that study of uplifting literature was one of the best means of attaining those ends. Another general aim was to stimulate initiative and the free play of individuality. With regard to voice training, the central purpose in all the schools was to free the voice from restricting habits and tension and to develop clear articulation and flexibility in the use of pitch, rate, volume, and quality. In action training the schools tried to help the student overcome habits which might interfere with the expression of thought and feeling; they tried to give exercises which would induce freedom and co-ordination. The aim in both voice and body training was to achieve responsiveness and technical facility.

The differences in aims were largely those of emphasis. Shoemaker, more than the others, stressed correct articulation, enunciation, and pronunciation. Both Emerson and his followers placed evolutionary progress through art at the top of the list of goals. Curry was anxious to develop what he called the natural languages (the vocal, the verbal, and the pantomimic), according to the laws of nature. Since the general aim of the Powers' school was more limited than the others, the specific aims were also more circumscribed. Powers, unlike the others, was little interested in educating teachers. His school was primarily to develop platform readers. The aims of each course were directed toward professional excellence. Powers' religious belief led him to advocate "dematerializing" the physical agents. Like Curry, however, who wanted the voice and body to be bridges over which thought and emotion pass, Powers sought to make the material media avenues, not barriers, to thought.

The methods used in the five schools were also very much alike. They agreed that in all phases of the work teachers should be helpful guides who encourage students by making them conscious of proper ideals and of their own accomplishments, however slight. In teaching all subjects the teachers must set problems to suit the students' needs and abilities. In oral interpretation the teacher should ask questions to cause the students to concentrate, to analyze, and to respond sincerely to the author's purpose. In voice training the teacher should demonstrate what cannot be explained on paper and guide the students' ear training. In body training the teachers demonstrated the exercises, gestures, positions, and bearings. They also used quotations and dramatic situations to stimulate responses.

There were more differences of method among the schools than in aims. The Shoemakers began teaching when they were very young; they were dedicated to no system so they changed their methods when they found what they thought might be an improvement. When they opened their school they taught gymnastics to develop health, vigor, and freedom. They also taught "position," that is walking and standing; movements of the head, arms, and legs in conversational, oratorical, and dramatic gestures; and finally unimpassioned and impassioned facial expression. Later Mrs. Shoemaker introduced aesthetic physical culture and Delsarte's action charts. The students practiced posing according to sentiment and gave demonstrations for public entertainments. Emerson and Curry always used Delsarte's principles and eventually attempted to use Delsarte methods. Emerson students also gave demonstrations with groups of girls gesturing together and assuming similar attitudes. The Currys were opposed to such methods, which Mrs. Curry called "statue posing." In voice training Emerson attributed to the nares the central place in tone production and attempted by some method not recorded to get his students to center their voices in the nares. More than any of the other teachers, Curry stressed the need to hold attention on one thought and to make quick transitions to the next point of concentration while reading. Curry is also the only one who, in print at least, discussed the details of eye-span training as an essential to oral interpretation. Possibly this is because Curry students usually held a book while reading in public; the other schools encouraged memorization. Powers demanded it; his students never appeared in recital using a book.

In a sense the schools anticipated the "progressive" educational movement whose method was to learn to do by doing. Like Froebel, they believed that education should be emancipation. Through studies resembling play, they believed that creative energies, especially the imagination, could be awakened. According to their theories and to the teaching methods they attempted to use, real education does not consist in acquiring facts; it consists in acquiring skill in execution. It was their contention that such skills could be acquired only if educational methods returned to nature and stimulated growth from within. They insisted that only if a person received accurate vivid impressions could he respond with true spontaneous expression.

Though all of these schools lagged behind the contemporary developments in psychology, they all attempted to encourage communication from subjective understanding and motivation rather than to inculcate a perfected technical display. Each school had peculiarities, some of them ridiculous by our present-day standards. But they were innovators and contributors to the movement which fostered a psychological approach to the teaching of speech.

Notes

1. Allan Nevins, *The Emergence of Modern America—1865-1878* (New York, 1927), p. 203.
2. *Ibid.*, p. 212.
3. Steele MacKaye came back from France in 1870 to raise money to aid French victims of the Franco-Prussian War by lecturing on Delsarte.
4. Samuel Silas Curry, *The Province of Expression, A Search for Principles Underlying Adequate Methods of Developing Dramatic and Oratoric Delivery* (Boston, 1891), p. 338.
5. William Joseph Farma, "A Study in Comparative Speech Forms of Delivery with Special Reference to Interpretative Reading," unpublished Ph.D. dissertation, Wisconsin, 1946, p. 451. Farma is quoting an article in *Werner's Voice Magazine*, III (1881), 143-144, reprinted from an article in the *Boston Herald*, n.d.
6. *Ibid.*, pp. 542-453; and *Boston University Yearbook*, 1873-1880, Vols. I-VIII.
7. Farma, *op. cit.*, p. 451, citing Fred Winslow Adams, "Boston as an Elocutionary Center," *Werner's Voice Magazine*, XVI (April, 1894), 114-115.
8. The Shoemakers are the only ones in the group of teachers being studied in this essay who were not directly influenced by Monroe.
9. *Catalogue of the National School of Elocution and Oratory for 1874*, p. 14.
10. *Catalogue of the National School, 1875*, p. 17.
11. Interview with Dora Shoemaker, June, 1950.
12. *Catalogue of the National School, 1874*, pp. 14-15.
13. In this period Moses True Brown of Boston, a former student of Lewis Monroe, joined the faculty and taught courses in Delsarte for two years.
14. *Catalogue of the National School, 1874*, p. 35.
15. *Catalogue of the National School, 1878*, p. 28.
16. "History of Emerson College," *Emerson College Magazine*, I (December, 1892), 2; and II (December, 1893), 2.
17. Untitled article quoting obituary in the *Boston Post, Emerson College Magazine*, XVII (December, 1908), 66-69.
18. "History of Emerson College," *loc. cit.*
19. *Emerson College Magazine*, III (December, 1894), 2-3.
20. *Ibid.*, XVII (March, 1909), 215.
21. Henry L. Southwick, "The Exceptional," *Emerson College Magazine*, XXVIII (November, 1919), 215.
22. *Annual Catalogue and Announcement of the Columbia School of Oratory, Physical Culture and Dramatic Art* (1895), p. 6.
23. See annual catalogs for the Columbia School, 1896-1927.
24. According to Binney Gunnison, an early graduate, later teacher, and dean of the School of Expression, Curry did not use his own name in the title because he hoped to find a benefactor who would endow the school. Curry believed that only an endowed school could operate successfully on a high educational plane.
25. *Catalogue of the School of Expression, 1906*, p. 5.
26. Not to be confused with the Boston School of Oratory which Emerson College acquired.

27. *Who's Who in America* (1920-1921).

28. *Annual Catalogue of the School of Expression,* 1899, p. 29.

29. Harry S. Ross, "Address," *Emerson Quarterly,* I (February, 1921), 71-76; and Samuel Silas Curry, "The Monologue as a Dramatic Form," *Expression,* II (September, 1896), 209-210.

30. Unsigned announcement, "The Graduate Course in Platform Art," *Emerson College Magazine,* X (May, 1902), n.p.; *Annual Catalogue of the School of Expression,* 1899, n.p.; and unsigned announcement, "Leland T. Powers," *Expression,* VII (Spring, 1899), n.p.

31. Interviews with Hortense Creede Railsback in 1944, with Adele Hoose Lee in 1945, and with Elizabeth Pooler Rice in 1945.

32. *Ibid.*

33. The conclusions in this section are based on a comparison of the books, articles, and published speeches of the schools' founders and of their colleagues and their immediate successors. Relatively complete files of the catalogs and other institutional publications were also studied. Other primary sources were interviews and students' notebooks. See particularly, Edyth Renshaw "Three Schools of Speech: The Emerson College of Oratory; The School of Expression; and The Leland Powers School of the Spoken Word," unpublished Ph.D. dissertation, Columbia, 1950.

34. *Practical Elocution for Use in Colleges and Schools and by Private Students* (Philadelphia, 1880)

35. *Ibid.,* p. 23.

36. *Ibid.,* p. 34.

37. *Ibid.,* p. 20.

38. *Ibid.,* p. 141.

39. *Ibid.,* p. 112.

40. *Catalogue of the National School of Elocution and Oratory,* 1889, pp. 9, 13; 1891, p. 9; 1893, p. 9; 1896, p. 17; 1900, p. 12.

41. Interview with Dora Shoemaker, June, 1950.

42. Mrs. J. W. Shoemaker, aided by George B. Hynson and John H. Betchel, *Advanced Elocution Designed as a Practical Treatise for Teachers and Students in Vocal Training, Physical Culture and Gesture* (Philadelphia, 1896).

43. *Ibid.,* pp. 13-15.

44. *Ibid.,* p. 276.

45. *Ibid.,* p. 17.

46. *Ibid.,* pp. 23-170.

47. *Catalogue of the National School of Elocution and Oratory,* 1895, p. 6.

48. *Advanced Elocution,* pp. 175-280. Most of the gestures described are the same as those usually attributed to Delsarte.

49. *Catalogue of the National School of Elocution and Oratory,* 1895, p. 11.

50. Charles Wesley Emerson, *The Evolution of Expression, A Compilation of Selections Illustrating the Four Stages of Development in Art as Applied to Oratory,* 4 vols., rev. ed. (Boston, 1892).

51. Charles Wesley Emerson, "The Cultivation of Voice," *Emerson College Magazine,* I (April, 1893), 94.

52. Charles Wesley Emerson, *The Sixteen Perfective Laws of Art Applied to Oratory,* 4 vols. (Boston, 1892).

53. Charles Wesley Emerson, *Psycho Vox or the Emerson System of Voice Culture* (Boston, 1897).

54. *Ibid.,* p. 100.

55. Charles Wesley Emerson, *Expressive Physical Culture or Philosophy of Gesture* (Boston, 1900), p. 17.

56. Henry L. Southwick, "The Scholastic Year of 1903-04," *Emerson College Magazine,* XII (May, 1904), 202.

57. See annual catalogs for the Columbia School, 1895-1903, for courses in "rendering."

58. *The Psychological Development of Expression* (Chicago, 1894), 4 vols.

59. *The Province of Expression* (Boston, 1891), p. 180.

60. *Ibid.*, p. 172.

61. *Lessons in Vocal Expression Processes of Thinking in the Modulation of the Voice* (Boston, 1895), pp. 14-15.

62. *Mind and Voice, Principles and Methods in Vocal Training* (Boston, 1910), p. 215.

63. *The Province of Expression*, p. 180.

64. Binney Gunnison, Interviews, August 1943 and 1944.

65. *Mind and Voice*, pp. 435-440.

66. *Ibid.*, p. 441.

67. *Foundations of Expression, Studies and Problems for Developing the Voice, Body, and Mind in Reading and Speaking* (Boston, 1920), p. 292; and "Pantomimic Expression," manuscript notes for 1897-1898, pp. 5, 19.

68. *Province of Expression*, p. 353.

69. In writing of certain general principles and abstractions which he believed to be universals, Powers always used capital letters. His practice will be followed in this essay.

70. *Talks on Expression* (Boston, 1917), pp. 66-67.

71. *Ibid.*, p. 69.

72. *Ibid.*

73. *Ibid.*, p. 104.

74. *Ibid.*, pp. 27-28.

75. *Ibid.*, p. 52; and Leland Powers and Carol Hoyt Powers, *Fundamentals of Expression* (Boston, 1916), p. 11.

76. Leland Powers, *Practice Book* (Boston, 1916), p. 28.

77. *Talks on Expression*, p. 82.

78. *Practice Book*, pp. vii-ix; and *Talks on Expression*, pp. 7-8.

79. *Practice Book*, pp. v, x, 1-4.

80. Interview with Elizabeth Pooler Rice, August, 1945.

81. *Fundamentals of Expression*, pp. 12-14.

82. *Ibid.*, p. 18.

83. *Ibid.*, pp. 28-35.

84. *Talks on Expression*, pp. 39-44.

85. *Practice Book*, pp. v-vii.

86. *Fundamentals of Expression*, pp. 29-30.

15 Phonetics and Pronunciation

BERT EMSLEY
CHARLES K. THOMAS
CLAUDE SIFRITT

••

American linguistic phonetics is a subject which has taken on added interest in the last generation or so as increased facilities for travel and communication have made Americans more conscious of their mother tongue. The roots of American phonetics, however, lie deep in the past, on both sides of the Atlantic. Our study, consequently, will deal with the background of scholarly investigation, chiefly American, but British where relevant, by which since the eighteenth century phonetics has made its gradually increasing contribution to speech education in America. Some great men and many lesser ones have made their contributions, but the present study deals more with movements than with men.

What do we mean by *phonetics?* The Merriam Webster defines it as the "science of speech sounds considered as elements of language," but narrows the meaning of the adjective *phonetic* to spelling, alphabets, and various kinds of symbolization "in which each letter always represents the same sound."

Phoneticians themselves use the adjective *phonetic* somewhat more elastically. Some use the term *phonemic* in referring to the basic units, or *phonemes,* which distinguish one word or utterance from another; and the term *phonetic,* or *allophonic,* to those variations in sound which do not distinguish, but which depend on contextual or personal factors. Thus the second sound in *skin* is the same phoneme as the first in *kin,* but a different allophone because of the different phonetic context. Other phoneticians use *phonetic* as a catchall term which avoids these subtleties. Here we are concerned, within practical limits, with all efforts to identify and indicate the speech sounds.

The plan of this entire work on American speech education sets our practical limits. First, we restrict the scope to American phonetics and pronunciation, except for immediate British and European backgrounds. Second, we exclude experimental, or laboratory phonetics, which is discussed in another chapter. Third, we shall touch only incidentally on intonation, for intonation in English is a feature of the phrase rather than of the word or the phoneme; it has more to do with interpretation than with pronunciation.

The linguistic limitation, however, involves something more than an analysis of sounds and symbols. There are significant historical, comparative, dialectal, and prescriptive problems. In the efforts to promote one or another acceptable form of American speech, some notable trends have been associated with phoneticians or orthoepists. We have all been influenced, in more ways than we realize, by Noah Webster's opinions. And to some extent William Tilly reaped where Joseph Worcester sowed.

Though we cannot hope for a complete record, we can hope to invite further study and give the reader some direction for it. With this in mind, we shall concern ourselves with the following natural historical divisions: British diacritics or orthoepy, mainly eighteenth century; American and British phonotypy, mainly mid-nineteenth century; American philology, mainly late nineteenth century; ideas reaching this country in the present century from the International Phonetic Association; and recent linguistic geography and phonemics from American sources, but of continental European inspiration. The field of Speech, although it has had little to do with the origination and shaping of these movements, has played an energetic part in assimilating, integrating, and adapting them to the needs of its teachers, scientists, and students.

I

English diacritical orthoepy may be described as orthography struggling to become phonetics. Says Sheldon: [1] "By the end of the 18th century the diacritical system for indicating the pronunciation had been developed almost to the stage now current in commercial dictionaries." Whether used in dictionaries, school readers, or elementary language books, the Webster key and its like are excellent eighteenth-century achievements.

For earlier periods the reader may consult Wheatley, Ellis, Lamport, Krapp, McKnight, and others.[2] We center on the eighteenth century because it was the period when the efforts to "fix" the language came to a head. Spelling was championed by Johnson's *Dictionary* of 1755, pronunciation by Sheridan's in 1780. With few exceptions the orthoepists dedicated themselves to standardizing the orthography, undisturbed by phonetic innovations. English pronouncing lexicography

SCHEME of the ALPHABET.

Number of simple Sounds in our Tongue 28.

9 *Vowels,*   à   á   ȧ   è   ȯ   ȯ.   é   i   ủ
               hall   hat   hate   beer   note   noofe bet   fit   but

               w   y
             short oo   short ee

19 *Confonants,*   eb ed ef eg ek el em en ep er es et ev ez etħ eth efh ezh ing.

2 *Superfluous,*   c,   which has the power of *ek* or *efs* ;
                   q,   that of *ek* before *u*,

2 *Compound,*   j,   which ftands for *edzh*.
                   x,   for *ks* or *gz*.

1 *No letter,*   h,   merely a mark of afpiration.

Confonants divided into Mutes and Semivowels.

6 *Mutes,*   eb ed eg ek ep et.

3 *Pure Mutes,*   ek ep et.
3 *Impure,*   eb ed eg.

13 *Semivowels,*   ef el em en er efs ev ez etħ eth efh ezh ing.

9 *Vocal,*   el em en er ev ez eth ezh ing.
4 *Afpirated,* ef efs etħ efh.

Divided again into

4 *Labial,*   eb ep ev ef.
8 *Dental,*   ed et eth etħ ez efs ezh efh.
4 *Palatine,* eg ek el er.
3 *Nafal,*   em en ing.

FIG. 7. Scheme of the Alphabet. From Thomas Sheridan, *A General Dictionary of the English Language* (London, 1780), p. 9.

began in this period. The titles of the following dictionaries, most of them long and unwieldy, are omitted, but their contributions are often the first of their kind:

1723: Thomas Dyche, accent marks
1740: Nathan Bailey, accent marks showing short and long vowels
1757: James Buchanan, occasional diacritic respelling
1764: William Johnston, diacritics and type variations
1766: James Buchanan, complete diacritic respelling, with omission of silent letters
1773: William Kenrick, vowels marked by numbers, syllables indicated
1775: William Perry, Italian *a*, acute and grave accents

1780: Thomas Sheridan, no new methods, but first great pronouncing dictionary with a descriptive tendency

1786: William Scott; pronunciation key line on vocabulary pages

1791: John Walker; synthesis of methods, prescriptive, most influential in America

In the nineteenth century American dictionaries, largely under the influence of Walker, became prominent. A few British dictionaries are listed with them because of their influence on Worcester, especially with reference to the intermediate *a* of such words as *ask*, which, says the *Dictionary of American Biography*, "was Worcester's one permanent contribution to lexicography and the English language in America."

1814: (4th ed.), George Fulton and George Knight, intermediate *a*

1828: (first ed. 1798?), Stephen Jones, intermediate *a*

1828: Noah Webster, Italian *a*, spelling reform

1830: (1829?), Joseph E. Worcester, intermediate *a*, general orthoepy

1836: Benjamin H. Smart, intermediate *a*, orthoepy

1847: Chauncey A. Goodrich, Italian *a*, orthoepy

The persistence of diacritical orthoepy in recent works is well known. Competent American scholars like Whitney, Funk, Kenyon, Greet, Thorndike, and Barnhart have been associated with dictionaries which contain at least one diacritical system, often the only one. The two Thorndike series, by reducing the number of diacritics indicating variation in pronunciation, have come closest to developing a genuine phonetic key; they were the first to introduce the phonetic schwa into general dictionaries, an innovation which has since been copied by at least two other dictionaries.[3]

In identifying sounds, that is phonemes, these dictionaries have been more expert than in indicating them through phonemic or phonetic symbols. A dominant trend, with some exceptions on the radio and elocutionary fronts, has been the enlightened recognition of reputable variants. Even in the eighteenth century there was much intelligent discussion of pronunciation, although the discussion was relegated to the not-widely-read introductions to the dictionaries. Sheridan, Walker, Nares,[4] and others also published similar material in separate orthoepical works. Let us note again that the more objective, "natural" Sheridan was less influential in the United States than the somewhat more arbitrary Walker.

Orthoepical publications of a less familiar sort are to be found in Buchanan's (anonymous) *British Grammar* of 1762, interesting for methods rather than for basic phonetic knowledge, and Murray's famous *Grammar* of 1795, which followed Walker closely. An earlier interest in phonetic analysis, spelling reform, and phonetic innovation shows in the writings of Smith 1568, Hart 1569, Bullokar 1580, Gill 1619, Butler 1634, Wallis 1653, and Wilkins 1668.[5]

A few survivals of this reform method carried over into the eighteenth century. In contrast to the dominant trend toward fixing and ascertaining language once for all, stood James Elphinston,[6] who tried respelling without new symbols in 1765, and Benjamin Franklin,[7] who produced a new alphabet in 1768. Joshua Steele [8] offered a few letters and honest sentiments toward the same end in 1775. Franklin set off a long series of American successors, some of them quite patriotic, culminating in Andrew Comstock's [9] remarkably phonetic and patriotic, alphabet of 1846.

Comstock, however, belongs in the following period, as does his master, James Rush,[10] who in 1827 worked out a system with definite phonetic terminology. But Rush and the great bulk of his followers neither invented nor adopted a phonetic alphabet. Early American elocutionists, like Ebenezer Porter 1824 and William Russell 1841, naturally followed the Sheridan-Walker orthoepic. This tradition is strikingly illustrated in the journals of elocution and the speech arts[11] as late as the period from 1892 to 1915, when all articles on pronunciation remained orthoepic except an occasional stray one on Visible Speech.

Schoolbooks, like grammars, are numerous from William Bullokar in 1580 and, in America, from Caleb Bingham in 1794. The schoolbooks still use diacritical methods even when reading experts call them phonetic. The Edgeworths[12] attempted a diacritic-phonetic alphabet in 1801, but fell back on the familiar markings.

Teaching apparently differed little from that of today. James Buchanan's *Complete English Scholar* of 1753 began with monosyllables, put together from the vowels and consonants, and taught spelling by the "power of the letters." These methods go back at least as far as the Port Royalists of 1660 and strangely resemble modern phonics and phonogram techniques.

When the orthoepists made phonetic analyses or recognized acceptable pronunciations they labored earnestly but not usually in agreement. Sheridan tallied 28 English sounds, Murray 36.[13] Sheridan in 1780 ignored the Italian *a* in words like *ask;* Walker in 1791 opposed it; whereas many less famous men from Marchant in 1760 to Barclay[14] in 1784 clearly recognized it. Nineteenth-century Americans were more nearly in agreement, for the change in fashion took place between the centuries. The intermediate *a,* already noted, was a compromise (except possibly in New England) then regarded more as medicine against the Italian *a* than against the "flat" *a* of *bad*.

Of *r* Sheridan (1780) says, "This letter has always the same sound, and is never silent." Marchant 1760, Franklin 1768, and Barlow[15] 1772 seem to agree. Grandgent[16] cites many New England orthoepists, including the early Webster, 1784, who said much the same, but gives lists of mistakes which betray the opposite tendency. Here also the change probably came between 1790 and 1820.

On "long *u*" pronounced as a diphthong in such words as *tune*, Sheridan supported a trend that is still favored in radio and among elocutionists, though most Americans outside the South use a simple vowel. This persistent diphthongal pronunciation is recognized in the first phonetic dictionary, of 1855, along with some other elocutionary features. On the other hand, Grandgent noted a New England fondness for the pure [u] vowel after alveolar consonants, as in *tune* and *duke*, going as far back as Franklin, 1768. Sheridan's assimilated *juke* for *duke* seems not to have had much vogue south of the Canadian border, but Walker's [djuk] was accepted by the elocutionists, and, moreover, became the normal Southern form.

Bronstein and Sheldon[17] have shown an eighteenth-century preference for [u] in *room, hoof, cooper, stood*, and *shook*. The vowel [u] emerged in the nineteenth century, becoming normal in *stood* and *shook*, normal for the South in *cooper*, occasional in *room*, and frequent in *hoof*.

Though our inclusion of phonetics in courses designed for the improvement of voice and speech marks a return to the eighteenth-century concept of orthoepy as a part of elocution, we must not forget that the orthoepists confused accent and quantity with syllabication and vowel quality, and thought that the placement of an accent mark was sometimes enough to reveal the pronunciation. Sheridan, for instance, placed an accent mark over the consonant at the end of a syllable containing a short vowel, but over the vowel when that was long. He did not, however, follow his system consistently, and later writers abandoned it. Sheridan's rules for accenting polysyllables are excellent, comparable to those of Ellis.[18] He also anticipated modern concepts of variation of vowel quality under reduced stress; unlike Walker, he cannot be held responsible for the unrealistic rule that unstressed vowels are never obscured or elided. But even Walker recognized three degrees of force: unaccented on particles, accented on significant words, emphatic with inflection on important words.

In looking back to the eighteenth century we must remember the orthographic handicap under which it labored. If the dictionary entries could be reproduced in phonetic respelling, without the misleading notion of the "power of the letters," we should get a more definite idea of the pronunciation of that day. Grandgent, as a phonetician, has been better able than most to interpret the diacritics and to draw heavily on the orthoepists for the backgrounds of New England speech. Similarly, if we could translate eighteenth-century terminology into present-day phonetic equivalents, we would probably discover efforts to solve the same problems that challenge us today. Surely these orthoepists were phoneticians before their time.

II

The next period, from about 1840 to 1860, was marked by a phonetic or phonotypic revolution, short lived, but amazingly successful. There were better tools to work with, better symbols and systems, and phoneticians like A. J. Ellis. Another factor was organization. The eighteenth century had been largely unorganized. Except for a few scattered groups and the help of their publishers, the orthoepists worked as individual writers, teachers, or advocates on their own. In the mid-nineteenth century, however, appeared the first phonetic societies with their own journals.[19] From this time on the movements have had organizations and opportunities for publication in phonetic type.

The term *revolution* is no exaggeration, though the watchword of the movement itself was *reform*. Excitement was in the air. Many of the leaders were visionary in other fields. Isaac Pitman was a Swedenborgian, vegetarian, dudodecimalist. Others professed phrenology, pacifism, and communism of the Brook Farm variety. Ellis abjured these irrelevant enthusiasms, but at that stage of his phonetic career he also was revolutionary. Orthography was branded heterography. Hardly a diacritic remained. The cleavage was complete.

It began when Pitman and Ellis got together, at first by phonographic correspondence, and decided to develop shorthand into phonetic type. Pitman's *Journal* became *Phonetic* in 1848 and so remained, except for a short lapse, throughout the century. Both Pitman and Ellis devised other systems, but their joint effort of 1846-1847 was endorsed by the British Phonetic Society and became the basis for the "American alphabet."

In 1851 Benn Pitman, one of Isaac's several indefatigable reformist brothers, settled in Cincinnati with the Longley brothers, another family of phonetic enthusiasts. *The American Phonetic Dictionary of the English Language,* the first of its kind, was published in Cincinnati. With an introduction by Ellis, it was larger than Jones or Kenyon-Knott, and the vocabulary, except for the first entry, was all in phonetic type. This and similar books were used in the schools of Greater Boston.

The Phonetic Alphabet.

Long Vowels.

written	printed	sounded as
Ĕ ĭ	Ɛ ɛ	ee in eel
Ę ę	E ę	ea . earth
A a	ʁa	a . ale
A ą	Aą	a . air
A ą	Aʠ	a . arm
O o	ϴ ϴ	a . all
O o	Ꙩ ꙩ	o . ope
O o	ꟿ ꟿ	oo . food

Short Vowels.

written	printed	sounded as
I i	I i	i . in
E e	E e	e . ell
A a	A a	a . am
A a	ɑ ɑ	a . ask
O o	O o	o . odd
U u	U u	u . up
U u	ꞟ ꞟ	oo . foot

Diphthongs.

written	printed	sounded as
Ĭ į	Ŧ į	i . isle
O ǫ	Ơ ơ	oi . oil
Ȣ ȣ	Ꝩ ꝩ	ow . owl
U ų	ꞟų	u . mule

Coalescents.

written	printed	sounded as
Y y	Y y	y . yea
W w	W w	w . way

Aspirate.

written	printed	sounded as
H h	H h	h . hay

Explodents.

written	printed	sounded as
P p	P p	p in rope
B b	B b	b . robe
T t	T t	t . fate
D d	D d	d . fade
C c	ℭ ç	ch . etch
J j	J j	g . edge
K k	K k	k . lock
G g	G ǥ	g . log

Continuants.

written	printed	sounded as
F f	F f	f . safe
V v	V v	v . save
th	Ꙩ ꝃ	th . wreath
dh	ꝺ ꝺ	th . wreathe
S s	S s	s . buss
Z z	Z z	z . buzz
ʃ	Ʃ ʃ	c . vicious
ʒ	Ʒ ʒ	s . vision

Liquids.

written	printed	sounded as
L l	L l	l . fall
R r	R r	r . for

Nasal Liquids.

written	printed	sounded as
M m	M m	m . seem
N n	N n	n . seen
ŋ	ꞥ ꞥ	ng . sing

Fig. 8. "The American Phonetic Alphabet." From *The American Phonetic Dictionary of the English Language* (Cincinnati, 1855), opp. p. 1.

The output of journals was amazing. The *British Phonetic Journal* lasted longest, and was supplemented for a time by smaller periodicals. The *Anglo-Sacsun* [sic], founded in Boston in 1847, and *The Phonetic Propagandist,* published in New York from 1850 to 1852, favored Pitman against Ellis when there was a difference. Cincinnati periodicals, which formed a regular series from *The Phonetic Magazine* of 1848 to *The American Phonetic Journal* of 1855-1858, supported Ellis.

Ellis's textbooks, *Alphabet of Nature* (1845) and *Essentials of Phonetics* (1848), stamped the young man as a phonetic genius who kept abreast of all the philological discoveries from Rask and Grimm to Willis and Wheatstone. With minor changes in terminology they could be used as textbooks today. Through these and later publications Ellis exerted great influence on Henry Sweet and thus on the International Phonetic Association. Hans Raudnitzky in *Die Bell-Sweetsche Schule* accords as much space to Ellis as to the men mentioned in the title. Among Americans interested in Ellis were J. C. Zachos and Richard A. Soule.[20]

Standing somewhat apart in phonetic history was Alexander Melville Bell's *Visible Speech,* projected in 1864, and supported by the British Phonetic Society, of which Bell was a member. His American following, both before and after he crossed the Atlantic, was not limited to teachers of the deaf nor to experimentalists. Rahe[21] found that Purdue in 1889 and the University of Indiana in 1890 taught Bell's system. Bell's system was essentially analphabetic; but most of the phoneticians retained Sweet's[22] romic (Latin) symbols and Bell's vowels as high, mid, low, and so forth.

The reformers published school books, probably in greater supply than demand, though Lamport cites books by Elias Longley[23] of Cincinnati, Andrew Comstock, and Edwin Leigh, which were presumably used. Comstock paid his respects to the Pitman-Ellis alphabet by producing an American version. This colorful Philadelphia elocutionist published such pioneer works as his *Phonology* of 1846 and his *Phonetic Magazine,* which ran from 1846 to 1848. The latter, though it had precursors,[24] was probably the first American journal to bear the phonetic title. Comstock was also probably the first American or English elocutionist to invent a phonetic alphabet. He followed Rush in his analysis, and his symbols were international, a daring venture for that time.

Edwin Leigh, one of the Boston phonotypic reformers, published a *Pronouncing Orthography* in 1864, and had a signal success, especially in St. Louis. He also edited McGuffey and Watson[25] in the new type and made a favorable impression on the French phonetician Paul Passy.[26] In one sense Leigh compromised with the past by indicating the sounds while preserving the orthography. In another sense he looked forward to the next period, which compromised on spelling while pursuing phonetic scholarship.

Much of the propaganda of the phonotypic period applies ambiguously to both phonography and phonetics. James Stone of Boston and Benn Pitman of Cincinnati were stenographers who advocated phonetics. A possible illustration of their success may be found in the fact that the Smithsonian report of 1856 named 35 colleges and schools, from Antioch to Yale, that taught phonography.[27]

The phonotypic movement gave the English-speaking world its first phonetic dictionaries, textbooks, readers, and journals, all explicitly so entitled. *Phonetics* and *phonetic* were slogans, applied to depots, institutions, festivals, councils, societies, soirees, even Sunday schools. Our use of the terms today comes down to us chiefly from this movement of a hundred years ago.

III

In 1877 the American Philological Association approved a new phonetic alphabet, at first designated by the letters APA, and at various later times by ADS, RSA, and NEA. The alphabet achieved its greatest popular success in 1893-1894, when Isaac Funk used it in the *Standard Dictionary*. During the period from 1904 to 1911 it was endorsed by the American Philological Association, the Modern Language Association, and the American Dialect Society; in 1911 it was adopted by the National Educational Association for use in the schools. Funk and Wagnalls used it in a *Standard First Reader*. This, however, was the beginning of the end. In the same year Guy Montrose Whipple hurriedly published *Relative Efficiency of Phonetic Alphabets*, reporting experiments that seemed to show the Webster key more effective educationally and psychologically than the NEA key; Whipple found the Funk and Wagnalls reader "pedagogically unfit." Though he was answered by Raymond Weeks, James W. Bright, and C. H. Grandgent, in *The N.E.A. Phonetic Alphabet* in 1912, the outcome may be guessed from the difficulty today of finding schoolbooks which use the NEA system.

Roughly contemporary with the *Standard Dictionary* was Whitney's *Century Dictionary* of 1889, which relied on diacritics, with a wealth of historical phonetics in the etymologies. In many ways Whitney was the father of American English phonetics. In his *Oriental and Linguistic Studies* of 1874 he gave an early frequency count for English sounds. He established a vowel triangle and classified the consonants from open to close. His observations in central New England show a mixture of eastern and western forms: he heard the New England "short *o*" in *coat* but had no patience with the "intermediate *a*" in *ask*.

Charles H. Grandgent, who published articles and books for over thirty years, seemed to be less aware of the east-west division in New England and more willing to hear an actual "intermediate *a*", although he deplored its elocutionary variety. He also recognized the pure [u] in *tune* as the natural Yankee pronunciation, the existence of different vowels in *hurt* and *hurry*, and the intrusive *r*. An expert whose work challenges modern phonetic analysis, albeit in non-technical terms, he brought a humane style and mellow humor to his work. He may be called the father of New England or Yankee phonetics.

The father of General American phonetics, on the other hand, was Oliver Farrar Emerson, whose *Ithaca Dialect* appeared in 1891. The speech of this central New York community was derived from New England, chiefly from Connecticut, in eighteenth- and even seventeenth-century form, and included "Western" pronunciations of such words as *ask, hot, true,* and *far*. Thus the theory that General American originated in older Standard English got a vigorous start. In his *History of the English Language* in 1905 Emerson presented a pioneer classification of American speech as Eastern, Southern, and Western, a classification which some present-day phoneticians still accept despite large additions to our stock of regional phonetic data. Emerson's methods, based on sound Middle English scholarship, were rigorous; his alphabet was essentially that of the American Philological Association.

The periodicals contained much phonetic material. The *Transactions of the American Philological Association* had such writers as S. S. Haldeman and George Hempl. The *Publications of the Modern Language Association* had A. M. Bell, Sylvester Primer, E. S. Sheldon, and others, and a phonetics section from 1887 to 1900. The Spelling Reform Association, which preferred amended to phonotypic spelling, published *Spelling* from 1887-1894 and issued various Bulletins.

The American Dialect Society [28] began publishing *Dialect Notes* in 1889; the present *Publication of the American Dialect Society* is a continuation of the same official organ. Emerson's *Ithaca Dialect* was first published in *Dialect Notes;* other early contributors were E. H. Babbitt on New York City, B. S. Monroe on upstate New York. E. S. Sheldon, and C. H. Grandgent. Somewhat later came W. A. Read on Southern, J. S. Kenyon on the Western Reserve, and Miles Hanley. Other American and German journals [29] were hospitable to phonetic articles.

The APA-NEA alphabet was a transition between the earlier phonotypy and the later phonetic approach of the International Phonetic Association. The symbols, which were intentionally *national*, survived long after the foundation of the IPA in 1889. George Philip Krapp's

Modern English (1909) and Godfrey Dewey's *Relative Frequency of English Speech Sounds* (1923, 2nd ed. 1950) are authoritative twentieth-century works using nineteenth-century symbolization. Yet the philological interest underlying the movement laid the foundation for present-day American phonetics and the study of American regional speech.

IV

The influence of the International Phonetic Association on American phonetics and pronunciation has been delayed. Only in the past two or three decades has it reached those Americans who did not aspire to speak with a British accent. *Le Maître Phonétique,* the official organ, is not widely circulated in this country. The letters IPA, which may mean either the Association or the Alphabet, are known chiefly in the latter sense; and the alphabet itself has been much modified for the recording of American speech. Yet both the early and later phases of the Association are important for Americans.

In 1886 Paul Passy, usually considered the authentic founder of the IPA, began publishing *Dhi Fonétic Titcer* [30] in a Pitman alphabet. In 1889 the IPA was formed, with new symbols based chiefly on Sweet's Broad Romic, which in turn drew heavily on Alexander Melville Bell, then a resident of Washington, D. C. Other pioneer members were philologists like Grandgent. Among American speech teachers, Henrietta Prentiss was a member by 1895, and Sarah T. Barrows by 1911.

Another American member was Robert Morris Pierce, who had joined the IPA by 1895. This independent scholar, spelling reformer, and language publisher, who advertised his "Alphagam" in the *Quarterly Journal of Speech* as late as 1927, should probably be credited with the first IPA dictionaries in English: the *International* of 1904, usually associated with Passy as French editor and George Hempl as American editor; the *Dictionary of Hard Words* of 1910; and the *Dictionary of Aviation* of 1911.

Some later dictionaries using IPA symbols are Michaelis-Jones (1913, British), Daniel Jones (1917 and many later editions, British), Palmer-Martin-Blandford (1926, British with American "variants"), James F. Bender (1943, NBC radio), Harold Wentworth (1944, American dialects), Kenyon-Knott (1944, American regional standards), Morris Needleman (1949, respellings, diacritics, and phonetics). These all use some form of IPA symbols, though the American works used extra symbols which the IPA did not declare official until after a good deal of prodding by Kenyon, W. C. Greet, and others. Most speech teachers prefer the system of symbolization used in Kenyon-Knott; the book, moreover, is the first dictionary to show, clearly and unmistakably, the pronunciation of the majority of Americans, call it General or, as the authors suggest, Northern.

Works other than dictionaries fall into three main groups. Those which use the form of the alphabet developed by Kenyon generally stress the General, Northern, or Central Western type of American Speech. Those which use the complex alphabet developed by William Tilly (of whom more later) generally stress Eastern New England or Southern British, and often try to fit the speech of New York City into one of these patterns. The third group varies.

In 1924 Kenyon published *American Pronunciation;* the tenth edition came out in 1950. After many years of memorializing the IPA to recognize the American *r*-colored vowels in *further,* Kenyon finally succeeded. In the meantime many Americans had adopted his special symbols for the obvious need they filled.[31] Some of the publications which closely follow the Kenyon alphabet are listed below under their short titles:

> Sarah T. Barrows, *Introduction,* 1928, elementary
> Samuel Moore, *Phonology,* 1929, historical
> Gray-Wise, *Bases,* 1934 special attention to Southern
> Hedde-Brigance, *Speech,* 1935, high school text
> Oma Stanley, *East Texas,* 1937, regional study
> Bender-Fields, *Transcriptions,* 1939, voice and diction
> Jane D. Zimmerman, *Transcriptions from American Speech,* 1939, radio
> Virgil Anderson, *Speaking Voice,* 1942, voice and diction
> Albert H. Marckwardt, *English Language,* 1942, historical
> Joseph S. Hall, *Great Smoky,* 1942, regional study
> Charles K. Thomas, *Introduction,* 1947, new regional divisions
> Allan F. Hubbell, *New York City,* 1949, regional, phonemic.

William Tilly was born in Australia, taught in Germany, had influence on Daniel Jones[32] in London, and began teaching at Columbia University in 1918. Ironically, he found Jones's symbols too broad, and added cumbrous diacritics which, in the hands of some of his students became symbols of orthodoxy rather than tools of fine distinction. He himself wrote little, but stimulated his students to publish. Among many such, the following may be noted: DeWitt 1924, Daggett 1928, McLean 1928, Davis 1933, Pray 1934, Daniels 1935, Raubicheck 1935, Mulgrave 1936, Darrow 1937, Lamers-Smith 1937, Barber 1939, Crawford 1941, Manser 1941.[33]

For a time the Tilly influence spread across America; today it is largely confined to the New York City school system. Critics have generally found the alphabet ill-favored and the regional attitude biased. While admitting the conscientious zeal of the Tilly followers, and the severity of the foreign-language problem in the New York City schools, critics outside the group have generally not been able to approve either methods or results.

, Some other American and British writers have used the IPA symbols, or symbols of their own, without committing themselves specifically to either the Kenyon or Tilly symbols. Daniel Jones [34] began in 1909 on intonation curves and elementary phonetics, but his many later books are better known. The Klinghardt dot system [35] for recording intonation found favor with the Tilly group. Palmer-Blandford and Armstrong-Ward [36] have also written on intonation, with accompanying recordings. Special attention should be called to the use of intonation markings in C. C. Fries's *An Intensive Course in English for Latin-American Students*, 1943-1944, and to Kenneth L. Pike's *The Intonation of American English*, 1945.

Among American phoneticians, George Philip Krapp deserves special notice. His *Pronunciation* of 1919 and his *English Language in America* of 1925 were the first of their kind. Like Kenyon, he had a special symbol for the *r*-colored vowels, and was probably the first to use the term "General American." [37] As a professor at Columbia he had a notable influence. Some others not specially influenced by either Tilly or Kenyon are listed below:

Sarah T. Barrows, *English Sounds for Foreign Tongues*, 1918
Anders Orbeck, *New England*, 1927, interpretation of written records
Edwin F. Shewmake, *Virginia*, 1927, regional study
Avery-Dorsey-Sickles, *Speech Training*, fundamentals
Leonard Bloomfield, *Language*, 1933, linguistic principles, special symbols
Kantner-West, *Phonetics*, 1933, 1941, kinesiological approach, special symbols
Snyder-Wilke, *Effective Speech*, 1938, transcriptions, recordings
Hans Kurath, *Linguistic Atlas of New England*, dialect maps
Harold Whitehall, *Middle English u*, historical development
R. H. Stetson, *Motor Phonetics*, 1945, syllables
R.-M. S. Heffner, *General Phonetics*, 1949, comparative
L. D. Turner, *Gullah*, 1949, African sounds in Negro speech.

The periodicals have multiplied. *Le Maître Phonétique*, as already reported, began in 1889; the *Quarterly Journal of Speech*, in 1915; *American Speech*, 1925; *Language*, 1925; *Journal of Expression*, 1928; *Speech Monographs*, 1934; *Speech*, 1935; *Journal of Speech and Hearing Disorders*, 1936; *Studies in Linguistics*, 1942; *Word*, 1945.

For some time *Dialect Notes* kept the old NEA alphabet, as shown by Kenyon's article on the Western Reserve in 1917 and official notation in 1918. By 1937 Simpson's study of Rhode Island used IPA symbols, and in 1944, when the *Publication of the American Dialect Society* replaced the older journal, the IPA-Kenyon system became official.

These periodicals review the progress of the Linguistic Atlas in detail from 1930 to 1939; thereafter the unpublished atlas material from outside New England has been reported on in occasional articles. The American Dialect Society plans a dictionary to supplement the special reports already issued in its publications, but no date has been set for the venture.

The IPA journal, *Le Maître Phonétique,* contains short articles, official business, and transcriptions, all in phonetic type. Essays on phonemics and the *r*-colored vowels helped to pave the way for American phonemics and for the official acceptance of Kenyon's symbols for the *r*-colored vowels. Regular American contributors have been Bloch, Bloomfield, deCamp, Joos, Kenyon, Trager, Voelker, and Wise, representing several schools of thought; the Tilly school, despite its devotion to the magazine, has contributed little.

The *Proceedings* of the International Congresses of Phonetic Sciences held in 1933, 1935, and 1938 contain materials on American speech teaching. The London congress of 1935 included contributions by the Americans Hanley, Kenyon, Kurath, Lowman, Russell, Wise, and Zimmerman.[38] The contents of these volumes include papers on phonemics, experimental phonetics, phonograph recording, and so forth.

The *Quarterly Journal* of the Speech Association of America (titles of both Journal and Association have been subject to change) began its phonetic career in 1921 with a resounding defense of British pronunciation by Windsor P. Daggett. In 1927 C. K. Thomas pointed out the limitations of this point of view and urged the collection of more factual material about American speech. A wide variety of related topics also appeared in the *Journal*: elementary speech, discussed by Poole and others; kinesiological phonetics by Kantner and West; objective testing by Jean B. Jones; affective phonetics, by Jon Eisenson and others; unstressed syllables by L. S. Hultzen; euphony by E. L. Thorndike, to give a general sampling. The *Journal* tried phonetic transcriptions in 1948-1949, shortly after *American Speech* had abandoned this activity. The major journal of the Speech profession has done well by phonetics, as the Knower index will show.

American Speech, however, has been the leading American phonetic periodical of the past quarter century. From 1933 to 1945 Jane D. Zimmerman edited a transcription section, mainly in Kenyon-IPA symbols, which are still printed on the inside back cover. Edited at first by

Louise Pound and Kemp Malone, the magazine acquired W. C. Greet as editor in 1933; Greet threw his influence behind Kenyon in the latter's efforts to get the IPA to recognize symbols for the *r*-colored vowels.

From the first the magazine attracted phonetic contributors. Marguerite DeWitt, the only Tilly follower, was promptly answered by Kenyon. Vance Randolph reported on Ozark pronunciation, Ayres and Greet on the Columbia University recordings, Allen Walker Read on local usage as the standard for place names. Claude M. Wise gave the first complete phonetic account of the Southern drawl. In 1934 S. N. Trevino began a phonetics bibliography.

Later came articles by Dobbie, Bloch, Heffner, Steadman, Shewmake, Wilson, Zipf, McDavid, Bronstein, and Sheldon, and others on matters geographical, articulatory, lexicographical. Steadman published a useful list of Tongue Twisters,[39] words that are really hard to say, without

Fig. 9. American Pronunciation. The pronunciation [ʌ] predominates east and south of the broken line; [ɜ], north and west. Reprinted by permission from C. K. Thomas, *American Speech* (April, 1946), p. 114.

any Peter Piper context. Thomas traced tentative cross-country isoglosses for *hurry* and *on*.[40] McDavid reported on the South Carolina Piedmont and the discovery that some Southerners, both lowland and highland, but not both low class and high class, reported the use of a Pennsylvania-background *r*. A new classification of regions, or at least a new need, began to appear.

In *Language,* organ of the Linguistic Society, articles on phonemics appeared from the start, with Sapir and Bloomfield breaking the ground. A modified IPA alphabet was adopted in 1927, but variations on it have always been freely used. Accounts of specific languages have been frequent in the magazine. Of special interest to speech teachers are such articles as those of Zipf on dynamic philology, Rositzke and Heffner on vowel length, Whitehall on Modern English [ɪ], Velter on Infant Language, Sheldon on dictionaries, and Hockett on linguistic continuity. Hockett, for example, argues that children associating with playmates away from conservative family influence, may be carriers of phonetic change. Here, as elsewhere, in a magazine to which speech teachers have contributed little, is rigorous and original thinking.

The Journal of Expression,[41] organ of the Curry School, has carried articles by Barrows, DeWitt, Prentiss, and other speech teachers. Except for Barrows, the point of view is mainly pro-British. The magazine used both IPA symbols and Webster diacritics.

Speech Monographs, the research journal of the Speech Association of America, has reported experimental phonetics freely, and linguistic phonetics occasionally. In 1942 Wilke and Snyder reported on speech preferences: the country as a whole favored types of speech which did not suggest the South, the East, or New York City too strongly. In 1948 Wise pointed out that Benjamin Franklin was a genuine phonetician rather than a random spelling reformer. In the same year Helene Blattner describes a pronunciation test with a list of a hundred words. In 1949 Arthur Bronstein described American nineteenth-century vowels and the emergence of [ɑ] in the early years of the century.

In *Speech,* an unofficial organ of elementary teachers, there is realistic consideration of classroom problems, and a balance between pro-British and pro-American views. Vida R. Sutton and the editor, Ellen Henderson, are the most frequent contributors.

The Journal of Speech and Hearing Disorders is the official organ of the American Speech and Hearing Association, a specialized offshoot of the Speech Association of America. Devoted more to speech science than to linguistic phonetics, it has nevertheless published such articles as G. Oscar Russell's plea for modified IPA symbols for scientific accuracy, Barker's articles on dynamic phonetics, Platt on Bell's *Visible Speech,* and Irwin and Chen on child speech.

Studies in Linguistics, an unofficial supplement to *Language,* features phonemics, linguistic geography, and bibliography. Writers and points of view resemble those of *Language,* but Speech has been represented by C. M. Wise. In June, 1945, Wise published a tentative report outlining graduate-student projects, plus an emerging pattern of such sounds as [ɜɪ] in *burn* and [ɔ] in *yard* in the Gulf coastal area.

Word is the organ of the Linguistic Circle of New York. Margaret Schlauch's 1946 article frees phonemics from behavioristic restrictions. Leopold writes on infant speech, especially bilingual. Bolinger's article on the phonestheme includes informal experimentation on affective and connotative aspects of sound groups. A rigorous statistical approach characterizes Reed and Hayden; the latter carries the analysis of relative frequency of English phonemes farther than Whitney, Dewey, or Voelker.

Phonetic printing remains a problem. The wide range of phonetic types offered by the Mergenthaler Linotype Company makes printing possible, but expensive. Dent and Dutton have served Jones and the Tilly group. Heffer in England, Pitman in New York, the Expression Company in the Boston Area, and Wahr in Ann Arbor have all taken risks in this hardy venture. The Varityper,[42] a development of the old Hammond typewriter, has inherited the Hammond phonetic font, which needs bringing up to date.

Within the past generation many recordings have been made, with a considerable range in acoustic and scholarly fidelity. Ayres and Greet, Armstrong and Ward, Barrows and Kraft, Daggett, Gardner and Skinner, Lloyd James, Daniel Jones, Kenyon, Raubicheck and Seals have all ventured into the field. Daggett is valuable historically, Barrows and Kraft for elementary instruction, Jones for the Cardinal Vowels. The Ayres-Greet series have made the shirker, Grip the Rat, famous for his *aunt, barn, loft, mind,* and *grass.*

V

The Linguistic Atlas of the United States and Canada began field work under Hans Kurath's direction in 1931. Six volumes of maps and a *Handbook*[43] for New England have been available since 1939. Most of the field work for the Middle and South Atlantic states has been completed, a considerable amount of field work has been done in the upper Midwest, and scattered work has been started as far west as the Rockies. Publication of the material from outside of New England has been delayed except for Kurath's *Word Geography of the Eastern United States* of 1949. Atlas studies show that New England divides into Eastern and Western areas. Kurath's *Word Geography* outlines Northern, Midland, and Southern main divisions, with numerous sub-regions. Whether these divisions apply to pronunciation as well as word usage is a question that must wait for the publication of additional Atlas material or material from other sources. Special studies of Atlas materials by Penzl for New England, McDavid for South Carolina, and Marckwardt for the Great Lakes area suggest an emerging pattern. The debt of the Atlas to the great European linguistic atlases is of course obvious and acknowledged.[44]

American phonemics is so new that it is difficult to evaluate. Terminology and symbolization are still in flux. The use of slanting lines for phonemes, and the restriction of square brackets to allophones is undoubtedly a useful distinction. But the practice of some phonemicists of using [y] for English [j] can lead only to ambiguity when it becomes necessary to refer to languages which have [y] vowels. Similarly, the use of [h] as a mark of vowel length leads to ambiguity in languages which have postvocalic [h]. Despite these vagaries, which are probably unavoidable in the establishment of a central tradition, the phonemicists should serve as a stimulus to the phoneticians, who often give too much preference to elementary teachable symbols. In alliance with the experimental phoneticians, moreover, the phonemicists are pioneering paths in what might be called the new visible speech, in their use of the new machines which give direct readings for sound analysis in place of the laborious system of Fourier analysis. The bearing of phonemics on phonetics is inescapable; unless we keep the distinctive sounds of any form of English in mind, we waste our time and our understanding in symbolizing a mass of trivia, as the Tilly school so often has done. As suggested by Hultzen,[45] phoneticians need to study and restudy the phonemic philosophy found in Bloch, Bloomfield, Hockett, Pike, Sapir, Trager, Twaddell, and the rest of the American structural linguists.[46]

VI

Though the role of the speech teacher in phonetics and pronunciation has been largely assimilative, there have nevertheless been original contributions. Barrows and Kraft have excelled in practical recording, Hultzen in symbol analysis, Snyder and Wilke in speech preferences, Zimmerman in radio pronunciation. Wise and Thomas have made extensive regional surveys, the former especially in Louisiana, the latter especially in New York.

A constructive development is the teaching of phonetics in speech departments. In 1927 Barrows found only a handful of such courses; today we may estimate well over two hundred. A similar trend appears in the textbooks of public speaking and fundamentals of speech, as distinct from texts on voice and speech correction. The IPA alphabet appears in Baird and Knower, Bender, Brigance and Immel, Crocker, Eisenson, Hibbitt, McCall, Murray, Oliver and Cortright, Painter, Thonssen and Gilkinson, Winans, Woolbert and Smith, and others. In dramatics, Albright and Dolman have followed the trend. Gray and

Wise have assimilated phonetic material all through their *Bases of Speech*.

VII

In summary, modern speech education is in debt to English eighteenth-century orthographical or diacritical phonetics; any general dictionary or elementary school language text will illustrate this indebtedness. The orthoepists conscientiously described the pronunciation of their time; Walker especially influenced American phonetic thinking.

Before 1850 Pitman and Ellis developed phonotypic *phonetics*, with a name that stuck. Comstock put Rush into symbols, journals appeared, and the reform even reached a few schools. The major effect, however, was to come later in the formation of the IPA.

In the later nineteenth century American philological phonetics began, and the ground was laid for later understanding of American regional speech. Learned societies and the journals were matched by the use of a phonetic alphabet in a famous dictionary. The schools almost went phonetic.

In the twentieth century the IPA developed an indirect but powerful influence. Many periodicals, including Speech journals, published phonetic materials. Rivalries developed over symbolization and, more basically, over acceptable standards of pronunciation, but seem now well on the way toward resolution with a clearer realization of phonemic principles and an emerging pattern of American regional speech.

In some ways, mainly in regional research, Speech has added to our understanding of the whole field. In other ways its leaders have gathered and synthesized facts and ideas from orthoepy, phonotypy, philology, the IPA, geography, and phonemics.

Notes

1. Esther K. Sheldon, "Pronouncing Systems in 18th Century Dictionaries," *Language,* XXII (January-March, 1946), 27. See also Sheldon's "Walker's Influence on the Pronunciation of English," *PMLA,* LXII (March, 1947), 130-146.

2. Henry B. Wheatley, "Notes on Some English Heterographers," and "Chronological Notices of the Dictionaries of the English Language," *Transactions* of the Philological Society, 1865; Alexander J. Ellis, *On Early English Pronunciation* (London, 1869), Pt. I, Ch. II; Harold B. Lamport, *A History of the Teaching of Beginning Reading* (Chicago, 1937); George P. Krapp, *The English Language in America* (New York, 1925), II, 273-284; Goold Brown, *Grammar of English Grammars* (New York, 1855), pp. xi-xx; Karl Brown and D. C. Haskell, *The Shorthand Collection in the New York Public Library* (New York, 1935); George H. McKnight, *Modern English in the Making* (New York, 1928); and Lester Thonssen, et al., *Bibliography of Speech Education* (New York, 1939), *Supplement* (1950).

3. *American College Dictionary* (New York, 1947); *The New American Webster Dictionary* (New York, 1951).

4. Thomas Sheridan, *Lectures on Elocution* (London, 1781), *The Art of Reading* (Dublin, 1775); John Walker, *Elements of Elocution* (London, 1781), *Rhetorical Grammar*, 2d ed. (London, 1787); Robert Nares, *Elements of Orthoepy* (London, 1784).

5. McKnight and Brown, *op. cit.*

6. James Elphinston, *Propriety Ascertained in Her Picture* (London, 1787).

7. Benjamin Franklin, "Scheme for a New Alphabet," *Works* (Boston, 1840), pp. 295-300. Claude M. Wise, "Benjamin Franklin as a Phonetician," *SM*, XV (1948), 99-120.

8. John B. Newman, "The Role of Joshua Steele in the Development of Speech Education in America," *SM*, XX (1953), 65-73.

9. Andrew Comstock, *Phonetic Magazine* (1846-1848).

10. James Rush, *Philosophy of the Human Voice* (Philadelphia, 1827); Lester L. Hale, unpublished Ph.D. dissertation, Louisiana State, 1942; Dan Scully, unpublished M.A. thesis, Louisiana State, 1951.

11. *Proceedings* of the National Association of Elocutionists (1892-1905), of the Speech Arts Association (1906-1916).

12. R. L. and Maria E. Edgeworth, *Practical Education*, 2d ed. (London, 1801).

13. Goold Brown, *op. cit.*, 162.

14. John Marchant, *New Complete English Dictionary* (London); J. Barclay, *Complete and Universal English Dictionary* (London).

15. F. Barlow, *Complete English Dictionary* (London).

16. Charles H. Grandgent, "Fashion and the Broad A," "The Dog's Letter," "New England Pronunciation," *Old and New* (Cambridge, Mass., 1920).

17. Arthur Bronstein and Esther K. Sheldon, "Derivatives of Middle English O. ...," *American Speech*, XXVI (May, 1951), 81-89.

18. A. J. Ellis, "Accent Laws," *Phonetic Journal* (Pitman's, 1848), 165-166.

19. British Phonetic Society, 1843; American Phonetic Society (Cincinnati), 1848. Elias Longley, *Manual of Phonography* (Cincinnati, 1853), v-vi and end. Pitman's *Journal* (1842—); *Phonographic*, 1842; *Phonotypic*, 1843-1847, 1849; *Phonetic*, 1848-1849, Feb., 1850—. Cincinnati: *Phonetic Magazine*, 1848-1849; *Phonetic Advocate*, 1848-1852; *Type of the Times*, interim; *American Phonetic Journal*, 1855-1859.

20. J. C. Zachos, *Analytic Elocution* (New York, 1861); Richard Soule, Jr. and Wm. A. Wheeler, *Manual of English Pronunciation* (Boston, 1861); S. S. Hamill, *Science of Elocution* (New York, 1879); Robert Kidd, *New Elocution and Vocal Culture* (Cincinnati, 1883).

21. Herbert E. Rahe, "Speech Education in Ten Indiana Colleges," unpublished Ph.D. dissertation, Wisconsin, 1939; Harry S. Houghton, *Elements of Public Speaking* (Boston, 1916); Glenn N. Merry, *Principles of Speech* (Iowa City, 1921).

22. Henry Sweet, *History of English Sounds* (Oxford, 1874); *Handbook of Phonetics* (Oxford, 1877).

23. Elias Longley, *Furst Fonetic Redur* (Boston, 1850); Andrew Comstock, *Phonetic Reader* (Philadelphia, 1847).

24. Andrew Comstock, *Phonology*, 2d. ed. (Philadelphia, 1855), pp. 9-12. Precursors: Franklin, 1768; Thornton, 1793; Ewing, 1798; Pelham, 1808; Embree, 1813; Kneeland, 1825, and others. Journals: M. H. Barton, *Something New* (Boston and Harvard, 1831); Wm. Beardsley, *Literary Reformer* (St. Louis, 1841).

25. *Leigh's McGuffey's New Eclectic Primer* (Cincinnati, 1864); *Leigh's Watson's National School Primer* (New York, 1873).

26. Paul Passy, *L'Instruction Primaire aux Etats-Unis* (Paris, 1885), p. 57; *Dhi Fonètic Titcer* (Paris, 1886), p. 1.

27. Townsend Sharpless and Robert Patterson, phonetic advocates, *Smithsonian Report* (Washington, 1857), pp. 277-280.

28. Louise Pound, "The American Dialect Society: A Historical Sketch," *Publications American Dialect Society* (April, 1952), pp. 3-28.

29. *Englische Studien* (1877—), *Modern Language Notes* (1886—), *Phonetische*

Studien (1888–), *Volta Review* (1889–), *Jour. of English and Germanic Philology* (1897–), *Modern Philology* (1903–), *English Journal* (1912–).

30. Recently reprinted by IPA; A. C. Gimson, Sec., University College, London W. C. 1.

31. Charles K. Thomas, "Symposium on Phonetics," *QJS*, XXXI (October, 1945). For a different view see Letitia Raubicheck, "A Footnote on Phonetics," *QJS*, XXXII (February, 1946).

32. Daniel Jones, "William Tilly," *Le Maître Phonétique* (October, December, 1935), p. 53.

33. M. de Witt, *Euphon English;* W. P. Daggett (handbook with recordings); Margaret P. McClean, *Good American Speech;* Estelle Davis and E. W. Mammen, *Spoken Word;* Sophie Pray et al, *Graded Objectives;* Fannie E. Daniels, *Good Speech Primer;* Letitia Raubicheck, *Teaching Speech;* Dorothy I. Mulgrave, *Speech for the Classroom Teacher;* Anne Darrow, *Folk Speech;* W. Lamers and M. E. Smith, *Making of a Speaker;* Sara M. Barber, *Speech Education;* Margaret E. A. Crawford, *Pathways to Tone;* Ruth B. Manser, *Conversations in Phonetic Transcription.*

34. Daniel Jones, *Phonetic Transcriptions* (Oxford, 1907); *Intonation Curves* (Leipzig, 1909); *Pronunciation of English* (London, 1909); *Outline of English Phonetics* (Leipzig, 1918); *The Phoneme* (London, 1950).

35. H. Klinghardt, *Übungen im Englischen Tonfall,* 2d. ed. (Leipzig, 1927).

36. Harold E. Palmer, *English Intonation* (Cambridge, Eng., 1924), with F. G. Blandford, *Everyday Sentences in Spoken English* (Cambridge, 1922); Lilias E. Armstrong and Ida C. Ward, *Handbook of English Intonation,* 2d. ed. (Cambridge, 1931).

37. *English Language in America,* I, 40; II, p. 230.

38. Miles Hanley—Linguistic Atlas recording; J. S. Kenyon—Ayres-Greet recordings; Hans Kurath—Linguistic Atlas; Guy Lowman-[au] in Virginia; G. Oscar Russell—Vowel Triangle; C. M. Wise—Comparative Pronunciations; Jane D. Zimmerman—Radio Pronunciations.

39. *Amer. Sp.,* XI (October, 1936), 203-204; *English Journal,* XXV (September, 1836), 573-588.

40. Thomas—April, 1946; McDavid—October, December, 1948.

41. *Journal of Expression* (June, 1927-1932?).

42. Vari-Typer, *Type Faces* (Chicago, 1943-1946).

43. Hans Kurath, *Handbook of the Linguistic Geography of New England* (New York, 1939).

44. Sever Pop, *La Dialectologie* (Louvain, 1950).

45. Lee S. Hultzen, "Phonetics, Phonemics, and the Teacher of Speech," *QJS* (April, 1947).

46. Bernard Bloch, "Postulates," *Language,* XXIV (January, 1948), 3-46; with George L. Trager, *Outline of Linguistic Analysis* (1942); Leonard L. Bloomfield, "Postulates," *Language,* II (1926), 153-164, and *Language* [book], (New York, 1933); Zellig S. Harris, *Methods in Structural Linguistics* (Chicago, 1951); Charles F. Hockett, "A System of Descriptive Phonology," *Language,* XVIII (January-March, 1942); Kenneth L. Pike, *Phonemics* (Ann Arbor, 1947); Edward Sapir, *Selected Writings* (Berkeley, 1949); George L. Trager and Henry L. Smith, *Outline of English Structure* (Norman, Oklahoma, 1951); W. F. Twaddell (Baltimore, 1935). For others see the periodicals: *American Speech, Language, Studies in Linguistics, Word.*

16 The Rise of Experimental Phonetics

JAMES F. CURTIS

....

The impress of science and the methodology of science on the patterns of our study and thinking has been felt in nearly every academic discipline. The importance of its influence in the study of speech, both on what we study and how we study and think, has been widely recognized. A recent article by Simon, for example, stresses the pervasive role of scientific method in the study of speech.[1] Many research studies employ experimental methods and quantitative procedures even in the fields of artistic performance.[2]

In shaping this trend toward the scientific study of speech, experimental phonetics has played a significant part. If we take the awarding of the Ph.D. degree in speech as evidence of academic majority, we see that experimental phonetics was exerting a substantial influence on graduate study and research when speech first came of age as an academic discipline. Two of the first four dissertations accepted for Ph.D. degrees in speech were studies in experimental phonetics.[3] From this beginning, growth has been steady, until today no national convention program of either the Speech Association of America or the American Speech and Hearing Association would be complete without at least one sectional program devoted to the reporting of research in experimental phonetics.

Nor has the influence of experimental phonetics been confined to the rarified atmosphere of graduate study. The undergraduate speech curriculum has also felt its force. In his 1950 analysis of the courses which make up the undergraduate major in general speech in American colleges and universities, Donald E. Hargis reports that fifty-three of two hundred institutions studied included a course in *voice science* as a part of the offering for this major.[4] It is almost certain that for specialized majors in speech correction and hearing rehabilitation the statistics would have been even more impressive. In fact, experimental phonetics is expressly listed in the Clinical Certification Requirements of the

American Speech and Hearing Association [5] as one of the areas of study from which the basic requirements must be met for any level or type of clinical certification. Furthermore, data derived from laboratory studies have application for general speech courses (e.g. fundamentals of speech, and voice and diction), and for the specialized courses in speech correction and hearing rehabilitation.

I

This chapter will try to trace the lines of development which have given rise to this branch of experimental science. At the outset, however, we confront the question: What is the scope of experimental phonetics?

The field is hard to define and circumscribe. This is, in part, because the term has had different meanings for different people, and, in part, because many of the important contributors to the field have been, and still are, persons who have not regarded themselves primarily as experimental phoneticians. Some of the most important contributions have come from physicists, psychologists, physiologists, and communications engineers, as well as from researchers in speech and linguistics. We are concerned with a borderline area, one which cannot be confined within the boundaries of any one of the older divisions of science. Some persons who have applied experimental techniques to the study of phonetics, such as Stetson in this country, have confined their investigations almost wholly to the physiological processes of speech production. But many others have found it impossible to restrict their interests to the physiology of speech. To them the data of speech physiology take on real meaning only as they relate to the physical characteristics of the sounds produced. Adequate understanding of such acoustical phenomena, in turn, demands that they be interpreted as language symbols which are recognized and assigned meaning by listeners. The processes of perception must likewise, therefore, be viewed as falling within the scope of experimental phonetics.

Still another difficulty in definition is that the experimenter finds it impossible to restrict his interest to those aspects of speech signals which are usually designated by the term *phonetic*. One cannot study speech sounds, either from the standpoint of their production or their acoustical properties, without realizing that a fundamental aspect of many speech sounds is vocal fold vibration. Hence, the student of experimental phonetics shortly finds himself concerned with a wide range of problems involving the human vocal apparatus as a sound generator. He thus brings within his scope of study many phenomena such as vocal pitch, voice quality, and so forth, which are not *phonetic* or *phonemic* in character, at least in English, but which are nevertheless important, both because they are significant aspects of speech behavior and because they constitute important variations in language signals which have meaning for listeners. In short, the experimental phonetician brings within his view all those phenomena that are sometimes classified by the label, *voice science.*

We may indeed question whether the division between *experimental phonetics* and *voice science* is not an altogether artificial one. For example, the publication by Giles W. Gray and his students of studies of the breathing process for voice production appeared under the title *Studies in Experimental Phonetics,*[6] although some might consider them as studies in voice science. On the other hand, *Voice Science* by Judson and Weaver [7] contains a considerable amount of material which is strictly phonetic. Moreover, sectional programs at national conventions entitled Experimental Phonetics have more often than not included papers which were concerned with such nonphonetic vocal phenomena as vocal pitch and intensity, vocal quality, studies of the vibratory motion of the vocal folds, and so forth.

The principal feature which seems to distinguish experimental phonetics from other branches of speech study is that it is an experimental science, and, to a large extent, a laboratory science. It is that branch of experimental, laboratory science which concerns itself with speech phenomena, that is to say, with speech signals, their production, and the processes by which they are perceived and interpreted.

II

In tracing the history and background of experimental phonetics, we shall first give attention to the backgrounds of *acoustic phonetics* and then turn to the development of *physiological phonetics* and *psychophysical phonetics.* We shall not carry our account of the historical backgrounds beyond 1930. By this date experimental phonetics may be said to have passed its infancy and attained some status as an experimental science. By this time, too, it was established within university speech departments. Lastly, by the end of the 1920's, the principal techniques and tools of experimental phonetics had either been well developed, or at least foreshadowed by such events as the rapid development of electronics during the twenties.

The first roots of experimental phonetics date back further than may be commonly realized. They spring from the new spirit of skepticism and inquiry of the seventeenth century. Faith and superstition were being challenged by a growing predilection to "try it and see." Present among the questions which piqued men's increasing scientific curiosity

FIG. 10. Physiological Positions for the Speech Sounds According to Wilkins.

were those concerning the mechanisms by which human speech is produced. As early as 1668 Bishop John Wilkins, an Englishman, published a book in which he attempted to describe and represent by anatomical diagrams the physiological positions for the various phonemes, and in which he presented a phonetic alphabet based on the presumed physiological characteristics of the sounds.[8] Figure 10 is a reproduction of page 378 of this book, showing what Wilkins believed to be the positions of the articulatory apparatus for eight vowels and twenty-six consonants. His phonetic symbols appear at the upper right of each picture. The insight into the physiology of speech production shown by these illustrations seems amazing for so early a date.

The first work of real scientific interest for acoustic phonetics came about a century after Wilkins' book and consisted of attempts to build speaking machines which could be made to simulate speech. In 1769 Wolfgang Ritter von Kempelen began work on his speaking machine, a task taking much of his time for twenty-two years and culminating in a mechanical speaking device capable of producing rather fair imitations, so we are told, of not only a considerable number of vowels, but of nineteen consonant sounds, and of connected speech combinations as long as five or six syllables. In 1791 von Kempelen published a 456-page book describing his experiments together with his conclusions concerning the physiology of speech production.[9] During this period other attempts to produce speaking machines were made, though none was on a comparable scale. The most notable was the work of Kratzenstein, who in 1779 was awarded the annual prize of the Imperial Academy of St. Petersburg for apparatus which would produce five vowels, [ɑ], [e], [i], [o], and [u]. He used five resonating tubes or cavities whose shapes were in part a rough imitation of the conformations of the human vocal tract for these vowels and in part, presumably, whose shapes were a result of trial and error experimentation.[10]

The speaking machines of von Kempelen and Kratzenstein were similar in certain respects. Both used vibrating reeds as sound generators and both depended upon the shaping of resonating cavities for the variations of sounds obtained. Von Kempelen's apparatus was the more elaborate and provided means of obstructing, restricting, and directing the air stream for consonant production. Both devices were the result of trial and error rather than systematic experimentation and there is little reason to believe that either of these men had any real conception of the physical principles which governed the variation in sound with which they experimented. Their work is nevertheless of acoustical interest since it may be taken as the beginning of a long series of experiments in synthesizing speech which are still being carried on and which have contributed much to our knowledge of the acoustical characteristics of speech.

It was well into the nineteenth century, nearly one hundred and fifty years after von Kempelen and Kratzenstein, before real progress began to be made in understanding the acoustical nature of vowel sounds. The work of Willis (1830) is the important landmark, since he may be said to have formulated the first scientific theory of vowel sounds stated in terms of definite physical principles deduced from substantial experimental investigation. Willis began with the work of Kratzenstein and von Kempelen, but went on to experiment with other forms of cavities and tubes, especially reed-organ pipes.[11] His work showed that it was not the form or shape, but rather the particular tuning of the cavity or pipe, which determined the vowel quality perceived by the ear. He concluded, therefore, that each vowel has a characteristic fixed pitch and that it is this fixed pitch or cavity tone which gives each vowel its peculiar sound. He found, moreover, that the pitch of the composite tone produced by his reed-organ pipes was determined by the vibration frequency of the reed, and since the frequency of the reed could be varied independently without disturbing the vowel quality so long as the tuning of the pipe remained the same, he further concluded that no necessary relationship need exist between them, i.e., the cavity tone could as easily be inharmonic as harmonic to the frequency of the reed. By analogy Willis' theory stated that the tone produced by the larynx of the human vocal mechanism served the double function of determining the vocal pitch and of exciting the cavity tone to which the supraglottal cavities of the vocal tract were tuned. Vowel quality, however, was thought to depend only on this cavity tone which bore no necessary harmonic relationship to the tone from the larynx. For this reason the cavity tone theory of Willis has come to be spoken of as the inharmonic theory of vowel quality.

Only a few years later (1837), Wheatstone, who like Willis duplicated and extended some of the experiments of Kratzenstein and von Kempelen, published his ideas on the acoustical nature of different vowel qualities.[12] It is of interest that Wheatstone apparently saw no fundamental disagreement between his concept and that of Willis, but seemed to regard his theory as mainly an extension and elaboration of the conclusions Willis had reached. Nevertheless, his statements laid the foundation of the cord-tone-resonance theory, or harmonic theory, and the relative merit of these two theories of vowel quality became the subject matter for a heated controversy which was to continue into the twentieth century. Wheatstone agreed with Willis that for each vowel there is a characteristic cavity tuning. However, he conceived of the cavities as resonators which sound in response to the vibrations produced in the larynx and which sound maximally when the resonant frequency of the cavity is harmonically related to the vibration frequency produced by the larynx. It is not clear that Wheatstone conceived of the cavities as amplifying selectively partials which were already present in the vocal fold tone. He seems rather to argue that the fundamental frequency of the vocal fold tone excites higher modes of the cavities when the necessary harmonic relationship is present. His theory thus laid the basis for the fixed-resonance theory which was to be more completely and elaborately stated by Helmholtz. Moreover, the view that the various partials of the complex vocal tone were necessarily harmonically related provided a theoretical basis for the application of harmonic analysis based on Fourier's Series. It was, indeed, the question of whether or not this method is applicable to resolving the complex vowel tone which lay at the basis of much of the controversy over vowel theories.

Perhaps the best-known, later exponents of the inharmonic theory of Willis are Hermann and Scripture. Hermann[13] quickly saw the possibilities of adapting the phonograph, which had been invented by Edison in 1877, for phonetic research, and in 1889 he began the publication of his research with that instrument. He found confirmation for the fixed pitch theory in the fact that vowel quality could be destroyed by increasing or decreasing the speed of reproduction of his vowel records. His study of vowel wave forms, obtained by means of phonograph recording, led him to the conclusion that the vowel tone was much more complex than Willis had conceived it to be, but he followed Willis in concluding that these wave forms did not show evidence of necessary harmonic relationships among the partials of the complex tone. He therefore rejected the application of Fourier analysis to their study. Hermann should apparently get credit for first applying the term "formant" to the characteristic partial frequencies of vowels, although he used it with reference to the inharmonic partials which he conceived to be characteristic of vowel quality, whereas modern usage of the term is more general.

E. W. Scripture also espoused the Willis-Hermann ideas and rejected the applicability of harmonic analysis to vowel study.[14] A large part of his 1906 book was addressed to this issue and to the explanation of procedures for "inharmonic analysis" which he had developed.

Throughout this period the harmonic, or cord-tone-resonance, theory of vowels also had staunch proponents. Probably the most famous of these was Helmholtz. Just prior to Helmholtz's important work in acoustics and audition, in fact while Helmholtz, as a young man of twenty-two, was studying to become a surgeon, Ohm published his *law of tone quality,* which systematized much of what was then known concerning complex tones.[15] Helmholtz devoted much of his work on acoustics to extending and elaborating this law. He developed the theory of summation and difference tones as well as the theory of the spherical resonators which have since been known as Helmholtz resonators. He did extensive work on both the analysis and synthesis of complex tones, including vowels.[16] His technique of analysis made use of tuned resonators as an aid to the ear in perceptually analyzing which frequencies in a complex tone produced the loudest sensation. In synthesizing tones, he employed series of eight or more harmonically related tuning forks and also tunable organ pipes. According to independent observers these latter experiments seem to have been only partially successful.[17] As previously indicated, his vowel theory followed closely the thinking of Wheatstone, but his fixed resonance theory was much more completely developed than Wheatstone's. Helmholtz held that vowels are characterized, not by single fixed pitches, but by fixed regions of resonance, determined by the vocal cavities, and that those harmonic partials of the laryngeal tone which lie within the region or regions of resonance for a particular vowel are selectively amplified by virtue of their favorable frequency location. Helmholtz also determined that the mouth cavity could act as a double resonator, i.e., could be simultaneously tuned to two resonant frequencies, and he believed that certain vowels were characterized by such double resonance, whereas others required only a single region of resonance.

Perhaps the most prominent name among twentieth-century proponents of the harmonic theory of vowels is that of D. C. Miller. His book, *The Science of Musical Sounds* (1916) is a classic, and his pioneering work in the application of harmonic analysis to vowels, as reported in this work, became the point of departure for much of the later work on vowel analysis. As verification of his vowel analyses, Miller also attempted the synthesis of vowel sounds. In these experiments he made use of organ pipes which were carefully tuned to reproduce the exact combinations of partials which he had found from his vowel analyses. Miller's interpretations of his results support the fixed-resonance, harmonic, theory of Helmholtz and he argued vigorously for the validity of this theory as opposed to the inharmonic, cavity tone, theory. Yet he apparently recognized that the matter was not completely settled. On page 215 of the 1922 edition of *The Science of Musical Sounds,* he wrote: "The tone quality of vowels has been more closely studied than that of all other sounds combined, and yet no single opinion of the cause of vowel quality has prevailed."

In recent years the controversy over vowel theories has apparently faded, or at least become less heated, although Scripture continued to argue vehemently against the validity of harmonic analysis well into the thirties.[18] Beginning with the work of Crandall most researchers seem to have adopted a more moderate point of view.[19] While recognizing that spoken vowels are only quasi-periodic and therefore that the existence of transient and inharmonic partials must be admitted, they have nevertheless considered the resonant character of these sounds to be well established, following the reasoning of Helmholtz and Miller. They have, therefore, generally believed that important data on the nature of vowel quality can be deduced from the results of Fourier Analysis and this method has been more widely applied than any other in vowel studies. Crandall's very important study of spoken vowels and consonants is a good illustration of this more eclectic position. He employed harmonic analysis to investigate the important regions of resonance, but he also studied the oscillographic records of wave forms, after the manner of Hermann, in an attempt to detect and measure any transient components which might be present with significant amplitude. Recently developed electrical analyzers, such as the sound spectrograph,[20] avoid the methodological aspects of the controversy over vowel theories quite successfully, since they resolve whatever energy is present in the complex acoustical wave, without regard to whether it is harmonic or inharmonic, transient or steady-state.

The story of vowel research and work on synthetic speech down to 1930 would hardly be complete without mention of the work of Paget in England.[21] Paget in many respects seems to hark back to von Kempelen and Kratzenstein for he, too, employed models consisting primarily of reed vibrators and cavities which were shaped in imitation of the vocal tract conformations. Unlike his predecessors of the eighteenth century, however, Paget employed his models, with cavities made from plastiscene and rubber, to deduce general acoustical principles concerning speech production. Paget's work on the resonances of vowels led to collaboration with W. E. Benton on the attempt at mathematical analysis of the vocal resonance system.[22] Although this attempt was only partially successful, it was a step along a road which has more recently been followed with greater success.[23]

Most of the recent work on synthesizing speech has made use of electrical analogues of the human speech apparatus consisting of electrical resonant circuits and electrical or electronic sound generators.[24] This work was foreshadowed during the period we are considering by the electrical analogue devised by J. Q. Stewart.[25] Stewart made use of the data on vowel resonances which had been obtained by D. C. Miller, whose research we have previously noted. With his apparatus he was apparently able to imitate not only normally voiced vowels and a number of semivowels, but whispered vowels as well.

From the standpoint of acoustical research on speech, perhaps the most significant development of the first three decades of our century was the embarkation on a long-range program of research in speech and hearing by the Bell Telephone Laboratories. Beginning midway in the second decade, it was inevitable that this program, supported by a large industrial laboratory which could maintain a team of highly trained specialists, would have an impact beyond that which could be achieved by individuals working alone in scattered university laboratories. Harvey Fletcher's *Speech and Hearing*,[26] which has become a classic in both acoustic phonetics and audition, summarizes the results of this program of research during the period here considered. We can hardly pass on, however, without at least highlighting the significant trends in research which were begun during this time. Crandall's analyses of the sounds of speech and Stewart's work on an electrical analogue of the vocal tract have already been mentioned. In 1922 Crandall and MacKenzie published data on the long-time, frequency-energy distribution for speech.[27] In 1925 and 1926, articles by Sacia[28] and by Sacia and Beck [29] reported measurements on the powers of the various speech sounds, consonants as well as vowels. Research on speech perception, which was proceeding simultaneously, will be mentioned later.

Thus far the discussion has dealt mainly with acoustical theories of speech and with research in the analysis and synthesis of speech. Going back to the middle of the nineteenth century, this paper will trace some of the equally important developments in apparatus and technique which have made such analytical studies possible.

Among the most important tools of acoustic phonetics have been devices for obtaining graphical records of sound waves. One of the earliest such devices was the phonautograph invented by Leon Scott.[30] This instrument consisted of a horn terminated by a diaphragm with a stylus which recorded the vibratory movement of the diaphragm on smoked paper carried by a revolving drum. Rudolph Koenig, one of the great names in acoustics during the nineteenth century, apparently made extensive use of Scott's invention. In 1862 Koenig invented the manometric capsule, a device in which the flame of a gas jet is made to vibrate in response to the pressure variations of a sound wave.[31] Although Koenig did not devise methods of securing permanent records with the manometric capsule, later investigators made improvements on it which permitted photographing the manometric flame records of vowels and spoken words.[32]

The invention of the phonograph by Edison in 1877 opened up new possibilities. In 1890 Hermann succeeded in making photographic enlargements of the groove modulation of a phonograph recording by

reflecting a beam of light onto film from a mirror carried on the repro-
ducing stylus.[33] Scripture's device for producing kymographic tracings
of phonograph groove modulations is completely described in his 1906
book.[34] These two devices may be considered the forerunners of later
equipment, e.g., the phonellegraph developed by Metfessel.[35] Probably
the most precise means of graphical recording of speech vibrations,
prior to the refinement of electrical oscillographic methods, was provided by the phonodeik of D. C. Miller.[36] This instrument consisted of
a horn and diaphragm of very thin glass which was connected to a tiny
mirror in such a manner that the mirror would oscillate in response to
vibrations of the diaphragm. The reflection of a fine beam of light from
this mirror to a photographic film produced an enlarged record of the
vibratory movements. This apparatus was constructed with exquisite
precision and was capable of recording frequencies above 12,000 cps.
During the 1890's an important development was the invention of the
string galvanometer by Duddell [37] and Blondel [38] which made possible
photographic recording of small electrical oscillations. However, the
application of this device to graphical recording of sound vibrations
had to await later refinements and the development of calibrated microphones and electronic amplifiers.

Among the other important developments which took place during
the late nineteenth century, Henrici's harmonic analyzer should be
noted.[39] This mechanical device for obtaining the coefficients of the
Fourier Series made harmonic analysis a more rapid and practical
technique for resolving the energy distribution of vowels, and thus
paved the way for the extensive vowel research of Miller as well as a
considerable number of later investigators.

Twentieth-century developments, besides those already noted, include the invention of the high fidelity calibrated microphones with
which the name of Wente [40] is closely associated, the refinement of the
string galvanometer oscillograph, for which Fletcher gives primary
credit to I. B. Crandall and C. F. Sacia,[41] and the many refinements of
audio frequency recording and measuring equipment which have come
with the development of electronic technology. Indeed, the character
of modern research tools in experimental phonetics, as in many other
branches of laboratory science, has been so changed by the rapid
developments in electronics of the last three decades that we may
appropriately speak of the "Electronic Revolution." Without the
vacuum-tube amplifier, the calibrated microphone and the string
galvanometer oscillograph would have been useless as tools of acoustical
research and there would be today no modern disc or magnetic tape
recording. Without the vacuum tube, there would be no oscillators, no
high-speed graphical level recorders, no cathode ray oscillographs.

III

The experimental method in physiological phonetics begins even earlier than in acoustic phonetics. The work of Kempelen and Kratzenstein, previously described, had at least as much physiological as acoustical interest and motivation. Indeed, Kratzenstein was a professor of physiology, first at Halle and later at Copenhagen. But physiological experimentation on the voice had started well before the career of either man. According to Metzger,[42] Anton Ferrein, who published his results in 1741, was the first to approach the physiology of speech experimentally. He experimented on the larynxes of cadavers as well as on the excised larynxes of dogs, pigs, and cows. Moreover, his attempts to simulate the larynx with elastic membranes may be considered the first experiments with laryngeal models.

Johannes Müller, however, in the fourth decade of the nineteenth century, was the first to experiment extensively and systematically with artificial models of the larynx.[43] His work was not limited to models, for he also made extensive observations on cadavers. He concluded that the vocal folds are essentially analogous to a pair of flat membranes and, further, that the supraglottal air is set in motion as a result of direct transmission of the up and down vibratory motion of these membranes, rather than as a result of modulation of the air stream into pulses by an opening and closing movement. These conclusions of Müller were rather widely accepted until late in the nineteenth century. In fact, a similar view, at least with respect to the flat membrane analogy, was held as late as the 1930's.[44]

Müller's views were unchallenged until the publication in 1855 of Garcia's theory of phonation.[45] Garcia is probably best known because in 1841 he became the first person to successfully observe the action of the living vocal cords by means of a mirror inserted into the oral pharynx,[46] although Moore mentions a number of previous unsuccessful, or only partially successful, attempts.[47] Garcia's theory of vocal cord action, based on his observations, is also important, for it is in the main very close to the view most prevalent today. Garcia apparently did not accept the flat membrane analogy, for he consistently uses the term *folds* and *lips* to refer to the vocal folds. Moreover, in opposition to Müller's views, Garcia believed that voice results from a series of explosive pulses which arise from the opening and closing movements of the folds. The following is taken from Metzger's quotation of Garcia's 1855 article in the *Philosophical Magazine:*

The ligaments of the glottis . . . close the passage, and present a resistance to the air. As soon as the air has accumulated sufficiently, it parts these folds and produces an explosion. But at the same instant,—by virtue of their elasticity, and the pressure from below being relieved, they meet again to give rise to a fresh explosion. A series of these compressions and expansions, or explosions, occasioned by the expansive force of the air and the reaction of the glottis, produces the voice .... It is not necessary to obtain the explosion of sound, that the glottis should be perfectly closed each time after its opening; it suffices that it should oppose an obstacle to the air capable of developing its elasticity.[48]

Garcia was strongly supported in his theoretical views by Merkel, who repeated Garcia's observations on his own voice and came to the same conclusions.[49]

Throughout the remainder of the nineteenth century and down to recent years experiments have continued, both with cadavers and with models of the larynx. During the last half of the nineteenth century, however, the results of experiments with cadavers began to be discounted, for the results thus obtained were not held to be valid for living tissue.[50] Consequently, this line of research gradually diminished, although progress continued to be made in experiments with artificial laryngeal models, and anatomical studies added to information concerning the morphology of the larynx.[51] Most laryngeal models continued to be made of thin membranes stretched across a tube and had little resemblance to the actual larynx, until Wethlo [52] and Ewald [53] constructed their cushion pipe models which they reported on in 1913. Ewald had earlier come to the conclusion that the living vocal folds were poorly represented by flat membranes. In his 1898 publication he had compared them to thick tissue cushions with rounded edges. The models which he and Wethlo built represented them by hollow inflatable cushions consisting of rubber stretched around a framework of glass or metal, the frame being constructed to produce the desired cushion conformation. Of these two, Ewald's model was superior, for it permitted separate variation of the width of glottal opening and of the intracushion air pressure. Hence, it provided greater flexibility for experiment. It was a model patterned after Ewald's which Carhart used for his later cushion-pipe experiments.[54]

In the meantime important developments were taking place in laryngeal viewing. This aspect of the history of laryngeal investigation has been well surveyed by Moore [55] and will only be highlighted here. Following Garcia the two principal lines of advancement were those of laryngeal photography and stroboscopic viewing. Early attempts were made to photograph the larynx almost as soon as Garcia's original technique had been improved to provide for relatively adequate illumination of the larynx. However, none of them seems to have been very successful until French devised his laryngeal camera employing a telescopic lens.[56] Moore credits him with having succeeded in taking some remarkably good pictures. Immediately following Garcia, attempts were made to improve on his technique by employing binocular viewing, so that depth might be added to the two-dimensional view. As a natural concomitant, attempts to obtain stereoscopic pictures were also made, and in 1899 Garel, employing a revised version of French's camera, apparently succeeded,[57] though Moore comments that the depth perception thus gained was slight.

Since the vibratory motion of the vocal folds is so rapid as to escape observation by the unaided eye, the attempt to apply stroboscopic illumination to laryngeal viewing was a natural development. The principle of stroboscopic illusion had been well understood for twenty years prior to Garcia's work. However, it was apparently not applied to laryngeal viewing until 1878, when Oertel made the first stroboscopic observations of the living larynx.[58] One of the difficult problems of strobolaryngoscopy was that of getting adequate illumination of the larynx. Oertel was apparently not satisfied with his early attempts at stroboscopic viewing of the living vocal folds, since most of his results are based on stroboscopic observations of models which he constructed, rather than on observations of the larynx itself. Although he published an article describing an improved strobolaryngoscope in 1895,[59] the illumination problem was apparently not solved in a satisfactory manner until Hegener constructed the apparatus which he described in 1914.[60] His strobolaryngoscope employed an arc light of great intensity together with a system of condensing lenses.

A year earlier Hegener and Panconcelli-Calzia had succeeded in taking stroboscopic motion pictures of the larynx.[61] These pictures, which were exhibited at the Phonetics Congress in 1914, were the beginning of the work which Panconcelli-Calzia continued through the twenties. His experiments resulted in much improved stroboscopic motion pictures of the larynx, and in making colored motion pictures of the larynx in 1929.[62] A year later Russell and Tuttle published their colored motion pictures of the vocal cords.[63] Thus, by 1930 the groundwork had been laid for the modern work with high-speed, motion picture photography of the vocal folds, beginning in the late thirties and continuing at the present time.

Study of the physiology of speech articulation owes much to the pioneering work of L'Abbé Rousselot, Professor of French Philology at Catholic Institute in Paris. Rosapelly had been the first to apply kymographic recording to the study of speech movements.[64] According to Stetson, however, it was Rousselot who "developed the methods and became the leader in the field of experimental phonetics and may be considered the founder of the science of experimental phonetics." [65] Rousselot's two volumes, published in 1897 and 1901,[66] constitute the first textbook to carry the words "experimental phonetics" in the title. This work must have been a monumental effort for it was the first attempt to bring together all of the widely scattered information on the subject. As Rousselot himself comments in his introduction, it was like trying to build an edifice from scraps and bits.

Rousselot's name is connected so closely with the development of physiological phonetics that it may come as a surprise to discover that his book devotes almost equal space to acoustic phonetics. He not only treats vowels, resonance, and intensity variations in speech, but he includes an appendix (Appendix IV, Vol. II) describing procedures for graphical analysis of sound waves by means of the Fourier Series, together with computational schedules. His greatest influence was without doubt on physiological phonetics. He was an ingenious builder of apparatus, and not only adapted many of the techniques of the physiological laboratory to the study of speech, but added refinements of his own. He devised original apparatus as well.

The turn of the century must certainly be noted as a special landmark in the history of experimental phonetics. In 1902, only five years after Rousselot published his first volume, Scripture, then at Yale, completed his voluminous (600 pages) *Elements of Experimental Phonetics*. Scripture's research interests were much more acoustical than physiological, but his book contains a full account of the physiological data and research methods of that day. For example, three chapters are devoted to palatographic methods and results, and many more palatograms were published than can be found in any other single reference up to that time.[67]

The most notable American follower of the Rousselot tradition has been Stetson. The first edition of his *Motor Phonetics* was published in 1928.[68] The second edition, which was published posthumously in 1951, summarizes his many contributions to the study of speech movements. Stetson, like Rousselot, made extensive use of kymographic methods and showed rare ingenuity in devising special types of equipment, including highly sensitive tambours, for recording speech movements, tongue contacts, and air pressure changes. His studies of the breathing movements of speech deserve to be much more widely studied than they are.[69]

In addition to the numerous variations of kymographic recording methods, two techniques which deserve special mention are X-ray photography and palatography. The application of X-ray techniques to phonetic study seems to have been tried very soon after their discovery by Roentgen in 1895. Russell [70] states that early attempts to study vowels with X-ray were made by a considerable number of investigators, including Grandgent, Weeks, Rousselot, Gutzmann, Stephen

Jones, and others. The double difficulties of expense and danger from overexposure curtailed many of these early efforts and no publications of findings resulted. In 1907 Barth and Grunmach were apparently the first to publish plates of a complete set of vowel tongue positions.[71] Shortly thereafter Scheier also published plates of German vowels and of two consonants, [m] and [l].[72] In 1914 Eijkmann published results of some X-ray study on vowels.[73] In this country, Russell was the first to employ the technique extensively and to publish a large number of X-ray photographs of vowel productions.[74] Russell combined palato-graphic techniques with his mid-sagittal X-rays to obtain lateral as well as antero-posterior and vertical measurements of the vocal cavities for the various vowels. Certain other investigators have questioned details of Russell's procedures and the interpretations he put upon his results,[75] but there can be little argument about the extensive nature of his investigations. He claimed to have taken over 3000 X-ray pictures on more than 400 subjects. The comprehensive nature of Russell's work is shown by the fact that his measurements were employed by Dunn in 1950 [76] for his theoretical calculations of vowel resonance. A number of other investigators both in Europe and the United States have also applied X-ray techniques to the study of vowels. Among American investigators, Holbrook's work [77] has probably been most extensive, next to that of Russell. Holbrook began his collection of X-ray photo-graphs of speech articulation during the 1920's, although his material was not published until some years later, following his death. He in-vestigated not only the variations in tongue positions among normally produced vowels, but also the effects of such variables as pitch change and head posture. In addition, he made studies of both consonants and vowels.

The other technique in physiological phonetics that deserves special mention is that of palatography. We have observed that Scripture treated the subject rather fully and that Russell made considerable use of palatograms. Both Rousselot [78] and Scripture [79] give credit for originating the technique to an Englishman by the name of Oakley-Coles. Shortly thereafter Kingsley [80] introduced the use of the artificial palate made from a plaster cast of the upper dental arch. He thus gave the technique the essential form in which it has come down to the present, although there have been many variations in the method of making false palates and of recording and representing the areas of tongue contact on the false palate. In his history of palatography, Moses credits Rousselot with having made substantial improvements in the technique [81] and apparently he used it considerably to study consonant articulation. Aside from Russell's work, the most extensive application of palatography, in this country during the period here considered, has been by Muyskens,[82] who used it to investigate areas of tongue-palatal contact and variability of tongue-palatal contact for certain consonants. The method has rather serious limitations, as Russell pointed out.[83] It is only useful for studying sounds produced by contacts of the tongue with either the hard palate or the lingual surface of the teeth. The method, moreover, severely restricts the phonetic context in which the sounds to be studied can be produced, so that the positions obtained may not be entirely representative of continuous speech. In addition, palatographic data are difficult to quantify. Nevertheless, uses for the method were still being found and improvements in technique were still being made as late as 1940.[84]

IV

The third principal division of experimental phonetics, *psychophysical phonetics,* is the most recent addition to the area. In 1902, Scripture recognized the importance of experimental research in the perception of speech sounds, although almost no such work had been done prior to that time. The three chapters which he devoted to perceptual problems are largely concerned with the structure of the ear, theories of hearing, and the problems in speech perception which, as Scripture saw them, needed investigation.[85]

Controlled experimental work in this area seems to have begun about 1920 as a part of the long-time research program of the Bell Telephone Laboratories, previously mentioned. The work done prior to 1930 consisted mainly in investigating the effects on the perception of speech of various factors, such as noise and distortion, which might act to degrade its intelligibility. The systematic investigation of frequency distortion was of particular significance to phoneticians because it provided data concerning the ranges of frequencies required to recognize the various sounds of speech, consonants as well as vowels. The effects of intensity variations on the recognition of speech sounds were also studied. In much of this work done during the period prior to 1930 the techniques and methods developed were quite as important as were the data which resulted. For example, the methods of speech testing which were devised set the pattern for much of the study of speech perception which has been carried on in more recent years. A very good summary of this early work at the Bell Telephone Laboratories has been given by Fletcher in *Speech and Hearing.*[86]

Much of the widespread activity and interest in speech perception which characterizes present-day research in experimental phonetics is a product of the last twenty years; the period since 1940 has been marked by an especially rapid acceleration in this development, stimulated in large measure by military communication problems. Hence, the greater part of this story lies beyond the scope of this paper. It is worth noting, however, that by 1930 the roots of this development were already well established by the Bell Telephone Laboratories.

In bringing to a close our account of the development of experimental phonetics, one other development needs notice. By 1930 experimental phonetics was definitely beginning to find comfortable living and working quarters within the graduate departments of speech which by that time had reached a state of flourishing growth. At Ohio State, Russell's laboratory was well established. At Wisconsin, Robert West was working vigorously. Through the efforts and foresight of Seashore and the vigorous support of Mabie, experimental phonetics was well established in the Speech Department at Iowa. The department at Michigan was supporting the work of Muyskens.

Experimental phonetics has never been a closely knit and unified field. The most casual reader of this chapter will observe that contributions to this field have come from persons who have had widely divergent professional specializations and training. Psychologists, physiologists, linguists, physicists, communications engineers—all have had a hand; all have contributed importantly to the growth and development of experimental phonetics. This is no less true today. So far as we can foresee this will continue to be the case, for no one group has a monopoly on interest and curiosity concerning speech processes and phenomena.

Research in experimental phonetics had been making progress for many years before the first department of speech was established. It would continue were all such departments to be suddenly abolished. Nevertheless, the affinity which has developed between speech education and a sizable part of experimental phonetics is surely no accident. The association was initiated, and has been encouraged and strengthened, because certain wise planners in speech education saw a need for the data which experimental phonetics could supply and because they understood that a complete program of study and research in speech required the laboratory methods and techniques which experimental phonetics had acquired. That the association between experimental phonetics and speech education has been mutually advantageous is amply attested to by experience. That it was already well established by 1930 is a tribute to the foresight of the founders of the speech education movement.

Notes

1. Clarence T. Simon, "Speech as a Science," *Quarterly Journal of Speech*, XXXVII (1951), 281-298.

2. See, for example, Edward C. Mabie, "The Responses of Theatre Audiences, Experimental Studies," *Speech Monographs*, XIX (1952), 235-243; and Grant Fairbanks, "Toward an Experimental Aesthetics of the Theater," *QJS*, XXVIII (1942), 50-55.

3. Franklin H. Knower, "An Index of Graduate Work in the Field of Speech from 1902 to 1934," *SM*, II (1935), 1-49.

4. Donald E. Hargis, "The General Speech Major," *QJS*, XXXVI (1950), 71-78.

5. "Clinical Certification Requirements of the American Speech and Hearing Association," *Journal of Speech and Hearing Disorders*, XVII (1952), 249-254.

6. *Studies in Experimental Phonetics*, ed. Giles W. Gray, Louisiana State University Studies, No. 27 (Baton Rouge, 1936).

7. Lyman S. Judson and A. T. Weaver, *Voice Science* (New York, 1942).

8. Bishop John Wilkins, *An Essay Towards a Real Character and a Philosophical Language* (London, 1668). Information concerning this book and certain other original materials which were not available to the author was drawn from a recent paper by Homer Dudley and T. H. Tarnoczy, "The Speaking Machine of Wolfgang von Kempelen," *Journal of the Acoustical Society of America*, XXII (1950), 151-166.

9. Wolfgang von Kempelen, *Mechanismus der Menschlichen Sprache nebst der Beschreibung seiner sprechenden Maschine* (Vienna, 1791). Information and citation taken from Dudley and Tarnoczy, *op. cit.*

10. Christian Gottlieb Kratzenstein, "Sur la Naissance de la Formation des Voyelles," *Journal de Physique*, XXI (1782), 358-380. Information and citation taken from Dudley and Tarnoczy, *op. cit.*

11. Wilfred Willis, "On Vowel Sounds, and on Reed-organ Pipes," *Trans. Camb. Phil. Soc.*, III (1830), 231-268; also, *Annalen der Physik und Chemie*, XXIV (1832), 397.

12. Sir Charles Wheatstone, *London and Westminster Review*, XXVIII (1837), 27-41; also *Wheatstone's Scientific Papers* (London, 1879).

13. L. Hermann, "Phonophotographische Untersuchungen, I," *Pfluger's Archiv für die gesammte Physiologie*, XLV (1889), 582; "Phonophotographische Untersuchungen, II," *ibid.*, XLVII (1890), 44; "Phonophotographische Untersuchungen, III," *ibid.*, XLVII (1890), 347.

14. E. W. Scripture, *Researches in Experimental Phonetics*, Carnegie Institute of Washington Publication, No. 44 (1906); and *Elements of Experimental Phonetics* (New York, 1902).

15. Georg S. Ohm, *Poggendorfs Annalen der Physik*, LIX (1843), 497. Cited in D. C. Miller, *Anecdotal History of the Science of Sound* (New York, 1935), p. 104.

16. H. von Helmholtz, *Sensations of Tone*, Ellis's translation from the 4th German edition of 1877 (New York, 1912).

17. See, for example, Lord Rayleigh, *The Theory of Sound* (London, 1877), p. 477.

18. E. W. Scripture, "The Nature of the Vowels," *QJS*, XXII (1936), 359-366.

19. Irving B. Crandall, "The Sounds of Speech," *Bell System Technical Journal*, IV (1925), 586-626.

20. W. Koenig, H. K. Dunn, and L. Y. Lacy, "The Sound Spectrograph," *JASA*, XVIII (1946), 19-49; also, L. G. Kersta, "Amplitude Cross-section Representation from the Sound Spectrograph," *JASA*, XX (1948), 796-801.

21. Sir R. A. S. Paget, "The Production of Artificial Vowel Sounds," *Proceedings*

of the Royal Society, CII (1923), 752-753; "The Nature and Artificial Production of Consonant Sounds," *ibid.,* CVI (1924), 150-174; *Human Speech* (New York, London, 1930).

22. Paget, *Human Speech,* pp. 275-298.

23. See, for example, H. K. Dunn, "The Calculation of Vowel Resonances, and an Electrical Vocal Tract," *JASA,* XXII (1950), 740-752; and T. Chiba and M. Kajiyama, *The Vowel, Its Nature and Structure* (Tokyo, 1941).

24. Homer Dudley, R. R. Riesz, and S. S. A. Watkins, "A Synthetic Speaker," *Journal of the Franklin Institute,* CCXXVII (1939), 739-764; and Dudley, "Remaking Speech," *JASA,* XI (1939), 169-177.

25. J. Q. Stewart, "An Electrical Analogue of the Vocal Cords," *Nature,* CX (1922), 311-312.

26. (New York, 1929).

27. I. B. Crandall and D. MacKenzie, "Analysis of the Energy Distribution of Speech," *Physical Review,* XIX (1922), 221-232.

28. C. F. Sacia, "Speech Power and Energy," *Bell System Technical Journal,* IV (1925), 627-641.

29. C. F. Sacia and C. J. Beck, "The Power of the Fundamental Speech Sounds," *Bell Sys. Tech. Jour.,* V (1926), 393-403.

30. Leon Scott, "Phonautographe et Fixation Graphique de la Voix," *Cosmos,* XIV (1859), 314.

31. K. R. Koenig, *Quelques Experiences d'Acoustique* (Paris, 1882).

32. E. L. Nichols and Ernest Merritt, "The Photography of Manometric Flames," *Phys. Rev.,* VII (1898), 93-101; and J. G. Brown, "New Records of Sound Waves from a Vibrating Flame," *ibid.,* XXXIII (1911), 442-446.

33. See Hermann, *op. cit.*

34. *Researches in Experimental Phonetics.*

35. Milton Metfessel, "Technique for Objective Studies of the Vocal Art," *Psychological Monographs,* XXXVI (1926), 1-40.

36. Miller, *The Science of Musical Sounds,* pp. 78-88.

37. W. D. B. Duddell, "Oscillographs," *The Electrician,* XXXIX (1897), 636-638.

38. A. Blondel, "Oscillographes: Nouveaux Appareils pour l'Etude des Oscillations Electriques Lentes," *Comptes Rendus,* CXVI (1893), 502-506.

39. O. Henrici, "A New Harmonic Analyzer," *Philosophical Magazine,* XXXVIII (1894), 110-121.

40. E. C. Wente, "A Condenser Transmitter as a Uniformly Sensitive Instrument for the Absolute Measurement of Sound Intensity," *Phys. Rev.,* X (1917), 39-63.

41. *Speech and Hearing,* p. 26.

42. Wolfgang Metzger, "The Mode of Vibration of the Vocal Cords," *Psych. Mon.,* XXXVIII (1928), 83.

43. Johannes Müller, "Von Stimme and Sprache," *Handbuch der Physiologie des Menschen,* 2 vols. (Coblenz, 1840).

44. See, for example, Robert West, "The Nature of Vocal Sounds," *QJSE,* XII (1926), 244-295; also, "A View of the Larynx through a New Stroboscope," *QJS,* XXI (1935), 455-461.

45. Manuel Garcia, "Observations on the Human Voice," *Phil. Mag.,* X (1855), 218.

46. Manuel Garcia, "Rapport sur Manuel Garcia, Mémoire sur la voix," *Comptes Rendus,* XII (1841), 638.

47. Paul Moore, "A Brief History of Laryngeal Investigation," *QJS,* XXIII (1937), 531-564.

48. Wolfgang Metzger, "The Mode of Vibration of the Vocal Cords," *Psych. Mon.,* XXXVIII (1928), 88.

49. C. L. Merkel, *Die Functionen des Menschlichen Schlundes und Kehlkopfes usw. nach eigenen pharyngolaryngoskopischen Untersuchungen* (Leipzig, 1862).

50. See, for example, J. R. Ewald, "Die Physiologie des Kehlkopfs," *Heyman's Handbuch der Laryngologie* (Vienna, 1898), I, 165.

51. See, for example, B. Frankel, "Studien zur feineren Anatomie des Kehlkopfs," *Archive für Laryngologie und Rhinologie*, I (1893), 1-24.

52. F. Wethlo, "Versuche mit Polsterpfeifen," *Parsow-Schaeffer's Beiträge*, VI (1913), 268-280.

53. J. R. Ewald, "Zur Konstruction von Polsterpfeifen," *Pfluger's Arch.*, CLII (1913), 171-186.

54. Raymond Carhart, "Infra-glottal Resonance and a Cushion Pipe," *SM*, V (1938), 65-96; "The Spectra of Model Larynx Tones," *SM*, VIII (1941), 76-84.

55. Paul Moore, *op. cit.*

56. Thomas R. French, "On a Perfected Method of Photographing the Larynx," *New York Medical Journal*, XL (1884), 653 ff.

57. J. Garel, "La Photographie Stereoscopique du Larynx," *Annales des Mals de L'Oreille*, XXV (1899), 702 ff.

58. M. J. Oertel, "Ueber eine neue Laryngostroboskopische Untersuchungsmethode," *Centralblatt für die medizinische Wissenschaft*, XVI (1878), 81-82.

59. M. J. Oertel, "Das Laryngo-stroboskop und die Laryngostroboskopische Untersuchung," *Arch. Laryng. Rhin.*, III (1895), 1-16.

60. J. Hegener, "Ein neues Laryngoskop," *Vox*, XXIV (1914), 1-10.

61. J. Hegener and C. Panconcelli-Calzia, "Eine Einfache Kinematographie und die Strobokinematographie der Stimmlippenbewegungen beim Lebenden," *Vox*, XXIII (1913), 81-82.

62. C. Panconcelli-Calzia, "Die Erforschung der Stimmlippentätigkeit der Kinematographie," *Deutsche Medizinische Wochenschrift*, LIX (1933), 891 ff.

63. G. O. Russell and C. H. Tuttle, "Color Movies of Vocal Cord Action," *Laryngoscope*, XL (1930), 549-552.

64. See P. J. Rousselot, *Principes de Phonetique Experimentale* (Paris, 1897), I, 98. Rousselot gives credit to Rosapelly for being first, but most writers since have credited Rousselot himself with being the first to make extensive use of kymographic procedures and to demonstrate their usefulness in phonetic study.

65. R. H. Stetson, *Motor Phonetics*, 2nd ed. (Amsterdam, 1951).

66. P. J. Rousselot, *Principes de Phonetique Experimentale*, I (Paris, 1897), II (Paris, 1901).

67. Chs. 21-23.

68. R. H. Stetson, *Motor Phonetics, Archives Neerlandaises de Phonetique Experimentale*, III (1928), 1-216.

69. R. H. Stetson and C. V. Hudgins, "Functions of the Breathing Movements in the Mechanism of Speech," *Archives Neerlandaises de Phonetique Experimentale*, V (1930), 1-30.

70. G. O. Russell, *The Vowel* (Columbus, 1927), p. 49.

71. E. Barth and E. Grunmach, "Roentgenographische Beiträge zur Stimmphysiologie," *Arch. Laryng. Rhin.*, XIX (1907), 396-407.

72. M. Scheier, "Die Bedeutung des Roentgenverfahrens f. d. Physiologie der Stimme und Sprache," *Arch. f. Laryngologie*, XXII (1909), 175.

73. L. P. H. Eijkmann, "Tongue Position in the Pronunciation of Some Vowels by Roentgen-Photographs," *Vox*, XXIV (1914), 129-143.

74. G. O. Russell, *The Vowel* (Columbus, 1927); *Speech and Voice* (New York, 1931).

75. See, for example, S. N. Treviño and C. F. Parmenter, "Vowel Positions as Shown by X-ray," *QJS*, XVIII (1932), 351-369.

76. H. K. Dunn, "The Calculation of Vowel Resonances, and an Electrical Vocal Tract," *JASA*, XXII (1950), 740-753.

77. R. T. Holbrook and F. J. Carmody, "X-ray Studies of Speech Articulation," *University of California Publications in Modern Philology*, XX (1937-1941), 187-237.

78. P. J. Rousselot, *Principes de Phonetique Experimentale*, I, 53.

79. *Elements of Experimental Phonetics*, p. 92.

80. Norman W. Kingsley, "Illustrations of the Articulations of the Tongue," *Internationale Zeitschrift für Allgemeine Sprachwissenschaft*, III (1887), 225-248.

81. Elbert R. Moses, Jr., "A Brief History of Palatography," *QJS*, XXVI (1940), 615-625.

82. John Henry Muyskens, "The Hypha," unpublished Ph.D. dissertation, University of Michigan, 1925.

83. G. O. Russell, "First Preliminary X-ray Consonant Study," *JASA*, V (1934), 247-251.

84. See, for example, Elbert R. Moses, Jr., *Interpretations of a New Method of Palatography* (Ann Arbor, 1940); also, R. H. Stetson, C. V. Hudgins, and E. R. Moses, Jr., "Palatograms Change with Rates of Articulation," *Arch. Neerl. Phon. Exper.*, XVI (1940), 52-61.

85. *Elements of Experimental Phonetics*, Chs. 12-14.

86. Part IV, Chs. 3-6.

17 Some Symbolic Systems for Teaching the Deaf

C. V. HUDGINS

....

Deaf children never acquire speech and language by the natural methods since they never hear the acoustic stimuli which normally guide the hearing child in his speech development. The absence of hearing, therefore, deprives the deaf child of the most vital sensory avenue for normal speech development. It is possible to substitute vision, touch, and the kinaesthetic sense for hearing, but special methods, special teaching skills, and special devices are necessary. Any remnant of hearing may also be employed to advantage provided that hearing aids and acoustic training are made available.

One of the essential devices for teaching speech to the deaf is a precise system of graphic symbols for accurately representing the speech sounds. Such a system is essential, first, because of the convenience in presenting to the child the sounds both individually and in combination, and second, because of the intimately related problems of reading. The more nearly the symbolic system approaches that used in the orthography of the language the better, because of the problem of making the transition from one to the other in reading. An ideal symbolic system is one that provides a unique symbol for each sound in the language. The idiosyncrasies of English orthography make it especially essential to employ a more precise system in teaching speech to the deaf. The problem is less acute for most of the European languages.

During the early stages of speech training the deaf child must learn to articulate each sound in the language. In addition he must learn to combine them into syllables, words, and phrases, a process that involves a smooth transition from one sound to another in an orderly sequence. A symbolic system that accurately represents the sounds becomes the medium of communication between the teacher and the child in speech teaching. Ultimately, however, it becomes necessary to make the transition from the symbolic system to the orthography of the language.

Since complete identity of the two systems is impossible in English, experience has taught us that a symbolic system the characters of which bear a close resemblance to those of the English alphabet is the most practical for use with deaf children.

The oral method of teaching the deaf was permanently established in America during the 1860's. Sporadic efforts previous to this time had been unsuccessful but it was not until the founding of the Clarke School at Northampton, Massachusetts, in 1867, that "oralism" became firmly established. Several other oral schools, including the Lexington Avenue School in New York, the Horace Mann Day School in Boston, and the Mystic Oral School in Mystic, Connecticut, followed in the late 1860's and early 1870's. Education of the deaf previous to the establishment of these schools had been conducted largely through the medium of the sign language, the manual alphabet, and reading and writing. The success of oralism as a method of teaching the deaf in Europe, especially in Germany and England had exerted little or no influence upon the education of the deaf in America prior to the establishment of the schools named above. The manual method of teaching was well entrenched by the time oralism was introduced. It had been brought to America by Gallaudet with the founding of the first American School for the Deaf at Hartford, Connecticut, which occurred in 1817.

From the beginning of oralism in America the need for an adequate symbolic system was felt. The early teachers were in a real sense pioneers; they found no readily usable methodology and were forced to improvise their own. The only symbolic system available at the time was the English alphabet and such diacritical marks as were available in dictionaries.

Visible Speech

The first systematic effort to apply a truly phonetic system to the teaching of speech to deaf children in America was the application of Melville Bell's Visible Speech Symbols. Graham Bell, son of Melville and thoroughly familiar with his father's system, had tried the symbols in two small English schools for the deaf with some success. In 1871 while lecturing at Boston University he was invited to lecture on the Visible Speech System at the Horace Mann School in Boston. Some of the teachers of the Clarke School attended these lectures and in the spring of the following year Bell was invited to Northampton for the purpose of introducing the system there. He spent the months of March and April, 1872, at the Clarke School lecturing and devoting four hours each day to instruction of the teachers and supervising the work of speech teaching in the classrooms. He also lectured to the teachers of the American School for the Deaf at Hartford during this period.[1]

• Bell was enthusiastically received and high hopes were held for the success of his method. At his suggestion an experimental program was inaugurated at the Clarke School in Northampton for testing the value of the Visible Speech System as a means of teaching speech to the deaf. The program, intended to extend over a period of three years, called for the entering classes to be trained first in the recognition and use of the Visible Speech Symbols, but the pupils were not to be permitted to talk during this period. Communication, meanwhile, was to be carried on by means of writing. Syllable drills and vocal exercises introduced by the Visible Speech Symbols were to be used until the pupils had become able automatically to reproduce at sight any combinations of sounds presented. At the end of this preliminary training period the transition from the written symbol to the spoken word was to be easily accomplished. It was expected that this transition would be immediate and simple. Familiarity with the symbolic system was all that was deemed necessary to bridge the gap between visual perception of the sequence of symbols and the combinations of speech sounds symbolized.

The method was not a success. The annual reports of the Principal of Clarke School on the progress of the experiment during the early stages were enthusiastic; later, there were expressions of considerable doubt especially as to the propriety of depriving pupils of speech during the preliminary period. The experiment was abandoned at the end of the three years. Visible Speech Symbols were used, however, for several years, and then discontinued in 1884.[2] In its place was substituted the system commonly known as the "Northampton Charts," which will be described later.

The Visible Speech System, meanwhile, was spreading to other schools. Graham Bell, who had been appointed Professor in the School of Oratory, Boston University, was deeply interested in the oral education of the deaf. In 1872 he published "Visible Speech as a Means of Communicating Articulation to Deaf Mutes." [3] This paper contains a rather complete explanation of the system and instructions for applying it in teaching speech to the deaf. Bell attended conventions of teachers of the deaf, lecturing and demonstrating the system. He also operated a small private school for the deaf children at Salem, Massachusetts, and continued to train teachers in his method. In 1874 Bell organized the Convention of Visible Speech Teachers, which held its first meeting in Worcester, Massachusetts, in January, 1874.[4] A second meeting was held in June of the same year.[5] By this time, according to the proceedings of this convention, the Visible Speech System had spread to six schools in addition to the Boston School where it was first introduced, and it was reported that thirty teachers had already been trained in the use of the system. The Organization of Visible Speech Teachers later became Articulation Teachers of the Deaf. There is no record of any further meeting of this group until 1884.[6] In that year, the convention was held at the Lexington Avenue School in New York City. According to the proceedings of the meeting, Visible Speech was no longer considered as the "white hope" of the articulation teachers. It continued to have loyal advocates, but it is of interest that at this convention Miss Alice Worcester of the Clarke School read her famous paper describing the system which had superseded Visible Speech Symbols at the Clarke School.[7] This, the "Northampton Chart System," was to become the most widely used symbolic system in America. It is still, in a slightly revised form, considered the most practical system available.

Bell's Visible Speech System was an attempt to express graphically the physiological aspects of the processes of articulation. The various articulators and the various areas of the vocal canal in cross section are represented by appropriate symbols (see Figures 11 and 13). Combinations of these symbols can be formed to represent any combination of sounds. Thus the system probably comes as near to being a universal alphabet as any in existence. It has serious limitations, however, in that it is unlike any known system of writing. It was later greatly modified by Sweet and others in the development of the International Alphabet.

Teachers of the deaf generally concede that Visible Speech is of considerable value to the teachers themselves in that it provides an accurate knowledge of the formation and development of the speech sounds. Hence, its usefulness in training speech teachers in the practical problems of teaching the deaf to speak is still acknowledged. As a transcription system, however, it is clumsy and impracticable. Its most serious limitation is that the symbols are totally different from those of English orthography. Deaf children who are taught to speak by means of the symbols must learn ultimately to translate them into the common English forms. This imposed an additional task which seemed in the end unnecessary.

A commentary on the application of the Visible Speech System in teaching speech to the deaf is supplied by Bell himself in the form of a summary of answers to a questionnaire which he sent out to seventy-six schools for the deaf in the United States and Canada in 1888.[8] Bell had been invited to appear before the Royal Commission appointed by the British Government to inquire into the condition of the deaf in England. He was asked to report on the education of the deaf in America. Among the questions in his lengthy questionnaire were the following: "Has Visible Speech been employed in your institution?" and "Is it still employed?" [9] Fifty-one replies were received from the seventy-six institutions canvassed. Of these, thirty-one reported that Visible Speech had been tried out in one or more classes. Eighteen schools reported that it was still being used. The remaining fourteen reported that it had been abandoned. Among these fourteen were Clarke School and the Horace Mann School in Boston where it had been originally initiated by Bell himself. Predominant among the reasons for abandoning it

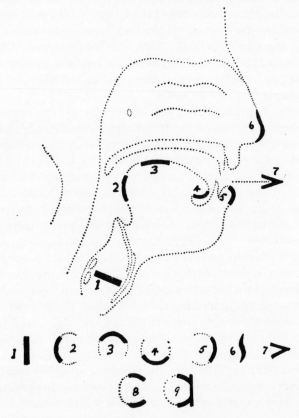

Fig. 11. Profile Cross Section of the Head and Neck with the Speech Organs Indicated by the Shaded Lines. From Bell's *The Mechanism of Speech*, p. 53.

were statements like the following: "The system seems to be too difficult to be understood by young pupils"; "We used it for two years, it was abandoned because it takes too much of the pupil's time"; "No longer used except in training teachers"; "Too complicated and easily forgotten."

A brief description of the Visible Speech Symbols is presented below. Figures 11, 12, 13, and 14 show the Symbols and the devices for explaining them to deaf children. These are the charts used by Graham Bell in a lecture delivered at the First Summer Meeting of the American Association to Promote the Teaching of Speech to the Deaf, in 1891. The lecture, "Visible Speech as Taught to the Deaf," was published in the "Report of Proceedings" of that meeting and later republished in *The Mechanism of Speech.*[10]

Figure 11 shows the profile cross section of the head and neck with the speech organs indicated by the shaded lines. The symbols below the profile represent the shaded lines independent of the drawing. These are the segments that make up the Visible Speech Symbols. They symbolize (1) voice, (2) back tongue, (3) front tongue, (4) point of tongue, (5) lip, (6) nose, (7) puff of air, (8) center aperture, and (9) shut position.

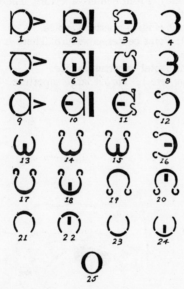

Fig. 12. Visible Speech Symbols Representing the English Consonants. From Bell's *The Mechanism of Speech*, p. 71.

Figure 12 shows the mechanism of the English consonants as explained to the deaf:

(1) *p (put, cup):* Lips shut, followed by a puff of air.
(2) *b (but, cub):* Lips shut, followed by voice.
(3) *m (man, came):* Lips shut, voice, nose.
(4) *f (file, huff):* Lips divided—aperture.
(5) *t (to, not):* Point shut.
(6) *d (do, nod):* Point shut, voice.
(7) *n (no, run):* Point shut, voice, nose.
(8) *v (vie, love):* Lip divided—aperture, voice.

(9) *k* (*key, sick*): Back shut, puff of air.
(10) *g* (*go, log*): Back shut, voice.
(11) *ng* (*lung*): Back shut, voice, nose.
(12) *wh* (*whet*): Lip center—aperture, back center—aperture.
(13) *l* (*lull*): Point divided—aperture, voice.
(14) *th* (*thin*): Point divided—aperture, front center—aperture.
(15) *th* (*then, with*): Point divided—aperture, front center—aperture, voice.
(16) *w* (*wet*): Lip center—aperture, back center—aperture, voice.
(17) *s* (*so, hiss*): Point center—aperture, front center—aperture.
(18) *z* (*zone, his*): Point center—aperture, front center—aperture, voice.
(19) *sh* (*she*): Front center—aperture, point center—aperture. Also occurs after point shut in *ch* (*church*).
(20) *s* (*measure*); *z* (*azure*): Front center—aperture, voice. Also occurs after point shut voice in *j* (*judge*).
(21) *h, gh* (*hue, few*): Front center—aperture. There is no English letter for this sound.
(22) *y* (*you*): Front center—aperture, voice.
(23) *r* in *pr* (*pry*): Point center—aperture. There is no English letter for this voiceless *r*.
(24) *r* (*run*): Point center—aperture, voice.
(25) *h* (*heat, hope*, etc.): Throat large—aperture.

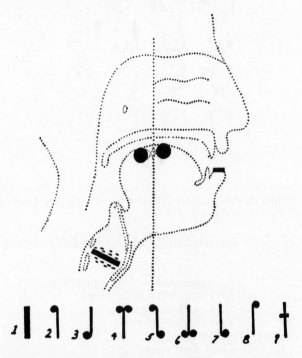

Fig. 13. Cross Section Profile Used to Explain the English Vowel System to Deaf Children. From Bell's *The Mechanism of Speech*, p. 64.

Figure 13 is designed to explain to the deaf the vowel symbols. The vertical line through the center of the profile divides front and back parts of the tongue and oral cavity. The dots on the right and left of the line indicate these parts. The dots appear on the symbols in connection with the "voice" symbol to indicate the position of the tongue in forming the vowel. A horizontal line through the "vowel" stem indicates that lip action is involved.

The symbols below the drawing indicate (1) voice, (2) back of tongue, (3) back of tongue, (4) both back and front of tongue (mixed), (5) back and front (mixed), (6) back and front (mixed), (7) front of tongue, (8) front of tongue, (9) lips.

Figure 14 shows the symbols that represent the position for the English vowels.

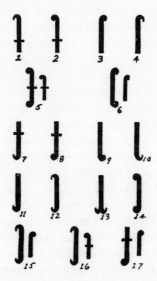

Fig. 14. Visible Speech Symbols Representing the English Vowels. From Bell's *The Mechanism of Speech,* p. 74.

(1) High back, wide, round: Vowel in *foot, put.*
(2) High back, round: Vowel in *pool, move.*
(3) High front: Vowel in *eel, eat.*
(4) High front wide: Vowel in *ill, build.*
(5) Mid back, round, glide towards "high back": Diphthongal vowel in *pole, coal.*
(6) Mid front, glide towards "high front": Diphthongal vowel in *ale, eight.*
(7) Low back wide, round: Vowel in *doll, what.*
(8) Low back round: Vowel in *all, paw.*
(9) Low front: Vowel in *shell, head.*
(10) Low front wide: Vowel in *hat, shall.*

(11) Low back wide: Vowel in *ah, father*.
(12) Mid back wide: Vowel in *ask, path*.
(13) Low mixed wide: Vowel in *her, pearl*.
(14) Mid back: Vowel in *come, rough*.
(15) Mid back wide, glide towards high back round: Diphthongal vowel in *cow, bough*.
(16) Low back round, glide towards high front: Diphthongal vowel in *oil, boy*.
(17) "The sound for *h* only occurs before the vowel . . . The deaf pupil is taught that the mouth positions for *h* is always the same as that of the succeeding vowel . . . for example: Contrast the *h* in *he* and *who*."

The Whipple Natural Alphabet

During the time that the Visible Speech System was being introduced as a method of teaching articulation to deaf children, a similar system although apparently developed independently, was being developed and used in a small family school in Connecticut. The author of this system, Zera C. Whipple, was the grandson of Jonathan Whipple who had gained notice forty years earlier for having successfully taught his own congenitally deaf son to speak and read the lips. The Whipple Home school was established at Ledyard, Connecticut, in 1871.[11] The pupils were taught orally, following the improvised methods devised by Jonathan Whipple in teaching his son forty years before. The teachers were members of the family, including the elder Jonathan, but responsibility for the project rested upon Zera Whipple. The latter, becoming dissatisfied with the methods and progress of the school, set himself to the task of developing a better system. During a session at the State Normal College at New Britain, Connecticut, he conceived the idea of a "natural phonetic alphabet" for teaching deaf children. Upon his return to the family school he developed and improved upon his original idea with the result that the "Whipple Natural Alphabet" became a successful device for teaching speech and lip reading. The system was successfully employed in the Whipple School from 1872 to 1879.[12] The number of pupils had increased when in 1874 the school moved to larger quarters in the town of Mystic. Zera Whipple was its director until his death in 1879. The school then changed hands and apparently the Whipple System was abandoned.

There is little evidence available to indicate that the system had any currency outside the Mystic School. One member of the family, N. F. Whipple, a former principal of the Mystic School, was appointed "Articulation Teacher" in the California School for the Deaf in 1887.[13] Apparently Zera Whipple, preoccupied with making the school a success, had little time for publicizing his system.[14] He did, however, issue a brief description of the method published first in the Report to the

Connecticut Board of Education in 1873, and later republished in *American Annals of the Deaf* (1891, XXXVI, pp. 288-291). Whipple appeared at few of the professional meetings of teachers of the deaf during the period he was successfully applying his system. He attended the Second Convention of Visible Speech Teachers held in Worcester in June 1874, and "... gave an account of the Natural Alphabet invented by himself for the purpose of teaching articulation and lip reading to deaf mutes. He also read a paper on lip reading." [15] It would be of historical interest to know further details concerning this meeting, and of the discussions that must have followed, for both the Visible Speech System of Bell and the Natural Alphabet of Whipple were presented at the meeting. The quotation above, however, taken from a summary of the Proceedings of the meeting is the sole reference available.

Aside from the quotation, the principal source of information concerning Zera C. Whipple and his system is contained in a paper written twelve years after his death by a former pupil. It was undertaken at the request of the American Association to Promote the Teaching of Speech to the Deaf, and published by that organization as: "Circular of Information No. 3, 1892." The title of the work is *The Whipple Natural Alphabet with a Memoir of the Inventor*. Its author, Miss Daisy M. Way, became a pupil of Whipple at the age of eight years. Miss Way describes the origin and development of the method, and gives a detailed analysis of it. She considers that her own mastery of speech and lip reading is a prime example of the efficiency of the Whipple method of teaching deaf children.

The Whipple system, like Visible Speech, is an effort to portray the formation of individual speech sounds by representing graphically the physiological positions assumed by the articulatory organs as the sounds are produced. Whipple made use of both the profile cross section of the oral cavity and the front view of the face. The symbols shown in Figure 16 were taken from a paper by Miss Way and represent a revised form of the Alphabet used in the later development of the system. [16] Mr. Whipple's own definition of the system from the same paper (page 211) follows:

The letters of the natural alphabet are pictorial of the organs of speech placed in relative positions, such as would be assumed by those organs in speaking the required sound. In other words, each letter of this alphabet is a reminder to the person who sees it to put certain parts of the mouth in certain positions relative to each other in order to produce a certain elementary sound of the language.

Figure 15 shows Whipple's physiological chart which he considered to be the basis for the symbols, primarily the consonants, that can be represented in profile view. He makes no effort to show any of the vowels in profile; instead, they are represented by the apertures made by the lips as seen directly from the front.

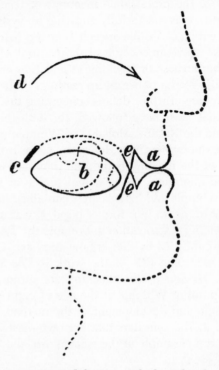

FIG. 15. Diagram Devised for Use with the Whipple Alphabet.

Figure 16 shows the twenty-six letters of the English alphabet written in the characters of the "Natural Alphabet." In addition are shown diagraphs, compound consonants, vowels, and diphthongs, which are not contained in the English alphabet and which usually require diacritical markings. The surd and sonant consonant series are indicated by light and heavy lines.

The Northampton Charts

Six years of experimentation with the Visible Speech Symbols convinced the teachers of the Clarke School of their impracticability. It was therefore relunctantly abandoned and in its place was substituted the system that has become known as the Northampton Charts. It was agreed that the Visible Speech Symbols were valuable in giving teachers an intimate understanding of the proper formation of the speech sounds, but that the system was not successful as a device for teaching

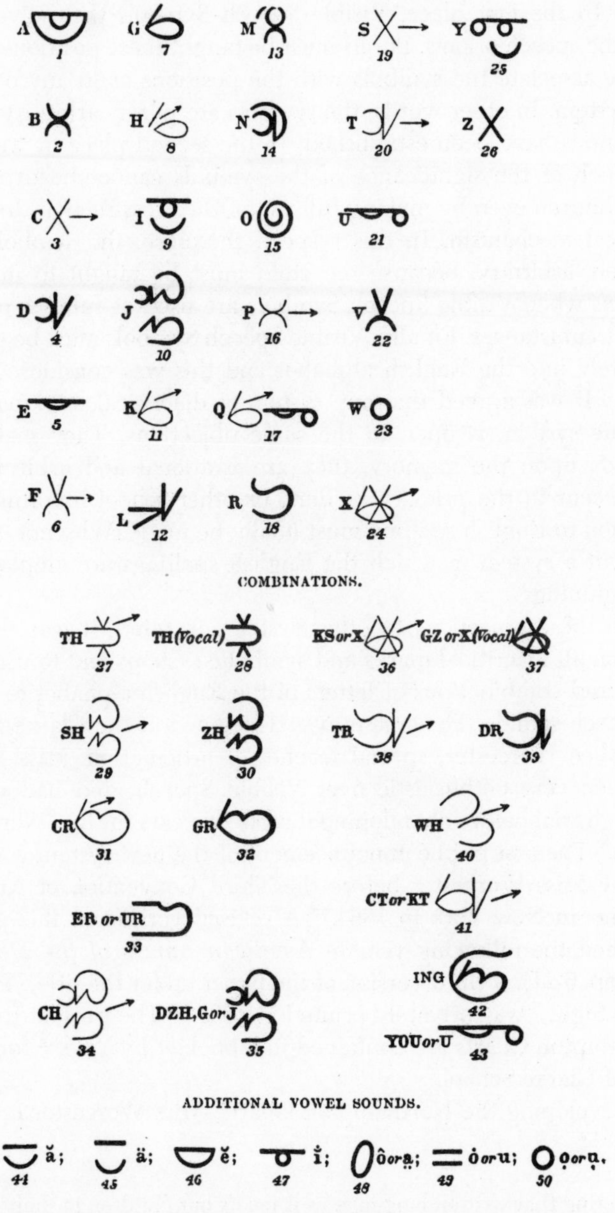

A 1 G 7 M 13 S 19 Y 25

B 2 H 8 N 14 T 20 Z 26

C 3 I 9 O 15 U 21

D 4 J 10 P 16 V 22

E 5 K 11 Q 17 W 23

F 6 L 12 R 18 X 24

COMBINATIONS.

TH 27 TH (Vocal) 28 KS or X 36 GZ or X (Vocal) 37

SH 29 ZH 30 TR 38 DR 39

CR 31 GR 32 WH 40

CT or KT 41

ER or UR 33

CH 34 DZH, G or J 35 ING 42

YOU or U 43

ADDITIONAL VOWEL SOUNDS.

ă; 44 ä; 45 ĕ; 46 ĭ; 47 ôorą; 48 ŏ or u; 49 ooru. 50

FIG. 16. Whipple's "Natural Alphabet" Symbols Used in Teaching Speech to Deaf Children. From *American Annals of the Deaf* (1892), p. 210.

speech to young deaf children. A number of reasons were given for its failure. In the first place, Visible Speech Symbols themselves do not direct the speech organs. Pupils must be taught these positions and then learn to associate the symbols with the positions as in any other symbolic system. In other words, the symbols are purely arbitrary until the associations have been established. In the second place, it was argued that much of the significance of the symbols cannot be explained to small children even by making full use of the cross-section drawings of the vocal mechanism. In this respect, therefore, the symbols remain relatively arbitrary, because the child must be taught to imitate the positions when Visible Speech Symbols are used as fully as under any other circumstances. Finally, Visible Speech Symbols must be translated ultimately into the English alphabet and this was considered a waste of time. It was agreed that any system of diacritical markings, or any symbolic system, is open to the same objections. They make undue demands upon the memory, they are irrational and arbitrary. They never occur in the primary readers, or other school literature; hence, transition to English spelling must finally be made. Why not, therefore, work out a system in which the English spellings are employed from the beginning?

With these objections to other systems in mind, it was decided to abandon all diacritical marks and symbolic systems and to use only the letters and combinations of letters of the English alphabet to represent the speech sounds. The system was developed at the Clarke School by Miss Alice Worcester, special teacher of articulation. Miss Worcester had been very enthusiastic over Visible Speech, and had given it a thorough trial before abandoning it after six years for the "Northampton Charts." The first public announcement of the new system was a paper read by Miss Worcester before the Third Convention of Articulation Teachers in New York in 1884.[17] A revised version of this paper was published the following year in *American Annals of the Deaf* (1885, XXX, pp. 6-21). A third version of the paper under the title, "Pronunciation at Sight," was privately printed in 1885.[18] The present form of the Northampton Charts are contained in a booklet by Yale,[19] former Principal of Clarke School.

In developing the Northampton Charts, Miss Worcester rationalized thus: [20]

Considering that written language as it meets our children in daily life comes only in the form of letters and combinations of letters, my effort has been to see how far it might be possible to lay aside all marks and symbols and to deal directly with the problem in the form under which it presents itself. It does, indeed, seem essential to have some standard representative for each

English sound. It is from this need, of course, that marks and symbols have arisen.

Then her explanation of the system follows:

I. As far, then, as I have been able to discover any unfailing letter or spelling which gives one of these sounds, I have used it as the foundation of work upon each. These stand first in each group upon the chart. [See Charts, Figs. 7 and 8.] Where not even one invariable representative has been found for a given sound, one of the most common is meant to stand in its place. But next, and more needful, has been the attempt—

II. To make letters *mark themselves* for pronounciation, to the greatest possible extent, by their position in words and their connection with other letters. Take for example the sound of long *a*. The simplest and most nearly invariable rule is that for monosyllables ending in "silent" *e*. When this vowel sound is taught as an element, therefore, it is first represented to the pupil in this way:—*a*—*e*. Work upon the combination at once fills these blanks with consonant letters in endless variety;

$$-a-e$$
$$c \quad k$$
$$-a-e$$
$$pl \quad t$$
$$-a-e$$
$$f \quad c$$
$$-a-e$$
$$n \quad m$$
$$-a-e$$
$$\text{etc.}$$

The quick teaching of the child's sight, which shows him that the relative position and connection of the '—*a*—*e*' remain unaltered, whatever the letters may be which fill the other places or however they may be changed, make its pronounciation a matter of established fact to him very speedily. Again *a* in a similar position without the *e*, has always its short sound. Representing this element, then, by the position of the letter which produces it,—*a*—, the child fills blanks as before:

$$-a-$$
$$c \quad t$$
$$-a-$$
$$m \quad n$$
$$-a-$$
$$th \quad t$$
$$-a-$$
$$\text{etc.,}$$

seeing more and more clearly, that the unchanging *a* is left always in a position which will, in future, carry its own pronounciation with it to him. . . . The child will see these letters in these relative positions all his life, where he will see neither marks nor symbols. He has no small advantage, then, in being independent of such helps. For just to such an extent that these rules apply, the pronounciation of written language is not an act of memory but of sight.

III. Of important letters and spellings having more than one sound, for whose pronounciation no fixed rules can be given, it is taught at once what and how many sounds each has to be remembered and decided between. So, if the pupil cannot be surely told, for example, when *ow* will have one sound and when another, he may at least know that it will have one of two, and that if his first pronounciation is wrong the second must be right. Such spellings are repeated on the chart, each one standing in groups under every sound it may represent. . . .

IV. The most common spellings of each sound are grouped so that they may stand clearly together before the eye. . . .

V. The attempt has been made to represent on such a chart just those rules for pronounciation which the elementary language of classes obliges them to learn as early as possible. . . .

VI. To connect them [rules] so intimately with the very sight of letters and act of speech that they shall not need to be remembered, but can be made the base of a continual addition in the shape of short lists of exceptions of rules that apply only to small classes of words.

CONSONANT SOUNDS

h—				
wh	w—			
p	b	m		
t	d	n	l	r—
k c ck	$\overset{1}{\text{g}}$	ng n(k)		
f ph	v			
$\overset{1}{\text{th}}$	$\overset{2}{\text{th}}$			
$\overset{1}{\text{s}}$ c(e) c(i) c(y)	z $\overset{2}{\text{s}}$		y—	
sh	zh $\overset{3}{\text{s}}$ $\overset{2}{\text{z}}$		x=ks	
ch tch	j $\overset{2}{\text{g}}$— —ge dge		qu=kwh	

FIG. 17. Northampton Chart Showing Symbols for the English Consonants. In examining the Chart it will be noted that the left-hand line is occupied by the English breath consonants. From Yale, *Formation and Development,* p. 10.

Before she decided upon the final letter forms of the charts Miss Worcester made an analysis of vocabularies found in elementary text-books to determine (1) the frequency of spellings that conformed to the rules as laid down for the charts; (2) the frequency of the spellings that required an additional rule; (3) the number that conformed to the charts by (a) crossing out a superfluous letter—for example the l in calf; (b) showing the double force of a letter, for example deer, and (c) showing the number that contradicts the charts, for example oe in shoe. It was found in the sample thus analyzed that 76 per cent of the words came directly under the rules of the charts; 5 per cent required

VOWEL SOUNDS

$\overset{1}{oo}$	$\overset{2}{oo}$	o–e	aw	–o–
(r)u–e		oa	au	
(r)ew		$\overset{2}{-o}$	o(r)	
		ow		

ee	–i–	a–e	–e–	–a–
$\overset{1}{-e}$	–y	ai	$\overset{2}{ea}$	
ea		ay		
e–e				

	a(r)	–u–	ur
		–a	er
		–ar	ir
		–er	
		–ir	
		–or	
		–ur	
		–re	

a–e	i–e	o–e	ou	oi	u–e
ai	igh	oa	$\overset{1}{ow}$	oy	ew
ay	–y	$\overset{2}{-o}$			
		ow			

FIG. 18. Northampton Chart Showing Symbols for the English Vowels. From Yale, *Formation and Development*, p. 11.

at least one additional rule; 10 per cent required either the crossing out of a letter, or showing the double force of a letter; and 10 per cent contradicted the charts.[21]

In 1942, a group of teachers made an analysis of more than 5,000 words to determine to what extent the standard English spelling of vowels contained in these words agreed with the Northampton Chart spelling.[22] The lists used were the International Kindergarten Union List, 2,596 words, and the Thorndike Word List, 2,500 words. The study was concerned only with the frequency of agreement with the primary Chart spellings; they thus ignored the supplementary rules designed to go with the chart. It was found that the IKU List showed an agreement of 75.2 per cent, while the Thorndike List showed an agreement of 74 per cent. This analysis agrees surprisingly well with the earlier analysis mentioned above by Miss Worcester. It may be presumed that had the supplementary rules been taken into account a similar agreement would have been found.

The present form of the Northampton Charts is shown in Figures 17 and 18. They have been revised only slightly since their original forms were worked out by Miss Worcester in 1884. A key to the sounds represented in the Charts is presented in Table 1.

TABLE 1
Consonants

p	pin, cup		zh	azure, rouge
b	bin, cub		ch	choke, rich
t	ten, bet		j	joke, ridge
d	den, bed		m	met, him
k	come, back		n	net, thin
g	gum, bag		ng	——, thing
f	fan, safe		l	laid, deal
v	van, save		r	raid, ——
th^1	thigh, bath		w	wet, ——
th^2	thy, bathe		y	yet, ——
s	seal, race		wh	when, ——
z	zeal, raise		h	ham, ——
sh	shore, rush			

Vowels

oo^1	stool, threw		ee	beet, ease
oo^2	wool, book		$-e-$	let, edge
$o-e$	pope, tone		$-i-$	sit, is
aw	awed, naught		$-a-$	pat, am
$a(r)$	part, alms		$a-e$	age, pay
$-u-$	sun, ton		$i-e$	bite, aisle
ur	urge, first		ou	out, power
$-o-$	hot, odd		oi	oil, boy
	$u-e$	fuse, few		

A quotation from Caroline A. Yale, former Principal of Clarke School, will serve as a description of the Charts:[23]

In examining the consonant chart it will be noted that the left-hand line is occupied by the English breath consonants; the second line by the voiced forms of the same sounds; the third by the nasal sounds. The horizontal arrangement classifies these sounds according to formation. A dash following a letter indicates that the sound is initial in a word or syllable.

In the vowel chart the upper line contains the scale of back round vowels (those modified chiefly by the back of the tongue and rounded aperture of the lips). The second line contains the scale of front vowels (those modified chiefly by the front of the tongue). The lowest line contains all of the diphthongal sounds, for *a* and *o*, although previously appearing in the scales to which their radical parts belong, are repeated here as being by their compound nature properly classified with diphthongs.

.... The number of secondary spellings given under some of these vowels might be increased, but in order to keep the chart from being cumbersome we have omitted all spellings except those covering large classes of words.

Since their inception the Northampton Charts have been widely accepted and employed in America wherever the oral method is used. The original form has been modified in the hands of other teachers, but the basic system remains the same, namely, that of using the letters of the English alphabet and a few secondary rules to represent all of the sounds of English speech. A survey made in 1942 [24] showed that of thirty-seven schools for the deaf with an enrollment of more than one hundred pupils all except two were using the Northampton Charts.

At present on the part of some teachers, there is a tendency to return to a system of diacritical marks. The movement has gained some support because lexicographers have adopted a standardized system of markings. It is argued that the employment of diacritical marks not only serves as an efficient symbolic system, but it also introduces the deaf child to the dictionary at an early age. Advocates of the Northampton Charts agree that the use of dictionaries is of great value, and that pupils should be taught to use them as soon as possible. The Charts, however, are of real value before pupils are able to use dictionaries, and as well after, for no diacritical markings ever appear in the readers or other textbook materials.

Notes

1. Caroline A. Yale, *Years of Building* (New York, 1931), p. 311.

2. *Annual Reports, Clarke School for the Deaf*, Nos. 5-16, 1872-1884.

3. A. G. Bell, "Visible Speech as a Means of Communicating Articulation to Deaf Mutes," *American Annals of the Deaf*, XVII (1872), 1-21.

4. "Proceedings, First Convention of Teachers of Visible Speech," *Amer. Ann. D.*, XIX (1874), 90-100.

5. "Proceedings of Second Convention of Articulation Teachers," *Amer. Ann. D.*, XIX (1874), 217-219.

6. *Proceedings of the Convention of Articulation Teachers of the Deaf* (Albany, N. Y., 1884), p. 162.

7. A. E. Worcester, "How Shall our Children be Taught to Read," *ibid.*, pp. 81-91. This paper was revised and published under the title, "Pronunciation at Sight," *Amer. Ann. D.*, XXX (1885), 6-21.

8. A. G. Bell, *Facts and Opinions Relating to the Deaf* (London, 1888).

9. *Ibid.*, p. vi.

10. A. G. Bell, *The Mechanism of Speech* (New York, 1906), pp. 51-75.

11. *Report of the Mystic Oral School for the Deaf*, 1896-1898, p. 9. I am indebted to Dr. Clara M. H. McGuigan, former Superintendent of the Mystic Oral School and cousin of Zera Whipple for making available a rare copy of the "Report,"

and also for pertinent information by personal correspondence concerning the development of the Whipple Alphabet.

12. Daisy M. Way, *The Whipple Natural Alphabet, with a Memoir of the Inventor.* Circular of Information, No. 3. American Association to Promote the Teaching of Speech to the Deaf (Washington, 1892).

13. *Amer. Ann. D.*, XXXII (1887), 62.

14. *The Whipple Natural Alphabet,* pp. 22-23.

15. "Proceedings of Second Convention of Articulation Teachers of the Deaf and Dumb," *Amer. Ann. D.*, XIX (1874), 217-219.

16. "The Whipple Natural Alphabet in Revised Form," *Amer. Ann. D.*, XXVII (1892), 206-214.

17. A. E. Worcester, "How Shall our Children be Taught to Read," *Proceedings of the Convention of Articulation Teachers* (Albany, New York, 1884), pp. 81-91.

18. A. E. Worcester, *Pronunciation at Sight* (Northampton, Mass., 1885), p. 17.

19. Caroline A. Yale, *Formation and Development of Elementary English Sounds* (Northampton, Mass., 1929), p. 43.

20. A. E. Worcester (*Pronounciation at Sight,* pp. 9-13; and Yale, *Formation and Development,* pp. 5-9.

21. Worcester, *Pronounciation at Sight,* p. 13.

22. Round Hill Round Table, "In Defense of the Northampton Charts," *Volta Review,* XLIV (1942), 487-490.

23. Yale, *Formation & Development,* pp. 11-12.

24. J. Utley and N. F. Walker, "Are the Northampton Charts Outmoded?" *Volta Rev.*, XLIV (1942), 485-487.

18 Development of Education in Speech and Hearing to 1920

CLARENCE T. SIMON

••

No historian can establish the exact beginning point of special consideration for those with speech and hearing handicaps. In fact, looking backward through the centuries of man's growing knowledge of himself and his ills, it seems impossible to say it actually began; in one form or another, it has existed always. Inevitably, human dependence on larynx and cochlea as communicative tools in the development of social organizations and cultures implies some effort to surmount handicaps and eliminate errors. Though to today's highly-trained and professionally-conscious therapists and educational experts, rehabilitation may seem as modern as radio and the dream of atomic power, in reality awareness of these difficulties and the need for help date from the beginnings of human expression. Extant references are as old as written records. Moses chose to rely on his more glib-tongued brothers,[1] the Ephraimites were detected by their inability to pronounce the sibilant *sh*.[2] Plutarch credits the Greek actor, Satyrus, with improving Demosthenes' harsh and monotonous voice as well as relieving his stuttering; [3] St. Mark reported the Master's cure of one "that was deaf and had an impediment in his speech." [4]

Though it seems impossible to establish an actual beginning point, the slow development of education for those with speech and hearing difficulties clearly lies within a framework formed by men, ideas, and events; procedures and programs in this special area follow the pattern of the changes in philosophies and concepts occurring with accumulated human experience. The perspective of time thus supports an historical hypothesis that this special form of education became an organized reality only when the social, scientific, economic, and educational climates were fortuitous; that its present form in the United States, as well as elsewhere, reflects the influence of a changing past.[5] Likewise, more than mere coincidence seems to have controlled the crystallization of these programs at the precise time in the changing pattern of man's culture when the need for their services reached a height unknown in earlier and simpler days.

While instances of sporadic, usually isolated, attempts to aid the handicapped are found in the records of all times and all civilizations, true educational programs are a phenomenon of the twentieth century. They came only with the merging of three great developments: appropriate social concepts, adequate knowledge, and an organismic approach. In view of this historical hypothesis, the various efforts and programs recorded in these pages thus merely pinpoint the broad philosophical changes occurring in a maturing civilization.

Historical Perspective

Appropriate Social Consciousness

Any student is well aware of the treatment accorded the handicapped in early civilizations.[6] Primitive societies valued their members mainly in terms of physical contributions to the welfare of the tribe. One who could fight, hunt, or build for the group was valuable; the one with a sensory or motor handicap was not. Man's worth was determined by his big muscle activity. Children who were potential hunters and fighters were cherished, others all too often were abandoned or destroyed. The inhabitants of ancient India threw their cripples into the Ganges, the Spartans tossed theirs from a precipice.[7] In both Greece and Rome there were periods when custom demanded the killing of the deaf.[8] Primitive society rejected the handicapped.[9]

A millennium before the Christian era, however, some bright but deservedly forgotten master of ceremonies discovered that the handicapped had some value as a source of humor for their more fortunate brothers. As a result, well into the Christian era, feasts and court ceremonies and country fairs were entertained and enlivened at least occasionally by the antics of the crippled buffoons and the stuttering fools. Though still rejected by society as useless and unfit, a few of the handicapped could trade rebuffs and ridicule for bread and butter.

Gradually through the centuries, however, the growing influence of the great religions of the world encouraged a tradition of pity for the unfortunate. Priests, monks, and leaders of many religions assumed greater responsibilities for the handicapped, giving them a right to life and, occasionally, to some measure of care through charity. A hospital for the blind was established by St. Basil at Caesarea, Cappadocia, in the fourth century; St. Lymnee of Syria founded a refuge a century later.[10] The first attempt to teach the deaf recorded in any European language was made by St. John of Beverly in the seventh century. The Venerable Bede tells how this bishop made a mute speak and was credited with a miracle.[11] Succeeding centuries recorded spasmodic instances of special attention to the handicapped. These, however, provided little more than asylum or refuge. It was far too early for attempts to alleviate handicaps, or to educate those possessing them.

Pity for the handicapped and unfortunate, nurtured in religious teachings, assumed new proportions in the thirteenth century. The concept of "charitable deeds," which influenced the treatment of the handicapped till relatively recent times, was established by the theologian and humanitarian, St. Thomas Aquinas. This remarkable scholar combined two lines, one from Aristotle through the Greco-Roman tradition and the other of Christian tradition and theology, to elaborate a classification of fourteen acts of charity—seven spiritual acts and seven corporeal acts. The seven spiritual were to Counsel, to Sustain, to Teach, to Console, to Save, to Pardon, to Pray. The seven corporeal acts were: I clothe, I give drink to, I feed, I free from prison, I shelter, I assist in sickness.[12] Subsequently, these acts became "good works" with definite rewards to the doer both in this world and in the hereafter.

Though the handicapped did gain greater sympathy and care, there was little concern for either rehabilitation or education of the unfortunate. Actually, with this motivation of pity and charity, handicaps assumed commercial value for begging. The records indicate that some children were maimed for exploitation, and the concentrations of beggars in public places, with their aggressive solicitations for alms, became a general nuisance. The subsequent establishment of asylums and homes, following the urgings of Hyperius of Ypres, may be regarded as an increase in the general welfare. In all likelihood, some of the handicapped achieved greater comfort; undoubtedly, the doer of "good deeds" was spared the sight of misery.

This system of charity, with its alms and asylums, improved the lot of the handicapped during the centuries of its influence. Unfortunately, however, it depended for its existence on immediate gain to the giver through heightened religious and social prestige in this world and his assurance of salvation in the next.[13] Adequate and enlightened public programs still were far in the future.[14]

Meanwhile, other events were contributing to the development of a broader view of the place and needs of the handicapped. The decline of feudalism, the signing of the Magna Carta, the Reformation, documented a growing philosophy of individualism and the significance of an individual life. The explorations of the thirteenth and fifteenth centuries and the later spread of scientific methodology and reasoning accompanied and fostered a break with the traditions of the past.

These, and many other events, foreshadowed the revolutions of the eighteenth century in politics, economics, and social theories.

Thirteen struggling colonies wrote a unique document that made strong and novel statements concerning the dignity and equality of man, and claimed for each individual certain inalienable rights. The people of France celebrated the fall of the Bastille. The English Georges surrendered much of their power to the Cabinet Council of the King, to give England at least the foundation of representative government. Bullets and ballots supported the new concept of the significance and the usefulness of the individual to the society of which he is a part. With this recognition of usefulness came the corollary that social and economic advantages impel training and special education, with the responsibility belonging not to the church, not to the philanthropist, but to society itself.

It is not by accident, therefore, that this revolutionary eighteenth century saw the beginning of publicly supported schools for the handicapped.[15] Not asylums or refuges, but schools as a public responsibility. Apparently Louis IX, of France, made the first public effort to aid the blind with the establishment of a hospital or refuge in Paris in 1260.[16] The first clearly defined school for the blind, however, opened in 1585, again in Paris.[17] Not until 1791, however, was this school taken under the protection of the state to establish the education of the blind as a public responsibility. The same year brought a public school in England; in Boston the Perkins Institution and Asylum for the Blind began its instruction in 1829.[18]

Early authenticated accounts of the teaching of the deaf date from the early sixteenth century,[19] growing in number, in both philosophical and medical literatures, to reach noteworthy proportions by the middle of the seventeenth. Apparently the earliest effective work in Europe was in Spain in the middle of the sixteenth century. Pedro Ponce de Leon, a Spanish Benedictine monk is reported to have taught the deaf "to speak, read, write, reckon, pray, serve at the altar, know the Christian doctrine, and confess with a loud voice." In England, following the publication of two tracts on deafness by Dr. John Bulwar (1644 and 1648), his friend, John Wallis, of Oxford, offered some practical instruction, but only two students are known.[20]

These attempts, though limited, foreshadowed the development of larger educational efforts which began during the eighteenth century. In 1760, Thomas Braidwood opened a school in Edinburgh, using secret, but largely oral methods. In 1783 he moved to London. About 1770, Abbé Charles Michel de l'Epee established a school in Paris which employed sign language and the manual alphabet. A few years later, 1778, Samuel Heinicke began instruction for the deaf and dumb at Dresden, using the oral method,[21] (moving later to Leipzig at the request of the government), thus establishing what some authorities name as the first *public* school for the deaf. "It is only after the middle of the eighteenth century that the deaf in Europe may be said to have come generally into the birthright of their education." [22]

Clearly then, modern political and social democracy dawned in the revolutionary eighteenth century. The handicapped—once rejected, then ridiculed, and later pitied—reached the dignity of accepted usefulness. Appropriate social consciousness opened the way for training and special education as a public responsibility.

Mere social consciousness, however, was not enough; training and education depend on adequate knowledge of man's structures and processes. Yet man's scientific study began far from himself, with the stars; astronomy is the oldest science. In the history of the sciences, physics has lagged behind astronomy and biology behind physics, with psychology late indeed.[23] Gradually, however, man began to know himself. Nineteenth and twentieth century research in anatomy, neurology, and psychology produced a constantly growing body of reliable knowledge as a basis for the design of educational programs and the extension of critical research.[24]

Organismic Approach

The modern approach to the education of persons handicapped in speech and hearing depended also on a concept of the human being as an organism, a functional entity—a concept developed only in the twentieth century, some time after the appearance of monistic theories in the natural sciences.

Early work in the natural sciences, following the philosophical assumptions of the Greeks, was dualistic in its premises and interpretations; the universe was composed of matter and energy. In the pattern of traditional philosophy, furthermore, scientific observations were guided by a concept of structuralism; knowledge and understanding were sought through analysis of natural phenomena into structures and substructures. Only in the beginning of the twentieth century were the researches of such men as Planck and Rutherford, and the logic of Einstein's equations sufficient to cast doubt on dualism and atomism as explanatory physical concepts.[25] Naturally, the later emerging sciences of physiology and psychology followed the pattern of their predecessors and at first viewed human behavior as resulting from the action of associated, but independent, structures.

Though in comparison to astronomy and physics the biological and medical sciences were late comers, they still ran far ahead of the studies of mental life. Furthermore, while psychology confined its study to the mind, and to mental phenomena, the medical and biological sciences ranged the realm of man's structures and processes, including his ills.

It is quite understandable, therefore, why the early work and published observations, particularly in speech, were largely the province of the physician or physiologist, with the explanations of human deviations and deficiencies being sought anatomically and physiologically in terms of the structure or functioning of specific organs.

Scientific literature of the late nineteenth century, however, contained a growing number of references to the "mind" and "mental factors." Not only were anatomists and physiologists increasingly exploring supposedly mental activity, but psychology enlarged its scientific observation, as it slowly but surely separated itself from philosophy and speculative analysis. Sir Charles Bell demonstrated the principle of differentiation of sensory and motor nerves in 1811; the middle of the century brought both the discovery of the two-point limen by Weber, and Fechner's psychophysical measurements. In 1869 Galton's *Hereditary Genius* [26] gave impetus to the study of individual differences with Wundt's laboratory (1879) and the study by Cattell and Farrand supplying additional and constructive emphasis.

Thus, in the latter part of the nineteenth century, through their greater attention to objective observations of individual differences, psychologists made a growing contribution to speech and hearing. With few exceptions,[27] however, these early psychologists followed the analytic techniques of physiology and natural science and analyzed the mind into a series of discrete substructures. "Structuralism," for example, as espoused by Wundt and Titchener [28] considered the three basic structures of the mind to be sensations, images, and affections—an analysis profoundly influential on both general and special education.

With the opening of the twentieth century, however, the accumulating results of experimental studies and the rapidly changing premises in philosophy, logic, and mathematics, combined to establish a theoretical view of the universe as a total process. Appearing first in the natural sciences, this concept spread rapidly to biology and, shortly after, to psychology and education. "Field Theory," the hypothesis that the behavior of parts is determined by the whole of which they are a part, was enunciated in the natural sciences, and became increasingly influential in biology and psychology.[29] Behaviorism, while stated more as method than as systematic psychology, was monistic in theory, though it followed the atomistic tradition in its observational methods.[30] Gestalt psychology, first announced in Germany in 1912,[31] was both monistic and organismic. The rapid fusion of its configurational hypotheses with current experimental data in the United States provided a psychological basis for a total educational approach.

Meanwhile, the field of education itself had not been static in these years. Jean Jacques Rousseau, called the father of modern education, insisted that children should be educated according to nature, which included the child's nature as well as the nature of things.[32] Pestalozzi followed the concept that education should be child-centered in his school at Stanz (1798) and in his views on education in *How Gertrude Teaches Her Children* (1801). Through the combined efforts of philosophers, psychologists and educators, the concept of a total approach to education became a reality in the early days of the twentieth century.

Developments In the United States

The framework for modern special education was relatively far along in its formative stages when the new nation was founded in the Western world. European interest in speech and hearing had brought a usable, though far from complete body, of knowledge; the new government itself was an evidence of an appropriate social consciousness. Though the later organismic view of education was still in the future, the pioneers held staunch beliefs concerning the need and value of publicly supported education for all.

Initial Delay

Educational work in speech and hearing, however, received little attention in the early days of building a nation in the wilderness. Such interest in speech training as did exist seemed confined to the rhetoricians and elocutionists, concerned with teaching their arts to the few college students.[33] Little educational effort, or publication, can be discovered on this side of the Atlantic prior to the nineteenth century.

Although the printing and publication of books began early in the Colonies,[34] Francis Green, of Boston, was the first American author to write concerning the deaf, but he published in England.[35] Dr. William Thornton, first head of the United States Patent Office and architect of the first Capitol at Washington, was the first to publish in America.[36] Early American references to stuttering appeared only as sections in larger medical or other scientific works, or as part of texts in Elocution.[37]

Since the work in this country began with the nineteenth century, it was extremely sensitive to the changes occurring elsewhere. There were wide variations in both theory and practice, with the beginning and close of the century representing different eras. The early years of the century may be labeled "physiological," with "psychological and educational" applying with increasing accuracy after 1850.

Early Nineteenth Century

Educational efforts in hearing and speech began practically simultaneously at the opening of the century yet the nature of the work done and the personnel involved differed markedly. Education of the deaf claimed more attention and expanded more rapidly; it passed more quickly through the era of temporary and isolated ventures to the establishment of permanent institutions on solid educational foundations. Furthermore, public responsibility for the education of the deaf was assumed a good half century before the public schools offered aid to the speech defective. Ministers and educators assumed a large rôle in the early efforts toward education of the deaf; speech remained with the physician and the elocutionist.

In contrast to the earlier but slower developments elsewhere in the world, the United States moved with amazing rapidity from early and temporary efforts to a solid program of permanent institutions and established public support. The first spur to education of the deaf apparently came from Francis Green of Boston with the publication of a census taken with the assistance of some of the ministers of the community. This 1803 survey found seventy-five deaf in Massachusetts, and estimated five hundred for the entire country. A few years later, 1810, a real though temporary beginning of education of the deaf occurred when the Reverend John Stanford found several deaf children in the alms house of New York and tried to teach them. While his work lasted but a short time, it paved the way for the establishment of a permanent school in 1817.[38] Other starts, beginning in 1812, were made by John Braidwood, of the English family controlling a secret oral method. His series of transient efforts in Baltimore, Goochland, and Chesterfield counties in Virginia, in New York, and again in Virginia, however, all ended in failure.[39]

The first permanent free school for the deaf [40] in the United States began at Hartford, Connecticut, in 1817. On the basis of a survey made with the assistance of a group of New England clergymen (1811-1812), Dr. Cogswell of Hartford estimated that there were 400 deaf in New England and 4000 in the United States. Led by Dr. Cogswell, friends of his daughter, Alice, organized and sent Thomas Hopkins Gallaudet,[41] a graduate of Yale and of Andover Theological Seminary, to Europe to prepare himself as a teacher of the deaf. Originally, his plan had been to study the oral method in London, but the Braidwood family, then in control, were reluctant to disclose their secrets.[42] Meeting this obstacle in both England and Scotland, Gallaudet accepted the invitation of Abbé de l'Epee at Paris and was instructed in the manual method.

Accompanied by Laurent Clerc, a teacher in the Royal Institution for the Deaf and Dumb in Paris, as an assistant, Gallaudet returned in August, 1816. Shortly before his return, the General Assembly of Connecticut passed an act of incorporation in accordance with the petition of sixty-three citizens of Hartford who were "formed into, constituted, and made a body politic and corporate by the name of the Connecticut Asylum for the Education and Instruction of Deaf and Dumb Persons." Under this charter and name, the school was opened April 15, 1817, using the sign language, manual alphabet, and writing.

This school, later known as the American Asylum, and now as the American School for the Deaf, was the forerunner, if not the exact model, for the great modern system of state supported schools. Though it had been initiated by private financial support, the Connecticut legislature, in October of 1817, appropriated five thousand dollars. Additional contributions came from other cities; in 1819, the United States government gave a substantial grant of land; and additional support in the New England states, Georgia, and South Carolina provided for the education of deaf pupils from a wider area.[43]

Similar schools followed in quick succession. The New York Institution for the Deaf and Dumb was incorporated April 15, 1817 [44] and opened in October of the next year; The Pennsylvania Institution for the Deaf and Dumb opened in Philadelphia, in the fall of 1820. In 1823, Kentucky marked a final step in public education. Not only was it the fourth state and the first away from the seaboard to establish free education for the deaf, but more significant to an historical account, the initial action was taken directly by the legislature, and the school was the property of the state from its inception. Thus, education for all, as a public responsibility, was established in the first quarter century. With these beginnings, new schools were opened at increasingly frequent intervals. Sixteen public schools, in as many states, had been established by 1854; by 1893 the total had reached sixty-one.[45]

Interesting to the historian is the fact that the education of the deaf in the first half of the nineteenth century depended almost entirely on the sign language and written instruction. Though the oral method was well known and frequently used in Europe at this time and had its staunch advocates in this country, the first school using the oral method was not started until 1866.[46] The slight appeal of the oral method usually is explained by the training of Gallaudet, and the continued reluctance of the Braidwoods to disclose their version of the oral method. Since other teachers than the Braidwoods were using oral methods, however, this may be an overly narrow view, for choice of method is influenced by dominant psychological and educational theories and the prevailing concept of the nature of speech.[47] In any event, changes in educational premises, coming originally from Europe, and a dawning view of speech as a part of the learning process coincided very closely with the increased use of the oral and combined methods in the second half of the century.

Of all the deviations of speech, stuttering received the major emphasis in the publications of the first half of the nineteenth century.[48] The various suggested causes and remedies for stuttering therefore most clearly indicate the sway of physiological concepts. It is only in the light of this physiological period, moreover, with its emphasis on the peripheral speech mechanism, that the modern student can understand the reported procedures and remedies, since some of them seem now to have a bizarre and even impossible flavor.[49]

The remedial procedures for stuttering in the first half of the nineteenth century fall rather clearly into three distinct approaches: drills, surgery, and the use of mechanical devices. With major blame placed on the peripheral organs of speech, varied and ingenious special exercises were designed for the tongue and lips, and for the breathing muscles. Stutterers were instructed and drilled in deep and regular breathing, repetition of the vowels, speaking, singing, arm swinging, and rhythmical movements of head, arms, or feet.

An early example of this drill procedure is given by the account of the "American Method," known also as "Mrs. Leigh's Method" and "The Leigh-Yates Method." Accounts vary concerning the origin and precise procedure of this method; since it was secret, the details must be gathered from indirect evidence, the proprietors making no statements. Warren gives the generally accepted information that the method was originated by a Dr. Yates, who opened the school in the name of his daughter's tutor, Mrs. Leigh, to avoid "the reproach of empiricism." [50]

Although there is some uncertainty concerning the exact methods employed,[51] there is none concerning the popularity and influence of the school and its methods. It was endorsed by prominent physicians and professors, stutterers flocked to its doors, and teachers came to study and to carry the methods back to their pupils. In 1828 this "American Method" was the subject of a report by Megendie to the French Academy, a report, however, which was expressed in something less than laudatory terms.[52]

In spite of many imitations, large numbers of students, and glowing testimonials, the original school and the "American Method" disappeared from the scene in time for Mr. Warren to report both the nature of the method and its demise in his article of 1837.

The physiological view of stuttering helps to explain the wave of attempts to cure stuttering through surgical intervention.[53] The early part of the nineteenth century brought a rapid development of surgery, with increasing attempts to cure both mal-functioning and deformities of trunk and limbs by this means. Although neither ether nor chloroform was yet in use, Dieffenbach, professor in the medical school at the University of Berlin, devised three operations on the tongue for stuttering, and performed the first one in January, 1841. His reasoning, though incomprehensible to the twentieth century, was not without its logic in the nineteenth. The numerous and optimistically-toned articles describing his work in France and England, as well as in Germany, brought large numbers of stutterers seeking this relief, and the surgeons responded to the demands.[54]

In the United States a few surgeons used variations of the original techniques. Dr. Alfred C. Post, of New York, apparently was the first, performing an operation on May 21, 1841. Dr. Schmidt, likewise of New York, reported surgery late in June. Before many operations were attempted, however, vigorous protest from members of the medical profession, and increasing evidence of fatalities brought this chapter in remedial attempts to a close as quickly as it had begun. The close of the year of its origin, 1841, brought the end of the surgical period.

Late in a half century that was still concerned mainly with the peripheral organs of speech, various appliances and mechanical aids were tried, in attempts to control the muscles and structures involved. Mrs. Leigh had recommended linen under the tongue; the pebbles of Demosthenes were not forgotten. The cork between the teeth, recommended by Charles Kingsley in 1859 was adopted by some American teachers. The most popular appliances, however, were three invented by Robert Bates of Philadelphia. These were patented, widely advertised, and sold for thirty-five dollars each.[55] Only from the view of the physiological concept of stuttering held at this time is it possible for the modern student to understand the endorsement of these appliances given by the "Committee on Science and Art" of Franklin Institute in 1854 and the award of the Scott Legacy Premium for these ingenious and useful inventions." [56]

Later Nineteenth Century

The early part of the nineteenth century had been one of growing but somewhat scattered efforts. The scientific spirit of controlled observation and criticism of both methods and results was only in the beginning stages. The second half of the century, however, brought increasing research, accumulation of knowledge, and further changes in educational and social concepts. Slowly, but clearly, this half century revealed the beginnings of the modern educational approach in speech and hearing. The young and vigorous science of psychology contributed more directly to educational theories; educators, more numerous and with increased professional consciousness, extended the possibilities and responsibilities of public education. New professional organizations fostered a sense of professional solidarity and power, while the ensuing conventions and journals increased the range and scope of educational planning. Simultaneously, larger school enrollments emphasized the responsibility of the public schools to provide comprehensive and realistic programs for all children, normal and handicapped alike.

Psychology, through most of its earlier history, had been concerned with a speculative search for universal principles, generalizations that would explain all activity of the human mind.[57] In the later years of this half century, however, the earlier search for ways in which all humans are alike yielded to the new awareness of individual differences and the need for more comprehensive educational programs became quite apparent.[58] The hallowed "Three R's" were not enough. The task of imparting information to the young, previously established according to "mental laws," became less simple. One child was not the duplicate of another.

These psychological changes, however, were only part of the developments occurring in this era. The concepts of Rousseau and Pestalozzi, Froebel's pioneer work with younger children,[59] and Horace Mann's [60] brilliant and energetic interest in public education all combined to outline and establish a new concept of the nature and responsibility of *public* education. Stimulated and validated by the philosophy of John Dewey,[61] and demonstrated in the "Progressive Schools," educational theory and practice moved to its modern concern not only for all children, but for each child as a whole.

In his occupation with formative theory and knowledge, however, the historian must not lose sight of the obvious and quite practical influence of increased school attendance, a growth particularly significant because it reflected a higher percentage of attendance on the part of children of school age in addition to a mere increase in the total population.[62] While numerous causes have been suggested for enlarged school attendance,[63] the greatest influence on the handicapped probably was exerted by the increasing agitation against child labor [64] and, particularly, the adoption of compulsory school *attendance* laws. The early compulsory education laws of this country had not required attendance, and the first of such legislation, established by Massachusetts in 1852, remained practically unenforced for a number of years. Actually it was only in the last three decades of this nineteenth century that compulsory school attendance, as known in Protestant

Continental Europe in the sixteenth century, really received much legislative attention.[65]

Obviously this increase in the school population brought a larger number of handicapped children into the public school system. These children, who in earlier years soon would have dropped out of school or never even appeared, forced a new awareness of the inadequacy of the traditional public school program to provide "equal educational opportunities for all."

The growth of professional organizations and learned societies in the late decades of the century likewise indicates a changing era. Members of these organizations not only met in conventions to discuss their mutual problems and to plan appropriate programs of action, but they published journals spreading the results of research and discussion, and pleas for action, to an ever longer roster of readers. A complete catalog of these organizations and journals would be neither interesting nor significant but a brief sample will make apparent the widening circle of shared knowledge and experience. Influential, with greater or less directness, on education in hearing and speech were the American Medical Association, founded in 1847, the National Educational Association (1857),[66] American Psychological Association (1892), and the Parent Teacher Association (1897).[67] More immediately concerned with the education of the deaf were the Convention of American Instructors of the Deaf (1850), Conference of Executives of American Schools for the Deaf (1868), the Volta Bureau (1887), the American Association to Promote the Teaching of Speech (1890),[68] and the Association to Promote Auricular Training of the Deaf (1894). Not all the organizations, however, were formed by the teachers and administrators. The membership of the National Association of the Deaf, founded in 1880, included deaf persons, especially those with an education. The National Fraternal Society of the Deaf (1901) is a fraternal and actuarial society, yet not lacking in its social aspects. Speech, however, as a separate area was represented in this period only by the Public Readers and Teachers of Elocution (1892), renamed a year later the National Association of Elocutionists.[69]

The work and influence of these organizations was extended through a growing list of publications represented by such journals as the *American Journal of Psychology* (1887), *Psychological Review* (1894), *Pedagogical Seminary* (1891), *Journal of Proceedings and Addresses, National Education Association* (1857), *Educational Gazette* (1869), and *Education* (1880). Special professional emphases came through the *American Annals of the Deaf* (1847), *The Volta Review* (1899), *The Voice* (1879),[70] *Emerson College Magazine* (1892), and the *Proceedings of the National Speech Arts Association* (1892).[71] This period likewise brought indexes, clear indications of growing scope and complexity in any area of research: *Index Medicus* (1879), *Psychological Index* (1895).[72]

No account of the educational developments in speech and hearing of this period would be complete without specific mention of Dr. Alexander Graham Bell, third in a family of distinguished scientists and pioneer educators. Alexander Bell, the grandfather, was a recognized early nineteenth century authority on diction and speech defects. His book, *Stammering and Other Impediments of Speech*, published in London in 1836, protested the cruelty of surgical operations and the quackery of those who have not studied the phenomena of speech, as well as outlining usable pedagogical methods. Alexander Melville Bell, the son, listed in the mid-forties in the City Directory of Edinburgh as a "Professor of Elocution and the Art of Speech," likewise achieved renown as an author [73] and teacher, and particularly for his system of alphabetics known as visible speech. When he was unable to accept an invitation to give a course to the teachers of the Boston School for Deaf-Mutes he sent his son, who had moved to Brantford, Canada, in 1870, for reasons of health. Subsequently, and fortunately for this country, Alexander Graham Bell decided to remain in Boston, and in 1872 opened a school of vocal physiology. In 1873 he joined the faculty of Boston University, and in 1875 offered what probably was the first university class for the instruction of teachers of speech correction and of speech for the deaf.[74] In spite of the demands on his time made by his research and his inventions [75] he retained his interest in speech, particularly for the deaf. Active as a teacher and a strong advocate of the oral method in the education of the deaf, in 1887 he established the Volta Bureau "for the increase and diffusion of knowledge relating to the deaf," with an original endowment of $100,000 [76] obtained through successful experiments at the "Volta Laboratory" [77] and the sale of basic patents on the phonograph-gramaphone. In 1908 he presented this treasure of educational scholarship, including its library, its research material, and the valuable case histories of many thousands of deaf persons, to the American Association to Promote the Teaching of Speech to the Deaf, which he had founded and endowed. Continuing his leadership and his staunch advocacy of the oral methods in all schools, he served as President of the Clarke School for the Deaf for the five years preceding his death, in 1922.

The life and work of this scientist, educator, and humanitarian fostered, if not actually originated, many of the concepts governing more recent educational procedures. As much as that of any other man, his work marked the beginning of a new era. Though dealing in terms of the knowledge of the times, his vision and principles were of the twentieth century. The fact that every telephone in North America was kept silent during his funeral was a tribute to only part of the contribution he made to future generations.

The work for the deaf in this latter half of the century may be described conveniently under four interrelated developments: first, an increase in the number of residential schools for the deaf; second, the extension of this instruction to public day schools; third, the growing number of deaf children attending school; and fourth, wider use of oral methods.

In the early years, the schools for the deaf in the United States had been associated with charity or benevolence—concepts ever present, and frequently dominant. Earlier accounts of these schools, and the statutes establishing them, frequently used such words as "care," "aid," "maintenance," or "support." Whether these words were stressed because they represented the major aim of the pioneers, or because their use facilitated the securing of donations is not our concern here. Undoubtedly, many of the early teachers were considerably concerned with deaf children who were found in conditions of poverty; yet at the same time, the major aim in establishing these schools seems to have been educational. In any event, by the middle of the century all schools were stressing the educational nature and importance of their work.

With mixed charitable and educational motives, groups of citizens had founded schools with funds from private donations. This tended to limit both the number of schools and the pupils who could be accommodated. Even when the state came to the aid of the schools, financial or geographical considerations limited attendance. Later, as the states established schools at their own initiative and expense, attendance still was limited either to a maximum number or to residents of stated areas.

The final step in the development of schooling for the deaf came with the complete acceptance of the educational motive and the removal of all restrictions of finance or place of residence. Instruction of the deaf, thus placed on the basis applying to all children, not only represented a culmination of centuries of development of a sense of public responsibility, but also encouraged the rapid growth in number of schools, teachers, and pupils, that occurred in the second half of the nineteenth century.

Of the forty-one public schools listed in the *History of American Schools for the Deaf*,[78] twelve were established before 1850, and twenty-nine of them between 1851 and 1893. The same publication lists eighteen private and denominational schools which were opened between 1869 and 1892. Volume III contains the names and addresses of 798 instructors of the deaf, ample evidence of the extent of the work that developed in this half century.

In the early part of this half century, Congress was asked to support an extension to the college level of the work done at the Columbia Institution for the Deaf and Dumb. While to a few the idea of higher education of the deaf seemed strange, actual opposition was slight. The appropriate legislation was enacted in 1864, and signed by President Lincoln, April 8. In June of the same year the National Deaf-Mute College was publicly inaugurated under the presidency of Edward Miner Gallaudet.

This college, in 1893 renamed Gallaudet College in honor of the pioneer teacher and its first president, extended the education of the deaf to the higher academic levels during the same years that brought accelerating growth of the work in the lower schools.[79] Thus, in this half century, the education of the deaf came to parallel general education, and to assume a place probably accorded to it in no other country.

Most of the earlier schools for the deaf had been residential institutions in which the pupils lived during the school year, the most likely development from current educational views and thinly populated areas. Beginning approximately in 1869, however, and with increasing rapidity following 1890,[80] day schools were established, which resembled more closely the regular public schools and were an integral part of state and civic educational programs. The conviction, accepted more widely by educators, that institutional life for children should be reduced to the lowest possible amount was fostered by clearer realization of the total needs of the child. The day school fitted the new demands in that it made possible the necessary special education of the child but without depriving him of the benefits of home life. Moreover, since many of the day schools were located in special classrooms in the general schools, it was easier for the deaf child to mingle with normal-hearing children.

Earliest of the day schools to show stable existence was the Horace Mann School of Boston, established in 1869 by the school board of that city, and named in honor of their pioneer educator. Subsequent growth was spasmodic, with many of the new schools existing for a short while only. Some were launched a number of times. While the arguments both for and against this type of school were many, and often vigorous, on the whole the growth was commensurate with that in general education and seemingly somewhat ahead of that in other special areas. As nearly as can be determined, day schools showing some measure of permanence, i.e., still in existence in 1920, had appeared in six states (California, Massachusetts, Michigan, Missouri, Ohio, and Wisconsin) prior to 1900; in five additional states by 1910, and in six others by 1920.[81]

Thus in a growing number of states they came to serve a part of the need formerly met by the state schools alone. Commonly they were aided by state legislation and financial support, but occasionally larger cities established day schools as part of the local system and quite independently of state support. The first full day school law was enacted by Wisconsin in 1885, preceded by general legislation in Pennsylvania in 1876 to establish schools for "defective" pupils in school districts of a certain size. Subsequent laws varied from permissive to mandatory, with some of them including proposals for special taxes. The majority of the states lacked any legislation in 1920.

In addition to the other changes, this period brought increasing attention to, and agitation for, the use of oral methods in the instruction of the deaf. Although the oral method received some consideration at the outset and the earliest proposals for schools intended the use of the oral method,[82] the leading schools used manual methods. Hence the oral method was able to make but slight appeal. Apparently reports of its successful use in Europe, particularly in Germany, made but little impression in this country. In 1843, however, Horace Mann, the Massachusetts educator, and Samuel Howe, Principal of the Perkins Institution for the Blind at Boston, visited Germany and returned to report favorably on the results of the oral approach. These recommendations aroused some enthusiasm, but representatives of other schools returned with conflicting views.

The middle of the nineteenth century, however, brought increased interest. The urgings of Mann and his colleagues, greater dissatisfaction with an educational procedure that tended to leave undisturbed the all too common label, "deaf and dumb," and increased knowledge of educational techniques all were probably influential. In 1864 there was an attempt to establish a small oral school in Massachusetts, but it was not successful. In 1866, however, a school was established at Chelmsford, which shortly moved to Northampton as the Clarke School for the Deaf; the first permanent oral school. Considerable, if indeed not the greatest, impetus was supplied in 1869, through the establishment of an oral day school by the School Board of Boston, the Horace Mann School. In general, the day schools which subsequently opened in other cities followed the pattern of this leader, with resulting extension of the oral method and an increase in the number of pupils so educated. There seem to be some indications likewise that the increasing dissatisfaction with the results of the manual methods operated, in turn, to promote the development of these day schools.

Certain special influences, however, should not be overlooked.

A number of organizations were formed to encourage the wider use of the oral method, the main one being the American Association for Promoting the Teaching of Speech to the Deaf.[83] The Volta Bureau, closely associated with this organization, was markedly influential. In 1868, the Conference of Principals of American Schools for the Deaf expressed approval of the oral method, though with definite qualifications, which were modified in 1886. Late in the century and continuing into the next, some of the states added legal force to the use of the oral method, one type of legislation requiring it in all schools, another in those that received state appropriations.

This second half century contains a clear record of some vigorous contention between the advocates of the two methods. In some respects this contention probably was unfortunate; in the longer view, however, it may well be that disagreement afforded a vigorous stimulation for expanding goals and conscientious work, and strong encouragement for objective review and evaluation of the various methods and procedures.

In any event, the record is clear that this second half century brought a remarkable increase in the number and calibre of the schools, a widened view of the responsibilities and the possibilities of the education of the deaf, with distinct improvement, educationally and economically, in the place of the deaf as citizens of the commonwealth. In this half century, the modern educational era found its true beginnings.

Speech correction, though subjected to the same influences, showed much less change and growth than the education of the deaf. The historian might surmise that this laggard development results, in part at least, from an unawareness of the detriment to education imposed by defective speech. Unlike the deaf child, the speech defective appears able to receive the elements of his education as they are presented by the teacher in the usual classroom. The less obvious fact, that his ability to profit from instruction may be impaired by his handicap in expression, did not emerge in an educational scheme based on dualistic psychology. With education aimed to train the "mind," stopped ears were seen to block the gateway; but the need for unhampered response, particularly in language, was not appreciated.

Under the dualistic tradition, speech [84] was considered mainly as a means of expression, a performance. The interest in delivery, and the separation of oral expression from rhetoric, apparently began in England in the eighteenth century with the change in instruction in the schools and colleges from Latin to English.[85] This concern with delivery to which Mason gave the name "elocution" [86] spread to the United States late in the eighteenth century and gained ground in the nineteenth. With emphasis mainly on the art of delivery, in both instruction and criticism,[87] the increase in speech activities,[88] particularly on the college level, tended to emphasize speech as an end product. Speech was a skill in addition to the educative process, but not part of it or of use in it.

This situation may help to explain a rather startling contrast between the rapid growth in the number of people professionally identified as "instructors of the deaf," and the enlarging number of organizations with the lack of such professional group in the field of speech. In the second half century instruction in the spoken word was given largely by public performers, the proprietors of private schools, and the itinerant "professor" of public speaking, many of whom were concerned with individual efforts and had little sense of affiliation with general education. The first professional organization, the Public Readers and Teachers of Elocution (a year later renamed the National Association of Elocutionists) organized in 1892, seems to have represented the professional rather than the educational view of speech.[89]

Since the educational loss inflicted by disorders of speech was not yet known, speech correction in this half century still was largely confined to stuttering and its dramatic symptoms. There were, however, distinct changes in the view of stuttering presented in the literature. Descriptions were concerned less with the peripheral organs of speech and more with physiological processes and remedial measures were suggested more frequently.[90] In this "physiological" period breathing exercises, loud talking, rhythmical utterance, and general hygiene were recommended more frequently, while a generally increased interest in the articulatory aspects pointed the way to the "drill methods" which were to continue in later years. Furthermore, elocutionists and educators were doing an increasing amount of the remedial work and the concept of stuttering as solely a medical problem yielded to the hope for re-education of the unfortunate speech habits.[91] Alexander Graham Bell's School of Vocal Physiology, in Boston, and the American Vocal Institute and the Bryant School for Stammerers in New York were typical of the growing attempts to retrain a mal-functioning mechanism through educational techniques.

Amid the diversity of approach, conflict of opinion, and controversy concerning the medical or educational nature of the problem, the most significant event of this half century seems to have been the increasing study of the stuttering person, using psychological methods and knowledge in an attempt to understand the individual as a whole. The observations of individual differences in the nature and manifestations of stuttering were a true harbinger of the scientific approach which characterized the twentieth century. In any event, at the end of the nineteenth century, the anatomical and physiological eras were drawing to a close, and the psychological period was well into its beginnings.

The Twentieth Century

The opening years of the new millennium were a blend of the old and the new. For this reason, some writers have seen the pre-war years as part of the preceding century. Yet there were real differences in concepts and events. There was a marked sense of quickening tempo with new facts and theories arriving in quick succession, and significant events occurring with increasing rapidity. These years brought, likewise, expanding research and the application of new mechanical and electrical instruments made observation more precise.

The greatest change, however, occurred in educational programs. As individual differences and the principles of learning became increasingly clear, both hearing and speech embraced a more comprehensive educational view.

Changes in the field of speech seem much more marked than those in hearing. With comparative suddenness, increased discussion and publication not only suggested new theories and procedures for stuttering, but also, and probably even more significantly, woke the schools to the real educational and social handicaps imposed by the seemingly minor and hitherto neglected disorders of voice and articulation. In brief, while the work in hearing was extended and modified, speech correction as an educational program came into being.

One of the marked additions to the work in hearing concerned children and adults with less than a total loss of hearing. Although some day schools had accepted hard-of-hearing children in the earlier years, provision for such separate classes was first made in Rochester, New York, in 1909. Since that date, educational facilities for hard-of-hearing children have been increased, either in special schools or in specialized classes within the regular public schools, with particular attention to lip reading and to the improvement of residual hearing and conversation.

Perhaps inspired by the broadened work for children, the early years of the twentieth century witnessed an increased demand by hard-of-hearing adults for instruction in lip reading. Apparently, however, the only instructors who attempted to use lip reading at all were some of the teachers of deaf children who seemed to have no settled teaching methods.[92] There is even some question whether anyone in these days really accepted lip reading as a necessity or believed it could be taught. In spite of his work as a teacher of speech and his interest in "visible speech," Alexander Graham Bell's first interest in lip reading seems to have come after the children at the Horace Mann School for the Deaf showed him they could understand his normal conversation.[93]

Shortly before 1900, Martha E. Bruhn, a Boston language teacher, threatened with the loss of her own hearing, studied with Julius Müller-Walle of Germany who had devised a system of teaching lip reading to adults. On her return, she began to teach lip reading to adults in 1902. Apparently just slightly earlier, Lillie Warren had opened a similar school in New York City to which Edward B. Nitchie came as a pupil, and remained for a short time as assistant. In 1903 this pioneer left the Warren School to open his own, using his individual method of teaching.[94] Teachers trained at these and other schools began similar work in other cities, thus extending even more widely this new educational opportunity.[95] Later, in 1913, public evening classes in lip reading for adults were started in the schools of Brooklyn and New York. Two years later, the same type of instruction was offered for children in special public-school classes in Lynn, Massachusetts, and Rochester, New York.[96] Thus the early years of this century not only brought modern methods for the teaching of the previously neglected skill of lip reading, but extended that teaching to a growing number of the newly recognized group of hard of hearing, both children and adults.

The early years of this century saw likewise a growth of research and the beginnings of co-operative work by men in several areas of study. Seashore's audiometer in 1897 and his testing of Iowa City school children a year later indicated greater accuracy and extended knowledge to come in both clinical practice and research. This promise was fulfilled abundantly by Bunch and Dean's pitch range audiometer in 1919, and the later phonograph audiometer resulting from the collaboration of Harvey Fletcher of the Bell Telephone Laboratories and Dr. Edmund Prince Fowler, an outstanding otologist.

The opening years of the twentieth century brought rapid changes in speech correction and considerable confusion in theories and procedures. The physiological concepts concerning stuttering were presented ably and clearly; so were the beliefs of those who tried to change poor speech habits through drill. Scientific study of the stutterer as an individual and observations of the results of therapy, however, sharply decreased the confidence formerly placed in both the physiological and elocutionary approaches to stuttering.

At this time, therefore, there was a real welcome for the introduction of the other half of the dual nature of man, "the mind." With a direct approach to the mind seeming possible, investigators held high hopes.[97] Their optimism, however, was soon tempered by the modern scientific demand for the modification of premises which fail to meet the test of observation and verification.[98] Nevertheless, conscientious students successively presented and applied the tenets of the various systems and "schools" of psychology. During these years, speech correction acquired accumulations from Structuralism, Freudianism, and Behaviorism; Social Psychology and Reflexology appeared in the post-war years with, still later, configurational and holistic theories.

Structuralism, with its concept of the division of the mind into the sub-structures of sensations, images, and affections, gave source and credence to the imagery theories. With stuttering seen as a mental phenomenon, it quite conceivably could be due to "visual center aesthenia," [99] or "transient auditory amnesia," [100] or, slightly later, "defective oratans" (i.e., defective kinaesthetic imagery).[101] Students of Freudian theory, the most optimistic of all, saw stuttering as rooted in the subconscious mind. Anxiety neurosis,[102] desire to express illicit feelings and suppress them too,[103] conflict between conscious control and unconscious fluency [104]—such theories were first advanced to suggest the significance of subconscious processes in stuttering.

Subsequently nearly all writers reflected some influence of the concepts of "inhibition," "conflict," and "ego involvements"; [105] a few used such concepts in building their theories.[106]

The influence of Behaviorism on stuttering theory was less distinct than is commonly supposed since it was essentially a method, not a school or a system of psychology. Its presentation of the monistic view, however, and its emphasis on environmental factors in determining behavior paved the way for greater attention to environmental factors and increased emphasis on conditioning and the possible rôle of laterality.

The suggestions concerning stuttering, however, were not limited to these few. Inheritance, [107] "asynergies" [108] and laterality [109] were proposed as possible causes or contributing factors. Nor was this confusion of theories lessened by later changes in both theory and description announced by some of the early contributors to the psychological view.[110]

In this interval of high hope and expanding knowledge, a number of schools or institutes were opened, on a day or residence basis, for intensive treatment of stuttering, using varying combinations of medical, psychological and elocutionary theories and remedial methods.[111] As a reflection of the current optimism rather than of growing scientific knowledge, there were even announcements of "new methods" for the self cure of stuttering at home, or by correspondence.[112]

Psychologists and physicians, however, were not the only ones active in the field of speech. Teachers of English, particularly in the public schools, were giving more attention to oral English and to deviations in articulation. The aim of their program, however, seemed limited to "speech improvement," or perhaps "betterment." An early article in the

English Journal, for example, used the word "speech" to mean good choice of words, correct grammar, and avoidance of slang.[113]

While speech correction undoubtedly was encouraged by more attention to oral English,[114] actual remedial work apparently developed from other sources. The contributions of psychologists, physicians, and educators were supported and extended by a new type of teacher of speech who was gaining familiarity with the acoustical, physiological, and psychological facts of speech production. Influential, likewise, was the simultaneous appearance of more articles by physicians and psychologists in the *Journal of the National Education Association,*[115] corrective programs in the public schools of several of the larger cities, surveys of the incidence of speech disorders in the public schools, and the establishment of university speech clinics.

Speech correction in the public schools apparently began with a New York City class in 1908, the work being prompted by the increased sense of responsibility for the handicapped which had led to the earlier establishment of "ungraded classes." Preliminary discussion of the appointment of a physician or educator to conduct the class was ended with the selection of a teacher, Dr. John F. Riegart, on the basis of his broad scientific training in speech, including the medical and pedagogical aspects.[116] Though known as a "Speech Improvement Class," [117] it included only children with speech disorders. Later the work was extended and Dr. Frederic Martin was appointed director of speech improvement in New York City in 1916, with the plan to develop a city-wide speech correction program.[118] Other cities soon followed the example if not the exact pattern of New York to establish the pattern of public school speech correction. Chicago in 1910,[119] Boston in 1912, with Detroit, San Francisco, Grand Rapids, and eight cities in Wisconsin by 1916 were early on the list.

The early years of the twentieth century likewise contained a new technique, the survey. Made by physicians, educators, and psychologists, surveys were a useful source of new data concerning the incidence of speech disorders and also a means of publicizing the need for more extensive speech correction work. Examples of the surveys conducted could well begin with Thorpe's preliminary work in 1903 and that of Conradi in 1904, and would include Ferreri in 1911, list McDonald, Blanton, Brown, and Wallin in 1916, and conclude with what was by no means the last of these pioneer surveys, Stinchfield's report on college students.[120]

Such surveys, combined with the growing attention to the need for speech correction in the sessions of the National Education Association [121] and expressed in the pages of its journals provided a sudden dissemination of information and a strong motivation for additional programs in the public-school system. It is possible, however, these public-school programs, necessarily on an operational level, might have become stagnant and routine without the extension of research and a source of adequately trained teachers provided by the university speech clinics appearing at this time.

Several of the early university speech clinics were established by psychologists with the work in speech correction considered an extension of psychological programs of retraining and rehabilitation. Scripture,[122] Twitmeyer,[123] and Martin[124] were among the pioneer psychologists to include speech correction within a clinical environment.[125] Blanton, a physician with considerable training and experience in speech[126] was appointed in 1914 by J. M. O'Neill, head of the Department of Public Speaking at the University of Wisconsin, to establish a speech clinic in this department. In the same year, 1914, Dr. Max Goldstein established the Central Institute for the Deaf in St. Louis, which made provision for hearing children with speech disorders in its second year and opened a free clinic for speech defects in 1926.[127]

Before World War I, therefore, the pattern of the university speech clinic as a teacher training and research center was established. Occasionally at the outset, and increasingly later, university clinics included education of the deaf and hard of hearing. Drawing on the resources of medicine, psychology, and speech, they set a new total educational program for the handicapped in speech and hearing.

There is real question concerning any immediate and direct effect of the war years on the work in speech and hearing. The indirect and derived influences, however, seem to have accelerated the educational development which had begun in more peaceful times. The invention and perfection of more sensitive and accurate instruments, wider areas of research, and more quantitative knowledge of the number and variety of speech and hearing disorders, and, perhaps even more, the subsequent "boom times," forced the growth of educational programs well started in earlier years.

In spite of expectations, few, if any, new remedial or teaching techniques emerged as the result of the work with service personnel.[128] In hindsight, the program seems to have been too hastily organized and sketchily administered to produce reliable clinical data. While disappointing, this situation was completely understandable in view of the limited knowledge concerning the probable case loads and an unavoidable lack of centralized professional guidance. In speech particularly, there was limited information concerning the frequency and types of disorders in the adult male population plus a marked lack of criteria for differential diagnosis. Carhart reported considerable variation in the diagnoses of both speech and hearing defects by the draft boards. The national ratio per 1000 of defects of the ear and defects of hearing was 7.69, but this ratio varied by states from 1.67 to 15.70. The number of men classified as speech defectives was relatively very small, with almost as many men reported as deaf mutes as were indicated to have defective speech. Defective speech was reported in a ratio varying from 2.3 to 0.02 per 1000 in different states. In the reports from the local draft boards cleft palate and harelip comprised almost half the total number of speech defects.[129]

Under the direction of the Surgeon General of the United States Army, the Division of Physical Reconstruction established to furnish rehabilitation service to disabled Army, Navy, and Marine personnel, included a section of Defects of Hearing and Speech, with Colonel C. W. Richardson as director. These facilities were housed in General Hospital 11, the hospital for head surgery at Cape May, New Jersey. The section was activated in July of 1918, and at the height of its service, employed ten speech reading and three speech correction teachers. Though the records are confusing, a minimum of 112 speech reading and 54 speech cases received treatment at Cape May.[130]

Colonel Richardson reports favorably on the work in both hearing and speech correction, though with percentages in one area and words in the other. Success in the speech-hearing section is reported as: Excellent, 53%; Good, 21%; Average, 14%; Fair, 6%; Poor, 6%. He further reports that "all the work in connection with speech correction has been a revelation to those who have not previously known its possibilities. It stands out as one of the most remarkable results attained by the Medical Corps in the history of the war." [131]

Better quantitative estimates of the accomplishments in speech probably are impossible. The training period was relatively short and the three speech correction aides dealt with disorders as various as aphasia, laryngeal wounds, and stuttering. Further, their services were used to teach English speech to soldiers with marked dialects and, interestingly enough, to teach illiterates to read.[132]

In the twentieth century, audiology and speech correction emerged as new professions to serve an educational concept only lately arrived. This concept found its early roots and growth in biblical times and the classic civilizations, was nourished by the basic teachings of the great religions, and came to full growth only when man's social consciousness, knowledge, and organismic concepts made possible a truly educational approach, as a public responsibility, for the handicapped in speech and hearing.

Notes

1. Exodus iv. 10-17.
2. Judges xii. 6. God instructed Moses, "Thou shalt not curse the deaf, nor put a stumbling block before the blind." Lev. xix. 14. Isaiah prophesied the curing of the deaf, lame, and blind. Isaiah xxix. 18; xxxv. 4-6; xliii. 8.
3. S. O. L. Potter, *Speech and Its Defects* (Philadelphia, 1882), pp. 41-42.
4. St. Mark vii. 32-37.
5. The desire to include perspectives and interpretations within limited pages seems to warrant the greater hazard to historical accuracy which is involved in presenting some generalizations instead of listing the historical facts in detail.
6. Cf. C. Van Riper, *Speech Correction* (New York, 1947), pp. 1-13.
7. *Ibid.*, p. 5.
8. Plato and Aristotle both mention the deaf. The latter apparently considered them practically uneducable because of the absence of the sense of hearing.
9. Obviously these are broad generalizations only, with many variations. Charity was well known long before the Christian era. The Greeks, for example, had a system of charity (sixth century, B.C.) involving emigration, supply of corn at reduced rates, and public relief. Rome provided public granaries in the third century, B.C.
10. Harry Best, *The Blind* (New York, 1919), p. 254.
11. Harry Best, *Deafness and the Deaf in the United States* (New York, 1943), pp. 374-375. For a brief description of the method, see abstract from Bede's *Ecclesiastical History*, Bk. IV, ch. 2, in E. F. Boultbee, *Help for the Deaf* (London, 1913), pp. 16-18.
12. Charles Stuart Loch, "Charity and Charities," *Encyclopaedia Britannica*, 11th ed., V, p. 876.
13. "Catholic charity is closely connected with the doctrine of poenitentia. The effect of alms giving on the soul of the donor was theoretically more important than its effect on the body of the recipient. This motive for charity did not cease with the Reformation: men have continued to give of their substance to the poor in recompense or contrition for the sin of their souls. It would hardly be possible to write about pre-Reformation philanthropy without considering this subject of motive. It is quite easy to do so for the post-Reformation period when, although this motive was still operative, it was ceasing to be explicit." B. Kirkman Gray, *A History of English Philanthropy* (London, 1905), p. vii.
14. At least one writer calls attention to the early inception of "public" in the sense of secular programs. "It becomes necessary to refute the general assertion that the church was the only charitable agency during the Middle Ages, or that charity was entirely administered by it...."
"Charity... was not merely the concern of church or monastery." Lynn Thorndike, "The Historical Background," *Intelligent Philanthropy*, ed. Ellsworth Faris, Ferris Laune, and Arthur J. Todd (Chicago, 1930), pp. 36-38.
15. With more obvious handicaps and apparent inability to learn or to perform in conventional ways, the blind and deaf received earlier and greater attention than those with speech difficulties.
16. An asylum originally for blinded Crusaders.
17. Founded by Valentin Haüy under the name, Institution Nationale des Jeunes Aveugles. Later the Société Philanthropique took the school under its patronage. Best, *The Blind*, p. 257.
18. Incorporated by the Massachusetts legislature as the New England Asylum for the Blind.
19. Accounts of earlier work consist of passing references; e.g., Rudolphus Agricola, who lived from 1443 to 1485, tells of a deaf mute who learned to read and write, but names neither the pupil nor his teacher. Girolamo Cordano, of Milan (1501-1576), believed that the education of deaf mutes was possible though

difficult, and stated the principle on which it depends. Edward Allen Fay, ed. *Histories of American Schools of the Deaf, 1817-1893* (Washington, D. C., 1893), I, p. v.

20. Best, *Deafness*, pp. 375-376.

21. The differing methods of these schools started a controversy which deeply affected the history of the teaching of the deaf in the United States as well as in Europe.

22. Best, *Deafness*, pp. 374, 379-381.

23. J. McKeen Cattell and Livingston Farrand, "Physical and Mental Measurements of the Students of Columbia University," *Psychol. Rev.*, III (1896), 618-648. (This is the first in the long line of studies using college students as more or less willing "guinea pigs.")

24. The first edition of Gray's *Anatomy* (1858) contained 750 pages and 353 illustrations; the 1948 edition, over 1400 pages and 1200 illustrations. *Psychological Index*, Volume I, listed 1312 articles; *Psychological Abstracts* for 1952 lists over 7000.

25. The Quantum Theory, 1900; the "smashing of the atom," 1919; Special Relativity, 1905; General Relativity, 1915.

26. Francis Galton, *Hereditary Genius* (London, 1869). Though Galton's interest seems to have grown out of Darwinism rather than psychology, his book greatly influenced the latter field.

27. Notably, Harald Höffding, *Outline of Psychology* (London, 1891).

28. Titchener coined the terms "structural" and "functional" to describe the two divergent views of the mind. See "Structural and Functional Psychology," *Philos. Rev.*, VIII (1899), 290-299.

29. "Field Theory" is illustrated in the physical sciences by Kepler's laws of planetary motion, Galileo's law of freely falling bodies, and their integration by Newton into the law of gravitation. For applications in psychology, see J. R. Kantor, "Current Trends in Psychological Theory," *Psychol. Bull.*, XXXVIII (1941), 31-38; also Kantor, "The Nature of Psychology as a Natural Science," *Acta Psychol.*, IV (1938), 1-61.

30. John B. Watson, "Psychology as a Behaviorist Views It," *Psychol. Rev.*, XX (1913), 158-177.

31. Max Wertheimer, "Experimentelle Studien über das Sehen von Bewegungen," *Zeitschrift für Psychologie*, LXI (1912), 161-265.

32. Jean Jacques Rousseau, *Emile* (Paris, 1762).

33. Rhetoric was included in the earliest educational programs. The first laws of Harvard College (1643) made provision for rhetorical study and practice; rhetoric (of Latin) was required in the courses of the colleges founded before 1730. The Spy Club for student speaking was founded at Harvard in 1719. English declamation was introduced at Yale in 1751; Pennsylvania had a Professor of English and Oratory as early as 1753; at Brown the laws made special provision for declamation and oratory in 1774. See Warren A. Guthrie, "The Development of Rhetorical Theory in America, 1635-1850," unpublished Ph.D. dissertation, Northwestern, 1940, pp. 28, 30, 76, 77-78.

34. Massachusetts in 1639 and Pennsylvania in 1685 were the leaders. The first spelling book bears the date of 1643 and the *New England Primer* appeared sometime between 1687 and 1690. R. Aiken, of Philadelphia, printed Burgh's *Art of Speaking* in 1775. This is listed as "fourth edition," but no earlier U.S. publication is discoverable. It was first published in London in 1761.

35. *Vox Oculis Subjecta—A Dissertation on the Most Curious and Important Art of Imparting Speech, and the Knowledge of Language, to the Naturally Deaf (Consequently) Dumb, with a Particular Account of the Academy of Messers Braidwood at Edinborough (by a Parent)* (London, 1783). (Green's deaf son had been a pupil at the Braidwood school.) This publication was reprinted in 1897 by the Boston Parents' Association for Deaf Children.

36. William Thornton, "Cadmus: A Treatise on the Elements of Written Language," with an appendix, "Essay on the Mode of Teaching the Deaf, or Surd, and Consequently Dumb, to Speak," *Transactions of the Am. Philos. Society*, III (1793).

37. For a comprehensive account of the literature of stuttering for the first half of the nineteenth century and earlier, see Pearl Bryant, "Speech Re-education in the Nineteenth Century," unpublished Ph.D. dissertation, Northwestern, 1941.

38. First named the New York Institute for the Instruction of the Deaf and Dumb and later the New York School for the Deaf. Best, *Deafness*, pp. 388-389, and Fay, *op. cit.*, I, x.

39. Whether the causes lay in the man or the circumstances, this is an unique record of five locations in as many years. There is some reason to believe that his presence in this country and his short-lived ventures contributed to the delay in the use of oral methods.

40. In fact, the first for any of the so-called "defective groups."

41. The present Gallaudet College in Washington, D.C., founded in 1864 as the National Deaf-Mute College, was named for him in 1893.

42. As noted above, John Braidwood was in the United States at this time. Fay states that the Braidwood family wished to establish a monopoly on the oral method in America as well as in Europe, and placed obstacles in Gallaudet's way. (*Op. cit.*, I, x.)

43. Job Williams, "The American Asylum," in Fay, *op. cit.*, I, 9-14.

44. The same day its predecessor at Hartford opened its doors.

45. Fay, *op. cit.*, I and III. The listing in these *Histories* of only eighteen denominational and private schools in this period (1817-1893) indicates the preponderance of public education.

46. At Chelmsford, Mass., in 1866. In 1867, with a liberal endowment, it moved to Northampton and was incorporated as the Clarke School for the Deaf. Gardiner Hubbard, first president of the Clarke School, reports the first attempt to obtain a charter for an oral school (1864) was opposed "by the friends of the American Asylum, on the ground that it was a visionary project and attempting the impossible." See his "Address" in Fay, *op. cit.*, II, 3-4.

47. The atomistic view tended to favor those methods of instruction using the smallest and most specific units. Furthermore, speech, viewed as an end-product separated from real education, could appear only as a desirable but not particularly necessary "extra" in the acquisition of language and the development of the mind.

48. Apparently its dramatic symptoms and occasional "cures" gave stuttering a place in the early medical and physiological literatures out of all proportion to its incidence. The student can only surmise concerning the work done by elocutionists, teachers, and the clergy, whose lay efforts were not reported in the relatively few technical journals.

49. In the absence of controlled observations, few limitations were placed on the nature of recommended methods or on the claims for their success.

50. J. Edward Warren, "Remarks on Stammering," *American Journal of Medical Science* (1837), p. 84.

51. Article "Athenaeum" gives some indication. Quoted by Lucille D. Schoolfield, "The Development of Speech Correction in America in the Nineteenth Century," *QJS*, XXIV (1938), 106-107.

52. Bryant, *op. cit.*, p. 61.

53. For a discussion of the development and events of this short era see Gray Burdin, "The Surgical Treatment of Stammering," *Journal of Speech and Hearing Disorders*, V (1940), 43-64.

54. In Berlin, by the middle of April, surgeons had operated on sixty patients; nearly two hundred were recorded in France within a year; on April 30, 1841, Yearsley of England reported on three hundred operations in five months.

55. Schoolfield, *op. cit.*, pp. 109-110.

56. *Ibid.*, p. 110.

57. The last systematic development of this point of view was the doctrine of "instincts," an explanatory concept which failed to meet the test of observations reported by psychologists (Dunlap, 1918-1919, Kantor, 1920, and Kuo, 1921), and economists and sociologists (Ogburn, 1923 and Bernard, 1924).

58. The rôle of experience and learning in determining the nature and performance of the individual was given additional emphasis by the work of the geneticists.

59. His first kindergarten, 1837.

60. Secretary of the Massachusetts Board of Education, his lectures and writings were strongly influential in the development of free public education in America. He established the first normal school in 1839, and in 1853 was elected the first president of Antioch College. The modern nature of his beliefs was demonstrated again when he made this college both coeducational and non-sectarian.

61. Professor of philosophy at the universities of Minnesota, Michigan, Chicago, Peking, and Columbia; consultant in the reorganization of the Turkish national school system. As Director of the School of Education at the University of Chicago he was noted for his educational principles and for his reforms in the public schools of Chicago.

62. Comparisons between the various years are apt to be confusing due to the varying bases of classification of the population. During the years in which comparisons are possible, however, the percentage of the population between the ages of five and seventeen enrolled in school rose steadily from 57% in 1870 to 68.6% in 1900, and 77.8% in 1920. U.S. Department of Commerce, Bureau of the Census, *Statistical Abstract of the United States,* 73rd ed. (Washington, 1952), p. 115.

63. Suggested reasons include a settled belief in the value of education, growth in urban populations, and the increase in available time accruing from mechanization and higher productivity in industry and agriculture. These reasons, however, may have had more influence on secondary and college enrollments.

64. Though child labor was opposed with increasing vigor and effectiveness from the days of the Civil War, this opposition was not reflected in permanent legislation. The first national law, passed in 1916, was declared unconstitutional. Legislation in 1918 proposing to tax the employers of child labor met the same fate. In 1924, Congress asked for a Constitutional amendment, but the states refused to ratify.

65. Arch O. Heck, "Compulsory Education," in *Encyclopedia of Educational Research,* ed. Walter S. Monroe (New York, 1950), pp. 290-300.

66. Its Department of Special Education, including instructors of the deaf, blind, and feebleminded, was organized in 1897.

67. First called the National Congress of Mothers.

68. This 1890 incorporation was preceded by earlier meetings beginning in 1874.

69. Somewhat later the name was again changed to the National Association for the Advancement of the Speech Arts and, finally in 1906, to the National Speech Arts Association, the title usually used to refer to the organization throughout its life.

70. Edited by Edgar S. Werner and devoted to voice and speech with considerable attention to stammering, it may well be considered the first speech correction journal. Its name was changed to *Werner's Magazine* in 1889; its last issue appeared in 1892.

71. Numerous and shorter lived publications appeared during this period and earlier. *The American Annals of Education,* e.g., began in 1826, merged with the *Education Weekly Reporter and Lyceum* in 1830, but suspended publication in 1839.

72. *The Proceedings of the N.E.A., 1857-1906* were indexed in 1907; the *Education Index* began in 1930.

73. *A New Elucidation of the Principles of Speech and Elocution* (Edinburgh, 1849); *Observations on Defects of Speech and Cure of Stammering and Principles*

of Elocution (New York, 1853); *Standard Elocutionist* (Edinburgh, 1860), with his brother, David C. Bell as co-author.

74. He continued his instruction here until the discontinuation of the College of Oratory in 1880. Schoolfield, *op. cit.*, p. 113, describes his courses as "Culture of the Speaking Voice," "Mechanism of Speech," "Visible Speech," and "Methods of Instructing Deaf Mutes in Articulation."

75. His inventions included not only the telephone (1876) but also the photo-phone, an apparatus by which sound could be transmitted 250 yards on a beam of light (never developed commercially), a graphophone which for the first time used wax records, an induction balance, and a telephone probe for bullet wounds.

76. Later benefactions increased his endowment to approximately a quarter million dollars.

77. This laboratory was so named because it had been established with the 50,000 francs of the Volta Prize. This award, established originally by Napoleon, was awarded to Bell for his invention of the telephone.

It might be observed, not entirely facetiously, that had Bell been a physicist instead of a teacher of speech he might never have invented the telephone; he would have known it was impossible.

78. Fay, *op. cit.*

79. In the interests of completeness mention should be made of the founding, in 1893, in Philadelphia, of the Garrett Home School for Little Children Before They Are of School Age, which admitted children at the age of two.

80. With perhaps ten starting prior to 1890, there were at least forty by the end of the century, and nearly eighty by 1920. Best, *Deafness,* p. 454.

81. Additional support for these schools came from the advocates of the oral method of instruction. Following the opening of the Horace Mann School with the oral method, the extension of the day school system became a focus for the rising protest against the non-oral methods which seemed to some to be fixed immovably in the residential schools.

82. The New York Institution for the Instruction of the Deaf and Dumb, for example, used it for some ten years before deciding to adopt what seemed then to be more successful techniques.

83. Bell's endowment increased considerably the resources and influence of this organization.

84. From the educational view of this study, the growth of speech correction is seen within the framework of speech; i.e., the speech correctionist is a teacher of speech with appropriate knowledge from medicine and psychology rather than a physician or psychologist turned to an interest in speech training.

85. Guthrie, *op. cit.*, pp. 232, 236.

86. John Mason, *Essay on Elocution* (London, 1748).

87. Barnett Baskerville, "A Study of American Criticism of Public Address, 1850-1900," unpublished Ph.D. dissertation, Northwestern, 1948, pp. 311, 318.

88. In terms of percentages of students participating in the exercises, the height of speech activities in American colleges and universities apparently occurred in the years 1840-1860, with intercollegiate debate and oratory continuing the emphasis on skill in speaking. Harold Monroe Jordan, "Rhetorical Education in American Colleges and Universities, 1850-1915," unpublished Ph.D. dissertation, Northwestern, 1952, p. 339.

89. There is some tendency among students of the history of speech education to see the "mechanics school" as the cause of the decline of elocution. There is much in this study to indicate more than the influence of one school, namely, the view of speech structured by the psychological theory of the time as a form of expression, a possible addition to, but not a part of, general learning and education.

90. Bryant, *op. cit.*, p. 280, reports 1820 as the date of the first appearance of published remedial procedures.

91. The 1840's had seen sharp and open conflicts between the physicians and elocutionists, particularly in England. See Bryant, *op. cit.*, p. 23.

92. Harriet Montague, "Lip Reading—A Continuing Necessity," *Jl. Sp. Dis.*, VIII (1943), 259.

93. Though there is no discoverable record of his prior use of lip reading in his teaching, his subsequent publications and activities clearly show his enthusiasm for its values and possibilities. See Montague, *op. cit.*, p. 260.

94. Warren H. Gardner, "History and Present Status of the Education of the Hard of Hearing," *Jl. Sp. Dis.*, VIII (1943), 228.

95. The arguments of the proponents of the oral method certainly were not strengthened by the existence of different methods of teaching lip reading. Bruhn and Nitchie used different systems; Cora Kinzie, of Philadelphia, announced a third in 1917. The Jena method was introduced in 1926.

96. Gardner, *op. cit.*, p. 228.

97. This "mental aspect" brought a wave of optimism concerning the cure for stammering that seems not to have been equaled elsewhere in the field of speech, though something of the same enthusiasm had prevailed in the work in hearing three-quarters of a century earlier.

98. "Notes," *QJSE*, VI (1920), 87, relates that the 1920 meeting of the Eastern Public Speaking Conference was enlivened by a challenge issued by Erastus Palmer, College of the City of New York, for anyone to cite a single instance of a stammerer who had been corrected and had stayed corrected for more than six months when not under the direct influence of his teacher. Apparently no one accepted the challenge for four years later "Editorial" commented, "He is still waiting. Is nobody going to take him up?" *QJSE*, X (1924), 271.

99. Walter B. Swift, "A Psychological Analysis of Stuttering," *Studies in Abnormal Psychology*, Series VI (1916), 225-235; and "The Developmental Psychology of Stuttering," *Studies in Abnormal Psychology*, Series VII (1917), 258-264.

100. Charles S. Bluemel, *Stammering and Cognate Defects of Speech* (New York, 1913).

101. Edwin B. Twitmeyer, unpublished lectures, 1930.

102. Edward W. Scripture, *Stuttering and Lisping* (New York, 1912).

103. Isadore H. Coriat, "Stammering as a Psychoneurosis," *Jl. Abn. Psychol.*, IX (1914-1915), 417-429.

104. Ernest Tompkins, "Stammering and Its Extirpation," *Pediatrics Sem.*, XXIII (1916), 153-174.

105. V. "A Symposium on Stuttering (Stammering," ed. Robert West, *Proc. Am. Soc. for the Study of Disorders of Speech*, I (1931).

106. E.g., Blanton.

107. Frank A. Bryant, "Influence of Heredity in Stammering," *Jl. of Heredity*, VIII (1917), 47.

108. J. M. Fletcher, "An Experimental Study of Stuttering," *Am. Jl. Psychol.*, XXIX (1913), 201-255.

109. P. B. Ballard, "Sinistrality and Speech," *Jl. Exp. Pediatrics*, I (1911), 298-310.

110. Fletcher, Bluemel, Blanton, as well as others, progressively modified their views.

111. Frank Augustus Bryant, *How Stammering May be Cured* (New York, 1890), "Details of the system used by the principal of the Bryant School for Stammerers"; *Some Speech Disorders and Their Treatment, Together with an Outline of the Methods Used in the Bryant School for Stammerers* (New York, 1913); *Questions and Answers About Stammering, Together with an Outline of the Methods Used in the New York School for Stammerers* (New York, 1916); Frank A. Reed, *The Reed Method for the Cure of Stammering* (Detroit, 1902); Samuel D. Robbins, *How to Stop Stammering* (Boston, 1921): "A discussion of stammering, its causes, effects, and correction, as embodied in the courses of private instruction for the correction of stammering as offered by the Boston Stammerers' Institute."

112. George Andrew Lewis, *Home Cure for Stammerers* (Detroit, 1907); E. R. Carswell, *Cause and Cure of Stammering and All Other Speech Defects; A Manual for School and Class Use and for Use in Correspondence Courses* . . . (Chicago, 1912).

113. Mary A. G. Mitchell, "Wanted: A Higher Standard of Speech," *English Journal*, I (1912), 284-286.

114. The Speech Improvement Weeks observed in the secondary schools, beginning late in 1915, grew out of a resolution to appoint a committee on speech training presented by John M. Clapp and adopted by the National Council of Teachers of English at its fourth annual meeting, November, 1914. "The NCTE," *Eng. Jl.*, IV (1915), 47-49.

115. The NEA did not include speech cases in its department for exceptional children established in 1907.

116. Dorothy Gertrude Kester, "The Development of Speech Correction in Organizations and in Schools in the United States during the First Quarter of the Twentieth Century," unpublished Ph.D. dissertation, Northwestern, 1950, pp. 192-193.

117. So named because he wished " 'to select a characterization that would indicate the class, not by its present status, but by its aim.' " Kester, p. 193.

118. Kester, p. 343.

119. Ten teachers in 1910, reduced to four for the next year, ". . . the assumption being that the number of children needing special attention had been reduced sufficiently to make ten teachers unnecessary but it has been found necessary to reinstate the original numbers!" Ella Flagg Young, *Annual Report of the Superintendent of Schools,* Chicago (1911). Quoted in Kester, p. 346.

120. Eliza J. Ellery Thorpe, "What Teachers Need to Know about Speech Impediments," *Jl. of N. E. A.,* XLII (1903), 1031-1036.

Edward Conradi, "Speech Defects and Intellectual Progress," *Jl. Ed. Psychol.,* III (1912), 35-38; 87,400 children in six cities—Kansas City, Milwaukee, Cleveland, Louisville, Albany, and Springfield (Mass.)—showed defects.

Giulio Ferreri, "Defects of Speech among Primary Pupils," *Volta Review,* XIII (1911), 31-33. In New York City, "a study of speech conditions in our public schools shows that 200,000 of the 800,000 children are affected with stuttering and speech defects." D. J. McDonald, *Addresses and Proceedings of the N. E. A.* (1916), p. 863.

Smiley Blanton, "A Survey of Speech Defects," *Jl. Ed. Psychol.,* VII (1916), 581-582, Madison, Wis.; Grace T. Brown, "Report of Corrective Speech Work in the Rochester Public Schools," *Volta Review,* XVIII (1916), 143-144; John Edward Wallace Wallin, "A Census of Speech Defects," *School and Society,* III (1916), 213-216, St. Louis; Sara M. Stinchfield, "Report on a Study of Speech Problems at Mount Holyoke College," *American Speech,* II, 148-152.

121. In 1900 a department of the deaf was represented by reports to the convention; stammering was added to the list of exceptional children in 1915.

122. Brill dates his interest in speech from his work with E. W. Scripture at the Vanderbilt Clinic, College of Physicians and Surgeons, Columbia University in 1908. (A. A. Brill, "Speech Disturbances in Nervous and Mental Diseases," *QJSE,* IX (1923), 129.) Mrs. Scripture reports 4,000 cases treated during the year 1915-1916. ("The Treatment of Speech Defects," *QJSE,* VI (1920), 1-16.)

123. Edwin Burkett Twitmeyer, Instructor in Psychology, University of Pennsylvania, 1914. Founded Clinic for Corrective Speech at University of Pennsylvania, 1914. (David J. Goodfriend, "News and Announcements," *Jl. Sp. Dis.,* VIII (1943), 185.)

124. He was director of the Psychological Clinic for Defective Speech at City College of the City of New York in 1915. "News and Notes," *Eng. Jl.,* V (1916), 141.

125. Credit for an earlier clinic should be given to Dr. G. Hudson Makeun, who was elected Professor of Defects of Speech in the Polyclinic Hospital and College

for Graduates in Medicine of the University of Pennsylvania in 1897. Mary Summers Steel, "How G. Hudson Makeun Treated Stammering," *Proc. Am. Soc. for the Study of the Dis. of Speech,* I (1931), 20. For his own report, see "Two Hundred Cases of Speech Defects at the Philadelphia Polyclinic Hospital," *Pa. Med. Jl.,* I (1897), 247-250.

The National Hospital for Speech Disorders established by Dr. James Sonnet Green seems to have been a more highly specialized institution. James Sonnet Green, "Releasing the Tongues of Men: How Speech Defects are Successfully Cured at a Free Medical Clinic for their Treatment," *Survey,* XLI (1918), 65-67; and "A Departure in Hospitals: The National Hospital for Speech Disorders," *Jl. Am. Med. Assn.,* LXXVII (1921), 1726-1728.

126. Blanton was a graduate of the Curry School, the Howard Theatre School in Boston, and Vanderbilt University, and the founder of the Cornell Dramatic Club. As an instructor at Cornell University his interest in speech led him to enroll in the Cornell Medical College for further study of the disorders of speech. He held the M. D. degree at the time of his appointment to Wisconsin. Kester, *op. cit.,* p. 279.

127. Mildred A. McGinnis, "Max A. Goldstein, M.D., L.L.D.," *Jl. Sp. Dis.,* VIII (1943), 208.

128. In the light of later events, this program may well be regarded as a "pilot study."

129. Raymond Carhart, "Some Notes on Official Statistics of Speech Disorders Encountered during World War I," *Jl. Sp. Dis.,* VIII (1943), 98-99.

130. *Ibid.,* p. 103.

131. C. W. Richardson, "Organization of Section of Defects of Hearing and Speech, Division of Physical Reconstruction, Surgeon General's Office," *Annals Otology, Rhinology, and Laryngology,* XXVIII (1919), 443.

132. Carhart, *op. cit.,* p. 105.

19   Some Teachers and the Transition to Twentieth-Century Speech Education

GILES WILKESON GRAY

....

The three decades from 1890 to 1920 were a period of transition in the development of American speech education. The changes that were taking place in these thirty years were perhaps more profound than in any other similar period since the founding of the first colonial schools. It was during these years that all the various aspects of oral communication were drawn together and integrated, under the common rubric of *speech*, into the beginnings of our present profession. Rhetoric, which for centuries had been thought of essentially as a matter of either style or literary criticism,[1] was by 1920 restored to its place as a substantial body of principles governing both oral and written discourse.

Work on the drama, heretofore primarily an extracurricular activity, was brought back into the classroom and given a prominent place in the speech curriculum. Delivery was elevated from the mechanized systems growing out of the philosophies of Diderot, Engel, Walker, Austin, Rush, and Delsarte, and made an integral aspect of the study of speech. *Pronuntiatio* again became the fifth canon of rhetoric.

In the oral reading of literature the mechanical, artificial, and exaggerated elocution of the nineteenth century was abandoned for the more rational and restrained interpretation of the twentieth. During these three decades, also, the first university clinic for both the correction of speech disorders and the training of competent therapists was established.

Before the close of the period speech finally became recognized as a dignified academic subject in itself. Courses had been offered for decades for the same credit as was given for other subjects; Chamberlain reported [2] that in one school elocution had "held a recognized place in the curriculum" for seventy-eight years; in another, sixty years; in one, "from the beginning"; in another, thirty years, and in still others, twenty-six and forty years. That courses in rhetoric (speaking) had been offered for generations is so well known as to call for no comment. By 1920 there were very few colleges or universities that were not offering at least a few courses, many of them permitting undergraduate majors, and a few even advanced work beyond the Bachelor of Arts degree. On April 28, 1911, more than sixty secondary school teachers of speech attended a conference at Swarthmore, called by Professor Paul M. Pearson.[3]

The academic independence of the field of speech was particularly marked by the establishment of autonomous departments throughout the country. These had in fact existed since 1841 and probably earlier; [4] by 1893-1894 fifty-two schools replying to an inquiry reported separate establishments. But such departments as the one at De Pauw in 1884, at Earlham in 1887, Cornell University in 1889,[5] Michigan and Chicago in 1892, Ohio Wesleyan in 1894, gave an impetus to the further setting up of similar ones elsewhere. Independent growth was, however, much more than the result of academic recognition already achieved; it engendered a still higher respect for the subject, with one result being the organization of graduate programs on a full scale at many of the major universities of the country.[6] It was only two years after the close of the period under discussion that the first doctorate in speech was granted.

Further evidence of academic independence may be observed in the professional associations that were founded during these three decades. Although there were scores of such organizations, mostly of local interest, three at least of national scope deserve mention. The National Association of Elocutionists, the first of the three, was established in 1892 and disbanded in 1916. To this organization belonged many men and women of high prominence in the field of speech. In 1910 the Public Speaking Conference of the New England and the North Atlantic States, commonly known as the Eastern Public Speaking Conference, was founded. It is still strong as the Speech Association of the Eastern States. The present Speech Association of America was organized in 1914 as the National Association of Academic Teachers of Public Speaking. It drew from the Speech Arts Association (the name adopted by the Elocutionists in 1905), according to Trueblood, "a lot of strength in numbers and activity." [7] The second and third of these three organizations particularly were founded on the basis of a profound belief in the essential integrity of the field of speech as a dignified, academic discipline in its own right.

Speaking contests had been known since the time of the Grecian Olympics; but during the three decades from 1890 to 1920 they became if possible more popular than ever. In December, 1911, Paul M. Pearson listed more than forty contest associations, with no suggestion that the list was complete.[8] Students from rival colleges had held debates since 1881;[9] but it was eleven years (1892) before a formal intercollegiate debate was held, and nine more (1901) before the nature of contest debating was clearly stated.[10] By 1920 the ensuing controversy had resulted in a full development of the principles involved; moreover, the function of the judge in a debate was established, and the patterns of present-day contest debating largely determined.

The changes that were taking place in American speech education are revealed, finally, in the character of the textbooks that were written and studied. Prior to 1890 there were no texts in interpretation as such; there was, however, a surfeit of books on elocution, a quite different thing. The writings on rhetoric were concerned with the written forms of communication, with little or no attention to the spoken word. Writers on rhetoric had forgotten that there were five canons originally, and having omitted *pronuntiatio* from their theory, they omitted with it the basis of any distinction between oral and written discourse. But by the end of the three decades Baker had written his *Principles of Argumentation*,[11] Laycock and Scales their *Argumentation and Debate*,[12] Foster his *Argumentation and Debating*,[13] Clark his *Interpretation of the Printed Page*,[14] Phillips his *Effective Speaking*,[15] Winans his *Public Speaking*,[16] and Woolbert his *Fundamentals of Speech*.[17] Scripture at Yale had published voluminously in the field of experimental phonetics,[18] Browne and Behnke their series of twelve articles on "Voice, Song, and Speech,"[19] and Alexander Graham Bell his *Mechanism of Speech*.[20]

In summary, then, the field of speech up to 1890 had been for the most part disorganized, and in the hands of the professional elocutionists, who apparently had no concept of the educational values in the subject. Rhetoric was essentially concerned with writing; and other aspects of speech were either neglected or unknown entirely. By the end of the three decades the professional organizations were taken over by academic teachers, not of elocution, nor entirely of public speaking, but of speech. The teaching of speech had moved from the itinerant elocutionist and the private schools, interested in public performance as a form of entertainment, to the high schools, the colleges, and the universities, and had become a respected academic discipline with a status equal to that of any other subject in the curriculum.

The thirty years were a period of transition and of integration. Will it be said that by the end of the next thirty years a period of disintegration had set in?

I

Even to mention all those who are known to have contributed, many of them in no small measure, to the development that took place during these three decades would obviously be impossible. But it is not unreasonable to expect that any account of the changes from 1890 to 1920 must inevitably include the names of a few without whose contributions those changes might not have taken place when they did, if at all. The available evidence indicates that these few were among the leaders, the pioneers in their respective fields, to whom their successors owe a profound obligation. Since it was in the colleges and universities that speech became more and more a genuinely educational discipline, this discussion is perforce limited to those who were specifically in the academic field.

In considering the rise of the academic teaching of speech during these three decades, one inevitably thinks of the name of Thomas Clarkson Trueblood of the University of Michigan. He was one of the few to begin his teaching career before the opening of the period, and to continue actively until well after its close.

Leaving Earlham College in 1878, he went to Jacksonville, Illinois, where he studied for a time with S. S. Hamill. While there he met and formed lifelong friendships with William Jennings Bryan and Robert Irving Fulton, the latter his collaborator in the writing of all their books. Later he went east and studied two summers with James E. Murdoch; he also had work with the Amherst rhetorician, Genung. In 1889, after some years with Fulton as itinerant teachers of elocution, and in their own school of oratory at Kansas City, he received an appointment in the Department of English at the University of Michigan. Three years later he was made full professor and head of the new Department of Elocution and Oratory, a position which he held until his retirement in 1926.

The first addition to his staff was not made until 1903-1904, when Merlin Ludlow Wiley was appointed Assistant in Elocution. In 1906-1907 R. D. T. Hollister was added. By the end of the year 1919-1920 he had seen his department grow from a program of three courses each semester to more than a dozen, and his staff included four persons besides himself. Whereas he had started by teaching Elocution, The Study of Great Orators, Shakespearean Readings, and Oral Discussions, by 1920 Elocution had become "Principles of Expression"; he had added courses in extempore speaking, advanced public speaking, debating, story telling, interpretive reading, play production, the theory of expression, speech correction, the oral reading of Tennyson and of Browning, and oral English.

He was instrumental in the founding of the National Association of Elocutionists in 1892, and was active in that organization until it disbanded in 1915. Although he himself taught elocution, he led the fight in 1905 to change the name of the Association. It was not elocution that was being repudiated, he pointed out: "most of us are ashamed of the 'ist'." One is led to the conclusion that Trueblood, a teacher of elocution, was not an elocutionist.

Two contributions seem to stand out above the general level of speech training of his time. In the first place, elocution was to him a quite different matter from reading, even public reading. He was both a teacher of elocution and an effective public reader; but he was not an elocutionist. He had grasped what few of his colleagues had been able to comprehend: that a wide gap exists between elocution as delivery of spoken discourse and elocution as an art form. To him elocution was a matter of delivery—of the use of the voice and body most effectively in speech, whether in reading or in original speaking. It was elocution as John Mason had used the term in 1748; as Thomas Sheridan had used it in 1762, and John Walker in 1781. It was the *pronuntiatio* of classical rhetoric, extended to include reading as well as speaking. The elocutionist, on the other hand, was a professional reader, usually in the exaggerated manner which grew out of the misinterpretation of the philosophies of Austin, Rush, or Delsarte. Trueblood himself was an adherent, through the teaching of Murdoch, to the theories of Rush, which, contrary to commonly held beliefs, were in his thinking anything but mechanical. At the same time, he was able to recognize the possible contribution of Delsarte. In his own teaching he drew from both: it took both, he said, to make a complete system of elocution.[21]

Elocution, then, meant to him delivery, whether of speaking or reading. The elocutionist as such was an anomaly—a practitioner, in theory, of the art of delivery: a sort of verbal Cheshire cat. Elocution was an essential part of interpretation, but it was only a part. The elocutionists themselves never saw that they were committing the error of taking the part for the whole. In Trueblood's thinking, reading was one thing; elocution was quite another. Both could be good, if neither was taken for the other.

The distinction which he made between elocution and reading was carried out in his departmental offerings. From 1892 to 1919 he offered courses in elocution—"the delivery of short extracts from masterpieces of orators." In his first year he also had a course in Shakespearean Readings, distinct from the course, Elocution. In 1910-1911 Hollister was teaching both Elocution and Interpretive Reading. The latter was continued throughout the entire period under discussion, but Elocution became "Principles of Expression," likewise a course in the principles of delivery, the use of the body and voice in speech.

It was not the teaching of Trueblood and of those who taught the same principles as he did, that brought elocution into disrepute. He held on to the term much longer than most academic teachers, for the simple reason that he felt that no term had yet been found that could quite take its place, to refer to the ancient Fifth Canon of rhetoric.

Trueblood's second major contribution to the teaching of speech consisted in his attitude toward academic standards. From the first days of his teaching he was insisting on the highest attainable standards. "... it is the duty of everyone in the profession," he was arguing as early as 1892, "to urge upon his students to get as much of a liberal education as is possible for them to acquire. ... We cannot have the standard too high." [22] "We must appreciate the necessity of education and general culture to the members of our profession," he said on another occasion; "we must also raise requirements for admission and strengthen our courses for graduation." [23] Never did he weaken in his insistence on the maintenance of the highest standards for the profession.

Although he started out as a teacher of elocution, and never lost his contact with it, he also developed strong interests in debating and oratory. He was influential in founding the Northern Oratorical League in 1890; his students proceeded to win seven of the first eight contests. In 1896 he read a paper on "Qualifications of the Orator"; [24] three years later he gave a paper on "The Educational Values of Sound Training in Public Speaking"; [25] and in 1911 he was writing on "Coaching a Debate Team." [26]

He was never able to understand why the seventeen founders of the present Speech Association of America could not have worked through the Speech Arts Association, in which he had been so active since its founding in 1892. Winans probably expressed the difficulty adequately when he said, "... it had little to offer to the teacher of public speaking, since its chief interest was entertainment." [27] Despite the fact that there were in the older organization many members, including Trueblood, whose interests were academic, and who emphasized the educational rather than the entertainment aspects of speech, Winans' evaluation was, on the whole, probably just.

II

Another famous teacher whose career more than spanned the thirty years from 1890 to 1920 was George Pierce Baker of Harvard University, later of Yale. He had been graduated from Harvard in 1887, and two years later received an appointment to the faculty in the Department of English, teaching forensics. The following year, however, he was teaching argumentative composition, and had taken over from Barrett Wendell the course in The Drama (Exclusive of Shakespeare) from the Miracle Plays to the Closing of the Theatres. In 1895-1896 he was elevated to an Assistant Professorship, was conducting courses in forensics and debating, as well as in dramatic history, and had published his *Principles of Argumentation,* the first modern textbook on the subject.

His earliest reputation was earned as a teacher of argumentation and debating, and of public speaking. The course in Forms of Public Address, which he introduced in 1900-1901, he continued to teach almost as long as he was connected with the work in public speaking. He believed intensely in the educational value of debating, and in what he termed "public discourse." [28] But debating, as he pointed out in 1901, was not "the most important part of our training in public discourse"; it was only a part of a larger whole. ". . . the teacher who insists that intercollegiate debating is simply a subdivision of a subdivision (oral discussion) of a larger field (public discourse) is the man who sees the truth." [29]

Several years before Theodore Roosevelt challenged the morality of requiring debaters to argue against their own personal convictions, Baker had encountered the problem, and in the article quoted here had disposed of it neatly and with dispatch. There is, he insisted, a great difference between teaching debating as training for persuasive argumentation, and coaching a team for the purpose of winning contests.[30]

According to Foster, himself the author of an excellent text on argumentation and debating, which in its several editions has been in use for more than forty years, "the first man to develop systematic courses of instruction in argumentation and debating was Professor George Pierce Baker of Harvard University. To his pioneer work all later books on these subjects seem much indebted." [31] His theories in this area of public discourse were, of course, incorporated into his textbook, *Principles of Argumentation.*

In 1900 he introduced his second course in dramatic history, The Drama in England from 1642 to 1900, which he continued to teach intermittently as long as he was in Cambridge. Although it was still some years before he abandoned the field of public discourse, his interest in the drama apparently overtook that in debating and public speaking. In 1905, the year he was elevated to a full professorship, he offered for the first time his English 47, which was destined to be "the most celebrated academic course in America." [32]

"English 47, English Composition.—The Technique of the Drama.

Lectures and Practice," was a course in playwriting, exclusively for graduate students. With the exception of two or three scattered years, when he was on leave, this course was offered every year at Harvard until 1923-1924. In 1916 he introduced his 47a, an advanced course in The Technique of the Drama. Along with his two courses in dramatic history, both 47 and 47a were "omitted" in 1924-1925; and although the first two of these were revived a year or so later, neither the 47 nor the 47a ever again appeared in a Harvard Catalogue.

Baker's course in playwriting, English 47, grew in popularity. It drew many students who later became famous playwrights. By 1911 Percy MacKaye could say, "Today, the study of the drama is more concentratedly alive at Harvard than at any other spot in America. . . ." [33] But though the students might write their plays, they had no certain way of knowing whether they were good drama or not. The test of good drama is audience response to an actual production. Baker "realized the necessity of studying dramatic technique in connection with the practical problems of production." [34] In 1912, therefore, he set up his 47 Workshop, "to meet a need steadily more evident in the course in dramatic composition." [35]

The 47 Workshop was in no sense a course, and no credit for the work was ever given toward a degree at Harvard. It savored too much of a technical course, which apparently did not fit into the Cambridge scheme. It was essentially a producing and acting company, to which anyone might be admitted who could meet rather rigid requirements. The main purpose of the organization was "to try out interesting plays written in the course in Dramatic Technique at Harvard University and Radcliffe College." [36]

It would be difficult to overestimate the contribution which Baker made to education in general, and to the development of the educational theatre in particular. He "brought writing for the stage into the educational field as a subject of practical instruction and greatly stimulated the 'little theatre' movement, then in its infancy." [37]

Although Baker initiated instruction in playwriting and although his 47 Workshop was undoubtedly the most famous university producing organization, it cannot be said that he first introduced dramatic (stage) technique into the college curriculum, or was responsible for its being introduced. It is difficult, often impossible, to fix upon either the institution or the date where and when the first of any kind of instruction was given. Percy MacKaye always felt that the lectures which his father gave at Harvard in 1881, and later at Cornell, Rochester, Syracuse, and elsewhere, were the original impetus that culminated in the introduction of such work, especially at Harvard.[38] Any such influence is certain to be nebulous. There is evidence that at the University of North

Dakota as early as 1905-1906 Frederick H. Koch was teaching the Elizabethan drama through "a dramatic rendering of scenes from these plays" as an "important feature of the work." [39] Similarly, at DePauw University in 1910 Harry Bainbridge Gough was assigning parts in the plays of Shakespeare in his Courses 5 and 6; and at Swarthmore Paul M. Pearson was giving a course, Acting Drama, which in 1912 was in its second year. [40]

Baker carried on his work at Harvard through the three decades under consideration, and beyond. It should be added that it was the persistent refusal of the Harvard authorities to recognize the value of his work or to give it academic credit that led in 1924 to his resignation and transference to Yale University. He established that "the classic treatment of the play as a mere branch of literature is inadequate.... Through his famous 47 Workshop at Harvard Professor Baker has become the 'foremost scholar of the theatre in this country.'" [41]

III

Earlier we remarked that in the oral reading of literature "the mechanical, artificial, and exaggerated elocution of the nineteenth century was abandoned for the more rational and restrained interpretation of the twentieth." Perhaps no one contributed more to that process than Solomon Henry Clark of the University of Chicago.

Clark began his career as a public reader and teacher of reading at the time when elocution was at its height. When he retired from active teaching in 1921 he had seen an almost complete repudiation of the excesses of the elocutionists. He was largely responsible for the adoption of the concept of *interpretation*—and the term—to replace the outworn and discredited *elocution*. He admitted to having been in his earlier days an elocutionist; but it was the "New Elocution" which he advanced, advocated, taught in his classes, and practiced in his own public appearances.

The only teacher to whom he ever acknowledged any indebtedness was Alfred Ayers, with whom he studied during the summer of 1888 (he was born in 1861). The teachings of George Lansing Raymond, whose *Orator's Manual* appeared in the fifth edition in 1886,[42] also deeply impressed him. Otherwise, he seems to have been essentially a self-taught man. He was at the organization meeting of the National Association of Elocutionists in 1892, gave two papers,[43] and entered into the discussions with great interest. The following year he gave another paper; [44] but his name soon disappeared from the roster of members. Perhaps he felt with Winans, that to the teacher of reading, as well as of public speaking, the Association had little to offer.

After some years teaching in Canada he went in 1891 to Chautauqua, New York, on his honeymoon, where he began his career as a reader and a teacher of reading. It was there that he came to the attention of William Rainey Harper, who was assembling a faculty for the new university being established at Chicago. When the University of Chicago opened in October, 1892, consequently, Clark was there as "Reader in Elocution," and as head of the Department of Public Speaking.[45] During his twenty-nine years at Chicago he built up a reputation as one of the ten best readers in America,[46] as well as one of the foremost teachers of interpretation. Vachel Lindsay always insisted that it was from S. H. Clark that he got many of his ideas of poetic structure, of "tone color," of poetry as an oral art.[47]

When he came on the scene as a reader and a teacher of reading, he saw what appeared to him to be "two hostile camps of extremists, each equally sure he was right and his opponent altogether blind. One is the so-called 'mechanical' school, with which the name of Diderot is associated; the other has been aptly called the 'impulsive' school." [48] The first of these, he felt, dealt entirely with externals; the latter with the inner being, the "psyche." Neither was by itself adequate. He believed that there was a "common ground on which all may stand."

Out of all the writings by and about Clark [49] it is possible to derive certain basic tenets of his philosophy of elocution, which contributed in large degree to the transition into the rational interpretation which he left when he retired from active duty as a teacher.

(1) Reading is an art, a re-creative art in much the same sense as music is an art.[50] The reader as an artist needs creative ability and technique. The "first requirement to artistic reading" is the intellectual and imaginative ability to understand a good play or poem in its entirety. As a re-creative art, the techniques of reading should be suggestive rather than impersonative. Clark himself relied almost entirely on his voice, which, by all accounts, was an "exceptionally magnificent organ." [51] He even insisted on using the actual book and desk: "the reader should actually read." [52] It was unnecessary either to set the stage for a reading, or to locate the characters always in the same place. "The reader ... performs, so far as this feature of the art is concerned, all that is required of him when he lets the audience know which character is speaking." [53]

(2) The thought is paramount. Technique is important and cannot be avoided, but it must be subordinated to the thought. The function of the reader is to get the thought to the listener, rather than to exhibit his virtuosity as a performer. "Appreciation of the meaning and beauty of literature," he says, "is the first requisite of a successful teacher of reading." [54]

Because of the prime necessity of getting the author's thought, reading becomes in itself an educative process. Vocal technique is useful as a means of getting the thought, but once the thought is grasped through the effective use of vocal technique, its expression should take care of itself.

(3) Elocution should be based on sound psychology. In addition to the cultural and mental training which derives from a study of psychology, the elocutionist needs it for two other reasons. First, "vocal expression is the outcome of complicated mental processes," to comprehend which an understanding of psychology is necessary. Second, it enables one to differentiate among the many "schools," and to reach something like an honest judgment.[55]

(4) The reader must feel the emotion he is trying to portray:

It is not enough to know that literature is primarily an appeal to the emotions through the imagination; that the purpose of literature is to arouse emotion in the reader; that an author frequently describes with great exactitude and detail the feelings of his characters. *One must himself, in kind at least, if not in fullest degree, experience imaginatively the same emotions or fail in whole or in part to receive from the author all that he has given us.*[56]

(5) The elocutionist must have a good education. He must be able to recognize, understand, and appreciate good literature.[57] He must be able to analyze the selections he is to read, and a part of the training of the reader involves learning how to make such analyses. Without an understanding of the criteria of literary criticism and analysis, and without a broad background of literature itself, such preparation would be impossible. Furthermore, an understanding of psychology is important in that it is of great aid in getting at the author's underlying intention.

Although Clark adhered to no particular "school" of elocution or expression, actually he taught most of the mechanics of speech, such as breathing, quality, time, emphasis, phrasing or grouping, and so on. It is not evident, however, that he taught any of these elements as ends in themselves. Always, in the final analysis, they were subordinate to the thought.

As Current points out, he made a significant contribution to the restoration of the prestige of interpretation as an artistic performance. "His chief contribution to interpretation as an art lay in what he did to restore dignity and standing to elocution as a profession. In all parts of the United States, he acted as an example of what sincerity and simplicity of presentation can do to make spoken literature a thing of beauty and pleasure."[58]

IV

Not all of those who contributed most to the transition that took place between 1890 and 1920 were active throughout the three decades. Many of them did not begin their professional services until well into the period. Particularly is this true of the last three men discussed in this paper.

James Albert Winans, born in 1872, received his Bachelor of Arts degree in 1897 from Hamilton College, which "for more than a hundred years ... has upheld the dignity of the spoken as well as of the written word." [59] Three years later he was awarded the M.A. degree. In 1899 he was appointed Instructor in Elocution and Oratory at Cornell University, being raised to the rank of full Professor of Public Speaking in 1914. In the Fall of 1920 he left Cornell and went to Dartmouth College, where he remained until his retirement in 1942.

From the beginning of his professional career Winans was a vigorous advocate of close association with others of similar academic interests. "Teachers of oral expression are much too isolated; they receive far too little of the stimulation and the broadening which result from contact with their kind." [60] He joined the National Association of Elocutionists, therefore, and attended the 1905 and the 1906 meetings. So far as is known, he never went back. It was at the first of these meetings that he spoke to the proposal to change the name of the Association, partly on the ground that a new name would attract more members from the colleges and universities: "I do not care a fig, which name we have. So long as the Association does not call itself the Association of Public Speakers, I am content: I shall fight that.[61] ... A good deal has been said about getting more members from colleges and universities. I do not think it will influence those institutions from the fact that the Universities and colleges know who you are and what you are doing. ... You will have to have something different to offer them rather than a different name." [62]

It is not surprising, therefore, that he should seek the fellowship of his colleagues who were academically minded in the field of public address. Consequently, during the school year of 1909-1910, as a result of conferences between himself and Wilbur Jones Kay, then of Washington and Jefferson, and Paul M. Pearson of Swarthmore, the Public Speaking Conference of the New England and the North Atlantic States was organized, and the first meeting held at Swarthmore in April, 1910. Winans was there, and was put on the Editorial Board of the *Public Speaking Review,* which began publication in September, 1911. He remained active in the Eastern Public Speaking Conference, as it came to be known, for almost a third of a century.

In 1912 the National Council of English Teachers set up an Oral English Committee, headed by James F. Hosic of the Chicago Teachers' College, to provide for programs in oral English at its annual meetings. But because the Committee could not appreciate the distinctive character of public speaking—to them it was simply another aspect of English—agitation was begun for the complete separation of the two disciplines. Winans actively supported O'Neill's contention that there was a definite dividing line between the two, and added that there were "practical reasons for separation." [63] Reporting on the third annual meeting of the Council in November, 1913, he was able to report that the teachers of English were becoming more and more aware of the fact that English is a spoken language, that they were beginning to see that "oral work, public speaking, is worth while for its own sake." [64] But he was consistently skeptical of any suggestion that the subjects could be successfully combined under a single discipline.

Consequently, he was one of the seventeen men who in 1914 seceded from the National Council and formed the National Association of Academic Teachers of Public Speaking, now the Speech Association of America. He was its second President, and until well past his retirement was a zealous participant in its activities.

Winans' most significant contribution to modern rhetorical theory lay in the use he made of current psychological thought. It cannot be said that he was the first to apply principles of psychology to rhetorical theory; even Protagoras knew the importance of "appeals to pity"; John Lawson, writing in 1759, had shown considerable understanding of these principles, and George Campbell in 1776 had made further application, especially with reference to the theory of persuasion. There is no evidence, however, that any of these had made a definite study of psychology as such in an effort to discover in what way it might be useful to the rhetorician or the public speaker.

Herein lay in part Winans' claim to originality. At the second meeting of the Public Speaking Conference in New York in 1911 he read a paper on "The Attention of the Speaker," [65] in which he quoted directly from E. B. Titchener and William James. In this paper he made use of the concepts of "voluntary" and "involuntary" attention, together with a third, as proposed by Titchener, the "secondary passive." From the standpoint of the speaker, the third was the most important of all. According to James, "what-we-attend-to and what-interests-us are synonymous terms"; but this over-simplification did not solve the problem for Winans; "...we attend most easily and steadily," he argued, "to those ideas and those statements which have for us the richest intellectual and emotional context. The more things we know about a topic, the more phases we have traced out, the more interests we have found the topic touches, the stronger is its grip upon our attention." For him attention and interest were not synonymous. We attend to that which interests us; but conversely, we are also interested in what we attend to.

One of the chief results to be desired is the effect on the delivery of such extensive preparation as is implied in the principle thus formulated:

We must think on our feet, think the full meaning of our words as we speak them and keep attention firm, no matter what the distractions. The clearer our understanding, the stronger the hold of the ideas upon our minds, the more nearly we have approached the stage of passive attention, the easier our task will be. . . . If we have thought the matter through repeatedly, with vigorous attention, the association of ideas will insure that our words shall represent large content. . . . At any rate, the speaker must make sure that he delivers his words with full and definite consciousness of meaning.[66]

Two and one half years later Winans extended his theory of attention to include "the modern theory of volition or will, as set forth . . . particularly well for our purposes by Professor James." [67] Briefly, James's theory of volition was that "what holds attention determines action. . . . One does not see any case in which the steadfast occupancy of consciousness does not appear to be the prime condition of impulsive power." [68] In applying this principle to persuasion, Winans then inquired, "Now taking James's statement as truth, is it not apparent that to persuade a man, in the sense of moving his will, is nothing more nor less than to secure and maintain his exclusive attention upon the desired action? According to this theory, if you keep your undivided attention upon an act, though it be murder, you will do the act."

The concept of the conversational manner, often attributed to Winans, was not original with him; it goes back into ancient rhetoric.[69] He did place more emphasis on the idea than had most previous writers; furthermore, he presented it in a textbook on public speaking which became so widely used that the concept itself received a far greater emphasis and currency than it had ever received before.

Winan's textbook, *Public Speaking,* first published in 1915, and running through many printings before being revised in 1938 as *Speech-Making,* embodied all these theories and many more both rhetorical and psychological. It was not the first modern textbook on public speaking; but, as evaluated by O'Neill:

No other book dealing with the problem of speaking has ever presented the results of so much and such accurate study in psychology. With "attention" as the "key-word," Winans has written a book at once sound psychologically, free from the common, external, mechanical approach to specific problems, and at the same time clear, simple, interesting. The book is probably not the last word on the psychology of public speaking. Its author neither claims nor desires it to be. But it is, it seems to me, the most authoritative word that has ever been spoken on this subject.[70]

Winans showed that rhetorical theory in order to be sound throughout must also be sound psychologically. His work constitutes an important contribution to the process of integration by which all branches of knowledge may ultimately be brought into complete and fundamental agreement. From 1915 on, no textbook on public speaking which was intended to be taken seriously could omit specific consideration of the psychological principles involved in the processes of influencing human thought and human behavior. Winans' *Public Speaking* was one of the few modern books to which the teacher or student of public speaking could turn for authoritative instruction on spoken discourse. It provided a body of principle, both theoretical and practical, that set the pattern for dozens of lesser books that were soon to follow. It may well be said that by 1920 his writings, with their strong psychological as well as rhetorical basis, had contributed largely to the restoration to academic status of the theory and practice of public speaking.

V

When Winans presented his paper on "Persuasion" he announced that at the following meeting of the Conference "Professor Woolbert is coming all the way from the University of Illinois to present his ideas, which I am able to assure you are decidedly novel. . . . He will maintain . . . that persuasion and conviction are the same thing, and attempt to beat down one of our proudly built division walls." The May, 1914, issue of the *Public Speaking Review* reports that Woolbert did read the paper, eliciting from Winans the hope that "he would soon treat the subject more amply in book form." It was thirteen years, however, before Woolbert's "novel" ideas on persuasion were given the treatment in book form that Winans had asked for.[71] His paper never appeared in the *Review,* but he did give his theories considerable development in a number of published articles.[72]

Charles Henry Woolbert, born in 1877, received his bachelor's degree from Northwestern in 1900, and his master's degree from the University of Michigan in 1909. After some years teaching at Olivet and at Albion Colleges, he went in 1913 to the University of Illinois, where he remained for thirteen years, attaining to the rank of professor in 1924. In 1926 he accepted a position in the Department of Speech at the State University of Iowa. He was there until his death in 1929.[73]

The paper which Woolbert presented to the Conference in 1914 was not the first statement of his beliefs. Two years before he had read a paper before the National Speech Arts Association [74] on "The Science of Persuasion," in which he seems for the first time to have repudiated the principle that conviction, as an appeal to reason, is any different from persuasion, as an appeal to emotion, or that the influencing of belief is essentially different from the influencing of action.

Throughout his utterances and his writings Woolbert drew heavily upon the principles of psychology, but upon a different psychology from that of Winans. He was a thoroughgoing behaviorist in his psychological beliefs, and made a constant and consistent effort to apply the tenets of behaviorism in his teaching of speech. Among these tenets were the hypotheses that mind is what the body is doing, and that the body tends to act, and at its most efficient does act, all in one piece, as an integrated whole. Everything that one does, therefore, may be thought of in terms of behavior, explicit or overt, or implicit or covert.

Furthermore, intellectual and emotional behavior differ mainly in that the one is characterized by a high degree of localization and control, whilst the other is diffuse, profound, and much less subject to conscious control. On this basis, then, if conviction is thought of as an appeal to belief and persuasion as an appeal to action, the distinction disappears, because both types of response are equally forms of behavior. If, on the other hand, conviction is considered as an appeal to the intellect and persuasion as an appeal to the emotions, once again the distinction disappears, since in reality both of these also are equally forms of behavior.

Conviction, then, is "mental action ... in *all* attempts of one mind to move another we are dealing with the same phenomenon of action." In argument logic is not enough in itself; the textbooks

... have no theory to offer why a man will listen to the best logic in the world and ignore it in his subsequent actions. They stake all on logic and reason, and naively blink at the fact that the most vital forces in inducing action are other than logical and rational. ... in the consideration of a science of persuasion that is fundamental enough to reach all cases and big enough to provide a real measure of results, we must give full consideration to *personality, personal attitudes, personal inclination, personal bias,* if you please. ... [75]

Ardent a behaviorist as he was, in one particular he departed from the strict behaviorist point of view: whereas one of the basic tenets of that school of psychology was objectivity, experimentation, Woolbert was no experimentalist. In fact, he could sometimes be somewhat impatient of experimentally derived conclusions, when those conclusions were in conflict with the results of his own subjective observations. The only experiment he ever performed, so far as is known, was the one required for his doctoral dissertation, and that one depended almost

entirely upon subjective evaluation. Paradoxical as it may seem, Woolbert was a subjective behaviorist.

The full development of his theory of persuasion took place over a
period of some fifteen years, from its first appearance in 1912 to its
final amplification in the 1927 revision of his *Fundamentals of Speech*.
But the series of articles in the *Quarterly Journal of Speech Education*
in 1919, together with his other presentations, made a profound impact
on the teaching of argumentation. One of the results of his development
was a reconsideration of the "general ends" of speech, which Phillips
had discussed in his *Effective Speaking* in 1908. Since there was no
distinction between influencing belief and influencing action, these two
were merged into one, which Woolbert called simply persuasion. But
what he did not see was that if acceptance of a belief was a form of
behavior, then understanding was no less so; hence there would be no
need of separating out information, or the securing of understanding,
as a distinct end of speech. In like manner all the other general ends
could be disposed of: since all the responses implied in those ends
were forms of behavior, the logical result of his theory would be the
insistence that actually there is but one general end of all speech,
namely, to obtain a response, and that any attempt to differentiate the
various types of response is contrary to sound psychological doctrine.

The second major application of his psychological beliefs was with
reference to the problem of delivery. His was the first attempt to
present a theory of delivery on the basis of the current academic psychology. His interest in this subject was revealed in the first volume of
the *Quarterly Journal of Public Speaking* in 1915, when he analyzed
and criticized a number of current "systems" of expression which were
being taught. After evaluating these different approaches he concluded:

The only way to get a pupil whose thinking does not guide him aright is to
take the thing apart and show him how it works . . . as a matter of teaching
it is the one best way—after the thinking of the thought has been done—of
developing the student's powers of self-criticism and of cultivating good
speech *habits*. . . . The ultimate way of doing this is to analyze tone. . . .
Meaning is carried by the *changes* in the elements; to get the right meaning,
choose and use the right changes in the elements.[76]

It was just such an analysis that he attempted to make in his doctoral
dissertation at Harvard.

The full development of his investigations were not published until
1927; however, even in his first edition of the *Fundamentals* in 1920 he
had set up, on the basis of the decreasing totality of behavior pattern
and of increasing specificity of control, the order in which the four
tonal elements should be studied.[77] This order arises out of the prin-

ciple that one must begin his study of speech by learning to control the grosser forms of behavior, and progress to the more delicate and refined. Therefore, in acquiring mastery over these elements, he would proceed in this order, "(1) Quality, (2) Force, (3) Time, and (4) Pitch. This will have the sound biological advantage of following the order in which our vocal mechanism grows; and it will tend to put the emotional and the intellectual aspects of speaking each in its rightful place."

But delivery meant more to Woolbert than voice alone. "A man speaking," he said, "is four things, all of them needed in revealing his mind to others. First, he is a will, an intent, a meaning which he wishes others to have, a thought. Second, he is a user of language, molding thought and feeling into words. Third, he is a thing to be heard, carrying his purpose and words to others through voice. Last, he is a thing to be seen, shown to the sight, a being of action to be noted and read through the eye." [78] Control over bodily action was necessary not only because meanings are read through the speaker's movements, but because general bodily control was the basis for the control of the other three aspects of speech, namely, voice, language, thought.

Delivery, then, involved both voice and action. But by no interpretation can delivery be thought of in his philosophy as a separate phenomenon. Delivery for him and the elocution of the elocutionists were worlds apart. Speech can be expressed only through voice and visible bodily action; it is a unified and integrated act, and although he had insisted that the elements could and should be studied separately when necessary, in actuality they could not be separated without destroying speech itself. Woolbert placed strong emphasis on delivery because to him delivery was as essential an aspect of speech as the thought itself; in fact, it was the effectiveness of the delivery which made effective communication of thought possible. Further, it was the delivery which completed and gave body to the thought.

It was in his insistence upon the inescapable unity of the whole speech process that Woolbert probably made his greatest and most enduring contribution to the transition that occurred from 1890 to 1920. The elocutionists had missed the point; there is little evidence that the writers on rhetoric, as applied to public speaking, were fully aware of it. Winans had the concept, but did not develop it. Although Woolbert's books did not appear until 1920, after that date scarcely a textbook on speaking was written that did not take into account many of the principles that he had advanced.

As Weaver pointed out in his excellent eulogy, "Woolbert had a profound and persistent belief in our manifest destiny as a profession. His was not a blind optimism. In pushing our frontiers forward and staking out new claims he met with as many discouragements as most of us have to meet. Yet he felt that a discipline as fundamentally useful as speech must somehow come into its own if we but toil and faint not." [79] There are relatively few people in the field of speech whose philosophies and teachings should be known to every serious student of the subject. Woolbert is one of these.

VI

As early as 1901 George Pierce Baker had suggested the contest nature of intercollegiate debating, comparing it with a game. The concept was further clarified by Foster in 1908. But it appears to have been fully developed only when James Milton O'Neill took up the problem and through a series of papers and controversies succeeded in crystallizing the specific nature of contest debating, and with it the true function of debate judges. Therein lies one of his most significant contributions to the development of speech pedagogy prior to 1920.

O'Neill was born in 1881, received his A.B. degree from Dartmouth in 1907, and did graduate work at Harvard University and the University of Chicago. After four years teaching at Hotchkiss School, he joined the faculty at Dartmouth in 1911, where he remained until 1915. In that year he was appointed head of the Department of Public Speaking at the University of Wisconsin. It was under his headship at Wisconsin that the first university speech clinic was established under Dr. Smiley Blanton, and the first doctorate specifically in speech awarded in 1922.

In the December, 1912, issue of the *Public Speaking Review* John Adams Taylor of the University of North Dakota had published a paper on "The Evolution of College Debating," in which he had pointed out some necessary qualifications for judges. Selection of judges for a debate, he suggested, was just like impanelling a jury for a trial. "Those who have not formed a strong opinion are more desirable; it is easier for them to determine which side gets nearer the truth." [80] Taylor's own confusion lay in the fact that while he implied that the function of the judges was to determine, as he said, "which side gets nearer the truth," he also advocated that decisions should be made, not on the merits of the question debated, but on the arguments of their presentation.

It was the basic concept of debating itself which could give rise to such a statement about judging to which O'Neill took vigorous exception.[81] Before we can determine what kind of judges we want, he pointed out, we must first decide what we want them for: "we do not want judges to 'determine which side gets nearer the truth,' but to

express an expert opinion as to which side does the better debating.[82]
. . . Of course we all know that the truth for any judge is the side of the
question that he believes in. . . . in any truth finding contest [the result]
must be that each judge will vote for the team that upholds the side
of the question that he happens to favor." The search for truth is an
admirable undertaking, O'Neill recognized; but intercollegiate debating and the search for truth are entirely different matters, and one
should not be confused with the other. It should then be obvious that
to serve as a judge one should know the principles and techniques of
debating, some of which are "probably not known to the man who has
never given time and attention to studying the art of debate—points on
which the keen business man, well known clergyman, or distinguished
college professor may have very unsound ideas or no ideas at all."

The controversy over the nature of contest debating, as distinguished
from either the search for truth or "debating as an academic study," in
which the purpose "is to teach students how to find and express that
which may truthfully be urged on *either* side of any question," [83] continued through the final issues of the *Public Speaking Review* and the
first four years of the newly founded *Quarterly Journal of Public Speaking*. Throughout the argument O'Neill never lost sight of the principle
that although contest debating partakes of the nature of a game, an intellectual sport, "classroom work in debating should certainly be training for 'real life'." "Of course," he insisted, "the purpose of all courses in
argumentation and debate is training for life and living." [84]

The argument over the nature of contest debating and the selection
of judges inevitably led to the question of the type of decision most
appropriate. According to Hugh Neal Wells, of the University of
Southern California, the decision should be rendered on the basis of
the preponderance of evidence—the "juryman's vote." Taylor had advocated much the same thing, but at the same time, paradoxically,
something like what came to be known as the "legislator's vote," in
which the decision rested on the judge's opinion as to which side came
more nearly to the truth, as developed in the arguments presented.
O'Neill himself urged the "critic's vote," in which the decision was given
on the basis of the merits of the debating. Since the "critic's vote" has
been adopted almost universally in the so-called "expert" judging of
debates, it is obvious that the present day attitude toward the basic
nature of contest debating and of the judges' decisions is due primarily
to the influence of O'Neill. A patent exception is in the case of the
"audience decision" in its various forms, to which he made little or no
contribution. Nor was he able to look with much favor on decisionless
debates, with which Woodward of Western Reserve had been experimenting.[85] The elimination of judges, he felt, was not a necessary

remedy for the ills that were occasionally encountered in contest debating.

Mention has been made of the secession from the National Council of English Teachers. O'Neill was in the thick of the events leading up to secession, and contributed significantly to the final outcome.

The crux of the matter seems to have been in the inability of the Oral English Committee of the National Council, under the chairmanship of Hosic, to recognize in public speaking anything more than another aspect of English. To present the other side of the argument, therefore, O'Neill presented a paper at the March, 1913, meeting of the Public Speaking Conference on "The Dividing Line between Departments of English and Public Speaking," in which he urged that there should be complete separation of the two lines of work, including choosing of the instructional force, the planning of courses, division of work, prerequisites, and the relation of the department to extracurricular activities in public speaking.[86]

On the following November 8, at the annual banquet of the National Council held in Chicago, O'Neill was asked to speak on "Public Speaking and English." In this paper he carried the controversy directly to his opponents. The deplorable condition of public speaking instruction, which he admitted, was entirely the fault of the English departments, which, having neglected the work that needed to be done, were now insisting that there was nothing worth teaching. In the only situations where public speaking was being taught effectively it was in those schools where it had been entirely separated from English. Nor was there any reason to expect that the situation would improve in the future. The work of the two departments should be coordinated, "but absorption of public speaking by departments of English is not to be thought of." [87]

Evidently the English Council was unwilling to accept his point of view, even in the planning of the public speaking programs; for at the very time of the meeting of the Council, which was attended by large numbers of public speaking teachers, serious thought was being given to the founding of an independent national organization.[88] The following November (1914), when the Public Speaking section of the Council met in Chicago, the question was again brought before the group. After one motion had been tabled, another was presented the following day and unanimously adopted to organize "The National Association of Academic Teachers of Public Speaking, for the purpose of promoting research and more effective teaching." [89] Among the seventeen who were registered as charter members were Winans, Woolbert, and O'Neill. Probably in recognition of his initiative, O'Neill was chosen the Association's first President, as well as the Editor of the

Quarterly Journal of Public Speaking, which was to be launched the following Spring. He was the only editor to serve two terms.

While it would obviously be unjust and incorrect to give to any one person the entire credit for the beginning of what has been one of the most significant single actions in the history of American speech education, O'Neill contributed to the consummation of that action probably more than any other one individual.

Like Winans, Woolbert, and others, O'Neill was possessed of a profound faith in the integrity of the profession, and in its future. As the first Editor of the *Journal* he set forth the essential function of the periodical, which was to be "a national organ owned and controlled by the public-speaking teachers of the whole country, of a character that will stand comparison with the professional journals of our colleagues in other departments." [90] His faith was further expressed in his Presidential Address at the first annual Convention, held in Chicago in November, 1915, in which he spoke on "The Professional Outlook": "It is toward educational achievement that we must set our faces. It was to educational achievement that this Association dedicated itself by the very resolution that brought it into being as a formal organization. It was formed 'for the purpose of promoting research and more effective teaching'." [91]

His ideals of speech pedagogy, to which he has adhered throughout his forty years of professional activity, were summed up early in his teaching at the University of Wisconsin, when he addressed the annual State Teachers' Association on November 2, 1917, on "Aims and Standards in Speech Education." [92] In four areas of speech training, "voice and the treatment of speech defects; second, debating; third, reading and declamation; and fourth, oratory or original speeches," he demanded that "standards of intelligent, agreeable, effective communication" be set up, rather than those of "spectacular, unreal exhibition," and that the program be extended to include not only the few gifted ones who need it least, but more important, the many who need it most, in all speaking, whether public or private, "for every day and for great occasions."

The aims, objectives, philosophies, even the basic concepts of speech education which were passed on from 1920 to succeeding decades were indeed quite different from those which had been inherited from the 1880's. Contributing to the changes that took place were many people and many influences. But it seems to be no exaggeration to suggest that of all those whose influence affected the course of development during this period, the contributions of the six persons discussed here were probably the most typical, even if one may be somewhat reluctant to insist that they were the most significant.

Notes

1. See, for example, George Saintsbury, *A History of Criticism and Literary Taste in Europe from the Earliest Texts to the Present Day*, 3 vols., 2nd ed., (Edinburgh, 1949). "Rhetoric long followed wandering fires," he says, "before it recognized its true star and became Literary Criticism." (I, 14.)

2. William B. Chamberlain, "Report of the Committee on Elocution in Colleges," *Proceedings of the National Association of Elocutionists* (hereafter cited as *Proceedings*, with the year of the meeting) *Third Annual Meeting*, June 25 to June 30, 1894, p. 147.

3. *Public Speaking Review*, I (September, 1911), 1.

4. Giles Wilkeson Gray, "Research in the History of Speech Education," *QJS*, XXXV (April, 1949), 156-163.

5. *Public Speaking Review*, IV (May, 1914), 31. "There has been an independent department for public speaking at Cornell for about twenty-five years." *Werner's Magazine* reported that "the chair of oratory" had been tendered to Mr. Duncan C. Lee, a graduate of Hamilton College in 1891. [XV (April, 1893), 143.]

6. Emerson College of Oratory had by 1893 established a course leading to the degree of A.M., embracing "studies equivalent to those required by any other college of high standing granting this degree." Winslow, "Shall Schools of Oratory Confer Degrees?" *Werner's Magazine*, XV (April, 1893), 128-129.

7. Personal letter from Thomas C. Trueblood, October 11, 1949.

8. Paul M. Pearson, "Intercollegiate Associations," *Public Speaking Review*, I (December, 1911), 119-120.

9. David Potter, *Debating in the Colonial Chartered Colleges, an Historical Survey, 1642 to 1900* (New York, 1944), p. 96.

10. George Pierce Baker, "Intercollegiate Debating," *Educational Review*, XXI (1901), 244-257.

11. (Boston, 1895.)

12. (New York, 1904.)

13. (Boston, 1908.)

14. (Chicago, 1915.)

15. (Chicago, 1908.)

16. (New York, 1915.)

17. (New York, 1920.)

18. Edward W. Scripture, *The Elements of Experimental Phonetics* (London, 1902), and *Researches in Experimental Phonetics. The Study of Speech Curves* (Washington, 1906) are but two of these.

19. *Werner's Magazine*, XVII (1895) and XVIII (1896).

20. (New York, 1906.)

21. *Proceedings* (1905), 235.

22. *Proceedings* (1893), 320.

23. *Proceedings* (1898), 27-38.

24. *Proceedings* (1896), 109-121.

25. *Proceedings* (1899), 14-26.

26. *Public Speaking Review*, I (November, 1911), 84-85.

27. John H. Frizzell, "Wilbur Jones Kay, 1873-1937," *QJS*, XXIV (October, 1938), 495-498.

28. "Intercollegiate Debating."

29. *Ibid.*

30. *Ibid.*

31. William Trufant Foster, *Argumentation and Debating* (Boston, 1908), Preface, p. ix.

32. "Yale Wins Again," *Nation*, CXIX (December 10, 1924), 616.

33. Percy MacKaye, "George Pierce Baker," *American Magazine*, LXXIII (December, 1911), 180-182.

34. "Yale Wins Again."

35. George Pierce Baker, "The 47 Workshop," *QJSE*, V (May, 1919), 185-195.

36. *Ibid.*

37. *National Cyclopedia of American Biography*, XXV, 28-29.

38. Percy MacKaye, *Epoch: The Life of Steele MacKaye*, 2 vols. (New York, 1927), II, 58 ff.

39. University of North Dakota *Catalogue*, 1905-1906.

40. Paul M. Pearson, "The Drama in the Curriculum," *Public Speaking Review*, II (1912), 7-12.

41. "Harvard's Loss is Yale's Gain," *Current Opinion*, LXXVIII (February, 1925), 202-203.

42. Chicago. An earlier edition was published in 1879.

43. "Psychology and Expression," *Proceedings* (1892), 31-35; and "Appreciation of the Aesthetic in Poetry as an Aid to the Reader," *ibid.*, 122-126.

44. "Marc Antony's Funeral Oration as a Study in Tact," *Proceedings* (1893), 221-232.

45. Personal letter from Mr. E. C. Miller, Registrar, University of Chicago, June 14, 1951. Although Mr. Miller writes of a Department of Public Speaking, the Catalogue for 1893-1894 lists it as the Department of Elocution. For our present purposes the distinction is unimportant.

46. Editorial, *Werner's Magazine*, XVII (February, 1895), p. 139. Even at the 1893 Convention it was reported that "Mr. S. H. Clark carried off the recitational honors of the Convention." "Notes on the Chicago Convention of Elocutionists," *Werner's Magazine*, XV (August, 1893), 283-285. See also the October, 1893, issue, p. 356.

47. Davis Edwards, "The Real Sources of Vachel Lindsay's Poetic Technique," *QJS*, XXXIII (April, 1947), 182-195.

48. "Psychology and Expression."

49. Lucille Mary Current, "A Study of Solomon Henry Clark as a Teacher of Interpretation," unpublished M.A. thesis, Northwestern University, 1938. Bibliography.

50. "Mental Technique and Literary Interpretation," in William B. Chamberlain and S. H. Clark, *Principles of Vocal Expression and Literary Interpretation* (Chicago, 1897), pp. 316-323.

51. Editorial, "S. H. Clark as a Reader," *Werner's Magazine*, XVIII (April, 1896), 351-353.

52. Current, p. 57.

53. "S. H. Clark as a Reader."

54. Current, p. 57.

55. "Elocution and Psychology," *Werner's Magazine*, XVIII (March, 1896), 203-210.

56. *Interpretation of the Printed Page* (Chicago, 1915), p. 283. *Italics in the original.*

57. "Education of the Elocutionist," *Werner's Magazine*, XVI (May, 1894), 169-171.

58. Current, p. 112.

59. James Albert Winans, *Public Speaking* (New York, 1915), Dedication.

60. "We Need to 'Get together'," *Public Speaking Review*, I (February, 1912), 185-187.

61. In presenting the arguments for changing the name of the Association, Fulton mentioned that the terms "Public Speakers" and "Public Speaking" had been suggested.—*Proceedings* (1905), 234.

62. *Proceedings* (1905), 249.

63. J. A. Winans, "Report of the March 24-25 Conference," *Public Speaking Review*, II (April, 1913), 227-231. (This was the Public Speaking Conference.)

64. *Public Speaking Review*, III (December, 1913), 108-112.

65. *Public Speaking Review*, I (October, 1911), 41-47.

66. *Ibid.*

67. J. A. Winans, "Persuasion," *Public Speaking Review*, III (March, 1914), 196-200.

68. *Ibid.*

69. See Norman Joseph Attenhofer, "The Development of the Theory of the Conversational Mode of Speech," unpublished M.A. thesis, Louisiana State University, 1951.

70. James Milton O'Neill, Review of Winans' *Public Speaking. Quarterly Journal of Public Speaking*, II (April, 1916), 213-215.

71. Charles Henry Woolbert, *The Fundamentals of Speech, Revised Edition* (New York, 1927). The first edition, published in 1920, made no mention of the problem of persuasion.

72. "Conviction and Persuasion: Some Considerations of Theory," *Quarterly Journal of Public Speaking*, III (July, 1917), 249-264; "Persuasion: Principles and Method," *QJSE*, V (January, 1919), 12-25; (March, 1919), 101-119; (May, 1919), 212-238.

73. Andrew Thomas Weaver, "Charles Henry Woolbert," *QJS*, XVI (February, 1930), 1-9.

74. This was, of course, the old National Association of Elocutionists.

75. "The Science of Persuasion," *Proceedings* (1912), 42-48.

76. "Theories of Expression: Some Criticisms," *Quarterly Journal of Public Speaking*, I (July, 1915), 127-143.

77. *The Fundamentals of Speech* (1920), pp. 154 ff.

78. *Ibid.*, p. 3. See also his "Analysis of the Phases of Speech," pp. 7-9.

79. "Charles Henry Woolbert."

80. John Adams Taylor, "The Evolution of College Debating," *Public Speaking Review*, II (December, 1912), 97-105.

81. "Judges for Intercollegiate Debates," *Public Speaking Review*, II (January, 1913), 135-138.

82. Woolbert had also presented this point of view in his paper on "The Science of Persuasion"; but Adams had indicated that the judges should do both.

83. J. M. O'Neill, "Game or Counterfeit Presentment?" *Quarterly Journal of Public Speaking*, II (April, 1916), 193-197.

84. *Ibid.*

85. Howard S. Woodward, "Debating without Judges," *Quarterly Journal of Public Speaking*, I (October, 1915), 229-233. See also J. M. O'Neill, "Judges Again," pp. 305-307, of the same issue.

86. *Public Speaking Review*, II (April, 1913), 227-231.

87. *Public Speaking Review*, III (January, 1914), 132-140.

88. J. M. O'Neill, "The National Association," *Quarterly Journal of Public Speaking*, I (April, 1915), 51-58.

89. *Ibid.*

90. *Ibid.*

91. J. M. O'Neill, "The Professional Outlook," *Quarterly Journal of Public Speaking*, II (January, 1916), 52-63.

92. "Aims and Standards in Speech Education," *QJSE*, IV (October, 1918), 345-365.

20 Origin and Development of Departments of Speech

DONALD K. SMITH

....

In 1900 there were no departments of "speech." Today there are hundreds of them, even if one excludes the related titles under which speech instruction is organized. In 1944 the United States Office of Education used its own survey of speech departments to assure the educational world that "the expressive arts have gained full recognition in college programs of study." [1] And in 1948, the American Council on Education began to use "speech" as a category for classifying graduate degrees awarded in this country. [2]

Our task here is to answer four questions:

1. What educational trends brought about the development of departmental structure in American higher education?

2. What specific circumstances account for the emergence of departments of speech as one of the many subdivisions of the modern curriculum?

3. When and where did speech departments develop?

4. What happened to the speech curriculum when speech acquired departmental status?

I

If departments of instruction are considered as a sort of pre-ordered division of the world of learning, they are very ancient. For a good many centuries the seven liberal arts—fortified as time went on by Aristotelian philosophic studies and by the classical languages and literature—constituted the curriculum of higher education. This was the curriculum of the arts course in England at the time of the colonizing in America, and it became the curriculum of the first American college at Cambridge. [3] Within this prescribed curriculum, however, departments of instruction had no administrative significance, and could not be said to exist in the modern sense of college departments.

447

The department in its modern sense came into being late in the nineteenth century when the structure of higher education underwent profound changes. The modern department not only designated a significant division of the world of learning, but it also assumed important administrative functions. The birth of departments at Harvard is typical. Commenting on the emergence of departmentalism, Herrick points out that the Harvard catalog of 1836-1837 showed "no visible departments; apparently this indispensable subdivision of higher education had not yet appeared. The department as Harvard knows it today seems to have sprung fully armed from the great administrative reorganization of 1889-1891.... After 1891, however, the department became the very focus of instruction at Harvard, 'issuing special pamphlets of its courses, discussing and arranging course programmes, planning assaults on the corporation for more money'." [4] Both Greene and Coulton place the development of the college department as subsequent to 1860, with the full realization of departmentalism coming near the turn of the twentieth century. [5]

Departmentalism resulted from the vast expansion of higher education during the nineteenth century. Expansion had many dimensions, both physical and philosophic. In retrospect, four of its aspects seem to have made a departmental structure for higher education all but inevitable.

The development of new learning, in the first place, produced a vast body of knowledge, and new methods for increasing knowledge, which made obsolete the comfortably prescribed boundaries of the old classical curriculum. For a time the prescribed curriculum met the flood tide of new knowledge in chemistry, mathematics, history, political science, economics, and the modern languages by inserting new courses into the old curriculum, and by shortening old ones. [6] Eventually this sort of stop-gap accommodation had to give way to fundamental administrative reform.

Second, the development of specialization forced the development of numerous and narrowly defined segments of the curriculum. American universities, much influenced by the practices of German universities, came to value specialization as an answer to the obvious impossibility of a single prescribed curriculum. [7] They developed the elective system so that students might choose among the many specialties. [8] Departments operated as administrative agencies to control the nature of studies offered within the various specialties.

Third, the concept that useful or practical knowledge was suitable to higher learning contributed to the expansion of courses and to the establishment of departments for administering the courses. Within a climate of pragmatic and utilitarian thought, the nineteenth century witnessed progressive deterioration of educational theories which would have maintained a comfortably prescribed curriculum. At Cornell,[9] and at the great state universities of the West, effort was made to provide university departments and courses which could answer the needs and aspirations of all the citizens of the state.[10]

The final catalyst of departmentalism was the expansion of college enrollments. College enrollments more than doubled in the last quarter of the nineteenth century.[11] This expansion added the pressure of numbers to the administrative burdens of higher education, thus placing more and more emphasis upon the importance of the college department.

The modern college department, accordingly, was born out of the pressures of new knowledge, specialization, new utilitarian concepts of the functions of education, and swelling enrollments. It judged the fitness of course offerings, the relationships of courses to one another; it set up prerequisites, and programs for majors and minors; it cultivated the expansion of knowledge in its own segment of the academic globe, and looked anxiously to unoccupied territory between itself and neighboring departments; it sought money and equipment, and made recommendations for appointments, promotions, and salary changes.

By the twentieth century, teachers in American colleges and universities found their individual aspirations and their aspirations for their instructional area increasingly involved with the sort of department within which they were working. It is understandable that men interested in the teaching of speech felt that the path of both hope and opportunity led from the establishment of an autonomous department.

II

The departmentalization of American education proceeded rapidly between 1860 and 1900. During this period, autonomous organization of speech instruction was a possibility, and actually took place in some institutions. In general, however, speech instruction became the responsibility of departments of English language and literature. Later, after the turn of the century, separate departments of speech appeared in a majority of American institutions of higher education, although the association with English persists to the present day in many institutions.[12]

Speech a Part of English

Teachers of speech have sometimes expressed surprise that the field of English literature led curricular instruction in the skills of writing and speaking into a new department of learning.[13] This did not happen in all institutions, of course. In some few institutions, departments of rhetoric, oratory, or elocution developed by the side of departments of English literature. In some schools departments of public speaking emerged from the departments of rhetoric or elocution without an interlude within a department of English. But the most important single growth of a department in the area of language and literature, at the end of the nineteenth century, was that which saw newly formed departments of English, with some variety of titles, assuming control over the teaching of writing, and such teaching of speaking as was included in the curriculum.

A number of forces doubtless influenced the linking of literature, writing, and speaking. Most important, perhaps, was the fact that the study of English literature appeared in the curriculum as the protégé of the venerable study of rhetoric. Rhetoric, with its traditional concern for the arts of discourse, had been an established part of the curriculum from medieval times. During the first half of the nineteenth century, however, the study of rhetoric both in England and America was increasingly identified with the study of literature and literary criticism. Potter calls Hugh Blair the "Father" of English literature in Britain, although there were scattered earlier lecturers.[14] The popularity of his *Lectures on Rhetoric and Belles Lettres* in this country is credited by Guthrie with giving impetus to the interest in criticism and literary taste which was to carry rhetoric into the field of English literature.[15] Guthrie also observes that the grouping of rhetoric with oratory in the early American colleges, had, by 1850, become more frequently a grouping of "Rhetoric and Belles Lettres," with attention to the practice of speaking, at least as involved in delivery, "now relegated to the tremendously popular 'Elocution'." In Guthrie's words:

... an examination of a few college catalogues will indicate the time and manner of the change.... In 1834 (at Harvard) when Whately replaces Blair for sophomores, the lectures given by the Boylston professor are no longer on rhetoric and oratory, but on rhetoric and criticism. ... In 1854 the rhetoric heading for lectures has disappeared, and the Boylston professor lectures on "English Language and Literature."

At North Carolina it was professor of "rhetoric and logic" in 1826, but of "rhetoric and belles lettres" in 1838. The Pennsylvania Professorship of Oratory and English Literature became a chair of "Rhetoric and English Literature" in 1834, and "Belles Lettres and English Literature" in 1855. ... At Yale Chauncey Goodrich was Professor of Rhetoric and Oratory in 1817, but ... in 1839, his replacement, William A. Larned, is listed as Professor of Rhetoric and English Literature.[16]

The movement of rhetoric toward the study of belles lettres is understandable if one recalls the form taken by rhetorical instruction in higher education—a form in which lectures about rhetoric, and the study of rhetorical models served as the curricular basis for practical exercises in discourse. Thus, the study of rhetoric in terms of orations may well have suffered from the fact that, as Professor Rarig has observed, "the taste for reading old orations had to be acquired." [17] The pleasures of studying imaginative literature seem to have stimulated an hegira by a number of famous American teachers from oratory to literature, and many persons joined newly formed Departments of English.

The development of the field of English at Harvard University was closely associated with the influence of Professor Francis J. Child, who moved from the Boylston Professorship to become in 1876 a professor of English. Bliss Perry's account of his own teaching career relates a similar transition, as he moved from an initial interest in elocution and oratory to literature and criticism. [18] At the University of Mississippi, where a chair of English literature appeared as early as 1858, the link between English literature and speech instruction was set in 1873, with the appointment of J. J. Johnson as "Professor of English and Provisional Instructor in Elocution." [19] At Cornell, the first catalog includes the name of Homer B. Sprague as professor of rhetoric, oratory and vocal culture, and his interest brought English literature into the curriculum. His successor in the chair of rhetoric and oratory, in 1870, was Professor Hiram Corson, whose primary interest was the English literature and language, and who moved within one year to be relieved from the "care of these less congenial branches [of rhetoric and oratory] leaving only that field of English language and literature which now received formal recognition in his title." [20]

Added to the historical and personal ties which bound literature to the skills of practical discourse was a certain lack of independent vitality within the area of rhetoric, i.e., the fields of elocution, oratory, and written composition. By the last half of the nineteenth century rhetoric was off on one of its periodic forays into dispersing and enfeebling itself. Part of its energy, some would say the better part, had gone into belles lettres. Its attention to the skills of discourse had become increasingly narrow, and closely identified with undergraduate theme writing. [21] Even in this narrow concern, it was increasingly a part-discipline, for the relatively recent field of English grammar also claimed the task of teaching students to write.

These two "part-studies" were ultimately to accompany one another into the desolate wastes of Freshman rhetoric, or Freshman English. The atmosphere which has surrounded discussion of beginning instruction in composition for more than half a century tends to indicate that one of the practical reasons for tying composition to literature has been the humane necessity for providing an avenue of hope for teachers of composition.

The development of college entrance requirements in English served to strengthen the bond between instruction in composition and literature. As early as 1874 Harvard had set up an entrance examination in English, but the move toward uniformity in such requirements came after 1888. In that year the New England Commission for Colleges "set a list of books for reading as the preparation for the [entrance] examination in English." In 1892 the famous Committee of Ten of the National Education Association called a conference on English at Vassar college, and recommended that literature and composition be unified in the high-school course. In 1893 the Association of Colleges and Preparatory Schools of the Middle States and Maryland set the pattern for the development of uniform college entrance examinations. These examinations tested the reading of a fixed list of English masterpieces, and knowledge about some aspects of English grammar and syntax.[22] Entrance examinations set a link between high-school work in English and beginning college work in composition which was to affect both, in that composition was linked with literature and skills in speech were largely ignored. An occasional voice was raised to protest the omission of speech.[23]

The elocutionary movement represented another aspect of dispersed rhetoric of the ninetenth century. As early as 1827 Ebenezer Porter observed that elocution had been taught for some years "in the most respectable school in the country," and predicted its general invasion of the college curriculum.[24] Actually academic attention to elocution was erratic. The coming or going of specially trained teachers determined its status. In schools of the Middle West, Trueblood observed that the teaching of public speaking in the seventies and after was largely in the hands of itinerant teachers, most of whom were, of course, trained in the tradition of elocution.[25] At the end of the century, however, with departmentalism growing in the college curriculum, both the title and the practices of elocution were sufficiently strong to secure the establishment of separate departments of elocution in a number of colleges.[26] There were certain complications apparent in the claims of elocution for departmental status in academic circles. For one thing, the teaching of elocution, like the teaching of composition, was by the end of the nineteenth century associating itself more and more closely with literary criticism and appreciation.[27] This association emphasized the claims of English departments to the whole field of language and literature. For another thing, the status of elocution, both as a word and as an instructional discipline, was in considerable question by the end of the century. It had ceased to be a required subject at Harvard in 1873.[28] By 1900 the new School of Oratory at Texas University was making explicit note in its announcement that its purpose was not training in "elocution." By 1915 college teachers of public speaking were inserting the word "academic" into the title of their new association to dissociate themselves with the "elocutionists" of the private schools. Some teachers of speech seemed anxious to escape the title of elocution.[29] The academic vitality of elocution, therefore, was considerably vitiated by its own internal problems of direction and depleted prestige.

In retrospect, neither the practice of rhetoric nor the practice of elocution, as it was conceived in the colleges in the last half of the ninetenth century seems to have possessed the status necessary for the general emergence of a department separate from English literature.

The Pressure for Separate Departments

English departments seem often to have been an early, if unpremeditated, experiment in welding into a single department the work of teachers of diverse interests. The ties between speech instruction and the English department appear to have been particularly tenuous. In some schools, as has already been noted, these ties were never achieved. In other schools, speech instruction perambulated through a variety of associations, only to lose curricular status once it was associated with English. The peripatetic nature of speech instruction is particularly well illustrated by its course at the University of Mississippi. There, from 1856-1868 formal instruction in elocution was given within the department of Belles Lettres, and Moral and Mental Philosophy; in 1868 it was moved to the department of Logic, Metaphysics, and Political Science; in 1873 it was joined with the chair in English, and in 1886 went into a separate department of Elocution. In 1905 a School of Rhetoric and Oratory made a brief appearance, but at the end of that year this school went into the new School of English, and instruction in oratory disappeared. In 1908 a new Department of Oratory was formed, whereupon speech instruction appeared once more within the curriculum.[30]

The movement in the field of speech for the establishment of departments separate from English grew, therefore, out of a background of departmental organization in which neither the place of speech instruction in the curriculum, nor the conditions of its association with English had achieved any measure of stability. Such a situation produced the immediate context for a separatist movement, but there were at least four specific sorts of pressures which were to give real impetus to separation: (a) the pressure created by the specialization of interest within English, (b) the outspoken discontent of speech teachers working in departments of English, (c) the claims of a neglected tradition and "new" types of course work for a sympathetic administrative home, and (d) the pressure of student interests for curricular recognition of speech.

Specialization of Interest Within English Departments

The opportunity for the development of the field of English came in the last half of the nineteenth century as science and utilitarianism were carrying on their successful assault upon the body of ancient classical education. As the hold of classical languages and literature upon the curriculum was broken, the study of the modern languages emerged, including a new emphasis upon the study of the English language and literature. Observing the nature of the pressure upon classical studies, one might expect that the new field of English would have been a little less militantly remote from the affairs of everyday life than had been the classics. Such an expectation would overlook both the massive conservatism of education and the entrenched prestige of great literature as the source of liberal learning. It would also overlook the fact that the men who were to become leaders in the new departments of language and literature were products of the linguistic tradition, and that many of these men derived their methods of study from German scholars. While the modern languages, including English, had fought with the classics in their search for recognition, it was a struggle in which they sought not to destroy the prestige of traditional linguistic education, but rather to take over and protect that tradition from the threatening spectre of utilitarianism.[31] Consequently the emerging field of English tended to emphasize not instruction in the practical skills of discourse, but intensive philological history and criticism.

Philology has been used to describe many academic pursuits. In a narrow sense the philological approach to literature involved the intensive study and interpretation of a text; in a broader sense it involved the study of a literary genre.[32] More recently philology has included linguistics, the study of the structure and development of languages. Both as linguistics and as intensive literary study, it identified the approach to the study of English which gained the greatest attention of English scholars in the last decades of the nineteenth century and the first decades of the twentieth. But whether English departments emphasized literature or linguistics, they found small place for teachers of speaking and writing.

The Discontent of Speech Teachers

The first important public demand for the separation of speech and English came from the Public Speaking Conference of the New England and North Atlantic states. On March 25, 1913, during its meeting at Yale University, the Conference passed this resolution:

Whereas, The principle and practice which are the foundation of excellence in public speaking form a unified body of material to a large extent separate and different from the content of the usual college department of English; and
Whereas, The best interest of the students are promoted by placing the instruction in all the elements of public speaking in the hands of a trained and organized department of specialists; be it
Resolved, That it is the sense of this conference that departments of Public Speaking in American colleges should be organized entirely separate from departments of English.[33]

A year later, the *Public Speaking Review,* which was being published by the Conference, carried an article by the editor, J. M. O'Neill, on "The Dividing Line Between Departments of English and Public Speaking." This article reported the chaotic condition of existing interrelations between English and public speaking departments, and sought to define the basis for division.[34] In 1914, the National Association of Academic Teachers of Public Speaking was launched, in the words of the National Council of Teachers of English, "by some of the more aggressive of the teachers of public speaking in the colleges."[35] In the recollection of the men who established this group, the "need" for departmental autonomy was one of the motives which prompted the interest of a number of these teachers in the new organization.[36] O'Neill's address to the association, as its first president, reaffirmed his belief in the necessity for separation from English. In the new *Quarterly Journal of Speech Education,* Professor C. E. Lyon, then head of the department of Public Speaking at the University of South Dakota, reported a survey of departmental organization in the English-speech areas. His survey of 60 institutions seems to have been concentrated on those which already had separate departments of public speaking. However, thirteen of the thirty-six institutions replying taught speech within the English department, and from the replies he found: "the most striking thing about the situation is that in eleven of the thirteen cases where they are not separated, those in authority (professionally) believe in the resolution favoring complete separation. And the two dissenting opinions are from professors of English."[37]

In the *Quarterly Journal of Speech Education* (1916) C. H. Woolbert, a member of the Department of English at the University of Illinois, argued that speech and English were "essentially different disciplines," that they differed in viewpoint and outlook, that speech was associated with the pure sciences of physics, physiology, anatomy and psychology, and that the attitude of the English scholar toward speech was "almost inevitably hostile, or at best luke warm." He observed that a practical difficulty faced the professor of speech whose closest associates spoke a different language and whose budget was controlled by scholars with different enthusiasms.[38]

The Claims of Subject Matter

In themselves, the aspirations of individuals within English departments would scarcely have added up to a movement for separatism. But by 1910 there was another, though related pressure for separation— a pressure alluded to in the New England resolution and by Woolbert. Speech teachers were asserting with increasing force the claims for a distinctive subject matter. One claim came from the ancient field of rhetoric and another from the contributions of science to the study of speech behavior.

Rhetoric, as has been observed, had fallen upon evil days after 1850. The unified study of speech-making, embracing concern for practical discourse as well as aesthetic, and for ideas and arrangement as well as for style and delivery, had never been completely forgotten. But as the teaching of written composition grew more narrow and as the distaste for elocution grew, the traditional rhetoric was reasserted. A curricular concern for practical, argumentative discourse became apparent in American colleges as early as the decade 1880-1890, with the introduction of course work in debate.[39] After 1900, courses in public speaking grew in number as courses in elocution dwindled. These courses reflected to some extent the comprehensive theory of practical discourse which had been the heritage of ancient rhetoric.[40]

The subject matter and purposes of public speaking courses could present a heritage as militantly classical as that of literature, while yet suiting the pragmatic temper of modern America. The field of public speaking, moreover, had sought new vigor from the modern sciences, particularly psychology, from which it derived material for the study of audience behavior. As a result, "composition" in the public speaking class embraced audience study and analysis, an emphasis not seen in courses in written composition within departments of English. Speech departments not only drew strength from the teaching tradition of classical rhetoric, they also served to establish scholarly study in the field of rhetoric at the graduate level, in both the study of rhetorical theory and the study of oratory. As early as 1915 the Northwestern

School of Oratory listed a course in The History of English Orations and Oratory, at the postgraduate level. A marked innovation was the course in Classical Rhetoric offered for the first time at Cornell University in 1923. By 1930 the field of rhetorical study had developed considerably at Cornell, with courses in British Orators, in The History of Rhetoric and Oratory, and a course in American Orators, which was listed but not taught until after that year. A course in American Orators was offered in 1930 at the University of Iowa.[41]

The uses of science to the study of speech inspired Woolbert's relocation of the field of speech in an area quite foreign to the interests of many English departments. The early affinity of scientists for speech, and speech teachers for science, had been somewhat erratically demonstrated in the elocutionary movement.[42] However, the second decade of the twentieth century saw the appearance of new courses in the correction of speech disorders, the anatomy and physiology of voice, and laboratory research into voice phenomena. These new courses were in general the product of specialization in autonomous departments of public speaking. These departments were also reaching into the field of phonetics, which was having problems of its own in finding a comfortable administrative home.

The growth of speech science may be observed in the appearance of a variety of courses. As early as 1910 the College of Idaho had a course entitled Anatomy, Physiology, and Hygiene of Voice and De Pauw was offering a course in The Psychology and Sociology of Oratory.[43] In 1914 a course in Voice Training and Phonetics was offered within the Department of Public Speaking at the University of Wisconsin, and in 1916 a course in the Psychology of Speaking and Reading was added. Professor Merry went to the University of Iowa in 1915 interested in studying speech phenomena experimentally, and offered a seminar in speech for graduate students in that year. By 1920 he was giving a course in The Psychology of Speech: Voice Science and Laboratory. In 1923 a course in Voice Science was offered for the first time at Wisconsin.

For the most part the curriculum for training speech correctionists developed after 1920, although as early as 1913 Professor Smiley Blanton gave a course on speech defects at the Cornell University Summer Session.[44] Dr. Blanton moved to the University of Wisconsin that fall to open what may have been the first clinic exclusively concerned with speech disorders, and to offer a course in the Correction of Speech Defects. A course in speech correction was also offered by Professor Scripture at Teachers College in 1919-1920. Michigan was offering a course in speech correction in 1918, but it appears from the catalog description to have been a remedial course for students with "vocal weaknesses," rather than for the training of specialists. Iowa listed a course in The Correction of Speech Disorders for the first time in 1922-1923, and at the same time announced the launching of a training program in the field of speech correction jointly with the Child Welfare Research Station of that university. Courses in the sciences of speech correction could claim as sanctions the enormous reputation of scientific learning. Moreover, they existed as a sort of living demonstration that the field of speech had boundaries quite remote at certain points from the centers of literature and composition.

Thus, the claims of old knowledge reasserted and the stimulus of new knowledge derived from the sciences helped establish the right of speech to departmental status.

The Demands of Students

A considerable portion of the practical training in speaking received by students in American colleges had always been through student activities, whether the activities took the form of required, faculty supervised declamations and orations, or whether they followed the voluntary path of the literary societies. Until the latter part of the nineteenth century, numerous institutions of higher learning provided through rhetorical exercises and the work of the literary societies an emphasis upon speech often far greater than that found today.[45] Under the pressure of expanding student enrollments and the reorganization of the college curriculum in terms of courses, rhetorical exercises were largely to disappear prior to the end of the century.[46] By the end of the century, also, the influence and activity of the literary societies were declining, although the societies persisted for varying periods of time in different colleges.[47] The disappearance of these traditional avenues for speech activity left little opportunity for speech training in many schools. This opportunity was to be re-established both by the development of course work in speech,[48] and the development of new forms of extracurricular speaking activity. The course work was often directly related to the activity. Intercollegiate debating, which developed generally after 1894 marked one new line of activity and by 1910-1920 course work in debate had become the most popular speech offering.[49] Intercollegiate oratory was another activity to develop and the appearance of the college theatre in the twentieth century claimed the interest of many students. Courses in theatre, after a few beginnings in the decade 1910-1920, developed spectacularly after 1920. These student activities, with their demonstrated appeal to student interest, were to form the basis, first, for the development of course work designed to give academic recognition to the educational significance of the activity, and second, for the formation of speech departments to direct both the activities and the courses associated with them.

The direct influence of student interest and pressure upon the formation of speech departments can be illustrated in the experience of a number of institutions. At the University of Michigan, Thomas Trueblood observed that after he had been given co-operation by the English Department and the Law School, in offering a course in elocution and oratory, pressure developed among the law students for granting of free tuition and credit for the course. A petition from the law students was granted, and a subsequent petition from the Literary College students was also granted. Thus it was that Professor Trueblood received a full-time appointment at the University of Michigan in 1889, to be followed in 1892 by the organization of a separate department under his direction.[50]

A similar experience is recorded at the University of Mississippi, where student petitions resulted in the re-establishment of the School of Oratory in 1908, after its merger with the Department of English in 1906 had eliminated instruction in oratory.[51] Lathrop credits the founding of the Department of Public Speaking at Louisiana State University in 1911 directly to the interests which had developed in debating in the decade preceding.[52] At Wabash College, agitation by the literary societies is credited with influencing the development of a department of public speaking in 1913.[53] And Gray's history of the University of Minnesota notes the growth of student interest in speech courses and activities which preceded the creation of an autonomous department at that institution in 1927.[54]

It would be a gross oversimplification of events to view speech departments as the direct product of student demand for speech instruction. Yet many of the courses from which they took their curriculum were the product of student activity and interest, and the men who directed student activities, or taught the related courses, were the teachers who sought academic status and administrative autonomy for speech.

The modern department of speech is a reflection of the forces which were shaping American higher education in the nineteenth and twentieth centuries. But not until the twentieth century did the impact of science and utilitarianism, of student interest and curricular specialization begin fully to be realized in the curricular area of the languages and literature. Speech departments, accordingly, came into being as an expression of the great forces which were changing the American educational scene, as these forces converged with the interest and energies of men who made the teaching of speech their profession.

III

Determining a specific date for the establishment of any speech department is complicated. The observation of Herrick, Greene, and Coulton that departments can scarcely be said to have existed in their modern sense prior to 1890 seems to place a sort of preliminary date on their establishment. Nevertheless, it is possible to observe earlier recognition of speech as an independent area of instruction in a number of institutions, and to see that this early recognition, with the administrative and disciplinary continuity it gave to the field of speech, doubtless hastened the widespread appearance of autonomous departments of speech in the twentieth century.

Perhaps no college in America has given more ancient and persistent emphasis to speech instruction than has Hamilton College. The history of speech at this institution deserves some consideration. It represents a development somewhat different from that in most schools; it influenced directly the development of speech in other institutions; and it illustrates the effect of a strong teacher and personality on the independent status of speech instruction within any college. The continuous tradition of speech training at Hamilton, extending to the academy which preceded the founding of the college in 1812, was given academic status after 1841, in which year Henry Mandeville went to Hamilton. *An Historical Discourse* by President Fisher of Hamilton College, delivered in 1862, observes that "the Department of Elocution and Rhetoric was organized under Dr. Mandeville, and has since been made very efficient in the training of students. Before this, instruction on these subjects was given by the President." [55] Of Mandeville, President Fisher recalls that he

... at once impressed himself on me as no common man. ... He came to this institution in 1841, and for eight years filled the chair of Elocution and Rhetoric. He found the department unorganized. ... He set himself to work to make it the power and give it the position to which its importance entitled it. He wrote here his system of Elocution, basing it on the principles enunciated by Walker, that the structure of the sentence controls its delivery— the only true philosophical idea of a sound elocution. ... He thus gave to this department its original form and impulse. [56]

The vagaries of departmental organization in early days were often determined by the interests and capabilities of particular professors. By 1860 the Hamilton catalog showed a professor of Logic, Rhetoric and Elocution, and Librarian, as one teaching post. By 1900, the department had become one of Rhetoric and Elocution, although Elocution, after the Mandeville system, was still the basic course of the department. It is interesting that the college Register for 1902-1903 lists this department first among the instructional divisions of the college, placing it before the department of Greek—a sort of eminence in listing which may be unique among the colleges of that period. The *Register* observes: "The work of this department has long made Hamilton eminent in its attention to the art of personal expression, both in utterance and in writing." The tradition has persisted. In 1947 Professor Marsh, head of the present Department of Public Speaking, was able to observe that "during its latest, as in its earliest days, Hamilton has required four years of speech training." [57]

It is not surprising to find a department with such continuity and tradition influencing the development of speech instruction in other institutions. In the case of Hamilton, its graduates played the primary rôle in the development of the department at Cornell University, where, with the appointment of Mr. Brainard Gardner Smith to the chair of oratory in 1887, the impress of a succession of Hamilton graduates was begun. Smith was succeeded at Cornell by Professor Duncan Campbell Lee, also a Hamilton graduate, and the succession to departmental chairmanship of Professors J. A. Winans, and A. M. Drummond, in this century, has continued the rôle of Hamilton men at Cornell.

There were other institutions at which early departmentalization of speech instruction has been noted, and some of these may be listed here, with no implication that the listing is exhaustive or final. Whitman College, in Washington, lists a department of Elocution in 1880,[58] and a department of Oratory and Elocution was organized in 1884 at De Pauw University, with a considerable offering under the direction of Professor Carhart.[59] Speech at De Pauw was associated with rhetoric in 1886, was neglected largely from 1887-1892, reappeared as a separate department in 1891, became a division of the English department in 1937, but again became a separate department of speech.[60] Boston University opened a School of Oratory in 1873, which survived for only four years. Earlham College had a department of Elocution in 1877-1878,[61] Baylor University a School of Oratory in 1890,[62] and note has already been taken of the Department of Elocution at the University of Mississippi, established in 1868.

The separate department of Elocution and Oratory, established at the University of Michigan in 1892 by Professor Trueblood, identifies the earliest department to maintain continuous autonomous organization for speech instruction in one of the great universities of the country.[63] The School of Oratory at Ohio Wesleyan, established in 1894, was also to maintain its separate administrative status; so did the School of Oratory at the University of Southern California, which was established in 1895.[64] And although the present School of Speech at Northwestern University was not linked to the arts college of that institution until this century, it descends in direct line from the Cumnock School of Oratory, which was established in 1878.[65]

One marks the turbulent status of speech training in the transition to departmental organization and the growth of course offerings in the last decades of the nineteenth century. A more comprehensive overview of the development of departmental associations for speech instruction is given by the research conducted by T. E. Coulton, who surveyed catalogs from a representative sample of American colleges and universities distributed over the entire nation. His data were taken from the examination of a catalog from each of the institutions within a series of time units, usually ten-year spans, and is therefore summarized as normative data from the existence of speech courses and departmental organization within decades in question.[66]

TABLE 2

DEPARTMENTAL TITLES IN TRANSITION

	1860-70	1870-80	1880-90	1890-1900	1900-10	1910-20	1920-30
No. Institutions Examined	97	97	111	116	118	118	118
No. dep'tal Headings for Speech Work	22	29	53	75	98	140	158
Significant Titles:							
English	7	17	40	45	51	69	69
Public spk.					5	31	33
*Public spk.						5	8
Speech							16
*Speech							4
Elocution				2	15	2	
Oratory				2	7	3	
Expression						8	2
Rhetoric	9	2		2	2	3	
Rhet. & speech			1	4	4	2	
Eng. & speech							6
Rhetoric & Eng.		3	4	2			
Dramatic arts							3

* Indicates the title as a subdivision of a larger department.

Coulton's data (Table 2) indicate both the rapid growth of curricular speech instruction during the period, and also places the movement for autonomous departments within the twentieth century. The data indicate that the movement for autonomy developed rather more slowly than would be indicated by other surveys. For example, in 1894 Chamberlain reported the results of his survey, begun in 1893, that there were fifty-two schools answering his inquiry which had distinct departments of elocution, and that in twenty-five of these, elocution was taught in connection with no other study.[67] Coulton shows only two departments of elocution in 116 colleges examined for that decade. Lyon's survey, reported in 1915, found departments of public speaking in well over half of the thirty-six institutions answering his inquiry,[68] but McLeod's survey in 1916 showed only twenty-eight out of sixty-six institutions in which there were separate departments of English and Public Speaking.[69] Percentage-wise, both of these surveys give a more advanced picture of autonomous departmentalization than the survey by Weaver of the catalogs of 356 colleges and universities for the years 1929-1930, which reported only eighty-six of these institutions with separate departments of speech.[70] All of the surveys are subject to obvious sampling errors, and the earlier ones made no normative claims, but it is likely that Coulton's study and Weaver's study, more extensive than the others, and attempting to sample the nation at large rather systematically, give a better picture of the status of the movement for departmental autonomy than the smaller surveys.

There is reason to believe, however, that the trend toward departmental autonomy for speech, clearly indicated by Coulton's study, has continued. So has the tendency toward a revision of departmental titles. Coulton indicates the appearance of "speech" as a departmental title after 1920, although at least one department had used the title prior to that time.[71] This title seems to have been the product of autonomy for speech instruction, and the corresponding expansion of the scope of speech; and it has achieved a sort of verbal triumph since 1920. Doubtless the title is also loosely descriptive, like "English."

A reasonably complete and recent indication of both the direction taken in naming speech departments and the extent to which autonomy has proceeded may be derived from an examination of the report of the American Council on Education on *American Universities and Colleges in 1948.*[72] In examining this volume it was possible to gather data on the departmental structure of 738 out of some 820 accredited American colleges and universities. The following is a summary of the number of independent departments of speech shown by this report, and a grouping of the titles used for these departments. Titles are grouped under a name most popular in the classification indicated, although each title would have a variety of specific forms (see Table 3).

There are few surprises in this tabulation. In general autonomous departments have developed most extensively in the universities, and least extensively in the teachers colleges and technological schools. Speech has become the most popular departmental title, but one marks the tendency toward the appearance of drama, both in conjunction with speech, or as a separate department. One notes also the extent to which

TABLE 3

DISTRIBUTION OF SPEECH DEPARTMENTS IN 738 COLLEGES AND UNIVERSITIES *

Categories	Universities	L.A. Colleges	Teachers Colleges	Schools	Totals
Total Autonomous Speech Depts.†	129	242	49	10	430
Total Without Autonomous Speech	52	177	71	33	333
Departmental Designations					
Speech	73	143	36	4	256
Speech and drama	15	34	1	1	51
Drama	14	20	x	2	36
Public speaking	7	9	1	1	18
Radio	8	1	1	x	10
Speech, radio & drama ..	2	2	x	x	4
Homiletics	1	x	x	x	1
English & speech	5	32	9	2	48
Communication	3	1	1	x	5
Rhetoric	1	x	x	x	1

* Data taken from American Colleges and Universities, ed. A. J. Braumbaugh, American Council on Education (Manasha, Wis., 1948), pp. 142-985.
† Departments listing both English and speech in the title have been included in this number. The total also includes twenty-three schools with two departments and one with three.

public speaking has disappeared as a departmental title, and the appearance of radio departments, of communications, and the variant combinations of English and Speech.

IV

It is possible to observe the various lines along which speech has developed as the field gained autonomous status. Turning again to Coulton's survey for an indication of curricular trends, it is apparent that the great expansion of course work in speech came after 1900. In the period from 1860-1870 such courses as forensics, declamation, elocution, oratory, logic, rhetoric, and extemporaneous speaking appear in the offerings of the few departments giving identifiable work in speech. The following decade showed as its major development the appearance of courses in debate, and of courses entitled "English" which were indicated as giving instruction in speaking. From 1880-1890 courses giving work in dramatic interpretation began to appear, such as those in the reading of Shakespeare, and similar courses continued to increase in number into the twentieth century. After 1890 there was an apparent increase in debate instruction, and near the end of that decade courses in public speaking put in their appearance. The real diversification of the curriculum came, however, after 1920, and must be considered a concomitant of departmental autonomy.

The following table summarizes data on course offerings from 1900-1935. Data has been grouped into the emerging lines of the curriculum represented by types of related course work. These groupings do not appear in the original data given by Coulton. The categorization of particular courses is to some extent arbitrary.

TABLE 4

CURRICULAR DEVELOPMENTS, 1900-1935*

(Figures indicate the number of semesters of instruction offered in 118 institutions studied.)

Course	Number of Semesters of Instruction in 118 Institutions			
	1900-10	1910-20	1920-30	1930-35
Public Address:				
Public speaking	58	152	164	171
Debate	182	229	153	156
Argumentation	x	x	105	101
Extemporaneous speech	x	50	42	41
Oratory	148	152	44	53
Rhetoric	195	35	7	5
Parliamentary law	x	7	11	13
Business speech	x	x	16	23
Drama:				
Production	x	x	176	186
Drama	50	89	91	136
Interpretation	37	104	167	202
Correction	x	x	34	39
Basic Sciences:				
Sciences	x	x	10	26
Phonetics	x	6	39	48
Radio	x	x	2	8†
Basic Courses:				
Elocution	289	107	4	4
Basic courses	x	x	118	115
Voice	58	43	49	50
Gesture	32	16	11	11

* Thomas E. Coulton, "Trends in Speech Education in American Colleges," unpublished Ph.D. dissertation, N.Y.U., 1935, pp. 46-52.
† The big development in radio courses came after 1935. The U.S. Office of Education reports surveys of radio courses in *Higher Education*, Federal Security Agency (Washington, 1944), pp. 30-31.

In interpreting the data in the table, it is worth noting that after 1920 courses in oratory are seldom performance courses, and would be grouped as rhetorical study in some institutions. Rhetoric courses also change from the study of rhetoric as practical instruction in composition, to the study of the history and criticism of rhetoric. The category of "basic courses" indicates the appearance of courses in fundamentals, or principles of speech. Such basic courses, supplanting earlier courses in elocution, constitute one of the significant curricular changes which occurred concomitantly with the development of speech departments.

These data do not indicate the beginnings of course work in two aspects of the developing speech curriculum: courses for teachers, and graduate courses.

Courses for Teachers

The appearance of courses for teachers appears to have been rather general in the decade 1910-1920 for six institutions examined.[73] In 1913 a course in Oral Reading and Oral English was listed at Cornell University, and was described as a "course for teachers." In the same year, Teachers College listed a course in the Teaching of Speech in the bulletin of its School of Practical Arts. Iowa listed a teachers course in its 1914 Bulletin and Michigan a course in Oral English, which was described as one for teachers. Wisconsin was offering a major in speech for high-school teachers in 1914-1915, and attention was being given to the problems of the high-school dramatics coach in the interpretation courses of the same period.[74] These courses are all directed at the high-school teacher, and seem to represent an early interest on the part of speech departments in the status of speech education at the secondary-school level.

There is evidence that such courses for teachers were not the first to be offered in this country. Indiana University listed a course in History of Elocutionary Methods in 1892, and a course in Teaching of Public Speaking in 1907.[75] A teachers course in Elocution was listed prior to 1910 at West Virginia University, as was a course in Methods of Teaching Reading, for which credit in elocution was given, at the University of Missouri.[76]

The Development of Graduate Study

The decade before 1910 saw seven M.A. degrees carried out under "an adviser in a department of speech." Three of these were granted at Iowa, in 1902, 1903, and 1904; three at Utah in 1906, 1907 and 1909; and one at Ohio Wesleyan University in 1908. There were three graduate degrees in speech given in 1918, but the real development of graduate study came after 1920.[77] Wisconsin, which had had its master's program approved in 1915, gave its first M.A. in 1920, and the first Ph.D. degree to be given in the field of speech in 1922.[78] Cornell, which had begun its graduate instruction in 1916 was to award its first

M.A. in 1922, and its first Ph.D. in 1926, in which year Iowa also granted its first Ph.D. degree. The first M.A. at Southern California was given in 1924, and Teachers College granted two Ph.D. degrees in speech in 1928. By 1936, Michigan, Iowa, Wisconsin, Northwestern, Teachers College of Columbia, Cornell, and Southern California had given 92 per cent of the graduate degrees awarded in speech to that date. By 1936, also, Stanford and Louisiana State offered graduate study in speech, and had granted the Ph.D. degree.

Autonomy brought its own internal logic to the developments within the field of speech. It saw the rapid expansion of the curricular offering in speech, the development of new courses, the revival of neglected types of study, the expedient reaching out for all types of course work dealing with the act of speech. It saw the development of specialization within speech, the growth of graduate study, the appearance of division within division. The field which took as its core the symbolic processes of direct discourse found this concept elastic enough to permit reaching into nearly all the major aspects of human learning. Specialists in the field of public address sometimes developed an affinity for the field of social studies, for the methodologies of historical research, and for the discourse of the citizen. Specialists in correction found an affinity with the natural and medical sciences, for the research methodologies of the exact sciences, and pathological discourse. Specialists in the drama and interpretation found their affinity with the humanities, and with the functions of literature and art in the modern world. As Professor Simon has said, the teacher of speech moves in many orbits.

Notes

1. U. S. Office of Education, *Higher Education*, Federal Security Agency (Washington, 1944), p. 30.

2. *American Colleges and Universities*, ed. A. J. Braumbaugh, American Council on Education (Manasha, Wis., 1948), pp. 58-59.

3. R. Freeman Butts, *The College Charts Its Course* (New York, 1939), p. 104.

4. Marvin T. Herrick, "The Departmentalization of Knowledge," *AAUP Bulletin*, XXXVI (Autumn, 1950), 465.

5. Evarts B. Greene, "Departmental Administration in American Universities," *Journal of Proceedings and Addresses of the Association of American Universities*, XIII (Chicago, 1911), 17-27; Thomas E. Coulton, "Trends in Speech Education in American Colleges," unpublished Ph.D. dissertation, New York University, 1935, p. 113.

6. Charles F. Thwing, *A History of Higher Education in America* (New York, 1906), pp. 300-311.

7. A personal account of the influence of German scholarship appears in Bliss Perry, *And Gladly Teach* (Cambridge, 1935), pp. 88-114.

8. Thwing, pp. 320-322.

9. For a discussion of the founding of Cornell, see Thwing, p. 433.

10. One of the best statements of the philosophy of these new Universities is found in the *Inaugural Address* of Charles Richard Van Hise, cited in Butts, p. 230.

11. Butts, p. 160.

12. Harold M. Jordan, "Rhetorical Education in American Colleges and Universities, 1850-1915," unpublished Ph.D. dissertation, Northwestern University, 1952, p. 104. Jordan summarizes the shift in departmental designations as follows: "(b) It was common practice to combine all rhetorical training under a single Department of English after 1890. (c) Many colleges and universities divided the subject-matter of Rhetoric into two departments designated as Departments of English Language and Literature and Departments of Rhetoric and Oratory, during much of the latter half of the nineteenth century. (d) Separate Departments of Public Speaking commenced to appear about the turn of the century, which took over much of the speech training before 1915."

13. See C. H. Woolbert's comment on this in his "The Organization of Departments of Speech Science in Universities," *QJS*, II (January, 1916), 64-77.

14. Stephen Potter, *The Muse in Chains* (London, 1937), pp. 107-114.

15. Warren Guthrie, "The Development of Rhetorical Theory in America," *SM*, XV (1948), 63.

16. *Ibid.*, p. 69.

17. From notes on a discussion of this shift with Frank M. Rarig, Minneapolis, 1951.

18. Perry, pp. 72-82, 128; 135-136; 160.

19. *Historical Catalogue of the University of Mississippi, 1849-1909* (Nashville, 1910), pp. 44-48.

20. Thomas Hewett Waterman, *Cornell University, A History* (New York, 1950), II, 34-36.

21. This shift has been frequently noted. One account is given by Donald Hayworth, "The Development of the Training of Public Speakers in America," *QJS*, XIV (November, 1928), 501.

22. "Report of the Standing Committee on Entrance Requirements," *School Review*, XVI (1908), 646-659.

23. F. B. Robinson, "Oral English as a College Entrance Requirement," *Public Speaking Review*, I (1911), 2-7.

24. Cited by Donald Hayworth, "The Development of the Training of Public Speakers in America," *QJS*, XIV (November, 1928), 495.

25. Thomas C. Trueblood, "A Chapter on the Organization of College Courses in Public Speaking," *QJS*, XII (February, 1926), 1-11.

26. Coulton, pp. 47-48.

27. Mary Margaret Robb, *Oral Interpretation of Literature in American Colleges and Universities* (New York, 1941), pp. 142-143.

28. Charles H. Grandgent, "The Modern Languages," in Samuel Eliot Morison, *The Development of Harvard University, 1869-1929* (Cambridge, 1930), p. 76.

29. Charles H. Woolbert, "The Teaching of Speech as an Academic Discipline," *QJS*, IX (February, 1923), 9-10. Also Woolbert, "Elocution Redivivus," *English Journal*, IV (1915), 179-180.

30. *Historical Catalogue*, pp. 44-48; 58-60.

31. A discussion of this struggle is given by C. A. Smith, "The Work of The Modern Language Association of America," *PMLA*, XIV (1899), 240-246. See also Grandgent, and Herbert Weir Smyth, "The Classics," in Morison, *op. cit.*, p. 34.

32. This definition is from Kemp Malone, "English Linguistics and the Ph.D." *EJ* (College ed.), XVIII (1929), 314-315. For a more thorough exploration of the "empire" of philology, see Albert S. Cook, *The Higher Study of English* (Cambridge, 1906), pp. 3-33.

33. Clarence E. Lyon, "The English-Public Speaking Situation," *QJS*, I (April, 1915), 46.

34. J. M. O'Neill, "The Dividing Line Between Departments of English and Public Speaking," *PSR*, II (1913), 231-238.

35. Note in *EJ*, IV (1915), 339.

36. J. M. O'Neill, "After Thirteen Years," *QJS* (April, 1928), 242-253.

37. Lyon, *op. cit.*, p. 45.

38. Charles H. Woolbert, "The Organization of Departments of Speech Science in Universities," *QJS*, II (January, 1916), 64-77.

39. Coulton, p. 46.

40. Coulton, pp. 49-50.

41. Data on specific courses unless otherwise noted, is taken from the appropriate catalog of the institution to which reference is made.

42. Robb, *op. cit.*, pp. 75-104.

43. Coulton, p. 97.

44. Note on this in *PSR*, III (April, 1914), 248.

45. Herbert E. Rahe, "The History of Speech Education and Ten Indiana Colleges," unpublished Ph.D. dissertation, Wisconsin, 1939, pp. 386, 410-411.

46. Rahe, p. 386. See also Helen Roach, "History of Speech Education at Columbia College (1758-1900)," unpublished Ph.D. dissertation, Columbia Teachers College, 1948, pp. 48, 136-137.

47. Rahe, p. 397.

48. Rahe, p. 386. See also Roach, p. 125.

49. A discussion of the rise of intercollegiate debating is given in a series of three articles: E. R. Nichols, "A Historical Sketch of Inter-Collegiate Debating," I, *QJS*, XXIII (April, 1937), 259-278; II, *QJS*, XXII (December, 1936), 591-602; III, *QJS*, XXIII (April, 1937), 259-278. See also Coulton, pp. 49-50.

50. Trueblood, *loc. cit.*

51. *Historical Catalogue*, p. 60.

52. Ruth Helen Lathrop, "A History of Speech Education at Louisiana State University, 1860-1929," unpublished M.A. thesis, Louisiana State, 1949, p. 141.

53. Rahe, p. 356.

54. James Gray, *The University of Minnesota*, 1851-1951 (Minneapolis, 1951), p. 467.

55. Samuel Ware Fisher, "Historical Discourse," in *A Memorial of the Semi-Centennial Celebration of the Founding of Hamilton College* (Utica, 1862), p. 82.

56. Fisher, pp. 87-88.

57. Willard B. Marsh, "A Century and a Third of Speech Training at Hamilton College," *QJS*, XXXIII (February, 1947), 23-27.

58. Coulton, p. 116.

59. Rahe, *op. cit.*, pp. 52-55.

60. Rahe, p. 82.

61. Rahe, p. 97.

62. Coulton, p. 116.

63. Trueblood, *op. cit.*, p. 69.

64. Alice Moe, "The Changing Aspects of Speech Education in the United States from 1636-1936," unpublished M.A. thesis, Marquette University, 1937, p. 128.

65. *Northwestern University; A History, 1855-1905*, ed. by A. H. Wilde (New York, 1905), IV, pp. 339-345.

66. The two charts in this paper, which are based on Coulton's research, are adapted from the data in his dissertation and do not directly reproduce any of the specific tables in his study.

67. William B. Chamberlain, "Report of the Committee on Elocution in Colleges," *Proceedings of the National Association of Elocutionists* (1894), pp. 129-137.

68. Lyon, *op. cit.*, pp. 47-48.

69. Alice M. MacLeod, "Majors and Credits in Public Speaking," *QJS*, II (April, 1916), 149-152.

70. J. Clark Weaver, "A Survey of Speech Curricula," *QJS*, XVIII (November, 1932), 607-612.

71. J. P. Ryan, "The Department of Speech at Grinnell," *QJS*, III (July, 1917), 203-209.

72. *American Colleges and Universities in 1948, op. cit.*

73. Unless otherwise noted, data on specific courses is taken from the catalog or register of six institutions: Cornell University, Northwestern University, Universities of Iowa, Michigan, Southern California and Wisconsin, and Teachers College of Columbia University.

74. Gordon J. Klopf, "A History of Speech Training at the University of Wisconsin, 1851-1941," unpublished Ph.D. thesis, Wisconsin, 1941, pp. 24-26.

75. Rahe, p. 394.

76. Coulton, pp. 130-131.

77. Franklin H. Knower, "An Index to Graduate Work in the Field of Speech, 1902-1934," *SM*, II (October, 1935), 1-49.

78. Klopf, p. 28.

21 Speech Education in Twentieth-Century Public Schools

HALBERT E. GULLEY
HUGH F. SEABURY

••

During the early decades of the twentieth century, speech found its place in the curriculum of the high school. Established first in extracurricular debate and dramatics, speech training in various forms gradually appeared in courses of study. The high school itself changed in these years from an institution which served the college-bound few to a center of educational activity which provided basic knowledge and training to almost every youngster in almost every township of the United States. Speech education kept pace with this growth. At the turn of the century it was available to the few in an occasional course, and as extraclass activity it was largely restricted to the superior student. By 1938, the approximate terminal date of this paper, it had become at least a small part of almost every school in almost every state. Some schools required a basic course and offered extensive electives. Speech served every student in the classroom, the talented in specialized events, and the handicapped in the clinic. Indeed, it prospered in any school which recognized subjects "in proportion to their relative importance for useful and successful living." [1] It found its way also into the elementary school.

George P. Baker in 1903, addressing the meeting of the National Education Association, called attention to the thriving debate societies in high schools, and deplored the scarcity of courses which alone could give students sound training and guidance in such pursuits. Younger teachers of English, he insisted, should "be required to give themselves such preparation as shall enable them to set standards for their pupils and to train them in right speaking and in proper delivery of their own work." [2] Many of Professor Baker's "younger teachers" were to become teachers of speech and their influence was to be felt across the nation.

471

Interscholastic Activities

By 1900, high-school debate societies were indeed thriving. In 1887, four schools in the Boston area were holding interscholastic debates.[3] The Lyceum Association of Wisconsin by 1895 had organized the first state forensic contests.[4] By 1902, high-school debate societies in Minnesota were sufficiently numerous for the state university to bring them to the campus for a meeting.[5] Iowa organized a High School Debating League in 1906,[6] Oregon the next year, North Dakota in 1909, Texas and Kansas in 1910, and Colorado in 1914.[7] By 1916, there was some kind of state organization for interschool debates in every state west of the Mississippi, and in ten states east of the river: Alabama, Georgia, North Carolina, and Virginia in the South; Pennsylvania and New Jersey in the East; and Ohio, Indiana, Illinois, and Wisconsin in the Midwest.[8]

The numbers of schools and debaters participating in each state were also impressive. In North Carolina, for example, schools in the league increased from 90 in 1913 to 325 by 1916.[9] During the 1914-1915 school year in Texas, 3,000 boys appeared in 2,096 debates before an aggregate audience of 99,100 people.[10] One director of debate estimated that the twenty-eight state associations had sponsored 54,041 debaters in 23,-663 debates before 2,602,745 persons in the period 1902-1916.[11]

Debate leagues prospered partially because interested teachers were trying to compensate for inadequate speech training within the school.[12] Some states compensated, also, by promoting activities other than debate. Texas included declamation, emphasizing selections of high merit and endeavoring to "checkmate the influence of the dramatic reader and the traditional elocutionist." [13] As the expansion of interschool debating continued, speaking events sponsored by the leagues became even more diversified. By 1930, Virginia had contests in reading, public speaking, and debate, while Wisconsin had added extempore speaking, extempore reading, declamation, interpretative reading, and play production.[14] *The Speech Bulletin* of the National Association of Teachers of Speech printed in 1931 a list of "known inter-school contests." There were ninety-five different leagues and associations conducting contests in debate, in humorous, serious, interpretative, and dramatic reading, in extemporaneous speaking, oratory, and declamation, in one-act plays, and acting.[15] The list reveals that there were more contests in the Midwest, West, and South than in the East, although some were reported in Maine, New Hampshire, Rhode Island, New Jersey, New York, and Pennsylvania.

Dramatics also came into the schools of the twentieth century as an extracurricular activity. Nearly all schools presented some kind of amateur theatricals to the community.[16] In 1915, the South Bend (Indiana) High School established the first little theatre in the public schools.[17] By 1931, eighteen states were holding interscholastic dramatic events.[18] By this date, if we may accept Macgowan's observations, dramatic activity within the school must have been fairly intensive:

A third of the 22,000 high schools of America are probably studying and applying production methods to a rather decent grade of play....[19] Some hundreds of thousands of young actors, designers, stage-hands, and managers are producing plays for an audience that runs into the millions. They have every sort of stage to work on, from auditorium platforms to plants so well equipped that the Theater Guild's Repertory Company plays there in preference to local halls or opera houses. In many places the students practice playwriting and scene design as well as acting, and indulge in state-wide tournaments.[20]

Two national honor societies for high-school students helped to foster enthusiasm for public speaking, debate, and dramatics. The National Forensic League, founded in 1925, furnished an appropriate reward for forensic achievement. In 1930, it had 289 chapters in schools of thirty-four states and had sponsored 14,500 contests in debate, oratory, declamation, and extempore speaking.[21] With much this same spirit for the advancement of speech training, the National Thespian Society began in 1929 to encourage dramatic arts in the high schools.[22] The National University Extension Association also contributed to speech education in this period by promoting interscholastic debate on a national level.[23]

Courses in Speech

During the first years of the century, then, speech education was within the orbit of the secondary school. Teachers of speech also sought to develop courses in the regular curriculum. James M. O'Neill had told the first convention of the National Association of Academic Teachers of Public Speaking in 1915 that "academic endeavor" must be their goal: "Non-academic and extra-curricular triumphs and victories must not be the most prized distinctions. The platform and the stage must give way to the study and the classroom as the scenes of our best and most important work and our richest and most enduring rewards." [24] The way was not always easy, even though extracurricular training had made favorable impressions on many administrators and influential citizens.[25] Indeed, the success of the Wisconsin debate association was attributed in large measure "to the increasing realization on the part of school principals and superintendents of the intrinsic value of the forensic activities sponsored by the League." [26] Yet many administrators regarded speech as "a frill of education, not an essential," [27] which could be acquired satisfactorily through extraclass experience. Gains in curricular recognition were slow; they were nonetheless inexorable.

Courses in subjects which we today label "speech" were offered by an occasional secondary school early in the century. As early as 1882, in fact, three schools in Cincinnati had included Elocution in the regular English program.[28] In 1903, the English syllabus for Greater New York high schools provided classes in argumentation the fourth and seventh semesters.[29] As Professor Baker expressed it, "some schools ... yielded to the inevitable and made debating a part of their curriculum." [30] Such offerings were few and scattered.

During 1910-1920, speech gained wider acceptance. Oral Expression was introduced as a course separate from English in Chicago high schools about 1912. Within seven years this subject, stressing reading, speaking, story-telling, technique of speech, and voice production, was being offered in half of Chicago's secondary schools.[31] Hunter College High School adopted Oral English in 1914, with emphasis on vocal and speech mechanics, pantomime, class discussion leading to informal debate, and the speaker's material, purpose, manner, and audience.[32] In 1912, a Berkeley, California, high school initiated a Shakespeare course which included student production of one play a year.[33] Steele High School of Dayton, Ohio, in 1916 organized a two-year course called Dramatic Art; it dealt with characterization, casting, voice development, simple impersonation, and history of the drama.[34] There were reports of oral work as a part of English classes in 1915,[35] and in 1916 of public speaking classes at Northwestern Academy.[36] The editor of the *Quarterly Journal of Public Speaking* could say in 1915: "Many normal schools, the leading private schools, and most of the large high schools have a definite part of their curricula in the hands of special teachers of public speaking." [37]

The need for speech training was pointed up during the period of the first world war. In the words of Alma Bullowa:

No greater stimulus could have been given to the work than the vast amount of public speaking that was being done the country round. ... Everyone who could speak in public did so, and those who couldn't tried to learn to do so, not for self-gratification, but as a means of serving. Thus public speaking became desirable, and good speaking an ideal to be achieved.[38]

Whether stimulated by war-time speaking, by the persistent efforts of teachers, or by a combination of these and other factors, speech offerings had greatly expanded by 1920. Textbook writers had contributed by furnishing high-school materials. A bibliography of 1918 recorded a book in public speaking written expressly for secondary schools, another in *Oral English for Secondary Schools,* five books in public speaking which could be adapted to high-school use, and seven of varying suitability for debate and argumentation courses.[39] A United States Bureau of Education survey on North Central Association schools commented, "it is doubtless contrary to general impression that nearly one-third of the schools make definite offerings" in public speaking.[40]

Of accredited schools in Montana, 52 per cent; in Indiana, 51 per cent; and in South Dakota, 50 per cent had some kind of course. Many states, of course, had none, although there were classes in the schools of Arizona, Colorado, Illinois, Iowa, Kansas, Missouri, Maine, Georgia, Texas, Utah, and New York.[41] Fifteen per cent of the 1032 schools in the North Central Association granted one-half unit for speech, 11 per cent a full unit, and 2.5 per cent two units.[42] Speech teachers should have been pleased that 30.3 per cent of the schools in this region included public speaking in their curricula, "since the teaching of any phase of Speech in the high schools is very recent indeed." [43] As Andrew T. Weaver observed:

A decade ago it seemed doubtful whether the importance of training in speech would ever be widely recognized. The situation is quite different today. There has come a growing conviction among school men everywhere that some sort of organized class work in Speech should be introduced into the high school curriculum. . . . We stand on the threshold of a new day.[44]

The new day was hastened by action of the National Association of Teachers of Speech. The Association appointed a special committee in December, 1923, "to study the situation and to recommend courses and procedures in speech training and public speaking for secondary schools." [45] This committee, ably headed by A. M. Drummond, was a successor to a Committee on High School Courses which in 1920 had advocated the introduction of a one-year foundation course in speech, wherever trained teachers were available, to be required in the second or third year. Specialized electives might be offered in elementary extempore speaking, debating, dramatics, and interpretative reading.[46] The Drummond committee and its forerunner built upon the work of an earlier National Joint Committee on English which had objected to English curricula that "practically ignored oral composition and subjects of expression drawn from the pupil's own experience." [47]

The Drummond committee called attention to "numerous well established high school courses," greater availability of teacher training in speech, and the demand for more training in Oral English made by the federal Bureau of Education and the National Council of Teachers of English. It recommended more speech in elementary schools, more and better speech clinics, more oral reading, and better teacher training. Following up its predecessor's suggestions, it presented courses of study for one-half to one unit of Speech Training or Public Speaking for the second or third year, and electives for juniors and seniors in public speaking, one-half to one unit; argument and debate, one-half or one unit; oral interpretation of literature, one-half unit; and dramatics, either oral interpretation or drama and production, one-half unit.[48] Published as a book containing helpful articles by many teachers, as well as its recommended study programs, the Drummond committee's report was a milestone. It helped to standardize curricula, clarify the planning of both speech and English teachers, and convince faculty and administration of schools without speech training that their offerings were incomplete. It continued to influence secondary-school speech education years after it appeared.

The National Association in 1928 again appointed a Committee for the Advancement of Speech Training in Secondary Schools, whose aims were "the expansion of speech education in all secondary schools now giving such training, and its introduction into those all too numerous schools which at present fail to offer instruction in speech subjects."[49] This committee published *The Speech Bulletin* as a supplement to the *Quarterly Journal of Speech* from 1929 to 1932, supplying surveys of the status of speech education and articles on developments in drama, debate, and interschool contests.

By 1932, speech courses were being offered in some of the high schools of at least thirty-three of the forty-eight states,[50] and in some of the other states where courses had not appeared, there were extracurricular speech programs. The attitude of many state superintendents toward speech at this time is partially revealed in a report by Dammon. In a questionnaire addressed to State Superintendents of Public Instruction, Dammon asked, "Do you feel that speech education is necessary to the better education of secondary school students?" Fifteen of the twenty-six who replied answered, "Yes"; five more responded affirmatively, with qualifications concerning the kind of speech education, and six answered, "No." [51] As these responses suggest, speech training was receiving more general approval in this period, and by the end of the decade, it was established in many more schools and in most of the states.

The area of the nation reporting the least speech training was New England and the East. Included in the list of states where speech was unreported in 1932 were Connecticut, New Hampshire, Rhode Island, Massachusetts, and Vermont.[52] Replies to the Dammon question from these states confirmed lack of classes devoted to speech training. Superintendent E. W. Butterfield, of Connecticut, thought there was "danger when Speech Education is segregated as a branch in itself," and the Vermont reply was: "There is no significant work being done in this field, and moreover, there is little probability of its development for a period of years on account of the local limitations, scattered population, small high schools with few teachers, limited finances." [53] By 1938, New York and New Jersey provided state courses of study in speech, Pennsylvania schools were offering some classes, and Vermont and Massachusetts were investigating the possibilities for extended programs. Reports from the Eastern states suggested that schools with few courses or none were becoming more interested in speech training, but, on the whole, the programs in this region were not as numerous as those in the rest of the nation.[54]

The South made rapid gains in this period, despite the late growth of its high schools,[55] and the tendency to leave what was considered specialized training in private or tutorial hands.[56] A 1928 Bureau of Education study on new courses in Southern schools listed the addition of thirty-one courses in public speaking, seven in dramatics, two in Expression, and two in Oral English. Alabama schools had added three, Florida six, Georgia three, Kentucky three, Mississippi one, North Carolina five, Tennessee one, and Texas twenty.[57] The phenomenal showing in Texas, which had some 800 high schools participating in interschool debate,[58] suggests that a thriving extraclass program contributed to curricular adoptions. During the next ten years, five of the thirteen Southern states adopted courses of study in speech—Florida, Louisiana, Oklahoma, Tennessee, and Texas. A survey by Harley A. Smith lists six others which included speech in English courses of study: Alabama, Arkansas, Kentucky, Mississippi, South Carolina, and Virginia.[59]

Examination of a speech education survey in Oklahoma [60] shows widespread interest in curricular speech. Of the 845 superintendents of schools questioned, 468 responded. Three hundred and ninety-three, or 84 per cent, reported speech courses in their schools. In order of popularity, they were: public speaking, dramatics, debate and parliamentary practice, and voice training and interpretative reading. Six hundred and ninety-two courses were given in these 468 schools, and administrators expressed a desire to offer 632 additional ones in dramatics, debate, voice training and interpretative reading, and public speaking. Three hundred and fifty-six administrators reported extracurricular activities, and 166 others said they would like to introduce speaking contests. Superintendents of schools giving no speech wanted to add a fundamental course in public speaking. Oklahoma schools, accordingly, seemed to recognize the values of speech training.

The Texas Department of Education revealed similar recognition of the values in speech education by permitting all high schools in 1938 to add three complete years of speech. Speech I, Fundamentals, was made a prerequisite to other courses, and electives included interpretation, dramatics, radio speech, public speaking, and debate.[61]

The South was not alone in promoting speech in these years; Western states also were extending speech education. Arizona, Oregon, and Washington published courses of study. Classes were provided in many schools of California, Colorado, Idaho, Montana, and Nevada. Utah and New Mexico stressed oral training in English courses, but were making plans to revise their programs to include more work in speech.[62]

In the Midwest, too, speech education was widely recognized by 1938. Extent of programs in the central states is suggested by these reports: [63]

Illinois. The Illinois School Directory for 1936-1937 reveals 303 high school teachers in the field of speech. Of this number 53 are classified in speech, 90 in public speaking, 140 in dramatics and 20 in debate. . . . Public Speaking, debate, and dramatics have in most of the larger schools won a place in the curriculum.

Missouri. The work of the Speech Association in Missouri, although extending over a period of only four years, has already achieved definite results in focusing greater attention upon the problems of adequately training teachers of English and Speech, of securing the proper emphasis upon speech training in the elementary curriculum and in the English curriculum of the junior and senior high schools, and of rewriting the state course of study in speech.

Kansas. The State Superintendent of Public Instruction reports: I believe that a large majority of high schools have some form of speech training. The subject is usually designated as public speaking or speech. A unit of speech training is approved in our program of studies. In a few schools two units are taught. This subject is offered in addition to either three or four units in English.

Nebraska. State Superintendent of Public Instruction: I would say that fully 50% of our Nebraska high schools are stressing speech training and many more are stressing it to some extent. We have a very fine high school debating league in Nebraska, and practically four-fifths of the schools in the state emphasize declamatory work. So I feel that our schools rank fairly well in the matter of speech training.

South Dakota. . . . there are 140 teachers of speech, 125 teaching speech as a major subject, and 15 . . . as a secondary subject. In the new English course of study, a semester, English III, 1, which is fundamentals of speech, is required of all accredited high schools.

Minnesota. A survey of speech education in public high schools of the state last spring showed that 39 percent of the larger high schools and 22 percent of the smaller offered at least one course in the study of speech . . . 75 percent of the school principals expressed real dissatisfaction with their speech programs. Most of these said they believed speech work sufficiently valuable to substitute speech for another course now in the curriculum. About 75 percent of these school principals were willing to indicate that they believed a course in fundamentals of speech should be required of high school students, and that as soon as possible, they would like to hire a teacher especially prepared to do this work.

Wisconsin. Thirty-four percent of the pupils of the state receive some speech training. The larger the high school, the greater the amount of speech training available. . . . The elements of speech training most frequently listed are gathering and organization of material, oral reading, extempore speaking, dramatics, voice, and impromptu speaking. . . .

There were extensive offerings also in Indiana, Iowa, Michigan, North Dakota, and Ohio.

Some idea of reasonably typical speech education programs in the central states may be found in an examination of those developed in Iowa. Well established as a curricular subject in many schools, speech received special emphasis in Creston, Davenport, Elkader, Fort Dodge, Iowa City, Ottumwa, and Sioux City. In addition, schools participated in declamation, debate, play production, original oratory, extemporaneous speaking, and so forth, as members of the Iowa Declamatory Association, and the Iowa High School Forensic League; they took part in the Iowa Play Production Festival, sponsored by the State University of Iowa, and in other speech and drama tournaments and festivals, such as the Invitational Tournament Festival at Drake University in Des Moines.

Schools representative of the development of speech education in the larger cities were those of Council Bluffs and Des Moines. Thomas Jefferson High School, Council Bluffs, at first was content with extra-class participation in forensics and dramatics. In September, 1928, it inaugurated a class in debate as an elective, meeting five periods a week each fall semester. A class in public speaking was scheduled each spring semester. Beginning in September, 1931, a course in Speech Improvement, required of all second-semester sophomores, was organized to meet five periods a week each semester. Dramatics was added in January, 1935, meeting five periods a week for one semester. By 1936, some speech work was being done in freshman English classes. Furthermore much emphasis was placed on discovery and preparation of talented students for successful participation in competitive forensic and dramatic activities. The apparent desire of the five speech teachers, other teachers, and the administrators of the school was to organize a speech program for all students.[64] Thus speech training in Council Bluffs was started.

The schools of Des Moines, by 1938, offered complete courses in speech and dramatics and provided for extensive extracurricular activities. After a careful diagnosis of speech needs, teachers designed a program of four courses. Speech I included classroom speaking and reading of poetry and stories. The second course called for parliamentary practice, panel discussion, short talks, story-telling, and speeches for special occasions. Public discussion, open forum debate, and radio speech were covered in Speech III, and in Speech IV, oral interpretation of poetry and stories, and oral reading of plays.[65]

As these reports from throughout the United States make clear, a sufficient number of secondary schools had adopted courses by 1938 to suggest that speech education had become a respectable component of the high-school curriculum.

Speech in Elementary Schools

As Emma Grant Meader points out in her book, *Teaching Speech in the Elementary School*,[66] many new movements in American education have had their beginnings in the lower grades and have moved upward to high school and college. Speech education in the twentieth century, however, was emphasized first in college departments, spread gradually to secondary schools, and appeared even more slowly in the elementary grades. The problem of deciding when speech training as such has been and when it has not been incorporated in elementary schools, of course, is considerably confused by terminology and emphasis. The early grades have not included subject matter labelled speech until recently, although the teacher could never avoid informal "instruction" in the oral use of the language. In reciting aloud, story-telling, reading lessons aloud, spelling-down, and the like, the child in the English class was of course "speaking." Yet the apparent intent was to teach reading and writing skills, not the skills of speaking. Teaching of speech in the elementary school, with emphasis directly upon oral communication, was a later and a new development.

Two examples selected at random may suggest the incidental, by-product nature of speech-in-English. A 1903 "Report on Courses of Study in English for Public Schools," [67] said that every course examined provided for "oral expression." By this was meant the reproduction of stories told by the teacher, reading of literature aloud or reciting the regular lessons, and narrating and reporting experience. The process was called oral expression, apparently, because the teacher listened and the student spoke. Outcomes which aided the child to express himself in speaking to others were incidental. Another curriculum study in 1916 spelled out the child's need for "clear, forceful, correct expression" in communicating with others for a purpose, but subject matter suggested to the teacher of English allowed only for "reading, writing, spelling, composition, grammar, and literature." [68] A later summary observed that in the elementary schools for many years the "written side of language has been taught ... oral reading has been stressed, grammatical mistakes have been corrected, and in recent years creative dramatics has been included, but the fundamental principles of speech, as such, have not been taught." [69] Alma M. Bullowa in 1922 reported: "Everywhere we are made to realize that ability to express thought in oral form, both adequately and excellently, has been neglected in the educational scheme . . . . speech training for normal children in the elementary schools [is still] incidental and occasional." [70]

Teachers became increasingly aware that the skills of speaking could, and should, be taught directly, especially after speech had found its place in colleges and secondary schools. In 1927, Teachers College of Columbia University established the "first class in direct speech education for the elementary school." [71] This course dealt with "basic principles underlying speech education . . . through a consideration of voice, phonetics, story-telling, oral composition, oral reading, and dramatics." [72] Encouraging also was the tendency in the 1930's for more elementary-school teachers to receive some speech training, so that every classroom could contribute to development of good speech. [73]

Signs of progress, too, were the courses of study developed for the elementary grades. Meader [74] cites examples in Michigan, New Jersey, and Minnesota. Dayton (Ohio) schools by 1935 were stressing articulation, pronunciation, and voice development; schools in Madison included training in bodily action, voice training, conversation, and dramatics. [75] The Washington State Speech Association prepared "An Integrated Course of Study in Speech" to be used "from the first grade through the high school." It was accepted by the State Department of Education in 1938. [76]

The kinds of learnings emphasized in this period are illustrated by a suggested speech program designed by Irene Poole Davis: [77]

Pre-school and Kindergarten
   Expression through bodily activity, relaxation, control of breathing: rhythmic games, dances, resting periods, pantomimic games.
   Appreciation of sounds, ear training for sound discrimination, vocal interpretations, accuracy in articulation of sounds: listening games, imitating sounds, guessing games of sound meanings.
   Co-ordinated expression for joy and delight, conversation, story-telling, dramatization: dramatized rhymes, jingles, songs, sharing experiences, repetitive stories told and played, spontaneous make-believe.
Grades 1, 2, 3
   (Much the same objectives, more advanced activities.)
Grades 4, 5, 6
   (Added:) Correct articulation, accepted pronunciation, vocabulary enrichment, correction of speech disorders.
   (Added under co-ordinated expression:) Oral reading (artistic sharing), original speaking (talks, reports, announcements, etc.), group movement (parliamentary activity in clubs, persuasion).

This type of training was not restricted to isolated schools in the thirties. Although the emphasis varied with the availability of trained teachers and administrative attitude, elementary-school curricula reflected the rapidly expanding concern with speech education. Gladys L. Borchers observed in 1936: "... today speech is a part of the daily training in the nursery school, it has its place in the program of the kindergarten, and it is an integral part of practically every revised elementary school curriculum...." [78]

Another innovation of the twentieth century which centered in the elementary school was the speech correction program. Educational philosophy by 1900 admitted a responsibility to atypical children,[79] and by 1910 Chicago public schools had a system of speech correction in operation. The Superintendent, responding to pressure from parents whose "stammering" children were lagging behind their classmates, brought in ten graduates of the department of expression, Chicago Teachers' College, who had shown ability and had some training in remedial speech to work with 1287 children listed by their teachers as "stammerers." They travelled from school to school, helping children wherever they were.[80] Remedial programs were established by city schools of New York [81] and Grand Rapids [82] in 1916, Cleveland,[83] 1918, and Madison,[84] 1923. In the next several years, acceptance of the public school's responsibility for aiding the speech-handicapped child became virtually universal.

Teacher Training

With the tremendous expansion of speech education during these decades came a persistent and difficult problem: the need for more teachers whose knowledge and professional preparation would enable them to teach effectively in the speech class, the speech-in-English classroom, and in extracurricular activities that demanded direct training in speech. Too often, extraclass activities and even courses were in charge of persons who were not educated in the teaching of speech in the same sense that instructors of history or mathematics were prepared in their disciplines; occasionally they had not taken a course in speech themselves! [85] Many earnest teachers of speech had attended colleges or normal schools whose offerings in their specialty were extremely limited. Throughout the period, accordingly, members of the profession endeavored to secure better training for teachers and to establish minimum standards for state certification of speech teachers.

Many colleges and universities, of course, had extensive departments of speech early in the century. In 1915, thirty-one of fifty-seven colleges questioned in one survey had separate departments of public speaking, elocution, oratory, and so forth.[86] By 1919, the University of Wisconsin was advertising courses for teachers of high-school speech in the *Quar-*

terly Journal of Speech Education, and within two years both Wisconsin and Iowa were granting the Ph.D. in speech.[87] The normal schools, on the other hand, were much slower to develop adequate training for speech teachers. Surveys of these institutions in 1918 and 1922 showed that they offered such courses as oral reading, play production, argumentation, advanced public speaking, dramatic interpretation, and applied drama and dramatic art; nevertheless they gave little or no attention to the *methods* of teaching speech. The inadequacy of their offerings as teacher training is suggested by the fact that 369 of the 379 courses offered in 115 schools were open to freshmen without prerequisite.[88]

Conditions had improved somewhat by 1930. A committee of the National Association of Teachers of Speech concluded after a study of teacher-training institutions:

The academic training of instructors has definitely improved since the survey of 1922 [by Rousseau]; there has been a decrease in the number of institutions offering work on a purely elective basis; one-half of the institutions offering speech work follow a system of prerequisites for advanced courses; in uniformity of nomenclature and standardization of approach there has been unmistakable improvement.[89]

Much of this progress, and of the continuing gains which were to follow, was due to the excellent work of the speech teachers' professional associations. The National Association of Academic Teachers of Public Speaking (later the National Association of Teachers of Speech and the Speech Association of America) called attention in the first issue of its journal to the need for properly qualified teachers in the field.[90] Membership in NAATPS, made up largely of college instructors, was opened at once to secondary-school teachers. As early as 1920, an Association Committee on High School Courses was asking that teachers of speech "be required to have the same general background" and the "special professional training required of those who teach other subjects."[91] Again in 1929, the Association demonstrated its concern with teachers' education and its constant attempt to contribute to a solution. The need for trained teachers was among the causes for the appointment of a Committee for the Advancement of Speech Training in Secondary Schools,[92] which publicized the needs of high schools in the period.

The state speech associations, too, worked diligently to secure minimum certification requirements for teachers of speech in the public schools. The obstacles encountered in this difficult undertaking are illustrated by the efforts of the Indiana Speech Association. About 1932, the Association persuaded the State Board of Education to issue a "speech teacher's license" for twenty-four hours credit in speech. It was possible in Indiana, however, for a teacher certified in English to teach speech if he had had *three* semester hours in *any* phase of speech. Naturally, there were few students who worked for the license in speech; unhappily, too, there were few schools in the state which could employ a full-time speech teacher. The Indiana Speech Association therefore urged that English teachers have twelve to fifteen hours of speech distributed in perhaps three areas before being allowed to teach it. The licensing requirement was changed in 1937, but still the English teacher needed only four to six semester hours of "oral composition" to teach speech.[93]

The Indiana experience was typical. In Illinois at the same time, the teacher of speech had to be qualified as a teacher of English and "have special preparation in the subject of speech to the extent of six semester hours of work." [94] The Missouri Speech Association by 1937 had succeeded only in bringing to the attention of the department of education and the accrediting agencies "the need of teachers especially trained in speech, and the need of speech training for all teachers." [95]

Despite such obstacles to the preparation of teachers, the diligence of the speech associations, national, regional, and state, was to be rewarded with progress in winning teacher certification. Curricular offerings of teacher-training agencies had improved through the years, and the trend was to continue. As more colleges established courses in speech, and as some began to require speech of all students,[96] teachers of all subjects in the schools were made more aware of the importance of the student's speech. The circle was evident: as opportunity for adequate training was increasingly available in colleges and universities and as speech became more important in the public schools, better teachers were demanded and obtained.

Professor Baker had suggested in 1903 that pupils should be trained in "right speaking." [97] The day he envisioned had not arrived by 1938, but it was much nearer than it was in 1900. Speech education was established from kindergarten to the doctorate. Secondary-school students were enrolled in speech fundamentals, public speaking, argumentation, radio speaking, oral interpretation, and dramatics courses in every region of the country; they appeared in thousands of debates and public speaking and dramatic performances. Many elementary-school children were acquiring basic speech skills, and hundreds of the speech handicapped were receiving the benefit of well-trained clinicians in their own school building. Speech education, one of the oldest disciplines in the western world, was firmly re-established.

Notes

1. John M. Loughran, "Oral English in the Secondary Schools," *Quarterly Journal of Speech*, XX (February, 1934), 72-80.

2. "The Teaching of Argumentative Discourse in High Schools," *National Education Association Journal of Proceedings and Addresses*, XLII (1903), 460-470.

3. Boston Latin School, Cambridge Latin School, Newton High School, and Dorchester High School. A. N. Levin and H. B. Goodfriend, *Harvard Debating 1892-1913*, p. 6, quoted in David Potter, *Debating in the Colonial Chartered Colleges* (New York, 1944), p. 96.

4. *The Speech Bulletin*, Supplement to *QJS*, III (December, 1931), 25.

5. According to James Leonard Highsaw, this was the first such invitational meeting at a university. "Interscholastic Debates in Relation to Political Opinion," *Quarterly Journal of Public Speaking*, II (October, 1916), 365-382.

6. *SB*, III (December, 1931), 18.

7. *Ibid.*, II (December, 1930), 46-60.

8. Highsaw, *op. cit.*

9. *Ibid.*

10. Edwin DuBois Shurter, "State Organization for Contests in Public Speaking," *QJPS*, I (April, 1915), 59-64.

11. Highsaw, *op. cit.*

12. Purpose of the Texas University Interscholastic League was "to foster in the schools of Texas the study and practice of public speaking and debating as an aid in the preparation for citizenship." Shurter, *op. cit.*

13. *Ibid.*

14. *SB*, II (December, 1930), 46-60.

15. *Ibid.*, III (December, 1931), 14-25.

16. J. Milnor Dorey, "Public Speaking and Dramatics in High Schools," *Education*, XXXIV (September, 1913), 31-38.

17. Wilhelmina G. Hedde, "A Brief History of High School Dramatics," *SB*, II (May, 1931), 2.

18. *SB*, II (May, 1931), 19-25.

19. Kenneth Macgowan, *Drama in the High School* (New York, 1929), p. 3.

20. Kenneth Macgowan, *Footlights Across America Towards a National Theatre* (New York, 1929), p. 169.

21. Bruno E. Jacob, "Work of the National Forensic League," *SB*, II (December, 1930), 18-21.

22. Karl F. Robinson, *Teaching Speech in the Secondary School* (New York, 1951), pp. 281-282.

23. Work of the NUEA was called "constructive." The first high-school debate "which determined anything like a national championship" took place in 1928 when Suffolk High School, Virginia champions, and Hartshorne High School, winners in Oklahoma, met before the House of Representatives in Washington. This debate led Professor Ted Beaird of the University of Oklahoma Extension Division to see possibilities in a nation-wide debate tournament. He presented the idea to NUEA and was named chairman of a committee to supervise the contest, which was later taken over by the National Forensic League. Arthur E. Secord and Ruth H. Thomas, "Speech in the Extracurriculum Program," *Bulletin of the National Association of Secondary School Principals*, XXIX (November, 1945), 117-119.

24. *QJPS*, II (January, 1916), 52.

25. Extensive high-school debating on a compulsory education law had been "in no small measure responsible" for the compulsory education law passed by the Texas Legislature. Shurter, *op. cit.* The Wisconsin State Legislature passed a resolution congratulating its successful high-school forensic association, and the Lieutenant Governor wrote: "I know of no single educational development in the past

forty years that is doing more to make good citizens." *SB,* III (December, 1931), 50-51.

26. *SB,* II (December, 1930), 46-60.

27. This was a statement made by a Dean of a College of Liberal Arts, quoted by W. Arthur Cable, "Speech, A Basic Training in the Educational System," *QJS,* XXI (November, 1935), 510.

28. The report available on this course was made in 1912, and then it had been in existence "for more than thirty years. At the time of the report, students attended one hour a week for four years (other hours were devoted to literature and composition) and were guided by "a regularly appointed teacher who has made a special study of elocution in its highest sense." At Walnut Hills High School, they studied voice physiology, articulation, breathing, poise of body, pause and emphasis, storytelling, and oral reading. They interpreted poetry, reproduced scenes from plays, and drilled on inflection, enunciation, vocal power, and facial expression. The fourth year was devoted to oratory and public speaking, which included argumentation and interpretation. The school had an extracurricular debating club open to junior and senior boys and a dramatic club for senior girls. Laura E. Aldrich, "Elocution in the Walnut Hills High School," *Public Speaking Review,* I (April, 1912), 242-246.

29. Charles S. Hartwell, "The Teaching of Argumentative Discourse in High Schools," *NEAJPA,* XLII (1903), 460-470.

30. Baker, *op. cit.*

31. Report of the Committee on Oral Expression of the Chicago High School Teachers Club, from Club *News,* April, 1919, quoted in *QJSE,* V (May, 1919), 301.

32. Alma M. Bullowa, "Speech Training in Hunter College High School," *QJSE,* VI (February, 1920), 24-32.

33. Macgowan, *Drama in the High School,* p. 5.

34. Grace H. Stivers, "A High School Course in Dramatic Arts," *QJSE,* IV (October, 1918), 434-437.

35. R. M. Lyman, "Oral English in the High School," *QJPS,* I (October, 1915), 241-259.

36. Andrew T. Weaver, "The Interschool Forensic Contest," *QJPS,* II (April, 1916), 141-148.

37. J. M. O'Neill, "The National Association," *QJPS,* I (April, 1915), 51.

38. Bullowa, *op. cit.*

39. *Public Speaking for High Schools* was written by Dwight E. Watkins and *Oral English for Secondary Schools* by William P. Smith. Elmer H. Wilds, "Speech Education in Secondary Schools—A Bibliography," *QJSE,* IV (March, 1918), 184-195.

40. Calvin O. Davis, "The Accredited Secondary Schools of the North Central Association," U. S. Bureau of Education *Bulletin,* No. 45 (Washington, 1919), p. 94.

41. Robert E. Williams, "A Survey of Speech Training in High Schools of the United States with Recommendations for its Improvement," *QJSE,* VIII (June, 1922), 224-255.

42. *Ibid.*

43. *Ibid.*

44. "The Content of a High School Course in Speech," *QJSE,* VII (February, 1921), 6-12.

45. A. M. Drummond (ed.), *A Course of Study in Speech Training and Public Speaking for Secondary Schools* (New York, 1925), p. v.

46. *QJSE,* VII (February, 1921), 76-78.

47. Drummond, *op. cit.*

48. *Ibid.,* pp. 6-9.

49. Rupert L. Cartright (sic), "Tomorrow's Bulletin," *SB,* I (November, 1929), 23.

50. Although the exact status of speech in each state is hard to determine from the reports available, since much depends on the interpretation of words used to describe "oral work" done in connection with English, etc., this figure seems reasonably reliable and is based on careful study of the following sources: Clara Krefting, "State Courses of Study in Speech," *SB*, III (May, 1932), 2-5; Orville C. Miller, "State Courses of Study in Speech in the Central States," *ibid.*, pp. 5-6; "Status of Speech Training," *ibid.*, pp. 7-12; Joseph Roemer, "Secondary Schools of the Southern Association," U. S. Bureau of Education *Bulletin* No. 16 (Washington, 1928); George S. Counts, *The Senior High School Curriculum* (Chicago, 1926), p. 31.

51. Clarence Dammon, "Attitude of State Superintendents," *SB*, III (May, 1932), 6-7.

52. Krefting, Miller, *et al., op. cit.*

53. The reply from Massachusetts was "Yes," from New Hampshire and Rhode Island, "non-committal." Dammon, *op. cit.*

54. Clara E. Kreifting, "The Status of Speech Training in the Secondary Schools of the Western and Eastern States," *QJS*, XXIV (April, 1938), 248-257.

55. The high school in the United States as a whole was a recent development, since in 1890 there were only 4,485 secondary schools, both public and private [Leonard V. Koos, *Trends in American Secondary Education* (Cambridge, Mass., 1927), p. 3]. The Southern high school was even newer: "Recuperation from the effects of the war between the States plus the mental set of the old South toward tutorial and private education retarded for several decades the growth and development of the modern high school in the Southern region. In fact the Southern high school dates from about the beginning of the second decade of this century." In 1896 there were 13 and in 1925, 756 schools in the Association of Colleges and Secondary Schools of the Southern States. Joseph Roemer, "Secondary Schools of the Association of Colleges and Secondary Schools of the Southern States," U. S. Bureau of Education *Bulletin*, No. 26 (Washington, 1927).

56. Attitude toward private and tutorial education and its influence on speech education was reflected in responses to Clara Krefting's survey. Alabama reported "A number of schools have arranged for private teachers of expression to train in public speaking those pupils who desire to follow it." The Georgia reply said: "Most courses in dramatics, debating and public speaking are paid for by parents of the persons receiving the training." Clara E. Krefting, "State Courses of Study in Speech," *SB*, III (May, 1932), 2-5.

57. Joseph Roemer, "Secondary Schools of the Southern Association," U. S. Bureau of Education *Bulletin*, No. 16 (Washington, 1928).

58. There may have been somewhat fewer than 800 schools in the years before 1928, but a report for the school year of 1929-1930 said there were "over 800" schools participating, *SB*, II (December, 1930), 58.

59. There was no report from Georgia, and that from North Carolina was not specific. "The Status of Speech Training in the Secondary Schools of the South," *QJS*, XXIV (February, 1938), 95-101.

60. *A Program of Speech Education for the Elementary and Secondary Schools and Junior Colleges of Oklahoma*, Speech Survey Project S-44, Works Progress Administration of Oklahoma (November, 1936).

61. "Teaching Speech in the Junior and Senior High Schools of Texas," *Bulletin*, The Texas State Department of Education (September, 1940).

62. Clara E. Krefting, "The Status of Speech Training in the Secondary Schools of the Western and Eastern States," *QJS*, XXIV (April, 1938), 248-257.

63. Clara E. Krefting, "The Status of Speech Training in the Secondary Schools of the Central States," *QJS*, XXIII (December, 1937), 594-602.

64. This desire culminated in the appointment of a committee to study the speech interests, needs, and abilities of students, and to suggest ways of developing student abilities. The result was to plan courses and experiences which would meet the needs of four groups: (1) entering freshmen; (2) students with no spe-

cial interests and abilities who had no serious speech defects; (3) students with serious speech defects; and (4) students with capacity and desire for specialized speech activities. Hugh F. Seabury, "Working Methods and Materials for the Diagnosis and Improvement of the Speech of Students in Thomas Jefferson High School," unpublished Ed.D. dissertation, Teachers College, Columbia University, 1938.

65. Earl S. Kalp, "A Summary of the Des Moines High School Speech Course of Study," *QJS*, XXIV (February, 1938), 90-95.

66. New York, 1928.

67. Mary C. Moore and Perley Horne, "Report on Courses of Study in English for Public Schools," *School Review*, XI (November, 1903), 746-776.

68. Mary D. Bradford, "Necessity of Changes in the Curriculum of the Upper Elementary Grades, both in Subject Matter and Content," *NEAJPA*, LIV (1916), 407-411.

69. Dorothy E. Sonke, "Speech Teaching in the Elementary Grades," *QJS*, XXI (November, 1935), 534-538.

70. "The Course of Study for Oral English in Hunter College High School," *QJSE*, VIII (November, 1922), 354-363.

71. Meader, *op. cit.*, p. 20.

72. *Ibid.*

73. In Missouri, for example, there was an increase of approximately 200 per cent in the number of classroom teachers taking courses in speech from 1937 to 1939. R. P. Kroggel, "Missouri Public School Speech Education Program," *QJS*, XXVI (April, 1940), 186-189.

74. *Op. cit.*, pp. 21-25.

75. "Suggestive Courses of Study Now in Use," *QJS*, XXI (November, 1935), 547-549.

76. Clara E. Krefting, "The Status of Speech Training in the Secondary Schools of the Western and Eastern States," *QJS*, XXIV (April, 1938), 253.

77. "A Speech Program for the Changing Elementary School Curriculum," *QJS*, XXII (October, 1936), 454-457.

78. "Co-ordination—Kindergarten through College," *QJS*, XXII (April, 1936), 246-249.

79. Paul Moore and Dorothy G. Kester, "Historical Notes on Speech Correction in the Pre-Association Era," *The Journal of Speech and Hearing Disorders*, XVIII (March, 1953), 48-53.

80. *Ibid.*

81. Source for the date is Moore and Kester, *op. cit.*

We should remark that speech training and speech correction in New York City schools presented a special problem. The New York population was polyglot; many pupils did not hear good American English consistently unless from their teachers. All prospective teachers were required to pass an oral examination, an examination which screened candidates not only for speech faults and defects, but also for deviations from good American-English usage. Speech clinics were provided for children with defective speech, and there were special classes for children who came from homes where a foreign language was primarily spoken. In addition to these special helps, there were classes to aid in the development and improvement of "normal" speech.

82. Pauline B. Camp, "Speech Treatment in the Schools of Grand Rapids," *QJSE*, VII (April, 1921), 120-138.

83. H. M. Buckley, "How Speech Training is Conducted in the Cleveland Public Schools," *QJS*, XXV (April, 1939), 200-203.

84. R. W. Bardwell, "How Speech Might Function in the Elementary School," *QJS*, XXV (April, 1939), 195-200.

85. A survey of speech in 123 Kansas high schools in 1931 showed that 100 schools offered training through extracurricular events; one in four of the teachers directing these activities was a teacher of speech and only five teachers worked

only in speech. *SB*, III (December, 1931), 49. In some schools, the Chicago High School Course in Oral Expression was taught in 1919 by teachers untrained in this field. Chicago High School Teachers Club *News*, quoted in *QJSE*, V (May, 1919), 301.

86. *QJPS*, I (April, 1915), 92.

87. *QJSE*, VII (November, 1921), 273, 385.

88. Elmer H. Wilds, "Speech Education in Normal Schools," *QJSE*, IV (May, 1918), 304-310; Lousene G. Rousseau, "Speech Education in the Normal Schools—A Survey," *Ibid.*, VIII (June, 1922), 209-217.

89. "Speech Education in Teacher-Training Institutions," *QJS*, XVI (February, 1930), 42-61.

90. J. M. O'Neill, "The National Association," *QJPS*, I (April, 1915), 51.

91. *QJSE*, VII (February, 1921), 76-78.

92. Cartright, *op. cit.*

93. H. B. Gough, "The Indiana Speech Teacher-Training Situation," *QJS*, XXII (December, 1936), 557-562.

94. Clara E. Krefting, "The Status of Speech Training in the Secondary Schools of the Central States," *QJS*, XXIII (December, 1937), 595-596.

95. *Ibid.*, pp. 598-600.

96. The State University of Iowa had made a course in public speaking compulsory for all Freshmen in 1919. *QJSE*, V (January, 1919), 58.

97. *Op. cit.*

22 National Speech Organizations and Speech Education

FRANK M. RARIG
HALBERT S. GREAVES

....

The late nineteenth century marked the beginning of organizations, national in scope, which succeeded in bringing together persons who sought to improve training in speech. By discussing their mutual problems, by looking critically at their aims and methods, these persons helped to secure the recognition and establishment of programs of speech education in the public schools and colleges. This essay is concerned with the record of events through the 1930's. By the end of the fourth decade of the twentieth century the principal organizations devoted to speech education seemed to have achieved stability and a considerable degree of professional maturity.

The National Association of Elocutionists

The National Association of Elocutionists was founded in 1892; its name was changed to the National Speech Arts Association in 1906; it ceased functioning in 1917. During the twenty-five years of its existence, speech education was gradually finding a place in the curricula of American high schools and colleges. Thus the life span of the Association and the pioneer period of speech education were nearly coterminous. To some extent the Association aided the development of speech education; nevertheless, individual members of the Association who were eminent teachers probably left as great an impact on speech education as the Association per se.

Periodically between 1882 and 1892 letters and editorials appeared in *Werner's Magazine* (at first called *The Voice*), urging elocutionists to hold a national convention or form a national association. But an organization was not achieved until 1892, when Hannibal A. Williams called for a convention which was held in New York City the entire week of June 27. Of approximately 2500 persons who were circularized, 373 attended. F. F. Mackay was elected president; Williams, vice-president, George R. Phillips, secretary; and Thomas C. Trueblood, treasurer. *Werner's Magazine* was named the official organ, and a constitution was adopted. A volume entitled *Proceedings* was published for this and for each subsequent convention.[1]

The name National Association of Elocutionists was adopted, although the word "elocutionists" met with heated opposition, for even then it was falling into disrepute.[2] Elocution was declining partly because public tastes were changing, partly because an academic approach to speech was being demanded by teachers and students alike, and partly because of doubtful practices of less skillful readers and "entertainers." Early in the history of the Association, educators were reluctant to grant college credit for elocution, but opposition slowly faded as speech education supplanted the entertainment motive, and as elocution broadened into speech arts. Elocution was largely entertainment characterized by the recitation of literature, usually memorized. The speech arts also embraced this type of performance, but went beyond it to include oratory, debate, public speaking, and acting.

Year after year convention speakers sang the praises and lauded the progress of elocution, yet decried the disfavor in which it was held by much of the public and by educators. The speakers candidly blamed entertainers who were guilty of a wide variety of objectionable practices including parlor recitation [3] and the "saying of pieces," [4] or, as F. Townsend Southwick wrote: "Any crank, any low comedian, any man or woman gifted or cursed by nature with what is vulgarly termed an 'elastic mug,' any school-girl with a few lessons from any sort of teacher, may step into our ranks and become at once a full-fledged elocutionist. ..." [5] In 1893, elocution was lambasted for tolerating "imitations of the cries of animals ... the blowing of whistles, ringing of bells, whirring of spinning wheels and other feats...." [6] In 1895, the "convention approved of statue-posing and musically accompanied recitations, but disapproved of bird-notes as a part of elocution." [7] College men did not have "any great amount of respect or care for elocutionary training," partly because they saw in it little but "the development of mannerisms in many of their pupils." [8]

In 1899, Mr. Henry Gaines Hawn censured certain objectionable practices, including inadequate training of many teachers and readers and the teaching of muscular development and grace of carriage. Public speaking and oral interpretation, however, he praised highly.[9] In 1904, as President, Mr. Hawn delivered an address full of "art anger," in which he denounced, among other things, "undignified advertisements ... absurd, pompous, flagrant and vulgar ..." such as "None

Better," "The Standard," "The Greatest Ever," and "The most successful reader before the public." He decried overemphasis on "one form of
the work, the 'saying of pieces.' We have made it seem that the art of
elocution is simply the memorizing of selections, and getting up before
the unoffending public, and reciting at them and for them." [10]

Reviewing progress in speech arts during the twenty years the Association had been active, President John P. Silvernail, in 1912, described
some conditions that had caused adverse criticism in the past and
sounded a strong note of optimism for the future:

> The press started in by ridiculing us in our national association and in state
> associations. We had the clapper of that "curfew bell" thrown at us; we were
> called stunt doers; we were called electrocutionists. . . . Well, long ago the
> press ceased to ridicule us and the public to look askance at us and educators
> to hold us at arms length. . . .
> Well, a revolution, a peaceful revolution, a bloodless revolution, has been
> taking place. The lowest form of the art—that merely of entertaining by com-
> ical recitations, is not now regarded as characteristic of our work.[11]

Opinions like these, taken from addresses delivered at conventions
between 1892 and 1912, reflect sentiments that were expressed at every
convention. They reveal three predominant ideas: (1) elocutionary
entertainment was in vogue during much of the late nineteenth and
early twentieth centuries; (2) although there were numerous well-
trained, competent, and sensitive elocutionists with high literary standards, there were also a great many who were guilty of the objectionable
practices outlined above; and (3) standards for elocutionary performance had improved slowly but steadily.

Against the preceding reports of the unfavorable attitude of the
listening public toward unskillful elocution must be balanced a discussion of the progress made by elocutionists in getting their art
accepted by the public and by schools. Mr. Silvernail hints at this
progress in the quotation above. Indeed, gaining wider acceptance for
the speech arts in colleges and high schools was a paramount concern
of virtually every annual meeting of the Association.

In 1892, the convention discussed the relation of elocution to college
and university education. Two college teachers reported very low salaries, two others high salaries. At Ohio Wesleyan, Robert Fulton, whose
fees for private lessons supplemented his salary, in a period of three
years earned by $400 more than twice as much as a regular professor.
The administration considered his services a good investment because
of the large number of students he brought to the school. At Michigan,
Trueblood was paid the same salary as other teachers, and his courses
were accredited with other subjects.[12]

Two years later, Franklin H. Sargent discussed "The Status of Elocution in the United States." His report was based on studies he had conducted in 1886 and 1893. Of the numerous statistics and many details covered, the following are most pertinent here: forty-three superintendents of public instruction replied to his questionnaires, and of this number "fourteen were favorable and twenty-nine unfavorable" toward the teaching of elocution, but of 162 colleges a ratio of four to one favored instruction in elocution. Salaries were low. In the public schools, for instance, they were lower by $500 than average salaries for other public school teachers, "i.e., less than $1000." [13]

Also in 1894, the Committee on Elocution in Colleges reported on the results of 440 questionnaires sent out, of which 102 were returned. Three conclusions of primary interest emerge from this report: (1) Most elocutionary instruction of the day was largely unacademic, "connected with oratorical or declamatory contests ... associated with some form of public rhetorical exercise; but only one ... specified original thought as an essential element." (2) The number of hours devoted to elocutionary study was generally low, varying from 35 to 144 hours per year. (3) "More work in our line has been established within the past ten years than ever before, 34 institutions reporting establishment within this later period, and only 9 prior to that." [14]

Reports more favorable than those of earlier years were made in 1898. Maud May Babcock stated that students at the University of Utah had petitioned for more work in interpretation. [15] Frederic Blanchard said the future was "bright with promise" because of growing favorable public sentiment; also, "Elocution is granted influence amounting to three percent of the whole.... I have in mind required elocution in the college. Where it exists at all, it requires about sixty out of the eighteen hundred or two thousand class-room hours in a college course." [16]

One of the most glowing and revealing addresses delivered at conventions was that of President Thomas Trueblood in 1898. He reviewed progress of the Association and of elocutionary work since 1878, and attributed much of the growth in college speech training to mounting interest in oratory and intercollegiate debating. In summary, he said:

1878 found three leading institutions in the East and four in the West with limited courses in oratory in their curricula; 1898 sees but few institutions of note that have not at least a year's work ... and many of our High Schools and Academies employing special teachers. 1878 witnessed the pioneers of our art going from college to college, where Presidents would deign to listen to them, and giving short courses to voluntary classes; 1898 sees these men occupying chairs of oratory in colleges and universities and devoting all their time to the advancement of the art. 1878 witnessed faculties strenuously opposing the introduction of elocution; 1898 sees extended courses offered which count with Greek, Latin and mathematics ... 1878 saw schools of oratory so few as to be numbered on the fingers of one hand; 1898 sees a prosperous school in every leading city, and department schools in two great universities.[17]

In view of the derogatory and pessimistic statements about elocution as entertainment and as education, these optimistic observations by Trueblood may seem somewhat paradoxical unless one remembers that they were made by a pioneer speech educator who desired nothing more than to see speech education become entrenched in college curricula. To him, in 1898, the establishment of speech departments in two great universities was a great achievement.

The high standards of some pioneer speech educators were excellently described by President Trueblood the following year, 1899, when he emphasized that education in expression develops "in a high degree the imagination, the literary faculty, the memory, the love of the beautiful. . . ."

[People] are not opposed to the right kind of elocution nor do they object to its teaching. Elocution is here and here to stay. It is entrenched in the high school, college, and university. If people do not like our work we must seek the cause, not in elocution but in ourselves. The uncultured will not stand false pretense and the most cultured will welcome genuineness and manliness. . . .

But in spite of Trueblood's high sentiments, the profession still had a long way to go, for "there are still colleges and universities and many high schools not yet supplied with teachers of expression. We must reach these by making our work too useful to be dispensed with. . . ." [18]

Robert Fulton, president in 1905, was as optimistic as Trueblood had been in 1898 and 1899: "When we organized this Association thirteen years ago, a college professorship was a rarity in our ranks. Today we cannot supply the demand for instruction in the high schools and universities. . . ." [19] Ironically, Fulton, who had been a leader in the fight to include the word "elocutionists" in the name of the organization, in 1905 led the fight to remove it. He was helped by several persons who forcefully decried the shabby reputation elocution had acquired. Trueblood asked the Association to "get rid of that abominable name 'elocutionists' that is down in the mud. . . ." [20] The name was changed to the Association for the Advancement of the Speech Arts,[21] and in 1906 to the National Speech Arts Association.[22]

Between 1905 and 1916, descriptions of "progress" were about the same: the speech arts had taken great strides forward; public esteem had increased tremendously; demand for teachers had never been so widespread; the number of students in high schools, colleges, and private schools had risen steadily. Nevertheless, the conventions recognized that much still remained to be done, for the speech arts had not yet acquired good standing with the faculties and administrations of most colleges and universities; there had been little standardization of subject matter, little uniformity of terminology, and but slight bibliographical accomplishment; literary taste of public and readers alike had not been elevated sufficiently; and membership in the Association had not increased.[23]

In 1916, George C. Williams was president, and although membership had dropped to 152 persons no address of any previous president had exceeded that of Mr. Williams in optimism. He forecast a rosy future for the speech arts and claimed that the Association had virtually eliminated the professional chaos of the late nineteenth century, the "multitude of pet theories, methods, short-cuts, or professional secrets." More than any other factor it had "been responsible for the remarkable development of public speaking in this country during the last quarter century." [24]

In 1916, Charles M. Holt was elected president and given power to designate the time and place for the next convention. There is apparently no record that such a meeting was held. Publication of *Proceedings* ceased with the volume for 1916,[25] and letters from several people who were active in the profession in 1916 have brought no information to indicate that a meeting was held in 1917.[26] The organization of the National Association of Academic Teachers of Public Speaking in 1914-1915 somewhat hastened the death of the Speech Arts Association, for the newer group attracted persons from the older association and offered a program of greater vitality and pertinence for speech educators. To a considerable extent, the birth of the one and the death of the other were parts of the same picture. Between 1892 and 1917 times and tastes had changed; as people became more interested in speech education they became less interested in elocutionary entertainment. Yet the Speech Arts Association did exert some favorable influence on the growth of speech education in America, for, as President Williams said in 1916, it succeeded in evoking widespread interest in all phases of speech education and it may have been the most influential single agency in raising standards of teaching and of platform performance. We are thus faced with the somewhat paradoxical conclusions that the National Speech Arts Association helped to bring about the improved conditions in speech education that made its own continued existence virtually impossible. But the paradox becomes explicable when we recall that it was an organization primarily for professional entertainers, that interest in listening to elocutionary entertainment was waning, and that many of the pioneer speech educators were also entertainers who had no other national association to cater to their needs for fellowship, interchange of ideas, and professional advancement until the National Association of Academic Teachers of Public Speaking was founded.[27]

The National Association of Academic Teachers of Public Speaking

That the Speech Arts Association itself recognized and participated in the transition from elocution to public speaking may be demonstrated further by noting that addresses on both practical and theoretical phases of public speaking received considerable stress in its last few convention programs. At its twenty-first convention in Minneapolis, Gaylord and Woolbert discussed the "science" of persuasion and the principles of public speaking.[28] H. B. Gislason spoke on "Debating as a Preparation for Life." [29] George L. Scherger's remarks point to the transition from elocution to public speaking: the professional man's "success or failure often depends on his ability to speak in public . . . . His training gives him a message but does not prepare him to deliver it. Let us acknowledge at once that mere elocutionary training of the traditional sort will not solve the problem." [30]

Two significant events in 1910 led to the organization of what is now known as the Speech Association of America and to the present broad program of speech education. In April, teachers of public speaking in colleges of Pennsylvania, Delaware, Maryland, New Jersey and southern New York met at Swarthmore College and formed the Public Speaking Conference. Their announced purpose was to become acquainted and to discuss common problems. To a second meeting in New York, April, 1911, the teachers in northern New York were invited. The members of this conference decided to publish "a periodical devoted to the interests of public speaking . . . and appointed a committee with power to act." In 1911, they produced the first number of *The Public Speaking Review*, declaring that the journal would be national in scope and would publish essays on all phases of speech:

The departments of the Review will be declamation, oratory, extemporaneous speaking, argumentation, acting drama, reading in schools, book reviews, criticism of speakers, and news items. The territory which the Review will represent is the entire country.[31]

At its fifth annual meeting, April 13 and 14, 1914, the Conference changed its name from *The Public Speaking Conference of New England and North Atlantic States* to *The Eastern Public Speaking Conference,* and announced that the *Review* should cease to be the publication of one conference only, but should represent all conferences in the United States.[32]

The second event of 1910 to foreshadow the founding of the SAA was the birth of the National Council of Teachers of English. The Council grew out of the work of a committee of the English Round Table, Secondary Department, of the National Education Association, at its meeting in Boston, July 1. The Table appointed a committee of schoolmen "to secure, as soon as possible, the judgment of its constituency upon the main question: 'Do the college-entrance requirements in English, as at present administered, foster the best kind of English work in the high schools?'" [33] On November 5, 1911, Chairman Hosic sent out the call for the first meeting to be held December 1 and 2, Chicago. Purpose of the meeting was "to create a *representative* body, which could reflect and render effective the will of the various local associations, and of individual teachers, and, by securing concert of action, greatly improve the conditions surrounding English work." On December 2 organization of The National Council of Teachers of English was effected. The first number of the *English Journal* is dated January, 1912.

Both of these movements were revolts. The English teachers rebelled against the type of scholarship and teaching fostered by the Modern Language Association, based largely on German requirements for the doctorate. To the meeting of the English Round Table at San Francisco July 12, 1911, Hosic presented *Questions at Issue:* "Should the children of the many be prepared for life and life's occupations," or should all be given the preparation of "the few for entrance to privately endowed colleges?" Oral expression was neglected. "The English course as a whole tended to formality, scholasticism, and over-maturity, and needed to be vitalized, redirected, and definitely related to the life of the present." [34]

Teachers of public speaking, whose work was "definitely related to the life of the present," found their teaching, wherever included in an English department, subordinated to English and themselves judged by traditional standards of scholarship irrelevant to what they were doing. Their discontent began to brew in various conferences. On December 27 and 28, 1912, twenty-two representatives of fourteen colleges in eight north-central states met at Northwestern University and discussed the relation of teachers of public speaking to the English Council, but reached no decision.[35] Representatives of twenty colleges comprising the *Ohio College Association* had somewhat earlier discussed the question, "Should our work be under the English Department, a separate department, or a school of Oratory?" [36]

The English Round Table had already taken action which was to make an important contribution to separate national organization of teachers of public speaking. Elmer W. Smith of Colgate University,

Chairman of the joint committee of the Eastern Conference and the Speech Arts Association, requested that "the N.E.A. Committee make provision for oral expression as a definite division of its work. The Round Table voted that this be done, and the Committee of which Mr. Smith is Chairman will join forces with the Committee of the Round Table." [37] This action created the Public Speaking Section of NCTE, the *first* mechanism, *national* in scope, to bring together teachers of public speaking. At the meeting of the Section in 1913, teachers took the initial step towards the formation of a national organization independent of NCTE.

The Eastern Conference, likewise, took action which pointed towards an independent association. The members of the Conference, at their fourth meeting at Yale University in March, 1913, adopted a resolution which declared that instruction in public speaking should be separated from departments of English. J. M. O'Neill of Dartmouth College launched the argument for separation. Having examined "about sixty college catalogues," he described what he had found, and declared, "the situation in our work throughout the country is in the unorganized, chaotic state that I have represented to you here." J. A. Winans gave practical reasons for separation: first, "Public speaking is made secondary to English"; second, "many heads of English departments will refuse to promote teachers of public speaking." O'Neill and Frederick B. Robinson prepared a declaration of independence which proclaimed that the principles and practices of public speaking were different from those of English, that students deserved public speaking teachers who were trained specialists, and that departments of public speaking should be entirely separate from departments of English.[38]

At the convention of the English Council, November 28, 1913, between fifty and seventy-five persons attended the meeting of the Public Speaking Section. Thomas C. Trueblood presided over an extended discussion, and a committee was formed to find out whether teachers over the country wanted an independent association.[39] The committee consisted of C. D. Hardy (Chairman), J. M. O'Neill (Secretary), and C. H. Woolbert.

At the banquet of the English Council, O'Neill laid out the issues dividing teachers of public speaking from departments of English. "The issue splits," he said, "on the rock of standards of scholarship. The German Ph.D. ideal is not for Public Speaking, which must have its own standards of scholarship and teaching. . . . The only hope for sane, sensible, academically respectable work in Public Speaking of any kind . . . lies in the general deliverance of this work from English Department control." [40]

Winans commented: "O'Neill's speech at the banquet started a good deal of thought on the future relations of teachers of public speaking to teachers of English. Professor Clapp of Lake Forest is strong for union but admits union is not for the immediate future, for he recognizes that in most English departments today, public speaking is likely to be assigned to underpaid men and treated with scant courtesy." [41] Events were moving toward culmination.

At the meeting of the English Council in Chicago the next year Chairman Hardy reported to the Public Speaking Section the results of the questionnaire his committee had sent out. Of 116 teachers who replied, 113 favored and 3 opposed a national association. After a long debate, when several strong supporters of a motion to organize had left the meeting, the motion was tabled by a vote of 18 to 16, and the meeting adjourned to the next day. Saturday afternoon, November 28, 1914, seventeen survivors of the Friday debate met in the Auditorium Hotel, and, emerged as charter members of the National Association of Academic Teachers of Public Speaking. Thus the issue over separation from English was settled. The founders had taken clear and positive action. The desirability of their action was soon confirmed by Lyon's report that teachers in twenty-seven state universities were almost unanimously in favor of a separate department.[42] The charter members were:

I. M. Cochran	Carleton College
Loren Gates	Miami University
J. S. Gaylord	Winona Normal
H. B. Gislason	University of Minnesota
H. B. Gough	DePauw University
Binney Gunnison	Lombard College
C. D. Hardy	Northwestern University
J. L. Lardner	Northwestern University
G. N. Merry	University of Iowa
J. M. O'Neill	University of Wisconsin
J. M. Phelps	University of Illinois
F. M. Rarig	University of Minnesota
L. R. Sarett	Northwestern University
B. C. Van Wye	University of Cincinnati
J. A. Winans	Cornell University
I. L. Winter	Harvard University
C. H. Woolbert	University of Illinois [43]

The decision to found an association for teachers of public speaking reflected wide and deep experience. The founders were sensitive to elocutionists and professional coaches of speaking who were not educationally oriented; hence, they were not welcomed into the fold at first, as the word *Academic* in the Association's name pointedly indicated and as made clear in the qualifications for membership in the first constitution. Thirteen of the seventeen founders, moreover, had contributed substantially to their profession—Winans as the most frequent contributor to the *Review,* member of its editorial board, and president of the Eastern Conference in 1913-1914; O'Neill as secretary-treasurer of the Conference during the same period, member of its editorial board, and instigator to revolt against domination of public speaking by English departments; Gough as associate editor of the *Review* and contributor to its pages; A. L. Gates as associate editor and as vice-president of the "Standardization Convention" of the Ohio Conference in 1912; Gates, Gislason, Hardy, Lardner, Sarett, Merry and Winter as contributors to the *Review;* Gaylord and Woolbert as authors of studies in the psychology of speech.

The decisive action of the men who framed the first charter of the Association led ultimately to the present program of speech education in America. The founders offered a new focus for the relatively random efforts of teachers and associations that had for twenty-five years or more striven, with occasional success, to unify, to place on a solid foundation, and to give academic stature to training in speech which was something more than "elocution." They were aiming at a balanced, well-developed program of speech education in both the high school and college. Deploring the abuses of elocution, they saw delivery, not as vocal and gestural display, but as voice and action tied to the meaning of ideas and giving effectiveness to thought. The principles of delivery, indeed, were equally valid for the actor, the reader and declaimer, and the public speaker. Discouraged by the attempts of teachers of English to teach "composition" chiefly in terms of grammar and style and to serve the ends of literary appreciation and writing, the founders felt they had to revolt. They believed that a speech of any kind was something more than a written theme or report repeated orally; they understood a public speech as practical, systematic communication whose ideas, organization, style, and presentation were a product of the speaker, his subject, his audience and occasion. They believed that public speaking, debate, and discussion were indispensable to the operation and success of a political and economic society founded on freedom of enterprise and freedom of debate. As teachers they were convinced that their subject could be taught effectively in the classroom, and that its principles and techniques could be steadily illuminated and advanced through scholarly study and research.

The new Association at once recognized the need for an organ of communication. O'Neill insisted that publication must coincide with the first year of the Association's life. Following his initiative, the group not only elected him its first president, but also, in recognition of his specific plans for a journal, handed him the responsibility of establishing the *Quarterly Journal of Public Speaking.* Without the official title of editor, and with the assistance of Winans, he assembled and edited the material for the three numbers of the volume of 1915.[44] The format, quality, and historical value of the contributions in this volume, the balance and proportion of its contents are the best testimonial to his industry, judgment, and foresight. Made official editor by action of the first convention,[45] he continued in that position for the next five years, survived many adversities, and handed to his successor, Woolbert, an established professional journal.

With the *Journal* provided for, the founders and early members of the new Association attacked these problems: Could public speaking be taught with English, under a label such as "Oral English"? Should public speaking and English be within one department or in separate departments? Around 1910-1912, most teachers of public speaking thought they could accept the framework of both the English department and the "Oral English" course. Elmer W. Smith of Colgate, chairman of NCTE's Oral English Committee, insisted that written and spoken English be taught in the same course.[46] Calvin Lewis of Hamilton College opposed separation into specialized departments. All teachers should teach English.[47] Public speaking teachers joined with English teachers in advocating tests of spoken English for college entrance and for programs of Oral English in high schools.

By 1914, teachers of public speaking by and large stood for autonomy in courses and in department organization. Lyon's report accurately reflected opinion in favor of departments distinct from English. Teachers understood, also, that a public speech was not the essay and theme of Oral English and that the spoken language did not always behave according to the prescriptive rules of grammar and pronunciation set forth in the Oral English classroom. After attending the third convention of NCTE, Winans asked the central question:

What is our work to be called in the future? Oratory? Public Speaking? Oral English? the last might be made to cover the ground best, but what does it really mean? Does it not seem to narrow our work to a matter of language? Does it suggest a virile public speech? [48]

A high-school teacher of Oral English during the same convention explained that the aim is "to make class room English the English of the street and the baseball field," and that the teacher proceeds by correcting idioms, by removing slang, by enlarging the vocabulary, correcting grammar and rhetorical structure in the sentence, the paragraph, and the whole composition. Effective expression, he said, is to be accomplished by drilling in distinct enunciation and correct pronunciation, supplemented by much reading aloud, declamations, and oral themes.[49] Of such a program Winans drily commented, "The need of arousing interest in literature was less emphasized than that of securing elementary correctness." [50] In November, 1913, Ohio teachers of public speaking concluded that "oral English should be done in the Department of Public Speaking; indeed ... [it] probably cannot be done intelligently elsewhere." [51] The immediate effect of the new association was to bring together persons convinced that public speech in all its forms and manifestations was practical, virile discourse and that it could and should be taught accordingly. Perhaps this conviction gave to the new Association greater strength, identity, and solidity than any other single belief.

The conviction that public speaking was something more than oral English was undoubtedly nourished by the long and wide experience with debate, oratory, and other speaking "contests" conducted largely on an extracurricular basis in both schools and colleges. Teachers, "coaches," and students alike well knew that the preparation and delivery of speeches for real audiences (often very large audiences indeed) went far beyond the average English teacher's preoccupation with themes and reports, with the elements of "correct" style and pronunciation. They knew, too, that intercollegiate speech-making dealt not with English literature, but with live questions on public affairs. From 1892 to 1914 the subject matter of orations and debates so directly reflected the political, social, and reform movements of the same period that an editorial in the *Public Speaking Review* raised the query:

It would be interesting to know what connection there is between oratory and debate work of this sort (intercollegiate) and the various political reform movements that are going on all over the country.[52]

The central conviction of the founders gave force and direction to the main lines of development in speech education for many years. Through its conventions, its publications, and its committees, and through its members who taught in scores of schools and colleges, the Association worked to establish the curricular study of speech in American education. Learning to speak well—or at least, acceptably—in any socially significant situation was regarded as an essential part of the individual's formal education; it should therefore be learned systematically, under specially qualified teachers, and merit the academic respect it had held for over two centuries under the name of "rhetoric." Two main trends can be discerned: (1) the organization of courses, including consideration of content and method, for both public schools and colleges; and (2) the attempt to shape extracurricular "speech contests" in ways that served educational goals, rather than competitive ends merely.

Perhaps the beginning of concerted effort to regularize college courses and their content was the "Standardization Convention" of the Ohio Conference in 1912. Twenty-two teachers from eight north-central states met twice, thoroughly canvassing their own courses, their purposes, and procedures.[53] To the NCTE convention in 1913, Fulton presented a college curriculum, with "Elocution: Man's Triune Nature" heading a list of ten courses. Among the "minimum essentials" in order of preference were Argumentation and Debate, Parliamentary Usage, Oratory, Rhetorical Criticism, Oratorical Seminar, Literary Analysis and Interpretation, and Shakespeare.[54] Trueblood proposed his speech program the next year; in 1916 Woolbert published his map of the field, "Speech Science and the Arts," along with a prospectus of courses for a department of speech.

The first complete and systematic syllabus for speech training in the secondary schools appeared in 1925.[55] It was the work of the Association's Committee for the Advancement of Speech Training in the Secondary Schools, led by A. M. Drummond. Published in book form the same year, together with a number of articles setting forth principles and points of view for all aspects of the speech program, the work doubtless stimulated speech training in the high schools and encouraged teacher preparation in the colleges.[56] In the early 1930's, the same committee supplemented and extended its pioneer work by issuing a series of special bulletins.[57]

As teachers of college courses in speech, members of the Association could agree that their goal was a sound education in speech—an education which offered the student both training in skills and techniques and knowledge of the principles which provided the rationale of skill. But about the character and content of specific courses, they argued vigorously. Mention of a few of their problems will have to suffice here. What, for example, should be the basic or "fundamentals" course in the college program? Trueblood, like Fulton, believed that "A *thorough* study of the principles of elocution should be the basis of all courses in public speaking." [58] Somewhat earlier, at the Ohio Conference, H. M. Tilroe argued for a foundation course in elocution, but met with sharp disagreement.[59] Persons, like Winans, who were skeptical of too much elocution wanted the basic course to concentrate on original, extemporaneous speaking, with a little declamation mixed in for special purposes.[60] Thus was started the debate over the "first" course; with ramifications, the debate has persisted to the present day.

As courses in public speaking multiplied, another question provoked sharp discussion: How should the college teacher handle the relationship between the substance or content of a speech, on the one hand, and form and technique, on the other? Should his course deal solely or primarily with processes and techniques? Should it incorporate a liberal amount of reading and discussion in timely political and social problems from which would be drawn the subjects and some of the "content" of student speeches? These were some of the questions of the O'Neill-Hunt-Sandford debate.[61] The questions, at first centered on pedagogy and method, ultimately involved the kind of preparation and background for the teacher of speech. How much specialization? How much liberal (or general?) education?

In 1917, Woolbert published his article, "Conviction and Persuasion." [62] It focused attention on the relationship between logical and psychological modes of proof, and for the twentieth-century teacher it helped to open up the kinds of contributions which the natural and social sciences might offer to public speaking and to the whole field of speech. On both theoretical and pedagogical grounds, Woolbert questioned the conventional distinctions between conviction and persuasion, as general ends of discourse, and argument and emotion, as means to the ends. Teachers of argumentation courses, debate coaches, and persons interested in the development of advanced courses in speech-making recognized the implications for both the content and conduct of their teaching. Mary Yost brought sociology to bear on argumentation.[63] A. P. Stone, teacher and professional writer and speaker, abjured the theories of Yost and Woolbert and stated the pragmatic position.[64] Rowell's "Prolegomena to Argumentation," published in four parts, concluded that while the traditional view of argumentative theory and principles is sound, the tradition should be *corrected* and *improved* by relating it to the great variety of "argumentative situations," to the contributions of modern logic and psychology; and should be shaped "not only to the student's search for skill and power but also to the general aims of education." [65] The problems thus raised have continued to interest large numbers of teachers.

The early years of the Association were marked by more than an interest in developing the academic study of speech. They were distinguished also by prolonged discussion over the values and methods of extraclass speech activities, especially those activities which entailed competition among schools and colleges. Although all "speech contests" were under scrutiny, the focal point was the interschool and intercollegiate debate. Had winning the debate, had intensive coaching of a few talented students, become so general a practice as to seriously hinder the realization of more comprehensive educational ends and methods?

The modern teacher of speech is familiar with "over emphasis" in athletics; he little realizes that many of the evils associated with highly competitive athletics today were also associated with competitive debate in the earlier 1900's. Few persons at first questioned the supreme importance of winning; the critics directed their shafts at the methods employed to insure victory. The first convention of NCTE noted "widespread hostility to debating in both colleges and universities on the grounds of dishonesty and plagiarism." [66] Lee Emerson Bassett observed: "To guard the interests of the college in intercollegiate debating and increase the prospect of winning, a system of professional coaching has grown up, which tends to relegate the activity to a place among intercollegiate sports." [67] Superintendent F. A. Welch of the Hampton (Iowa) public schools deplored the training of a few students to the neglect of the many, declaring that schools outside the state debate league achieved a better educational product than the schools in it; he announced unqualifiedly, "We want teachers, not coaches." [68] As the controversy wore on, the critics sometimes gained notable converts. James M. O'Neill, for example, was at first willing to defend intercollegiate debating as "a college sport, no more and no less . . . honesty in coaching and competent judges, skilled in debate could qualify debating as an intellectual sport purely as a student activity." [69] Twelve years later, O'Neill could say:

Both for those who participate and those who listen, contests in debate should be helpful toward higher standards, better ideals, greater ability in this field. Their function is properly educational, and they should not be allowed to be diverted from their really great educational end. When we neglect their possibilities as educational agencies and prostitute them to mere advertising and cheap "sporting" ends, we are committing an offense as great as any of the outrages that characterized the worst days of athletic rivalry. [70]

The controversy over ends and means in debate continued from time to time, generating changes aimed to make contests more of a genuine enterprise in communication and education. Competitive debate practices were modified in various ways: use of the expert critic judge, the judgeless debate, decision by the audience, the open-forum debate, and the Oregon Plan. Both coaches and teachers in increasing numbers could subscribe sincerely to the values of debate as expressed by a distinguished classical scholar, Charles Sears Baldwin:

. . . a college training broad enough to interpret and energize a wide range of studies, to give zest to learning and mastery to the learners, and so to show what the intellectual life of the college is actually worth in making men intellectually efficient among their peers. . . . the sheer knowledge of public affairs displayed is worthy of any platform; and it cannot be acquired without methods of study that are of far wider use. [71]

Interscholastic debating made great strides when the National University Extension Association in 1928, through its committee on discussion and debate materials, provided a mechanism through which the representatives of the state debate leagues could meet annually for the discussion of common problems, for the selection of the national debate question, and for the annual publication of two volumes of authoritative materials aimed to furnish students, at low cost, with a thorough background and understanding of the facts and opinions essential to intelligent discussion and debate of the nation-wide topic. (Parenthetically, it may be observed that speech contests were not securely put within an educational frame of reference until 1951 when SAA published "A Program of Speech Education.")[72]

The founders and leaders of the new association understood early the need for scholarly research and the academic respectability which surrounded it.[73] Primarily teachers of elocution and public speaking, members had received relatively little training in the discipline of the scholar. The Association promptly set up a Committee on Research to encourage the study of public speaking as a "scholarly subject with a body of verified knowledge and a professional tradition and ethics. . . ."[74] The first editor of the *Quarterly Journal* announced that he would give "the right of way over all other material to articles giving the results of research which come to us through the chairman of the committee on research."[75] Although the editor's policy touched off a controversy over the merits of research and of teaching as ways to academic advancement and status,[76] the Association steadily encouraged scholarship. When the volume of research material had become too great for the *Quarterly Journal of Speech, Speech Monographs* started publication in 1934 and endeavored to print all worthy articles which were the products of historical, critical, and experimental study. *Monographs* was made financially possible by inaugurating Sustaining Memberships in the Association with annual dues of $10.

The importance of bibliography for both teaching and research was recognized early. The first bibliography on speech education for secondary-school teachers appeared in the fourth year of the *Quarterly Journal of Speech Education;*[77] it was soon followed by Blanton's bibliography for the beginner in speech correction.[78] Two years later Baird published his selected bibliography of American Oratory,[79] and in 1929 appeared McGrew's pioneer bibliography on rhetoric and related subjects in sixteenth- and seventeenth-century England.[80] In 1937, O'Neill offered a basic bibliography to graduate study in speech,[81] and in the same year Ewbank prepared the first classified bibliography on radio speaking and writing.[82] The comprehensive *Bibliography of Speech Education* was published by the H. W. Wilson Company in 1929 under the editorship of Thonssen and Fatherson.

Through the years the Association has shown remarkable growth. In 1916 its regular members numbered 160 and the budget was slightly over $1300; in 1949 its membership numbered over 5100 (including

1300 Sustaining Memberships) and its annual budget was $41,000. Sixty persons attended the first convention in 1915; at the Chicago convention in 1949 over 2100 registered. The programs of the convention strikingly illustrate the development of manifold special interests within the field of speech. The first two conventions provided for no section meetings, the convention of 1950 had well over 100. As its members developed diversified interests, the official name of the association underwent change. Starting out with the National Association of Academic Teachers of Public Speaking, it soon dropped the adjective *academic* and welcomed to its membership any worthy private teacher of public speaking. Later, the name became the National Association of Teachers of Speech; still later the Speech Association of America.

American Academy of Speech Correction [83]

Initially the Association attracted and made welcome all teachers interested in established activities to which speech was central—persons interested in dramatics, in the oral interpretation of literature, in voice training, in phonetics and in remedial or corrective speech, as well as persons concerned mainly with public speaking and debate. But within ten years of its founding, the Association felt the impact of science and specialization which World War I brought with it. Special interest groups emerged from the parent organization. The two major ones to assume permanent shape within the time span of this volume were the American Academy of Speech Correction and the American Educational Theatre Association. (The history of the second group is briefly sketched in another article in this volume.)

At the 1925 convention of the National Association of the Teachers of Speech, Robert West proposed the following:

Be it Resolved that the Association favors the organizing, within its group, of semi-autonomous daughter organizations having memberships limited by the special arts and sciences represented by the Association.[84]

Although the Association took no action, West's resolution reflected the opinion of teachers and professional workers in speech correction that they would welcome an organization which served their special interests. West, joined by Sara Stinchfield of Mt. Holyoke College, met informally with a group of speech correctionists "in the interests of a new organization to include workers in the field of speech correction who might best promote the interests of a national organization and best represent the new movement." [85] With West as temporary chairman the group discussed the purpose and standards of membership, and, among other things, suggested that the new society be allied with NATS as an auxiliary part of that organization but with restricted membership.[86] The topics settled upon for discussion at their next meeting indicate the immediate interests of the group: classification and terminology in the field of speech correction, "research on success and failure of stutterers," foreign accent problems, phonetic mechanisms of "careless speech," case history and records, and bibliographies in speech correction.[87]

By December, 1926, the American Academy of Speech Correction was a fact. Its purposes, stated in the original constitution, remained the same for many years:

To stimulate among educators, physicians and others of the general public a deeper, more intelligent interest in problems of speech correction.
To raise as rapidly as possible existing standards of practice among workers in the field of speech correction.
To secure public recognition of the practice of speech correction as an organized *profession*.
To furnish this new profession with responsible and authoritative leadership.
To make this leadership generally respected by our good work, i.e., by our scholarly research work, publicity work and administrative skill.
To make membership in our organization a coveted recognition of merit and in this way furnish workers in the field of speech correction with a powerful incentive to greater achievements.[88]

Robert West was elected President; Lee Edward Travis, Vice-President; Sara Stinchfield, Secretary; and Richard Borden, Treasurer.[89]

In the same December, NATS decided that it could encourage and support any responsible group of members who wished to band together for the advancement and study of their specialty. Its resolution to this effect was worded as follows:

That the National Association put itself on record as being favorable toward the inclusion and due recognition of groups or organizations having as their purpose within the general field of speech or Public Speaking, the investigation, discussion and standardization of special or technical phases of our work; but that such groups or organizations shall first submit for the approval of the National Association a definite statement of their aims, policies and basis for membership.[90]

The new organization, renaming itself the American Society for the Study of Speech Disorders, was finally endorsed at the Cincinnati convention of NATS December, 1927. The two organizations recognized, as Robert West said, that "their purposes, requirements and organizational structures are so different that they complement each other rather than compete." [91] A sizeable number of persons held membership in both organizations and both groups continued to meet in joint annual convention for many years.

As knowledge accumulated about the behavior of the speech-handicapped person and as both the public and educators became aware that the child with a speech difficulty could be helped, the public schools began to demand qualified teachers and therapists. Colleges and universities started special courses and professional curricula. The new association devoted much of its attention to standards of professional practice and to the number and content of courses designed to train the correctionist. It insisted, moreover, upon a basic code of professional practice, namely, a pledge to help the handicapped person to come as close to normalcy as could be, and to abide by the standards of training his peers determine appropriate. It did much also to stimulate research into all phenomena of speech and hearing and to related areas of learning as well. Its official publication, the *Journal of Speech Disorders* (now the *Journal of Speech and Hearing Disorders*), first appeared in 1936; its *Monograph Supplements,* reporting at length upon significant research, is published irregularly. Now known as the American Speech and Hearing Association, its membership includes 2800 persons.[92]

Honor Societies

Honor societies were founded to confer distinction on students who have shown unusual ability in public address.

Delta Sigma Rho

The idea of an honor society for the recognition of excellence in intercollegiate debate and oratory occurred simultaneously to Henry E. Gordon, of the University of Iowa, and to E. E. McDermott, of the University of Minnesota. They enlisted Thomas C. Trueblood in the enterprise, and two years later, the three men, together with five or six others from midwest universities, met in Chicago on April 13, 1906, and founded Delta Sigma Rho, the first of the honor societies. On McDermott's insistence, participation in intercollegiate contests was made the sole condition necessary for membership. This condition excluded the founders.[93]

The first president was George T. Palmer of Northwestern; its first secretary, Gustavus Loevinger of Minnesota. It now has chapters in 77 colleges and universities.[94]

The purpose of the fraternity is to encourage "sincere and effective public speaking," and it grants the DSR key as an award of distinction to speakers in contests arranged by colleges and universities. Today it holds occasional national student congresses for the discussion of issues of broad public policy but holds no contests. Each congress is organized as a legislative assembly and formulates proposals for laws. Its official organ is *The Gavel.*

Tau Kappa Alpha

Tau Kappa Alpha, organized by Oswald Ryan while a student at Butler University, April 13, 1908, "as an honorary society which would in a way do for public speaking in American colleges what Phi Beta Kappa does for scholarship," [95] now has 187 chapters in thirty-six states which are arranged in seven *Regions,* each with its governor. At its national conferences, the eleventh of which was held in March, 1951, it stages discussions and debates, and to outstanding speakers awards the Wachtel Plaques. Applications for membership are limited to candidates in the upper 35 per cent of scholarship in their college class, after two years of participation in intercollegiate debate and discussion or a speakers' bureau. Special features are close co-operation with faculties; provision for civic chapters on petition by alumni members; *Annual Speaker-of-the-Year Awards* to honor public personages who, by their "effective, responsible, and intelligent speech," foster these ideals of TKA and make "outstanding contributions to American and world society." [96] Its publication is *The Speaker.*

Pi Kappa Delta

Pi Kappa Delta ("the art of persuasion beautiful and just")[97] was organized in 1912-1913 through the co-operation of John A. Shields of Ottawa University, Edgar A. Vaughn of Kansas State College, and E. R. Nichols of Ripon College. Instead of making the state the unit of organization, as had Tau Kappa Alpha in the beginning, the founders made the whole nation its territory and divided into nine provinces under as many governors. It has orders of debate, oratory, and also of instruction, so that each chapter may have the benefit of the counsel of teachers. Another distinguishing feature is its award of degrees of merit in the various orders: *Fraternity* for membership, *Proficiency, Honor, Special Distinction,* and since 1936, the degree of *Grand Distinction* for national tournament winners.[98] In 1949 it had 129 chapters in 36 states. Its organ is *The Forensic,* published since 1915.

Phi Rho Pi

Phi Rho Pi, the National Honorary Forensic Society for Junior Colleges, was founded in 1928 by Roland Shackson, coach of forensics at Grand Rapids Junior College, Michigan. Its purpose:

To promote the interests of debating, oratory, extemporaneous speaking, and other speech activities, in the junior colleges by affording a means of fellowship and cooperation among them, and by rewarding their deserving candidates with a badge of distinction, graduated according to achievement. Phi Rho Pi shall not be a secret society.

Its three classes of membership are Active, Graduate, and Honorary; the three Orders of membership: debate, oratory, extemporaneous speaking and public speaking. Its three degrees of achievement are Fellowship, Honor and Highest Achievement.[99] In 1950 the society had 67 chapters and was still growing. The programs of its inter-school, district-regional, and national meets include debate, radio, all forms of forensics, declamation, oratory, poetry, Bible, and story-telling.[100]

In 1950 the executive council of SAA revised the organization and procedure of its Committee on Intercollegiate Discussion and Debate to provide a representative from each of the four co-operating forensic fraternities—Delta Sigma Rho, Tau Kappa Alpha, Pi Kappa Delta, and Phi Rho Pi—and one member to represent unaffiliated colleges. One purpose was to enable these representatives to select a national question for college debate and also topics for discussion. More significant for the cause of speech education was a second purpose, namely, to provide a meeting place for the evaluation of intercollegiate debate and discussion standards, methods and materials. "The intention," so SAA stated, "was to bring debate and discussion into coordination with educational and ethical standards discussed in conferences of teachers since 1910." [101]

The National Forensic League

Organized as a "High School Honor Society" in 1925, the League has its national tournaments held under the sponsorship of universities. It holds extensive programs of debate, original oratory, extemporaneous speaking, oratorical, dramatic, and humorous declamations, and radio announcing. Its awards to student speakers are for honor, excellence, and distinction. Its membership includes alumni and honorary members, and numbers 60,000. *The Rostrum,* its official publication, has now reached Volume VII. NFL has grown from 11 National Districts in 1925 to 25 Districts in 1950, and from 24 to 532 chapters in the same period.

The League is outstanding among honor societies for the number and variety of its awards. Besides awards to student speakers, it confers its Diamond Key on deserving coaches, its Bronze Plaque on individual chapters, the Distinguished Service Key for effective promotion of its work, and its Leading Chapter Award each month to two chapters in each District. Since 1936 the *Tau Kappa Alpha* Award has been given for "year after year excellence in national speech tournaments."

To commemorate twenty-five years of service to the high-school speech program, the League in 1950 published a handsome volume, *1925 NFL 1950* in which are chronicled "some of the achievements of the League's members and chapters."

The last sixty years have seen the birth of national professional groups dedicated to the advancement of speech education in the high school, college, and university. By and large, these groups have in the twentieth century tried to place speech training in a framework of recognized educational aims and methods, seeking to secure for it academic basis and status and removing it from the unpredictable influences of the nonacademic teacher and "coach" and from the circumscribed environment created by the tradition of study in English language and literature.

Notes

1. "Origin and Preliminary Meetings of the First National Convention of Public Readers and Teachers of Elocution and the National Association of Elocutionists," *Proceedings*, I (1892), 138-146. Cf. "Report of Committee on Permanent Organization," *Proceedings*, I (1892), 101-106; and Edgar S. Werner, "History of the National Association of Elocutionists," *Werner's Magazine*, XVIII (1896), 489-519.

2. *Proceedings*, I (1892), 103.

3. Henry Gaines Hawn, "Needed Reforms in Elocutionary Instruction," *Proceedings*, VIII (1899), 154-174, passim.

4. H. G. Hawn, President's Address, *Proceedings*, XIII (1904), 20-29, especially 26-27.

5. Letter by F. Townsend Southwick to Edgar S. Werner, printed in *Werner's Magazine*, XVIII (1896), 516.

6. May Donnally Kelso, *Proceedings*, II (1893), 158.

7. Editorial, *Werner's Magazine*, XVII (1895), 615.

8. Statement by H. W. Smith in a discussion of a report submitted by the Committee on Colleges, *Proceedings*, IV (1895), 107.

9. "Needed Reforms...," *Proceedings*, VIII (1899), 154-174, especially 159-160.

10. *Proceedings*, XIII (1904), 20-29, especially 21 and 26.

11. President's Address, *Proceedings*, XXI (1912), 17.

12. William B. Chamberlain, "The Relation of Elocution to College and University Education," *Proceedings*, I (1892), 86-92; discussion printed on pp. 92-95, remarks by Fulton and Trueblood on p. 93.

13. *Proceedings*, III (1894), 149-152, passim.

14. W. B. Chamberlain, "Report of Committee on Elocution in Colleges," *Proceedings*, III (1894), 131.

15. *Proceedings*, VII (1898), 54.

16. "The Place of Elocution in the College Curriculum," *Proceedings*, VII (1898), 61.

17. President's Address, *Proceedings*, VII (1898), 30-31.

18. President's Address, *Proceedings*, VIII (1899), 21.

19. President's Address, *Proceedings,* XIV (1905), 25.

20. *Proceedings,* XIV (1905), 248.

21. *Proceedings,* XIV (1905), 250. The discussion of the proposed change in name will be found on pp. 230-250.

22. *Proceedings,* XV (1906), 11.

23. These themes may be found in almost any volume of *Proceedings,* particularly in the addresses delivered by the various presidents. A particularly good elaboration of most of the themes may be found in the address by President Adrian M. Newens in 1910, *Proceedings,* XIX (1910), 11-22.

24. President's Address, *Proceedings,* XXV (1916), 12-16, passim.

25. *Union List of Serials* (New York, 1943), p. 1913.

26. Letters to the author from:

Lee Emerson Bassett, March 16, 1949; and November 21, 1951. (Professor Emeritus, Stanford University)

James L. Lardner, February 3, 1949; and December 3, 1951. (Former Professor of Speech, Northwestern University)

Lew Sarett, February 2, 1949; and November 8, 1951. (Professor of Speech, Northwestern University)

Thomas C. Trueblood, February 20, 1949; and March 3, 1949.

Dwight E. Watkins, April 17, 1950. (Former Professor of Speech, University of California)

James A. Winans, January 31, 1949; and November 27, 1951.

27. During the early part of this century the term "public speaking" was widely used to designate the subject matter areas that would now be loosely included in the expression "performance areas of speech."

28. See J. S. Gaylord's address in *Public Speaking Review,* II (October, 1912), 50-51. Woolbert's address was not published.

29. *PSR,* II (October, 1912), 40-42.

30. "Public Speaking for the Professional Man," *PSR,* IV (December, 1914), 97-103.

31. *PSR,* I (September, 1911), 1-2.

32. *PSR,* III (April, 1914), 2.

33. *Reorganization of English in Secondary Schools,* comp. James Fleming Hosic (Government Printing Office, Washington, 1917), p. 18.

34. *Reorganization of English in Secondary Schools,* pp. 20-21.

35. *PSR,* II (February, 1913), 180-182.

36. *PSR,* I (March, 1912), 210-212.

37. "The National Education Association Conferences," *EJ* (September, 1912), 52-53; *PSR,* II (October, 1912), 52-53.

38. "The Dividing Line Between Departments of English and Public Speaking," *PSR,* II (April, 1913), 228; 231-238.

39. "The National Association," *QJS,* I (April, 1915), 51-58.

40. "Public Speaking and English," *PSR,* III (January, 1914), 132-140.

41. "The Convention of the National Council of English Teachers at Chicago," *PSR,* III (December, 1913), 111.

42. C. E. Lyon, "The English-Public Speaking Situation," *QJS,* I (April, 1915), 44-50.

43. O'Neill, "The National Association," *QJS,* I (April, 1915), 51-58.

44. Letter from J. M. O'Neill, December 11, 1950.

45. H. S. Woodward, "Secretary's Record of the First Annual Convention," *QJS,* II (January, 1916), 87.

46. "Oral English as a College Entrance Requirement," *PSR,* I (October, 1911), 78-84.

47. "Oral English Again," *PSR,* I (January, 1912), 145-155.

48. "The Third Meeting of the NCTE in Chicago," *PSR,* III (December, 1913), 111.

49. B. E. Heagle, "Oral English in the High School," *PSR*, II (November, 1912), 84-85.

50. *PSR*, II (November, 1912), 95.

51. J. A. Winans, "The Convention of the National Council of English Teachers at Chicago," *PSR*, III (December, 1913), 108-112.

52. Editorial, *PSR*, II (October, 1912), 56.

53. H. R. Pierce, "Standardizing Public Speaking Courses," *PSR*, III (May, 1913), 15-18; Northwestern University Conference, *PSR*, II (February, 1913), 180-182.

54. "College Courses in Public Speaking," *PSR*, III (March, 1914), 205-209.

55. "Report of Syllabus Committee," *QJS*, XI (April, 1925), 107-123.

56. *A Course of Study in Speech Training and Public Speaking for Secondary Schools,* comp. & ed. A. M. Drummond (New York, 1925), pp. 83-86; rev. by Gladys Borchers, *QJS*, XII (February, 1926).

57. *The Service Bulletin for Teachers of Speech,* Supplement to Vol. XV, *QJS* (1929); *The Speech Bulletin,* I, 2 (May, 1930); II, 1 (December, 1930), *Debate;* II, 2 (May, 1931), *Drama;* III, 1 (December, 1931), *Contests;* IV, 2 (May, 1932), *Course of Study.*

58. Thomas C. Trueblood, "College Courses in Public Speaking," *QJS*, I (April, 1915), 260-265; see also "A Chapter on the Organization of College Courses in Public Speaking," *QJS*, XII (February, 1926), 1-11.

59. "The Place of Declamation in the College Curriculum," *PSR*, I (January, 1912), 136-138.

60. "The Practice at Cornell," *PSR*, I (November, 1911), 99-103; letter to author, September 20, 1950, commenting on Winans' early course.

61. Benjamin P. DeWitt, "The Use of Current Topics in the Class-Room," *PSR*, III (May, 1913), 1-5; J. M. O'Neill, "Speech Content and Course Content in Public Speaking," *QJS*, IX (February, 1923), 25-52; W. P. Sandford, "The Problem of Speech Content," *QJS*, VIII (November, 1922), 364-371; Everett Lee Hunt, "Adding Substance to Form in Public Speaking Courses," *QJS*, VIII (June, 1922), 256-265; Herbert A. Wichelns, "Our Hidden Aims," *QJS*, IX (November, 1923), 315-324; J. M. O'Neill, "Foot Notes on Form and Content," *QJS*, X (April, 1924), 174-180.

62. *QJS*, III (July, 1917), 249-264; see also "The Place of Logic in a System of Persuasion," *QJS*, IV (January, 1918), 19-39.

63. "Argument from the Point-of-view of Sociology," *QJS*, III (April, 1917), 109-124.

64. "Novelties, Real and Fancied, in the Teaching of Argumentation," *QJS*, IV (May, 1918), 247-262.

65. Edward Z. Rowell, "Prolegomena to Argumentation," *QJS*, XVIII (February, 1932), 1-13; (April, 1932), pp. 224-248; (November, 1932), pp. 585-606 (Quotation, p. 606).

66. J. A. Winans, "The Convention of the NCTE at Chicago," *PSR*, I (March, 1912), 211-212.

67. Lee Emerson Bassett, "Intercollegiate Debates and Debating Leagues," *PSR*, II (January, 1913), 129-135.

68. F. A. Welch, "Our Debating and Oratorical Leagues," *PSR*, II (January, 1913), 138-143.

69. J. M. O'Neill, "Debating as a College Sport," *PSR*, II (February, 1913), 161-165.

70. As quoted by G. Rowland Collins, "Problems in Teaching Debate," *QJS*, VII (June, 1921), 268-269.

71. "Debate That Talks and Tells," extracts from Charles Sears Baldwin's "Intercollegiate Debating," (*Edinburgh Review,* 1911), *PSR*, II (February, 1913), 191-193.

72. "A Program of Speech Education: Recommendations of the Contest Com-

mittee of the North Central Association with Respect to Speech as Submitted by the Speech Association of America," *QJS*, XXXVII (October, 1951), 347-358.

In March, 1950, the Contest Committee of the North Central Association adopted a resolution which recommended that interscholastic contests be discontinued. This recommendation by a widely influential accrediting agency whose Criteria, Policies, and Standards lay down the conditions by which colleges and secondary schools may receive, or be denied, academic rank aroused the officers of the SAA to positive action. The President appointed a Special Contest Committee which a year later presented its report at a meeting of the Commission on Secondary Schools of the NCA in Chicago. The Commission adopted the report, and L. B. Fisher, Chairman of the Contest Committee, commended it to school authorities for optional consideration and use as "a complete speech program for secondary schools presented officially by the Speech Association of America."

The contents of the report make it clear that the SAA Committee considered its responsibility to be that of correcting a distorted view of speech work brought about by overemphasis and publicity given to speech contests in some communities, and by a failure to publicize an authoritative statement of the whole program of speech education which had developed since 1914. This document makes good both deficiencies. It suggests procedures by which contests may be replaced with less competitive programs, and all such activities kept in their proper relationship with classroom instruction. The report goes farther and presents a comprehensive philosophy of speech education and the relationship of each of its specialized divisions to that philosophy.

In recent years, also, SAA, together with AETA, ASHA, and the Association for Education by Radio, has made available to high-school principals information about speech training and speech programs. Under the direction of special editorial committees, the following volumes of the *Bulletin* of the *National Association of Secondary School Principals* have appeared:

The Role of Speech in the Secondary School, XXIX (November, 1945), 9-160; *Speech Education for All American Youth*, XXXII (January, 1948), 9-22; *Dramatics in the Secondary School*, XXXII (December, 1949), 1-272; XXXIV (November, 1950), 7-139.

73. J. A. Winans, "The Need for Research," *QJS*, I (April, 1915), 17-23.

74. "Research in Public Speaking," *QJS*, I (April, 1915), 17-32; J. M. O'Neill, "The Quarterly Journal and Research," *ibid.*, pp. 84-85; Editorial, "On Speaking Out," *ibid.*, pp. 76-77; Wilbur Jones Kay, "Esprit de Corps," *ibid.*, pp. 89-90.

75. Editorial, *QJS*, I (April, 1915), 84-85.

76. Everett Lee Hunt, "The Scientific Spirit in Public Speaking," *QJS*, I (July, 1915), 185-193; "General Specialists," *QJS*, II (July, 1916), 253-263; C. H. Woolbert, "The Organization of Departments of Public Speaking in Universities," *QJS*, II (January, 1916), 64-77; "A Problem in Pragmatism," *QJS*, II (July, 1916), 264-274.

77. Harry Emerson Wilds, "Bibliography—Speech Education in Secondary Schools," *QJS*, IV (January, 1918), 184-195.

78. Smiley Blanton, "A Workable Bibliography for the Beginner in Speech Correction," *QJS*, X (February, 1924), 37-41.

79. Albert Craig Baird, "A Selected Bibliography of American Oratory," *QJS*, XII (November, 1926), 352-356.

80. J. Fred McGrew, "Bibliography of the Works on Speech Composition in England During the 16th and 17th Centuries," *QJS*, XV (June, 1929), 381-412.

81. James M. O'Neill, "A Bibliographical Introduction to Graduate Work in Speech," *QJS*, XIII (February, 1927), 39-48.

82. Henry L. Ewbank, "Classified Bibliography on Radio Speaking and Writing," *QJS*, XXIII (April, 1937), 230-238.

Some additional bibliographies:

Alfred R. Root, "The Pitch Factors in Speech—A Survey," *QJS,* XVI (June, 1930), 320-41.

Dayton D. McKean, "A Bibliography of Debating," *QJS,* XIX (April, 1933), 206-210.

Robert T. Oliver, "A Working Bibliography on Conversation," *QJS,* XX (November, 1934), 524-535.

Irene Poole Davis, "Short Reference Lists for the Elementary Teacher's Bookshelf," *QJS,* XXI (November, 1935), 549-553.

Lyman Spicer Judson, "After Dinner Speaking—A Bibliography," *QJS,* XXIV (April, 1938), 220-227.

Henry Lee Ewbank, "Bibliography of Periodical Literature on Debating and Discussion," *QJS,* XXIV (December, 1938), 634-641.

Edwin Duerr, "Book List for the Graduate Student in Theatre," *QJS,* XXVIII (April, 1942), 169-173.

A Bibliography of Theatre and Drama, comp. and ed. by Committee on Research of AETA, John H. McDowell, Chairman and Editor, *SM,* XVI (November, 1949), 1-124.

Harry Caplan and Henry H. King, "Italian Treatises on Preaching; A Book-List," *SM,* XVI (September, 1949), 243-252; "Spanish Treatises on Preaching: A Book-List," *SM,* XVII (July, 1950), 161-171.

Abraham Tauber, "A Guide to the Literature on Speech Education," *QJS,* XX (November, 1934), 507-524.

Giles Wilkeson Gray, "Research in the History of Speech Education," *QJS,* XXXV (April, 1949), 156-163.

83. Special thanks for the material in this section are due to Dorothy G. Kester and Paul Moore.

An obscure and short-lived organization antedated AASC. *The Quarterly Journal of Speech Education* (May, 1918), carried this announcement:

Dr. W. B. Swift announces that *The American Journal of Speech Disorders and Correction,* the official organ of the National Society for the Study and Correction of Speech Disorders, will start publication in July, 1918.

"In February, 1920, the *NEA Bulletin* published the program for the convention of the National Society for the Study and Correction of Speech Disorders which was scheduled to meet that same month in Cleveland. The president, Walter B. Swift, was then temporarily affiliated with the School of Education, Western Reserve University. No copies of the journal have been found, and there are no evidences of meetings beyond 1921. Evidently the organization ceased operation in that year." [Moore and Kester, "Historical Notes on Speech Correction in the Pre-Association Era," *Journal of Speech and Hearing Disorders,* XVIII (March, 1953), 52.]

84. "Resolutions at the 1925 Convention of the National Association of Teachers of Speech," *QJS,* XII (February, 1926), 74.

85. From official minutes in the office of the Executive Secretary, ASHA.

Persons present at the meeting:

Mary A. Brownell, *University of Wisconsin*
Elizabeth Dickinson McDowell, *Teachers College, Columbia University*
Jane Dorsey, *Smith College*
Alvin C. Busse, *New York University*
Richard Borden, *New York University*
Robert West, *University of Wisconsin*
William J. Farma, *New York University*
C. K. Thomas, *Cornell University*
Jane Bliss Taylor, *Vassar College*
Thyrza Nichols, *Bryn Mawr College*
Sara M. Stinchfield, *Mount Holyoke College*

86. Official minutes.

87. *Ibid.*

88. *Ibid.*

89. By December, 1926, the following persons had qualified as charter members:

Robert West	Eudora Estabrook
Richard Borden	Mary A. Brownell
Alvin Busse	Sara Stinchfield
Lee E. Travis	Dr. Smiley Blanton
Dr. Elmer L. Kenyon	Mrs. Margaret Blanton
Thyrza Nichols	Pauline Camp
Frederic Brown	Mrs. Lacey
Lavilla Ward	C. K. Thomas
Mrs. Mable Gifford	Samuel Robbins
Mrs. Elizabeth McDowell	Jane Dorsey
Jane Taylor	Sine Fladeland
Ruth Green	

90. "Report of the Resolutions Committee," *QJS,* XIII (April, 1927), 187.

91. Dorothy G. Kester, "The Development of Speech Correction in Organizations and in Schools in the United States during the First Quarter of the Twentieth Century," unpublished Ph.D. dissertation, Northwestern, 1950, p. 135.

92. ASHA asserts officially that "the purposes of this organization shall be to encourage basic scientific study of the processes of individual human speech and hearing, promote investigation of speech and hearing disorders, and foster improvement of therapeutic procedures with such disorders; to stimulate exchange of information among persons thus engaged, and to disseminate such information." (*By-Laws,* Art. II.)

Its members fall into two classes: (1) "Members," who are required to hold at least Bachelor's degrees in the general area of the Association's interests; and (2) "Associates," who are required to meet general academic requirements.

The Association carries on a program of clinical certification in Speech and in Hearing. Certification is on two levels: "Basic and Advanced. A Basic Certificate indicates that the holder thereof is capable of performing general clinical duties under supervision and guidance; an Advanced Certificate indicates that he has demonstrated ability to conduct clinics, train others in the arts and skills of the profession and is a fully trained professional worker. A qualified Member may be certified in both areas, Speech and Hearing, although joint certificates are not issued. Such a Member may hold a Basic Certificate in one area and an Advanced Certificate in the other, or the levels may be the same."

93. "Delta Sigma Rho," *PSR,* I (September, 1911), 28-30; *PSR,* II (February, 1913), 180; Egbert Ray Nichols, "A Historical Sketch of Intercollegiate Debating, II," *QJS,* XXII (April, 1936), 591-602.

94. *The Gavel,* XXXV (May, 1953), inside cover and 74-77.

95. Oswald Ryan, "Tau Kappa Alpha," *PSR,* I (September, 1911), 30.

96. See *The Constitution of Tau Kappa Alpha* (mimeographed pamphlet, pp. 1-8), and *Tau Kappa Alpha, National Honorary Fraternity* (mimeographed pamphlet, pp. 1-2).

97. *The Constitution of Pi Kappa Delta* (1949), Art. I.

98. See "The History of Pi Kappa Delta," *The Forensic,* XXXIV (March, 1949), 69-77.

99. *Constitution of Phi Rho Pi.*

100. Letter from Glenn L. Jones, President of Phi Rho Pi in 1950.

101. *The Rostrum,* XVII (May, 1953), 2.

PART III

The Educational Theatre

23 Educational Dramatics in Nineteenth-Century Colleges

JOHN L. CLARK

....

1698–1800

The circumstances which surrounded the beginnings of college dramatics in this country are uncertain, and the records are woefully incomplete. The first documented evidence of collegiate interest in the drama is found in the cryptic entry in Harvard President Increase Mather's diary for October 10, 1698: "examined the Scholars about the comedy, etc." [1] William and Mary's famous "pastoral colloquy" of 1702, and a performance in 1736 by "the young Gentlemen of the Colledge" of "the tragedy of Cato," [2] are generally accepted as the first and second dramatic performances by college students in what is now the United States, but the bare, unadorned newspaper announcements constitute all that is known concerning them. The account in the diary of John Blair, November 16, 1751, shows that William and Mary students had not lost interest in the drama:

This evening Mr. Preston (professor of moral philosophy), to prevent the young gentlemen of the college from trying at a rehearsal in the dormitory how they could act "Cato" privately among themselves, did himself act the "Drunken Peasant," but his tearing down the curtains is to me very surprising. [3]

It may be surmised that some sort of continuity in college dramatics existed in Virginia between 1736 and 1751, but lack of evidence prevents certainty.

John Crowne, the English Restoration playwright who was "the first Harvard man who succeeded in making a living by practising a recognized form of literature," [4] attended Harvard College from 1657 to 1660, but it seems doubtful that his playwriting talent received any encouragement while he was there. Cotton Mather's *Suggestions on Points to be Inquired Into Concerning Harvard College,* submitted to

521

the Overseers in 1723, indicates the suspicion with which the theatre was viewed:

> Whether the scholars have not their studies filled with books which may truly be called *Satan's Library*. Whether the books mostly read among them are not plays, novels, empty and vicious pieces of poetry. . . .[5]

In calling plays "vicious," Cotton Mather was not, in the eyes of early eighteenth-century Massachusetts, meddling in matters which did not concern him. The mingling of the functions of state and church in New England colonial government was taken for granted, and although education was thought to be a function of the secular arm,[6] Mather's position as a minister of Boston automatically made him an Overseer of the college.[7] The early presidents of the New England colleges were chosen from the ranks of eminent Protestant divines; the piety of the students was as much a responsibility of their instructors as was their proficiency in their studies.[8] Cotton Mather's concern that the students might read plays arose from his concern for the state of their souls; condemnation of the stage was traditional in the history of Puritanism. This antagonism was to affect college dramatics in America until after the Civil War.

It may well be that American Protestant opposition to the stage had its antecedents in such controversies as that which took place at Oxford in 1592 between William Gager, the Christ Church dramatist, and Dr. John Rainolds of Queen's College.[9] Rainolds attacked the performance of Gager's plays on grounds which were to become familiar later in both England and America. His main charges were that the Scriptures (Deuteronomy xxii, 5) forbade the wearing of women's clothes by men; that acting had been proscribed by civil law; that the performances wasted hours for both participants and audience which could be put to better use; and above all, plays were often presented on the Sabbath, a most flagrant violation of divine law. Gager defended what had been a tradition in the schools of England for three centuries past.[10] After denying that his amateurs were subject to the charges made against professional actors, he asserted:

> We contrarwise doe it to recreate owre selves, owre House, and the better part of the Vniversitye, with some learned Poem or other; to practyse owre owne style eyther in prose or verse; to be well acquantyed with *Seneca* or *Plautus* . . . your goodwill I doe and ever will most gladly embrace, and your judgment toe, in this cause so farr, as you wryte in the generall agaynst Histriones. . . .[11]

Gager did not undertake to defend the professional stage, but he pled for an exception in the case of the college plays.[12] It was as such an exception that dramatic performances appeared on the American Puritan college campus. "The extent to which acting flourished in the days of our fathers is very remarkable," says a nineteenth-century college historian.[13] Officially, the Puritan colleges adopted the Rainolds position; in practice it was often that of Gager which prevailed.

The Reverend John Witherspoon, sixth president of the College of New Jersey (later Princeton), was clearly on the side of Rainolds. While still in his native Scotland, he had written *A Serious Enquiry into the Nature and Effects of the Stage* (1757). He found the "Nature and Effects" to be most undesirable, and he stated unequivocally, "We hope to abolish the theatre just as much as other vices." [14] When it is remembered that as late as 1824 Yale President Timothy Dwight was to announce, in his *Essay on the Stage,* "An evil so great, contagious, and extended, ought to meet universal opposition," we are not only surprised that acting "flourished," but that it was able to exist at all!

Administrative disapproval of the drama does not always seem to have been consistent, however, even in the eighteenth century. When President Ezra Stiles of Yale visited the College of New Jersey in 1754, New Jersey President Burr saw that he was entertained by "two young gentlemen of the college [who] acted Tamerlane and Bajazet, &c." [15] On the other hand, an early mention of the drama is to be found in a memorandum from the faculty judgments at Yale under date of January, 1756:

> Whereas it appears that a play was acted at the house of William Lyon [a tavern-keeper on State Street] on the evenings after the 2d, 6th, 7th and 8th days of January instant, and that all the students (excepting some few) were present at one or other of those times, and many of them continued there until after nine of the clock, and had a large quantity of wine, and sundry people of the town were also present. And whereas this practise is of a very pernicious nature, tending to corrupt the morals of this seminary of religion and learning, and of mankind in general, and to the mispence of precious time and money.[16]

The students who had been present were fined eight pence, and the actors (who were all students) were fined three shillings each. Dartmouth's first definite code of college laws, formulated in 1782, took notice of "public entertainments"; since holding them "by students of this college is detrimental to their morals ... such entertainments are prohibited under penalty to $5 fine to anyone who participates." [17] In addition, no student was allowed to take a female part in any dramatic entertainment.

We are indebted to the diary of Nathaniel Ames, a Harvard student of the class of 1761, for an account of a comparatively intensive program of undergraduate drama in the years 1758 and 1759. These selected entries [18] will suffice:

1758, July 3, Cato a Play acted at Warrens Cham . . . July 6, Cato to perfection . . . Cato more perfect than before.

1759, April 20, Went to see the Drummer acted at Hows . . . April 21,
The Orphan acted ye 13th inst. . . . June 20, The Recruiting Officer acted by
ourselves then Public.

Four years after he graduated, Dr. Ames made an entry which indicates
that the college actors had gone too far:

1765, Nov. 20, Scholars punished at College for acting over the great and
last day in a very shocking manner, personating the Jude eterat Devil, etc.

This incident was to achieve international notoriety, and a letter from
a Bostonian in England (Dennys DeBerdt to Stephen Sayre, tentatively
dated 1766) shows the seriousness with which this offense was regarded:

Your mentioning Cambridge reminds me that I have concerning the scholars there, they were so proph. as to act the Day of Judgment with a mock
Solemnity, pray inquire into the fact, for if it be true & the prophane wretches
not expelled there is nothing to be expected from that Colledge.[19]

Whether or not Ames' *Diary* reflects a typical picture of student theatrical activity, it is apparent that Cotton Mather's earlier fears were
justified. Ames tells us that in August of 1762 he went to Providence to
see the Douglass Company, which was performing plays in that city.[20]
It is evident that the determination of the college students to see and
even to produce plays had grown to such an extent that for the first
time it became necessary, in 1767, to take official notice in the laws of
Harvard of this pernicious habit:

Chap. IV Of Misdemeanours and criminal Offences XVIII. If any undergraduate shall presume to be an actor in, a Spectator at, or any Ways concerned in any Stage Plays, Interludes or Theatrical Entertainments in the
Town of Cambridge or elsewhere, he shall for the first Offence be degraded
—& for any repeated Offence shall be rusticated or expelled . . . Provided,
That this Law shall not prevent any Exhibitions of this kind from being performed as Academical Exercises under the direction of the President and
Tutors.[21]

The restrictions and prohibitions listed above will serve to demonstrate that the Gager-Rainolds controversy was not yet dead—at least in
American colleges. Witherspoon's *Enquiry* contained most of Rainolds'
objections, including the excessive time required by plays. Yale's judgment against the play at Lyon's tavern repeats this complaint, although
the objection seems to be as much to the public nature of the performance, the lateness of the hour, and the "large quantity of wine," as to
the play itself. Dartmouth's law against acting feminine roles is obviously related to the Scriptural edict concerning the wearing of women's

clothing. The Harvard law is most interesting for the severity of the penalty, and for the loophole which is left by the reservation in the final sentence. The rather frequent performance of plays in eighteenth-century colleges could have been possible only where a somewhat greater tolerance to the drama existed than is evident at first glance. The concept that the college drama contains positive educational values was thus given official college sanction in the colonial period, and it is in the restricted area of Gager's stipulations concerning the academic drama that college theatricals began in America.

"To Be Well Acquantyed with Seneca or Plautus"

There is evidence to show that the play as "academical exercise" had some currency at eighteenth-century Harvard. The *Faculty Records* for this period indicate the rigid control which was maintained over such performances. The authorities were self-conscious about allowing any kind of stage play, and performances for which official approval was given were very carefully supervised:

1762, April 28, This day was the Public Examination, the Com*tee* of the Overseers being present, after w*ch* Oliver & Huntington were allow'd to exhibit a Scene in Terrence before the Com*tee* they desiring it, but in Private in the Library none being present but the Com*tee*, the President and Tut*rs*.[22]

In non-Puritan Virginia, William and Mary could afford openly to encourage the use of the drama as an educational device, even to the point of adapting student recreation to that end. The statutes of that college as codified and published in 1738 contained this provision:

... And if there are any sort of Plays or Diversions in Use among them, which are not to be found extant in any printed Books, let the Master compose and dictate to his Scholars colloquies fit for such sorts of plays, that they may learn at all Times to speak Latin in apt and proper Terms.[23]

The Harvard faculty, too, had taken it upon themselves by 1781 to compose dramas for the furtherance of culture among the students. At least the *Faculty Records* for November 16 of that year have this entry: "Voted—That To-morrow evening, some Scenes of Busiris, a Tragedy written by Dr. Young, be exhibited in the Chapel, as an academical exercise, by a number of the Students." [24] The final relevant entry in the *Records* would indicate that some thought was paid to the way in which the actors were dressed: "December 7, 1781. Voted—That a number of the Junior Sophisters who are to exhibit, this evening a piece from Pope's *Illiad*, be permitted to appear habited." [25]

These specific references to performances which were primarily "academical" seem to be to exhibitions which were unusual in one way or another. Other evidence, largely negative in nature (Yale censured its students for a public performance, Dartmouth's law warned against similar practices) would seem to indicate that these isolated instances represent a fairly common practice: making the study of the classics more palatable by simple dramatic presentations. There were productions, however, which cannot be explained by any such pedagogical motivation.

"To Recreate Owre Selves and the Vniversitye"

It is difficult to reconcile the common concept of the early New England colleges as cold, cheerless temples of learning [26] with the frequent excursions into the drama made by the Yale literary societies, Linonia and Brothers in Unity. Fortunately, the fairly complete records of these societies have been preserved, and offer a very interesting insight into the college drama at Yale in the latter half of the eighteenth century.[27] Yale's "literary society" drama, along with isolated instances at other institutions, seems to have been an extracurricular activity, quite in the modern sense of the term. These societies (Linonia was known as the "Honorable Fellowship Club" until 1772) were the most successful and durable of the early societies at Yale. "They were seriously meant, by those who founded them, to supply a kind of literary culture which the curriculum did not furnish, and they well-fulfilled this office for three-quarters of a century." [28] They offered an opportunity for the students to engage in debate, make speeches, and in general to confront an audience from the platform. To these forensic pursuits were soon added humorous dialogues, light comedies, and farces, for an entry in the records of the Honorable Fellowship Club dated February 6, 1767, speaks of an "especial meeting" at which "a number of Freshmen were admitted, a play and actors appointed for the anniversary." [29] The dramatic presentations soon assumed a major role in the clubs' activities. Acting "not only enlivened their weekly gatherings, but it was the main feature of the exhibitions in which the anniversary of the 'Venerable and Illustrious Society' was celebrated." [30]

When college authorities objected to plays, "dialogues" were substituted at various places in the community. "The Court-house, the State-house, the 'old auction room,' Moss's school room, and especially the 'Sandamanian Meeting house' were the scenes of their activity." [31] Some of the plays were written by the members; however, the repertoire of the early American professional acting companies was not neglected. Thus, The Toy Shop, The Beaux' Stratagem, The West Indian, and

Love Makes a Man are titles which were familiar to the audiences at Yale and to those of the Hallam company as well. As was customary with professional companies well into the nineteenth century, a double bill was often presented. At the anniversary celebration of Linonia in 1780, the program consisted of a tragedy, *Ximena,* followed by a farce, *Love Makes a Man.* The audiences on these occasions were often composed not only of members of the societies, but also of townspeople, and in 1782 interest had risen so high that spectators were admitted by ticket. At the anniversary celebration of 1773, Linonia presented the first part of the *Lecture on Heads,* a form of entertainment frequently offered by Lewis Hallam and other early professional actors in America. This was followed after dinner (the meeting was held at the house of Thomas Atwater) by a performance of *The West Indian,* and the record of this day includes a description of the costumes. "The whole received peculiar Beauty from the Officers appearing dressed in Regimentals and the Actresses in full and elegant suits of Lady's apparel." [32]

There is no doubt that these plays were produced at Yale with the knowledge of the officers of the college. Occasionally, it is true, there is a record of "authority of the college interfering," as in 1783, but for the most part the programs of the literary societies seem to have been unmolested. An entry in the diary of President Ezra Stiles for April 6, 1782, indicates a general tone of disapproval, but hardly one of censure:

> There are two academic fraternities in college, the Linonian and the Brothers in Unity . . . their entertainments and dramatic exhibitions have become of notoriety no longer to be concealed. The general sense of the members of both has been against carrying dramatical exhibitions to the greatest length. Others have been zealous for the whole drama . . . .[33]

Stiles' disapproval of this "notoriety" was eventually to result, in the fall of 1789, in the prohibition of public exhibitions.[34] The records of the societies for the spring of 1790 mentioned the performance of a comedy and a tragedy. These were apparently the last plays by the societies.[35]

That literary societies were not peculiar to Yale is well known. They were part of the college community at Harvard, Princeton, Dartmouth, and other colleges. Not at every institution did they put such emphasis on the drama; Princeton's American Whig and Cliosophic Societies, for example, were famous for the excellence of their forensics, as were the Peithesophian and Philoclean Societies at Rutgers. Out-and-out dramatic clubs were not known at the colleges in this period, but the literary societies which produced plays seem to have prepared the way for such clubs. The Social Friends and the United Fraternity of Dartmouth extended their dramatic activities into the nineteenth century.[36]

Nathaniel Ames' diary records plays at Harvard in the extracurricular tradition.[37] Although one writer says, "Evidence of the performance at the College of New Jersey of plays other than dialogues is lacking," [38] Wertenbacker presents evidence which has been overlooked:

In 1782 the students presented the tragedy *Ormisinda and Alonzo,* in which the "rich and elegant" costumes excited admiration and the acting was so real "that it caused the tears to flow from many a compassionate mind and made them feel for the characters in distress." This was followed the next year by the *Rival Queens, or Alexander the Great,* acted before a very large and enthusiastic audience.[39]

Jared Sparks' *Life of John Ledyard* [40] gives an amusing picture of the American explorer acting in *Cato* while he was a student at Dartmouth in 1772. Ledyard apparently brought "theatrical materials" with him to college, including calico for curtains. There is evidence of a little-known performance at Rutgers in an invitation somehow preserved since 1783:

> The students of Queen's College solicit the
> company of Dr. Ryker and Lady at an exhibition
> of a Tragedy on Wednesday 19th Instant at
> 6 O'Clock in the Evening.
> > Brunswick   Admittance will be
> > 7 March   obtained by this card [41]
> > 1783

The College of Philadelphia (later the University of Pennsylvania) numbered among its original trustees one William Plumstead, familiar to students of the American drama as the owner of "Plumstead's Store," in which the pioneering Murray and Kean Company first played in 1749.[42] This college, founded in 1755, was prompt in beginning its dramatic activities. The students, "having from Time to Time . . . acted Parts of our best dramatic Pieces," [43] performed the *Masque of Alfred* during the Christmas holidays of 1756-1757. "The first dramatic production composed and acted by college students," [44] this play was produced in the college building. The *Masque of Alfred* was an adaptation, but Quinn calls it original because of the introduction of many new scenes and the addition of more than two hundred original lines.[45] Thomas Godfrey, the author of the first American tragedy to be produced on the professional stage (*The Prince of Parthia*), was a pupil of the college provost, William Smith, who sponsored and directed the *Masque of Alfred.* With friends of the drama in high places among the officers of the college, it is not surprising that the College of Philadelphia occupies a prominent position in early college drama.

"To Practyse Owre Owne Style"

The societies at Dartmouth (which may have been inspired by those at Yale, according to one writer)[46] appear to have depended almost wholly upon their own members' resources for such plays as they produced. Otherwise, their activities followed much the same pattern as the Yale societies. The meetings of the Social Friends (founded 1783), and the United Fraternity (1786), were held weekly. The anniversary celebrations at Dartmouth were soon observed with public performances at commencement. The first of these was held by the Fraternity on the day before commencement in 1787, and consisted of an oration and an original tragic dialogue. Competition was keen between the two societies, and soon both were presenting dramatic programs on these occasions. In 1790 "an original drama, entitled 'The French Revolution'" was produced, also by the United Fraternity. This play was printed, and apparently was also produced at Windsor, Vermont.[47] "An entertaining comedy" plus an oration, was the fare at commencement in 1792, this time by the Social Friends. Although the commencement celebrations were suspended in 1800, they were revived in 1811, with an original play by a member of the society apparently still a feature.[48]

Current affairs were watched with keen interest by college students of the Revolutionary period. The successive titles of "dialogues" at various commencement exercises probably reflect current opinion fairly accurately. The College of Philadelphia paid its respects to England at the commencement of 1761 with "An Exercise containing a Dialogue and an Ode Sacred to the Memory of his late Gracious Majesty, George II," and followed with a similar exercise in 1762 on the accession of George III.[49] The titles, unfortunately, are not specific for the period of the Revolution; the 1775 and 1776 commencements each produced "An Exercise Containing a Dialogue and Two Odes." These "Exercises" were apparently printed,[50] but I have been unable to see them. It would be interesting to know what students at "Ben Franklin's College" had to say, dramatically, on the eve of Howe's occupation of Philadelphia!

Freneau and Brackenridge wrote political dramatic exercises for Princeton's commencements, as will be seen later. In the years immediately following the Revolution, the societies at Yale produced strongly patriotic plays which were written by members. The interest which these societies took in their new government may be inferred from some of the titles. *Arnold's Conquest of the New London Fort* (1786), *The Disturbances in Massachusetts* (evidently Shay's Rebellion, since the play was produced in 1787), and *The Conspiracy of*

Arnold (1789), are some of the provocative subjects. In the year of the Constitutional Convention, 1787, the names of the characters of *The Disturbances in Massachusetts* as listed in the records of The Brothers of Unity reveal the political bias of at least one college playwright. "True-heart and Manly" are described as "Gentlemen in favour of the Constitution," while "Puff, Wronghead, Obstinate, Sneak, Sulky and Underbrush," are the names given to the anti-federalists.[51]

The College of New Jersey had a young tradition of commencement dialogues which had begun in 1760 with an *Ode to Peace*. The commencement of 1762 featured *The Military Glory of Great Britain*, of which the *Pennsylvania Gazette* for October 21, 1762, had this to say: "... a Poetical Entertainment given by the candidates for Bachelor's degree, interspersed with choruses of Music, which with the whole performance of the day, afforded universal satisfaction to a polite and crowded auditory." [52] In 1771 Hugh Brackenridge and Philip Freneau, well-known literary figures of the Revolutionary period, collaborated on a commencement dialogue which was entitled *The Rising Glory of America*.

College playwrights were found by no means only in the student body. Provost William Smith and "Dr. Young" of Harvard have already been mentioned. John Smith, Professor of Learned Languages at Dartmouth, wrote dialogues which were apparently presented at the commencements of 1779 and 1781. These dialogues, entitled *A Dialogue Between an Englishman and an Indian,* and *A Little Teatable Chitchat, alamode,* seem to be fairly typical of the form. They are topical in their subject matter, and show only rudimentary attempts at dramatic action. The first has only two characters, and although the second has a cast of five, two of them have only a line or two. At the close of each dialogue, however, "the curtains fall," indicating that the author was writing for some sort of stage.[53] A letter by Smith to John Phillips which accompanied these dialogues shows that more than passing interest in the dramatic form was maintained by this faculty member:

As you have been pleased, heretofore, to grant me your attention to productions of this kind, I rely on your candor, even without an apology.

The first mentioned dialogue was acted pretty naturally, as a real Aboriginal defended the part of the Indian. The other incurred no censure; and passed for a humor.[54]

It is evident that the college playwright, then as now, concerned himself with such matters as type-casting and audience reaction.

Hugh Brackenridge became master of the Somerset Academy in Maryland after he graduated from the College of New Jersey. That he did not forget the possibilities of the drama as a weapon in the battle for freedom "is proved by the dramatic piece written by him for his scholars, and which after due preparation they exhibited. . . . It was called Bunker Hill, composed shortly after the battle." [55] *The Battle of Bunker Hill* is "A Dramatic Piece of Five Acts, in Heroic measure. . . . The principal characters are well-known officers in the British and American Armies." [56] Brackenridge followed this play with *The Death of General Montgomery in the Storming of the City of Quebec*, in 1777. His note to the public is of interest here, for it shows the traditional suspicion of the professional theatre, and the rigid dichotomy which was maintained between the professional and the academic stage:

It is my request that the following Dramatic Composition be considered only as a school piece . . . . It is intended for the private entertainment of gentlemen of taste and martial enterprise, but by no means for exhibition on the stage.[57]

There seems to be no record of the occasion of the performance of these plays at Somerset Academy, but it is probable that they were a part of the graduation exercises. Evidence of school performances in this period is even more rare than for the colleges. Earle records a performance of an exhibition or "showing-off" at a girls' school in New York in 1784. "The 'Search after Happiness' by Mrs. More, 'The Milliner,' and 'The Dove,' by Madame Genlis were performed." Such exhibitions were common at girls' schools at the close of the school year, and may have provided the major opportunities for school drama during this period.[58]

"I Will Gladly Embrace Your Judgement Agaynst Histriones"

Brackenridge's classmates did not all share his implied rejection of the professional theatre, for Samuel Greville, the first American professional actor, apparently chose to follow his profession shortly after leaving the College of New Jersey. His new career was viewed with mock horror and quizzical interest by at least one former classmate, William Paterson (later Governor of New Jersey), in a letter to John MacPherson, Jr., dated January 26, 1767:

Poor Greville, what a noble subject on which to moralize, "in truth 'tis pitiful, most wondrous pitiful." Sam's fate reached Princeton long ago, before he appeared on the stage. You might have been more particular, and informed me what induced him to take that unhappy course. Was it because his finances were reduced to a low ebb, or was he smitten by an actress, as is not uncommon? [59]

There is little evidence of play production in American colleges before 1750, although William and Mary witnessed some sort of dramatic activity almost a half-century before. The traditional Puritan opposition to the drama effectively prevented plays at most of the colonial colleges prior to the middle of the century. Although antagonism to the professional theatre remained implacable, there was a noticeable increase in collegiate dramatics in the latter part of the century.

The drama appears in the colleges of this period in several well-defined forms. As "academical exercises," the performance of classical plays seems to have been used to stimulate student interest in and to aid in the study of Latin. Extracurricular plays were not lacking, however, as is proved by the comparatively extensive program of plays presented by the early literary societies, especially those at Yale. Even where literary societies did not produce plays, student initiative overcame the difficulties on occasion, and plays were presented. A general interest in the drama by college students is evidenced by entries in letters and diaries of the period. Commencement plays and "dialogues" constitute a third category of eighteenth-century college drama.

Although acting as a profession did not attract college men, both faculty and students were eager to write plays. These were written for commencement exercises as well as for less formal occasions. Brackenridge's preface to a play written for his students at Somerset Academy shows disdain for the professional stage; yet Thomas Godfrey seems to have drawn no censure for *The Prince of Parthia* after his death.

1800—1861

No sharp line divides the eighteenth century from the nineteenth in American collegiate dramatics. We find less mention of plays in the colleges during the first part of the nineteenth century. It would appear that this is because the performance of such plays was considered less "newsworthy" than it had been in earlier years. It is true that Yale President Dwight's condemnatory *Essay on the Stage* appeared in 1824, and that the Yale societies had stopped their dramatic activity by the end of the eighteenth century; yet Wegelin records the production of *Zamor*, a tragedy, which "formed part of the commencement exercises at Yale College in 1815." [60] Amherst's first commencement, in 1822, featured two dialogues and a colloquy, as well as three orations, a salutory in Latin, and a prayer by President Moore. [61] In some instances, new literary societies followed the lead of those at older colleges in claiming the drama as their province. The Adelphic Society of Union College presented an exhibition in 1808 which included a play, *Pulaski*, written by member Henry Warner. John Howard Payne, then a student, played the only female role, Lodoiska. [62] Wake Forest's first play, written by a Professor Armstrong, was the contribution of the Euzelian Society to the Fourth of July celebration in 1836. [63] The University of

Virginia appears to have produced no plays prior to the Civil War, although there is reason to suppose that the student body was interested in acted drama:

[1831] A Thespian Society had already been organized in the town. . . . Several students were accused of joining the society, but they all denied personal connection with it. At least one, however, John Leitch, was known to have participated in a theatrical performance that took place in the town; but this may have been a drama staged by an obscure company in the course of a tour.[64]

A play, *Traconi*, written by College Chaplain Walter Colton, was given in 1826 as part of the celebration of the sixth anniversary of the founding of Norwich University in Vermont. Another faculty member wrote the 1837 commencement play, which satirized "Grahamism" (a contemporary vegetarian fad) among other things.[65]

The Litchfield, Connecticut, school for girls produced plays written by the head mistress, Miss Sarah Pierce. The Litchfield Female Academy, as it was called after its incorporation in 1827 (the school opened in 1792), presented these plays at the end of the school term, evidently in the tradition of the college commencement plays. The plays themselves, to judge from the three Vanderpoel has printed in her *Chronicles of a Pioneer School*,[66] were highly didactic, moral pieces. The subject matter of two of them is taken from the Old Testament, while the plot of the third revolves on the duty of parents to bring up their children so that they will be virtuous and "free from vanity." A rather surprising characteristic of the productions is that "the young men of the town were often invited to take part." [67]

Elocution programs in the schools also offered an opportunity for a kind of dramatic exercise. The Lancastrian School at New Haven, Connecticut, was in the habit of presenting these programs once or twice a year between 1818 and 1850. The programs, which began at six in the evening and lasted "several hours," consisted largely in the delivery of declamations by the pupils—often famous historical speeches, but "There were also a few dramatic selections from *Douglas, Bertram,* and the *Castle Spectre,* in which the pupils exhibited their declamatory skill in portraying the characters." [68]

It seems clear, however, that if no sharp decline can be traced in the academic drama during this period, that this activity had ceased to be as significant a part of the college scene as it had been during previous years. It was a period of rapid acceleration in the growth of higher education in this country, and no longer was the American college to be a monopoly of the eastern seaboard states. The church continued to be the major influence in the founding of new colleges (150 denominational colleges were founded between 1800 and 1861, as compared to eighteen state institutions),[69] and the concept of the colleges as a "nursery of ministers" continued, if anything, stronger than before.[70] The greatly increased number of colleges and the varying circumstances under which they were operated in this period make it unwise to generalize about administrative policy toward extracurricular drama. The rise of evangelism, for example, seems to have strongly affected play-giving in some colleges, whereas in others it made little difference. "The forces of orthodox religion, after a temporary setback during the Revolution, regained their ascendancy over the cultural life of this country at the turn of the century. . . . This ascendancy was maintained in large part up to the time of the Civil War." [71]

The determination of the trustees and faculty of the College of New Jersey to impose this orthodoxy on the students is blamed by Borgers for the complete disappearance of plays at that institution between 1783 and 1874. The single reference to the drama at that college during this period of one hundred years is found in the diary of student John Buhler, who wrote a tragedy which was rehearsed but not produced in 1845.[72] This regimen was not imposed on New Jersey students without a struggle. While other eastern colleges also were having trouble maintaining the absolute control which had been possible in the eighteenth century,[73] the College of New Jersey seems to have adhered rigidly to the wishes of the church until well after the Civil War.

Despite the religious revivals which swept the colleges intermittently during the first decades of the nineteenth century,[74] there was no lack of interest in the theatre by college students. The extension of the railway system increased the opportunity for Princeton students to attend the theatre: John Buhler's diary in 1846 happily noted that a change in train schedules made it possible for students to get to Philadelphia in time for evening performances.[75] An anonymous letter to President Kirkland of Harvard sometime in the 1830's drew his attention to the fact that from sixty to one hundred tickets were "sold every play night to young men from Cambridge." [76] This interest by college students seems to reflect the general growing toleration for the theatre in the country as a whole.

With the exception of classical comedies, tragedy was the dramatic form most acceptable to the faculties of American colleges in the early nineteenth century. When students were able to carry out their own wishes, on the other hand, the usual preference seems to have been for light comedy or farce. English comedy did not have much literary standing during this period, at least at the University of Virginia. In the University Library is found the statement:

Shakespeare gained an entrance under the head of Tragedy, but no English author enjoyed the like distinction under the head of Comedy. As the plays of Sheridan, Goldsmith, and Congreve could claim no higher usefulness than an ability to tickle the sense of amusement, they were rejected, and the Latin Humorists were enthroned in their stead.[77]

Youngerman says the "theatrical activities at the University [of Wisconsin] were preceded by years of student rhetoricals and elocution." [78] In 1856 the elocution courses were using the Greek drama for class exercises, and the German drama was added in 1858.[79] But comedy was valued in the classroom for neither its literary nor its elocutionary possibilities. Outside the classroom, however, English farce and comedy found a welcome. The early programs of Harvard's Hasty Pudding Club reflect the students' preference in the drama when they were not restrained by faculty supervision.

The Hasty Pudding Club did not begin its prominent role in American college dramatics until 1844, although it had been founded in 1795. In its early years it had been "a rather jolly amalgam of literary, convivial, and patriotic elements," [80] which soon became the largest of the college societies. The interest of the society after 1800 centered in debates on "questions of literature, morality, and politics," which followed society suppers. Later activities were burlesque trials on such matters as Dido *vs.* Aeneas for breach of promise.[81] These trials foreshadowed, in the late 1830's, the activity which was to bring fame to the Hasty Pudding Club; for it became customary to enliven the proceedings "by costuming the court, bar, and witnesses." [82] In the records of the club, in accordance with the traditional obligation for the secretaries to write their minutes in verse, appears this entry in 1844:

> At the termination
> Of the initiation
> The Club received an invitation
> To a theatrical representation,
> Of Pudding rules an innovation,
> And of college regulation
> A most flagrant violation.[83]

The "theatrical representation" referred to was a performance of *Bombastes Furioso,* organized by Lemuel Hayward, of the class of 1845, and presented in his room at the regularly scheduled meeting.[84] This production was the first of a series which was to continue each year to the present date, interrupted only by national emergencies. In 1849 the club was granted two rooms in one of the dormitories, but it did not boast a stage until 1871.[85]

The plays presented by the Hasty Pudding Club prior to the Civil War were largely stock farces from the professional stage.[86] Limited production facilities made small casts essential, and in consequence plays which met the requirements were played again and again. Examination of the record between 1844 and 1860 shows six performances of *Bombastes Furioso;* five of *Lend Me Five Shillings;* four of *Slasher and Crasher* and of *Box and Cox;* and three each of *Chrononhotonthologos* and *The Dead Shot.* We may assume that the plays were adapted to the needs and taste of the club, but the extent of such changes is difficult to determine. In 1855 Fielding's *Tom Thumb* was set to music by a club member, but no totally original play was produced in this period. *Tom Thumb* represented the club's first musical play, the precursor of the extravaganzas which were to be the trademark of the Hasty Pudding in later years. From the earliest time this club showed an unchanging preference for farce and burlesque, never attempting serious drama.

In the early days of the club, performances were frequent, sometimes as often as once every two weeks. The first plays were obviously not elaborate productions:

> The audience sat in a small room, without a stage or footlights, save a circle of tallow dips or lamps, at one end of which the play was performed with an Elizabethan spirit that made up for lack of illusion. The music, what there was of it,—sometimes only a flageolet,—was furnished by the Company; while, partly for secrecy, partly for economy's sake, the cast of the play was placarded about the walls. . . .

From this small beginning there grew an organization which was to be of great importance in the development of extracurricular dramatics in American colleges and universities. For us, the significance of the early Hasty Pudding Club lies in the continuity of the early performances. Its major influence, in the field of musical burlesque, will be discussed later.

College dramatics in the period from 1800 to 1861 continued in the directions which had been indicated in the earlier years. Although the number of colleges increased greatly during this period, there seems to have been no proportional increase in college play production—this, despite evidence which shows that college students were increasingly interested in the theatre, and went to see professional performances whenever possible.[87] Plays continued to be presented at commencements and other celebrations, and often these plays were written by faculty members. English tragedy was recognized as a worthy literary study by the colleges, whereas English comedy was relegated to the realm of "mere" entertainment by the college educators. When students had the chance to make their own choice, they usually chose to present farce or burlesque. The Harvard Hasty Pudding Club began its long play-producing career in this period, foreshadowing later dramatic clubs.

The Civil War to 1900

According to Samuel Eliot Morison, Harvard's historian, "from the Civil War to the World War Harvard undergraduates had an insatiable thirst for theatricals." [88] The thirst was by no means confined to Harvard. It was during this period that college plays took their place on the American campus as a major extracurricular activity. The moral censure of the stage which had militated against the academic drama in previous eras had largely disappeared. The commercial theatre's growth had stimulated interest in the acted drama. The extension of the railway system to the west made performances by road companies available to communities which had formerly been strangers to the theatre. Most large towns had their own stock companies, and the hamlet was remote indeed which had not witnessed a minstrel show or a performance of *Uncle Tom's Cabin.* College students all over the country became interested in plays, and began producing and acting in them. The student playwright was again in evidence, and the first plays at a college were often "originals."

A new phenomenon appeared in college theatricals shortly after the Civil War. For the first time, students banded together in organizations whose primary purpose was the presentation of plays. One of the earliest was the Thalian Dramatic Association, founded at Brown in 1866.[89] Vassar's Philaletheis was formed in 1866, but was originally a literary society of the older type which occasionally put on plays.[90] Fordham's St. John's Dramatic Association was founded in 1871, and the Williams Dramatic Association in 1872. The Cornelian Minstrels were founded at Cornell in the same year, and 1875 saw the first performance of the university's Amateur Dramatic Association.[91] The Tufts Dramatic Club was formed in 1876.[92] A performance by Lawrence Barrett of *Hamlet* in 1879 led to the formation of the Barrett Club at the University of Michigan in 1880.[93] A "Dramatic Club" was founded at the University of Wisconsin in 1885;[94] the Princeton College Dramatic Association was founded the same year, after a previous "College Dramatic Association," formed in 1882, had proved not to be permanent.[95] The Shakespeare Society at Wellesley presented an open-air performance of *As You Like It* in 1889, and the Wellesley Dramatic Association was founded in 1896.[96] The University of Utah's Dramatic Club gave its first performance in 1897,[97] and Dartmouth's Dramatic Club, which had been giving annual performances since 1886, changed its name in 1898 to The Buskin.[98] In 1899 a women's dramatic club, The Red Domino, was founded at the University of Wisconsin; this club was later organized on a national basis.[99] The above list is not intended to be exhaustive; rather it is designed to show the spread of the dramatic-club idea through the colleges in this period.[100]

The dramatic clubs (with the exception of the musical comedy organizations) lacked continuity. The extracurricular drama at individual institutions seems to have run in cycles; clubs were founded and flourished for a few years, only to disappear when those students graduated who were most interested. The leading spirit of the Tufts Dramatic Club in 1876, for example, was J. H. Bradbury, later a comedian on the professional stage. Ten years later a new organization, The Stuft Club, was founded, only to disappear from the campus when John Burgess Weeks, later stage manager for Otis Skinner, left college in 1892. By 1895 a new group, the Modjeska Club, was giving performances; and so it went.[101]

The last half of the nineteenth century was a period of expansion of the extracurricular aspects of college life. Play production increased as did college athletics, glee clubs, social fraternities, and similar activities. The production of plays was by no means confined to "dramatic clubs," for other organizations often found it both enjoyable and profitable to "put on a play." The "benefit performance" was common, and many campuses were first introduced to college theatre by the presentation of a play whose primary purpose was to make money. In 1874 Norwich University students presented two plays, *Neighbor Jackwood* and *Loyal Mountaineers*, in the local concert hall for the benefit of the "Northfield Cornet Band."[102] At Amherst in 1870 the "Naval Dramatic Association" was formed to present an "Exhibition"; the profits from this performance went to help form a crew to participate in intercollegiate rowing contests.[103] The junior and senior classes at Brown University were presenting comedies about the same time, for the benefit of "baseball and boating." [104] Horticultural Hall at Harvard was the scene of performances by the athletes themselves; the University Boat Club and the Baseball Club gave public performances during the seventies.[105] Illinois College presented *The Old Flag* (by Samuel Nichols, an alumnus) in 1891, in order to raise money for the athletic association's effort to build a cinder running track.[106] After producing minstrel shows for several years, the athletic association of the University of Illinois produced, in 1895, *The Rabbit's Foot*, an original play by W. E. Shutt of Springfield, Illinois.[107] Mount Holyoke's production of *The Ghost of a Chance* in 1897 "made possible ... the customary Junior Prom." [108] The Ladies' Self-government Association at the University of Wisconsin gave a play and a musical program in 1900 to raise funds for an art exhibit.[109] At Goucher College it was forbidden for many years to give entertainments for which admission was charged; consequently at this college the benefit idea worked in reverse. "Oc-

casionally a fortunate class made enough on its publication of Donny-
brook Fair [the college annual] to defray cost of production of its most
expensive production, the senior play, but that did not happen
often." [110] The college drama program sometimes helped with the
finances of functions vital to the institution itself. Norwich's Cadet Theatrical Club, for example, donated the receipts of its production of
The Spy of Atlanta to the college library in 1883.[111] Mount Holyoke's
plays in the nineties were usually given in the cause of the college
endowment fund.[112] The high school at Madison, Wisconsin, presented
"an entertainment" to raise funds for the school library in 1884, indicating that "benefits" were not restricted to higher education.[113] The
whole picture of the late nineteenth-century academic drama indicates
that the college and school amateurs found in the drama a pleasing
and efficient money-maker. Indeed the "benefit" play remained characteristic of high-school theatre into the twentieth century.

It remained for the oldest of all the clubs presenting plays in the
nineteenth century, Harvard's Hasty Pudding, to establish a custom
which was to influence the founding of clubs in other colleges for a
specific kind of dramatic performance—the musical burlesque. As has
been seen, the emphasis in the Hasty Pudding before the Civil War
had been simply on producing plays. There are few signs of attempts
at playwriting. The first original plays of which there is any record are
the burlesques Bluebeard and Babes in the Wood, written by club member Edward J. Lowell and produced in June, 1866. Henry Cabot Lodge
and Henry W. Smith wrote the burlesque of Don Giovanni which was
produced in 1871.[114] Owen Wister's opera-bouffe Dido and Aeneas,
produced in 1882, "gave the club a national reputation ... [and] from
'82 to the present time, not a class has failed to produce an original
play." [115] The production of 1891, Obispah, was the first for which original music was written; prior to this date, the music had been found
"through an old custom of ransacking the pages of others; Offenbach,
Lecoq, Suppé, Sullivan, Bizet, Meyerbeer and Wagner were among
those to whom [the Musical Manager] ... had recourse." [116] With the
addition of an original score, the pattern was complete for a peculiarly
American phenomenon: the male undergraduate dramatic club which
produces musical comedy (though it was not until 1906 that the Hasty
Pudding plays were billed in this way).[117] The custom of men playing
women's parts was almost a necessity in those colleges where no women
were enrolled; but the tradition was adopted in coeducational institutions as well. The Haresfoot Club at the University of Wisconsin,
founded in 1899, was to set its precedent of all-male casts in 1907, and
its motto, "All our girls are men, yet every one's a lady," became familiar
wherever its productions were presented.[118]

Pennsylvania's Mask and Wig (founded 1892) and Princeton's Triangle Club (named in 1893, though not otherwise altered from its previous year) were the next such groups to be formed.[119] A revision of John Brougham's burlesque of Indian plays, *Po-ca-hon-tas, or the Gentle Savage,* produced in 1891 with added music by the Princeton College Dramatic Association, led student Booth Tarkington to write a farce, *The Honorable Julius Caesar,* for the 1892 production. This set the pattern for future Triangle Club plays, a pattern described by Borgers as "the annual presentation of an original comedy with original music, characterized by an improbable plot, low-grade humor, female impersonation, and a large chorus." [120] The Princeton College Dramatic Association changed its name in 1893 to the Triangle Club in response to an objection by the faculty to the use of the word "dramatic" in describing the activity.[121]

Characteristic of these societies were the performances "on the road." The performances of *Tom Thumb,* Hasty Pudding's 1854 musical play, were given at private homes in Cambridge, Brookline, and at Chickering's in Boston.[122] This marked the first time that a Hasty Pudding Club play was shown before outsiders, but the "trip" became common in later years, and when other college clubs began to produce such plays, alumni far from the campuses were given the opportunity to see the performances.[123] *Dido and Aeneas* was shown by the Hasty Pudding in 1882 in New York, Philadelphia, and Boston, taking those cities "by storm"; this established the real precedent which has since been followed by the musical clubs.[124] The Hasty Pudding Club writers grew so expert that its 1892 production of *The Sphinx,* with libretto by David Gray and music by Lewis S. Thompson, was later presented on the professional stage.[125] An idea of the lavishness of some of these productions may be gathered from their expense. L. Guernsey Price, writing in 1903 of the Columbia Varsity Show of the year before (*The Mischief Maker*), estimated that it had cost $2,500, while the annual burlesque of Pennsylvania's Mask and Wig "cost something like $5,000, over half for scenery." [126]

The "musical comedy society," which was to be a spectacular part of the campus scene at so many American colleges and universities in the years to come, became firmly established at a few institutions before the end of the century. It seems to have varied little from campus to campus, although allowances must be made for differences in talent from year to year. The organizations were run by the students, with only nominal supervision by the faculty, and may be said to have been extracurricular in every sense of the term.

The general quickening of the college drama was marked by the renascence of an old tradition, the production of foreign language plays.

These performances, in both modern and classic languages, were sponsored by the various language faculties, apparently with the same end
in view that had prompted the original "academical exercises." The
"Scene in Terrence" exhibited "in private in the library" in 1762 at
Harvard, had anticipated by more than one hundred years the performance of Terence's *Adelphi* by Michigan's sophomore class in 1882
under the direction of Professors C. M. Gayley and R. P. De Pont,
although *Adelphi* was advertised as "The first Latin play ever given in
this country." [127] In 1890 Professor J. H. Koch of the same university
directed Plautus' *Menaechmi*, and this production was so successful
that it was later taken to Chicago for a performance at the request of
the alumni of that city.[128]

To Harvard, the home of so many "firsts" in the college theatre, goes
the credit for another significant beginning. The production of *Oedipus
Tyrannus* at Harvard in May, 1881, was remarkable in many ways.[129]
It was probably the first Greek tragedy presented in the original Greek
in America. Perhaps never in the history of the college theatre has so
much time and care been lavished on a single production. The play
was in rehearsal for over six months, and all details were carefully
supervised by the professors of the Greek department. No pains were
spared to insure all possible historical accuracy, although some modifications were made in an attempt to make the play more sympathetic to
the contemporary audience. Music was composed especially for the
production by Professor J. K. Paine of the Music Department, while
costuming was the responsibility of Mr. F. D. Millet, who "made a
prolonged study of costume from the historical and artistic points of
view." The latter attended many rehearsals in order to instruct the
players in the proper handling of the unfamiliar garments. George
Riddle (Harvard A. B., 1874), an instructor in elocution at Harvard,
played the leading role and later attempted it on the professional
stage.[130] It is perhaps significant that of the remaining seven principal
actors, five were members of the Hasty Pudding Club. The dramatic
chorus was composed of fifteen members of the Harvard Glee Club,
while a forty-piece orchestra and a "supplementary chorus of sixty
voices" made up the company. The production was staged in the
Sanders Theatre, and was apparently an unqualified success:

The play was witnessed by six thousand people; on the occasion of the first
performance, by an audience which, for literary distinction, has probably
never been equalled in America; many persons were unable to obtain seats,
although ten times the original price was freely offered; it was reported by
every considerable newspaper in the country, and the news of its performance
was not only telegraphed to Europe, but was even inserted in the local papers
there. . . .[131]

The enthusiasm and publicity which attended the Harvard production stimulated other colleges to follow suit. Notre Dame had planned a production of *Oedipus Tyrannus* in 1879, but a fire forced postponement until 1882.[132] In all, Pluggé lists thirty-seven performances of Greek plays at American colleges between 1881 and 1900.[133] Beloit College's production of *Antigone* in 1885 marked the beginning of a tradition. With the exception of 1893, that institution produced a Greek play every year until 1903, and intermittently thereafter.[134] There seems to have been only one recorded performance of a Greek play in a high school during the nineteenth century. The Gloversville, New York, high school produced *Iphigenia in Tauris* in 1896.[135]

Departments of Greek sponsored all of the Greek plays at the college level in this period, but they were often presented in translation. There were eighteen performances in English between 1881 and 1903, while fifteen were presented in the original language.[136] At Beloit, the translations, in meter, were made by the sophomore class in Greek; while each member of the cast of *Antigone,* presented by Drury College in 1897, translated his own role as part of his work in advanced Greek.[137] This marks an early example of the invasion of the curriculum by the acted drama. The production of Greek plays had the approval and often the assistance of the college authorities in the late nineteenth century.

French and German plays—although performances do not appear in numbers until somewhat later than the Greek plays—were common in the last two decades of the century. They were most often produced under the auspices of the French and German clubs which grew up about this time. Although Gafflot says the productions of *Le Misanthrope* in 1888 and a "modern play by Labiche" in 1889 by Harvard's Cercle Français were "the first performance of French drama in any college or university since the expulsion of the Jesuits from France in 1762," there was a performance of Racine's *Les Plaideurs* at Michigan's commencement in 1882.[138] The high school at Ann Arbor, Michigan, had produced a "French play" in February, 1872.[139] There may have been a friendly rivalry between the French and German Departments at Goucher College, for 1884 marks the first plays in both French and German. *Le Premier Roman* and scenes from *Minna von Barnhelm, Sappho,* and *Die Jungfrau von Orleans* were produced in that year.[140] The Deutsche Gesellschaft at Northwestern produced *Eigensinn* and *Der Dritte* in 1895, and observed the Schiller festival with a scene from *Wilhelm Tell.*[141] The Cercle Français of the University of Illinois produced Labiche and Martin's *Le Poudre aux Yeux* in 1896, while in 1900 that institution's Deutsche Verein presented *Einer Muss Heiraten.*[142] The University of Wisconsin's Germanische Gesellschaft took advantage of the large German community in nearby Milwaukee to bring to

Madison from that city professional companies producing plays in German. *Minna von Barnhelm* was sponsored in 1901, and *Wilhelm Tell* for the Schiller Day festival in 1905, "so that the student might have an increased knowledge of German drama." [143] Harvard's German department installed the Conreid Company of New York on the stage of the Sanders Theatre in 1899-1900, to produce plays by Goethe and Lessing. [144] In 1897-1898 Harvard's French Department produced Racine's *Athalie,* with Mendelssohn's music and "impressive choruses." [145]

The foreign language play, as may be seen, was closer to the curriculum than any other kind of college dramatic activity during this period. In most instances the faculties of the various language departments were the instigating forces behind the plays, producing, directing, and in at least one instance writing the play. [146] An unusual production at Stanford in 1903, however, found the Spanish Club presenting *Calderon contra Ramsey* in Spanish, written by two students. [147] Modern language plays began to be produced frequently during the last two decades, although Cassidy says that French and Spanish plays were sometimes part of the commencement program at Catholic colleges prior to 1850. [148]

The foreign language play, associated with departments of instruction, doubtless helped to merge curricular and extracurricular drama. Departments and professors of elocution and oratory also became interested in dramatic materials and production. For example, although no course in "dramatic presentation" was offered at the University of Wisconsin until 1906-1907, [149] *Macbeth* and *Othello* were used for class exercises in elocution beginning in 1884 by Professor David Frankenberger, head of the Department of Rhetoric and Oratory. [150] In 1892 Frankenberger directed *Othello* when it was presented by the University Dramatic Club. [151] By 1898, with the object of stimulating "activity and study along theatrical lines," cash prizes of fifty and thirty-five dollars were being offered to "the best two casts . . . Casts were trained by members of the Department of Rhetoric and Oratory." [152] The "college elocution course" at the University of Utah in 1896, taught by Professor Maude May Babcock, divided the class time equally between "reading and study" of *Julius Caesar,* and extemporaneous speaking and oratory. [153] Professor Babcock is credited by Engar with supplying the "drive and organizing ability to commence a sustained program in [extra-curricular] dramatics." [154] In 1899 Shakespeare's birthday was celebrated at Mount Holyoke with a semi-dramatic performance. Elocution instructor Laura A. Rose read the texts while twelve Shakespearean scenes were presented in tableau. [155]

Shakespeare's were not the only "literary" plays which were to be seen. Professor C. A. Corson at Cornell, together with his wife, directed the Cascadilla Dramatic Association in a production of Oliver Gold-smith's *She Stoops to Conquer* in 1880. Mrs. Corson's presence was salu-tary. She was "an excellent actress, her enthusiasm, knowledge of foreign theatres, and general interest in dramatic art had an inspiring influence." [156] Professor R. M. Maulsby of Tufts College directed *Ralph Roister Doister,* which was presented in the college gymnasium in 1895.[157] Elizabethan drama was produced by the Delta Upsilon fra-ternity at Harvard—the plays of Dekker, Beaumont and Fletcher, and others were presented under the direction of the famous George Pierce Baker beginning in 1900.[158] Gilbert and Sullivan operettas found a responsive audience on American campuses, as they did all over the English-speaking world. *Pinafore* was presented at Princeton on April 24, 1879, "hardly a year after its completion," [159] and was given at Dart-mouth the following year.[160] Michigan's *Iolanthe* company, which per-formed in 1883, was made up of both students and faculty.[161] The appeal which Gilbert and Sullivan have always had for high schools manifested itself early; *Trial by Jury* was performed by the Madison, Wisconsin, high school in 1879.[162]

American women's colleges in this period were not behind the rest of the college world in the production of the classics of the drama. Vassar, whose Philalethean Society presented a scene from *Henry VIII* in celebration of the second anniversary of the society in 1867, seems to have set a standard for play production at that college. "The students of the first decade established the tradition for good plays, for 'The Rivals,' 'She Stoops to Conquer' and 'The Taming of the Shrew' are typical of the plays given." [163] The first "play" at Goucher College could hardly have been more sedate, for it consisted of tableaux with readings from Tennyson's *Dream of Fair Women.*[164] Wellesley's Shakespeare Society was for many years a branch of the London Shakespeare So-ciety, and devoted itself to "the study and dramatic presentation of Shakespeare." [165] Smith College's production of Sophocles' *Electra* was the first Greek play at a women's college,[166] but Wellesley [167] and Vassar [168] followed before 1900. Although Doyle says that some play producing groups at women's colleges were "entirely independent of faculty assistance or direction," [169] it is clear that they were not free from faculty supervision, to judge from the rules which applied to the productions themselves. College girls acting the male roles, for example, were hindered by a rule which seems to have arisen from an early prejudice against higher education for women, on the grounds that it tended to unsex them. They were forbidden to wear men's clothes, and the expedients which were resorted to are amusing in retrospect, as they must have been to an objective observer at the time. Goucher College "men" wore gymnasium costumes, long ulsters, or raincoats over their skirts.[170] At Mount Holyoke "prior to [1918] . . . bloomers, instead of trousers . . . lent a hilarious touch to many a scene," [171] while dark skirts were the convention which indicated masculinity in Vassar plays.[172]

The change in the attitude of the colleges toward the professional theatre in this period is most clearly shown by the appearance on the college lecture platform of professional theatre men. The actor, playwright, director, and student of Delsarte, Steele Mackaye, appeared "in the 1870's" at Princeton under the auspices of the Student Lecture Association. His subject was "The Mystery of Emotion and its Expression in Art." [173] In the eighties the public lectures at Harvard reflected interest in the drama. The English actor Henry Irving lectured in the 1884-1885 season; the German scholar Kuno Francke gave three lectures on the contemporary drama in 1887-1888.[174] Bronson Howard, the American playwright who "represents the . . . establishment of the profession of the dramatist in this country," [175] lectured at Harvard in 1886. His subject was "The Autobiography of a Play," a description of the successive revisions of his popular *Banker's Daughter*.[176] In 1897 Joseph Jefferson, sponsored by the Oratorical Association, lectured at the University of Michigan on "The Actor and His Art." [177] The fact of these lectures is clear evidence of the respectability to which the drama had attained in American colleges in the space of a hundred years.

We can conclude that dramatic activity in American schools and colleges prior to 1900 reveals several discrete influences. The colonial and Revolutionary periods are marked by an antagonism toward the theatre on the part of the Puritan schools and colleges, tempered by recognition of the educational values of the drama. This antagonism lasted well into the nineteenth century at some institutions. Despite this opposition, the literary societies at Yale in the last decades of the eighteen century engaged in an intensive program of extracurricular dramatics, and were imitated at several other colleges. Although there were isolated instances of performances (usually in Latin) which were officially recognized by the administrators of the colleges, the only dramatic activity which approached the literary society performances in quantity were the commencement odes and dialogues, which were presented in at least a semi-dramatic form.

The period from 1800 to the Civil War was one which saw a great increase in the number of colleges, but there does not seem to have been a corresponding growth in college theatricals. Many of the new colleges were founded by evangelical religious sects, and the religious revivals which intermittently swept the campuses may have affected the drama adversely. College men in the eastern states had more opportunity to attend the professional theatre, and the first Hasty Pudding Club play was inspired by such attendance. The history of this club is important, for it foreshadowed the formation after the Civil War of dramatic clubs whose only function was to produce plays. During the later period almost every college and many schools had some sort of dramatic program presented at irregular intervals by dramatic clubs (often short-lived), or by other organizations which found play production a means of raising money. The musical comedy organizations modeled after the Hasty Pudding Club became traditional on many campuses. They enthusiastically presented musical burlesques and *operas bouffes* which were often expensively mounted and which played to audiences of alumni and the general public as well as to the student body.

The theatre attracted the interest of college and university faculties, and the college drama was given real impetus by the various language departments. Plays in French, German, Spanish, Latin, and Greek began to be presented quite regularly. Since adaptations of foreign plays had long been popular on the professional stage, it may be that this innovation helped to make the drama more respectable, academically speaking.[178] Beloit and Drury Colleges made the Greek play a part of the course-work in Greek, and elocution courses in many colleges were using dramatic literature for training. With the appearance of professional theatre men on the lecture platform of American universities the way was prepared for the acted drama to take its place as part of the curriculum.

Notes

1. Quoted in Samuel Eliot Morison, *Harvard College in the Seventeenth Century* (Cambridge, Mass., 1936), Part II, p. 464.

2. *Virginia Gazette*, September 10, 1736, quoted in Lyon Gardiner Tyler, *Williamsburg, The Old Colonial Capital* (Richmond, Va., 1907), pp. 224-225.

3. Tyler, quoting, p. 228.

4. George Winship, *The First Harvard Playwright, A Bibliography of the Restoration Playwright John Crowne* (Cambridge, Mass., 1922), p. 3.

5. See Josiah Quincy, *History of Harvard University* (Boston, 1860), I, 559.

6. Evarts B. Greene, *Religion and the State in America* (New York, 1941), p. 44.

7. Barrett Wendell, *Cotton Mather, Puritan Priest* (Cambridge, Mass., 1926), p. 202.

8. The extent to which American colleges were "organized, supported, and in most cases controlled by religious interests" up to the time of the Civil War has been indicated by Donald Tewksbury in *The Founding of American Colleges and Universities Before the Civil War*, Teachers College, Columbia University, Contributions to Education, No. 543 (New York, 1932). See especially pages 55-56. Of the twenty-seven permanent colleges founded in this country prior to 1800, all but three (the Universities of Georgia, North Carolina and Vermont were state institutions from the beginning) were founded by religious groups; eighteen of the

remainder were organized and operated by dissenting churches. Moreover, the early colleges, almost without exception, were founded to provide an educated ministry for the religious interests they represented. President Thomas Clap of Yale, writing in a pamphlet published in 1754, might have been speaking for the founders of each institution when he wrote, "The great design of founding this School was to educate Ministers in our Own Way."

9. Frederick S. Boas, *University Drama in the Tudor Age* (Oxford, 1914), p. 220. A full account of the incident may be found in this book. See also E. N. S. Thompson, *The Controversy Between the Puritans and the State,* Yale Studies in English, XX (New York, 1903), 95-100.

10. See James L. McConaughy, *The School Drama,* Teachers College, Columbia University, Contributions to Education, No. 57 (New York, 1914), Ch. I.

11. Boas, pp. 235-236, 241.

12. Samuel Eliot Morison, in *The Puritan Pronaos* (New York, 1936), pp. 18, 19, has drawn attention to the influence of the English universities upon the intellectual leaders of the early New England communities—including the men responsible for the establishment of the colonial colleges. "[This] was the standard to which the New England puritans attempted, however imperfectly, to attain. . . . The great, absorbing intellectual interest in the Oxford and Cambridge and Dublin from which the founders of New England came was . . . ecclesiastical controversy."

13. Edward B. Coe, "The Literary Societies," *Yale College, A Sketch of Its History,* ed. William L. Kingsley (New York, 1879), p. 308.

14. Quoted by Edward W. Borgers, "A History of Dramatic Production in Princeton, New Jersey," unpublished Ph.D. dissertation, New York University, 1950, pp. 24-25.

15. Quoted in Thomas Jefferson Wertenbacker, *Princeton 1746-1896* (Princeton, New Jersey, 1946), p. 29.

16. Quoted in Franklin Bowditch Dexter, *Student Life at Yale in the Early Days of Connecticut Hall* (Reprinted from Vol. VII of the *New Haven Colony Historical Society Transactions, 1907*), p. 295.

17. Leon Burr Richardson, *History of Dartmouth College* (Hanover, N. H., 1932), I, 272.

18. Quoted in Albert Matthews, "Early Plays at Harvard," *Nation,* XCVIII (March, 19, 1914), 295.

19. Quoted in *Publications of the Colonial Society of Massachusetts* (Boston, 1912), XIII, 320. DeBerdt was an agent in London of the Massachusetts House of Representatives from November, 1765, to April, 1770.

20. Matthews, *op. cit.*

21. "The Laws of Harvard College (1767)," ed. Allyn Bailey Forbes, *Publications of the Colonial Society of Massachusetts* (Boston, 1935), XXXI, 358.

22. Matthews, *op. cit.*

23. *William and Mary Quarterly Historical Magazine,* XXII (April, 1914), 288.

24. Matthews, *op. cit.*

25. *Ibid.*

26. For example, Marjorie I. Smith, "Dramatic Activity Before 1800 in the Schools and Colleges of America," unpublished M.A. thesis, Cornell, 1948, pp. 98-99: "Only the purest Calvinism was permitted in the teaching of Yale students and only those principles of behavior [which] closely adhered to the Puritan way of life."

27. Edward B. Coe's chapter (see note 13) and Ota Thomas' article, "Student Dramatic Activities at Yale College During the Eighteenth Century," *Theatre Annual, 1944* (New York, 1945), offer good secondary sources for those to whom the records of the society are not available.

28. Coe, p. 308.

29. *Ibid.*, p. 316.

30. *Ibid.,* p. 311.

31. *Ibid.,* p. 309.

32. *Ibid.,* p. 312.

33. *Ibid.,* p. 314.

34. Marjorie I. Smith, *op. cit.,* p. 110.

35. *Ibid.*

36. John King Lord, *A History of Dartmouth College 1815-1909* (Concord, N. H., 1913), pp. 525-526.

37. Matthews, *loc. cit.*

38. Smith, p. 125.

39. Wertenbacker, *Princeton 1746-1896,* p. 197. He quotes from Princeton Library MSS, Am 8796 and Am 11288.

40. *Library of American Biography,* XXIV (1847), 23.

41. Recorded in William S. Demarest, *A History of Rutgers College* (Princeton, New Jersey, 1924), p. 149.

42. Arthur Hobson Quinn, *A History of American Drama from the Beginning to the Civil War* (New York, 1946), p. 9.

43. *Ibid.,* p. 18.

44. Thomas R. Birch, *The First One Hundred Years of the Zelosophic Literary Society* (Philadelphia, 1929), p. 87. See, however, Smith, *op. cit.,* p. 142, who contends that William Smith is the adapter of this play, and that he, not the students, made the additions which caused this play to be classified as an original composition.

45. Quinn, *op. cit.,* p. 18.

46. Lord, *op. cit.,* p. 514.

47. *Ibid.*

48. *Ibid.*

49. Arthur Hobson Quinn, "The Early Drama, 1756-1860," *The Cambridge History of American Literature,* p. 215.

50. Oscar Wegelin, *Early American Plays 1714-1860* (New York, 1905), p. 13.

51. Coe, "The Literary Societies," p. 318.

52. Quoted in Smith, *op. cit.,* p. 114.

53. Harold G. Rugg, "The Dartmouth Plays, 1779-1782," *Theatre Annual, 1942* (New York, 1943), pp. 55-69. This article contains photostats of the complete manuscripts, as well as the accompanying letter.

54. *Ibid.,* p. 58.

55. H. H. Brackenridge, *Modern Chivalry* (Philadelphia, 1856), II, 154.

56. Wegelin, p. 22.

57. Borgers, "The History of Dramatics at Princeton," pp. 36-37.

58. Alice More Earle, *Child Life in Colonial Days* (New York, 1899), pp. 115-116.

59. W. J. Mills, ed., *Glimpses of Colonial Society and the Life at Princeton College 1766-1776* (Philadelphia, 1903), p. 30.

60. Wegelin, p. 66.

61. Claude Moore Fuess, *Amherst: The Story of a New England College* (Boston, 1935), p. 56.

62. Willis T. Hanson, Jr., *Early Life of John Howard Payne* (Boston, 1913), p. 110.

63. An interesting description of this open-air performance may be found in George Washington Paschal's *History of Wake Forest College,* I, 154 ff.

64. Alexander Bruce, *History of the University of Virginia* (New York, 1920), I, 57-58.

65. William A. Ellis, *Norwich University, 1819-1911* (Montpelier, Vt., 1911), I, 57-58.

66. Sarah Pierce, "Ruth," "The Two Cousins," and "Jepthah's Daughter," *Chronicles of a Pioneer School from 1792 to 1833,* compiled by Emily Noyes Vanderpoel (Cambridge, Mass., 1903), pp. 84-145.

67. Vanderpoel, *Chronicles of a Pioneer School*, p. 84.

68. Esther Alice Peck, *A Conservative Generation's Amusements*, University of Maine Studies, 2nd Series, No. 44 (Bangor, Me., 1938), p. 11.

69. Tewksbury, *The Founding of American Colleges and Universities*, pp. 32-54.

70. *Ibid.*, pp. 83-84.

71. *Ibid.*, p. 57.

72. Borgers, "A History of Dramatics at Princeton," pp. 47-48.

73. Wertenbacker, *Princeton, 1746-1896*, quotes letters from the presidents of Harvard, Union, and Yale, congratulating the trustees of the College of New Jersey for their action after the riot of 1807, and implying that "impatience of control" on the part of college students was a national problem.

74. Wertenbacker, p. 166, and Tewksbury, pp. 66-67.

75. Wertenbacker, p. 249.

76. C. E. Walton, *An Historical Prospect of Harvard College, 1636-1936* (Boston, 1936), p. 35.

77. Bruce, *History of the University of Virginia*, II, 188.

78. Henry C. Youngerman, "Theatrical Activities: Madison, Wisconsin, 1836-1907," unpublished Ph.D. dissertation, University of Wisconsin, 1940, p. 127.

79. *Ibid.*, p. 157.

80. Samuel Eliot Morison, *Three Centuries of Harvard College* (Cambridge, Mass., 1937), pp. 182-183.

81. *Ibid.*

82. Lloyd McKim Garrison, "The H. P. C. Theatre, An Historical Sketch," *An Illustrated History of the Hasty Pudding Club Theatricals*, ed. Theodore Chase, *et al.* (Cambridge, Mass., 1933), no pagination.

83. *Ibid.*

84. *Ibid.*, "The First Pudding Play."

85. Garrison, *op. cit.*

86. The information and the quotation in the next two paragraphs come from the Garrison article.

87. Garrison, *op. cit.* Hayward got the idea for the first Hasty Pudding Club play from having seen *Bombastes Furioso* presented by a company in Boston.

88. *Three Centuries of Harvard*, p. 431.

89. Walter C. Bronson, *The History of Brown University, 1764-1914* (Providence, R. I., 1914), p. 348.

90. Agnes Rogers, *Vassar Women* (Poughkeepsie, N. Y., 1940), p. 348.

91. Waterman Thomas Hewett, *Cornell University, A History* (New York, 1905), I, 139.

92. *History of Tufts College*, ed. Alaric B. Start (Cambridge, Mass., 1896), p. 69.

93. Wilfred Shaw, *The University of Michigan* (New York, 1920), p. 222.

94. Youngerman, "Theatrical Activities: Madison, Wisconsin," p. 128.

95. Borgers, "A History of Dramatic Production in Princeton, New Jersey," p. 80.

96. Florence Converse, *Wellesley College 1875-1938* (Wellesley, Mass., 1939), p. 153.

97. Keith Engar, "History of Dramatics at the University of Utah From Beginnings Until June, 1919," unpublished M.A. thesis, University of Utah, 1948, p. 20.

98. Richardson, *History of Dartmouth College*, II, 644, 731.

99. Youngerman, p. 132.

100. The University of Illinois seems to have been an exception, for the literary societies, Philomathean and Adelphic (founded in 1868) were "for the first thirty years of the university the chief sponsors of undergraduate [dramatic] activity." (Mary Elizabeth Homrighaus, "A History of Non-professional Theatrical Production at the University of Illinois from its Beginnings to 1923," unpublished M.A. thesis, University of Illinois, 1949, p. 3.)

101. Start, *op. cit.*, p. 69.
102. Ellis, *Norwich University 1819-1911*, I, 168.
103. Fuess, *Amherst: The Story of a New England College*, p. 199.
104. Bronson, *The History of Brown University*, p. 379.
105. Morison, *Three Centuries of Harvard*, p. 431.
106. Charles Henry Rammelkamp, *Illinois College, A Centennial History 1829-1929* (New Haven, Conn., 1928), p. 371.
107. Homrighaus, *op. cit.*, p. 16.
108. Arthur C. Cole, *A Hundred Years of Mount Holyoke College* (New Haven, Conn., 1940), p. 229.
109. Youngerman, *op. cit.*, p. 133.
110. Anna Heubeck Knipp and Thaddeus P. Thomas, *The History of Goucher College* (Baltimore, 1938), p. 460.
111. Ellis, *op. cit.*, I, 185.
112. Cole, p. 229.
113. Youngerman, p. 126.
114. Garrison, "The H. P. C. Theatre, An Historical Sketch."
115. *Ibid.*
116. Owen Wister, "The First Operetta."
117. *An Illustrated History of the Hasty Pudding Club Theatricals.*
118. Youngerman, p. 131.
119. Borgers, "A History of Dramatic Production in Princeton, New Jersey," p. 95.
120. *Ibid.*
121. *Ibid.*, pp. 94-95.
122. Garrison, *op. cit.*
123. See Borgers, p. 96.
124. Morison, *Three Centuries at Harvard*, p. 426.
125. Garrison, *op. cit.*
126. L. Guernsey Price, "American Undergraduate Dramatics," *The Bookman*, XVIII (December, 1903), 380.
127. Clara Marie Behringer, "A History of the Theatre in Ann Arbor, Michigan, from its Beginnings to 1904," unpublished Ph.D. dissertation, University of Michigan, 1950, p. 124.
128. Shaw, *The University of Michigan*, p. 223.
129. Henry Norman, *An Account of the Harvard Greek Play* (Boston, 1882), p. x. These details have been taken from this interesting and valuable account of the play. The remarkable photographic plates of the production are particularly rewarding for students of the college drama.
130. *The Development of Harvard University Since the Inauguration of President Eliot*, ed. Samuel Eliot Morison (Cambridge, Mass., 1930), p. 76.
131. Norman, p. 13.
132. Domis E. Pluggé, *History of Greek Play Production in American Colleges and Universities from 1881 to 1936*, Teachers College, Columbia University, Contributions to Education, No. 752 (New York, 1938), p. 5.
133. *Ibid.*, pp. 14, 16.
134. *Ibid.*
135. *Ibid.*, p. 5.
136. *Ibid.*, pp. 107-108.
137. *Ibid.*
138. Cf. Morison, *Three Centuries at Harvard*, p. 342; and Shaw, *The University of Michigan*, p. 222.
139. Behringer, "Theatre in Ann Arbor," pp. 70 f.
140. Knipp and Thomas, *The History of Goucher College*, pp. 463-464.
141. Arthur Herbert Wilde, *Northwestern University, A History* (New York, 1905), pp. 84-85.
142. Homrighaus, "Theatrical Production at the University of Illinois," p. 16.

143. Youngerman, "Theatrical Activities: Madison, Wisconsin," pp. 133-134.
144. *The Development of Harvard University*, p. 97.
145. *Ibid.*, p. 98.
146. Knipp and Thomas, p. 464. In 1899 Goucher College presented an operetta, *Schneewittchen*, the "book" written by Froelicher, the songs by Reinicke, of the Goucher College faculty.
147. Price, "American Undergraduate Dramatics," p. 375.
148. Francis Patrick Cassidy, *Catholic College Foundation and Development in the United States* (Washington, D. C.), p. 95.
149. Youngerman, *op. cit.*, p. 107.
150. *Ibid.*, p. 158.
151. *Ibid.*, p. 129.
152. *Ibid.*, p. 131.
153. Keith Engar, "Dramatics at the University of Utah," p. 20.
154. *Ibid.*, p. 8.
155. Cole, *A Hundred Years of Mount Holyoke College*, p. 200.
156. Hewett, *Cornell University, A History*, I, 140.
157. Start, *History of Tufts College*, p. 69.
158. Morison, *Three Centuries at Harvard*, p. 432.
159. Borgers, "Dramatic Production in Princeton," p. 52.
160. Richardson, *History of Dartmouth College*, II, 644.
161. Shaw, *The University of Michigan*, p. 222.
162. Youngerman, "Theatrical Activities: Madison, Wisconsin," p. 126.
163. James M. Taylor and Elizabeth H. Haight, *Vassar* (New York, 1915), p. 100.
164. Knipp and Thomas, *The History of Goucher College*, p. 460.
165. Converse, *Wellesley College, 1875-1938*, p. 153.
166. Pluggé, *A History of Greek Play Production*, p. 16.
167. Converse, p. 154.
168. Pluggé, p. 16.
169. Sister Mary Peter Doyle, *A Study of Play Selection in Women's Colleges*, Teachers College, Columbia University, Contributions to Education, No. 648 (New York, 1935), p. 4.
170. Knipp and Thomas, p. 458.
171. Cole, *A Hundred Years of Mount Holyoke College*, p. 308.
172. Rogers, *Vassar Women*, p. 65.
173. Borgers, "Dramatic Production in Princeton," p. 68.
174. Morison, *The Development of Harvard University*, p. 94.
175. Arthur Hobson Quinn, *A History of the American Drama from the Civil War to the Present Day* (New York, 1936), I, 39.
176. *Ibid.*, I, 43.
177. Behringer, "Theatre in Ann Arbor," p. 244.
178. Professor Alfred Hennequin, who taught courses in the French drama at the University of Michigan, grew so much interested in the theatre that he gave up his teaching in order to devote himself entirely to professional playwriting and play "doctoring." In 1888 Bronson Howard had visited one of Hennequin's courses in "the principles of dramatic construction." When he returned to the East, Howard made known his approval in a letter to the *New York Herald* (May 8, 1888). "One hundred students were present and they evinced the closest possible interest.... I ... learned many things which would be of service to me hereafter.... If any young man in the United States seeks a liberal education, desiring to become a dramatic critic ... or a dramatic author, he has no choice at present but to go to the University of Michigan." (Behringer, "Theatre in Ann Arbor," pp. 166 ff.)

24 The Private Theatre Schools in the Late Nineteenth Century

FRANCIS HODGE

Professional theatre schools to train actors did not appear in this country until the last quarter of the nineteenth century. They met a need and provided a fresh impulse at a time when the American theatre was changing radically and extensively. The study of their origin and growth is the study of the beginnings of a new theatre and the passing of the old, for the schools reflected new points of view in theatrical management and in theories of acting and production. In these early schools many of the ideas that later came to flower in the university theatre were first introduced. The schools believed, for example, that acting can be taught in the classroom. This idea they developed fully because they were primarily schools of acting and not the all-inclusive schools of theatre arts we know today.

The story of the first professional acting schools, important as it is, has not been set down except in isolated fragments. Like many innovations, the theatre school was lightly regarded and the victim of much buffeting during its early years. Yet as we look back from the vantage point of today, its significance grows and we recognize the acting school as one of the important links between nineteenth- and twentieth-century theatre.

The appearance and growth of acting schools during the 1880's and 1890's was a natural result of a series of changes that sharply altered the face of the American theatre after the Civil War. For most of the century the travelling star system, with its emphasis on individual style and the relative independence of leading actors, had dominated a theatre whose backbone was the resident stock company. At first this system was thought to be the most efficient method of showing distinguished actors to many audiences, but it soon developed many evils. With a succession of visiting stars, the best of whom demanded high guarantees, local managers found they could make a profit only by sacrificing the quality of the resident stock company. By mid-century, therefore, leading actors began touring with supporting players of their own choosing, a condition which inevitably led in the 1860's to the combination system or the hiring of actors for a single play, the method still employed today. With the combination system New York became the unquestioned theatrical center because road companies were made up there.

Most important to the actor in this managerial shift was the loss of his primary training ground—stock company repertoire. Playing a handful of parts during a season, as the actor did under the combination system, was scant training compared to playing the many and various roles required by the frequent change of stock bills. Where, then, could new actors hope to learn their craft? At the same time, the problem was intensified by the steadily increasing need for low-salaried performers to fill road company jobs.[1] During the mid-fifties the minstrel show and such family plays as *Uncle Tom's Cabin* had proved popular, and large numbers of people gained the taste for and habit of theatre-going; and by the eighties, with the Puritan restraints of the church largely relaxed, several thousand theatres were in need of a continuous supply of entertainment. Some method of satisfying this demand with actors who had learned at least the rudiments of their trade had to be devised.

But the advent of the combination system and the growth of the audience were not the only important changes in the theatre. The retreat behind the proscenium, the appearance and growth of the realistic play, the new emphasis on ensemble acting, and the new prominence of the stage director were slowly shaping a new style of theatre art. The new style required a radical change in acting. The traditional method of stock actors, of passing interpretation in lines and business from one generation to another, did not satisfy the demands of the new realism which required the actor to "go to life" for his model. Instead, he needed to master those fundamentals of acting which he himself as actor-artist would find applicable to new roles under new conditions.[2]

I

The beginning actor's training in this country before the advent of formal schools of instruction was haphazard. Success in the profession was won in a contest of the survival of the fittest, and a sound start often depended on the novice's connections with the theatre. If he was fortunate enough to be born into an acting family, his training literally began while he was still in arms, since he was likely to be carried on the stage for those scenes in which a baby was called for. Later on as he gained the experience of children's parts, he began to pick up the rudiments of stage discipline, and often, as in the case of the Bateman children and Julia Dean,[3] might even receive formal tutoring from his father or other members of the acting family as they moved from town to town in an endless series of stock engagements. This constant practice instilled a basic knowledge of the theatre. Others who were not born of theatrical families began on the amateur stage and either worked their way into companies as supers or, on occasion, paid for the right to appear before an audience on a benefit night. But however he found his way into a company, the stock actor had to be versatile and this demanded hard study and rigorous training. Such actors as Edwin Forrest, John Drew, and Anna Cora Mowatt took lessons in fencing for general body development, and Forrest studied acrobatics and boxing.[4] Months before Mrs. Mowatt made her debut she exercised daily with dumb-bells "to overcome the constitutional weakness of her arms and chest"; and for four hours every day she wore a voluminous train, as Fanny Kemble had before her, "to learn the graceful management of queenly or classic robes." [5]

In addition to body training many actors sought formal study in elocution to prepare them for a stage life dominated by Shakespeare and other verse drama.[6] Edwin Forrest, James E. Murdoch, and John McCullough worked with Lemuel G. White, a frustrated actor, so Lawrence Barrett claims, and an exponent of the Garrick-Kean school; [7] and Murdoch went on to become not only a first-rate actor but a celebrated teacher of elocution [8]—"one of the few artists," commented Joseph Jefferson, "who were both professed elocutionists and fine actors." [9] Katherine Sinclair and Mary Anderson both studied with George Vandenhoff,[10] a prominent English actor long on the stage in this country and author of The Art of Elocution. On the other hand, many actors, as Murdoch observed, considered the study of elocution unnecessary and regarded the teachers of the art with a suspicious eye.[11] However, the actor did not always have the last word. "Any gump can learn stage technique and the business of a part," argued vitriolic Alfred Ayres, a prominent teacher of elocution and acting, "but there is only now and then a person that can, try as he may, learn to read really well." [12]

As he advanced in his profession, the actor naturally followed the English tradition, a tradition requiring that he turn to the models on the stage and adopt not only conventional interpretations of certain parts but whatever was effective in acting styles as well. Thus Edwin Booth copied his father; James H. Hackett imitated the elder Charles Mathews; and Forrest followed Kean.[13] Notions about traditional stage behavior were likely to be derived not only from first-hand observation but by working with others long familiar with the old stage ways. Charlotte Cushman learned much about Mrs. Siddons' acting from Mr. Barton, stage manager at the St. Charles in New Orleans,[14] and Mrs. Mowatt studied with W. H. Crisp,[15] a leading actor at the Park Theatre in New York. John Drew during the rehearsal of old plays "always talked over" both the play and his part with his mother because "she knew the stage business which had been tried and found successful." [16] But this traditional hand-me-down system of playing led to trite and shallow acting unless dominated by an actor's cultural and intellectual equipment. "Original conception grafted upon knowledge of the past is the true method of evolution in stage art," argued John McCullough.[17] He was supported by Helena Modjeska who maintained that "the general cultivation of the mind, the development of all the intellectual faculties, the knowledge of how to think are more essential to the actor than mere professional instruction." [18]

The stock company, of course, was the primary training ground. One writer estimates that a competent beginner could play as many as one hundred bit roles in a season.[19] Thus there was opportunity to establish essential disciplines; yet the actor was left to his own devices, and he perished or survived on what he could pick up from more experienced actors. Olive Logan tells a story about a famous American actor who was distracted at rehearsal by the inattention of a young member of the cast with whom he was playing a scene. "My young friend," he said, "if you desire to progress in your profession, you should be more attentive. A rehearsal is *your school,* sir, and inattention to what's going on on the stage, while you are engaged in the scene, is wrong, sir." [20]

If the run-of-the-mill stock company was a haphazard training ground, the same could not be said of a few companies like Augustin Daly's, where training the apprentice actors was a primary occupation of the master himself. Intensely interested in the performance of the ensemble, Daly demanded thorough rehearsal with meticulous attention to detail. William Dean Howells, a leader in the late-century movement to raise American artistic standards, labeled Daly's theatre "the nearest approach to a national school of acting," [21] while John Rankin Towse called it "the only true school of acting in the United States." [22] Others thought it "the most wonderful school of acting," [23] and Daly a great teacher;[24] it was "a school from which many actors graduated to become stars," [25] a "rare schooling," [26] and a "thespian academy." [27] Daly not only provided the basic nourishment for beginning actors, but he also furnished the salt to season the work of his advanced performers. No one was spared during rehearsal period, and many an actor looked back on his Daly apprenticeship as the cornerstone of his later success.

Daly's stage direction, however, was the exception. Other important companies, although lacking the guidance of such an expert teacher,[28] worked out limited training programs that included occasional classes in fencing, dancing, walking, and grace.[29] But formal schooling in the ordinary stock company never went beyond these techniques, and in most of them the rehearsal period was the usual time for any brief instruction considered necessary. Most of the time the beginner worked alone, and what he could not manage singlehanded simply went undone. Playing too many parts in a season often resulted in blindness to error, resort to expediency, and reliance on old tricks which meant both poor playing and poor training. Undoubtedly such a system was beneficial to some players, but it was all too frequently detrimental to others. Minnie Maddern Fiske decided that stock training might help the beginning actor only if he kept telling himself, "This is all wrong, wrong, wrong."

With this background in mind it is not hard to understand the controversy that arose among professional actors of standing when the idea of the formal school of acting was first broached. The older methods of learning acting—primarily the "doing" method—had convinced many professional actors that in spite of its evils, it was the only possible way for a beginner to learn his trade. Acting simply could not be taught in the classroom. During the seventy years or so which have elapsed since the early efforts of Steele MacKaye, Franklin Sargent, and other school advocates, we have so wholeheartedly accepted the concept that it can be taught and proved it by the widespread growth and general acceptance of theatre schools that we tend to underestimate the strong feeling against the school idea in its first years. But in the 1880's such responsible actors as Jefferson, Barrett, Boucicault, and Modjeska warmly argued the question.

"Could acting be learned from others, or must it be self-acquired?" was a problem for which there was no ready answer except the prejudice of personal experience. "The study of gesture and elocution, if taken in homeopathic doses and with great care, may be of service," was Joseph Jefferson's guarded opinion.[30] But Lawrence Barrett—who later, ironically enough, performed enthusiastically with apprentice actors at the New York School of Acting[31]—did not beg the question: "No school of elocution, no training outside the theatre can I regard as at all valuable. All teachers of elocution come to the theatre for their models; why should the pupil go out of it for his? . . . The theatre is the school of the actor."[32] Maggie Mitchell was in full agreement. "I do not think novices reap any practical benefit from private lessons. . . . The stage itself is the best, in fact, the only school for actresses. . . . Mere oral advice, or training in elocution or gesture counts for very little."[33]

Helena Modjeska, on the other hand, thought that something could be learned from a properly chosen private instructor although the "best school of acting seems to me to be the stage itself," [34] and with the latter opinion William Warren found easy agreement. One writer estimated that nine out of ten actors would tell beginners that the stage was the best teacher.[35] Another damned elocution as "injurious" to dramatic students, arguing that "criticism and the stage director have made more competent actors and actresses in a day than elocution schools will put forth in a lifetime." [36] In a pro and con discussion of the question conducted by *The Idler Magazine* in 1893 and printed under the title, "Shall We Have a Dramatic Academy," [37] many were still in substantial agreement with a committee composed of Henry Irving, Hermann Vezin, Henry Neville, Dion Boucicault, and others who, a decade earlier, had decided that "acting could be taught only on the stage, as swimming can be taught in the water, and riding on horseback. All chamber tuition is worthless." [38]

On the other hand to refute the often-voiced negative opinion was the positive support for the school idea exemplified in the Paris Conservatoire.[39] Over many decades this celebrated institution had trained leading actors for the French stage, and, with its reorganization in the 1870's, the theatre "department" won new prominence. Such well-known actors as Regnier, Got, Delaunay, and Worms were regular members of the faculty. Others such as Constant Coquelin continually supported it and praised its merits. "Whatever success I have had as an actor I attribute entirely to training," wrote the first actor of the French stage.[40] "Every detail of my performance and delivery is the result of training, study and preparation. I leave nothing to inspiration.... One has always the need of a conservatoire. All art has need of a school. Every artist must be schooled. There is no art possible without training." Here was the positive rebuttal to those who maintained that acting could not be taught. "The Conservatoire gives the grammar of the art—the orthography of acting, if one may say so—the ABC, in short," argued Coquelin. "The period that the pupil passes in its walls is a period of germination.... It gives style, and without style there is no good acting." In 1900 Bronson Howard would argue that the Conservatoire, although excellent of its kind, was only a small "department" operating on the "old system of teaching by great masters individually," and that America had established the first fully organized school of acting in the world.[41] But in his eagerness to claim the best, Howard overlooked the influence of the Paris institution on MacKaye and others when they were trying their early experiments in the seventies and eighties. The proof of its success was apparent in its steady contribution to the French stage.

This was the background and the climate of opinion, then, out of which the first formal schools of acting were born in America.

II

Since early experimentation and practice reveal basic ideas and frequently the innovating mind—first the artist, then the organizers, observed Gordon Craig—a look at the beginnings of theatre schools in this country is significant. But beginnings are often difficult to trace, and the problems here are the usual ones—a scarcity of readily accessible records, claims and counterclaims, and confusion in terminology, of which the most pertinent to our discussion is what was meant by "school." The story must be pieced together from many sources.

There is little doubt that Steele MacKaye was the most important single influence in the establishment of formal actor training in this country.[42] He is so frequently cited as an innovator in theatrical art, an inventor of machines, as a playwright, and as a theatre manager, that it is easy to forget that at the beginning of his career he was an actor, and that the study and practice of acting was his first important work in the theatre. In the late sixties, MacKaye came under the tutorship of François Delsarte [43] and soon reached such wholehearted agreement with the French master's theories of expression that spreading his own interpretation of these theories became an extraordinary mission. Whatever MacKaye personally may have accomplished in his study of Delsartism or whether he fully understood it is open to debate, but clearly he was a teacher who could inspire others beyond their ordinary capacities. Within a few years he had won a number of important students to Delsartism, as he interpreted it, and had begun a series of experiments in classroom teaching that were to reach a climax in the Lyceum Acting School of 1884.

In his earliest writings and lectures after his contact with both Delsarte and the Paris Conservatoire, MacKaye asserted that a theatre school was essential to the foundation of a responsible art theatre. He began his campaign late in 1871 with the publication of a prospectus setting forth his plans to open an acting school at the St. James Theatre, his first venture in theatrical management.[44] He argued:

> There can never be a healthy vital drama until there is a safe and sure school where the dramatic aspirant may go as a student, and where he will be guaranteed the best social and moral associations, as well as the most thorough practical and aesthetic preparation for the profession.

He further claimed to be the "only living pupil in this country" of François Delsarte, whose teachings were to be followed. How MacKaye conducted this first school has not been recorded. It lasted only a few months, and apparently there was little enrollment beyond the members of his acting company. But probably as stage manager he gave instruction while directing plays, and, in addition, arranged special tutoring sessions. Despite its short life, the St. James project was an important step toward that goal which MacKaye had hoped for in the prospectus: the founding of a Free Conservatory of Art.

Continuing to teach privately and to lecture wherever he could, MacKaye launched a second enterprise in 1877, the School of Expression on Union Square. In his prospectus for this project, MacKaye again pleaded for a theatre that would fulfill its inherent function of "instructing and elevating society beyond merely entertaining it." But a new worry was evident. He was seriously concerned over the decline of acting, the life blood of dramatic art; he feared that its decline had led to a theatre relying on "sensational stage attire rather than the dramatic ability of the company." As a remedy he urged the training of disciplined actors to replace those dilettantes who "threatened the deterioration of the stage." As in the St. James "school," MacKaye was again the sole teacher. His studio was equipped with a small stage where students could perform the exercises of Delsartian instruction. This system of training, MacKaye defended thus:

[It] develops the student's faculty to feel by a scientific exposition of the natural facts and laws governing the manifestation of human emotions. It develops his faculty to express by thorough discipline in practical Pantomime, Stage Business, and Vocal Gymnastics. Thus it aims to equalize and increase the activity of these complementary faculties, ultimately rendering their cooperation so complete and instructive as to endow the art of the actor with the crowning characteristic of genius,—spontaneity.[45]

Of the several students actively engaged on the stage who sought MacKaye's help at this time, the best known was John McCullough who declared that MacKaye "has taught me more in three months, than I could have learned otherwise in twenty years, and I don't care who knows it."[46]

Like his first venture at the St. James, the Union Square School was of brief duration. But MacKaye soon took over the management of the Madison Square Theatre, where he hoped "to show in his actors the result of training according to the ideas of Delsarte."[47] In this new project MacKaye had a first-rate theatre at his command for the first time. But the conservative Mallorys, the Madison Square owners, restricted his activities, and he withdrew to head a most ambitious undertaking, the new Lyceum Theatre. MacKaye's management of this house lasted but a few months, yet his work here was the most significant of all his school ventures, for it saw the founding of the Lyceum

Acting School which has survived to the present day as the American Academy of Dramatic Arts.

The Lyceum Theatre School was a fitting climax to MacKaye's efforts. For a decade he had worked persistently and had attracted only minor interest and few converts. But the Lyceum School apparently struck at an opportune moment and was conceived in a size calculated to excite public attention. Whether Franklin Sargent in the Spring of 1884 first broached the idea of an amateur dramatic academy to Mac-Kaye,[48] as Sargent claimed, and MacKaye quickly embraced the plan, found financial support, and moved forward with a big scheme of professional dimensions, need not be settled here.[49] The fact remains that it was obviously MacKaye as the head of the Lyceum project who gave it vital leadership and staunch purpose. Here was MacKaye's art theatre almost fully realized. No other manager in the American theatre was able to boast of such complete organization and facilities as the Lyceum, with its special stage devices, quality stock company, and theatre school to train its potential personnel. Since MacKaye's best efforts as a stage director had been realized where he could work with a permanent acting company subject to his daily supervision and instruction, it was only natural that he should conceive of a school capable of fulfilling these artistic demands. His experience with Regnier and the Théâtre Français several years before had taught him the value of an apprentice training program in conjunction with a professional company.

The school project also appeared to be a sound business proposition. Charles Frohman, the Lyceum's business manager, had set up a tuition plan that would permit the school to pay its own way, and in spite of an initial, limited enrollment of one hundred students, $32,000 was immediately made available to the Lyceum treasury. This income was, of course, earmarked for instructional salaries; but since it became part of the theatre's operating income, it could be diverted to other needs of the theatre. Within a few weeks after the school had opened, the tuition money became a subject of contention: MacKaye and Frohman were accused of misappropriating these funds into other departments of the theatre and in this way preventing the prompt payment of the faculty and the proper administration of school activity. It is true that the opening of the theatre had been delayed, a circumstance which placed heavy financial burdens on the management, and this fact undoubtedly gave support to the strong suspicions voiced in the attack. Both Mac-Kaye and Frohman vigorously denied the charge.[50] Despite this misunderstanding, the venture revealed the possibility of co-ordinating school and theatre financial arrangements. In addition, the school was a most practical investment in the future. Here was a way of supplying

the low-salaried apprentice actors needed for the Lyceum's road companies as well as for the bit parts in the New York productions.

Unfortunately profits cannot wait on artistry. Within a few months
after the School had opened, MacKaye, pushed to the wall by unfore-
seen difficulties in getting the new plant into operation, was forced to
abandon the management of the Lyceum and revert to private teaching as a means of livelihood. Reorganized, the Lyceum School came
under the sole control of Franklin Sargent, the Harvard-educated
teacher and organizer whom MacKaye had won as a Delsarte convert
in 1878 [51] while delivering a lecture at the Boston School of Oratory.[52]

Although MacKaye had headed the Lyceum project and undoubtedly
had much to do with determining the size and scope of the school,
Sargent had been hired to administer the practical details of training
and had made some of the advance arrangements.[53] In the actual
instruction, Sargent supervised classroom activity while MacKaye
worked with the student actors in stage productions. Sargent had
brought to the Lyceum job a backlog of experience from the Madison
Square Theatre where he had gone in 1882 as a coach to help prepare
new actors for the many road companies dispatched by that organization under MacKaye's management. With MacKaye's departure from
the Lyceum, Sargent inherited not only complete control of the school
but also one of its chief instructors, David Belasco, who had also followed MacKaye from the Madison Square to the Lyceum. If its reigning
genius was lost, the school had fallen into careful and respectful hands,
for Sargent's subsequent record as director is a testimonial to his artistic
integrity and strong purpose.

III

Although MacKaye's Lyceum Theatre School was the first formal
school that could boast a varied curriculum, a fair-sized faculty, and a
large student enrollment, spot sources of information, such as periodical
advertisements and directories,[54] reveal that others were making
attempts to offer dramatic training. In New York the Lawrence School
of Acting claimed a beginning in 1869. Undoubtedly this school's early
emphasis was chiefly on elocution, although by 1892 acting was the
dominant study. In 1878 the New York Conservatory of Music was
advertised as a "School of Elocution, Oratory and Dramatic Action."
The following year saw the founding of James E. Frobisher's College of
Oratory and Acting where teaching was based on its founder's text,
Acting and Oratory. In Boston, a School of Elocution and Dramatic
Art was active as early as 1867. The endorsements of Edwin Booth,
William Warren, and Joseph Jefferson were claimed for Rachel Noah's

Petersilea Academy (1871), and the Delsarte School of Oratory and Dramatic Art (1881) on Tremont Street offered "direct stage practice under professional management." But the rapid growth in number and the size of enrollment of dramatic schools waited on the success of the Lyceum venture. During the late 1880's and early 1890's a rash of schools appeared—one or two of which, like the Lyceum, have survived until the present day, a few more lasted a brief span of years, but most led short lives as one-man studios rather than full-scale schools of acting.

Among the "schools" opening in New York between 1884 and 1900 were: The Alviene Master School of the Theatre (1894); Mrs. D. P. Bower's School of Dramatic Instruction (c. 1892); The Empire Theatre Dramatic School (1893); The Grand Conservatory of Music of the City of New York (c. 1887); Rose Eytinge's Only School of Acting (c. 1892); the E. J. Henley Dramatic School (c. 1897); the Madison Square School of Instruction (1887); the McKee Rankin School of Acting (c. 1897); National Dramatic Conservatory (c. 1899); Proctor's School of Acting (c. 1892); and The Stanhope-Wheatcroft Dramatic School (1897).

In Chicago, among others, were the American School of Dramatic Art (c. 1892) directed by E. Z. Vezina, and the Chicago School of Acting (c. 1892) located in the Schiller Theatre Building, with Hart Conway as director. Boston could boast not only the schools mentioned earlier, but the Bijou Dramatic School (c. 1885); Bickford's School of Elocution, Oratory and Dramatic Art; the Bliss School of Elocution; the Boston School of Acting; and probably the best known of the group because of its survival to the present day—the Curry School of Expression, now Curry College. Philadelphia had the Edwin Forrest School (c. 1899), and was near enough to New York to be solicited by an occasional agent for the American Academy. In St. Louis, Grahame's Stage School and Dramatic Agency (1866) advertised frequently, and in Cincinnati the Schuster-Martin School (1900) offered training for the actor.

Undoubtedly there were many other schools, but this list shows not only how rapidly formal instruction in acting had spread but also how it was administered. Many of these schools were privately operated, but a number followed the Lyceum tradition and were closely associated with producing theatres. In New York these included such important theatres as the Empire, Proctor's, the Madison Square, the Murray Hill (McKee Rankin), and Palmer's (Mrs. Bower's School).

A large group of private instructors also promised in their advertisements the best tutelage. A few like Ada Dow, the teacher of Julia Marlowe, were professional actors and offered an extensive course of training, including gymnastics, voice culture, elocution, stage deportment, and, most important of all, analysis and special work on many plays that could equip the student with a repertoire.[55] Among others whose names may possibly be remembered were Emma Waller, Harry Pepper, Rosa Rand, and Parson Price. Perhaps the best known of the group in New York was Alfred Ayres [56] who had worked professionally with Steele MacKaye and later at the Lyceum School where he had come into conflict with Sargent over teaching methods. The author of *Actors and Acting* (1894) and an earlier volume titled *The Essentials of Elocution* (1886), Ayres early lost faith in dramatic schools because, so he claimed, they failed to pay attention to stage delivery which was the very core of acting to his way of thinking. Adept at straight talk, that often received publication in the *New York Dramatic Mirror*, he blasted the schools at every opportunity. "A candidate for the stage might profit quite as much by being a member of an amateur dramatic association as by being a pupil of any one of these so-called schools, a good half of which are mere confidence schemes," he wrote.[57] If Ayres's ranting made him sound something like a sorehead, undoubtedly he was only one of many who saw that the art of elocution and the elocution teacher would play an even smaller role in actor training as the new schools with their specialized curricula found favor. Yet the elocutionists still played a direct part in the training of professional actors, and in every city throughout the country their special services were available.

A significant number of stage "names" were associated with the schools. A few of these early teachers such as David Belasco,[58] Henry DeMille, Rachel Crothers, and May Robson are still well remembered. Among others were George Cable, George LeSoir, F. F. Mackay, Madame Michels, Rosa Rand, McKee Rankin, Adeline Stanhope, Nelson Wheatcroft, Fred Williams, and William Seymour. Not only had Belasco, Williams, and Seymour been actors before they undertook the responsibilities of the classroom, but they were also successful stage managers. Wheatcroft, F. F. Mackay, DeMille, McKee Rankin, and Miss Stanhope were recognized actors of standing. And all of them, like Steele MacKaye, brought through-the-mill backgrounds to their work. Of the many instructors connected with these early schools, Franklin Sargent, although not a professional actor, looms next to Steele Mac-Kaye as the most important. His integrity, his scholarship, his devotion to teaching as an art, his conviction that theatre had a higher mission than mere entertainment and its artists a special obligation to society, gave a responsible leadership to this new approach to actor training. To Sargent, the development of personal character was essential in making the artist, and proper instruction was "condensed experience plus disciplined faculties and an established art creed." [59]

IV

What theories and methods of acting were taught in the schools? What methods of teaching were used? To answer such questions only a limited amount of firsthand material is readily available.[60] It must be carefully sifted, for it is tinged with the strong idealism of those who believed that classroom training was superior to the haphazard stock company method.

At the outset, the classroom approach implied not only that acting could be taught profitably in the group, but that the student would learn more quickly under the watchful eye of a trained instructor. As one school head who had been brought up in the hard knocks of stock company training put it, "I know that a year in a dramatic school will teach the young aspirant for stage honors what it took me at least ten years to learn." [61] Teaching had its first impetus from MacKaye, an apostle of the Delsarte system, and this system, variously interpreted and adopted, permeated the schools of acting. Of MacKaye's many pupils who spread Delsartism—Lewis Monroe, S. S. Curry, Genevieve Stebbins, and Franklin Sargent—Sargent was undoubtedly the most important. As head of the American Academy, he could well claim by 1900 to have provided, either from his staff or student body, the leadership of most of the important dramatic schools in the country. The line from Delsarte was direct, even if the theories and practice were watered down and modified over the years. The claim in 1887 that "there is hardly a professor of note in America who does not include Delsarte's principles in his teachings" [62] was probably exaggerated, but it is clear that after MacKaye's first introduction of this new approach to acting, the Delsarte system—or what was called that—enjoyed a wider and wider vogue.

Helena Modjeska said that imitation is the "worst method in art as it kills the individual creative power, and in most cases, the imitators only follow the peculiar failings of their model." [63] Franklin Sargent maintained that acting could not be properly taught by imitation or coaching. "No teaching can give anything—it can only draw out and encourage or discourage tendencies in the pupil," he argued.[64] Had their worlds crossed intimately, he might have been talking in perfect agreement with Joseph Jefferson, who thought that dramatic instructors fell into the error of teaching too much. This celebrated actor reasoned that the teacher could best learn what to teach only by first allowing the novice to exhibit his special quality and thus set his own course of instruction. Dogma "pounded" into the actor could only result in smothering innate ability.[65] Like Jefferson's, Sargent's method was one of creative growth in which the actor would slowly overcome his weaknesses and gain eventual command of himself as an expressive instrument.

It was inevitable that the new ideas should come into conflict with the old. Scarcely four months after the founding of the Lyceum School, Sargent dismissed such qualified instructors as Madame Michels, Mrs. George Vandenhoff, Max Freeman, William Seymour, and Professor Alfred Ayres on the charge that they were "old-fashioned" in their methods.[66] "The Delsarte system was the foundation, and no departure will be recognized," Sargent wrote in defense of the dismissals. Yet, at the same time, he retained David Belasco who was no Delsartian. Sargent often argued that stage managers were the best teachers of acting, and undoubtedly he saw something unusual in Belasco, regardless of his notions on acting or his methods in the classroom. Actors made very poor teachers, Sargent insisted, because they could not easily devote themselves exclusively to the needs of the student. Teaching required great humility and was a special art in its own right. A stage manager was the true servant to creative production and was thus well qualified to guide the beginner.

Methods of instruction were not the only problems facing the new schools. What should be taught was even more important and from the first received the most careful attention. A wide curriculum of specialized studies was soon developed. When the Lyceum School opened its first session in October, 1884, course work included training of the body, the art of mute expression or pantomime, the training of the voice, the art of vocal expression, the art of imitation or mimicry, the study and understanding of plays and dramatic situations and effects, the study of character, and practical lessons in acting.[67] In 1886 special studies added were: "Action, Diction, Stage Effect, Make-up, Elementary Dance and Ballet Steps, Fencing and Lectures on all subjects relating to the culture and improvement of actors." [68] In the nineties, the study program involved two terms of six months each, with the first comprising technical training in all basic essentials, and the second advanced classroom study and the production of plays.[69] First term work covered three major areas: Action, Diction, and Stage Work, with training in Action consisting of Physical Training, Dancing, Fencing, Pantomime, and Life Studies, while Diction instruction followed the special subjects of Vocal Training, Phonetics, Elements of Vocal Expression, English Language, and Dramatic Literature. Completing the Junior course was Stage Work, which introduced the student to Stage Mechanics, Make-up, Costuming and Art Decoration, Stage Business, Stage Rehearsals, and Complete Performances. Before entering the Senior year and the Academy Stock Company, the student had to pass a comprehensive examination. Once over this hurdle, he continued class study in several areas although the primary emphasis was placed on the study of roles and on performance. Among the important courses that continued during the two-term period was Life Study, with its emphasis on "going to life" for material to use in creating a realistic representation. This was considered basic study, for if the author drew from life, "should not the actor study that life also, that he may the more justly portray it?" [70] Bronson Howard commented:

All the students belong to this class. They are expected to observe their fellow human beings and afterwards to illustrate their actions and speech on a platform in the school: beginning with the mere movement of the hand, or head, or other parts of the body, under the various circumstances of every-day [sic] life; then constructing little scenes for themselves, based on their own observation, even bits of unwritten plays, after they have become sufficiently skilled in the minor work. [71]

Since the plays of Ibsen, Maeterlinck, and other modernists were performed by the students, the new acting approach to them was necessary.

In contrast to this elaborate curriculum, Nelson Wheatcroft, Director of the Empire Theatre Dramatic School, which in 1899 was to be merged with Sargent's Academy, rather pointedly stated in his prospectus that "energies will not be diffused by attention to extraneous subjects, but will be devoted only to that work which is constantly in requisition on the stage itself." What he meant by this is not clear. Was he implying that other schools, the Academy for instance, were confusing the student with irrelevant material in teaching technique through a system of acting like Delsartism? More than likely, stock-actor Wheatcroft was an adherent of the traditional hand-me-down method of actor training and could see no good in the new approach. At any rate, the Empire School was much smaller than Sargent's American Academy and could not boast the faculty necessary for an extensive curriculum. Three or four instructors taught Modern Dramatic Art, which, of course, could be very inclusive but probably involved the acting of recent plays, Shakespeare and the classics, Melodrama and Comedy. [72] In addition, every two weeks a criticism class was held, at which the students gave a résumé of their work before the entire school and received the criticism of faculty and students. For a small enrollment this curriculum might be quite satisfactory, and it certainly was a practical method for preparing the beginning actor in a short time.

In sharp contrast to these curricula with their specific interest in active production was the more conservative academic approach exemplified by the Curry School in Boston. [73] Make-up, costume, and business were ignored, and stage properties and scenery were reduced to an absolute minimum. Professor Curry, unlike others who operated in close association with producing theatres, considered the environment of stage life and all theatrical equipment harmful. "The pupil must imagine all; must concentrate his mind exclusively upon characterization and the dramatic situation." And so the curriculum was said to be based on that of the Paris Conservatoire with "rigorous training in aesthetic gymnastics, movements which are modifications of the so-called Delsartean system, slow and thorough voice-building, and a general acquaintance with English, French, and German dramatic and poetic literature." On play days the pupils sat in a circle around the stage to watch their classmates perform.

Curry did not stand alone in this point of view. Professor Ayres of New York might well have been bred in the same school, for he took pride in advertising: "No stage with which to amuse the pupil and squander his time. Begin with rehearsals when trees begin to grow at the top; when architects begin with the house and follow with the foundation." How much like a direct attack on Sargent's methods the Ayres's advertisements sound: "He that begins with rehearsal never gets far," he cautions, and then ends with a barbed warning: "Essentials are never taught by those who do not themselves know them." [74]

The classroom curriculum in most schools, however, was not all-important. If Curry and Ayres frowned on the trappings of the stage, other school directors certainly did not. Public performance was often part of the over-all training, and occasionally the novice actors appeared with established members of the profession. Not only were beginners given a chance to be seen by managers, but undoubtedly the public performances were intended to substitute for those practical experiences the beginning actor would have received under the old stock company system. MacKaye had this specifically in mind when planning the Lyceum School. As an adjunct to the theatre, the classroom was the training ground for future members of the performing companies, and MacKaye, as author-director, worked with the student bit-players in the first Lyceum offering—his own play, *Dakolar*. From that point on, students of the Lyceum School were given regular performance opportunities, and the production of high quality plays became the policy. Franklin Sargent shortly won fame as the outstanding producer of Greek plays in this country. During these early years he also staged Maeterlinck's *The Blind;* a program including *The Intruder,* choruses from *Antigone,* and three scenes from *Oedipus;* Molière's *Les Précieuses Ridicules* and *Tartuffe;* Congreve's *Love for Love;* and a mixed evening that included Royall Tyler's *The Contrast* and Rinniccini's *Euridice.* Sophocles' *Electra* was given in collaboration with David Belasco and Henry DeMille. And to keep pace with the moderns, Ibsen's *Pillars of Society,* Musset's *Un Caprice,* and Shaw's *The Man of Destiny* were given full scale stagings.[75] At the Empire

School, Nelson Wheatcroft made a regular practice of presenting students on the stage of the Empire Theatre in bills of short plays, many of which were being performed for the first time. A few years later, Mrs. Wheatcroft, as head of her own school, gave acting-instructor Rachel Crothers the opportunity not only to "jump in and act a part" but also to present her own original plays.[76]

Although information concerning early curricula is sketchy, it is probably representative. There were differences, of course, in acting theory and how it should be taught, and the size of any curriculum was often dependent on the number of teachers who could be hired and the quality of instruction they could give. One important point, however, must not be overlooked: the early theatre schools were by need and intention acting schools. The inclusion of "Stage Work" in the curriculum at the Academy was more the exception than the rule, for technical production, as it is taught today in our theatre schools, had gained little attention. Thus acting—with its general literary background as well as its specific technical aspects—was the dominant study.

V

By the turn of the century, the theatre schools were firmly established. The largest and best-known ones were in New York, because it was the center of professional production, but nearly every important city had one or more. The American Academy alone had graduated over three hundred students.[77] Graduates of the schools were finding employment in the theatre. Franklin Fyles, writing in 1899, declared that not only were managers no longer prejudiced against the school-trained actors but actually preferred them to actors equipped only with haphazard experience acquired on the stage.[78]

Clearly the schools satisfied a vital need. Although more and more actors were needed for steadily increasing theatrical production, the long run was replacing the repertory system, and the combination company was rapidly replacing the resident stock company which had always been the training ground for the beginning actor. By 1900 the theatre school had largely assumed that function of the stock company.

Other factors appear to have contributed to the rise of the theatre school and to have given it the particular character it eventually took. The new realistic drama emphasized the ensemble rather than individual virtuosity, and it required that the actor go to life for his models rather than to stage tradition as represented by the characterizations of established actors. The techniques required for ensemble acting and for creating from life could be more effectively taught in the classroom than in actual production. In some schools, the new techniques were taught from the beginning; in others the old method of individual tutorship in traditional stage business continued. The curricula reflected not only the changing style in acting but also the change from the conception of theatre art as primarily the art of acting to the conception of theatre art as the art of production.

Thus the theatre schools appeared, grew, and flourished in America as a result of a fundamental change in the organization of the American theatre, and they took their particular form as a result of fundamental changes in the style of production and in the conception of theatre art in general.

Notes

1. George Blumenthal, *My Sixty Years in Show Business* (New York, 1936), p. 11.
2. Bernard Shaw, *Dramatic Opinions and Essays* (New York, 1907), I, 206.
3. Olive Logan, *The Mimic World* (Philadelphia, 1870), pp. 32, 47.
4. William R. Alger, *Life of Edwin Forrest* (Philadelphia, 1877), I, 158; John Drew, *My Years on the Stage* (New York, 1922), p. 9; Anna Cora Mowatt, *Autobiography of an Actress* (Boston, 1853), p. 219.
5. Logan, pp. 41-42.
6. For a brief listing see Alfred Ayres, *Acting and Actors* (New York, 1894), p. 148.
7. Lawrence Barrett, *Edwin Forrest* (Boston, 1881), p. 14.
8. For a discussion of his theory and observations on the elocutionary art see James E. Murdoch, *The Stage or Recollections of Actors and Acting* (Philadelphia, 1880). Also see Mary Margaret Robb, "Rise of the Elocutionary Movement and its Theorists," in this volume.
9. Joseph Jefferson, *Autobiography* (New York, 1889), p. 152.
10. Mary Anderson gives a brief description of a lesson with Vandenhoff in her autobiography, *A Few Memories* (New York, 1876), pp. 43-44.
11. Murdoch, p. 273.
12. Ayres, p. 145.
13. *Actors and Actresses of Great Britain and the United States: Macready and Forrest; and Their Contemporaries,* ed. Brander Matthews and Laurence Hutton (New York, 1886), p. 272.
14. Murdoch, pp. 237-238.
15. Mowatt, pp. 218, 383.
16. Drew, p. 17.
17. Joseph Jefferson and others, "Success on the Stage," *North American Review,* 135 (1882), 581. Hereafter cited as "Success on the Stage."
18. *Ibid.,* p. 583.
19. For a detailed discussion of training at the Boston Museum, as well as a general evaluation of the stock company as a "school," see Edward Mammen, *The Old Stock Company School of Acting* (Boston, 1945). David Belasco thought this discipline so valuable that in training Mrs. Leslie Carter for the stage, he insisted that she learn twenty-eight roles in the same manner she would have, had she been a stock company actress. For a detailed account of his training of this actress see David Belasco, *The Theatre Through the Stage Door* (New York, 1919), pp. 95 ff.
20. Logan, p. 67.
21. Augustin Daly Scrapbooks, *Robinson Locke Collection,* New York Public Library.
22. J. Rankin Towse and George Parsons Lathrop, "An American School of Dramatic Art," *Century Magazine,* LVI (1898), 261-275.

23. *Ibid.*

24. Frederick Bond, "Casino Comedian's Reminiscences of Augustin Daly," *New York Evening Telegram,* July 31, 1907.

25. Gustav Kobbe, "Augustin Daly and his Life Work," *Cosmopolitan,* XXVII (1899), 413.

26. Deshler Welch, "Augustin Daly—Dramatic Dictator," *Booklovers,* III (1904), 495.

27. Owen Barry, "The Augustin Daly Alumni," *Green Book,* VIII (1912), 890-896.

28. William Seymour at the Boston Museum also has been lauded as an expert teacher of beginning actors. See Mammen, pp. 60-61.

29. *Ibid.,* p. 49.

30. "Success on the Stage," p. 586.

31. Philip G. Hubert, Jr., "New York's Lyceum School for Actors," *Lippincott's Magazine,* XXXV (1885), 483-488.

32. "Success on the Stage."

33. *Ibid.*

34. *Ibid.*

35. Cora Maynard, "Art and the Actor," *North American Review,* CXLVII (1888), 175.

36. F. H. McMechan, "Acting versus Elocution," *The Theatre,* I (1901), 17-19.

37. "Shall We Have a Dramatic Academy," *The Idler Magazine,* III (1893), 568-576. For further discussion see "A School of Dramatic Art," *The Spectator,* LXVI (1891), 169-170; Hamilton Aide, "A Dramatic School," *The Theatre,* V (1882), 73-76; Hamilton Aide, "A New Stage Doctrine," *Nineteenth Century,* XXXIV (1893), 452-457.

38. Dion Boucicault, "My Pupils," *Clipping File,* New York Public Library Theatre Collection.

39. For a detailed account of work at the Conservatoire together with a brief review of its past history see A. Strobel, "A Visit to the Paris Conservatory," *The Theatre,* IV (1888), 444-449.

40. "A British Dramatic Academy—Interview with M. Coquelin the Elder," *The Daily Graphic,* January 21, 1891.

41. Bronson Howard, "Our Schools for the Stage," *Century Magazine,* LXI (1900), 28-37.

42. The best account of MacKaye's participation in the school movement is, of course, in the biography by his son, Percy MacKaye, *Epoch,* 2 vols. (New York, 1927).

43. For a discussion of "MacKaye and the Delsartian Influence," see the essay under that title by Claude Shaver, in this volume.

44. This brief pamphlet bears the title, "A Plea for a Free School of Dramatic Art." A copy of the pamphlet is available in the New York Public Library. For mention of the St. James opening, see George Odell, *Annals of the New York Stage* (New York, 1927-1949), IX, 194.

45. MacKaye, I, 268.

46. *Ibid.,* 271.

47. *Werner's Directory of Elocutionists, Readers and Lecturers,* ed. Elsie M. Wilbor (New York, 1887), p. 259.

48. According to Blumenthal, p. 11, Sargent had suggested that a school be established at the Madison Square Theatre where he was employed as a training coach for road company actors in 1882-1883.

49. Percy MacKaye discusses this significant controversy in *Epoch,* I, 463. He maintains, and perhaps justifiably, that his father never received full credit for his important work in founding the project.

50. For more complete accounts see the *New York Dramatic Times,* January 20, 1885, and the *New York Mirror,* January 31, 1885.

51. MacKaye, I, 291.

52. *Ibid.*, 289.

53. Unidentified newspaper clipping for July 31, 1884. "Lyceum Theatre," *Clipping File,* New York Public Library Theatre Collection.

54. Since much of the material in this section has not been previously collected, the writer used a wide variety of sources. Much work still remains to be done in obtaining and sorting material in this area of the study. Undoubtedly on-the-spot investigations in such cities as New York, Boston, Chicago, Philadelphia, and San Francisco would turn up much more detail. Among the sources used for this brief view are: Garrett H. Leverton, *The Production of Later Nineteenth Century American Drama* (New York, 1936); Percy MacKaye, *Epoch,* 2 vols. (New York, 1927); Dexter Smith, *Cyclopedia of Boston and Vicinity* (Boston, 1886); Steiger's *Educational Directory of 1878* (New York, 1878); *Werner's Directory of Elocutionists, Readers and Lecturers* (New York, 1887); *New York Dramatic Mirror; Chicago Record; St. Louis Republic; Philadelphia Inquirer; The Theatre Magazine.*

55. Lewis C. Strang, *Famous Actresses of the Day* (Boston, 1899).

56. Alfred Ayres was a pseudonym for Thomas Embley Osmun.

57. Ayres, p. 149.

58. For Belasco's views on early theatre schools see David Belasco, "Dramatic Schools and the Profession of Acting," *Cosmopolitan,* XXXV (1903), 359-368; William Winter, *The Life of David Belasco* (New York, 1918), I, 348 ff.

59. Franklin H. Sargent, "The Preparation of the Stage Neophyte," *New York Dramatic Mirror,* July 19, 1911.

60. The only school in this early period that has been well documented is the American Academy.

61. "Adeline Stanhope Wheatcroft," *New York Dramatic Mirror,* June 19, 1897.

62. *Werner's Directory,* p. 259.

63. "Success on the Stage," p. 586.

64. "Franklin H. Sargent," *New York Dramatic Mirror,* March 21, 1896.

65. Jefferson, p. 448.

66. "Another Lyceum Complaint," *New York Mirror,* January 24, 1885. See also: "A Lyceum Revelation," *New York Mirror,* January 31, 1885.

67. "A School for Actors," *The Nation,* XXXIX (1884), 195.

68. "The School of Acting," *The Theatre,* II (1886), 48.

69. This material has been drawn from the *Catalogue of the American Academy of Dramatic Arts* for 1899 which outlines the work in detail. For additional discussion of acting theory and technique see *Dramatic Studies,* a publication of the Academy which first appeared in 1893. Much of the material taught at the Academy is illustrated here with detailed exercises and explanations.

70. *Dramatic Studies,* I (November, 1893).

71. Bronson Howard, "Our Schools for the Stage," *Century Magazine,* LXI (1900), 32.

72. "Nelson Wheatcroft," *New York Dramatic Mirror.*

73. Marianna McCann, "Two Schools of Acting," *Harper's Weekly,* XXXV (1891), 999 ff.

74. *New York Dramatic Mirror,* October 15, 1892.

75. For reviews of several Academy plays see Norman Hapgood, *The Stage in America,* 1897-1900 (New York, 1901), pp. 291-303.

76. Henry James Forman, "The Story of Rachel Crothers," *Pictorial Review,* XXXII (1931), 56.

77. *Catalogue of the American Academy of Dramatic Arts* for 1899 contains a list of those graduated from the Academy.

78. Franklin Fyles, *The Theatre and Its People* (New York, 1900), pp. 24-25, 31.

25 College and University Theatre Instruction in the Early Twentieth Century

CLIFFORD EUGENE HAMAR

••

Well before 1900 there were rumblings and stirrings which foretold the coming of significant changes in college and university treatment of dramatic art. The continuity of thought and practice which linked the nineteenth with the twentieth century may be indicated by a few instances.

As early as 1886, William O. Partridge, sculptor, novelist, and professor of fine arts at Columbia University, made an eloquent plea for college departments of drama before a national meeting of social scientists.[1] College catalogs show clearly that a number of professors were teaching theatrical techniques in college courses some time before 1900.[2] Possibly a considerable number of teachers gave such training under vague or misleading catalog titles. Henry Frink, professor of oratory at Hamilton College, complained in 1892 that the word "oratory" was being "usurped and turned from its original usage" by schools for the technical training of dramatic readers.[3] As subsequent evidence will show, theatre courses often entered the college curriculum through the offerings of semi-independent schools of oratory and elocution which later became full-fledged collegiate departments.

A single brief chapter does not allow scope for reviewing the general changes in American cultural institutions and in American higher education which occurred during the late nineteenth and early twentieth centuries, important as these factors are for understanding why and how theatre training entered the college curriculum. It is essential to note, however, that even before 1900 educators were beginning to accept the idea that the theatre has a basically serious role in our culture, that the theatre is an instrument for the moral uplift of man.[4] The principle that the drama is a fine art which must be witnessed by an audience in the theatre to be appreciated, today universally accepted, was already gaining ground. This fact in turn led to acceptance of two corollary principles: that one must pursue understanding of the drama in the theatre, in the workshop where part of the essential creative process occurs; and that modern and contemporary drama and the "living" theatre constitute appropriate subjects for academic attention.

That such ideas have become commonplace today may be due, in large measure, to the efforts of a few key figures in the history of our educational theatre; for example, George Pierce Baker, Frederick Koch, Thomas Dickinson, E. C. Mabie, Thomas Wood Stevens, Kenneth Macgowan, Gertrude Johnson, and Alexander Drummond. For their effective advocacy of the laboratory approach to the drama, these men and women are justly honored by theatre teachers everywhere. It is important to remember, however, that the prestige of the laboratory method of instruction was growing in many departments of the college and university during the late nineteenth and early twentieth centuries. Possibly the most conspicuous tendency in higher education was away from bookish learning toward the technical and practical.

Because studies of the development of theatre training in the college and university have usually focused upon the larger and better known institutions, it is possible that we have overemphasized the impact of particular individuals on the development of instruction in practical techniques of the theatre. It is customary to date the beginning of American college and university theatre instruction from Baker's introduction of a playwriting course at Radcliffe in 1903. Was Baker entirely original in this? I doubt that Baker himself would have claimed as much. In 1899-1900, Charles H. Patterson at the University of West Virginia required practice in the writing of plays and study of contemporary drama in a credit course.[5] Professor Lucius A. Sherman, a graduate of Yale, required playwriting in connection with his course in "The Principles of Dramatization" at the University of Nebraska in 1900-1901.[6] Did college and university instruction in the staging of plays begin with the establishment of the "47 Workshop" at Harvard in 1905-1906?[7] This event was a landmark, but "English 47" at Harvard was not the first university course to devote attention to the physical production of plays. Thomas Dickinson gave instruction in the "staging" of plays in a course at Baylor in 1901-1902, although his course was short-lived, it is true.[8]

With his series of textbooks entitled "Chief Contemporary Dramatists," Dickinson may have done more than any other single teacher to encourage the growth of college courses devoted to the study of living playwrights. At Wisconsin between 1909 and 1916, he fought valiantly, against various forms of "academic repression," for the new point of view toward the study of drama. He failed to persuade his colleagues in the English department, however, and diverted his efforts to the development of the Wisconsin Dramatic Society off the campus.[9] Gertrude Johnson and James M. O'Neill participated also in the fight for academic recognition of theatre instruction at Wisconsin, and Johnson succeeded in winning faculty approval for a course in "Dramatic Production" in 1916-1917.[10] By this time, however, at least seven other colleges and universities offered play production courses.[11] The Harvard faculty did not recognize Baker's "47 Workshop" as a legitimate, academic activity, either before 1921 or later. Mabie at Iowa and Drummond at Cornell were just coming into national prominence around 1919-1920; their wide influence upon educational theatre was felt between World Wars I and II. As the director of a professional theatre school in a technical institution, Thomas Wood Stevens stood outside the current of curricular change in the liberal arts college and university. Koch was chiefly known before 1921 for his advocacy of instruction in the writing of folk-plays. College "dramatics" was effectively making its way, and gradually a considerable number of drama and theatre enthusiasts on college faculties succumbed to it.

A complete history of the American educational theatre of course will carefully weigh the contributions of such giants as Baker, Dickinson, Koch, Mabie, and Drummond. Indeed the work of some of our great teachers of theatre already has been described in print. My primary task here is to present the general picture of collegiate theatre instruction. Specifically, I shall attempt answers to the following questions: (1) To what extent were discrete courses in various types of theatre instruction offered at the turn of the century? (2) What types of discrete courses invaded the curriculum between 1900 and 1920-1921? (3) Was the growth (or decline) of specific types of theatre instruction gradual or abrupt? (4) Where did the most significant developments occur, in terms of geographical areas and particular institutions? (5) What were the principal trends in course aim, content, and method, in theatre instruction as a whole and in particular types of courses? (6) Who were the individuals most active in the early twentieth-century development of theatre instruction, not as propagandists but as teachers of new types of courses? and (7) What institutions, or types of institutions, trained a significantly large number of the pioneer teachers of theatre in the college?

Such questions embrace instruction in the formal curriculum only. I am obliged in this essay, for practical reasons, to ignore the important subject of extracurricular dramatics and their relationship to formal instruction. I have limited the investigation, as far as possible, to curricula of college-level institutions which required a certificate of graduation from a secondary school for entrance and granted a bachelor of arts degree, or the equivalent, for four years of resident study. The primary evidence, accordingly, is drawn from the courses open to all undergraduates which were listed in the annual catalogs of degree-granting institutions.

I have relied mainly on the primary sources for any historical study of the college curriculum, i.e., upon the official catalogs, registers, year-books and similar publications of the relevant institutions. The "theatre" courses described in the catalogs of American colleges from 1899-1900 through 1920-1921 appear to fit, with a minimum of overlapping, into the following rough classifications: (1) Dramatic interpretation (with two sub-divisions, Shakespearian and general); (2) Play presentation (with two sub-divisions, Shakespearian and general); (3) Acting; (4) Directing and "Coaching"; (5) Play production; and (6) Theatre history. A more precise description of the nature of courses placed in these categories will be presented as each of the types is discussed.

The evidence comes from more than 3,000 separate publications issued by 180 institutions of various sizes, denominations, and geographical locations. The median number of catalogs examined for each of these 180 colleges and universities was 13 and the average number 16.7. In each of the possible catalog-years from 1899-1900 through 1920-1921, the median number of publications examined was 144 and the average number 136.7.[12]

Since standardization in American higher education had scarcely begun at the turn of the century, statistics on any very large number of institutions have limited validity, of course. I have attempted to select representative institutions. Whether or not the colleges and universities covered here were truly "representative," the reader may judge for himself from the list of them in the notes. Of the 180 institutions surveyed, 128 were located east of the Mississippi river and only 52 west of the Mississippi. This fact should be noted particularly in connection with later remarks on the geographical trends of theatre instruction.[13]

Dramatic Interpretation

Shakespearian

Among the 180 colleges and universities surveyed, 26 listed in one or more catalogs a course devoted primarily to the oral reading or declamation of passages from Shakespeare. Eleven such courses were described in catalogs of 1899-1900 and 1900-1901; namely, at Wooster, Northwestern, Oberlin, Washburn, State U. of Iowa, U. of Washington, Michigan, Smith, Allegheny, U. of Colorado, and Yale. Certain of these institutions, Northwestern for example, unquestionably offered the course well before 1900. Somewhat later in the first two decades of the century, 15 colleges and universities seem to have introduced courses of this type.[14] A great majority of the 26 courses, 18 of them, remained in the curricula of the colleges offering them through 1920-1921.

From this data it does not appear that instruction in the oral reading of Shakespeare was ever widely popular. In proportion to the number of colleges which offered such courses around the turn of the century, the growth of the course during the first two decades of the century was insignificant. The years immediately following the first World War were a period of rapid expansion in the curriculum generally and for certain other drama and theatre subjects, but these were not years of growth for instruction in the reading and declamation of Shakespeare.

Five of the early courses of this type were offered in Ohio institutions, a rather high proportion for one state. Otherwise, the geographical location, size, and type of the institution appear to have had little bearing on the incidence and growth of the course.

A number of the catalogs gave significant clues concerning aim, content, and method. The course introduced at Otterbein in 1906-1907, perhaps typical of instruction in this subject during the first decade of the century, required analytical study of Shakespearian plays and "rendition of principal scenes." [15] Some teachers of the subject, even in the first decade, stressed the point of view, generally accepted today, that the drama must be understood as an art not fully realized except in the theatre before an audience. The course in "Reading Shakespeare" at DePauw, for example, devoted attention to "conditions of production and presentation." According to the university bulletin for 1904, the course was an "attempt to see the plays from the standpoint of an Elizabethan audience."

In general, the qualitative information on such courses in annual publications from 1899-1900 through 1920-1921 suggested that the advocates of Shakespearian reading and declamation looked upon it as a method for helping the student realize the literary and dramatic values in Shakespeare's plays more fully than he normally did in the classroom devoted to lectures, quizzes, and weekly themes. The evidence indicated further that the tendency in procedure was away from individual declamation of scenes toward group reading of scenes. In some instances, a course devoted to presentation of Shakespearian plays upon the stage evolved gradually out of the reading course.

Although instruction in oral interpretation was generally given in semi-independent departments of oratory, elocution, or expression in the first years of the century,[16] Shakespearian interpretation was not uncommon in English departments. The catalogs, furthermore, indicated that a number of the early instructors of this course held advanced degrees; namely, from Amherst, Earlham, Wesleyan, and Taylor. Two were graduates of the Columbia College of Expression and one of the Philadelphia National School of Oratory.

General

Courses in the oral interpretation of miscellaneous dramatic literature, including the classics but not predominantly Shakespearian drama, were also evident in the colleges. Thomas Coulton discovered from an examination of 1890 catalogs and earlier publications that only six of 139 colleges prior to 1900 "mentioned dramatic interpretation, and then as but a part of courses given over principally to either elocution, declamation, or voice culture." He noted also a very rapid increase in this subject from 1900 to 1910 and a still greater increase between 1910 and 1935.[17]

This investigation was in agreement with Coulton's in noting a substantial number of new courses in dramatic interpretation, a total of thirty-seven, in catalogs from the turn of the century through 1909-1910. In publications from 1910-1911 through 1920-1921, however, we found new courses in dramatic interpretation in only sixteen institutions. In other words, the evidence confirmed the growth of the subject but pointed to a decline in the *rate* of growth. The discrepancy between these findings and Coulton's was due, apparently, to the fact that Coulton placed many courses in this category which I have classified under the headings of "acting," "play presentation," and "play production."

General courses in dramatic interpretation were listed in catalogs of 1899-1900 through 1901-1902 at Kansas, Wisconsin, St. Louis, Albion, Whitman, Mount Holyoke, Nebraska, State U. of Iowa, Southern California, Adrian, Illinois Col., Syracuse, and George Washington. Some of these courses were certainly introduced before 1900. From 1902-1903 through 1920-1921, as far as this study could determine, forty other colleges and universities introduced work in dramatic interpretation.[18] Of the total of fifty-three courses of this type identified, approximately thirty-five seem to have remained in the curricula of the respective institutions through 1920-1921. It is noteworthy that no new courses of this type were introduced from 1916-1917 through 1919-1920.

Although the subject appears to have been introduced into a wide variety of types of institutions, the small coeducational colleges of the West and South were especially well represented. Eighteen of the thirty-seven colleges which offered this course prior to 1910-1911 were in the West, a rather high percentage in view of the preponderance of eastern institutions among those surveyed. Another ten of these thirty-seven colleges were in the South and in the mid-western states, Wisconsin, Michigan, Illinois, and Ohio.

In spite of general opposition to theatre training from the academic faculty, a representative state university, Wisconsin, seems to have given a course in dramatic interpretation throughout the first two decades of the century. The 1906-1907 catalog of the university described the course at that time as devoted to "conduct of Rhetoricals, contests and plays" and to "Repertoire." The suggestion of training in directing should be noted. In 1914-1915, under Gertrude Johnson, the course at Wisconsin became "Dramatic Personation," and was described as follows: "Designed for those who show marked dramatic ability, and who wish to specialize in dramatic platform work. Advanced study of pantomime with gesture. Character impersonation. Stage direction and business." Miss Johnson was struggling at this time to develop speech and theatre courses whose content would compare favorably with other academic courses, and she stressed principles fundamental to various speech activities while at the same time providing activities which might appeal to students chiefly interested in play-acting.[19]

At St. Louis University at the turn of the century drill in "Elocution" was required in all classes of the college. To judge from the catalog, the drill consisted largely of declamatory rendition of dramatic selections by individual students. The work of each class was broken down into two units, one in "Vocal Culture," and one in "Gesture Drill." In 1903-1904, the course was revised somewhat to put greater stress on the drama. According to the annual catalog, the work after this date consisted of "interpretation and rendition of various species of dramatic selections; Tragedy, Comedy, etc. Dialogues and Scenes." As in other Jesuit universities at this time, the work terminated in the public presentation of a play at commencement.

Lectures on "analysis, mind, concentration, imagination, memory, scene-building and interpretation" constituted an important phase of the course at Florida State College for Women, 1902-1903. Under the title "Vocal Expression and the dramatic instinct," the course in 1908-1909 and later was devoted in part to "dramatic thinking; voice modulations, pantomimic expression." The aim, according to the catalog, was "exclusively" to "secure a solid foundation for conversational delivery"; that is, the course concentrated upon interpretation of drama for non-dramatic purposes. The influence of Curry may be detected, perhaps, in the foregoing references to "dramatic instinct" and "dramatic thinking."

Harvard's course in "Dramatic Interpretation," 1904-1905, included "public presentation of characters in classic drama." In the course at Alfred University, 1903-1904, and perhaps earlier, consideration was given to "modern drama" as well as to Shakespeare. An untitled course at New Mexico, in 1904-1905 and "Dramatic Interpretation" at Temple, 1905-1906, also made a special point of the inclusion of "modern drama." In the course at Temple, part of the program of the "junior year" leading to a teaching certificate in the School of Oratory, the students gave "One-act Plays"; that is, the procedures included some practice in "play presentation."

Professors Arthur Priest and Maynard Daggy at the University of Washington offered two courses in "Dramatic Reading" beginning in 1904-1905. The university catalog announced the instruction as follows: "The study of the classic drama from the point of view of vocal expression. Representative plays . . . are read, and selected scenes are acted by members of the class. . . . Topics and critiques on various phases of dramatic art." Priest and Daggy, both DePauw graduates, were enthusiastic promoters of acted drama at Washington, especially in the extracurriculum.[20]

At Stanford University, Lee Emerson Bassett's course in "Vocal Interpretation of Dramatic Literature," introduced in 1906-1907, required individual and group reading of scenes from Shakespeare and from modern plays. As taught by Elizabeth Buckingham after 1918-1919, the course involved "the study of short plays, of literary and dramatic merit, for presentation before the class." Parts were assigned.

Yankton College, where the Department of Elocution was semiautonomous until about 1914-1915, offered a sub-course in "Modern Drama" after 1909 under the general heading "The Principles of Dramatic Art and Dramatic Interpretation." The college bulletin stressed "perfect naturalness" as the keynote of all instruction. In the catalog of the State College of Washington for 1909, a two-hour-per-week course in "Dramatic Art" was described as follows:

Preliminary to the study and presentation of plays a series of lesson in Life Study and Personation . . . is given, followed by character studies from Dickens with physical representation of the same. Dramatic scenes are then given, together with a study of stage etiquette, deportment and business. Later more advanced work in modern drama and scenes from Shakespeare are presented.

This item remained in the catalog substantially unchanged through 1918-1919. The early theatre instruction at the State College of Washington appears to have been modeled after that in the Columbia College of Expression, where all of the instructors were trained.

Accordingly, in the early twentieth-century college course in dramatic interpretation, we observe a definite movement away from individual declamation toward group performance as a method for learning dramatic values and dramatic techniques. Increasing use was made of "modern drama" for study materials, although the classics were by no means neglected.

The college catalogs contained information on the training of seventeen of the fifty-three teachers who introduced courses of this type into college curricula. Of these, three were alumni of Columbia University. The majority (fourteen) were graduates of schools of oratory, such institutions as the Columbia College of Expression, the National School of Elocution and Oratory, the Boston School of Expression (or Curry School), the Northwestern School of Oratory (or Cumnock School), and Emerson College. Here and throughout the investigation the evidence indicated that the better-known eastern and middle-western schools of oratory, through their graduates in college departments, had much to do with the early growth of theatre instruction in the college curriculum and even more to do with the shaping of course content and method. For instance, the textbooks of S. S. Curry, founder of the Boston School of Expression, were fairly common and his influence was apparent in a number of catalog descriptions of courses.

Play Presentation

Shakespearian

Many courses seemed to be concerned primarily with rehearsal and performance of plays, although not with problems of technical production (scenery, lighting, costuming, and so forth). There are indications that college credit was occasionally given for Shakespearian presentation prior to 1900. Latimer Obee, in a study of dramatics at Adrian College, found that the first play publicly presented there was "given in Downs Hall, June 8, 1897, by the Shakespeare Reading Class." [21] In the catalogs of the 180 institutions covered by this investigation, thirteen new courses of this type were listed.

West Virginia, Colorado, Notre Dame, and St. Ignatius (now the University of San Francisco) apparently offered instruction in the presentation of Shakespearian plays in the years 1899-1900 and 1900-1901 or earlier. It may be significant that two of these four institutions were Jesuit colleges. Nine institutions inaugurated courses of this type in the years from 1904-1905 through 1920-1921.[22] Only five of the total of thirteen colleges and universities continued to list the course in catalogs through 1920-1921. It appears from this evidence that instruction in the presentation of Shakespearian plays obtained no very firm foothold in the college curriculum generally from 1900 to 1920. Interest in such courses was actually declining sharply during the second decade of the century.

A check on geographical distribution indicated that eight of the thirteen courses were introduced in western or mid-western schools and only one in the East, at West Virginia.

The course of this type first listed in the catalog of Southern California was entitled the "Shakespeare Club" and later the "Dramatic Club." Only students in the semi-independent College of Oratory received academic credit for the instruction. Otherwise the course was open, according to the catalog of 1906-1907, to "all regular students of the university." The club devoted itself to "Interpretation and presentation of the drama" and to "a study of dramatic law." "Shakespearian Reading" at the University of Notre Dame, 1900-1901 or before, involved the reading of two Shakespeare plays "with stage action." The catalog stated, "The students present the play by scenes before the class." A public performance may have been given. At St. Ignatius in the same year the work of the "Elocution" class led to public presentation of *Julius Caesar,* in a local theatre, as part of the annual exercises of the college.

John Quincy Adams's course at the University of Illinois, 1904-1905 and perhaps earlier, involved "Critical study and presentation of two Shakespearian plays." As taught by Thatcher Guild, according to the university register of 1906-1907, the course led to "public presentation of a Shakespearian play or special scenes." At Miami, in 1910-1911, Arthur L. Gates devoted his course entitled "Studies in Shakespearian Drama" to "discussion of the means of realizing, both in oral expression and in stage presentation, the dramatic values of the scenes studied."

The Washburn College catalog, 1911-1912, described a new course in "Dramatic Reading" as follows: "Lectures on stage business and the laws of acting. One tragedy and one comedy [both Shakespearian] are studied, the principal scenes committed and worked out on the stage. The aim is to cultivate an intimacy with Shakespeare, and to develop responsiveness of mind, body and voice through dramatic representation." It may be observed that instruction in the technique of acting was frankly a part of this course.

The bulletin of Yankton College for 1917 made the following announcement concerning a course in the Department of Expression:

English 16. The Annual Shakespeare Play. In connection with the regular work in Shakespeare, and with training in the department of expression, there is carried on each year a special study of an Elizabethan play, with a view to presenting the same in public in a manner approximating the conditions of the Elizabethan stage.

That Shakespearian presentation formed a part, at least, of some English courses devoted to Shakespeare in the early twentieth century is indicated in Walker's account of Frederick Padelford's work at the University of Washington. According to Walker, "Dr. Padelford's sophomore English class, in 1908, began work on two Shakespearian plays, with the purpose of performing them in the spring." A similar experiment the preceding year had been "exceedingly successful." [23]

In general, it appears that critical and literary study of the plays preceded rehearsal in a majority of the courses devoted to presentation of Shakespeare. Public performance served, in part, as motivation for the bookish study. Some teachers of the course, however, advocated rehearsal and performance as a superior way of coming to understand the dramatic values in the plays.

The data on the background of early teachers of this course was rather meager. Gates at Miami and G. H. Durand at Lawrence held A.M. degrees, the former from Columbia University and the latter from Harvard. Patterson at West Virginia was graduate of Tufts and a former student at the Paris *Conservatoire*.

General

Perhaps the nearest synonym to "general play presentation" in the modern college catalog would be "rehearsal and performance." Discrete new courses devoted chiefly to this activity were noted in the catalogs of twenty-seven institutions. West Virginia, Oregon, and Tufts listed such courses in the catalogs of 1899-1900 and 1900-1901; the remaining twenty-four schools inaugurated credit courses in play presentation later in the first two decades of the century. [24] Until 1917-1918, instruction in this subject appears to have spread at a fairly constant rate. Fourteen new courses were observed in catalogs of the first decade and thirteen in catalogs for the years 1910-1911 through 1916-1917. After the latter year, no new courses were observed. Approximately two-thirds of the general play presentation courses located, sixteen out of twenty-seven, appeared to remain in the curricula through 1920-1921.

In the incidence and growth of this course, the type and location of the college seem to have had definite significance. Play presentation for credit was evidently commonplace in Jesuit colleges around the turn of the century. There was scarcely any such thing as an extracurriculum or an elective system in the Jesuit college, however; all courses were prescribed and all activities closely supervised. Of the fourteen courses in general play presentation offered in the first decade of the century, eleven were in institutions west of the Mississippi. The spread of the course in general was from West to East.

The catalogs contained much more data on aims, content, and method than can be presented in this essay. Patterson's course at West Virginia, listed in the 1899-1900 catalog, was entitled "Dramatic Presentation." The catalog stated: "Six plays will be cast and rehearsed. Possible production of a play." For his course in "Interpretation of the Drama" at Oregon, in 1900-1901, Irving M. Glen announced that at least one play would be "publicly presented." Archibald Reddie, at Oregon beginning 1913-1914, continued the course in "the practical study of the drama." His students presented three plays during the year under the auspices of the University of Oregon Drama League. Under Reddie, the course at Oregon included attention to elements of technical production, "costume, period decoration, architecture, manners and customs, musical themes, stage carpentry, lighting and color effects." In other words, "play presentation" became "play production" at Oregon in 1913-1914.

In three of the Jesuit schools, St. Ignatius, Santa Clara, and St. Louis, courses of this type were very similar. The year's work in elocution was directed toward preparation of a classic play for public performance. Santa Clara appears to have had one of the best equipped college theatres in the country near the turn of the century.[25]

The course in play presentation introduced at Drake in 1903-1904 (in the School of Oratory) sought to develop "directness of address" and to induce "sympathetic identification with a variety of characters." Drake's annual announcement of courses for 1905-1906 indicated that the Delsarte system was taught in the theatre courses and that all such courses included intensive physical training. Edwin and Florence Evans, who taught the courses in play presentation at Drake after 1914-1915, seem to have stressed the theories and methods of Curry, with special emphasis upon cultivation of the "dramatic instinct."

Fred Wesley Orr at Pacific University in Oregon, in 1906-1907, introduced a course entitled "Drama" which involved careful planning of "business," rehearsal of scenes and "presentation of scenes before the class." In the second semester, the course required the writing of a "short original play." Orr's successor in 1911-1912, William G. Harrington, an "Honor Graduate" of the Emerson College of Oratory, introduced instruction in "acting" in the course entitled "Dramatic Art." Also he taught the following: "Platform deportment, stage business. Preparation and presentation of short plays, ... costuming, grouping, tableaux; make-up; lighting and color scheme; stage management, rehearsal and performance." Under Harrington, obviously, the course became "play production," perhaps the first such course in an American college.

"Life Study and Personation," introduced at South Dakota in 1909-1910, required "the Presentation of short plays and scenes from the classics and modern drama." The course also involved "training in stage deportment and stage management." Re-titled "The Department Play" in 1910-1911 and simply the "Mask and Wig Play" in 1913-1914, this course still gave two hours of credit for each of two semesters' work. The merger of the college dramatic club with the formal curriculum at South Dakota was indicative of a growing tendency, particularly in western colleges and stage universities, in the second decade of the century.

To summarize, a number of American colleges, especially in the West, offered credit-courses in "play production" prior to 1920-1921. In general, the instruction was designed primarily to train public readers and teachers of expression and dramatics. Very early in the second decade of the century, as we have noted in the instruction at Pacific University, courses in "play production" began to invade the curriculum with the addition of training in technical production to activity in rehearsal and performance. Some catalog descriptions of courses indicated a tendency away from the relatively mechanical and analytical methods of Delsarte toward the more subjective and intangible methods of Curry. There was clearly a tendency in the second decade of the century to offer instruction in "play presentation" in regular departments of the college for credit toward the B.A. degree rather than in semi-independent schools of oratory for the teaching certificate only, the frequent situation prior to 1910. The departments of oratory were either disappearing or gaining legitimate status in the college. The majority of the teachers who first taught play presentation were graduates or former postgraduate students of special schools of oratory, expression, or elocution.

Acting

An "acting" course is difficult to define and even more difficult to separate from other types of theatre courses. Instruction in rehearsal and performance, or in play presentation, might include training in acting. In this study only courses are so classified which aimed explicitly at giving instruction in "acting" or which seemed, from the course descriptions, to be devoted primarily to particular techniques of the actor, for instance, movement on the stage, gesture and pantomime, and use of the voice in the theatre.

At least twenty-nine colleges and universities offered some instruction in "acting" between 1899-1900 and 1920-1921. In the years 1899-1900 and 1900-1901, Wittenberg, Idaho, Kansas, Smith, St. Ignatius, and Wesleyan offered courses of this type. From 1901 through 1920-1921, similar courses were given perhaps for the first time in an additional twenty-three institutions.[26] At least twenty out of the total of twenty-nine courses seem to have persisted in the curriculum once they were offered.

The introduction of instruction in "acting" by 29 out of 180 institutions over a twenty-year period does not indicate universal acceptance of the value of such training in the college curriculum, but it does show that courses of this type were gaining a place in higher education before 1920.

Even more strikingly than in the development of general play presentation, instruction in acting seems to have entered the curriculum first in coeducational institutions of the West, and especially in state universities and colleges. Of the fourteen schools offering such courses before 1910-1911, ten were located west of the Mississippi and two in the Mid-West, in Wisconsin and Ohio.

The courses I have regarded as "acting" bore a great variety of titles, for example, "Dramatic Action," "Pantomimic Training," and "Technique of Dramatic Expression." Such titles as "Dramatic Art for Actors," "Acting as an Art" and "Play Acting" began to appear in college catalogs comparatively late in the second decade of the century.

Reference to a few of the catalog descriptions will suggest the nature of the courses. At Wittenberg, in 1899-1900, the study of "Theory," under a graduate of Curry's school in Boston, involved elaborate training in gesture, "dramatic work," and "Stage movement positions." "Pantomimic Training" at the University of Idaho, in the same year, stressed "elements of Delsarte's philosophy of bodily expression." Professor Vickrey at the University of Kansas, in 1899-1900, also used the methods of Delsarte in such a course. Under the heading "Dramatic Action," his students gave "costume impersonations with accessories." Probably all such courses were similar in content and procedure to "Dramatic and Pantomimic Action" offered at the University of Washington between 1894 and 1896, the first theatre course at that institution, according to Walker.[27]

One of three courses for seniors in the Elocution Department of Smith College, 1900-1901, was entitled "Gesture and Pantomimic Action." The work consisted of "Dramatic Expression" and "Scenes from Plays." Training in the "presentation of dramatic materials" appeared in the Smith curriculum in some form from the turn of the century through 1920-1921. Wilford O. Clure, another graduate of the Curry school, introduced a series of courses at Lawrence in 1903-1904 with the titles: "Assimilation and Dramatic Instinct," "Pantomimic Expression," "Pantomimic Training," "Dramatic Training," and "Impersonation." The catalog of the college for 1908-1909 stated explicitly that these courses were intended to train the student in the "art of the actor."

Instruction in "Acting Drama" at Carleton College, 1911-1912, afforded "practice in acting plays and scenes from plays." The course at Macalester College, in 1913-1914 or earlier, emphasized "Physical presentation of emotions, including facial expression, gestures and attitudes." It was entitled "Action." At Pennsylvania State College, training in "Dramatic Expression," introduced in 1913-1914, aimed explicitly at training in "the technique of the actor." The catalog stated: "Scenes from standard dramas will be rehearsed and a finished production will be staged." Charles von Neumeyer at California introduced a course in "Dramatic Technique" in 1916-1917, described in the university's annual announcement of courses as "A study of the psychology of acting." The course aimed "at cultivation and development of the dramatic instinct through character portrayal."

In summary: (1) Reliance upon the Delsarte system for the teaching of acting was common in the first decade but declined sharply in the second decade; (2) The influence of Curry was apparent in content and method throughout most of the twenty-year period; (3) The assumption that training in acting meant cultivation of the "dramatic instinct" was widespread, a factor due not only to Curry's stress upon "Imagination and Dramatic Instinct" but also, perhaps, to the "instinct psychology" of the day, popularized by William James, Edward Thorndike, and others; [28] (4) While a considerable number of teachers aimed explicitly at training in "acting," the instruction was usually justified upon the ground that incidental values were derived from it for all students, for example, training in conversational speech; (5) In the second decade, instruction in acting consisted less frequently of individual drill and more frequently of group rehearsal, so that the border line between "acting" courses and "play presentation" or "play production" courses became increasingly vague.

A majority of the early teachers of acting courses, for whom background information was given in the catalogs, received some or all of their training in schools of oratory, mainly in those institutions which have already been mentioned in this essay. The graduate schools of the University of Chicago, Columbia University, Michigan, and Ohio State also trained some of the teachers. Three, for instance, had studied at Chicago.

Directing and "Coaching"

The catalogs of twelve institutions, from 1899-1900 through 1920-1921, listed courses designed to give training in the techniques of play directing or to prepare future teachers for the coaching of plays. All such courses were evidently brought into the curriculum in response to a demand for teachers qualified to supervise dramatics in the public schools.

The first discrete course of this type noted, in the catalogs available, was offered at Hamline in 1912-1913. In the same year, however, Miss

Latham in the Teachers' College of Columbia University offered a course in "The Teaching of Oral English" which included "study of the educational values" of dramatics. Subsequently eleven other colleges and universities introduced instruction in directing, or coaching.[29] Eight of the twelve institutions in this group were located in the West or Middle West, especially in the larger western cities. It may be inferred, accordingly, that the high schools of certain western states, for example Nebraska, Kansas, Iowa, and Oregon, were giving considerable attention to dramatics before 1920.

The course entitled a "Dramatic Seminar" at Hamline was devoted to study of the theory of coaching plays, but afforded no practice in it as far as the catalog descriptions revealed. Nebraska's course, introduced in 1913-1914, was a mixture entitled "The Writing of Dramatic Criticism and the Coaching of Plays." Possibly the two subjects were regarded as complementary. Drake introduced a course in "The Coaching of Plays and Pageants" in 1914-1915, but replaced it the following year with a general course in play production. Apparently the contents of the two courses were similar. The University of Utah, in 1918-1919, offered six semesters of work in play production. The emphasis depended upon whether the student registered for "Dramatic Art for Actors" or "Dramatic Art for Directors." The "Teachers' Course in Play Producing," first given at Oregon in 1914-1915, was practically identical in content with the general course in "Play Production" offered the same year, and the former was dropped from subsequent catalogs.

It was apparent from the catalog data on the whole that a number of colleges and universities between 1912-1913 and the first World War were experimenting with the kind of instruction that might provide the best general background for the high school teacher of dramatics. The choice gradually settled upon general "play production," the topic of the next section of this essay.

No significant new information on the background of the teachers who introduced directing or coaching courses was available in the catalogs.

Play Production

The division between "play production" and "play presentation" is of course, not clear cut. The courses to be discussed below are those which seemed either to divide the instruction about equally between matters of technical production and rehearsal and performance, or to place emphasis upon the technical.

Reference was made earlier to an abortive effort by Thomas Dickinson to introduce a course in the "staging" of plays at Baylor, in 1901-1902. As we have also noted, Pacific University in Oregon in 1911-1912 may have been the first institution to offer a course in play production which persisted in the curriculum. Twenty-seven other American colleges and universities introduced training in this branch of theatre from 1911-1912 through 1920-1921.[30] In addition, courses which devoted some attention to matters of technical production were offered in eight colleges and universities,[31] all for the first time evidently between 1916-1917 and 1920-1921.

Accordingly it is apparent that "play production" grew comparatively rapidly in the college curriculum in the second decade of the century and especially after about 1916-1917. Of the twenty-eight institutions which clearly gave courses in play production, twelve were located west of the Mississippi and another nine were in mid-western states; Ohio, Wisconsin, Illinois, and so on. Only seven were in eastern colleges.

Quotations and citations from a few of the catalogs will indicate the general nature of the early twentieth-century training in play production. The course at the University of Illinois, introduced by Charles H. Woolbert in 1915-1916 and described fully in the 1916-1917 catalog, involved "stage action; staging and acting of several one-act plays." The course was given "especially in the summer session. The catalog of Washington and Jefferson for 1915-1916 described a new course in "Dramatic Art" as follows:

Three plays will be used each year as the basis of this course. Parts will be assigned for impersonation. Instruction will be given for staging amateur plays which should aid those who teach English in public schools and any others who may wish to aid in community development.

The course in "Stagecraft and Production of Plays" first offered at Mills in 1917-1918 included careful study of the history of stage production and laboratory work on plays. Smith and Vassar also stressed the "history of play production" in such courses. The work at Smith, as of 1919-1920, aimed to "arouse appreciation of the art of the theatre and to prepare students to put on school and community plays." Students were given "practice in the organization of committees necessary in stage production, in modelling stage settings and in directing rehearsals."

In the study of "The Acted Drama" at Ripon, 1917-1918, the student was "introduced to the history of the drama and of the stage, and ... made acquainted with authors and plays of representative schools" as background for the "actual work of staging a play." "Dramatic Production," which entered the curriculum of the University of Kentucky in 1918-1919 with the addition to the faculty of E. C. Mabie, was described in the university catalog as follows:

Studies of community drama, dramatic personation and interpretation, organization and technical work of the theatre and the presentation of plays. A practical laboratory theatre will be operated in connection with this course. The purpose is to promote appreciation of dramatic literature and to prepare students for work as directors and supervisors of high school and community dramatics.

Mabie introduced a similar course at the State University of Iowa in 1919-1920.

At Stanford University, in 1920-1921, Gordon Davis was the instructor in a new "Theatrical Workshop," described in the university register as follows:

A theatrical laboratory for advanced students in the production of one-act plays for public presentation. Particular attention will be given to the construction and designing of stage scenery, and to costuming, lighting, acting and stage direction.

Howard and Brigham Young Universities also made a particular point of offering training in the design and construction of scenery in 1920-1921. Of course the Department of Drama in the Carnegie Institute of Technology, excluded from this study because of its "professional" purpose, had a discrete course in the designing of stage scenery as early as 1913-1914. In so far as could be ascertained from the catalogs available, the elements of production, costuming, make-up, design, and so forth were studied in the college before 1920 only in connection with general courses in play production. The only exceptions noted were courses at Carnegie and a separate course in make-up given in the School of Dramatic Art at Drake in 1914-1915.

The largest number of teachers who introduced play production courses into the college curriculum, as well as other types of theatre courses, seem to have been trained primarily in independent schools of oratory. Harrington at Pacific and Reddie at Oregon, two of the earliest teachers of this course in the American college, were both graduates of the Emerson College of Oratory. Maud Babcock, an active promoter of the drama at Utah from 1905-1906 through 1920-1921, was an alumna of the National School of Elocution and Oratory in Philadelphia and of the University of Chicago. Some of the early teachers of this course, however, were trained in well-known university graduate schools. For instance, Woolbert of Illinois studied at Michigan and Harvard.

Theatre History

From the turn of the century, teachers of dramatic literature were paying increasing attention to the historical development of the physical theatre as background for the understanding of drama. As early as

1902-1903, for instance, L. M. Harris in the English Department at the College of Charleston included "consideration of the Globe Playhouse" in his course on Shakespeare. It would be possible to cite numerous instances of this kind.[32] One sign of the increasing interest in theatre history during the early twentieth century was the establishment of a "Dramatic Museum" at Columbia University in 1911, through the influence of Brander Matthews. As the preceding discussion has indicated, a number of colleges before 1920 taught the history of the physical theatre in connection with training in play production.

The first discrete course in theatre history noted in this study was given in the Greek Department at Illinois College in 1913-1914. It was evidently limited to the evolution of the Greek theatre. In 1914-1915, the Department of Elocution and Dramatic Art at Nebraska introduced a course devoted to the history of the theatre from ancient to modern times. Similar courses were first given at Pittsburgh, 1915-1916, and Stanford, 1920-1921. The latter was "an historical survey of the origin and development of the theatre, its social function and significance, and a study of various kinds of theaters." A course introduced at Iowa in 1919-1920 seems to have been devoted to the development of the "contemporary stage." Again, it may be observed, the majority of these courses appeared in western and mid-western institutions.

Summary

To what extent were discrete courses in various types of theatre instruction offered at the turn of the century? The answer appears to be that a quite insignificant number of colleges offered training for the theatre around 1900. The subjects taught were chiefly dramatic interpretation, play presentation, and "acting."

The new types of courses which appeared and the approximate years of their introduction into the college curriculum seem to have been as follows: play production, 1911-1912, with Dickinson's experiment at Baylor excepted; directing and the training of teachers for play-coaching, 1912-1913; and theatre history, 1913-1914.

Curriculum changes affecting theatre training were clearly quite gradual. Each type of course evolved slowly with the discarding of worn out content and procedures and the gradual adoption of new materials and new methods. Innovations came with gradually changing conditions and needs.[33] In no single year did more than a handful of institutions introduce new courses of a particular type. The decline of certain types of courses, especially of dramatic interpretation, was also gradual.

The relative rate of growth of various types of courses may be seen in the following tabulation:

TABLE 5

Type of Course	New Courses 1899-1910	New Courses 1911-1921	Total
Dramatic Interpretation:			
Shakespearian	19	7	26
General	37	16	53
Play Presentation:			
Shakespearian	8	5	13
General	14	13	27
Acting	14	15	29
Directing and "Coaching"	0	12	12
Play Production	0	28	28
Theatre History	0	5	5
TOTAL	92	101	193

Such statistics would have more significance, of course, if it were possible to compare them with data on the rate of growth of other subjects in the curricula of the same 180 institutions. It is well known that the development of the elective system brought a great increase in the number of college courses of all kinds. The evidence here probably confirms what is already a matter of common belief, that theatre instruction did not constitute a major factor in higher education at any time during the early twentieth century.

Our inquiry aimed, among other things, to discover where the most significant developments in theatre instruction occurred in the early twentieth century. The geographical evidence has indicated that a larger number of new courses appeared earlier in institutions west of the Mississippi and in the Middle West rather than in the East. State institutions and colleges in the large western cities were especially active in the development of theatre instruction from 1900 to 1920. Of the various types of institutions discussed, Jesuit colleges seem to have given most attention to "theatre" instruction at the turn of the century.

In so far as one may generalize from incomplete evidence, the aims of early twentieth-century theatre instruction were consistently practical as well as cultural. In response to changing social and educational demands, colleges sought to train public readers, lecturers, entertainers, instructors in elocution and physical education, and finally, teachers and supervisors of dramatics in the lower schools. At the same time, the instruction aimed to develop understanding and appreciation of dramatic and moral values through methods conceived to be more dynamic and effective than those prevailing in the traditional academic class-room. The historically dominant aim of the American college, to mould character according to the accepted ideals of the time and place, was always present in the background.

Theatre instruction in the early twentieth century made constantly greater use of modern and contemporary drama for study and drill material, although the classics were not neglected. The favored pro-cedure in college "theatre" classes during the first decade of the cen-tury appears to have been individual drill in reading and in declama-tion from memory; the trend after 1910 was toward group performance in play presentation and play production courses. Attention to Del-sartean theory and method virtually ceased by 1915, but Curry's phi-losophy of "Imagination and Dramatic Instinct" exerted a strong in-fluence upon content and methodology throughout the first two decades of the century.

The relative importance and influence of men and institutions cannot be measured accurately, of course, from quantitative data alone, and it should be remembered that this study has excluded the growth of dramatic literature in the curriculum. It is evident that the source material covered does not provide absolutely firm ground for statistical generalizations. On the other hand, so far as I can discover, no prior study of the subject has gone so extensively or intensively into the primary sources.

Notes

1. See his "Relation of the Drama to Education," *Journal of Social Sciences,* No. 21 (September 18, 1886), pp. 188-206.

2. For example, Robt. M. Cumnock at Northwestern. See university catalog for 1892-1894, p. 43. Phillip N. Walker describes a course at the University of Washington in 1884-1885 which included "study of the plays of Shakespeare and public practice in their rendition." See Walker's "A History of Dramatics at the University of Washington . . .", unpublished M.A. thesis, University of Washington, 1947, p. 6.

3. In "Rhetoric and Public Speaking in the American Colleges," *Education,* XIII (November, 1892), 497-509.

4. For statements of this view, see article by Partridge and also the following: Charles Klein, "Religion, Philosophy and the Drama," *Arena,* XXXVII (May, 1907), 492-497; B. O. Flower, "The Theatre as a Potential Factor for Higher Civilization," *ibid.,* 497-502.

5. See description of course in "The Drama" in university catalog for that year, p. 117.

6. Listed with offerings of English Department in university calendar, 1900-1901.

7. "English 47" first appeared in the Harvard catalog in 1905-1906.

8. Course listed in university catalog as "Dramatic Recitation." In a letter dated November 16, 1951, to the author of this study, Dickinson states that "rumbles of opposition and even of outrage" greeted his innovation. Baylor, he says, was still "under the control of a rather rigorous religious temper."

9. In the term "academic repression," I am again quoting Dickinson's letter.

10. O'Neill became head of the public speaking department in 1915. Miss Johnson's course is listed in university catalog for 1916-1917. In a letter, November 18, 1951, to the author, she describes earlier efforts to incorporate work of the university dramatic clubs into academically sound courses.

11. They were Pacific University, Oregon, Michigan, North Dakota, Illinois, Washington and Jefferson, and Drake.

12. To list the specific catalogs examined is not practical in this volume. The following summary of the number of catalogs checked for each of the 22 catalog-years may assist the reader in evaluating the data, however.

Year	Catalogs	Year	Catalogs
1899-1900	56	1910-1911	144
1900-1901	121	1911-1912	152
1901-1902	136	1912-1913	162
1902-1903	138	1913-1914	152
1903-1904	138	1914-1915	146
1904-1905	136	1915-1916	144
1905-1906	125	1916-1917	149
1906-1907	131	1917-1918	147
1907-1908	135	1918-1919	152
1908-1909	144	1919-1920	147
1909-1910	148	1920-1921	104
Totals	1,408	Totals	1,599

Grand Total: 3,007

A catalog bearing the date of a single year rather than an academic year, e.g. 1900, was counted as the catalog for the academic year beginning with that date, i.e., as the catalog for 1900-1901.

13. The findings of the study are necessarily given in summary only. The reader who wishes to examine the evidence in greater detail is referred to my doctoral dissertation for Stanford University (June, 1951) entitled "The Rise of Drama and Theatre in the American College Curriculum, 1900 to 1920." The dissertation discusses early twentieth-century trends in the teaching of playwriting, dramatic theory, and other branches of dramatic literature, as well as "theatre" instruction.

14. 1902-1903, Mills, Boston University, DePauw; 1905-1906, Utah; 1906-1907, Otterbein; 1907-1908, Illinois Wesleyan; 1908-1909, State College of Washington; 1909-1910, Denison; 1911-1912, Hiram; 1912-1913, Louisiana State; 1914-1915, Brigham Young, Monmouth; 1915-1916, Pennsylvania State College; 1917-1918, Berea, Simpson.

15. This and other quoted passages may be found in the catalog, yearbook, or similar publication of the indicated date. Since publications of this kind are fugitive material and largely inaccessible to the average reader, the page numbers are not given.

16. See Hamar, "Rise of Drama and Theatre," Ch. VI.

17. "Trends in Speech Education in American Colleges, 1835-1935," unpublished Ph.D. dissertation, New York University, 1935, p. 94.

18. 1902-1903, Illinois, Willamette, Florida State College for Women; 1903-1904, Drake, Alfred, Tufts; 1904-1905, Harvard, Cumberland, Washington, New Mexico, Milwaukee-Downer; 1905-1906, Temple, Idaho, Denison, Stanford, Kenyon; 1907-1908, Alabama, Colorado, California; 1909-1910, Yankton, State College of Washington, Bates, Macalester, Vassar; 1910-1911, Adelphi, Earlham, Carleton, Smith; 1911-1912, Simpson, Otterbein, Hamline; 1912-1913, Trinity (Washington, D. C.), Pennsylvania; 1913-1914, Baylor; 1914-1915, Pittsburgh; 1915-1916, Colgate, Maryville; 1916-1917, Mills; and 1920-1921, Brigham Young, and University of the South.

19. Miss Johnson refers to these struggles in a personal letter. See note 10, *supra.*

20. Walker, pp. 61 ff.

21. "A History of Dramatics at Adrian College," unpublished Senior thesis, Adrian, 1934 (in possession of Harold Obee, Dept. of Speech, Ohio State University), p. 10.

22. 1904-1905, Illinois; 1905-1906, Rockford; 1906-1907, Southern California; 1909-1910, Chattanooga; 1910-1911, Miami (Ohio); 1912-1913, Louisiana State, Washburn; 1917-1918, Yankton; and 1920-1921, Drake.

23. Walker, p. 62.

24. 1901-1902, St. Ignatius; 1903-1904, Santa Clara, St. Louis, Drake; 1906-1907, Oklahoma, Pacific; 1908-1909, Illinois; 1909-1910, State College of Washington, Southern California, New Mexico, South Dakota; 1910-1911, Swarthmore, Miami; 1911-1912, Georgetown; 1912-1913, Otterbein, Wisconsin; 1913-1914, Lawrence, Pennsylvania State, Willamette; 1914-1915, Kansas, Vassar; 1915-1916, Cumberland; and 1916-1917, Montana and Missouri.

25. See description of it in Santa Clara College Catalogue, 1906-1907, pp. 132-133.

26. 1901-1902, Yankton; 1902-1903, Macalester; 1903-1904, Lawrence; 1905-1906, South Dakota; 1906-1907, Oklahoma; 1908-1909, New Mexico, Drake; 1909-1910, Iowa; 1911-1912, Carleton; 1912-1913, Hiram, Pennsylvania State; 1916-1917, Alfred, Whittier, Utah, Montana, California; 1917-1918, Vassar; 1918-1919, Beloit, Alabama; 1919-1920, Washington; and 1920-1921, Brigham Young, Kentucky, Indiana. Some attention was given to acting techniques in earlier courses at Washington and Vassar, at Temple (1902-1903), and at Knox (1908-1909).

27. Walker, pp. 6-7.

28. See John S. Brubacher, A History of the Problems of Education (New York, 1947), p. 201.

29. 1913-1914, Nebraska; 1914-1915, Drake, Oregon; 1915-1916, Louisiana State, Washington and Jefferson; 1916-1917, Washburn; 1917-1918, City College of New York, Southern California; 1918-1919, Utah; and 1919-1920, Indiana and Maine.

30. 1913-1914, Oregon; 1914-1915, Michigan, North Dakota; 1915-1916, Illinois, Washington and Jefferson, Drake; 1916-1917, State College of Washington, Wisconsin; 1917-1918, Yankton, Mills, Ripon; 1918-1919, Utah, Kentucky; 1919-1920, Indiana, Lawrence, Smith, Maine, Minnesota, Iowa; and 1920-1921, Northwestern, Pennsylvania State, Brigham Young, Monmouth, Stanford, Miami, Vassar, and Howard.

31. Utah, Grinnell, Alabama, North Carolina, Missouri, DePauw, Washington, and Bucknell.

32. Again see Hamar, "Rise of Drama and Theatre," Ch. VI.

33. Miss Johnson stresses in her letter to the author, note 10, that particular courses must be considered "in the complete backgrounds of the era in which they were set."

26 Dramatics in the High Schools, 1900-1925

PAUL KOZELKA

....

In 1900, dramatics was entirely co-curricular in American high schools, although music and art were fully accredited. The plays produced at the time were on the whole lacking in literary merit, and the directors or coaches were volunteer teachers, enthusiastic but untrained. "Amateur theatricals" were considered a pleasant and harmless activity with little educational value for either the participants or the audience. By 1925, however, dramatics was an important part of the program in the secondary schools of America. We propose to look at those twenty-five years and to direct attention to the values and objectives of dramatics, the kinds of dramatic activity, the acceptance in the curriculum of courses in theatre arts, the resources available to the teacher in charge of play production, and finally, typical stages and equipment of the period.

Values and Objectives

In the early years of the twentieth century, the primary objective of play production in American high schools was to raise money. Before long, however, some teachers recognized the educational potentialities inherent in dramatic activity. In 1912, Miss Adelia Cone, of the Oxford (Ohio) High School staff, advanced the claim that dramatics in the small town high school had great value, not only for the community by raising standards of drama and diminishing the popularity of plays like *The Fatal Wedding* and *Queen of the White Slaves* as performed by professionals in the Town Hall, but for the student as well, by teaching him co-operation and better voice habits, by enriching his life, and by inspiring him to greater learning.[1]

In the same year, Mr. J. Milnor Dorey, teaching in the Trenton (New Jersey) High School wrote that it was the duty of the schools not only to train the mind but also to develop live, forceful, attractive personalities. School dramatics, he said, could develop three desirable qualities: resourcefulness, which is acquired by studying and memorizing a part in a play; knowledge of human nature, which comes by studying contrasting roles such as the liar, thief, or hypocrite; and altruism, which comes out of the team-work involved in play production. He therefore asked that dramatics be given formal recognition in education. Mr. Dorey, whose dramatics group had raised $3000 for the school fund in the previous seven years, believed that the income from ticket sales was an important by-product of school dramatics and could be spent on athletics, school equipment or maintenance, special lectures, and books.[2]

Other people besides educators recognized the possible values of dramatic activity and helped to change prevailing attitudes toward "amateur theatricals." Eleanor Robson (Mrs. August Belmont), who co-operated in establishing the Educational Dramatic League in 1913 for the purpose of raising standards and helping play production in schools, churches, and settlements, said: "To produce a play educationally means that the preparation, not the production, is the most important thing—not imitation, but natural development."[3] Mrs. Belmont believed also that the new eight-hour day would create more leisure time during which working people could take part in dramatics and could "assume heroic characteristics" by acting noble and heroic characters.

Thatcher Guild of the University of Illinois, however, found that the prevailing objectives of high-school dramatics in 1913 were frankly "fun and funds." His information was based on the replies to a questionnaire sent to 125 high schools in the United States. Other aims listed in the replies were "to vitalize English work, develop taste and imagination, give speech training, learn self-discipline and utilize the dramatic instinct."[4] Educational service to the community was mentioned occasionally. Guild found that there was slight relationship between classroom study in English courses and play production, even though 86 per cent of the 125 schools gave plays regularly and 20 schools had produced plays and pageants written by students.

After World War I, some people made such exaggerated claims for dramatics as a miracle solution to behavior problems that in 1921 John Dolman felt he had to defend play production as an art whose greatest single value lay in teamwork, not in incidental therapy.[5] In 1924, Clarence Thorpe of the University of Oregon further clarified aims and objectives when he stated that through dramatics teachers could more easily motivate the study of literature and create interest in the manners and customs of the past; dramatics provided drill in speech, in mental and physical coordination, and in discipline; it had a socializing influence and developed better taste in theatre-going; and finally, it was preparation for better living.[6]

Other teachers in the twenties, either individually or through organizations, tried valiantly and often successfully to reconcile dramatics with the currently popular aims of secondary education: to promote good health and good citizenship, to provide training for a vocation and a command of fundamental processes, and to develop ethical culture, constructive use of leisure time, and "worthy home membership."[7] In 1928, Dina Rees Evans analyzed the returns of 1100 schools to a questionnaire she had distributed, and found that personal development was the most frequently stated objective of play production.

Values and objectives attributed to dramatic activity during this quarter-century were altered and clarified as educators gradually recognized the universality of the dramatic instinct and learned how to channel its varied expressions into constructive, fruitful creation. Accepted as a harmless and sometimes a trivial pastime at the beginning of the century, dramatics was recognized by 1925 as a worthwhile field of endeavor with clearly-defined goals and values.

Types of Dramatic Activity

The most common form of dramatic activity in this period, as it is today, was the production of long and short plays. Pageants and festivals, however, were very popular between 1910 and 1920, and dramatization was widely used as a teaching device.

The titles of 436 plays given in high schools between 1900 and 1925 are included in a note.[8] The great variety and range of the plays reflects the varying abilities and standards of the teachers who were in charge of play production. Plays written for the amateur market predominate, although Broadway successes appear in the list. Before World War I playwrights hesitated to release their latest plays because amateurs were not so conscientious about royalties as they are now. Charles Coburn, for example, brought suit against three amateur groups for unlicensed performances of *The Yellow Jacket*.

Amateurs presented *Esmeralda* and *Green Stockings* more frequently during this period than any other plays from the professional theatre. *Esmeralda*, written by F. H. Burnett and William Gillette, opened at the Madison Square Garden Theatre on October 29, 1881, where it played 350 performances. The Samuel French catalog for 1910 says: "This celebrated play has been produced with tremendous success by amateurs in general all over the United States. It stands high in favor with principals of high schools." *Green Stockings*, written by A. E. W.

Mason, was Margaret Anglin's starring vehicle in 1912. It was released to amateurs in 1915.

Although a director had a fairly large selection of long plays from which to choose, relatively few one-act plays were available before 1915, and these were mostly farces of the William Dean Howells type. After 1915 Barrett Clark and a few other leaders translated and published significant one-act plays by European authors for the educational theatre.

The majority of the 436 plays appearing in the footnote are contemporary plays, but there is also a respectable scattering of classics. Some schools, such as East High School, of Columbus, Ohio, presented classical plays exclusively. At this school in the years around 1903, Miss O'Lemert gave complete versions of *Ralph Roister Doister, Midsummer Night's Dream, As You Like It, Comedy of Errors, Taming of the Shrew, Love's Labour's Lost, Twelfth Night, Robin Hood,* and MacKaye's *Canterbury Pilgrims.*[9] Many schools celebrated the Shakespeare Tercentenary in 1916 with a Shakespearean play. Others observed the occasion with an original pageant based on episodes from Shakespeare's life and including scenes from his plays. At the Kansas City High School, for example, 250 students participated in an outdoor pageant called *King Poet,* for which the students prepared text, music, and costumes.[10]

Pageants and festivals supplemented the production of plays. The exact distinction between pageant and festival is clearly made by Professor Azubah Latham, who defined a pageant as first, last, and always a spectacle, generally produced by a professional, whereas a "festival is not an exhibition, but it might well take the place of school exhibitions; it must be a community product, not the work of one or two geniuses; it is essentially a celebration of some feeling, day or other thing that we wish to celebrate; and the impulse must be spontaneous and the operation must be democratic."[11] Miss Latham is credited with being the first person to use central staging in America,[12] when she produced a festival in 1914, *The Masque of Joy,* in the center of a gymnasium. Members of the audience came in special costumes and joined in the singing and dancing.

The historical pageant, a kind of civic celebration directed and prepared for various communities by such outstanding men as Thomas Wood Stevens, Percy MacKaye, George Pierce Baker, and Garnet Holmes, was a very popular form of dramatic activity from 1910 to 1920.

Students participated in or observed pageants and festivals in teacher-training institutions, and then created similar productions in their own schools. These ranged from Arbor Day celebrations to historical epics and Christmas pageants.

Informal dramatics, under the name of dramatization, educational dramatics, or improvisation, flourished during this twenty-five year period in elementary and high schools. This teaching device, directly related to creative dramatics of the present day and possibly to modern role-playing, claimed a respectable pedagogical heritage in 1908.

If you try having a child act a thing, especially in his own words, with his own improvisations . . . will he not take the story into his nerves and muscles? The dramatic method is the "play" method, the actively illustrative method, for the inspiration to which we are indebted to Froebel and his compeers.[13]

Alice Minnie Herts, who founded her Educational Theatre for Children and Young People in New York in 1903, objected to the usual practice of giving the best role to the brightest child and letting the same child play the same role over and over again. She felt strongly that:

. . . dramatic instinct is too often confused with dramatic talent and ignorance of the laws relating to education and life is almost universal. . . . The object of all dramatized lessons is to create in the unexpressive child through the cultivation of its imagination in relation to the assumed part, a something which did not previously exist for the child.[14]

Emma Sheridan Fry, who supervised dramatic work at the Educational Alliance from 1904 to 1914, explained her philosophy and method, *Educational Dramatics* (New York, 1913), to help those who worked with adolescents. By understanding the three zones of a personality, Mental, Emotional, Vital, "the Educator may present contacts (stimuli) and regulate the resulting sequence of life processes towards Expression." Mrs. Fry claimed that a "professional coach may produce good plays but the educational profit of dramatics is not the entertainment value to an audience but the value of the preparation to the players." At about the same time, another book appeared, *The Dramatic Method of Teaching* (Boston, 1912), written for the teachers of America by Harriet Finlay-Johnson. It described how the English author had taught history, literature, geography, arithmetic, composition, and even nature-study by means of dramatizations. Miss Maude Frank, a teacher in the DeWitt Clinton High School, New York, explained the values of dramatization in teaching literature as an aid to self-expression, to development of imagination, and to vocabulary building. She liked the method because everyone in the class could participate, but especially because it "made the literature belong to the boys." [15]

One teacher stated that too much dramatization might overdevelop the imagination and the emotions, and too much acting might lead to affectation and bluffing,[16] but many teachers firmly believed in a shibboleth of the day, "the fact acted out is the fact remembered," and enlivened their classes with simple dramatizations.

The production of a standard play for an audience was the most prevalent and accepted form of dramatic activity, but dramatization in the classroom gave many more students the opportunity to participate in the dramatic process. Festivals and pageants brought theatre experience to more students than could appear in a play. It was a rare student who finished his high-school training without having had some direct experience in dramatics.

The Place of Dramatics in the High-School Program

In the early years of the twentieth century the production of plays was an entirely extracurricular activity directed either by a volunteer English teacher untrained in theatre work or by a professional coach hired from outside the teaching staff. Furthermore, the study of any of the theatre arts was not considered important enough for academic recognition; school administrators did not realize the need for qualified teachers to direct dramatics, nor did any institutions of higher learning provide opportunities for young teachers to acquire background and experience in theatre arts.

Personal experience of teachers active during this period reveals significant changes in attitude toward dramatics. Between 1900 and 1908, Mabel Hay Barrows produced plays and pageants in private schools, settlement houses, and universities from New England to California. She adapted plays from Greek and Latin sources and also wrote original masque-plays. Some of her productions were directed by correspondence only, and some by another person who used Mrs. Barrows' notes and instructions. Mrs. Barrows discovered:

Almost everywhere . . . faculty and students agreed on the great advantage of the training to the actors. Where the parts were thrown open to competition there were often three or four competing for each part. I would frequently have fifty or sixty students practicing the dancing, though all knew that not more than fifteen or twenty could be chosen. It was usually surprising to the faculty to see how many of the students they had not specially noticed were "brought out." [17]

Miss Mary A. Thomas, who taught in a high school in upstate New York from 1909 to 1913, recalls that she was engaged to teach English and history and "do all you can to help the children socially."

The academic session closed at one-fifteen p.m. . . . I began at once to organize a dramatic group. It was all extra-curricular; no courses in drama. The students took to it as soon as they saw it was fun and not just another class. We taught technique as the occasions arose. I regret to have to admit that the plays were, on the whole, inconsequential, except for *She Stoops to Conquer, Dear Brutus, The Old Lady Shows Her Medals,* and a few scenes from Shakespeare.

Not more than two long plays were given in a school year, but the students had experience in all branches of production. I did all the directing—certainly not professional, with a student assistant. In our school, there were no courses in elocution, expression or dramatics. No academic credit was given.[18]

Miss Wenona L. Shattuck describes her experiences in Vermont around 1910 in the following excerpt:

The school produced one play annually as part of the graduation exercises. The plays were trivial: *A Strenuous Life, Professor Pepp, Shore Acres* among them. The casts were chosen from members of the senior and junior classes. The principal of the school and an English teacher, both entirely untrained, acted as directors. The "productions" were given in the high school auditorium with costumes and properties borrowed from townspeople and with "sets" borrowed from the local "opera house." Lighting came from the regular auditorium facilities with a spot or two supplied by a local light company. Proceeds helped finance graduation expenses. I taught English at St. Albans High School where we did *The Rivals* and *The Importance of Being Earnest.* I assisted as director with no other experience or training than that received in high school and college drama clubs.[19]

One teacher, in an article on techniques of directing, advised that when rehearsals came to that point or "deadspot" where everyone hates the play and each other, the "coach must lose her temper and flay right and left."[20] She also should use a "sad, discouraged and disgusted air for dress rehearsals."

A healthier climate for work in dramatics is apparent soon after the First World War. Clare Slick recalls:

... in 1919 I took my first teaching job, directly out of college. I was engaged as a speech instructor in a western high school at a salary of $1000, which was considered a goodly sum. Two full-time instructors were employed. All Freshmen students were required to take speech. The course was really a fundamental course, designed to promote greater reading efficiency. Beyond this requirement, speech courses were optional, but full credit was given for advanced courses. Interpretation and literary appreciation as well as dramatic literature were included in the advanced work. Every high school lad aspired to recite with fervor "Gunga Din" and the "Cremation of Sam McGee." During the school term, we were required or expected, barring fatalities, to present six one-act plays for the assembly period, one operetta, and one Senior play.[21]

Dina Rees Evans' experiences around 1924 are significant. She arrived at Bozeman (Montana) High School to find the little theatre movement in full swing:

The effects of summer sessions at Wisconsin, Minnesota and Northwestern, together with the influence of the little theatre and the inspiration of *Theatre*

Arts Monthly . . . made me revolt against the painted interiors and the exterior provided us by the school board, to be held sacred through the years against any violation of change. In our zeal, the students and I built and painted sets with our own hands. It was revolutionary. In Bozeman, I taught accredited classes in dramatics and . . . with my high school club called "The Parrots"—the stage crew was known as "The Perch"—I produced *Seven Keys to Baldpate, The Goose Hangs High, The Road to Yesterday* and *You and I.* There was a pent-house production of *Twelfth Night.* We won the state contest at Missoula with *The Valiant.*[22]

All through this quarter-century there is evidence that administrators approved of dramatic activities in their school programs. Early in the century Thomas Davidson said:

That dramatic work should form a branch of common school education, I have not the slightest doubt. So long as the theatre forms one of the chief amusements of the great body of our people, it is most essential that they should be taught in school to appreciate a good drama and to reject a low-toned inartistic one. . . . The reason that so many people seek low pleasures and coarse sensual delights, is that our schools, by neglecting their aesthetic education, have left them without means of finding amusement and delight in a rational way.[23]

In 1915, Mr. W. F. Slocum, principal of the Carl Schurz High School, said that drama provided "the very last finishing touch of the art-culture of a school." On the other hand, one principal when replying to a questionnaire on how dramatics contributed toward citizenship, said:

Not at all. . . . Such work is trifling, non-productive, appeals to cheap egotism of a few pupils. The time and energy of pupils should be directed to work of lasting value. One play each term given by members of the Senior Class gives quite adequate opportunity to any real talent and more than enough for poor abilities. Elocuters are trying to create jobs for themselves by boosting for Dramatic Training.

In 1925, Dr. William M. Davidson, superintendent of Pittsburgh schools, said in the preface to a book of plays:

But what is of far greater significance to me than the recreational and, in the narrow sense, educational advantages to be derived from the production of plays in schools, is the humanitarian aspect of the whole matter. By this I mean that I am convinced that drama is much more than a school "subject": it is a manifestation of life and character. . . . Drama seems to me one of the most important factors in modern education.[24]

In some communities an outstanding dramatic production helped to change the attitude of administrators and general public alike toward dramatics as a curricular subject. The Shakespeare Tercentenary in 1916 was observed in many schools by excellent productions on modified Elizabethan stages. As one teacher explained it, presenting Eliza-

bethan plays in the original style made dramatics academically acceptable by creating a favorable attitude toward theatre in a community.
He believed also that the current widespread popularity of Shakespeare was the result of emphasis which university professors were
placing on advanced study of Shakespeare "from an acting point of
view," the increase in popular knowledge of the theatre, and, finally,
the great interest in various forms of dramatic activity both for instruction and recreation.[25]

Another factor, albeit a negative one, in the struggle to win academic
recognition for dramatics was the growing dissatisfaction with the
work of professional coaches. Professor H. J. Riverda, of Cornell University, claimed that a professional coach did not tie the play in with
classwork, he did not understand the routine of the school and he was
too dependent on the financial success of the play. "Even if there is
something lost in actual finish of a play, the evils of using an outside
coach are so great that the idea cannot be endorsed." [26]

The situation is vividly described in Clare Slick's letter:

> Our class work was so heavy (180 students per day), that another pro-
> fessional director was called in to assist us on the extra-curricular activities.
> This practice was employed in the middle west, I recall as a student. For our
> class plays and declamatory contests a special coach came from Des Moines
> to train us for these events. I think all small high schools followed this prac-
> tice. I know of several coaches who were assured of fairly steady work all
> during the school year. They traveled from town to town and did this "coach-
> ing." Of course if a regular instructor could be induced to take on this extra
> load, the expense of a professional was not deemed necessary unless they
> were anxious to surpass a rival town. . . . Most of the plays were comedies,
> with little literary merit I should say. One hundred dollars a week was the
> top price paid for such work. Two weeks was generally the allotted time,
> but smaller schools often engaged a professional for the last few rehearsals
> only, expecting him to do the miraculous.

Gradually during this twenty-five year period administrators and
curriculum supervisors recognized the educational potentialities of
dramatics under the guidance of qualified, full-time teachers rather
than outside coaches. By 1925 only one out of 47 California schools had
a professional coach, and in 1929 only one out of 177 Kansas high
schools had a non-faculty dramatics director. At the same time, dramatics was gradually introduced as a full-time, curricular study rather
than as an annual or semiannual event isolated from classroom activity.

The slow process of establishing accredited courses in theatre arts
began in 1915 and, of course, has not ended yet. In 1917 a notice in the
English Journal asked members of the association to urge their principals to give credits in English for dramatics.[27] By 1915 thirty-five

schools in southern California were offering from one-half to four credits for dramatic classes, and colleges and universities had begun to give
entrance credit for courses in dramatics which included certain stipulated material. Nevertheless, some teachers objected strenuously to
giving credit for play production. Mr. Frank Tompkins of the Central
High School in Detroit believed that this kind of course should be in
the English department solely, that only good, historical plays should
be read and produced occasionally if they did not consume too much
time or distort the true academic aim of the course. He believed that
no credit in English should be given for production or the arts of the
theatre. He knew of one boy who "got English credit for two hours of
face make-up and history of costume to present to an Eastern university. This is deplorable." [28]

Space does not permit a full description of how individual teachers
and principals all over the country began to develop courses in dramatics, at first in the English department and, after 1917, in separate
speech departments. We can only point to some of the important milestones. In 1915 a course in dramatics and a little theatre were established in the high school at South Bend, Indiana. In 1916 a two-year
course was inaugurated at a Dayton, Ohio, school; it included history
of drama, stage phraseology, playwriting, voice development, and
simple impersonation.[29] An elective course in play-reading, acting, and
playwriting was offered in 1917 in the University of Chicago High
School.[30] In this same year the Senior class of seventeen students of the
Chisholm, Minnesota, school had as a year project the co-operative
writing, staging, and publishing of a regional or folk play.[31] At the
1920 Convention of the National Association of Teachers of Speech, the
complete separation of dramatics from the English field was urged by
the committee on high-school courses. The Texas Speech Arts Association was organized in 1921. In the *English Journal* the same year,
Miss Mary Rodigan declared that dramatics should be a curricular
subject, because it had so many possibilities for personality development; it presented a large body of facts; and it could be taught scientifically. "We are applying a psychological law when we capitalize the
play instinct." Miss Rodigan described a two-year course in dramatics
covering historical, literary, artistic, and mechanical aspects of the
theatre which she was teaching at the Racine (Wisconsin) High School
even though she had no stage.[32]

Dramatics won academic recognition toward the end of this era for
several reasons. Qualified teachers rather than outside coaches showed
how participation in dramatic activities developed personalities and
prepared students as well as any traditional course of study, and sometimes better. Administrators realized that a student should be given

credit for an activity which could help him mature and into which he poured large amounts of time and energy. The general public saw how the production of plays growing out of continuing course work gave to dramatic activities a new perspective and stability that had been lacking in the early years of the century.

Resources

Where could the teacher responsible for producing a play turn for help to solve the many problems of play production, rehearsing and acting, and of scenery and lighting? Where could the director get new ideas, inspiration, and encouragement?

Not only the plays but ideas for staging them often came from the professional theatre. Around 1904, the Ben Greet players began their regular tours of America and presented *Everyman* and Shakespearean plays out-of-doors or on bare stages of schools and theatres. This practice of presenting Shakespeare on Elizabethan-type or semi-bare stages begun in the nineteenth century in England by William Poel was successfully carried out by Mr. Floyd Bartlett, principal of the Auburn (New York) Academy High School during the 1890's and early 1900's. Mr. Bartlett used a flexible, open stage to present the annual class play, always chosen from Shakespeare.[33]

Magazines and books explained and illustrated the ideas of Gordon Craig, Reinhardt, and other European leaders of the "new movement" in stagecraft. Hiram K. Moderwell's *The Theatre of Today* and Sheldon Cheney's *The New Movement in the Theatre* appeared in 1914. College and "Art" or "Little" theatres adapted many of the new ideas to their productions. Walter H. Nichols, a teacher in the Pasadena (California) High School, introduced some of these ideas to fellow English teachers in an article on high-school dramatics. Mr. Nichols explained Gordon Craig's emphasis on simplicity of scenery and his methods of synthesizing all the elements in a production. Describing Craig's production of *Hamlet* at the Moscow Art Theatre in 1914, Mr. Nichols says: "Craig revealed hitherto undreamed-of possibilities in simple monotone screens, differently arranged and lighted for different scenes and moods of the play. Professor Reinhardt has accomplished wonders along similar lines in his Berlin production." Mr. Nichols explains how the Irish Players, who toured America in 1911, achieved effective, simple scenic effects solely through lighting.[34]

The professional theatre provided plays for the high-school theatre as well as ideas on how to simplify scenery artistically. However, finding just the right play for a particular group of students, then as now, was a difficult problem. Among the resources available to a teacher were play lists, magazine articles, a few books, and certain university departments. Mr. Thatcher Guild, in 1913, wrote that since 70 per cent of college freshmen had taken part in amateur dramatics, the high-school coach should choose a play not only because it was entertaining but because it gave the actors something worth doing. Mr. Guild suggested that teachers find plays with good themes by (1) buying plays from publishing houses (they cost only fifteen or twenty-five cents each at that time), (2) writing to the Agency for Unpublished Plays, (3) following the bulletins of the Drama League, and (4) reading the Dramatic Index, which had begun to appear in 1908.[35]

After 1911 the teacher could turn to the lists of plays distributed by six publishing houses and three women's organizations. The play publishers included Samuel French, Inc., Walter H. Baker Co., Dramatic Publishing Co., Penn Co., Dick and Fitzgerald Co., and the Eldridge company. The Samuel French catalog in 1910, for instance, lists the names and sometimes the descriptions of 600 new plays, most of which are one-acts; 1,820 standard plays; and 350 in the category of "minor drama." In the Baker catalog of 1912 the royalty for *Wedding Bells* is listed as only five dollars, but for Langdon Mitchell's *The New York Idea,* a recent Broadway success, it is quoted as twenty-five dollars. Pinero's *The Profligate* is described as being "not suited for amateur performances or permitted to them" and his *The Second Mrs. Tanqueray* is also prohibited because, according to the publisher, it "cannot be played by amateurs." In the same catalog there are eleven pages of comedies and minstrel sketches for female characters and four pages for men; and there are lists of operettas, tableaux, statuary episodes, charades, mock trials, and pantomimes.

In 1908 Elizabeth McFadden and L. E. Davis published *A Selected List of Plays for Amateurs and Students of Dramatic Expression in Schools and Colleges.* Lists of plays and notices of current theatrical activity were widely distributed by the American Drama Society (founded in 1909), the MacDowell Club (1910), and the Drama League (1911). When the first volume of the *Quarterly Journal of Public Speaking* appeared in 1915, it contained a list of available European and English one-act plays prepared by Alexander Drummond. Other pioneer teachers who prepared lists of plays for various publications were E. C. Mabie, Frederick Koch, Clarence Stratton, Sarah Trainer Floyd, and Gladys Tibbetts. Information on available plays began to appear regularly in the *English Journal* and in the bulletins of the American Library Association. Several universities, among them Utah, North Dakota State, Cornell, and North Carolina, established rental libraries and circulated thousands of plays. Over twenty anthologies of plays were published between 1915, when the first edition of Thomas Dickinson's *Chief Contemporary Dramatists* appeared, and 1925, when Frank Shay published *Twenty-Five Short Plays*.

Books on the technique of directing plays were extremely rare before 1917. One book (1890) gave this kind of advice:

Have every actor recite Collin's "Ode on the Passions" before a mirror and practice the expression of all the passions from anger to wonder with proper gestures, tone of voice and facial expressions. Select the play for the strongest members of the group. Arrange act endings or tableaux to form appropriate living pictures with the leading people as centers of interest. For a play of average length, plan at least six rehearsals but twelve would be good. Buy paper scenery at Art stores for interior settings. Paste the following rules inside your hat: Be letter perfect. Speak clearly and slowly. Don't interrupt. Be appropriately dressed. Stand still. Face the audience. Underact rather than overact. Choose easy plays or secure the services of a professional coach. That is all.[36]

Another book (1916) treats carefully such problems as dramatic values, emphasis, triangular grouping and other aspects of picturization, tempo and rhythm, scenery, costuming, and lighting. The author also insists that the student actor be given sides only, never a full script. Then he will never be distracted and also "he can form no independent (and possibly mutinous) notions about how the play should be conducted as a whole." [37]

More useful and popular books on the arts of the theatre and on the specific problems of play production in high schools began to appear in 1916 and were used by teachers as references or as texts. The best known in this group include Arthur Krows' *Play Production in America* (1916), Barrett Clark's *How to Produce Amateur Plays* (1917), Louis Calvert's *Problems of the Actor* (1918), Arthur Hopkins' *How's Your Second Act?* (1918), Gertrude Johnson's *Choosing a Play* (1923), and Helena Chalmer's *The Art of Make-Up* (1925).

By 1926 a teacher could select a textbook for a class in dramatics from among Andrews and Weirick's *Acting and Play Production*, Alice E. Craig's *The Speech Arts*, Crafton and Royer's *The Process of Play Production*, Milton Smith's *The Book of Play Production for Little Theatres, Schools and Colleges*, Claude Wise's *Dramatics for School and Community*, André Smith's *The Scenewright*, and Roy Mitchell's *The School Theatre*. In some courses one or two anthologies of plays were used in addition to these technical books.

Theatre Arts magazine, beginning as a quarterly in 1916, became indispensable to the teacher in charge of dramatics, and other professional magazines began to carry stories and illustrations of activities connected with play production in schools. An entire issue of *School Arts Magazine* (1924) was devoted to articles on costuming, lighting, equipping a stage, rehearsals, and puppetry and the use of other departments in the school.[38] In another magazine, *Industrial Arts* (1924), Philip Burness, a shop teacher in Lindblom High School, Chicago, showed how all the different shops in a technical school could work on the scenery, lighting, and publicity for a play. He believed that if dramatic work was directed by the proper teachers it could "encourage more cultural thought and accomplish more technical training than much of the ordinary classroom work."[39]

Guild, in 1913, in the article referred to above, said that the dramatics coach could teach acting best by imitation if she could assume the various characters. He believed that a reasonable equipment for the coach was dramatic instinct and the opportunity to observe good acting. He advocated the study of recordings, motion pictures, and the photographs of scenes from plays in the catalogs of the Byron Company. These were ways of self-help. Soon institutions of higher learning began to offer courses and practical experience in theatre arts.

Teachers College of Columbia University in 1913 commenced courses in the techniques of festivals, pageants, and dramatization. A check of available catalogs shows that courses in dramatics for teachers were offered during the summer sessions of 1914 at State College of Washington, in Pullman, and the University of North Dakota. The University of Texas offered a round table discussion for no credit, at which "Problems of Expression in Public Schools" were analyzed and solved. In 1915 summer courses labeled "High School Dramatics" or "Practical Instruction in Staging Plays" or "Interpretation of Dramatis Personae" were given at Cornell University, the University of California at Los Angeles, and at Berkeley, the University of Wisconsin, DePauw University, the University of Iowa, Iowa State College, and Pennsylvania State College. Teachers enrolled in courses given by specialized schools such as the American Academy of Dramatic Arts in New York, the Columbia College of Expression in Chicago, and the Emerson College of Oratory, the Leland Powers School of the Spoken Word, and the School of Expression (Curry) in Boston. In 1921 Professor Frederick Koch reported to the convention of the Drama League of America that 398 courses in dramatics representing 998 academic hours were being given in 164 institutions of higher learning.[40]

Beginning in 1917 and continuing through 1928, all students at Hunter College were required to take a course which included dramatics and speech development. By 1929 all prospective teachers of high-school English in the state-supported institutions of West Virginia were required to take a course in play production.

A new type of resource for the teacher of dramatics became available in the 1920's, when graduate schools encouraged students to undertake research in the area of high-school dramatics. By 1930 at least eight graduate students had investigated various aspects of the subject, bringing large amounts of organized material to teachers, administrators and the public. Ruth Damon wrote on "Some Tendencies in the Field of Speech," [41] Mary Margaret Robb's study was entitled, "Aims and Methods of Dramatic Work in Secondary Schools." [42] Elizabeth F. Keppie, basing her study primarily on replies to her questionnaire from forty-seven California schools, wrote on "Dramatics in the High School." [43] Gilbert T. Gustafson, using the replies to his questionnaire returned from 127 schools, wrote on "The Status of Extra-Curricular Activities in Iowa High Schools for the School Year of 1925-26." [44] Dina Rees Evans' investigation was entitled, "A Preliminary Study of Play Production in Secondary Schools." [45]

Wilhelmina G. Hedde, in 1929, prepared "A Survey of High School Dramatics in the School System of Cities of Population Over 30,000." [46] The report begins with a brief description of each of the milestones in the progress of dramatics from 1899, when a course called Oral English was established in the Oakland (California) High School, to 1927 and the Drama League Report of that year which, among other things, gave basis for the statement that there were over three million students eager to participate in dramatic activities in high schools. Miss Hedde includes the course outlines used in the dramatics courses of eight schools and describes fully the findings of her own questionnaire. Bertha Luckan Wilson investigated "The Status of Dramatics in the Senior High Schools of Kansas—1929-1930," [47] and in the same year, 1929, E. Turner Stump described "A State Program of Educational Dramatic Activities for West Virginia." [48]

A teacher in charge of play production at the beginning of the twentieth century often had an innate sense of good theatre, enthusiasm, and a willingness to learn by experience, but there was no large body of plays from which to make a selection and it was difficult if not impossible to get any help from teachers or books. As interest in supervised or educational dramatics grew, authors and publishers increased the number and quality of plays, qualified workers wrote valuable books on acting and production techniques, and colleges and universities introduced at first single courses and later extensive programs in all theatre arts to meet the needs of young teachers.

Production Problems

The stages for high-school plays were, as a rule, hopelessly inadequate in both size and equipment. In the early years of the century there were a few good stages and auditoriums in certain high schools, but more often the stage was a lecture platform or a temporary construction of platform and curtains. Mr. Nichols, of Pasadena, complains in 1914 of the way school boards and architects continued to provide poor stages with no wing space but large aprons, and very deep orchestra pits.[49] He suggests a room for the cast to study their homework during rehearsals with only one door which leads directly on-stage. The chaperon (a member of the faculty) could thus carry out her work more easily. Mr. Nichols asks for a good switchboard because beautifully lighted stage pictures are "all powerful in impressing art standards on students."

Some schools were built without stages so that play-giving (the work of the devil) would be impossible. For instance, the high school in Tacoma, Washington, was built in 1907 with an auditorium but no stage. At one end was a platform, but to prevent its use as a stage, rows of steps were erected for the chorus. The 1800 students demanded a play, however, and in 1908 one was given; the next year there were two, and in 1910 a stage was built.[50] Some schools rented the Town Hall, or occasionally the nearest regular public theatre. The high school at East Columbus, Ohio, gave some of its plays outdoors and had an indoor stage 14' x 25' surrounded with neutral muslin.

Scenery was rented, improvised, and occasionally built by the students. When Miss Charlotte Herr gave *She Stoops to Conquer* in 1908, at the high school of Idaho Springs, Colorado, the problem of scenery was left to near the end of the rehearsal period. The play was presented in the town theatre and "under the direction of a young college man who had some experience in the production of plays at Harvard, the senior boys set to work in the manual training building, and in a few days they had constructed the frames." [51]

At Tacoma (Washington) High School, sixteen performances of eight plays were given in 1915. Only two settings were available for all productions; one small set was painted by the art students and one elaborate set was done by a professional scenic artist who charged five cents per square foot. Both sets cost sixty dollars. Proceeds from the twenty-five cent admission charge went to the stadium fund or for paintings to hang in school corridors.

High-School Dramatics Today

In some respects the picture of high-school dramatics has not changed since 1925; in other respects it has greatly improved.

Today the problems of producing a play are better understood by administrators and architects and unusually fine facilities have been provided in some schools. To achieve flexible lighting, the trend now is to install spotlights and dimmers in place of the general lighting units and switches of long ago. Some schools have small studio theatres for dramatic work in addition to a larger auditorium. The old practice of using the same set of scenery for every play and even circulating the same flats year after year among several schools in one area is still followed in isolated regions, but the usual procedure today is to have students design, build, and paint scenery for every new production. In this way students can participate more completely in the entire process of producing a play.

Similarly, the resources available to a good teacher of dramatics today have grown to such an extent that one organization, the National Thespian Society, is concerned exclusively with the problems of high school dramatics. The American Educational Theatre Association, the Speech Association of America, and the American National Theatre and Academy, like the National Thespian Society, sponsor drama conferences and festivals and promote committees and publications. Some colleges and university extension divisions offer in-service training courses. Although the problem of choosing the "right" play is no easier now than it was twenty-five years ago, there are more plays from which to choose. Publishers and play agents are more liberal in their royalty arrangements and more playwrights are writing exclusively for the high-school market. Such factors tend to make the preliminary work of play production easier for the teacher than it was in the first twenty-five years of the century.

Dramatics is not yet universally accepted as a curricular subject nor do admissions offices of institutions of higher learning accept all dramatics courses equally. The subject will be more widely recognized, however, as good teachers multiply and course content improves. Twenty-five years ago there were relatively few trained teachers to handle high-school dramatics, but today almost every college can offer specialized courses in the theory and practice of theatre arts to young people who plan to teach.[52] In some large high schools the demand for dramatic activity is so great that several full-time instructors are needed to supervise the directing, mounting, lighting, and costuming of plays and operettas, and to teach specific courses.

There are more kinds of dramatic activity in high schools today than there were in the first twenty-five years of the twentieth century. Many groups prepare special productions for children and participate in regional drama festivals and in the celebration of International Theatre Month. Interesting experiments with arena staging, choric dramas, and living newspaper techniques illustrate the creative vitality of the modern high-school theatre. Some groups tour their productions, bringing living theatre to larger audiences and giving actors and stage crews further experiences in adjusting to new conditions.

The values and objectives of dramatics remain fundamentally what they were twenty-five years ago, except that more teachers in all fields are aware of how important dramatic activity can be in developing a student's personality. Educators and parents today look upon high-school dramatics as a priceless opportunity to encourage avocational activity, and to teach standards of appreciation.

Whatever status dramatics may have in the secondary-school program today, it is the result of the vision, ability and enthusiasm of many teachers and students who laid permanent foundations in the first quarter of the twentieth century. Often working in isolation and under incredible difficulties, teachers in charge of the early dramatics programs brought dignity and artistic integrity to "amateur theatricals" and made the study and practice of the arts of the theatre an important tool in the education of American youth.

Notes

1. Adelia W. Cone, "The Value of Dramatics in the Secondary School," *Ohio Educational Monthly*, LXI (1912), 462-464.
2. J. M. Dorey, "A School Course in Dramatics," *EJ*, I (September, 1912), 425-430.
3. Eleanor Robson, "The Theatre and Education," *Outlook*, CXV (March 7, 1917), 412.
4. Report of the Committee on Plays in Schools and Colleges, J. M. Dorey, chairman, *EJ*, IV (January, 1915), 34-40.
5. John Dolman, Jr., "Educational Dramatics," *QJSE*, VII (April, 1921), 158-161.
6. Clarence D. Thorpe, "The Educational Function of High School Dramatics," *QJSE*, X (April, 1924), 116-127.
7. The place of dramatics can also be justified in a recent program aiming to create better intergroup relations through education. The program appeared in *The New York Times*, September 2, 1951, Section 4, p. 7, and presents the following goals: To teach the moral worth of all people, to equalize as far as possible, in school and outside, the conditions of free-enterprise competition, to promote positive co-operation across racial, creedal and other barrier lines, to apply these objectives primarily in the education of young people as agents of change, to provide leadership in school and community co-ordination and to use the techniques of the psycho-social sciences in experimental efforts to change behaviors.
8. The plays in the following list, both three-act and one-act, come from articles, books, and personal letters, but primarily from a questionnaire the late Ernest Bavely sent to all Thespian Troupes in 1950. The seventy-six troupes which returned the questionnaire are distributed all over the United States (with the majority in Ohio) and in Hawaii and Puerto Rico. The articles "A" and "The" have been omitted when they constitute the first word of the title.

Aaron Boggs; Above the Clouds; Adam and Eva; Admirable Crichton; Adventures of Miss Brown; Advertising for a Husband; Alabama; Albany Depot; Alcestis; Alexander Hamilton; Alice in Wonderland; All Aboard; All A Mistake; All-of-a-

Sudden Peggy; All-of-a-Sudden Smith; All on Account of Polly; All Smiles; All's Well That Ends Well; Along Came Nancy; Always in Trouble; Amazons; Am I Intruding; Among the Breakers; An American Citizen; Anchorhold; Angela Merici; Ann of Old Salem; Arrival of Kitty; As You Like It; At the End of the Rainbow; At the Movies; At the Sign of the Shooting Star; Aunt Maggie's Will.

Bachelors' Congress; Back Again Home Town; Back to the Farm; Barbara Frietchie; Barrett Cox and Co.; Bashful Mr. Bobs; Beau of Bath; Beauty and the Jacobin; Believe Me, Xantippe; Big Idea; Bird's Christmas Carol; Birthday of the Infanta; Bishop's Candlesticks; Blossoming of Mary Ann; Blue Bird; Blue Stockings; Blundering Billy; Boomerang; Box and Cox; Box of Monkeys; Brewster's Millions; Brown of Harvard; Brown's In Town; Buddies; Burglar; By Way of the Secret Passage.

Cabin Courtship; Cabinet Minister; Calico Cat; Camouflage of Shirley; Canterbury Pilgrims; Cappy Ricks; Captain Jinks of the Horse Marines; Captain Letterblair; Captain of Plymouth; Carrots; Case of Suspension; Cathleen Ni-Houlihan; Caught in the Act; Chanticleer; Charley's Aunt; Charm School; Church Bazaar; Christmas Carol; Christmas Chimes; Christmas Freedom; Christopher Jr.; Claim Allowed; Clarence; Close to Nature; Co-Eds; College Days; College Town; College Widow; Colonel's Maid; Comedy of Errors; Come Out of the Kitchen; Comus; Contrary Mary; Converting Bruce; Cooks and Cardinals; Cool Collegians; Copperhead; Corner of the Campus; County Chairman; Country Minister; Courtship of Miles Standish; Cousin Kate; Cricket on the Hearth; Crazy Idea; Crisis; Cupid at Vassar.

Daddy Long Legs; David Garrick; Deacon Dubbs; Dear Boy Graduate; Dear Brutus; Dear Departed; Delegates from Denver; Dictator; Dido the Phoenician Queen; Doin's at Titusville; Dolls; Dorothy's Neighbors; Down in Dixie; Dream that Came True; Dried Pair of Suspenders; Drum Major; Dummy; Dust of the Road.

Eliza Comes to Stay; Elopement of Ellen; Emancipated Ones; Esmeralda; Everyman.

Fabiola; Family Affair; Fanchon the Cricket; Fanny and the Servant Problem; Feast of Dido; Feast of the Little Lantern; Fifi of the Toy Shop; Fifty-Fifty; Fighting for Freedom; First Lady in the Land; First Thanksgiving; Flight of Aeneas; Florist Shop; Flower of Yeddo; Flying Wedge; Fool; Fortune Hunter; Four Little Spiggots; Four Seasons; Freshman; Fudge and the Burglars; Full House.

Galliger; Genius; Gift of the Magi; Girl With the Green Eyes; Girls Over Here; Glass Slipper; Glorious Girl; Goldbug; Golden Days; Green Stockings.

Half-Back Sandy; Hamlet; Hattie Makes Things Hum; Heart of Pierrot; Henry V; Hiawatha; Hiawatha's Childhood; Hicks at College; Higbee of Harvard; His Majesty Bunker Bean; His Model Wife; His Molly; His Uncle John; His Uncle's Niece; Honor Bright; Hoodoo; Hottentot; Hot Water; Hour Glass; Houseboat on the Styx; House Next Door; Hurry! Hurry! Hurry!; Hyacinth Halvey.

Icebound; Ici On Parle Français; Importance of Being Earnest; Ingomar the Barbarian; In India; In Old Madrid; Iron Hand; Isle of Chance; Is Your Name Smith; It Pays to Advertise.

Jeanne D'Arc; Joan of Arc; Joint Owners in Spain; Judsons Entertain; Julius Caesar; Just Like Judy.

Kentucky Belle; Kicked Out of College; Kiss in the Dark; Kingdom of Hearts; Kleptomaniac.

Lady Bantok; Lady of Lyons; Lady of the Lake; Land of Night; Lend Me Five Shillings; Lettre Chargée; Lion and the Mouse; Little Fowl Play; Little Game With Fate; Little Teacher; Little Tycoon; Look Out for Paint; Lost, A Chaperone; Lost Paradise; Lost Word; Love's Labour's Lost.

Macbeth; Maid of Yokohama; Maker of Dreams; Mammy's Lil' Wild Rose; Man from Home; Manikin-Minikin; Man on the Box; Maneuvers of Jane; Man Who Married a Dumb Wife; Mary Jane's Pa; Mary's Millions; Masonic Ring; Me and Otis; Melting Pot; Men, Maids and Matchmakers; Merchant of Venice; Merchant of Venice Up-to-Date; Merely Mary Ann; Mice and Men; 'Mid Cherry Blossoms;

Midsummer Night's Dream; Milestones; Miss Civilization; Miss Dalton's Orchid; Miss Fearless and Company; Miss Hobbs the Private Secretary; Missing Miss Miller; Miss Nobody Else; Miss Somebody Else; Miss Topsy-Turvy; Mistaken Identity; Modern Ananias; Mousetrap; Mr. Bob; Mrs. Bumpstead-Leigh; Mrs. Pat and the Law; Mrs. Temple's Telegram; Mrs. Tubbs Does Her Bit; Mrs. Wiggs of the Cabbage Patch; Mrs. Wiggs of the Poultry Yard; Much Ado About Nothing; My Lord in Livery.

Nathan Hale; Necklace; Neighbors; Nevertheless; New Administration; New Co-Ed; New Lead; New Poor; Niobe; Night Off; Nothing But the Truth; Number 728.

Obstinate Family; Officer 666; Old Lady Shows Her Medals; Olives; One Must Marry; One of the Eight; On Plymouth Rock; Our American Cousin; Our Aunt from California; Our Boys; Our Country Cousin; Our Mrs. McChesney.

Pair of Sixes; Pa's Picnic; Passing of the Third Floor Back; Path Across the Hills; Peg o' My Heart; Pennant; Penrod; Percy Pendleton's Predicament; Perplexing Situation; Phantom Tiger; Phyllis' Inheritance; Pied Piper of Hamelin; Pierre Patelin; Piper; Pipes o' the Hills; Playgoers; Polly in Politics; Pomander Walk; Pride and Prejudice; Prince Chap; Prince Charming; Princess; Private Secretary; Professor's Mummy; Professor Pepp; Promoters; Proposal; Prunella; Pygmalion. Quality Street; Queen Esther.

Ralph Roister Doister; Rebecca of Sunnybrook Farm; Ready Money; Red Lamp; Rejuvenation of Aunt Mary; Return of Hi-Jinks; Rip Van Winkle; Rivals; Robin Hood; Rollo's Great Adventure; Romancers; Romantic Age; Romeo and Juliet; Rosalie; Rosberry Shrub, Sec; Rosemaiden; Rose of Plymouth Town; Ruggles; Runaways; Ruth in a Rush.

Safety First; Sauce for the Gosling; Savageland; School for Scandal; School Mistress; Scientific Country School; Scrap of Paper; Secret Service; Senior; Señor Pecan; Serious Situation in Burleigh's Room; Seven Keys to Baldpate; Seventeen; Sham; She Stoops to Conquer; Sherwood; Silent Detective; Sisterhood of Bridget; Six Who Pass While the Lentils Boil; Sleeping Car; Smilin' Through; Sophomore; Spring Spasm; Star of Bethlehem; Stop Thief; Strenuous Life; Strongheart; Sunday, Sunset; Superior Miss Pellender; Suppressed Desires; Sweet Girl Graduate.

Tailor Made Man; Taking Father's Place; Taming of the Shrew; That Parlor Maid; Things That Count; Thread of Destiny; Three Chauffeurs; Three Crooks and a Lady; Three Wishes; Tiger House; Time of His Life; Tom Harrington; Tommy's Wife; Tom Pinch; Too Much Johnson; Too Much of a Good Thing; Toreadors; Touchdown; Toymaker of Nuremberg; Trouble at the Satterlees; Trust Emily; Trysting Place; Tweedles; Twelfth Night; Twelve-Pound Look; Twig of Thorn; Two Little Rebels.

Uncle Jimmy; Uncle John's Private Secretary; Uncle Josh's Folks; Uncle or Nephew.

Valley Farm; Varsity Coach; Virginian Romance.

Wappin' Wharf; Wedding Bells; Wee Willie Winkie; What Happened to Jones; When a Feller Needs a Friend; When a Man's Single; When Love is Young; When Smith Stepped Out; When You've Earned Enough to Marry Dear; White Butterfly; Whose Little Bride are You; Whole Town's Talking; Why the Chimes Rang; Why Smith Left Home; Wonder Hat; Workhouse Ward; Wrong Mr. Right; Wurzel-Flummery.

Year's Misinterpretations; Ye Olde District Skule; You Never Can Tell; Youth.

9. Helen O'Lemert, "Classical Play for High Schools," *EJ*, II (August, 1913), 386-388.

10. News and Notes, "In Honor of Shakespeare," *EJ*, V (1916), 516.

11. Azubah J. Latham, "The Making of a Festival," *Teachers College Record*, XVI (1915), 248-264.

12. Margo Jones, *Theatre-in-the-Round* (New York, 1951), p. 38.

13. Anne Throop Craig, "The Development of a Dramatic Element in Education," *Pedagogical Seminary*, XV (March, 1908), 78.

14. Alice Minnie Herts, "Dramatic Instinct—Its Use and Misuse," *Pedagogical Seminary*, XV (December, 1908), 553-554.

15. Maude Frank, "Dramatization of School Classics," *EJ*, I (October, 1912), 476-481.

16. E. L. Norton and L. A. Ashleman, "Dramatics in the Teaching of a Foreign Language," *Elementary School Teacher*, VI (1906), 33-39.

17. Quoted by Elnora Whitman Curtis, "The Dramatic Instinct in Education," *Pedagogical Seminary*, XV (September, 1908), 326.

18. From Miss Thomas' letter to the writer, Nov. 20, 1950.

19. From Miss Shattuck's letter to the writer, September 15, 1950.

20. Laura G. Whitmire, "The Class Play," *QJSE*, VII (1921), 138-148.

21. From Miss Slick's letter to the writer, September 12, 1950.

22. "Fifty Years in the High School Theatre," speech by Miss Evans at the 1950 Convention of the American Educational Theatre Association.

23. Quoted by Elnora Whitman Curtis, *op. cit.*, p. 314.

24. Olive M. Price, *Short Plays from American History and Literature for Classroom Use* (New York, 1925).

25. Franklin P. Baker, "Shakespeare in the Schools," *EJ*, V (May, 1916), 299-309.

26. Harding Jordan Riverda, *Extra-Curricular Activities in Elementary and Secondary Schools* (New York, 1928), p. 44.

27. *EJ*, VI (March, 1917), 197-198.

28. Frank G. Tompkins, "The Play Course in High School," *EJ*, IX (1920), 530-533.

29. Grace H. Stivers, "A High School Course in Dramatic Art," *QJSE*, IV (October, 1918), 434-447.

30. Ernest F. Haines, "The Drama Course in the University High School," *School Review*, XXIX (December, 1921), 746-757.

31. A. Bess Clark, "An Experiment in Problem Teaching," *EJ*, VI (October, 1917), 535-538.

32. Mary V. Rodigan, "Dramatics in the High School," *EJ*, X (June, 1921), 316-326.

33. From a personal letter from Professor Alexander M. Drummond, February 23, 1953.

34. Walter H. Nichols, "The High School Play," *EJ*, III (December, 1914), 620-630.

35. Thatcher H. Guild, "Suggestions for the High School Play," *EJ*, II (December, 1913), 637-646.

36. Charles Townsend, *Amateur Theatricals* (New York, 1890).

37. Emerson Taylor, *Practical Stage Direction for Amateurs* (New York, 1916).

38. *School Arts Magazine*, XXIII (May, 1924).

39. Philip Burness, "Stagecraft—An Extra-Classroom Activity," *Industrial Arts*, XIII (April, 1924), 152-154.

40. Carol McMillan, "The Growing Academic Recognition of Dramatic Production," *QJSE*, X (1924), 23-29.

41. Unpublished M.A. thesis, Northwestern, 1923.

42. *Ibid.*, Iowa, 1924.

43. *Ibid.*, Southern California, 1926.

44. *Ibid.*, Iowa, 1927.

45. *Ibid.*, 1928.

46. *Ibid.*, Northwestern, 1929.

47. *Ibid.*, Kansas, 1930.

48. *Ibid.*, Iowa, 1930.

49. See Walter H. Nichols, "High School Play."

50. O. B. Sperlin, "The Production of Plays in High School," *EJ*, V (March, 1916), 172-180.

51. Charlotte B. Herr, "The Value of Dramatic Work in the Teaching of English," *Journal of Education*, LXVII (January, 23, 1908), 95-97.

52. Unfortunately, many college students cannot foresee the exact nature of the teaching they will do and when, as teachers, they are given the job of directing a play they cannot do it or themselves justice because of insufficient training. See "The High School Dramatic Director," an article by Opal Wigner Boffo, *Educational Theatre Journal*, III (May, 1951), 119-125, for a description of inadequate working conditions and poorly trained teachers in 151 schools of northeastern Ohio.

27 Professional Theatre Schools in the Early Twentieth Century

FRED C. BLANCHARD

> The elocutionist, orator and actor have one power in common to possess before success can be reached. Our aim is to give this secret power. Our work is altogether new, scientific, wonderful. The results are instantaneous, marvelous. Terms lowest in country until we are known.

The above advertisement appeared in 1902 in a widely circulated professional magazine. The "School of Oratory" which thus so modestly invited attention to its services was in a small city with a population of 28,757, far from the commercial milieu of Broadway or any other theatrical producing center where, it is likely, secret powers could be cultivated in contemplative quiet. But this frank statement of purpose reveals many of the major problems faced by the philosophers and practitioners who conducted American Professional Schools of Acting and Theatre during the first quarter of the twentieth century.

The teachers and proprietors of the well-known professional schools of the period under discussion, in their pedagogy and organization, exhibited the same concerns as their provincial competitor. They too believed that their instruction would benefit almost any prospective student, regardless of his vocational aims. They wanted their products to succeed, theatrically and otherwise. They were inclined to believe in the inherent powers of the individual, and were, of course, confident that their own systems and methods could develop those powers. Like their cut-rate colleague, they had to provide the kinds of services which would enable them to stay in business.

I

By about 1900, the young actor was discovering that opportunities for training were becoming more and more difficult to obtain. With the completion of the railroad system and the organization of theatre as a national big business, the "road" had become a profitable enterprise. Producing became concentrated in a few large cities, especially in New York. The old type of stock company training, so well exemplified in Mrs. John Drew's company at the Arch Street Theatre in Philadelphia and at the Boston Museum, was no longer readily available to the beginner. Franklin H. Sargent, founder of the American Academy of Dramatic Art, wrote in 1899 that the stock companies, which he regarded as schools of acting, were practically obsolete.[1] There seems to be little doubt that the old stock company was indeed a school for actors in many ways. Stock provided regular experience under conditions of actual productions; special rehearsals were conducted for the young "walking ladies and gentlemen" of the company to instruct them in the skills, graces and deportment of the stage. Memoirs and autobiographies are full of testimony that stage managers and older actors were often patient and effective tutors. Lester Wallack placed high value on the disciplines of stock company rehearsal and performance.[2] Mrs. Gilbert recalled many instances of informal teaching by older actors in the companies.[3] Frederick Warde described the thorough training given to the young members of stock companies.[4] A long apprenticeship was expected of the young actor before he would be entrusted with a responsible line of parts.

It seems clear also that by 1900 the once well-established method of private coaching to supplement experience had been generally discarded. Sargent, in the article already cited, noted that private teachers were plentiful in earlier days and that many well-known actors also had assumed the responsibility of teaching a few students. Some, like James E. Murdoch, George Vandenhoff, and F. F. Mackay, eventually became better known as teachers than as actors, and sought to organize and formalize their methods of instruction. But by the end of the nineteenth century, few actors of high reputation were either willing or able to teach. The kind of theatrical organization in America which had made possible the training of stage aspirants by the traditional master-pupil method, still associated with the teaching of other arts, was in the process of change. The difficulty experienced by the young actor or actress in obtaining adequate training was being recognized and frequently discussed. Professional schools in the late nineteenth and early twentieth centuries stepped in to fill the roles of the private teacher and the actor-teacher.

Other forces also contributed to the founding and growth of theatre schools. The interest in declamation and vocal expression had not abated. The development of the platform reading of entire plays by gifted performers like Leland Powers may have brought the stage and the platform nearer together. The scientific methods of Darwin and

Spencer led to the desire to organize all kinds of knowledge. The institutionalizing of theatre, especially in France, and the formalizing of instruction by Delsarte and his followers led to eager imitation in America. The ardent discipleship of Steele MacKaye carried the theories of Delsarte into many theatrical schools, popularizing a so-called "natural" system of training allegedly much unlike the older Rush-Murdoch method which was being criticized as stilted and artificial. Post-Ibsen playwriting and post-Belasco staging turned from nineteenth-century practice. The cult of the everyday and natural was in the ascendant. The teaching of the art and craft of theatre was bound to be affected as new schools were founded.

II

What should we regard as a professional school of acting and theatre? An accurate and simple definition is this: Any school which has as one of its major purposes the preparation of its students for the vocation of acting or some other form of theatre practice. Within the scope of this definition, the selection of appropriate schools for study is difficult. A few schools held vocational theatrical training as their principal and almost sole aim; they are no problem. The many schools of "oratory" and "expression" can hardly be excluded because preparation for the professional stage was considered an important though not the only aim of their training. Universities and colleges we shall observe only in passing. For the most part, their development as "professional" or "vocational" schools of theatre practice came near the end of the period of study or in later years. We shall take notice of schools of other kinds when they seem to have moved in the direction of specific training for theatre practice.

III

Although professional theatrical production became more and more centralized, professional schools as here defined were located in all parts of the country. By way of example, advertisements and news items in theatre magazines from 1900 to 1925 mention schools located in New York, Philadelphia, Boston, Chicago, Detroit, Cincinnati, Cleveland, Pittsburgh, Kansas City, Washington, St. Louis, Denver, Los Angeles, San Francisco and Seattle. There were, of course, many others in cities large and small. Such geographical distribution of schools is evident throughout the entire twenty-five years under consideration. Many schools suddenly appeared and quickly died; a few have survived all vicissitudes. The professional studio-school is still with us, and despite the great development since 1925 of the colleges and universities as centers of professional instruction, it is likely to remain for many years to come.

Some rough classification of these many schools is possible, grouped according to their origins and their stated or apparent purposes at the time of their founding.

Theatrical Schools

The "theatrical" schools, for want of a better term, were founded by theatrical practitioners or other persons who were close to the professional theatre. They did not grow out of other kinds of organizations; they were schools from the beginning. They were begun with the clearly stated aim of providing preparation for work in the professional theatre. In the case of those schools which survived until 1925 or later, the professional aim has remained the primary one, although the curriculum has often been modified to include other social and professional purposes.

The School of Acting under the guidance of Dion Boucicault, founded more than a decade before the period of this study, may well be typical of the school which is closely connected with the professional theatre. Constance Morris, a one-time pupil of the school, described its method of operation.[5] It was formed in the old age of Dion Boucicault—actor, playwright, director, and theatre leader through many years in England and America.

Boucicault was backed in the venture by two leading theatrical managers of the period, A. M. Palmer and Augustin Daly, among others. The stated purpose of the planned three-year course was to discover and train young people of talent. No tuition was to be charged, and placement in the theatre was expected. Constance Morris describes the try-outs for membership, which were held before a committee of Boucicault, Palmer, Daly and others. Out of one hundred aspirants, fifty-three were chosen for the course. These were divided into two groups according to ability and accomplishment, the first group to be taught by Boucicault and the second by Theodore Corbett. Frequent assignments of individual roles and parts of scenes were made, and the student performances were then criticized and corrected by the teachers, probably much in the manner of the old stock company stage manager. Well-known actors and actresses gave demonstrations and lectures. Semi-annual examinations were conducted at the Madison Square Theatre, before such Broadway stars as John Drew, James Lewis, Ada Rehan, Helena Modjeska, Otis Skinner, Wilton Lackaye, Rose Coghlan and Mrs. Gilbert, some of whom would act as judges. According to Miss

Morris, the successful student performers were placed in professional companies.

The American Academy of Dramatic Arts in New York has maintained a close relationship with the professional theatre from its first year in 1884 until the present time. Although its founder and long-time president, Franklin H. Sargent, had early training at Harvard and in the Boston University School of Oratory, he soon became employed in professional theatre activities, and was engaged in the instruction of young actors at the Madison Square Theatre in 1883. In 1884, he was associated with Steele MacKaye and Gustave Frohman in operating the Lyceum Theatre School, which became the American Academy of Dramatic Arts in 1885. In 1897, the Academy joined with the Empire Theatre School, and for a number of years special student performances were given at the Empire. The purpose of the Academy as stated in 1900 was to give "a broad and practical training to those desiring to make acting their profession," an aim which has apparently remained constant.[6] The school has received the support and encouragement of professional theatre leaders; its Board of Trustees and Advisory Board from 1900 to 1925 included such names as Charles and Daniel Frohman, John Drew, William Gillette, David Belasco, Bronson Howard, Augustus Thomas, Winthrop Ames, and William H. Crane. Among its staff members from 1900 to 1925 may be noted such familiar names as Charles Jehlinger, Eva Alberti, May Robson, William T. Price, William C. DeMille, William J. Dean, Algernon Tassin, Helena Chalmers, Philip Loeb, and Donald Oenslager. Like other schools of its kind, it has sought to provide a professional showcase for its advanced students.

The Alvienne Academy in New York was founded in 1894 by Claude M. Alvienne, actor and director, and is now under the management of Mrs. Neva Alvienne. In current brochures, this school is referred to as the Alvienne Academy, School of Theatre and Stock Company. It is asserted that "the Alvienne was one of the first leading Dramatic Schools to introduce the stock theatre system for production experience." [7] Although an early catalog describes the school as "a co-educational institution dedicated to the promotion of expression arts and culture," the idea of professional training was apparently uppermost.[8] It should be noted that courses during its early years included stage dancing, vaudeville, and instrumental music, and Mrs. Alvienne states that the fundamental emphasis at the school has always been professional.

The National Dramatic Conservatory was founded in New York in 1898 by F. F. Mackay, character actor since 1863 at such famous theatres as the Arch Street in Philadelphia, the Globe in Boston and the Union Square in New York. Mackay taught at the conservatory until a few months before his death in 1923, at the age of ninety-one. His work was certainly directed toward professional theatre participation, and his book on acting technique, long regarded as a standard, still has much of interest for the actor of today.

In 1900, the Stanhope-Wheatcroft Dramatic School in New York conducted private and class lessons in practical theatre subjects, and was clearly interested in the professional careers of its students. Alfred Ayres, well-known as a critic and writer on acting as well as a teacher, offered instruction in dramatic art and elocution. The actress, Rose Eytinge, prepared pupils for "stage, platform, pulpit and parlor."

One highly specialized school was the American School of Playwriting, conducted by William T. Price, critic and writer on playwriting. Later New York schools for actors included the Theodora Irvine Studio and the Alberti School, both well known for professional coaching.

Other early schools emphasizing professional theatrical training include the Hart Conway School of Acting in Chicago, affiliated with Chicago Musical College, later conducted by J. H. Gilmour; and also in Chicago, the Alden School of Acting. The Edwin Forrest School of Dramatic Arts in Philadelphia was directed by Robert C. McGee; the department of Dramatic Art of the Hayward School of Cincinnati was managed by Thomas Jefferson Wheatley, formerly of the Daly Company; the Robert Hickman Dramatic School was operated in Washington, D. C.

Mrs. Bessie V. Hicks, well known as an actress in her native Philadelphia, founded a School of Dramatic Arts under her name in 1919, and was its active director until her death in 1951. Mrs. Hicks believed in the encouragement and development of stage talent in young people, a policy continued by the present administrator of the school, John A. Bowman. The practical application of principles is stressed in radio, television and theatre courses. In a recent interview, Mr. Bowman pointed out that although the school offers many courses not designed for professional theatre aspirants, the practical vocational aspects of the program continue to be a chief concern of the school. Again, opportunities for professional placement are provided. In 1946, the school was reorganized as a nonprofit institution, the American Foundation of Dramatic Arts, but is still identified as the Bessie V. Hicks School of Dramatic Arts.

The Dauphin School of Arts in Philadelphia was not founded until 1928, later than the period being considered, but its inception was somewhat earlier, and stemmed directly from pioneering work in commercial radio broadcasting. The professional nature of the school is indicated by the recent statement that "courses are designed to enable the student to establish himself without delay in his chosen field of art." [9] Mariam Howlett, director of the school, is herself a teacher of dramatic art, music, and dance.

Almost at the end of the period, a professional school was founded which was to begin a "movement" of importance in theatrical training. During the season of 1922-1923, the Moscow Art Theatre appeared in New York with a considerable repertory and a company which included its leading players. Within a year, Richard Boleslavsky, trained at the Moscow Art Theatre, was in the American theatrical capital announcing the opening of the Laboratory Theatre School, the aim of which was the founding of "a Creative Theatre in America." (Capitals not mine.) The Laboratory Theatre combined a school and a working theatre, with all students, in addition to scheduled courses, taking part in every production. The theatrical invasion was on in full force, and Stanislavsky and Nemirovich-Danchenko soon became easier to pronounce than Booth and Belasco. An advertising page in a drama magazine, otherwise filled with theatrical announcements, prominently displayed an advertisement of a Russian restaurant, with appropriate food and music. Russian fare, artistic and culinary, was about to become a regular part of the menu.

Stock Company Schools

Several instances are found of schools which were operated in connection with regularly producing commercial theatres. These are, of course, clearly professional schools, but are unlike any thus far considered. The formation of schools in connection with such professional theatres comes late in our period.

Among the best known of these was the Henry Jewett School of Acting operated in conjunction with the Boston Repertory Theatre. Mr. and Mrs. Henry Jewett directed a professional repertory company at the Copley Theatre from 1916 to 1924. The Jewetts obtained sufficient support to build their own playhouse, which opened in November, 1925. In the new theatre, a school of acting, design, and playwriting was conducted.

The Detroit Civic Theatre, under the management of Jessie Bonstelle, had its inception in regular commercial stock. Reorganized as a civic, nonprofit enterprise, it operated a theatrical training school as well. The Stock Company of the old and honorable Elitch's Gardens in Denver, founded in 1893, also operated a school from time to time.

The School of the Theatre of the Threshold Playhouse in New York was founded by Mrs. Clare Tree Major in 1921. The stock type of experience was anticipated for students before their graduation. By 1923, Mrs. Major was placing much emphasis on the professional production of plays for children, a field in which her companies have gained reputation.

The Mae Desmond School of the Theatre in Philadelphia was derived from a professional theatre group, the Mae Desmond Players, who were well known in Philadelphia, in other Eastern cities, and on the road. The School, founded by Miss Desmond and her associates in 1938, in recent years has been combined with a professional company which tours with plays for children.

The Washington Square Players and the Theatre Guild also were briefly in the school business. Whether these and the other stock company schools have had any great effect on the teaching of theatre art in America is impossible to say. It is likely that the theatres have been more important than the schools in their impact on our theatrical scene.

Schools of Expression

Many of the institutions first known as schools of Expression or Oratory cannot be excluded from this study. The widespread interest in mastery of the spoken word and the expressive body is amply illustrated by the numerous schools and private teachers of expression, by the great popularity of platform reading, by the inevitable "reader" in Chautauqua and other lyceum circuits, by journals devoted to the subject, by associations and conferences of elocutionists and "expressionists." The files of *Werner's Magazine* from 1892 to 1902 show the extent and diversity of these "expression" activities. Many teachers and directors of dramatic art, of amateur groups in particular but of professionally oriented organizations as well, were graduates of the schools of expression. Professional theatre training came to be an important and even a major aim of their programs.

The study of oratory and expression was not, in 1900, any innovation in American education. Indeed, it had gained a place of widely recognized importance. Boston was for many decades the center of instruction for this kind of training, and three Boston schools were particularly important—Emerson College of Oratory, the School of Expression, and the Leland Powers School of the Spoken Word.

As Edythe May Renshaw points out, the founders of these schools—Charles Wesley Emerson, Samuel Silas Curry, and Leland Powers—were all students of Prof. L. B. Monroe at Boston University School of Oratory.[10] Franklin H. Sargent, founder of the American Academy of Dramatic Arts, was also one of Monroe's pupils. Monroe was interested in the theories of Delsarte and Steele MacKaye, and was well known as a platform reader.

In 1880, Charles Wesley Emerson founded the school first known as the Boston College of Oratory, renamed the next year as the Monroe Conservatory of Oratory in honor of Emerson's former teacher. By 1886, the conservatory was incorporated as the Monroe College of Oratory and had a faculty of a dozen teachers. In 1890, the name was again changed, this time to Emerson College of Oratory, by which title it was known for almost forty years. In 1889, Henry Laurence Southwick, known for many years as a lecturer and interpreter of Shakespeare, joined Emerson in the administration of the school. Mrs. Jessie Eldridge Southwick and William Howland Kenny became officers of the institution. On Emerson's retirement in 1903, William James Rolfe, Shakespearean scholar and writer, became the second president, to be succeeded by Southwick in 1908. President Southwick held the post until his death in 1932. The college gradually moved in the direction of formal academic recognition. A four-year course was established in 1913; the right to confer the degree of Bachelor of Literary Interpretation was granted by the Massachusetts legislature in 1919. The B.L.I. from Emerson soon became familiar in the profession of speech arts teaching. In 1936, the college was granted the privilege of awarding the B.A. degree; the M.A. degree was added in 1941. In 1939, the phrase "of Oratory" was deleted from the title, and from then on the school has been officially known simply as Emerson College.

Current Emerson College publications acknowledge and reassert some of the fundamental theories of its founder—his conviction that the power of oral expression transcends any practical use to which it may be put, his aim to develop personality and character as well as speech, his belief in education through self-development. The liberal arts aspects of the program are today similar to those of most American colleges. Particular fields of concentration in this specialized institution are now Broadcasting (Radio and Television), Drama, and Speech. Many courses are of a practical, vocational nature, and the workshop kind of experience is provided in each field. This is to be noted not only in the regular college, but in the numerous courses of the evening extension division. The college places considerable emphasis on teacher training, but is also clearly interested in the placement of its graduates in the professional theatre. A recent pamphlet, for example, points out the high proportion of the graduates of the radio division now professionally employed. Emerson College began as a school of oratory and expression; it has become a degree-granting institution, although still a specialized one. But it has been a professional theatre school as well.

Samuel Silas Curry succeeded Lewis B. Monroe as Professor of Oratory at Boston University. His assumption of this post and his conducting of private classes may be said to comprise the informal founding of the School of Expression. Three years later Curry married Anna

Baright, who was already conducting her own School of Elocution and Expression. Their classes were merged, and a prospectus was issued the next year. Thus was begun the institution to be known for fifty years as the School of Expression. The stated aim of its founder was "to supply to all who use the voice, a course of instruction in all branches of Expression as scientific and thorough as can be found in any phase of education." Curry continued to hold his position at Boston University until 1888, but from then until his death in 1921, he was the active head of the School of Expression. The School acknowledges the encouragement, during the years of Curry's administration, of many prominent people. Dr. Curry was himself a minister, and among the patrons of the school were several well-known churchmen of Boston and other cities. Others who have been cited include Henry N. Hudson, Alexander Graham Bell, Alexander Melville Bell, Charles W. Eliot, William Dean Howells, and Joseph Jefferson. Like Emerson College, the School of Expression became a degree-granting institution; in 1939, the Commonwealth of Massachusetts granted the School the right to award the degrees of Bachelor of Science and Master of Science in Oratory. The name was changed to Curry School, and since 1943 it has been officially designated as Curry College. In 1952, the college was moved from Commonwealth Avenue in Boston to a campus in nearby Milton.

The list of graduates who have become speech and drama educators and theatre performers is a long one. Recent course offerings show subject matter concentrations in Speech, Stage Arts, and Radio, many of a vocational nature. The interests of Curry College, the onetime School of Expression, have not been far removed from professional theatre practice.

Still another Boston institution of wide reputation is the Leland Powers School, which has followed a pattern quite different from that of Emerson College and Curry College. It has become a completely professional school. The school was founded in 1904 by Leland Powers and his wife, Carol Hoyt Powers. Leland Powers had been a student of Monroe and had later taught with both Emerson and Curry. He was highly regarded as a platform reader, especially of the impersonated play; he was an artist with the Redpath Lyceum Bureau for many years. Mrs. Powers was a graduate of Emerson School and a member of the Emerson faculty. She was also a professional platform reader, and well known as a teacher of Bible reading. The purpose of the school at its founding was training in the "Art of Expression through the Spoken Word." Indeed, it was first called a "School of the Spoken Word." According to Haven W. Powers, now Principal of the school, students were trained for both the professional and educational fields.[11] He states that at present most graduates prepare for a professional career.

Mr. Haven Powers observes that the basic teachings and policy of the school have remained the same. Certain fundamental courses are now required of all students, such as the Speaking Voice, Diction, Expressive Movement, Literary Interpretation, and Philosophy of Expression. Course descriptions indicate that the books of Leland Powers are still the primary texts for some of these courses. However, the school has been alert to change with changing theatre forms. It became a School of Theatre and Radio, and now is known as a School of Radio, Television, and Theatre. It provides facilities for practice in production, and most of the courses in the two-year curriculum are planned for vocational theatre training.

Many members of the faculty of the Powers school have been professionals in some form of theatre practice. Among these have been Leland Powers and Carol Hoyt Powers, Rachel Noah France, Phidelah Rice, Elizabeth Pooler Rice, Maude Scheerer, John Craig, Arthur Holman, and Alan Mowbray, known as readers, actors, or directors. Today the president of the corporation of the school is Moroni Olsen, actor, producer, and director. A long list of recent graduates now engaged in theatre work attests to the interest of the school in professional placement. Leland Powers School, then, founded as a "School of the Spoken Word," has had an active interest from the first in professional theatre training. Today it is definitely a professional school.

As has already been indicated, interest in expression, oratory, the spoken word—call it what we may—was widespread. During the early years of the period being considered, many schools other than those in the "Hub" of expression are to be noted. A few examples will here suffice. The New York School of Expression directed by F. Townsend Southwick and Genevieve Stebbins, the Columbia College of Expression in Chicago, the Hayward School of Expression and Dramatic Art in Cincinnati, the Greeley School of Elocution and Dramatic Art in Boston, and the Morse School of Expression in St. Louis—these and many others were conducting training which was in part planned for aspirants to the theatrical profession.

Community Theatre and Art Theatre Schools

A considerable number of the producing organizations of that part of the theatre somewhat patronizingly called "Off-Broadway" or "Tributary Theatre" developed schools as an integral part of their organization. Nearly all of these community or art theatres were started before the terminal date of this investigation, but did not form schools until after 1925. Some began as amateur organizations during a period of protest against the alleged evils of the commercial theatre; others sought as amateurs to provide dramatic fare to communities bereft by the near-disappearance of local stock companies and the decline of the road. As they achieved stability and success, they acquired buildings and real estate and found themselves in the professional or near-professional theatre business. It is true that the schools attached to these organizations were not functioning until after 1925. However, the parent theatres were well within our period, and the prominence which some of them achieved, not only as theatres but as highly successful schools, may warrant at least brief acknowledgment here.

The Cleveland Playhouse began under the guidance of Raymond O'Neill as an amateur producing society in 1916. It made its first step toward professionalization in 1921, when Frederic McConnell assumed direction. His work gave rise to regular productions by a professional company and to the building of an excellent theatre plant. Another result of his efforts was the formation of a school for instruction in all branches of theatre art. For a number of years, the Playhouse has also conducted classes and a theatre program as a part of the Chautauqua summer program. As theatre and school, the Cleveland Playhouse has achieved high repute.

The Goodman Theatre was established in Chicago by the Chicago Art Institute with the aid of a gift from Mr. and Mrs. William O. Goodman in 1924. Thomas Wood Stevens left Carnegie Institute to direct the theatre. Organization of a theatre school was an early development. B. Iden Payne and Whitford Kane soon joined the staff. Under the later direction of Maurice Gnesin, the Goodman Theatre School has continued to maintain high standards as an institution for training in theatre.

In Califor   , the Pasadena Community Playhouse was founded in 1917 by Gilmor Brown. Mr. Brown is still the Supervising Director; Charles F. Prickett, now the Executive Vice-President, has been associated with Brown in the playhouse enterprise since 1918. This long and highly successful partnership has resulted in a community theatre and school, excellently housed and well staffed. In 1927 and 1928, the Playhouse conducted summer sessions in conjunction with the University of California Extension Division. It began its own school on a year round basis in the fall of 1928.

Another interesting theatre and school was that founded by Miss Nellie Cornish in Seattle in 1918. Its inclusion in this section is perhaps inappropriate, for it was the outgrowth of the School of the Arts, including Music and Dance, which Miss Cornish had begun in 1914. According to Miss Cornish, theatre was added to the program of the school with the specific object of giving the ballet pupils a theatre background.[12] But for many years the Cornish School served as a community theatre for Seattle, with regular productions of modern and classical plays. In pleasant and efficient housing, the Cornish Theatre was a definite part of the cultural life of the city. Performers included staff members, advanced students, and occasional guests. Among the well-known members of the faculty were Maurice Browne, Ellen Van Volkenburg, Moroni Olsen, Burton and Florence James, Herbert Gellendre, Jacques Mercier, and Alexander Koiransky. Miss Cornish retired from her position as director of the School in 1939. Soon thereafter, theatre instruction was dropped from the program of the school. But for almost twenty-five years, the Cornish Theatre had provided theatre training of professional calibre.

New York City has not furnished fertile ground for the flowering of the community or art theatre type of school. Such schools have appeared from time to time; they have usually had exciting but short lives. One of the most successful and the hardiest of these is The Neighborhood Playhouse School of the Theatre. The Neighborhood Playhouse began as an amateur diversion at the Henry Street Settlement. Under the patronage and guidance of Alice and Irene Lewisohn, it soon became a professional company, appearing in a varied repertoire during the years from 1915 to 1927. Although the company conducted classes in speech, movement, and allied arts, teaching was always related to the problems of specific performances. In 1927, the Lewisohns gave up their producing at The Neighborhood Playhouse on Grand Street, and turned it over officially to the Henry Street Settlement.

Doris Fox Benardete has assessed the work of the 1915-1927 period in a detailed study.[13] In 1928, the Lewisohns established the School of the Theatre in an uptown location. Whereas the older organization was a producing theatre, the new one was a theatre school from the first. The school is now directed by Rita Wallach Morgenthau; the faculty includes Martha Graham, Sanford Meisner, and Paul Morrison. According to a recent publication, "the curriculum is based on the professional experience of The Neighborhood Playhouse in its years of experimental productions—productions which reflected the concept of theatre as an organic expression of life interpreted through a fusion of the arts." [14] Its courses in Movement, Acting, Make-up, and Voice are planned for the aspirant to professional theatre work.

Another form of theatre enterprise should at least be mentioned here, though the principal development did not occur until the 1930's. The summer theatres—amateur, semi-professional and professional—often conducted schools as well as theatres. Usually for a fee, these companies offered instruction and training in acting, staging, and management. Though sometimes abused, this apprenticeship system of professional education has no doubt given valuable experience to many beginners.

Colleges and Universities

Although theatre instruction in colleges and universities is beyond the scope of this study, one must recognize that in a few institutions, theatre training took a professional turn. Usually beginning as extra-curricular activity or as a minor part of academic work in departments of English, theatre work in many institutions has moved strongly in the direction of professional training. Among the colleges and universities supplying special theatre training and experience before 1925 were Wisconsin, North Dakota, North Dakota State, North Carolina, New York University, Iowa, Northwestern, Washington, Cornell, and Harvard. There were others, of course. As courses multiplied and became intensive, theatre education and production in such institutions had mixed aims—partly informational and cultural, partly professional. Yale's Department of Drama, established in 1925 with George Pierce Baker as head, attracted many students with definite professional aspirations.

Unique among the colleges engaged in theatre work is Carnegie Institute of Technology in Pittsburgh. The Department of Drama there, opened in February, 1914, with an incomplete theatre and eighteen students, had a strongly professional purpose from the first. According to Elizabeth Kimberley, Assistant Head of the Drama Department, "it rendered a pioneering service in this country by recognizing the theatre as an art which demanded of its practitioners the same type of systematic and progressive technical training and the cultural background demanded of workers in other arts." [15] This purpose is still held. Unlike other pioneers in the university theatre field, Thomas Wood Stevens was able to provide a complete four-year degree curriculum in Theatre and Allied Arts at once and to have the use of a building and equipment designed to carry out its purposes. Carnegie was a technical institute; the new department became a division of the School of Applied Design. As Stevens wrote soon after his theatre opened, "Carnegie Institute had already established a four-year course to the B.A. degree, with a long list of general studies, severe training in technical practice, and an emphasis on the cultural as well as the scientific—an appreciation and historical knowledge as well as an application of paint to canvas." [16] The curriculum shows many courses which were professional or vocational in nature. Under Stevens and later B. Iden Payne and Chester Wallace, and with a faculty including Woodman Thompson, Theodore Viehman, and Alexander Wyckoff, Carnegie's school of theatre soon became a training and proving ground for professionally minded students. Many of its graduates are leaders in some aspect of theatre and today nine-tenths of its students are headed for professional theatre work. It can surely be considered a professional theatre school; the same might well be said of some other university departments of later years.

IV

A general view of the courses taught in the professional schools from 1900-1925 can be sketched adequately by focusing upon course listings of the American Academy of Dramatic Arts. Complete catalogs and course descriptions are on file, and have been made available for study.

In 1900, the curriculum in the first, or Junior, year of the two-year course was divided into three parts, referred to under the titles of Action, Diction, and Stage Work. "Action" courses were given in Physical Training, Dancing, Pantomime, Fencing, and Life Studies; "Diction" consisted of work in Vocal Training, Phonetics, Vocal Expression, English Language, and Dramatic Literature; "Stage Work" included Stage Mechanics, Makeup, Costuming, Playwriting, Art Decoration, Stage Business, Stage Rehearsals, and Performances. The first year was known as the Technical Training School. The second, or Senior, year was devoted to advanced classroom studies, rehearsal of practice plays, and the production of plays by class members. The work apparently proceeded from study and practice of basic techniques to their application and use in production.

The courses at Mackay's School in 1900 included Vocal Gymnastics, Technique of Speech, Dancing, Fencing, Swedish Gymnastics, Analysis of Emotions, Reading and Rehearsing of Plays, and General and Dramatic Literature. Another dramatic school offered Acting, Recitation, Voice Production, and Fencing among its courses. At about the same time, a perhaps typical school of Oratory was giving courses in Elocution, Oratory, Physical Culture, Voice Culture, Rhetoric, Psychology, Literature, and (under the Bell influence) Visible Speech. Another school listed studies in the fields of Oratory, Physical Culture, Literature, and Dramatic Art. A School of Expression offered courses in Oratory, Voice Culture, Breathing, Physical Culture, Dancing, and Fencing, and observed that stammering and defective speech were positively corrected. Titles of the courses above suggest that the schools gave emphasis to the technical training of voice and body.

From 1900 to 1925, courses at the American Academy did not greatly vary. In 1910, new courses appeared in Dramatic Reading and Dramatic Analysis, dealing with the development of the imagination and individual creative powers. These courses were grouped in a separate

Department of Conception. No playwriting course was offered. Bulletins for 1910 make a strong point of the production of standard dramatic works of various periods, such as Maeterlinck, Jonson, Goldoni, Congreve, Ibsen, Shaw, Rostand, Echegaray, Strindberg, Tolstoi, and Shakespeare. Other schools similarly show few changes.

At its beginning in 1914, the Department of Drama at Carnegie Institute of Technology required the study of Dramatic Literature, French, History of Theatre, Drawing, Scene Design, Costume, Dancing, Diction. Rehearsal and Performance and a strong fourth-year theatre specialization. Among its courses in 1916, the Columbia College of Expression included Platform Presentation, Interpretative Dancing, and Festival and Pageantry.

In 1920, the American Academy bulletins show considerable rearrangement, but no important changes in course offerings. An Alvienne School publication of about this date shows an organization of courses somewhat similar to that of the American Academy. The Alvienne curriculum was divided into two departments, Technical and Expressional. The Technical Department courses included Physical Training (Health, Posture, Gesture, Fencing, and Dancing), Voice Training (Breath Control, Diction, Resonance, Phonetics), and Stage Training (Business, Costume, Make-up). The Expressional Department courses were in Physical Expression (Pantomime, Life Study, Characterization), Oral Expression (Interpretation, Delivery, Line Reading, Dialects), and Theatre Practice (Rehearsals, Productions). The Columbia College of Expression in 1921 listed courses in Voice Development, Selection of Plays, Pantomime, Modern Drama, Interpretation of Prose and Poetry, Directing, Stage Decoration, Costume Design, and Community Drama.

Cornish School in Seattle in 1922 was teaching Voice and Diction, Phonetics, Play Reading, Pantomime, Dalcroze Eurythmics, Dancing, Fencing, Music and Art Appreciation, Costume and Scene Design, Make-up, and Play Rehearsal and Performance. Among its courses in 1921, the Morse School of Expression in St. Louis listed Physical Training, Story Telling, Vocal Expression, Dramatic Art, Stage Technique, and (with an apparent bow to Percy MacKaye whose Civic Masque had been produced in St. Louis in 1914) Pageantry. The Grace Hickox Studios in Chicago offered such courses as Expression and Dramatic Art, Dalcroze Eurythmics, Story Telling, Playwriting, and Stagecraft. Other school announcements show an interest in Children's Dramatics, Pageantry, and Community Drama.

Again in 1925, bulletins of the American Academy showed few changes in course offerings. Summer courses for teachers were being advertised, based on the regular curriculum, and several courses had already been given under the auspices of the Extension Division of Columbia University. By 1925, the "Art Theatres" were engaged in teaching, usually by informal workshop methods, but with specific courses like Dancing, Music, Choral Speech, Diction, and Stagecraft. As has been already noted, Boleslavsky had begun his Laboratory Theatre School in 1923, under the announced workshop plan of active participation in all phases of production.

Many of the courses offered in 1900 are still being taught today, sometimes under slightly different titles. The nature and direction of change in the quarter-century are signified by such courses as Dalcroze Eurythmics, Community Drama, Pageantry, and Children's Theatre. The Dalcroze system was becoming known in America; the "Little Theatre movement" had begun and was growing; community drama had been encouraged by the work of Percy MacKaye and national and local cultural societies. There is, toward the end of the period, greater emphasis on staging rather than acting. This, too, might well be expected, as new ideas were being brought into theatre by the designers and directors. Although the professional schools seem to have held to many of the theories of their founders, they made changes to suit new conditions.

V

The listing of courses taught may have some interest but little meaning, for courses with the same title can well be taught with quite opposing aims. The theories held by teachers of acting are accordingly a matter of valid concern. Some categorizing of the underlying ideas of the teachers of acting at about 1900 must be attempted, although the classification of methods of acting cannot be iron bound. In actual practice, it is likely that most good teachers used a combination of methods.

First, the successful professional actors who became teachers seem to comprise one group. It must be remembered that the typical nineteenth-century organization was that of the stock company, with long runs the exception. Actors were expected to maintain a repertory of standard parts and to be able to prepare new roles on short notice and with little rehearsal. This meant that good actors were required to develop skills, graces, and accomplishments which could be easily transferred from one role to another. In experience and training, young actors were presented with graded tasks, increasing in difficulty, until they could be entrusted with important roles. Following the advice and example of their preceptors, they sought to master the methods established by experience and tradition. The good actor became a master of audience effect, fully able to create the semblance of emotion through controlled voice and body symbols clearly understood by theatre-goers.

Many stage managers and master actors were able to transmit their theories, derived from experience, to their pupils. It is likely that Boucicault, always a master of stage effect, was a pragmatic and practical teacher of acting. George Vandenhoff was probably another teacher of the same kind. His book on elocution, in considering such matters as articulation, pause, inflection, emphasis, and intonation, is full of definite examples.[17] F. F. Mackay's textbook on acting of a later period is replete with exact advice about specific roles and the problems inherent in the acting and presentation of certain plays.[18] Mackay insists, too, on the thorough control of emotions and passions. There was nothing esoteric about the theories of these actor-teachers; communication of the playwright's intentions in understandable terms was their primary aim. Their teaching methods, however, fell into disfavor; perhaps imitation became the principal means of instruction. It is certain that when reasons for action are forgotten, when problem solving is left out of the teaching process, sound and fury signifying nothing are the eventual result. Whatever the reason, the traditional techniques of training for the stage came to be regarded as stilted and artificial.

Some teachers became dissatisfied with the established methods. James Rush was one of the first who attempted to develop a new system of instruction in voice and elocution. He is the principal exemplar of a second group, the exponents of a "scientific" method. He studied the physical aspects of speech, and sought to establish sound, scientific bases for instruction. Virgil A. Anderson has recently pointed out Rush's importance as a teacher, particularly of voice:

Speech teachers in general and voice scientists in particular owe more to Rush than is usually acknowledged, because he not only pioneered in applying the scientific method to the study of voice and speech production but also offered a sound approach and keen observations to demonstrate that the expressive action of the voice can be described, if not explained, in relatively precise, objective terminology. In a day when teaching was done largely by precept, "hunch," and imitation, Rush did much to establish speech and voice training upon a firm basis.[19]

As Anderson notes further, Rush had a great influence upon a number of well-known and influential teachers.

James E. Murdoch, famous actor-teacher, was an adherent to the theories of Rush, and no doubt was more responsible than any other individual for introducing them into the teaching of acting. Other influences on Murdoch perhaps modified his use of Rush's doctrines. He was a pupil of the elocutionist and teacher, Lemuel White, known for his emphasis on *emphasis,* lessons in which were apparently never forgotten by his onetime student, Edwin Forrest. Murdoch was a successful stage performer. As an elocutionist and reader, he entertained the troops during the Civil War, some eighty years before Charles Laughton provided the same kind of one-man entertainment for the G.I.'s of World War II. The success of modern readers like Laughton and Emlyn Williams who browse in the long green pastures of the platform derives from a rediscovery of an old and honorable branch of the actor's art. Murdoch was also a distinguished leading man on the stage; his practice could not have been too much different from that of his contemporaries. The Rush-Murdoch "scientific" school, however, met the fate which seems to be in store for most systems, and itself came to be regai led as mechanical and "unnatural."

Those teachers who objected to the so-called scientific method adopted a considerably different point of view. To quote Anderson again:

> These individuals were in the vanguard of the inspirational or "think-the-thought" school of elocution. The contention of this school was that if the voice is only left free, it will respond naturally to the inner dictates of thought and feeling. The main concern was to free the voice, as a part of total bodily expression, as a medium for an outward manifestation of inward activity. Little formal voice training was believed necessary.[20]

The influence of this theory on elocution and stage training from 1900 to 1925, and today for that matter, seems beyond question.

A belief in man's possession of inherent qualities which, by proper training, can be freed for the purpose of full expression was crucial to this group of teachers of acting and allied forms of communication. Most important among them were the founders of the three Boston schools—Curry, Emerson, and Powers. Although their theories, which they expressed in many books, articles, and lectures, were not identical, many beliefs in common can be observed.

It was probably no accident that Boston was the center of this school of expressional philosophy and practice. Faith in man's inner power was congenial to New England transcendentalists. Monroe, teacher of the founders of the Boston schools, was regarded as a transcendentalist. The religious bent, always present and apparent in elocution teaching, was being intensified by the deep interest in the "revelations" of Swedenborg; Monroe was also interested in Swedenborgianism. The mysticism inherent in much of Delsarte's teaching was not difficult for the Boston teachers to accept, although many aspects of his "system" were rejected. Man was regarded as possessed of great, God-given powers. The freeing of these powers by training was to be the task of teachers of expression.

One of the best known of S. S. Curry's many books was *Mind and Voice,* but he appeared to have been more interested in mind than voice. Some of Curry's statements in another book may be of interest here:

As the leaf manifests the life at the root of the tree; as the bobolink's song is the outflow of a full heart; so all expression obeys the same law; it comes FROM WITHIN OUTWARD, from the centre to the surface, from a hidden source to outward manifestation. However deep the life, it reveals itself by natural signs.

Expression in man is governed by the same law. Every action of face or hand, every modulation of voice, is simply an outward effect of an inward condition. Any motion that is otherwise is not expression.[21]

Curry goes on to criticize any manipulation from without, any imitation. Such methods he regards as artificial and mechanical. The voice and body, through misuse and bad habit, are unable to respond freely to the inner impulse. It is the function of training, he asserts, to create conditions for natural expression. Exercises, he says, may be technical or psychic. Both are needed, but the psychic (or specific practice of that mental action which tends to cause the right expressive action) is safer for individual or class use. Most important to Curry were mind and spirit, particularly mind; but technical systems of training must be devised for mind to function properly. He gave some credit to other systems of training, but in general rejected them, including the Delsartian, as invalid. His own methods of training became highly detailed and, to the uninitiated, seem complex.

Charles Wesley Emerson, too, believed in the mental and spiritual basis of expression. He maintained that man is capable of self-improvement, that such self-improvement must start from within. Voice and body express the soul, he held; but he too developed complicated theories of training and technical drills and exercises. He used also some body training based on Delsarte. Mechanical perfection, however, was not the aim, but always the mental and spiritual.

Leland Powers seems to have been a mystic and a transcendentalist; he strongly believed in man's possession of all needful power and knowledge. To evoke man's power should be the principal task of the teacher of expression. He shared the view that voice training was a matter of "freeing," and developed a set of principles and training methods for the purpose. Powers accepted the "trinities" of Delsarte, and many of Delsarte's ideas and methods. He acknowledged this, but noted changes in his own use of them.

The followers of Delsarte might be regarded as another group which had great influence during much of the period from 1900 to 1925. Steele MacKaye, near-genius in all aspects of theatre practice, became an enthusiastic adherent of the "natural acting" theories of François Delsarte, with whom he had studied in Paris. Delsarte, too, believed in the actor's inner powers, and in the trinity of man as mental, physical, and spiritual. His theory of "trinity" led him to develop an intricate system of training and exercises. His theory of the control of muscles to create emotional states was later carried to the point of excess and consequent ridicule. These principles and practices of Delsarte, MacKaye promoted in the United States with persuasive zeal. Though already being discredited, Delsarte's ideas were still strongly held by many teachers of acting during the 1900-1925 period.

The last clearly identifiable class of teachers of acting consists of those who followed the example of the Moscow Art Theatre and the principles enunciated by Constantin Stanislavsky. These theories were derived from long practice and were apparently intended for the use of a mature, disciplined company, but were soon ardently and hopefully studied by many amateurs and some professionals in America. Stanislavsky's idea of emotional recall and his emphasis on mood and ensemble playing seemed fresh and original. Stanislavsky and his colleagues were certainly fine, expert actors who knew their craft and art, both of which they sought to enrich. The high reputation of the actors, directors and writers associated with the Moscow Art Theatre gave ready authority to the adherents of the so-called Stanislavsky "method" of acting. The influence of the Moscow Art Theatre was not important until the end of our period.

From the beginning of the quarter-century, performances of plays were a part of the program of the professional schools, although probably to exhibit the results of actor training. But the center of interest began to shift away from the actor. As the theories of Craig and Appia became known, there was an increasing concern with the production aspects of theatre. Art theatres, amateur drama groups, little magazines for advanced thinkers encouraged the "movement." Reinhardt's spectacles needed space and machinery, not skilled performers. Community historical pageants, popularized by Percy MacKaye, needed livestock and live Indians, not trained actors. The director was coming to be regarded as the major interpreter of the dramatist. The appearance of a new group of interesting and important playwrights after World War I operated still further to turn interest away from the actor. More and more, theatrical criticism ignored, or nearly ignored the actor. All the emphasis on "naturalness" of script and production mistakenly led to inadequacy of training for the individual. The old actor practiced more and rehearsed less than his modern counterpart. At present, the actor is likely to practice little, and rehearse to the point of exhaustion. But from the standpoint of the actor-artist and his teachers, good ensemble is not enough. The individual actor still needs training.

The professional schools probably did not turn as far away from the problems of the actor as did amateur organizations. They still worked with individuals who paid the bills, and who wanted to develop the skills to get and hold professional jobs. And it is unlikely that any such school altogether neglected the individual for the group. The curricula and organization of the schools, however, do reflect the changing theatrical world.

Franklin H. Sargent, in the 1899 article about the American Academy of Dramatic Art, wrote: "The School followed plans suggested by the Paris Conservatoire, modified by methods of German schools, and to a lesser extent, the Italian and English ways of stage education." [22] Elsewhere, Sargent indicated his interest in Delsarte, and Steele MacKaye was associated with the Academy in its formative years. We know, too, that Sargent was a student of Monroe in Boston. These observations are not meant to imply that Sargent did not know what he was doing; but they do suggest that he was ready to use theories and methods from many sources. This pragmatic approach may have been characteristic of the teaching of theatre in the first quarter of the twentieth century. It has been shown that some schools followed the old "professional" approach, that others looked to Delsarte for inspiration, that the schools of "expression" continued to adhere to the principal theories of their founders, that the influence of the Moscow Art Theatre became noticeable at the end of the period.

To discover what specific methods teachers actually used in the classroom or rehearsal hall has not been possible on the basis of the available material. There was formal instruction, individual and group, in separate subjects. Play rehearsals and completed productions were a part of training during our entire period, though it has been noted that the "work-shop" plan increased in use. Practical experience was stressed from the first. More information would be needed, however, to make more than general declarations regarding the translation of theory into teaching method and technique.

Several dichotomies run through the theatre education conducted by the professional schools. Leaders and teachers of many schools believe in the innate, "natural" powers of the individual; they develop systematic methods of developing such powers. They believe in personality development and also in technical proficiency. The schools have alleged professional aims; they also assert that they can serve general educational purposes. They believe in art; they know that they are in business. Reconciliation of these discrete purposes is, of course, not impossible. It may not be impertinent to remark also, that these recurring problems are not peculiar to professional schools of acting and theatre. Each school and teacher has to face some of them, and solve them at least well enough to meet proper standards of integrity.

VI

In considering schools which purport to give training for professional work, it is pertinent to ask what happened to their graduates. Responses to this inquiry show considerable variation. A former officer of one reputable school no longer in operation replied that few students made the jump from "art to commerce"; another administrator answered that about a third of the students went into professional work, that another third became teachers and that the fate, however happy, of the rest was unknown; another observed that all but a tenth of its graduates went into some form of theatre activity. The visitor to any professional school will be readily provided with long lists of former students who have been or are employed in the theatrical profession. Even though such lists are prepared for publicity purposes, there is no reason to doubt their accuracy; many of the names mentioned are well known to American theatre-goers. Others, though not in lights, no doubt represent competent persons making a living in the theatre. There is always the implication that "you, too, can succeed"; the schools are proud of their distinguished graduates; their officials and teachers believe, of course, that their training has been helpful. They seek professional placement for their pupils. To make any allegation about a possible cause-and-effect relationship between the training in the schools and later professional employment would require long and controlled study, even if all data were available. In this sampling, no conclusions can be reached and no invidious comparisons made. But the evidence is impressive enough to provide support for the stated professional aims of the several schools. There seems to be little doubt that their graduates have made a definite impact on the American theatre of yesterday and today.

What of the professional schools today? Their present aims are still professional, although they offer many non-vocational courses. Curricula have been modified to suit new developments in the theatre business; courses in radio, television, and motion picture have largely supplanted those in vaudeville and platform reading. Some professional schools have become degree-granting colleges. Others which have not taken this step regard their offerings as capable of providing a satisfactory personal and professional education. Some hold firmly to the ideals and principles of their founders; others shift with the changing breezes of theatrical theory. The worst of them will be condemned, as in the past, for all the sins of opportunism; the best of them will continue to hold a respected and respectable place in education and theatre.

Notes

1. Franklin H. Sargent, "Stage Training," *Dramatic Studies*, II (April, 1899), 3-7.

2. Lester Wallack, *Memories of Fifty Years* (New York, 1889).

3. *The Stage Reminiscences of Mrs. Gilbert* (New York, 1901).

4. Frederick Warde, *Fifty Years of Make Believe* (New York, 1920).

5. Constance Morris, "Dion Boucicault's School of Acting," *Green Book*, VI (August, 1911), 401-407.

6. American Academy of Dramatic Arts *Bulletin* (1900).

7. Alvienne School *Bulletin* (1952).

8. Alvienne School *Bulletin*, n.d.

9. Dauphin School *Bulletin* (1952).

10. Edythe May Renshaw, "Three Schools of Speech," unpublished Ph.D. dissertation, Columbia Teachers College, 1950. In this excellent study of the three schools mentioned, the theories and methods of each are described and compared.

11. Letter from Haven W. Powers, March 2, 1953.

12. Letter from Miss Nellie Cornish, March 2, 1953.

13. Doris Fox Bernardete, "The Neighborhood Playhouse in Grand Street," unpublished Ph.D. dissertation, New York University, 1949.

14. Neighborhood Playhouse School of the Theatre *Bulletin* (1952).

15. Letter from Elizabeth Kimberly, March 17, 1953.

16. Thomas Wood Stevens, "A School of the Theatre Arts," *Drama*, IV (November, 1914), 635.

17. George Vandenhoff, *The Art of Elocution* (London, 1862).

18. F. F. Mackay, *The Art of Acting* (New York, 1913).

19. Virgil A. Anderson, "A Modern View of Voice and Diction," *QJS*, XXXIX (February, 1953), 27.

20. *Ibid.*

21. *Foundations of Expression* (Boston, 1920), p. 10.

22. Sargent, *op. cit.*, p. 5.

28 National Theatre Organizations and Theatre Education

WILLIAM P. HALSTEAD
CLARA BEHRINGER

....

Only in the United States and only during the twentieth century have educators accepted theatre training as subject matter for the academic curriculum. True, schools had officially produced plays earlier, but they had employed such production chiefly as a device for teaching other subjects—the Greek and Latin languages, the Bible, diction, literature. It follows naturally, then, that national organizations concerned with the pedagogy of theatre should first appear in this century and in America.

The succession of these organizations reflects the growth and change in theatre activity itself. In the early decades of the century, play production was extracurricular in most colleges and secondary schools; hence, the first national academic organizations exclusively concerned with theatre were honorary fraternities designed to give recognition to the participants in extracurricular productions.

Concurrently, theatre was creeping into the curriculum through the teaching of drama and "speech" in the English departments. Accordingly, the first educational association to take an interest in the curricular study of drama and in extracurricular activity in theatre was the National Council of Teachers of English.[1] Just as theatre training left the English departments along with speech training, so teachers of theatre became members of the National Association of Teachers of Speech when it organized in 1914 as a splinter group of the English association.[2] However, since neither of these organizations evidenced more than perfunctory interest in the teaching of theatre, they served only as transitional agencies; therefore, this chapter will discuss them only incidentally in relation to the associations subsequently organized.

For a number of years, NCTE and NATS satisfied the needs of teachers of theatre. However, as outstanding pioneers arose in the

641

educational and community theatre, they led their groups to a level of serious endeavor and technical excellence—a level which left theatre leaders unsatisfied with NATS Convention sections planned for the beginners and the untrained. They felt the need for smaller conferences with their peers; they achieved that objective in 1931 with the formation of the National Theatre Conference.

As increasing numbers of high schools and colleges admitted theatre work to the curriculum, more and more individuals were prepared for co-operative effort on a high level. NTC did not meet this need and opportunity by expanding its membership; NATS failed to recognize adequately the growth of this phase of speech work. Therefore the American Educational Theatre Association appeared in 1936 as an organization for co-operative effort in raising the standards of educational theatre and its status in the curriculum. Within the short life of AETA, curricular theatre has expanded tremendously, and a new emphasis on theatre research has appeared. The services of AETA reflect these trends.

Before the establishment of NTC and AETA, however, specialized groups had felt the need for sharing ideas and experiences not satisfied by the general conventions and publications of the NATS. The first association of Negro colleges emerged in 1930 to administer festivals and exchanges of plays. Similar specialized needs resulted in the organization of the Catholic Theatre Conference in 1937.

Space limits this discussion to organizations whose origins or present activities are primarily linked with schools. However, not even the most casual student of education would maintain that dissemination of information and stimulation of appreciation lie wholly within the province of educational institutions. Consequently, although their histories cannot be detailed, note must be taken here of three organizations and a magazine which performed important educational functions as a part of their concern with the American theatre as a whole. These include the Drama League of America, the American National Theatre and Academy, the Theatre Library Association, and the *Theatre Arts* magazine.

The Drama League was formed in 1910 as an association of theatregoers interested primarily in raising the standards of professional productions, and only secondarily in encouraging productions by nonprofessionals. As noncommercial productions increased in number and improved in quality and as the professional road and stock companies dwindled, the Drama League expanded its interest in the amateur theatre.

Similarly, when ANTA was chartered by the Congress in 1935 with the intention of operating one or more professional repertory theatres, the founders had no thought of the noncommercial theatre. But when ANTA finally became active in 1946, its interest included all types of theatre activity.

Organized in 1937, the TLA reflects the new emphasis on theatre research. Formed to encourage the establishment and growth of theatre collections in libraries and museums, TLA does not limit membership to college libraries, although a large proportion of the membership derives from collegiate institutions.

Throughout most of the period, *Theatre Arts* magazine, edited by Edith J. R. Isaacs and later Rosamond Gilder, reflected the changing attitude toward noncommercial theatre and gave important guidance and stimulation to the noncommercial as well as the commercial theatre.

This chapter provides a brief history of educational theatre organizations. Since this volume deals chiefly with the history of speech education only until about 1925, the emphasis is placed upon the initiation and formative years of each organization; the later development is sketched briefly except when significant changes took place. The organizations are discussed in the chronological order of their founding. When several organizations are treated together, the earliest founding date among the organizations determines the group's position in the chronology.

National Honor Fraternities and Societies

Of the national organizations interested exclusively in theatre, the first to take root in academic life were the national dramatic honor fraternities. The idea of honoring students for achievement in theatrical activity originated in the colleges, then spread to the high schools and junior colleges. Several organizations grew up, and although they differed in some ways, they showed marked similarities in scope, purpose, operation, and educational achievement.

The college honoraries emerged from two types of activity. Some sprang from college play producing units, either temporary or permanent; [3] others from the earlier professional societies and honorary fraternities of the several academic fields. [4]

Some of the professional and honorary fraternities specifically included dramatics as one of their areas of recognition. Zeta Phi Eta, a professional fraternity for women founded in 1893, encompassed both speech and drama, as did Phi Eta Sigma, begun in 1901 and later combined with Zeta Phi Eta. [5] Phi Alpha Tau, an honorary for public speakers and actors, followed in 1902, [6] and Phi Beta, a professional fraternity for women in music and drama, appeared in 1912. [7] Such

organizations have doubtless made contributions to drama education. Nevertheless, since they were not concerned exclusively with
drama, they do not fall within the compass of this study.

Three organizations comprise the college-level group of honoraries
concerned exclusively with the theatre field: National Collegiate
Players, Theta Alpha Phi, and Alpha Psi Omega.

The first of these, NCP, resulted from a combination of Associated
University Players and Pi Epsilon Delta, in 1922. Associated University Players originated in 1913 when Mask and Bauble, a producing
unit at the University of Illinois, promulgated the idea of a national
organization of university dramatic clubs. AUP established chapters
at the Universities of Ohio, Washington, and Oregon.[8]

Pi Epsilon Delta, the other component of NCP, began operating in a
capacity similar to AUP at the University of Wisconsin, June 8, 1919.
The founding students organized the fraternity because they felt the
need for recognizing distinction among upperclassmen in the dramatics
area.[9] Roy E. Holcombe served as the first president; Lawrence W.
Murphy, as the first vice-president. Murphy composed the ritual and
Frances Ellen Tucker designed the key. At the invitation of the charter
members,[10] faculty members joined PED;[11] one of these, Gertrude
Johnson, in the following years devoted so much time and effort to the
organization that it became identified with her. Members carried on
three types of activity designed to bring petitioners to the organization: campus visitations, initiation of visiting students and faculty
during summer sessions at Wisconsin, and colonization—institution of
chapters on different campuses by Wisconsin students who transferred
to them. These activities quickly established chapters at Washington
University (St. Louis), University of Minnesota, and Northwestern.[12]

When AUP and PED merged in 1922 they chose a non-Greek name
—National Collegiate Players—and designated chapters by numbers
rather than by Greek letters, but they accepted PED's objectives.[13]

These objectives, stated as purposes in the NCP Constitution, included representing the college and university in national movements
for the betterment and welfare of drama and theatre in the United
States, and raising the standards of college and university theatres by
recognizing the most worthy individual and group efforts in the creative arts of the theatre.[14]

How did the organization go about achieving these ends, and to
what extent was its activity beneficial educationally? NCP limited
membership to juniors and seniors and established a "B" average as a
requirement, thus furnishing incentive for better scholastic work.
Through a qualifying point system it provided motivation for increased and higher quality participation.[15] In 1924 NCP began publi-

cation of *Players Magazine,* an organ of collegiate theatre that has progressed from four to eight issues annually and has achieved international circulation.[16] Through it members are provided with the latest information on all phases of theatrical activity and with a medium for exchange of ideas with other NCP units.

Trailing the founding of AUP by six years and that of PED by six months, Theta Alpha Phi was organized at a meeting of the National Association of Teachers of Speech held in Chicago in December, 1919.[17] John R. Pelsma of Oklahoma A. and M. College was active in the founding.[18] Finding it difficult to induce students to accept bit roles and to participate in technical work, Pelsma conceived TAP to motivate a greater interest in all theatre activities.[19] At the organizational meeting, Charles Newcomb of Ohio Wesleyan University became the first national president.[20] Pelsma, who was elected secretary-treasurer, designed the pin and wrote the ritual.[21] Chapters instituted in 1919 include Oklahoma A. and M. and Ripon Colleges and Ohio Wesleyan, Louisiana, John B. Stetson, and Bucknell Universities.[22]

According to the constitution, the purposes of TAP are "to increase interest, stimulate creativeness, and foster artistic achievement in all of the allied arts and crafts of the theatre.[23]

The organization employed the following means to implement these purposes. It restricted membership to students of the sophomore, junior, and senior classes who fulfilled participation requirements in the acting, directing, writing, business or technical aspects of public production.[24] To facilitate the exchange of information, TAP began publication of *The Cue,* a quarterly magazine, in 1921 under the editorship of Pelsma.[25] The organization has sponsored annual conventions at which specialists in theatre lecture and meet with students for discussion of problems of the theatre worker.[26]

The youngest and largest of the three college dramatic honoraries is Alpha Psi Omega, founded August 12, 1925, at Fairmont State College, Fairmont, West Virginia. Desiring to establish an honor society for its theatre workers, the Masquers, Fairmont's dramatic club, applied to NCP and TAP for affiliation; neither application was accepted. NCP seemed to limit its roll to the major universities; TAP appeared to prefer liberal arts colleges as members; Fairmont was a teachers college.[27] The Masquers, under the guidance of Paul F. Opp, then set up Alpha Psi Omega as the local honorary. Interest among neighboring colleges called almost immediately for formation of a national organization.[28] Opp and E. Turner Stump of Marshall College composed the first drafts of constitution and ritual. They were the first national officers of the organization and continued as officers as late as 1952.[29]

In addition to Fairmont and Marshall, Washington and Lee and Acadia (Canada) established chapters during the founding year.[30]

The stated purposes of APO are to encourage student participation in college dramatics and to reward serious effort.[31]

Have these purposes elicited the same educational achievements cited for the other two collegiate dramatic fraternities? Like the others, APO has employed a publication, in this case *The Playbill,* to furnish information and the inspiration for intercollegiate contacts. Like them, it has established a qualifying system; however, this system requires that points be earned in technical fields as well as in acting, thus attempting to insure a rounded theatre experience. APO has attempted to raise the level of production among its member schools by empowering the national office to act as a service organization— performing such tasks as helping with the royalty problem and securing discounts on stage equipment and supplies.[32]

In the Spring of 1929, four years after the founding of APO, the National Thespian Society, an honorary organization of high-school students, appeared. The idea originated with Earl W. Blank, then a teacher in Natrona County High School at Casper, Wyoming. Observing the National Forensic League in operation, Blank felt that a similar national association of dramatic groups could serve the educational theatre. Blank wrote Opp of APO to inquire as to the feasibility of the plan,[33] with the result that the national officers of APO—Opp, Stump, and Russell Speiers of Colgate—voted a gift of five hundred dollars from APO to NTS to start its work.[34] The Casper school became Troupe No. 1, and Blank served as national president for thirteen years. Because the clerical work was done at Fairmont State College, that school was designated the place of founding.[35]

NTS set out to accomplish two general aims: to establish and advance standards of excellence in all phases of dramatic arts, and to create an active and intelligent interest in dramatic arts among boys and girls in the high schools.[36]

To implement these aims, NTS, like the college groups, has published a magazine to acquaint directors and students with the activity in other high schools and to disseminate information on all aspects of production. Begun as an annual, *The High School Thespian* [37] evolved into *Dramatics,* a magazine of eight issues a year, which attained a circulation of over twenty thousand by 1950.[38] Coast-to-coast hookups over a national broadcasting chain also have stimulated interest.[39] The organization has sponsored four National Dramatics Arts Conferences at Indiana University; one thousand students and teachers attended the 1952 sessions.[40] To further encourage participation and raise standards, NTS has sought to aid its chapters financially, through royalty reductions,[41] a library loan service, discounts on stage equipment, and complimentary publications,[42] and through a placement service for faculty sponsors.

The two dramatic honoraries on the junior-college level arose as a result of the fact that the constitutions of the college fraternities made no provision for chapters in the two-year schools, which were repeatedly petitioning for admission.[43] Generally speaking, they resemble in form and function the senior honoraries from which they sprang.

The older of the junior college fraternities, Delta Psi Omega, began in 1929. Mrs. Irene Childrey Painton, director of dramatics at Modesto, California, Junior College, presented the idea and plan for the organization to Opp of APO. Opp designed the badge and drew up the constitution for the junior fraternity. DPO also admits to membership unaccredited four-year colleges that have equivalent programs of production.[44]

It was twenty years later, in 1949, when the second of the junior-college groups, Junior Collegiate Players, was established. A committee from NCP, headed by Earl Seigfred of Ohio University, worked out the details of founding.[45] The general scholastic average required for membership in JCP is the minimum required for participation in extracurricular activities in the given school.[46]

In summary, the dramatic honor societies share a common aim—recognition of demonstrated ability in the theatre arts—and have, by working toward that aim, been of benefit to education by making thousands of students theatre conscious [47] and by motivating higher-quality participation in dramatic activity. Beyond these points of agreement, the paths diverge markedly, with some of the societies assuming the capacity of service organizations to their member groups. These services, too, contribute to the general cause of education in the theatre area.

Negro Dramatic Associations

As shown in the preceding section, the early dramatic honor societies and fraternities originated with students and emphasized student membership, although faculty members were, of necessity, largely responsible for continuation of the fraternities' programs. The Negro educational theatre associations, in contrast, were faculty-inspired, but as they developed, they included students as an integral part of the groups.

To understand the struggle for existence and the educational contributions of the Negro organizations, it is necessary to examine briefly the place of theatre activity in the Negro colleges. In these colleges dramatics began slowly,[48] but after World War I, two developments outside the educational picture furnished impetus to the school theatre. First, Negro little theatre groups in larger cities gained recognition.[49] Second, prominent dramatists turned out widely acclaimed and commercially successful plays which presented Negro life and problems sympathetically.[50] During the twenties and thirties, dramatic organizations mushroomed in colleges for Negroes.[51] These dramatic clubs prepared the way for the gradual inclusion of theatre courses in the curriculum.

The efforts of one man, S. Randolph Edmonds, provided the stimulus for the organization of the Negro dramatic associations. It is noteworthy that he organized the first association a year before the National Theatre Conference was established.

On March 7, 1930, representatives from five colleges—Howard University, Hampton Institute, Morgan State, Virginia Union, and Virginia State Colleges—met on the Morgan campus at the invitation of Edmonds. These schools constituted the charter membership of the Negro Inter-Collegiate Dramatic Association. (The name was changed to Inter-Collegiate Dramatic Association in 1947.) Delegates elected Edmonds to the presidency, an office he retained for five years.[52] Several college organizations applied for membership in the new association each year, but growth was slow. NIDA required that the member groups exchange plays, and distance between schools often prevented such exchange. After seven years the membership list included only ten schools.[53] NIDA held annual conferences until World War II caused suspension of the meetings. President J. Newton Hill of Lincoln University and Secretary Felicia Anderson of Virginia State worked to keep the organization alive, and in 1946 regular meetings were resumed with one held at Bennett College.[54]

Having removed to Dillard University at New Orleans, Edmonds founded the Southern Association of Dramatic and Speech Arts for schools of the southern area. Nineteen colleges and one community theatre responded to Edmonds' call for a meeting at Dillard, February 26-27, 1936.[55]

Permanent organization was not attempted until the 1937 meeting at Florida A. and M. College. The charter member list included: Alabama State, Alcorn, Lane, LeMoyne, Morehouse, Morris Brown, Prairie View, Shorter, Spelman, Talladega, Tougaloo, Wiley, and Winston Salem State Teachers Colleges; Atlanta, Dillard, and Fisk Universities; and Tuskegee Institute.[56] Edmonds was elected president.[57]

The next year the organization divided into three units geographically—southwestern, south central, and southeastern [58]—to promote more frequent and closer contacts among members.[59]

In 1941, 137 delegates gathered for the yearly meeting, but by 1942 the pall of the war years settled over the organization. Edmonds was serving with the U. S. Army; Thomas E. Poag, a former student of Edmonds, became president. From Cornell University, where he was studying for a doctorate, Poag issued news letters, which held the membership together until the group could meet at his own school, Tennessee A. and I. State College, April 10-12, 1946.[60]

The *SADSA Encore*, official publication of the association, first appeared in 1948 under the editorship of Lillian Voorhees.[61]

SADSA changed its name to National Association of Dramatic and Speech Arts on May 5, 1951, at Alabama State College. The change was made because both the membership and program had become national in scope, and because a majority of the members wished to remain an affiliate of the American Educational Theatre Association with representation on its Advisory Council.[62] NADSA reached its maturity and national status under the leadership of Poag, who served as its president for nine years (1942-1951),[63] and of Voorhees who was executive secretary of the organization for ten years (1937-1942; 1947-1952).[64]

Some members of the two Negro associations have suggested a merger of the groups. A committee from SADSA appointed in 1949 to investigate the suggestion recommended co-operation and interchange of materials between the organizations but opposed the merger. The committee believed that neither group yet desired affiliation and that each organization has a clear geographical function.[65] Further, SADSA planned to work itself out of existence as the Negro becomes integrated into American life.[66] A merger was held to be inimical to that goal.[67]

Although they remain separate organizations, the two associations share some goals. The need for a system of play exchanges and of contact among directors, the desire to raise the standards of production, and the hope of hastening the inclusion of theatre courses in curricula, motivated their formation.[68] These objectives, however, were but the immediate and concrete expression of a broader vision and aim. Edmonds saw that almost every major area of study in the schools had its professional organization; specifically he noted that athletics had not attained its prominence through isolated intermural programs. Logically it followed that an intercollegiate association might stimulate interest in theatre. Further, Edmonds noted that as a result of shifting interest and personnel, few of the many community theatres which sprang up from time to time managed to achieve permanence. The stability and hardiness of college educational programs suggested that in this field might lie the hope of a continuing Negro theatre.[69]

The two organizations, working separately but co-operatively, have contributed in large measure to the welfare of educational theatre in Negro colleges. They stimulated activity which resulted in markedly increased production,[70] provided for interchange of ideas among directors, and supplied laboratory experience that resulted in improvement of standards.[71]

IDA and NADSA have employed a variety of methods to achieve these ends, first trying exchange of plays among the member colleges. Even during World War II colleges located sufficiently near each other managed an occasional exchange.[72] At the early annual conferences, play tournaments served as teaching devices, with experienced theatre persons such as Frederick Koch, Alexander Dean, and Edith J. R. Isaacs judging the entries; [73] by 1938 the tournaments gave way to the festival plan.[74] Conference lectures and forums aimed at informing and stimulating the members. The organization sponsored playwriting contests, favoring themes centering around Negro life. Authors retained the rights to their plays, but members of the association could produce them royalty free.[75]

Throughout these activities, the associations emphasized student participation. Speaking for NADSA, Voorhees claims that student membership has proved an excellent training ground for leaders in the field.[76] Students served to bring new life into the organization, as, passing from student to faculty capacities, they have taken their places with their former teachers to help achieve the goals of the Negro educational theatre organizations.

National Theatre Conference

Formally organized in 1931, one year after the Negro Inter-Collegiate Dramatic Association, the National Theatre Conference answered a need felt by many active workers for at least a decade before its founding. Its history reveals that NTC brought together some theatre practitioners of experience whose co-operative efforts benefited education in theatre.

Many educational and community theatre workers recognized the need for a "meeting of minds" during the twenties. In 1925 Walter Prichard Eaton called for "some central Little Theatre Organization." [77] About the same time an anonymous little theatre director cried in *Theatre Arts,* "We are working practically in isolation." [78] Edith J. R. Isaacs in 1932 stated that "for ten years, the idea of some sort of union or federation of little theatres ... has been in the air." [79]

The annual conventions of the National Association of Teachers of Speech and of the National Council of Teachers of English permitted some interchange of ideas, though these organizations limited their sections devoted to theatre and often designed them for the beginning teachers rather than for the active, experienced leaders.[80] Informal state, regional, and national conferences showed the same tendencies.[81]

B. Iden Payne and Chester Wallace called a "Conference on the Drama in American Universities and Little Theatres" at Carnegie Institute of Technology on November 27-28, 1925.[82] The invitations said, "The purpose of the conference is to review the situation" of the "regenerative forces at work in the American theatre ... in the Little and Community Theatres and dramatic activities of the universities and colleges ... to obtain a just estimate of what has so far been accomplished, and, finally, to endeavor to give cohesion to the movement." Payne, Otto Kahn, Brock Pemberton, Otis Skinner, Samuel H. Church, Richard Boleslavsky, George Pierce Baker, Thomas Wood Stevens, Edward C. Mabie, S. Marion Tucker, Kenneth Macgowan, and Frederic McConnell spoke, and Arthur Hopkins attended as a spectator.[83] McConnell refers to this as "the first meeting of NTC and its inception." [84] Though it is not legally accurate, this is true in spirit because there was continuity of purpose from this conference to the eventual formal organization.

Fifteen months later, three hundred persons attended a "second annual conference of representatives of the nonprofessional theatres" called by Baker at Yale, February 11-12, 1927.[85]

The next year Macgowan visited the noncommercial theatres of the country under a grant from the Carnegie Corporation to the American Association for Adult Education, and reported his observations in *Footlights Across America*. In this book [86] and in an article in *Theatre Arts*,[87] Macgowan stressed the need for an organization to give structure to the theatre of the nation. Eaton had earlier stated the need for help on royalties; Macgowan, in addition, recommended that the organization serve the theatre through giving technical and business advice, awarding scholarships, holding conferences, publishing a yearbook, and conducting an employment register.

Macgowan continued to agitate for a "National Theatre Council" [88] and in 1931 secured another grant of twenty-five hundred dollars from the Carnegie Corporation through AAAE to pay all expenses for thirty leaders of community and university theatres to meet and find a basis for a national federation.[89]

At the ensuing three-day conference at Northwestern University in June 1931, the delegates "decided that such a federation was essential

to the development of a national theatre in America, and to the progress of the educational theatre"; and in spite of marked differences
they finally appointed a committee of fifteen to serve as a Council for
an organization to which they gave the name National Theatre Conference.[90] At subsequent meetings at Iowa City and New York, the
Council drafted a constitution and elected as officers: Baker, president; Gilmor Brown, first vice-president; Mabie, second vice-president;
and Isaacs, secretary-treasurer. These officers continued until the
death of Baker, January 6, 1935, when Brown became president, Mabie,
first vice-president, and Allardyce Nicoll, second vice-president.[91]

The early promotion literature described NTC as "a co-operative
membership organization to serve collectively the interests of the
American theatre." [92] *Theatre Arts* described it a little more specifically:

The National Theatre Conference hopes to remain, as its name implies, a
not-too-heady and not-too-definite organization, but rather a medium for the
exchange of ideas and of collective service between the leading organized
theatres of all kinds throughout the country; a gesture in the direction of
wiping out that sense of distance and aloneness which adds so much to the
difficulty of the American director or playwright who works far away from
New York.[93]

NTC initially offered two types of membership.[94] The principal
executive of a community or college theatre producing three or more
full-length plays during a year could be an active member. Any junior
college, high school, club, organization, or individual interested in
NTC's purposes could be an associate member, receiving more limited
services.[95] In 1934 the organization added library memberships.[96]

The budget submitted to the AAAE for 1932-1933 estimated that
five thousand dollars would be received in dues, on the basis of one
hundred active and two hundred fifty associate memberships.[97] But at
the end of the year there were only thirty-three of each category,[98]
and they increased slowly. This has been ascribed to the lack of an
appropriation for promotion,[99] but the inability to promise specific
services undoubtedly contributed; when, in 1934, NTC reduced membership dues and offered more definite services, membership grew
rapidly, reaching three hundred in June 1935.[100]

NTC's financial career was checkered. In addition to exhibit fees and
the sale of publications, annual grants of approximately five thousand
dollars from the AAAE supplemented the dues.[101] The AAAE intended to withdraw its support in 1935, but it made an "emergency
grant" of two thousand dollars for 1935-1936 because of the burden
of the NTC help to the Federal Theatre and the belief that dues and
publications might carry NTC if it had one more year in which to

grow.[102] However, another deficit occurred in 1935-1936. Rosamond Gilder, half-time editorial secretary almost from NTC's beginning, took an editorial position with the Federal Theatre Project in order to remove herself from the NTC budget, to continue similar work, and to be able to carry on NTC work without salary.[103]

Mabie and others proposed that the New York office be closed to save money, that "the work of the secretary-treasurer be separated from tasks which might be assigned to another person as New York representative," [104] and that in other ways the activities be curtailed to keep within the anticipated income. A questionnaire ballot submitted to the Council [105] offered as alternative that individual members of the Council underwrite NTC to the extent of three to five hundred dollars each. The vote favored the closing of the New York office.[106]

Negotiations with the Rockefeller Foundation, begun by Isaacs [107] and others, became promising at about the same time. At Council Meetings in New York, December 27-28, 1936, the constitution was tentatively revised (formally adopted in 1937) to conform to the general policy of the Foundation in making grants.[108] Sawyer Falk made the clearest statement of this policy in 1945:

The Rockefeller Foundation is committed to a policy of aid on a university level and not on a general educational level. It is interested in sowing its seed in definitely fertile soil and not scattering it to the winds. Hence NTC is, perforce, an organization made up of certain selected leaders in the field of drama and not of anyone and everyone who has the urge to be identified with it.[109]

The Foundation further required that the secretary and the treasurer remain in office during the period of a specific grant. The rewritten constitution put the business of the Conference in the hands of an executive committee (trustees of the fund) of five including a permanent secretary,[110] and limited the total membership to twenty-five, with the current members of the Council becoming the initial members. Isaacs was so strongly opposed to the reduction in membership that she resigned as secretary-treasurer.[111] NTC received a series of grants from Rockefeller totalling more than two hundred thousand dollars,[112] beginning in 1937 and terminating in 1950. It is now in the process of adjusting its services and goals to the more limited funds provided by dues alone.

What contributions has NTC made to theatre education? To discover the most valuable services which could be supplied by NTC, Isaacs in 1933 made a questionnaire survey of the noncommercial theatre of the country on an AAAE grant of four thousand dollars.[113] Her summary of the survey provided the specific early goals of the Conference:

Almost all the work indicated as within the scope of the National Theatre Conference can be handled by an organized exchange of information and ideas by four [sic] methods:

(1) CONFERENCES—local, regional, and national. The literal "meeting of minds" which is, especially in the arts, the most creative and energizing form of exchange.

(2) INFORMATION BUREAUS—regional and national, chiefly to make known the best sources of information.

(3) PUBLICATIONS—The printing, reprinting, and distribution of books, brochures, articles, etc., which are of special interest and use to workers in the theatre, and teachers of the theatre arts, or such as may stimulate a larger and finer audience interest in the theatre.

(4) NEWS LETTERS—to members.

(5) EXHIBITIONS—A visual presentation of the best standards of theatre production, design, architecture, books, costumes, etc.[114]

Some aims were never implemented because AAAE earmarked its grants for publications and other projects in which it was most directly interested; [115] for others there were insufficient funds. Some of the goals were too large to be attacked directly, and the possible indirect influence cannot be evaluated with so many other agencies working toward similar objectives.

But the record shows some accomplishments. In the early years, especially, was NTC's publication record notable. The list includes Gilder's A Theatre Library (1932), Stanley McCandless' A Method of Lighting the Stage (1932), Henning Nelms' Lighting the Amateur Stage (1932), Boleslavsky's Acting, the First Six Lessons (1933), Dorothy Coit's Kai Khosru and Other Plays for Children (1934), Behind the Magic Curtain: Eight Folk Scenes (1935), the Neighborhood Playhouse promptbook for The Little Clay Cart (1934), Isaacs' Architecture for the New Theatre (1935), and Gilder and George Freedley's Theatre Collections in Libraries and Museums (1936). A number of booklets and many leaflets of speeches, play lists, and so forth, supplemented these major publications.

During the same period, a number of special projects benefited the theatre as a whole. The first was Isaacs' Survey. In 1934-1935 NTC made a survey of four hundred "stock towns" in order to demonstrate to the Dramatists Guild that these no longer contained stock companies, and that there was therefore no reason for delay in the release of plays to noncommercial theatres in these areas.[116] In November 1934 the Theatre Code Authority of the Federal Government attempted to place the nonprofessional theatre under the terms of the Professional Theatre Code, but Isaacs, Gilder, and Boyd Smith spearheaded a successful campaign to prevent this.[117] About the same time Actors Equity prepared to rule that the Pasadena Community

Playhouse (and by implication many other community theatres) was a commercial theatre and that, therefore, Equity members must receive their minimum salaries when they played there.[118] NTC intervened and persuaded Equity to delay action until Brown flew to New York and, with NTC assistance, demonstrated the noncommercial status of the theatre by proof of government exemptions from income taxes, and so forth.

In this early period NTC continued conferences—though they were often limited to the Council,[119] prepared exhibitions which it rented to members,[120] and published—albeit irregularly—a "Newsletter" which kept members informed of NTC activities.

The planning in the early years emphasized regional organization, but although NTC appointed regional directors,[121] this activity never assumed importance.[122] However, the 1934-1935 report of NTC states that the Federal Theatre plan of operation stemmed essentially from the regional planning of NTC,[123] and Hallie Flanagan Davis, director of the Federal Theatre Project, confirms this.[124] The 1950 regional planning of the American National Theatre and Academy [125] followed a similar pattern.

After reorganization, NTC continued some general services, but the policy of the Rockefeller Foundation necessitated emphasis on the training of outstanding individuals. NTC published books,[126] pamphlets, and a quarterly *Bulletin;* [127] operated a placement register; promoted and supported regional conferences by subsidizing costs of preliminary organization, running expenses, and speakers' fees; conducted a Veterans' Counseling Service; [128] arranged for royalties by "block buying"; [129] secured release of plays to its members prior to Broadway production (Saroyan's *A Decent Birth, a Happy Funeral* [130] and *Jim Dandy*,[131] Flavin's *In the Good Old Summer Time,* and Anderson's *The Eve of St. Mark*); [132] and helped to organize the Army theatre program.[133] The group expended most of its funds on playwriting scholarships,[134] playwriting prizes for the armed forces,[135] grants for study, travel, and artist-in-residence programs, a touring acting company at Indiana University,[136] and a "show-case" in New York for recent college graduates.[137]

Probably the most valuable service of the NTC to its members throughout its existence has been the opportunity it afforded through its annual conferences, for a group of the leaders of the noncommercial theatre to meet for a few days and exchange ideas and viewpoints. This is the justification for the limitation of the membership. An unfortunate aspect of this, however, is that theatre workers (nonmembers of NTC probably more than the members) have come to look upon membership in it as a recognition of ability, and failure to gain membership as a slight upon their achievements. This feeling of slight was less strong and widespread when NTC rigorously held itself to twenty-five members than it seems to be now that the membership is nearly a hundred. Yet the intimacy of the organization is its essential value, and this would be lost if it expanded membership appreciably.

Except for the scholarship and conference type of activities, the broad scope of NTC's educational work had decreased with the years; it has assumed the specialized aspect of "adult education" for its membership. This is a natural result of the policy of the Foundation to limit membership to those with considerable experience. It is probable that the noncommercial theatre generally profits from the discussions held within NTC, for ideas expressed there inevitably permeate through participation by members in the meetings of larger national organizations, through their participation in regional conferences, and through their teaching.

American Educational Theatre Association

Because the small group of pioneers in universities and community theatres who set up new standards of production and goals higher than those of previous "amateur dramatics" had felt the need to refresh themselves by exchange of ideas with others on their level of experience, the organization of NTC had been inevitable. The emergence of an educational theatre organization out of the general speech association was almost as inevitable.

A survey of the educational theatre situation in the thirties will reveal why this was so. Theatre teaching increased rapidly in the twenties and thirties.[138] The quality of college and high-school productions improved: in the colleges, dramatic work shifted from extracurricular to academic status; in high schools, the attitude toward plays became more serious and some offered dramatics courses. Many teachers were devoting full time or major emphasis to this work, often without being specifically trained for it; they needed extended conferences, committee work, and more publication of scholarly and pedagogical writings. NTC could have filled this need, but it held few open conferences; it was basically a service organization which did not encourage active committee work, and the reorganization of 1936 prevented increase of its membership. NATS could have filled the need, but most of its officers were from the public speaking field, and they underestimated the needs. Theatre people found it administratively difficult to work through them to expand the theatre phase of the convention program, committee organization, and publication. Consequently teachers of theatre felt neglected and slighted.[139] Had the NATS taken the initiative by establishing a theatre section with some freedom to do its own planning and to organize its own activities, a permanent relationship might have continued, but in the absence of this, the American Educational Theatre Association started as a "functioning" section of the NATS,[140] then dropped all reference to NATS in the revision of the Constitution in 1941, and in later years has planned to hold conventions apart from the parent organization.

The story of AETA's founding and growth reveals the enthusiasm and earnest purpose of the men and women who comprise its membership. An educational theatre organization had been discussed by E. C. Mabie [141] and others for several years, but the final impetus came with the reduction in the membership of NTC. Mabie, having taken the leadership in the NTC reorganization in New York on December 28, 1936, also led in organizing AETA at the NATS convention in St. Louis two days later.

Theatre teachers were called together on the morning of December 30, the last day of the NATS convention, at the Hotel Statler in St. Louis. With Mabie as temporary chairman the assembly voted to form an association, and a committee drafted a constitution which was adopted that afternoon.[142] The constitution stated that the association intended to act as a functioning section of NATS.

Officers elected at this meeting were President, Mabie; Vice-President, Alexander M. Drummond; Secretary-Treasurer, Donald Winbigler; Executive Council: F. A. Buerki, Lester L. Hale, Jessie T. Casebolt, Dina Rees Evans, Claude L. Shaver, Florence B. Hubbard, Barclay Leathem, Lee Norvelle, and Katharine Ommanney.[143]

Constitutional changes have been necessary from time to time. In December, 1941, AETA adopted a new constitution [144] which eliminated all reference to NATS. A major revision in 1945 specified that "the name of the Vice-President each year shall be submitted by the Nominating Committee as candidate for President" [145] in order to insure more continuity of administration. In 1947 AETA altered the nominating procedure to provide a more democratic method of selecting the Nominating Committee and to permit ample time for consideration.[146] In 1949 the association created the office of Administrative Vice-President to relieve the President of some supervisory duties. Jack Morrison was the first to hold this office.[147]

AETA's membership grew slowly in the first years, dropped slightly during the war years, and increased rapidly in the years immediately following the war, rising from 185 in 1944 to 2192 in 1950.[148]

Spending nearly all its income each year,[149] AETA has remained a nonprofit organization, risking bankruptcy with every major publication venture.[150]

AETA has made major contributions to education in theatre. Probably its greatest service has been to make teachers of theatre aware of their status as a professional group, and to fuse them into a cohesive body working for an improvement in the quality and an increase in the stature of theatre studies in the curriculum. The size and representativeness of AETA's membership have given it the right to speak for the teachers of theatre of the country; national and international agencies, including ANTA, the State Department, the Veterans Administration, Senators and Representatives, the International Theatre Institute of UNESCO, and the British Society for Theatre Research, seek its advice.[151]

Through its conventions, AETA has raised standards of production and scholarly activity and has stimulated curricular study of theatre in the secondary schools. The association held annual national conventions in conjunction with the NATS (later renamed the Speech Association of America) except for 1942 and 1944.[152] The convention program expanded rapidly to a pattern of approximately four general sessions, twenty sectional meetings, and fifteen project meetings for the years 1949-1952.[153] Sections treated acting; directing; stagecraft and design; the specialized pedagogical problems at the levels of children's theatre, secondary schools, colleges, and graduate studies; and the specialized forms of theatre such as cinema, television, and radio drama. Starting with the 1948 Convention, planned by Hubert C. Heffner, the emphasis on the scholarly side of theatre work increased with separate sections on theatre history, dramatic literature, and criticism. In addition sections from time to time are devoted to specialized topics such as playwriting, student problems, audio-visual aids, adult education as a community theatre function, guidance, architecture, conferences and festivals, theatre libraries, and extracurricular theatre.

The organization took the leadership in arranging AETA meetings in connection with the regional speech associations, thereby increasing the number of theatre sections offered at these meetings, and serving many teachers who seldom attend national conventions. Several more limited regional conferences also have been arranged under the stimulus of AETA—the first ones being the Southern California Section of AETA spearheaded by Morrison, and the Northwestern Conference organized by Horace Robinson at the University of Oregon.

Further, AETA has encouraged the children's theatre workers to weld themselves into an active, cohesive group. It sponsors an annual Children's Theatre Conference (designated as Convention starting with 1951) [154] which meets in the summer. Winifred Ward called an organizational meeting in 1944 at Northwestern University; [155] AETA sponsored annual conferences, beginning with one at Seattle in 1946.[156] This project, designated Children's Theatre Conference in 1950, and Children's Theatre Division in 1952 [157] has officers and a council of its own, and has become an autonomous division within AETA.

Through its publications, too, AETA has contributed materially to education. As with the conventions, publications have served to raise production standards, and to stimulate curricular study in theatre. In addition, the publications have served to disseminate all types of theatre information, scholarly and pedagogical.

Almost from the time of its organization AETA sought to issue a journal devoted to educational theatre. In 1940 Heffner, as chairman of the AETA Publications Committee, supported an NTC request to the Rockefeller Foundation for a quarterly publication, under the impression that it was to be a joint AETA-NTC project,[158] but when the grant was made NTC considered it a grant in support of the NTC *Bulletin*.[159] Richard Ceough then offered to finance personally a theatre journal if AETA would help to launch it. It was to start as an annual and eventually to become a quarterly. The Advisory Council approved this plan in 1941,[160] but the AETA sponsorship did not eventuate, and Ceough alone inaugurated *Theatre Annual* with a 1942 issue.[161]

Meanwhile AETA began a mimeographed "AETA Newsletter" in 1942,[162] with Valentine Windt as its first full-time editor after a year of committee editorship. Irregularly published at first, it soon appeared eight times a year and continued until the launching of the *Educational Theatre Journal*.[163]

This long-sought quarterly began publication in October 1949 with Barnard Hewitt as editor.[164] The first issue was devoted to reports from committee efforts known as Work-Projects. Editor Hewitt stated, "... the *Journal* will continue to publish the results of such group efforts. In addition, however, the editors hope soon to publish individually written articles, both popular and scholarly.... Our purpose is to make the *Educational Theatre Journal* of the greatest possible use to students, workers, and teachers of educational theatre and drama in all aspects and at all levels." [165]

AETA has from its origin put emphasis on co-operative group work. Its projects and committees have been the core function. In 1938 its projects numbered only eight.[166] These have increased and changed until, in 1952, there are twenty-five, in addition to a number of con-

tinuing committees and specialized investigations under the projects.[167]

Reports from these projects comprised the chief publications of
AETA until the *Journal* was established. The pamphlet reports in-
cluded: *Syllabus for a Proposed Course in Dramatics at the High
School Level* (three editions, 1940, 1943, 1946, the last edition in co-
operation with NTS), *A Selected List of Painting, Music, and the
Dance Useful to Theatre Workers* (n.d., about 1943), *Research in
Drama and the Theatre in the Universities and Colleges of the United
States, 1937-1942* (1944), *Teaching Dramatic Arts in the Secondary
Schools* (1950), *Drama Festivals* (1945), *Records for Use in the
Teaching of Dramatics* (1946), *A Selected Bibliography on Theatre
and the Social Scene* (1946), *16mm Films for Use in the Teaching of
Dramatics* (1947), *A Selected Bibliography and Critical Comment on
the Art, Theory, and Technique of Acting* (1948), *National Directory
of Drama Festivals and Contests Held in the United States during the
School Year 1946-47* (1948), *Directory of Children's Theatre* (1948,
with supplements, published by ANTA for AETA), *A Suggested Outline for a Course of Study in Dramatic Arts in the Secondary Schools*
(1950, reprinted from March 1950 *Journal*), as well as annual directories of members and mimeographed compilations of reports from
projects.

AETA accepted an invitation, extended through SAA, to prepare
copy for a special issue of *The Bulletin* of the National Association of
Secondary-School Principals on "Dramatics in the Secondary School."
This appeared in December 1949 under the editorship of Hugh W.
Gillis.[168] A booklet entitled *The Educational Theatre in Adult Educa-
tion* was prepared under the editorship of Robert Gard.[169]

The Research Project, with John H. McDowell as chairman, prepared *A Bibliography on Theatre and Drama in American Colleges
and Universities, 1937-1947.* This repeated the work of the previous
bibliography because the initial five-year study was out of print.
Since AETA was unable to finance the publication alone, the SAA
printed it as a special issue of *Speech Monographs,*[170] with AETA un-
derwriting a portion of the cost.[171] The Bibliography Project is at
work on a 1948-1952 continuation of this study.[172]

The above list of projects and publications includes several which
were the result of co-operation with other organizations. AETA's
Advisory Council includes representatives of almost all the active
theatre organizations, thus facilitating co-operation with one or more
of them in large-scale programs for the betterment of educational
theatre and of the theatre in general.

Catholic Theatre Conference

By 1937 there were firmly established several organizations serving the needs of educational theatre in general, but apparently the special needs of some groups were not being met. Directors and sponsors of Catholic theatre groups formed their Theatre Conference in 1937 to "provide a channel for the exchange of inspiration and information among groups and individuals interested in fostering and spreading Catholic Theatre." [173]

Most of the problems arising during the founding and growth of CTC are similar to those revealed by the older organizations in the field of educational theatre; some problems and their solutions are markedly different.

Emmet Lavery, dramatist, film scenarist, and former Director of the National Service Bureau of the Federal Theatre, furnished the impetus for the movement through an article in *America*, December 5, 1936.[174] Two meetings resulted from that article. Rev. George A. Dinneen, S.J., pastor of St. Ignatius Church, Chicago, and Mr. Charles Costello, director of the Loyola Community Theatre of that parish, invited interested parties to attend the first National Catholic Theatre Conference in Chicago, June 15 and 16.[175] The Blackfriars Guild, headed by Rev. Urban Nagle, O.P., arranged for a convention for August 7 and 8 at Catholic University in Washington.[176]

From twenty-eight states, 416 delegates came to attend the Chicago meeting.[177] The delegates approved temporary organization with Lavery as Chairman to serve until the Washington convention,[178] at which time Rev. John H. Mahoney of the Catholic Theatre Guild, New York, was elected president.[179] CTC set up official headquarters in September, 1937, at Catholic University.[180]

CTC established a policy of holding national conventions on alternate years. Travel restrictions occasioned by World War II resulted in a "convention by mail" in 1943, although simultaneous meetings were held in some conveniently located metropolitan areas.[181] At the 1947 convention, the name of the organization was changed from National Catholic Theatre Conference to Catholic Theatre Conference.[182]

As the Conference grew, regional division became necessary. Twelve divisions emerged, closely corresponding to those set up by ANTA in 1950.[183] The West Central region organized with the Wichita Diocesan Theatre Unit as a center. This and other diocesan units, because of their strong independent development, for a time posed a threat to CTC. With the assistance of members of the Hierarchy, the Conference convinced the diocesan units of the advisability of accepting the national organization's leadership.[184]

Financial insecurity has plagued CTC. From time to time donations have taken care of deficits. In 1949 members of the convention agreed to send proceeds of special benefit performances to the national office. An anonymous donor in 1943 began contributing funds to pay a salary for full-time services of the national secretary.[185]

What did CTC propose to do? The members who attended the early meetings represented diverse interests in the theatre; they included parish priests, theatre directors, professional actors, professional playwrights. Their needs varied: suggestions for play selection, assistance with technical problems, pre-Broadway training grounds, markets for new scripts. The diversity was reconciled by a common purpose as ultimately expressed in the Constitution, June, 1945, in Article II, Section I:

1. To promote Catholic truth and principle through dramatic art and to promote dramatic art in harmony with Catholic truth and principle.
2. To unite Catholic dramatic groups in Catholic thought and action and to encourage the creation of new groups eligible for such union.
3. To afford service to its members.[186]

Catholic leaders have seen in such general purposes more specific goals. Dr. Roy J. Dederrari, Dean of Catholic University's Summer Session, 1937, felt that CTC would become a great collaborator in the project of Catholic Education.[187] Cardinal Mooney, Archbishop of Detroit, viewed the Conference as an agency for Catholic Action.[188] Father Dinneen, one of the founders of the Legion of Decency, looked to the association as a complement to the Legion, as a force to encourage the creation of worthwhile plays.[189] Father Mahoney regarded it as a force that might serve as an "antidote to subversive and un-American propaganda," as well as a significant step in "the gradual decentralization of the American theatre." [190]

To realize its goals CTC employed both methods that older associations had tried and methods peculiar to its own group. From the year of its founding, CTC has boasted official publications. Under the editorship of E. Francis McDevitt, a monthly *Bulletin* appeared for the first time in November, 1937. Beginning with November, 1938, a quarterly, *Catholic Theatre*, served as the official organ until it was replaced in 1941 by the more economical monthly *Production Calendar*.[191] From 1945 to 1951 CTC published an annual production *Bulletin* with photographs from the various schools and guilds, augmented by articles.[192]

CTC early urged its members to organize play cycles. Under this plan, six producing units combined to provide at a given theatre, a week of Catholic drama—a different play by a different group each night. Each group financed its own production. Such cycles were produced in the New York and Chicago areas.[193]

The Conference has aided its members by maintaining a play reading library of over 2000 titles and by providing a frequently revised list of recommended plays suitable for production by Catholic groups.[194]

CTC has encouraged playwriting through two awards: the Bishop Shiel award in 1946 offered a prize of five hundred dollars to the winner; the Dinneen Fellowship the same year granted the winner fifteen hundred dollars for the study of playwriting at Rosary College.[195]

Through services to a special group of educational and community theatres, CTC has contributed to the general cause of educational theatre.

The national educational theatre organizations have endeavored, first of all, to spread knowledge of theatre arts and appreciation for them. Toward this primary goal, they have achieved much. The increase in the number of plays produced in educational institutions, for example, cannot be unrelated to their efforts. Some of the associations, notably the honoraries, the Negro groups, and the Catholic Theatre Conference, have contributed to this increase through encouragement of extracurricular activity. These same organizations have joined with the American Educational Theatre Association and the National Theatre Conference to win a place for theatre in the curriculum. This has led to even more production; and increase in the number of productions has meant increase in the number of persons participating. Recognition of achievement, provided specifically by the honoraries, has stimulated such participation. A portion of the general increase may be attributed to emphasis on specialized types of production, such as children's theatre. Fostered by AETA,[196] children's theatre has grown to the status of a major division of educational theatre activity.

Whether intended for children or adults, a surplus of good scripts has never existed. Most of the theatre organizations have taken steps to augment the small body of American drama through encouragement of new authors; NTC's grants for playwriting fellowships and AETA's Manuscript Play Project are well-known examples.

Not only has the quantity of production increased, but the quality of production has improved also. Here again the educational theatre organizations have contributed. In no area of achievement have the organizations' efforts been more numerous than in that of improvement of teachers. Conventions and publications have informed the beginner and inspired the veteran. Meetings and writings concerning methods and dramatic forms have stressed both the mastery of traditional concepts and the need for experimentation. Nor have these efforts reached only a limited group of enthusiastic educators. The growth in membership of educational theatre organizations indicates that the number of professionally minded theatre workers has increased.

As teaching improved, it was to be expected that standards for student performance in all areas would rise correspondingly. In addition to this indirect influence, the educational theatre organizations have addressed themselves to students through publications and special meetings.

Most of the organizations help improve the quality of production by specific services for members, such as National Thespian Society's list of supply dealers or NTC's effecting royalty reductions.

So that teachers and students may continue to grow in knowledge of theatre, past and present, research in the field must proceed. Publications of the various organizations give encouragement to research by disseminating its findings, but in addition AETA has prepared bibliographies and conducted surveys of productions.[197]

Dedication to worthy ideals and corresponding sincere effort to achieve them have brought general recognition. The combined efforts of many earnest teachers have raised curricular and extracurricular work in theatre to a position of stature and dignity.

As the organizations have gone about the task of helping the educational theatre to produce more significant drama than ever before and to produce it better, they have made progress toward other related goals. First, the associations have grown in membership until they now constitute bodies of individuals capable of unified action. AETA and NTS, for example, can raise voices to which legislators have shown a willingness to listen. NTC, too, is effective through its prestige. Secondly, the theatre organizations have recognized their obligation, as educational units, to promote good international relationships. AETA, NTC, and NTS, which have welcomed memberships from all parts of the world, have eagerly accepted opportunities for the exchange of ideas.[198] All these groups have sent representatives to international conferences, and AETA is compiling information on educational theatre throughout the world.

It is important to note that the achievements toward the organizations' primary goals and achievements toward the related goals are interactive. As a result of international liaison and a capacity for potent unified action, the task of spreading information about, and esteem of, the theatre is facilitated.

But achievement alone does not characterize the history of educational theatre organizations; there are areas distinguished by lack of progress. On the secondary-school level, in particular, much remains for the educational theatre to accomplish. Its organizations have been largely ineffective in raising the standards of high-school play selection. Examples of high-school theatre programs of quality may be cited, it is true, but in general, significant drama is infrequently chosen for production on the secondary level. In spite of several excellent studies in secondary-school curricula, there has been no concerted campaign to introduce theatre studies into the secondary-school curriculum. Further, only recently have studies been undertaken to set standards for the high-school director.

Curricular studies on the college level are long overdue. There is little examination of requirements for undergraduate degrees in theatre or of standards for graduate work.

Evaluation of the past in terms of failure and achievement indicates that the educational theatre organizations cannot relax their efforts in the future. The outlook for the groups can be examined from the individual and from the collective point of view.

Considering the groups individually, it would appear that AETA, CTC, the Negro associations, and NTS embrace relatively clearly defined programs which are within the power of the groups to carry out, and as a result it is likely that these groups will continue to grow in membership and in service. In the case of honor societies other than NTS, the diminishing activity of chapters at institutions where curricular theatre obtains suggests that the societies will become less important. NTC is experiencing a period of reorganization, and its future is not predictable.

In general, it seems likely that the groups which continue to function will co-operate more closely, engaging in joint efforts and performing services for each other. At present, an avenue for co-operation exists in representation on AETA's Advisory Council.[199]

Notes

1. Dina Rees Evans, "A Preliminary Study of Play Production in Secondary Schools," unpublished M.A. thesis, Iowa, 1929, pp. 3, 18-23.

2. *Ibid.*, pp. 23-28. At the time of founding, the organization was called National Association of Academic Teachers of Public Speaking.

3. The producing groups, in turn, evolved from "annual exhibitions" of the college literary societies. As illustrative of the development of producing units the authors suggest the Yale University Dramatic Association. See *The Memorial Quadrangle*, comp. Robert Dudley French (New Haven, 1929), pp. 57-59; William Lyon Phelps, "Culture Comes to Yale," *Yale News* (50th anniversary issue, 1929), p. 44; L. G. Price, "American Undergraduate Dramatics," *Bookman*, XVIII (December, 1903), 373-388.

4. *Baird's Manual*, 13th ed. (Menasha, Wis., 1935), pp. 1-2, 4, 396, 440, 442.

5. *Ibid.*, p. 558; *Prospectus of Zeta Phi Eta* (1947).

6. *Ibid.*, 9th ed., p. 590. Phi Alpha Tau's listing in *Baird's Manual* continues through the 12th ed. (1930); thereafter it does not appear.

7. *Ibid.*, 13th ed., p. 568.

8. *History and Scope of the National Collegiate Players*, pamphlet issued by the national office. The U. of Washington did not join NCP at the time of the merger. *Baird's Manual*, 15th ed., also lists chapters of AUP at U. of Chicago,

Northwestern U., and U. of Wisconsin. In an interview January, 28, 1952, Lawrence W. Murphy, a freshman at Wisconsin in 1914 (the year of the University's supposed establishment of a chapter), recalled a visit to the campus of AUP representatives for the purpose of such establishment. Lack of interest met the organizers. Individual producing groups were not ready to co-operate with each other, much less with groups from other schools. Murphy concedes the possibility that individuals may have taken out membership, but does not recall the establishment of a chapter.

9. Interview with Lawrence W. Murphy, January 28, 1952.

10. According to Murphy, charter members included Fred Bickel (now known as Frederick March), Janet Durrie, Julia Hanks, John McPherrine, Eleanor Riley, and Helen Colby.

11. E. B. Gordon, Gertrude Johnson, J. M. O'Neill, and Andrew T. Weaver.

12. Interview with Murphy.

13. *History and Scope of NCP.*

14. *Constitution and By-Laws of National Collegiate Players,* pamphlet prepared by national office.

15. Personal letter from Delwin Dusenberry, August 14, 1951.

16. *History and Scope of NCP.*

17. *Baird's Manual,* 13th ed., p. 436.

18. Portions of a letter circulated by Pelsma soliciting members are reproduced under "A Dramatic Fraternity" in the *QJSE,* V (October, 1919), 379.

19. Personal letter from Pelsma, July 28, 1952.

20. Personal letter from R. C. Hunter, August 19, 1952. Notes from the TAP office at State College, Pa., received January 19, 1953, list subsequent presidents, including Maud May Babcock, U. of Utah; C. L. Menser, vice-president of NBC; Irving C. Stover, John B. Stetson U.; Lee Norvelle, U. of Indiana; and R. C. Hunter, Ohio Wesleyan U.

21. Letter from Pelsma. Arthur C. Cloetingh, Pennsylvania State College, became secretary in 1928 and held the office for twenty-five years.

22. *Baird's Manual,* 13th ed., p. 436.

23. *Constitution of the Theta Alpha Phi,* issued by the national office, n.d.

24. *Ibid.*

25. Personal letter from Cloetingh, c. January 25, 1953.

26. Notes from TAP office.

27. Personal letter from Paul F. Opp, June 22, 1951. Notes from the TAP office state that TAP chapters "are limited to Class A Colleges and Universities."

28. *Baird's Manual,* 13th ed., p. 433.

29. Personal letter from E. Turner Stump, May 21, 1952.

30. *Baird's Manual,* 13th ed., p. 433.

31. Paul F. Opp, "Alpha Psi Omega," *Southern Speech Bulletin* (March, 1941), pp. 91-94.

32. *Ibid.*

33. Personal letter from Earl Blank, June 21, 1951.

34. Letter from Stump.

35. Letter from Blank.

36. The *National Thespian Society* (rev. 1949), pamphlet issued by national office, p. 3.

37. *Ibid.,* p. 15. Harry T. Leeper was the first editor. Ernest Bavely took over as editor in 1935, at which time bimonthly publication was undertaken.

38. Personal letter from Leon C. Miller, May 22, 1952.

39. *NTS,* p. 15.

40. Letter from Miller, July 1, 1952.

41. Ernest Bavely, "Aims and Purposes of the National Thespians," *The High School Thespian,* V (October, 1929), 11.

42. *NTS,* p. 4.

43. Letter from Opp.

44. "Delta Psi Omega," typed ms. issued from DPO national office.

45. Interview with Karl Windesheim, June 23, 1952. The committee also included Windesheim and Campton Bell.

46. *Constitution and By-Laws of Junior Collegiate Players,* pamphlet issued by national office.

47. In 1953 the cumulative membership figures were as follows: NCP—6,575 in 54 chapters; TAP—1,572 in 55 chapters; APO—22,122 in 303 chapters; NTS—190,000 in 1256 troupes; DPO—11,580 in 200 chapters; JCP—68 in 2 chapters.

48. Singer A. Buchanan, "The Development of the Educational Theatre in Negro Colleges and Universities from 1925 to 1949," unpublished M.A. thesis, Tennessee A. and I., 1949, pp. 10, 12. Mr. Buchanan's thesis was the first to be accepted by any Negro college as partial fulfillment of the requirements for an advanced degree in Speech and Drama.

49. Frank Yerby, "The Little Theatre in Negro Colleges," unpublished M.A. thesis, Fisk, 1938, pp. 2-4. Examples include the Ethiopian Art Theatre of Chicago, The Negro Art Players of New York, the Gilpin Players of Cleveland.

50. Notable among the group stand Eugene O'Neill's *All God's Chillun Got Wings* and Marc Connelly's *Green Pastures.*

51. Yerby, pp. 4, 6-10, notes the founding of twelve specific groups in the 1920-1929 period and sixteen in the 1930-1937 period. Many were named for popular Negro stage personalities. The plays of Paul Green and Willis Richardson constituted an important part of their repertory.

52. Buchanan, p. 20. Current president (1953) is Fannin S. Belcher.

53. Personal letter from Randolph Edmonds, June 12, 1952.

54. Ethlynne Thomas, "Common Goals," *SADSA Encore* (1948), 25.

55. Letter from Edmonds.

56. *Ibid.*

57. Carrie Pembroke, vice-president; Lillian Voorhees, secretary; Lois P. Turner, treasurer.

58. Buchanan, p. 24, lists the components of the areas.

59. Lillian W. Voorhees, "SADSA Yesterday and Tomorrow," *SADSA Encore* (1948), p. 12.

60. Buchanan, pp. 26, 28.

61. *Ibid.,* p. 31.

62. Personal letter from Thomas E. Poag, August 18, 1951; "Minutes of AETA Advisory Council Meetings, December 27-30, 1950," item 16. The Council voted to interpret the AETA Constitution more strictly, and to limit representation on the Council to Organizational Members with a nationally distributed membership, could appoint a member to the Council.

63. James O. Hopson became president of NADSA in 1951.

64. Personal letter from Lillian Voorhees, May 25, 1952.

65. Buchanan, p. 35, fn. 9.

66. "Minutes of AETA Advisory Council Meetings, December 26-29, 1951," item 48. James O. Hopson reported that during 1951 Poag was elected President of the interracial Southeastern Theatre Conference, that Tenn. A. and I. College was elected to chapter membership in Theta Alpha Phi, and that Negro memberships were accepted in the Southern Speech Association.

67. Buchanan, p. 35, fn. 9.

68. *Ibid.,* pp. 12, 20, 22.

69. Randolph Edmonds, "The Negro Little Theatre Movement," *The Negro History Bulletin* (January, 1949), p. 92.

70. *Ibid.*

71. Buchanan, p. 37.

72. Thomas, p. 25.

73. Buchanan, p. 21.

74. Thomas, p. 25.

75. *Ibid.;* Buchanan, p. 22.

76. Letter from Voorhees.

77. *Theatre Arts,* IX (September, 1925), 587. Special issue on Little Theatres.

78. *Ibid.,* IX (November, 1925), 762. Other references to national organizations occur especially in X (March, May, 1926), "Editorially Speaking" column in advertising pp.; X (September, 1926), 578.

79. Edith J. R. Isaacs, *The American Theatre in Social and Educational Life: A Survey of its Needs and Opportunities* (New York: NTC, 1932), 5 (Gilder files). "Gilder files" refers to materials examined December, 1950, in Rosamond Gilder's personal files stored at Theatre Arts Books, then at 270 Madison Ave., NYC. Copies of most of these materials are filed with the National Theatre Conference, Western Reserve U., Cleveland, Ohio (confirmed by personal letter from Barclay Leathem, September 12, 1951), and with the NY Pub. Lib. (confirmed by personal letter from Paul Myers, September 5, 1951).

80. Evans, p. 3.

81. *Theatre Arts,* passim, especially X (May, 1926), advertising pages; XI (June, 1927), 463; XVIII (April, 1934), 238; XVIII (July, 1934), 564; XXIII (July, 1939), 536.

82. *Ibid.,* IX (December, 1925), 840; Angela Guidry, "A History of the Drama League of America," unpublished M.A. thesis, Louisiana State University and A. & M. College, 1949, p. 97.

83. *Ibid.,* X (January, 1926), 58.

84. Personal letter from Frederic McConnell, October 18, 1951.

85. *Theatre Arts,* XI (January, 1927), 74; XI (March, 1927), 217; XI (April, 1927), 307. Personal letter from Boyd Smith, November 15, 1951, following a study of Baker's correspondence files, states, "There is considerable correspondence here following this conference, between Mr. Baker and various other persons for the purpose of holding regional conferences and I find definitely four were held. These were at North Carolina, Iowa, Pasadena, and Dallas. These followed within the next two, three, or four years this conference at Yale."

86. Kenneth Macgowan, *Footlights Across America* (New York, 1929), pp. 311-325.

87. "A Dozen Rubicons," *Theatre Arts,* XIII (July, 1929), 480.

88. A sample is a four-page mimeographed prospectus for an organization similar to NTC issued by him "revised-March 26, 1930" from the producers' office of Macgowan and Joseph Vernor Reed, 122 East 42nd St., N. Y. (Wyckoff files). "Wyckoff files" refers to materials in the personal files of Alexander Wyckoff, 170 Prospect St., Leonia, N. J.

89. Rosamond Gilder, "National Theatre Conference Report of Funds Received and Expended," May 13, 1935. Carbon copy of typewritten report (Gilder files).

90. Isaacs, *Survey,* introductory pages. The Council consisted of Baker, Gilmor Brown, Jasper Deeter, Glenn Hughes, Isaacs, Frederick Koch, Garrett Leverton, McConnell, Mabie, Boyd Martin, Macgowan, Stevens, Tucker, and Wyckoff. Rupel Jones was added to the Council by a telegraphic vote initiated by Isaacs November 16, 1932 (Gilder files).

Bulletin, National Theatre Conference, passim, and other sources give NTC officers (as of June 1, 1953)—Presidents: Baker (1932-35), Brown (1935-40), Paul Green (1940-42), Lee Norvelle (1942-44), Sawyer Falk (1944-); Executive Secretaries: Isaacs (1932-36), Frank Fowler (1936-37), Leathem (1938-); Treasurers: Isaacs (1932-36), records incomplete for the transitional period, McConnell (1939-). Personal letter from Leathem, February 20, 1952, states that officers never received salaries.

Though others—notably Macgowan, Mabie, Isaacs, and Koch—were active in initiating NTC, innumerable sources speak of Baker as organizer and early leader: personal conversations with Gilder, December 24-26, 1950; "NTC Newsletter" (February, 1934); *Theatre Arts* XIX (February, 1935), 85; XIX

(July, 1935), 538; "Report of the February 22-23, 1935, Council Meeting at Yale" (Wyckoff files).

91. "Minutes of Council Meetings, February 22-23, 1935" (Wyckoff files).

92. "Membership Circular of 1933" (Gilder files).

93. *Theatre Arts,* XXXI (October, 1947), 10. See also *Bulletin,* IX (April, 1947), 21; Mary Morris, "Tryout Studio in New York," X (July, 1948), 46.

94. "Membership Circular of 1933."

95. Gilder, "NTC Report, May 13, 1935"; "Tentative Revision of Constitution, December 28, 1936"; "Minutes of National Meeting, December 27-30, 1937." (Copies of all in Gilder's files.)

96. Gilder, "NTC Report, May 13, 1935."

97. "NTC Newsletter" (November 19, 1932). (Gilder files.)

98. *Ibid.* (February, 1934).

99. *Ibid.*

100. "NTC 1934-35 Report to AAAE" (September 19, 1935). (Carbon copy in Gilder files.)

101. "NTC Newsletter" (November 19, 1932). (Gilder files.)

102. "NTC 1935-36 Report to AAAE" (September 15, 1936). (Carbon copy in Gilder files.)

103. Personal conversation with Gilder, December 24, 1950.

104. Questionnaire sent by Mabie to Council for vote, April 16, 1936 (Wyckoff files).

105. Letters from Mabie to Wyckoff, January 7 and April 16, 1936 (Wyckoff files).

106. "NTC Newsletter" (June 17, 1936). (Wyckoff files.)

107. On instructions from the NTC Council, Isaacs had requested a grant from Rockefeller Foundation in April, 1935. "Minutes of Council Meeting, December 29-30, 1935" (Wyckoff files) record that Isaacs stated "nor was there any indication of a grant from the Rockefeller Foundation."

108. Copy of letter from Mabie to Brown, January 6, 1937 (Wyckoff files) states that at the December 27, 1936, Council Meeting, NTC voted to dissolve, but that Mabie secured assurances from David Stevens, an official of Rockefeller, that he would recommend grants for five years. See also David Stevens, "Historical Notes," *Bulletin,* XII (December, 1950), 39.

109. *Bulletin,* VIII (March, 1946), 45.

110. "Constitution of December, 1937," Art. V, Sec. 1, 2, 3 (copy in Gilder files). The Executive Committee consisted of Brown as President, Nicoll and Mabie as Vice-Presidents, and Leathem and McConnell as elected members. The last two became the permanent secretary and treasurer respectively.

111. Personal conversation with Gilder, December 24, 1950.

112. These grants include $5000 for May 15, 1937-May 14, 1938 for operating expenses, study of the royalty problems, and Gilder's library study; $25,000 for fellowships June 30, 1940-June 30, 1944; $155,000 "for general administration, postwar fellowships and rehabilitation, publications, and developmental projects" for the five years beginning January 1, 1946; $10,000 for fellowships December 1949-December 1950; $7,500 for regional conferences June 1949. See *Bulletin,* VII (January, 1945), 50; VII (April, 1945), 30; VIII (March, 1946), 50; XI (August, 1949), 55; *Theatre Arts,* XXIX (July, 1945), 44; letter from Brown to Wyckoff, June 15, 1937 (Wyckoff files); and personal letter from McConnell, March 10, 1952.

113. Gilder, "NTC Report, May 13, 1935."

114. Isaacs, *Survey,* 55.

115. NTC mimeographed letter to Regional Directors, January 28, 1933 (Gilder files).

116. "There's Millions in It," *Theatre Arts,* XIX (May, 1935), 343.

117. "NTC Newsletter" (April, 1934) (Wyckoff files) states that at the hearings, Frank Gillmore, President of Actors Equity, suggested "two or three

methods of curtailing what his committee considered unfair competition on the part of the Little Theatres throughout the country." See also *Equity* (November, 1934), p. 5.

118. "NTC 1934-35 Report to AAAE" (September 19, 1935).

119. *Bulletin,* passim, and *Theatre Arts,* passim. NTC Conferences were held spasmodically on invitation in the first few years, some being open and some limited to the Council. A few were held at the same time as SAA and AETA conventions. A Thanksgiving meeting in N. Y. became traditional after 1940.

120. Early touring exhibits included original Callot engravings of Commedia dell' Arte, T. W. Stevens' drawings for *From Athens to Broadway,* and "Sketch to Stage," an exhibit prepared by Yale University showing the successive types of working drawings transforming a designer's sketch into a completed setting. *Theatre Arts,* XVIII (January, 1934), advertising pages.

121. "NTC Newsletter" (January 3, 1933). (Gilder files.)

122. "Minutes of Council Meeting, December 29-30, 1935" (Wyckoff files) record that the regional plan "had actually not been put into operation at all."

123. Gilder, "NTC Report, May 13, 1935."

124. "Federal Theatre Project," *Theatre Arts,* XIX (November, 1933), 865.

125. "Resolutions Adopted by the National Theatre Assembly, January 2-4, 1951," No. VII. (Distributed by ANTA.)

126. *Organizing a Community Theatre,* ed. Samuel Selden (1945); *Are You Going to Build a Theatre?,* ed. Paul Baker and George Freedley (1947); Roy Stallings and Paul Myers, *Guide to Theatre Reading* (1949).

127. *Bulletin,* passim. Initiated in April, 1939, as *Quarterly Bulletin,* the title was shortened in January, 1944, in the hope that more frequent publication might take place; this never occurred. Publication was discontinued December, 1950, after a total of forty-six issues. McConnell was permanent editor.

128. Robert C. Schnitzer, "Players Well Bestowed," *Bulletin,* VIII (March, 1946), 11; VIII (June, 1946), 31. Run by Schnitzer, the agency served fifteen hundred to two thousand by mail, phone, or personal conference.

129. *Theatre Arts,* XXIII (January, 1939), 75; XXIII (November, 1939), 837; *Bulletin,* VI (January, 1944), 43; VI (April, 1944), 60. Approximately one thousand reductions were secured.

130. *Bulletin,* VI (April, 1944), 35.

131. *Theatre Arts,* XXV (November, 1941), 777.

132. *Ibid.,* XXVI (November, 1942), 666; XXVII (July, 1943), 392. A commercial production of *The Eve of St. Mark* was arranged, and the producer exercised his right under the Dramatists Guild contract to withdraw it from amateur production.

133. *Ibid.,* XXIII (November, 1939), 839.

134. *Bulletin,* VII (January, 1945), 50; VI (October, 1944), 50; VI (April, 1944), 30; VIII (June, 1946), 54; IX (October, 1947), 54; X (April, 1948), 47; XI (March, 1949), 51.

135. *Ibid.,* VI (January, 1944), 43; VII (April, 1945), 30; VII (August, 1945), 47; *Theatre Arts,* XXIX (October, 1945), 549. The first contest distributed $1020 in prizes, the second $1500 plus promises by colleges of postwar fellowships, and the third, $1500. In the second contest, the largest, 697 scripts were submitted.

136. Lee Norvelle, "NTC Touring Company," *Bulletin,* IX (April, 1947), 64; IX (October, 1947), 33; X (November, 1948), 75.

137. *Theatre Arts,* XXXI (October, 1947), 10; *Bulletin,* IX (April, 1947), 21; Mary Morris, "Tryout Studio in New York," X (July, 1948), 46.

138. Evans, passim.

139. This viewpoint is generally confirmed by a personal letter from Lee Norvelle (June 1, 1950), who, with Mabie, attended preliminary meetings preceding the public organizational meetings.

140. 1936 Constitution of AETA.

141. Personal letters from Evans, June 4, 1951, from Barclay Leathem, June 1, 1950, and from Wallace A. Goates, August 10, 1953.

142. "Minutes of Meetings, December 30, 1936."

143. "Minutes of Second Meeting of December 30, 1936." Minutes of Annual Business Meetings, *passim*, give the subsequent officers: Presidents, Leathem (1938), Norvelle (1939), Evans (1940), Marian L. Stebbins (1941), James H. Parke (1942), C. R. Kase (acting after Parke entered military service, and continuing into 1943 since there was no business meeting at which to elect new officers, and with Stebbins serving as presiding officer of the 1943 meeting of the Advisory Council, since Kase in turn had entered military service), Herschel Bricker (1944, and continuing in 1945 because of no business meeting for election), Valentine Windt (1946, after serving for Bricker when he entered the Army Education Program), Kase (1947), H. Darkes Albright (1948), Hubert C. Heffner (1949), Monroe Lippman (1950), Lee Mitchell (1951), William P. Halstead (1952), Barnard Hewitt (1953). Vice-Presidents: Gertrude Johnson (1938), Evans (1939), Stebbins (1940), C. Lowell Lees (1941), Kase (1942), Windt (1944 and part of 1945), Kase, (1946), Albright (1947), Heffner (1948), Lippman (1949), Mitchell (1950), Halstead (1951), Hewitt (1952), Horace Robinson (1953). Administrative Vice-Presidents: Jack Morrison (1950-1953), Lillian Voorhees (1954-1955). Executive Secretaries: Winbigler (1937-1939), John W. Hulburt (1940-1946, two terms and an extra year), Halstead (1947- 1949), Norman Philbrick (1950-1952), Mouzon Law (1953-1955).

144. "Minutes of Business Meeting, December 29, 1941."

145. "By-Laws" (1945), Sec. 4(b). Other changes include transfer of responsibility for the convention program from President to Vice-President.

146. "Minutes of Business Meeting, December 30, 1947."

147. "Minutes of Business Meeting, December 29, 1949." The Administrative Vice-President is elected by the Advisory Council for a two-year term; he is not in the automatic succession to presidency. His chief function is to administer the Work-Projects (see fn. 167).

148. Membership figures compiled from Annual Financial Statements.

149. Originally ("By-Law No. 1") dues for regular membership were $3.50 ($1.00 for those with NATS membership) and for sustaining members, $10.00. Beginning with 1942, dues for regular members rose to $2.50 for all; with 1948, to $3.50; with 1952, to $4.50. Also in 1952, sustaining membership rose to $12.50. (See "Minutes of Business Meeting, December 29, 1941; December 30, 1947; December 29, 1950; December 30, 1952.")

150. Total expenditures suggest the extent of activities. For example, annual Financial Statements show $311.06 expended in 1944 and $10,728.14 in 1950. Small deficits existed 1948-1950, though a stock of publications on hand partially balanced them.

151. Hubert C. Heffner, "President's Report," *Educational Theatre Journal*, II (March, 1950), 72; "Minutes of Advisory Council Meetings 1949, 1950, 1951"; "Report of International Liaison and ITI Project, 1951."

152. The numbering of annual conventions became confused by variation in terminology and by numbering them in a fixed relationship to SAA conventions. "Minutes of AETA Advisory Council, December 26-29, 1951" officially numbered its conventions as follows: (1) N. Y., 1937; (2) Cleveland, 1938; (3) Chicago, 1939; (4) Washington, 1940; (5) Detroit, 1941; (6) N. Y., 1943; (7) Columbus, 1945; (8) Chicago, 1946; (9) Salt Lake City, 1947; (10) Washington, 1948; (11) Chicago, 1949; (12) N. Y., 1950; (13) Chicago, 1951; (14) Cincinnati, 1952. Convention programs bear other numbers.

153. Convention Programs, 1947-1951.

154. "Minutes of Advisory Council, December 27-30, 1950."

155. Personal letter from Winifred Ward, May 30, 1952.

156. Pre-Convention Memo, December 6-9, 1950 from Ex. Sec. Philbrick: The Seattle Conference was originally designated as the "first" AETA conference. In

1950 this was recognized as misleading, so the conferences were renumbered: (1) Evanston, 1945; (2) Seattle, 1946; (3) Bloomington, Ind., meeting with NTS, 1947; (4) Denver, 1948; (5) N. Y., sponsored by ANTA, 1949; (6) Minneapolis, 1950, with a U. of Minnesota Workshop for 150 of the 400 delegates preceding the conference; (7) L. A., 1951, with a UCLA Workshop; (8) Madison, with a U. of Wisconsin Workshop, 1952; (9) Garden City, N. Y., with an Adelphi College Workshop, 1953.

157. "Minutes of Advisory Council, December 27-30, 1950; December 28-31, 1952."

158. Memo from Heffner to AETA Committee on Publications, May 14, 1940, and letter of same date to Evans (in Heffner files). Heffner's full files on this are not available. He loaned them to Richard Ceough and then went into military service. Ceough died during this period, and the files have not been located.

159. Personal letter from Heffner, June 7, 1950.

160. "Minutes of Advisory Council Meetings, December 28-31, 1941." Heffner reported to the Council that there were enough promises of subscriptions to make possible the projected *Theatre Quarterly* with the Theatre Library Association. "Minutes of Advisory Council Meeting, December 27, 1943": it was voted to give "every support to *Theatre Annual.*" At the death of Ceough in January, 1947, *Theatre Annual* was taken over by Blanche A. Corin as publisher, with William Van Lennep as editor.

161. Published in May, 1943. Personal letter from Blanche A. Corin, May 26, 1952.

162. "Minutes of Advisory Council Meetings, December 28-31, 1941." Savage, Bricker, Lippman, Windt, and Foster Harmon, with Kase as chairman, were appointed a committee to edit issues in turn. Single editorship began in 1944: Windt (1944-1945), Hewitt (1946-1948), David W. Thompson (1949).

163. "Minutes of Advisory Council Meetings, December 27-30, 1948."

164. Albright was Assoc. Ed. and Winship, Mng. Ed. (all 1949-51). Mouzon Law replaced Winship when he reentered military service. Albright was elected Editor, 1952-1954.

165. "Editor's Foreword," *ETJ*, I (October, 1949), 1.

166. "Minutes of Advisory Council Meetings, December 27, 1938."

167. Norman Philbrick, "Notes from the Meetings of the Advisory Council," *ETJ*, V (March, 1953), pp. 69-70: Audio Visual Aids, Bibliography, Board of Research, College Curriculum, Conferences, Contests and Festivals, Graduate Project, Counseling, International Liaison and ITI, Junior and City College, Manuscript Play Project, Motion Pictures, Opera, Production Lists, Radio, Secondary Schools, Stage Movement, Summer Theatre, Teacher Training, Television, Theatre and Adult Education, Theatre Architecture, Touring, Veterans Administration Hospital.

168. *The Bulletin*, NASSP, XXXIII, No. 166, 182 pages.

169. *The Educational Theatre in Adult Education*, Robert Gard, ed. (Washington, Division of Adult Education Service of NEA, 1951).

170. *SM*, XVI (November, 1949), 124 pages.

171. Personal letter from Albright, June 24, 1952.

172. "Minutes of Advisory Council Meetings, December 26-29, 1951."

173. Sister Mary Xavier Coens, B.V.M., "The Origin and Development of the Catholic Theatre Conference, 1937-1949," unpublished M.A. thesis, Catholic U., 1951, p. 1.

174. Emmet Lavery, "The Catholic Theatre: New Thoughts on an Old Dream," *America*, LVI (December 5, 1936), 197-199.

175. Coens, p. 3.

176. *Ibid.*, p. 4. Unaware of the simultaneous activity for the Washington convention, Lavery joined Dinneen and Costello in laying plans for the Chicago meeting. In a letter to Lavery (January 22, 1937), Nagle suggested subordinating the Chicago meeting to the Washington one, pointing out, ". . . geographical ad-

vantages can not compensate for the interest of the Hierarchy in the activities of their Catholic University." Since the Chicago group did not deem the subordinating advisable, both meetings were held, as consecutive ones of the same organization.

177. Euphemia Van Rensselaer Wyatt, "A National Catholic Theatre," *Catholic World*, CVL (September, 1937), 723. Coens (p. 50) indicates that membership grew from 1937 to 1949, to 524, over 300 of these being producing groups, thus bringing the estimated number of participants to approximately 6000. Canada, New South Wales, Australia, England and thirty-nine states sent convention delegates. High-school unit memberships grew from 4 in 1941 to 202 in 1950.

178. Coens, pp. 8, 9. Other temporary officers included Rev. John H. Mahoney and Father Dinneen, vice-chairmen; E. Francis McDevitt, secretary-treasurer. A noteworthy resolution passed by delegates to this meeting was that which expressed appreciation to the WPA Federal Theatre Project for its compilation of a list of Catholic plays.

179. Coens (pp. 54-55) lists all the officers, 1937-1951. Ensuing presidents include Dinneen, Lavery, Costello, Rev. James J. Donahue, Rev. Karl Schroeder, Joseph F. Rice, Walter Bamberger, and Theresa M. Cuny.

180. *Ibid.*, p. 10. The office was moved to 316 W. 57th St., N. Y. in 1941 and to 120 Madison Ave. in 1949. In 1952 it was located at 22 Park Place, and in 1953 at Cudahy Library, Loyola University, Chicago.

181. *Ibid.*, pp. 22-23. The same cause limited attendance at the 1945 convention to the Executive Board and members from the Chicago area.

182. *Ibid.*, p. 25. The word "National" was regarded as too restrictive in view of international membership. Another objection lay in the possibility of confusion with NTC.

183. *Ibid.*, p. 50.

184. *Ibid.*, pp. 33-34, 50.

185. *Ibid.*, pp. 18, 29-30; personal letter from Coens, May 20, 1952. Helen Purcell, who had given generously of her time to the secretaryship, assumed full-time capacity and continued until 1947, at which time Margaret Passmore took over. Townley Brooks replaced Passmore from August, 1951, to April, 1952, at which time Passmore resumed her duties as Secretary protem. In August, 1952, Patricia Bradley became secretary-treasurer.

186. Coens (pp. 64-67) includes the entire constitution.

187. *Ibid.*, p. 8.

188. *Ibid.*, p. 12.

189. *Ibid.*, p. 10. Dinneen was responsible for the inclusion of the Motion Picture Committee as one of the permanent committees.

190. *Ibid.*, p. 11, quoted from "Statement by the President," *Bulletin*, I (November, 1937), 4.

191. Wyatt, "The National Catholic Theatre Conference," *Catholic World*, CLIX (September, 1944), 552. In an earlier article, CLV (August, 1942), 601, Mrs. Wyatt credits Purcell, the first editor, with *Production Calendar's* success.

192. Personal letter from Wyatt, June 13, 1952.

193. Coens, pp. 39-41.

194. *Ibid.*, pp. 44-45.

195. *Ibid.*, pp. 25, 46, corrected by letter from Wyatt.

196. The Drama League and ANTA have contributed to the growth of children's theatre.

197. TLA, too, has exerted influence in this field by devoting itself to specific research projects.

198. ANTA has assumed responsibility for the American Centre of the International Theatre Institute.

199. An opportunity for representation exists, too, at the National Theatre Assemblies called by ANTA.

INDEX

DATE DUE